The Jesus Movement

THE JESUS MOVEMENT

A Social History of Its First Century

Ekkehard W. Stegemann
Wolfgang Stegemann

Translated by O. C. Dean, Jr.

FORTRESS PRESS   MINNEAPOLIS

IN MEMORY OF

OUR BELOVED PARENTS

Martha and Wilhelm Stegemann

THE JESUS MOVEMENT
A Social History of Its First Century

First English-language edition published by Fortress Press in 1999

Translated by O. C. Dean, Jr., from *Urchristliche Sozialgeschichte. Die Anfänge im Judentum und die Christusgemeinden in der mediterranen Welt*, published by Verlag W. Kohlhammer, Stuttgart, Germany, copyright © 1995.

The publication of this book was aided by a grant from Inter Nationes, Bonn, Germany.

Jacket design: Eric Lecy Design
Interior design: Peregrine Graphics Services

Scripture quotations, unless otherwise indicated, are from the New Revised Standard Version of the Bible, copyright © 1989 by the Division of Christian Education of the National Council of the Churches of Christ in the United States of America, and are used by permission.

The Library of Congress has catalogued the hardcover edition as follows:

Stegemann, Ekkehard.
    [Urchristliche Sozialgeschichte. English]
    The Jesus movement : a social history of its first century /
Ekkehard W. Stegemann and Wolfgang Stegemann ; translated by O.C.
Dean.
        p.   cm.
    Includes bibliographical references and index.
    ISBN 13: 978-0-8006-3009-6
    1. Sociology, Christian—History—Early church, ca. 30-600.
2. Sociology, Jewish—History. 3. Women in Christianity—History—
Early church, ca. 30-600. 4 Mediterranean Region—Social
conditions. I. Stegemann, Wolfgang, 1945– . II. Title.
BR165 S79513   1999
270.1—dc21   98-50392
                                      CIP

Manufactured in the U.S.A.   AF 1-3425

CONTENTS

ABBREVIATIONS

AGAJU	Arbeiten zur Geschichte des antiken Judentums und des Urchristentums
AJAH	*American Journal of Ancient History*
ANRW	*Aufstieg und Niedergang der römischen Welt*
ANTZ	Arbeiten zur neutestamentlichen Theologie und Zeitgeschichte
ATANT	Abhandlungen zur Theologie des Alten und Neuen Testaments
BA	*Biblical Archaeologist*
BASOR	*Bulletin of the American Schools of Oriental Research*
BETL	Bibliotheca Ephemeridum Theologicarum Lovaniensium
Bib	*Biblica*
BibS	Biblische Studien (Neukirchen)
BJS	Brown Judaic Studies
BK	*Bibel und Kirche*
BTAVO	Beihefte zum Tübinger Atlas des Vorderen Orients
BTB	*Biblical Theology Bulletin*
BWANT	Beiträge zur Wissenschaft vom Alten und Neuen Testament
BZ	*Biblische Zeitschrift*
CBQ	*Catholic Biblical Quarterly*
CIG	*Corpus inscriptionum graecarum* (1828-77)
CII	*Corpus inscriptionum iudicarum* (1936-52)
CIL	*Corpus inscriptionum latinarum* (1862-)
CPJ	*Corpus papyrorum judicarum* (1957-64)
EDNT	*Exegetical Dictionary of the New Testament*
EKKNT	Evangelisch-katholischer Kommentar zum Neuen Testament
EvErz	*Evangelische Erziehungen*
EvT	*Evangelische Theologie*
EWNT	*Exegetisches Wörterbuch zum Neuen Testament*
FRLANT	Forschungen zur Religion und Literatur des Alten und Neuen Testaments
GBS	Guides to Biblical Scholarship
HNT	Handbuch zum Neuen Testament
HNTC	Harper's New Testament Commentaries
HTKNT	Herders theologischer Kommentar zum Neuen Testament
HTR	*Harvard Theological Review*
HUCA	*Hebrew Union College Annual*
ICC	International Critical Commentary
IEJ	*Israel Exploration Journal*
IGRR	*Inscriptiones Graece ad res Romanas pertinentes* (1901-27)
ILS	*Inscriptiones Latinae selectae* (1892-1916)
Int	*Interpretation*

JAAR	*Journal of the American Academy of Religion*
JAC	*Jahrbuch für Antike und Christentum*
JBL	*Journal of Biblical Literature*
JJS	*Journal of Jewish Studies*
JR	*Journal of Religion*
JRH	*Journal of Religious History*
JRS	*Journal of Roman Studies*
JSHRZ	Jüdische Schriften aus hellenistisch-römischer Zeit
JSJ	*Journal for the Study of Judaism*
JSNT	*Journal for the Study of the New Testament*
JSPSS	Journal for the Study of the Pseudepigrapha Supplementary Studies
JTS	*Journal of Theological Studies*
KHA	Kölner historische Abhandlungen
KJV	King James Version
LXX	Septuagint
MGWJ	*Monatschrift für Geschichte und Wissenschaft des Judentums*
NIV	New International Version
NovT	*Novum Testamentum*
NRSV	New Revised Standard Version
NTAbh	Neutestamentliche Abhandlungen
NTD	Das Neue Testament Deutsch
NTOA	Novum Testamentum et Orbis Antiquus
NTS	*New Testament Studies*
OBO	Orbis biblicus et orientalis
OBT	Overtures to Biblical Theology
OTL	Old Testament Library
PRE	*Paulys Real-Encyklopädie der classischen Altertumswissenschaft*
QD	Quaestiones Disputatae
RAC	*Reallexikon für Antike und Christentum*
RGG	*Religion in Geschichte und Gegenwart*
RIDA	*Revue internationale des droits de l'antiquité*
SBLDS	Society of Biblical Literature Dissertation Series
SBLSBS	Society of Biblical Literature Sources for Biblical Study
SBT	Studies in Biblical Theology
SCS	Septuagint and Cognate Studies
SEÅ	*Svensk Exegetisk Årsbok*
SIG	*Sylloge Inscriptionum Graecarum*, 3d ed. (1915-24)
SJLA	Studies in Judaism in Late Antiquity
SNTSMS	Society for New Testament Studies Monograph Series
ST	*Studia Theologica*
STDJ	Studies on the Texts of the Desert of Judah

TDNT	*Theological Dictionary of the New Testament*
ThBei	*Theologische Beiträge*
TLZ	*Theologische Literaturzeitung*
TRE	*Theologische Realencyklopädie*
TWNT	*Theologisches Wörterbuch zum Neuen Testament*
TZ	*Theologische Zeitschrift*
VC	*Vigilae Christianae*
VT	*Vetus Testamentum*
WD	*Wort und Dienst*
WG	Wege der Forschungen
WMANT	Wissenschaftliche Monographien zum Alten und Neuen Testament
WUNT	Wissenschaftliche Untersuchungen zum Neuen Testament
ZNW	*Zeitschrift für neutestamentliche Wissenschaft*
ZTK	*Zeitschrift für Theologie und Kirche*
ZWT	*Zeitschrift für wissenschaftliche Theologie*

ABBREVIATIONS OF ANCIENT SOURCES

Dead Sea Scrolls

1QapGen ar	Genesis Apocryphon
1QH	Hymn Scroll
1QM	War Scroll (1Q33)
1QpHab	Commentary on Habakkuk
1QS	Community Rule
1QSa	Messianic Rule (a) (1Q28a)
4QMMT	Halakhic Letter (4Q394)
4QFlor	Florilegium (4Q174)
4QpNah	Commentary on Nahum (4Q169)
4QOrd	Ordinances (4Q159)
4QpPs37	Commentary on Psalm 37 (4Q177)
11QMelch	Melchizedek (11Q13)
CD	Damascus Document

Pseudepigrapha

Ep. Arist.	*Letter of Aristeas*
Jos. As.	*Joseph and Asenath*
Jub.	*Jubilees*
Ps.-Phoc.	*Pseudo-Phocylides*
Test. Job	*Testament of Job*
Test. Mos.	*Testament of Moses*

GRECO-ROMAN SOURCES

Agr.	Philo, *De Agricultura* (On Agriculture)
Ann.	Tacitus, *Annales* (Annals)
Ant.	Josephus, *Antiquities of the Jews*
Ant. Rom.	Dionysius of Halicarnassus, *Antiquitates Romanae* (Roman Antiquities)
Anthol. Pal.	Antipater of Thessalonica, *Anthologia Palatina* (Palatine Anthology)
Ap.	Josephus, *Contra Apion* (Against Apion)
B. Civ.	Caesar, *Bellum Civile* (Civil War)
Bell. Civ.	Appian, *Bella Civilia* (Civil Wars)
Ben.	Seneca, *De Beneficii* (On Benefactions)
Cat.	Lucian of Samosota, *Cataplus* (Landing)
Cels.	Origen, *Contra Celsum* (Against Celsus)
Decal.	Philo, *De Decalogo* (On the Decalog)
Dom.	Suetonius, *Domitian*
Ep.	Pliny the Younger, *Epistulae* (Epistles)
Ep.	Seneca, *Epistulae* (Epistles)
Ep. Arist.	*Letter of Aristeas*
Epigr.	Martial, *Epigrammaton liber* (Epigrams)
Flacc.	Philo, *In Flaccum* (Flaccus)
Fug.	Lucian of Samosota, *Fugitivi* (Fugitives)
Fug.	Philo, *De Fuga et Inventione* (On Flight and Discovery)
Hermot.	Lucian of Samosota, *Hermotimus*
Hist.	Herodotus, *Historia* (History)
Jos.	Josephus
Leg. Gai.	Philo, *De Legatione ad Gaium* (On the Embassy to Gaius)
Leg.	Plato, *Leges* (Laws)
Leg. Agr.	Cicero, *De Lege Agraria* (On the Principles of Agrarian Life)
Migr.	Philo, *De Migratione Abrahami* (On the Migration of Abraham)
Nat. Hist.	Pliny the Elder, *Naturalis Historia* (Natural History)
Off.	Cicero, *De Officiis* (On Offices)
Oik.	Xenophon, *Oikonomicus* (On the Household)
Or.	Dion of Prusa (aka: Dio Chrysostom), *Orationes*
Pereg. Mort.	Lucian of Samosota, *De Morte Peregrini* (On the Death of Peregrinus)
Pol.	Aristotle, *Politica* (Politics)
Quis Her.	Philo, *Quis rerum divinarum Heres sit* (Who is the Heir)
Quod Omn. Prob.	Philo, *Quod omnis Probus Liber sit* (Every Good Man is Free)
Phaedr.	Plato, *Phaedra*
Praef.	Cornelius Nepos, *Praefatio* (Preface)
Ran.	Aristophanes, *Ranae* (Frogs)

Sac.	Philo, *De Sacrificiis Abelis et Caini* (On the Sacrifices of Abel and Cain)
Sat.	Horace, *Satirae* (Satires)
Sat.	Juvenal, *Satirae* (Satires)
Sat.	Lucian of Samosota, *Saturnalia*
Satyr.	Petronius, *Satyricon*
Spec. Leg.	Philo, *De Specialibus Legibus* (On the Special Laws)
Thes.	Aristophanes, *Thesmophoriazusae*
Verr.	Cicero, *De Verrem* (On Verrus)
Virt.	Philo, *De Virtute* (On Virtues)
War	Josephus, *War of the Jews*

EARLY CHURCH WRITINGS

Adv. Iud.	Justin, *Adversus Iudaeos* (Against the Jews)
Apol.	Justin, *Apologia* (Defense)
Apol.	Tertullian, *Apologicus* (Defense)
Barn.	*Epistle of Barnabas*
Cels.	Origen, *Contra Celsum* (Against Celsus)
De mort. pers.	Lactantius, *De morte Persecutorum* (On the Death of Persecutors)
Dial.	Justin, *Dialogue with Trypho*
Did.	*Didache*
Haer.	Epiphanius, *Haereses* (On Heresies; aka: *Penarion*)
Hist. Eccl.	Eusebius, *Historia ecclesiastica* (Church History)
Ign. Eph.	*Ignatius, Letter to the Ephesians*
Ign. Mag.	*Ignatius, Letter to the Magnesians*
Ign. Phld.	*Ignatius, Letter to the Philadelphians*
Ign. Smyrn.	*Ignatius, Letter to the Smyrnaeans*
Man.	*Shepherd of Hermas, Mandates*
Mart. Pol.	*Martyrdom of Polycarp*
Nat.	Tertullian, *Naturalis Historia* (Natural History)
Or.	Tatian, *Oratio ad Graecos* (Oration against the Greeks)
Scorp.	Justin, *Ad Scorpius* (Against Scorpius)
Sim.	*Shepherd of Hermas, Similitudes*

RABBINIC SOURCES

Abod. Zar.	*Abodah Zarah*
B. Bat.	*Baba Batra*
Ber.	*Berakot*
Deut. Rab.	*Deuteronomy Rabbah*
Exod. Rab.	*Exodus Rabbah*
Ḥull.	*Ḥullin*

Lam. Rab.	*Lamentations Rabbah*
m.	Mishnah
Ma'aś.	*Ma'aśerot*
Midr. Gen.	*Midrash Genesis*
Meg. Ta'an.	*Megillat Ta'anit*
Men.	*Menahot*
Mo'ed Qat.	*Mo'ed Qatan*
Pesa.	*Pesahim*
Pesiq. R.	*Pesiqta Rabbati*
Sanh.	*Sanhedrin*
Shabb.	*Shabbat*
Sheb.	*Shebi'it*
Sheq.	*Sheqalim*
Sot.	*Sotah*
b.	Babylonian Talmud
t.	Tosephta
Ta'an.	*Ta'anit*
y.	Jerusalem Talmud
Yad.	*Yadaim*

LIST OF MAPS, TABLES, AND FIGURES

PREFACE

Only in exceptional cases will readers want to attempt to read from start to finish such a comprehensive work as the following overview of the social history of early Christianity. Therefore we offer here some suggestions for reading, in the hope of making the book more accessible in parts.

The book is so arranged that each of the main sections can be read by itself. Thus those who are initially interested only in "The Land of Israel, the Social History of Judaism, and the Followers of Jesus" can begin immediately with Part Two. Cross-references are made to important presuppositions that in this case are presented in detail in Part One—say, on the economics of antiquity as a whole or on our model of the social stratification of Mediterranean societies. Indeed, it is possible in principle to turn intentionally to an individual chapter, whether it is—to name two examples—Chapter 13 on "Women among the Followers of Jesus in the Land of Israel" or Chapter 11 on "External Conflicts of Believers in Christ with Gentiles and Jews in the Diaspora."

We also intentionally decided to place the notes at the end of the book in order not to encumber the reading of the text. Since the overwhelming majority of the notes simply involve references to biblical or other ancient sources or to secondary literature, they are not necessary for a direct understanding of the text itself.

In individual cases we also mention Greek, Latin, and Hebrew or Aramaic terms, which are always presented in transliterated form. Greek words are written with *ē* for *eta* and *ō* for omega as needed.

Because of the highly detailed table of contents, we have omitted a subject index. At the end of the book, however, there is an Index of Ancient Sources.

We have dedicated this book to the memory of our parents. Along with many others, they taught us to see the reality of human beings concretely in their particular social context.

Ekkehard W. Stegemann
Wolfgang Stegemann
Basel and Neuendettelsau
March 1995

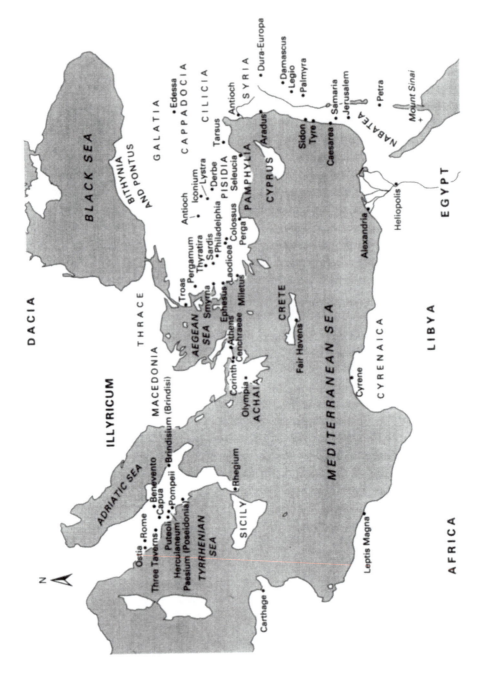

Eastern Mediterranean in the First Century

INTRODUCTION

This book attempts to offer an overview of the economic and social living conditions of the groups and communities in the New Testament who are either connected with the historical Jesus or confess the risen Christ. Hence it deals with the period of about one hundred years after the beginning of the reckoning of time, in which the twenty-seven books of the New Testament came into being and in which the conditions they describe prevailed. We will attempt a synthesis that incorporates many individual studies. The overall picture of early Christian social history will be sketched against the background of what is known about contemporary Mediterranean societies in general. Thus it is not a question here of a history of the politics and events of early Christianity. Related historical circumstances will be mentioned only tangentially.

The Term Early Christian

The term *early Christian* (Ger. *urchristlich*) is retained here for pragmatic reasons.[1] On the one hand, it refers to the various phenomena of Jesus' following in the land of Israel, that is, to the oldest Jesus movement—the Jerusalem primitive church and the "churches of Judea" mentioned by Paul—and to messianic groups in Israel in the period after the destruction of the second temple in 70 C.E. On the other hand, it refers to the Christ-confessing communities in various cities of the Roman empire outside of Palestine and especially to the Pauline churches and others that are still recognizable in the New Testament writings after the year 70.[2] In this sense we can also speak of a *New Testament* social history.

Geographical Limitation

Thus the *historical period* of the social history of early Christianity treated here can be relatively precisely defined as the first century after the birth of Christ. Somewhat more difficult is an exact *geographical* delimitation. Frequently we have no direct information about the place of origin of the New Testament. This is especially true of the Gospels but also applies to some letters. We are better informed about Paul and his extensive journeys, which led him to many important cities of the Roman empire (for example, Antioch, Damascus, Ephesus, Thessalonica, Corinth, Rome), where the churches he founded are also to be sought. Naturally, Jesus and his followers can be located more precisely.

1

They came from a rural region of Galilee in the vicinity of the Lake of Gennesaret (or Sea of Galilee, Sea of Tiberias). And after the crucifixion of Jesus in Jerusalem, a stable community of confessors of Jesus developed there, the so-called early Jerusalem church, whose influence gradually radiated into the surrounding area and apparently even to Syrian Antioch. But where was the Letter to the Hebrews written? Where did its addressees live? Where was the home of the author of the Letter of James? This letter is addressed to the twelve tribes in the Diaspora (Jas 1:1) and thus in principle set its sights on the whole inhabited Mediterranean world. This comprehensive geographical perspective also commends itself for the following presentation. For even with all the uncertainties about details, we can make one fundamental statement: the authors and addressees of the New Testament scriptures all lived in the Roman empire.

Socio-Geographic Classification

Hence these New Testament authors and addressees belonged to societies that were subject in a more or less intensive way to the political, military, economic, social, and cultural influences of a social system that had its center of power in Rome and its emperors.[3] *Socio-geographically* this means the area around the Mediterranean Sea.[4] More precisely, as seen from Rome, this includes Italy, the coast of Greece and Asia Minor, and finally Syria and the land of Israel (Palestine), as well as—around the end of the first century and the beginning of the second—Bithynia in northwestern Asia Minor.[5] Further to the southeast the boundary was formed by Arabia (Gal 1:17). The map on p. xxii gives an overview.

Christ-confessing Communities as Part of the Mediterranean World

Thus the world of the New Testament is the Mediterranean world of the first century. In terms of social geography, this is a region for which comparative ethnological and (cultural and social) anthropological studies have demonstrated remarkable commonalities.[6] These works have also been applied to the New Testament, especially through the lead of Malina.[7] With respect to culture, the societies of the Roman world were linked by commonalities of various kinds. This can also be said of political and socio-economic conditions. For however great one may judge the similarities among the various regions within the *Imperium Romanum* because of Roman rule, similar factors seem on the whole to have shaped the economic and social structures of urban and rural areas. For our purposes we may assume that aside from all special circumstances, in the cities and in rural areas of the Greco-Roman world and also of the land of Israel, the economic and social living conditions around the

Mediterranean Sea were *structurally* similar. This means that they can be classified under one *social type:* they are *advanced agrarian societies* (see Chapter 1). We are not at all asserting here that the conglomerate of societies around the Mediterranean Sea that were ruled by Rome amounted to something like a unified society.[8] For us it is a question here first of the "overarching elements" of the economic and social order.[9] In this connection, Alföldy points to the "expansion of the Roman legal system," which was connected "with the sanctioning of forms of social independence according to unified principles and with the constitution of 'Roman' elites according to very similar economic, social, political, and ideological criteria."[10] Thus we can say with Alföldy:

> Regarded as a whole, the Roman Empire was marked by a unified economic and social system in such a way that, depending on province or region, this system either was clearly established or at least represented the aim of the economic and social development process, without really clear alternative models being available.[11]

In a similar way, modern western industrial societies also resemble each other, even if distinct differences between the United States and Germany or France can be ascertained. Taken as a group, however, modern industrial societies are different from agrarian societies with newly developing industry, such as those presently found in many countries of eastern Asia and Latin America. Thus a *social history of early Christianity* belongs in the context of the social history of the Mediterranean societies of the first century. The direct and indirect statements of the New Testament regarding economic and social conditions took shape within this larger context. At the same time they themselves can also be drawn upon as a source of contemporary living conditions. Hence a social history of early Christianity also has the task of providing an overview of the economic and social conditions of the Mediterranean world of the first century. This task will be completed in the first part of the present work.

The Basic Differentiation of the Societies Represented in the New Testament

A basic distinction is made here between *Jesus' followers in the land of Israel* and *Christ-confessing communities* outside of Israel *in the urban regions of the Roman empire*. Especially characteristic here are regional peculiarities regarding the economic, social, and religious situation of Judaism in Israel, which also had their influence on Jesus' followers in Israel. Expressed differently: the followers of Jesus were part of the predominantly Jewish society of Palestine, whereas the Christ-confessing communities in urban residential areas outside

Israel lived in the context of a predominantly Gentile society. Moreover, we will also consider the ethnic-religious context of groups of followers of Jesus in the land of Israel in contrast to that of the Christ-confessing communities outside Israel. The latter groups were characterized by religious and social fellowship between members of the Gentile social majority and Jews of the Diaspora, and indeed the participation of formerly non-Jewish members gradually became predominant. By contrast, the groups of Jesus-followers in Israel were made up primarily of Jews; Gentiles come into the picture at best marginally in the last third of the first century. Thus the followers of Jesus in the land of Israel are to be understood here socio-historically and religiously as a phenomenon of Judaism in the land of Israel. Under the concept *followers of Jesus* we include the actual Jesus movement, the so-called early Jerusalem church, and the messianic groups in the land of Israel that in our view are represented by the Gospels of Matthew and John. We will examine these groupings in Part Two, which gives an overview of the socio-economic condition of the land of Israel and its significance for the religious situation. By contrast, the Christ-confessing communities outside Israel—even with all their affinities with Jewish religious tradition—are no longer a phenomenon of Judaism, above all for sociological reasons. This is seen first in the fact that they existed beyond the synagogues of the Diaspora, the representations of Judaism outside Israel. Moreover, in their self-understanding the Christ-confessing communities distinguished themselves not only from Judaism (in Israel or in the Diaspora) but also from the Gentile social majority (see the introduction to Part Three). In Part Three we will present the social history of these urban Christ-confessing communities. In Part Four, finally, we go into the special situation of women in the Mediterranean world in general, as well as in the Jesus movement and in the Christ-confessing communities inside and outside the land of Israel.

PART ONE

Economy and Society
in the Mediterranean World
of the First Century

1

THE TYPE OF ANCIENT
MEDITERRANEAN SOCIETIES

In this chapter we will determine the type of ancient Mediterranean societies and distinguish the social model that we feel is appropriate from some others (1.1). The second section then discusses structural factors of agrarian societies in order to give an overall impression of this type of society (1.2).

1.1 Advanced Agrarian Societies

Here we subsume the societies in question under the basic type *agrarian societies*. This expresses the fact that, on the one hand, from the standpoint of production, farming shaped Mediterranean societies but, on the other hand, the distribution of a society's goods was subject to the controlling power of a small social group. Thus the term *agrarian society* shows that the economic backbone of these states was agriculture.[1] It also implies that the overwhelming majority of the population lived in the country and by agriculture. It includes above all free farmers, tenant farmers, day laborers, and their families, as well as slaves. In this sense, the designation also implies a basic statement about the social structure: agrarian societies are rural societies.

The term *agrarian society*, however, does not express the economic importance of *cities*, especially in the areas of skilled labor and trade, and as the consumers of agricultural production. Socially and politically, however, cities also shaped the character of Mediterranean agrarian societies, since in them lived the elite, who as owners of property and wealth, and as possessors of social control, ruled both country and city. This detailed definition of the agrarian type of society can call attention to the fact that agricultural production—and not it alone—was subject to a political and social governance system that through *redistribution* concentrated the wealth of society in the hands of a small number of the elite. Naturally, all of this means also that the mode of production of these societies was *preindustrial* (see p. 10).

A Slave-holding Society?

Thus our determination of the type of Mediterranean societies places the emphasis on *agricultural production* and on a particular *redistribution system*. Here we see the two fundamental determinants that are typical of these soci-

7

eties. Other models ascribe this role, for example, to "slave labor" as the "typical form of dependent work," which is at the same time the "foundation of agricultural and urban production."[2] In accordance with this judgment, the type of Mediterranean societies is expressed with a term such as *(highly developed) slave-holding society*.[3] This characterization seems inappropriate to us first of all because without doubt it places too high a value on the contribution and importance of slave labor. Thus Brunt estimates the number of unfree people in the population of Italy at only somewhat more than one-third, which means that even in purely quantitative terms, slave labor can hardly have been the predominant element of production.[4] Moreover, slave labor was concentrated in the central area of production, agriculture, in certain regions (above all Italy and Sicily) and was no doubt hardly the decisive production factor in urban regions. There slaves, liberated slaves, and those born free worked side by side as skilled laborers and craftsmen. Nor was slavery the predominant element in trade connected with the crafts or in the whole commercial sector generally. Kippenberg correctly says:

> For a long time there has been too great a concentration on slavery as the primary source of economic well-being, and we have lost sight of the fact that ancient cities rested on an agrarian base and were each surrounded by large areas of agricultural land, from which the well-being of the citizens derived.[5]

It would be much better to say that the most important production factors of Mediterranean societies lay in the possession of land and in the labor of more or less economically dependent small farmers, leaseholders, and wage earners. In this context, naturally, slavery also played an important—but not absolutely crucial—role.

The Level of Technology and Social Power as Determinants?

In addition to the production factors of land and agricultural labor, the social structure and above all the distribution of the controlling power over property and people are also of fundamental importance for the determination of type of society. Other social theories ascribe a defining role to the level of technology or the exercise of social power. Thus Sjoberg, in his view of the history of social forms, distinguishes three different types on the basis of the central independent variable *technology*: folk or society, feudal or preindustrial societies, and industrial-urban societies. Yet he also recognizes that the particular technological level puts its special stamp on the named social types only in connection with specific social structures and their influence on other variables (such as the city, cultural values, and social power).[6] In accordance with his classification, the societies of the ancient Mediterranean world that interest us belong in the category of feudal, preindustrial societies. J. H. Kautsky, by contrast, distinguishes three phases of "social history":[7] primitive societies, traditional aristocratic kingdoms, and modern (commercialized or industrialized) societies.[8] In his view, the aristocracy is the ruling class in an agrarian society; it does not participate in work itself but lives entirely or primarily off the labor of the peasants. He holds that this type of society is represented best by ancient Egypt and by Mesopotamian and early medieval societies—but not by the Roman empire, because with its high degree of commercialization, it was, according to Kautsky, a forerunner of the type of modern societies.[9] While in aristocratic societies relative importance is to be given to the commercial sector, Kautsky recognizes that in the Roman empire aristocrats relinquished a portion of their power to tradespeople or even went into business themselves. Thus the application of his social model to the Mediterranean world of the first century presupposes a close connection of the political elite with a central economic realm and in particular a decision about the economic importance of the commercial sector in these societies. Nonetheless, it is at least controversial whether agriculture or trade and business were more important economically in these societies.[10] Here we are inclined toward the view advocated, for example, by MacMullen. In his opinion, the land was by far the most important producer of wealth, but at the same time the cities had a close symbiotic relationship with the rural regions.[11]

However the type of society is determined,[12] it seems advisable to us not to make any one-sided deterministic statements but to place the technological level, the social structure or controlling power, and the basic conditions of production side by side. Yet the conceptual delineation of social types requires a decision as to which of the named factors will, as it were, give its name to a type of society and defines its most important characteristics in comparison with other types of society. In this regard, the term *agrarian society* appears sensible to us, since it can express two fundamental factors of the ancient Mediterranean social form. The term *agrarian society* also implies a statement about technological level, as we will soon see.

The Development and Spread of Agrarian Societies

In the macrosociological studies of Lenski, agriculture is distinguished from the earlier type of horticultural societies on the one hand and the later industrial societies on the other.[13] According to Lenski it was the result of a "social revolution" that was set in motion by "a series of inventions and discoveries that led to great improvements in production, transport, and trade."[14] Thus, seen macrohistorically, technological innovations strongly favor the development of this type of society. In this respect we must in any case agree with the just-mentioned model of Sjoberg. Here the invention and production of the iron plow and the use of animal power in agriculture seem to have been especially important. The invention of the wheel and the sail also eased and improved the conditions of transport. These and other "innovations laid the common foundation for the subsequent development of a new type of society," which above all in regard to the "character of its subsistence system" is to be called an agrarian society. Such agrarian societies first became established between 5000 and 6000 years ago in the Middle East, then spread from there into the whole Mediterranean world, and were the predominant social form almost everywhere in Europe and North Africa until the latter part of the fifteenth century. If the agrarian societies replaced the horticultural, then they were in turn largely pushed aside by (modern) industrial societies, which were shaped by, among other things, revolutionary developments in the realms of technology and production, the development of many new sources of energy and an enormously increased consumption of energy, considerable improvements in the means of transport and trade, increased expansion of markets and regulatory mechanisms, and also a fundamental social transformation.[15]

The Term Preindustrial

Thus the agricultural type of society is on the one hand posthorticultural and on the other preindustrial. Accordingly, the present-day observer can regard this type of society as a progressive improvement over previous types or judge it from the perspective of modern industrial societies. Thus Garnsey and Saller,[16] for example, characterize the ancient economy of the Roman empire from the perspective of modern industrial societies as a preindustrial and underdeveloped political economy. For the overwhelming majority of the population who worked in agriculture, it was purely a subsistence economy. It especially lacked macroeconomic entities, such as markets for goods and labor, and regulatory mechanisms, such as the regulation of money by state authority. Lack of technological development hindered productivity in agriculture, as well as in trade and business. We will examine this aspect of ancient economics in more detail below (see 2.1). Yet we must not overlook the fact that this description is oriented toward the experiences of a modern political economy and on this basis focuses especially on the *deficiencies* of the ancient economy. This perspective is entirely legitimate, since it allows modern contemporaries to evaluate the economy of antiquity, which, based on their experience, is underdeveloped. Nevertheless, it is also meaningful to understand the economic and social conditions at the beginning of the Roman imperial period as an *advance* in the history of societies, when one compares them with earlier types of society. Not only is the modern perspective thereby relativized, but the economy and society of this epoch can be placed in a history of types of society. Furthermore, a macrosociological analysis offers the opportunity to consider structural factors in ancient economic and social history. These macrosociological structures will now be sketched, as we refer above all to the appropriate studies by Lenski.[17]

1.2 Central Factors of Advanced Agrarian Societies

The following central macrosociological factors are among the most important ones to consider in examining an advanced agrarian society:

Technological Level

Improvements in the realm of technology, especially the spread of the iron plow, lead to increased productivity in comparison with the earlier horticultural type of society. This also makes it possible to achieve a greater economic output while at the same time expending less human energy to guarantee subsistence. Yet technological innovations slow down in advanced agrarian societies. Also *military technology* is more progressive and characterized by a division of labor, since the individual alone is no longer capable of manufacturing the more complicated weapons.

POWER STRUCTURE

One important consequence is that the ruling power in agricultural societies becomes stronger and better organized. Professional armies come into being. In this way it also becomes possible to administer larger domains. Agrarian states are also *conqueror states,* but conquests also have consequences. On the one hand, as in many agrarian societies, various ethnic groups lived in the Roman empire. On the other, war becomes almost a chronic state. Similarly, a multitude of internal struggles must also be endured. In the period from Augustus to Romulus Augustulus, who was deposed in 479 by Odoacer, 79 Roman emperors reigned; of these 31 were murdered, 6 were driven to suicide, and 4 were violently deposed.[18] Agrarian societies tend to have *monarchical* regimes. The fact that this form of government was not able to prevail against the Roman republic is related to the special conditions of Roman society. The institution of the consulate fulfilled the most important purpose of monarchical sovereignty: the concentration of military power in the hands of one person.

POPULATION DENSITY

In agrarian societies population numbers increase considerably compared with earlier types of society. Yet the higher birthrates are accompanied by high infant mortality. Catastrophes (famines, floods) also lead to a high rate of mortality. Lenski estimates the population of the Roman empire at 70 million at the beginning of the third century.

ECONOMY

The economy is characterized by increased division of labor and a chain of command, but not by supply and demand. It is divided into two sectors: (1) the rural agrarian economy and (2) the urban commercial and (at most) beginning industrial economy. The conditions of the rural agrarian economy are subhuman, marked by peasants and slaves who are forced by the ruling class to serve urban economy, slaves in households, beggars, prostitutes, and wretches. The burdens of taxes, religious and political imposts, and rents increase and benefit the upper stratum. The lower classes largely remain only at a subsistence level. The debts of the lower stratum become an important factor.

CITIES

Also typical of agrarian states is the spread of urban municipalities. They increase in comparison with earlier types of society, and the population in cities also grows. Sjoberg names three basic presuppositions for the development of urban centers: favorable ecological conditions (climate, soil, water supply, and the meeting of various cultures, which allows an increase in technological skills), advanced technology in agricultural and nonagricultural production (more people can be supported by less agricultural labor, and thus some can be liberated from agricultural production), and a well-developed social organization, especially in the political and economic spheres (the political structure makes it possible through tax and tribute to draw on the agricultural surplus for the support of the urban population).[19] Yet even if the proportion of urban dwellers in an agrarian state is clearly greater than with earlier social forms, it remains a relatively small part of the overall population; Lenski estimates about 5 to 10 percent. In any case, the rural population comprises the overwhelming majority. Nevertheless, the predominance of the urban centers is exercised politically, economically, religiously, and culturally. This is related to the fact that wealth and political power are concentrated in the cities. Markets develop, and a variety of vocations and activities is also a key part of the urban situation. In the urban population are, among others, officials, priests, scholars, scribes, merchants, servants, soldiers, artisans, workers, and beggars. In addition, there is a small number of elite, people who derive their living from their property and/or from political offices.

INCREASED DIVISION OF LABOR

Noteworthy is the increasing division and specialization of labor. There is a high degree of differentiation, for example, in handicrafts. Yet we must observe that only seldom in the Roman empire and only to a limited extent was there anything like manufacturing, in which several workers or artisans were occupied.[20] Artisans are organized in guilds. Certain municipalities are known for their specialization in various crafts. In addition to the division of labor there was also a regional specialization in certain economic sectors. North Africa and Spain were known in the Roman empire as providers of dried figs and olive oil. Gaul, Dalmatia, Asia Minor, and Syria as producers of wine; Spain and Egypt supplied the market with salted meat; and Egypt, North Africa, and Sicily were the main producers of grain.

TRADE AND BUSINESS

The specialization in crafts naturally leads to increased trade and business, which provides for transportation and the distribution of wares:

> The economic surplus in agrarian societies was normally brought to the ruling classes and their dependents, which led all advanced agrarian societies to resemble a tree or a plant with a gigantic system of supporting roots spreading out in all directions, drawing off the surplus and moving it in stages to the end user, the municipal population. On the outer edges of this system were thousands and hundreds of thousands of small peasant villages, each with a few hundred inhabitants. They brought their surplus to the nearest market town, where a portion remained for the local population while the rest moved on to the provincial capital. Again, a portion remained there while the remainder went to the capital of the state.[21]

MONEY AND WRITING

The inventions of money and writing are crucial milestones in the improvement of the economic system of agrarian societies. Yet it is important to note that money and writing both become instruments of social domination, since money is present in the cities, and writing is found more in the province of the urban minority than the rural majority.[22] In this way the gap between city and country is broadened.

THE CONTRAST BETWEEN CITY AND COUNTRY

It is precisely the contrast between city and country that also shapes the ancient form of society.[23] If it is true of modern industrial societies that in them cities are not to be understood as a construct beyond a regional system but rather as an urbanization of the whole society, then this social and geographic separation is especially decisive for the preindustrial city in ancient agrarian societies.[24] Although ancient cities were dependent on the agrarian hinterland for their supply of basic foodstuffs, the hinterland was at the same time controlled by the urban elite and also financially oppressed by a system of religious or political taxes. Thus city and country were separated not only geographically but also socio-economically. In the cities a small group of specialized workers produced goods for the consumption of the elite. On the whole, the quantitatively small urban portion of the population and the correspondingly low need drew only a little labor into the cities; indeed, through legal restrictions most agrarian societies even prevented the rural population from living in the cities.[25]

SOCIAL INEQUALITY

In agrarian societies a notable social inequality prevails, with large differences among people in regard to the distribution of power, the enjoyment of privileges, and prominence in society. Governmental institutions are the primary source of inequality. The ruling class sees the state as its plunder. Political power is concentrated in the cities and centrally executed; the administrative apparatus continues to grow. As a consequence of the concentration of power, there is a great accumulation of property and wealth. Confiscations, appropriations, taxes or demands for tribute, compulsory labor, and the payment of rent all enrich the rulers. After one war Sulla is supposed to have demanded a tribute of 480,000,000 sesterces from the residents of Asia Minor.[26] Confiscations—the forced appropriation of foreign assets—are the result of conquests. Similarly, the same Sulla is supposed to have raged against his internal enemies in Rome and put to death around 2300 rich equestrians (*ordo equester*) and 90 still richer senators, whose property he appropriated.[27] Many Roman emperors or rulers proceeded in a similar way, including Augustus, Tiberius, Caligula, Nero, and Domitian. The concentration of sovereignty in the ruling class leads to exploitation, especially of the rural population. From its ranks come increased protests and revolts against the rulers. The *ruling class* comprises between 1 and 2 percent of the total population. Lenski includes in this class the highest state officials in both the civil and military sectors and also the slaves and freed slaves who served the elite in elevated positions. Belonging to this class made enrichment possible, for example, when high officials such as proconsuls in the provinces allowed themselves to be bribed by residents. When Cicero was proconsul of Sicily, he rejected bribes, according to his own account.[28] Because he was so "honest," during his proconsulate these sums amounted to "only" 2,200,000 sesterces (=550,000 denarii). By contrast, Verres is supposed to have withdrawn 40,000,000 sesterces (=10,000,000 denarii) during the three years he was in office.[29]

2

THE ECONOMIC SITUATION
OF ANCIENT MEDITERRANEAN SOCIETIES

In this chapter we will discuss the problems of the theory of the ancient economy (2.1). Then we will sketch the economic boundary conditions of ancient societies (2.2). Finally, the characteristics of their structure will be clarified (2.3). It should be noted that here we can provide only an overview and a selection of topics. This seems to us justified, since the multiplicity of problems of ancient economics has already been discussed in detail elsewhere in a number of more detailed studies, to which we will refer.[1]

2.1 The Economy of Antiquity

Anyone who attempts to describe the economy of antiquity runs into a variety of difficulties. First there is the shortage of detailed traditions and especially of statistical information. What we have is indirect sources: archaeological, inscriptional, numismatic, papyrological, and other literary testimonies,[2] from which we must then develop economic data. Thus what we call *economy* and expand with a number of terms such as *production, labor, capital, market,* and the like has no equivalent in ancient languages. In addition, antiquity itself developed no comprehensive economic theory. It lacked, to be sure, not only the appropriate terminology but also the presuppositions for such a theory. The reason for this, as Finley has shown, lies hardly in the inability to abstract but in the ancient economy itself and its perception by the people of antiquity:

> Naturally, they worked as farmers or traders, manufactured goods, and worked in mines; naturally, taxes were raised and money coined; funds were received and deposited; naturally, people made a profit or went broke in their enterprises. But they did not see all these individual activities as a single entity, as a "differentiated subfunction of society" in the terminology of Parsons.[3]

Yet in a certain sense the people of antiquity could also distinguish subareas of the economy, for example, the production of goods (*technē*), the meeting of need (*chreia*), the exchange of money (*nomisma*) at the market (*agora*), and the distinction between private household (*oikos*) and public needs (*politeia*).[4] Yet reflection on all these needs and activities occurred not in the sense of economic theory but as political, philosophical, and ethical phenomena.[5]

15

Oikonomia

Although it is true that the term *economy* is derived from the Greek word *oikonomia*, in ancient Greek linguistic usage it means the "operation of a household" or, in general, "administration" or "organization." Thus the Greek *oikonomia* is not identical with our word *economy*. Naturally, economic matters are implied, but only in the sense that the administration of an ancient household *also* involved economic tasks. Beyond this, however, *oikonomia* included things that we can by no means classify as economic. It concerns, namely, the rights and powers that a "head of household," *oikodespotēs, paterfamilias*, held with respect to his "assets," that is, his wife and children, his grandchildren and slaves, and his personal property.[6] Similarly, ancient primers that give advice for the administration of a household are not interested only in economic questions. Thus the *Oikonomikos* of Xenophon (early fourth century B.C.E.), which has the form of a Socratic dialogue, contains not only sections on agriculture, which is seen as the only honorable economic activity, but also, for example, statements on the relationship of husband and wife, and on the virtues that a head of household should possess. Therefore, Finley says that the *Oikonomikos* is "basically . . . a book on ethics."[7] At the same time he points out that well into the eighteenth century, following this ancient tradition, economic questions were not treated together as a separate field. In addition to Finley, the pioneering studies of the economic historian and anthropologist Polanyi[8] have especially influenced the discussion of the theory of ancient economics.

A. THE TERM *ECONOMY*

In the modern economic sciences *economy* is usually understood in principle as the division of scarce means among competing ends, and one assumes that people behave "economically"; that they divide the scarce resources available for achieving certain goals in such a way that the use of these resources remains as small as possible. Polanyi's economic theory, however, distinguishes between a formal and a substantive meaning of economy. He also points out that only in modern economics do the two aspects come together, for the ancient form of economy is comparable with the modern only in the substantive aspect. This substantive meaning of economy means a "regulated process of cooperative effort between people and their surroundings that produces an ongoing provision of material means for the purpose of satisfying needs."[9] Here it is to a certain extent a question of an ethnological concept of economy, as shown, for example, by its acceptance by the cultural anthropologist M. Harris. He understands economy as "the sum of all actions that are responsible for the provisioning of a society with goods and services."[10] In connection with our own interest in the ancient economy, this "ethnological" concept of economy seems to us more meaningful than the modern one, since it does not presuppose a constant human economic interest, as it were, but assumes, among other things, that traditional cultural values always go into concrete economic "actions" for the provisioning of a society.

Economic and Cultural Values

Polanyi points out, for example, that in the course of human history the possession of a horse has repeatedly been seen as desirable. Yet this was not so much because of the special capability of this animal for work, "but for the sake of the horse, which was connected with social rank and so forth."[11] The cultural aspect of the economy can also be explained through ancient dealings with "capital." In principle we can distinguish three possibilities for dealing with capital. Large quantities of money were either loaned at interest, hoarded as treasure, or invested in land.[12] The decision for one of these forms of investment was dependent on cultural values and membership in one of the ancient strata, not on an interest in maximizing profit. Thus, for example, Cicero (see p. 25), as a representative of the upper class, recommends to businessmen who have acquired a considerable income, especially through the shipping of large quantities of basic foods, to invest this in real property. Connected with this was a great deal of honor but hardly the greatest economic usefulness. Totally ineffective in the sense of rational economics was the hoarding of money as "treasure," which was widespread, for example, among the peasants (when they possessed surplus financial means at all). In this way they wanted not only to avoid the risk of lending money but also to be the envy of their neighbors.

We may also note in this connection Jesus' parable of the talents (Matt 25:14-30; Luke 19:12-27). It offers a surprising message, for it is clearly interested in a maximization of profit. One can say that it tramples on the values of the rural population.[13] For the slave who buries the sum of money entrusted to him by his master (and thus hoards the capital) is sharply criticized. By contrast, the master approves of the behavior of the two other slaves, who "work" (thus literally Matt 25:16) with the entrusted capital. This extravagant feature of the parable contradicts the norms of solidarity of peasant societies, as well as the prohibition of the Torah against accepting interest, whose meaning was apparently to counteract the impoverishment of broad segments of the peasantry.[14] For the everyday behavior of the rural population was determined by reciprocity, by mutual economic behavior that resulted, economically speaking, in a zero sum balance (see 2.2.2). Making a profit at the expense of a neighbor was not part of the reciprocal system of distribution of village neighbors. It was achieved above all by way of redistribution, which was based on sovereignty and aimed at control over others. This is seen, by the way, in the Lukan version of this parable, in which the faithful servants are rewarded with sovereignty over ten and five cities, respectively (Luke 19:17, 19).

Thus in ancient societies it was hardly economically rational when money was stored at home as treasure instead of "working" with it. And it is also doubtful whether a wholesaler, who realized his income from the ocean transport of large quantities of foodstuffs, was well advised economically to invest the proceeds in agriculture. He would without doubt have reaped a greater profit from investment in real estate. Thus economic behavior does not have to be rational and calculating but can also be connected with a variety of cultural values independent of financial gain. Yet the ancient economy is distinguished from modern rational economies not only by the named cultural values. Polanyi has called attention above all to the problem of the "embedding" of ancient economic activity in social institutions and distinguished it from the modern detached form of economy.[15]

B. THE EMBEDDING OF THE ECONOMY IN THE SOCIAL STRUCTURE

For Polanyi this "embedding" of economic activities in social institutions and events as a whole is the primary characteristic of ancient economics. It is basically distinguished from modern economics, which is "detached" or "disembedded" in relation to society and represents a separate realm:

> The disembedded economy of the nineteenth century stood apart from the rest of society or, more especially from the political and governmental system. In a market society the production and distribution of material goods in principle is carried on through a self-regulating system of price-making markets. It is governed by laws of its own, the so-called laws of supply and demand, and motivated by fear of hunger and hope of gain. Not blood-tie, legal compulsion, religious obligation, fealty, or magic creates the sociological situations which make individuals partake in economic life, but specifically economic institutions such as private enterprise and the wage system. . . . [In premodern "marketless" societies, by contrast, the] elements of the economy are . . . embedded in non-economic institutions, the economic process itself being instituted through kinship, marriage, age-groups, secret societies, totemic associations, and public solemnities.[16]

The most important ancient social institution in which economic behavior was embedded is without doubt the *household*. This embedding of economic activities in the social structures of ancient societies resulted, on the one hand, in the fact that in principle the economically crucial factor *land*, which essentially belonged to the upper stratum, set stratum-specific boundaries for the accumulation of wealth. On the other hand, the household economy as subsistence economy within a household, in which all members of the family worked for self-sufficiency (including necessary tools and clothing), restricted the development of appropriate markets. Thus what we call "economy" and what constitutes its own area of study in the national economy presuppose a comprehensive concentration of all economic activities and to a certain extent the independence of these activities.[17] This makes it clear that a description of the ancient economy must take into consideration the fact that it is dependent on categories and theories that come from the study and analysis of modern, market-oriented forms of economy.

C. A BRIEF OVERVIEW OF THE HISTORY
OF THE THEORY OF ANCIENT ECONOMICS

The foregoing insight was first called a problem by the economist K. Bücher at the end of the nineteenth century. He determined that the ancient economic order cannot be designated a *national economy* (in the sense of a modern market economy), since it largely lacked the fundamental conditions, for example, production for market, exchange of products and services, manufacturing output, market-oriented commerce, and independent labor.[18] He called the ancient economy—following Rodbertus, who spoke of an *Oikenwirtschaft* (household economy)—a *closed household economy* and thereby distinguished it from the medieval form of economy, the urban economy (*Stadtwirtschaft*), because the ancient economic cycle of production and consumption essentially took place within the house. Although Bücher did not overlook the fact that in ancient societies there was trade and that to some extent large quantities of manufactured goods were produced for export, this was, nonetheless, the exception, not the rule.

At first the views of this specialist in economics did not make much impression on the study of antiquity. Its scholars followed, rather, the views of their own expert, E. Meyer, who refused to subscribe to a progressive model of economic history, such as that of Bücher, and accepted instead the idea of cyclical stages of development within the various epochs. In this way he justified his description of the ancient economy in analogy to a modern national economy.[19] He drew parallels, for example, between the Greece of the seventh and sixth pre-Christian centuries and the fourteenth and fifteenth centuries of our time. He pointedly talked of an "industrialization of the Greek world" and of Corinth and Megara as "commercial and industrial cities."[20] Meyer's view of things prevailed for a long time, reinforced not least of all by the epochal study of M. Rostovtzeff on the social and economic history of the Roman empire, a work likewise oriented toward modern capitalist and market-oriented economic categories.[21] Another discouraging element in the debate was the false alternative between the characterization of the ancient economy as "primitive" or "archaic" and that of recent economies as "modern" and "highly developed."[22] Yet supported especially by Weber, Hasebroek,

Oertel, Heichelheim, and the already mentioned economic historian Polanyi,[23] the view inaugurated by Bücher has been largely confirmed—if in part also considerably modified and corrected—by the more recent economic historical works on antiquity by scholars such as Jones, Duncan-Jones, and above all Finley.[24] This history of research cannot be examined more closely here,[25] but the following special points will suffice to indicate the results of that research.[26]

D. BASIC CONCLUSIONS IN THE STUDY OF THE ANCIENT ECONOMY

1. In the Roman empire agriculture had a preeminent position economically.
2. Business and trade were not market-oriented but rather were based on scarcity. The high costs of land transportation in particular permitted trade essentially only in wine, oil, and other easily transported goods of great value. The cheap and high-volume shipment of grain was possible in ships only when a fruitful hinterland (North Africa, Egypt) had easy access to a seaport.
3. In antiquity there were no markets in the modern sense. Ancient markets were locally concentrated and dominated by the privileged few who could produce a surplus beyond the subsistence of the household. The lack of buying power among the majority of the rural population stood in contrast to the growth of market structures, whose increasing spread made a certain expansion possible.
4. Technically and economically, the workshops were not suited for mass production. Moreover, the mass transport of goods was not possible. The few workshops were the businesses of families (including slaves) and specialized in certain mass goods (pottery, bricks, bricks and tiles, textiles, and weapons).
5. Cities were usually oriented toward consumption, not production.
6. The financial economy was not developed.
7. The great majority of the population worked in agriculture and existed on a low subsistence level. Their production was oriented toward what they consumed and as a rule permitted no surplus. Moreover, these population groups were often dispossessed by the ruling class. The requirements of peasants for food, clothing, and implements were in principle met within their households.
8. Of economic significance is the fact that economic activities were "embedded" in the social structures of society. That is to say, in addition to the self-sustaining household economy, the central factor of the ancient economy—namely, land (not capital)—was bound by fixed power and property structures to the upper class. Thus in this sense the accumulation of wealth was restricted and concentrated socially. Exceptions were (per-

haps) wholesale trade and tax collection. Likewise, in principle it was also possible only for members of the elite to receive a large income through high government office.

2.2 Economic Boundary Conditions in Mediterranean Societies

Every economic system presupposes certain *boundary conditions* that (1) shape *production* in agriculture and business, as well as the rendering of services, (2) regulate the *distribution* of products or exchange of goods, say, through transport and trade or through markets, and (3) influence the *consumption* or use of products. In this connection Kloft speaks of *interdependencies,* which include geographical space, population density and social stratification, technology, and fundamental governmental or legal conditions.[27] Of fundamental importance for the realm of production are, for example, the technological standard and the type of organization of work; for the realm of consumption, the development of means of transport and the exchange system or *money.* Yet consumption is also determined by cultural modes of behavior and social rules. Likewise, in addition to *geographical* factors, *political* ones influence the economic system. While the geographical conditions are largely set by the natural situation in certain regions, the achievable standard of technology shapes the intensity of agricultural and commercial production as well as the conditions of work and transport. Furthermore, political conditions, which were set, say, by the imperium, played an important role in economic expansion and the circulation of goods. In addition to the securing of property and ownership rights,[28] these included the development and security of ways of transport. Also of great importance was the fact that in a certain sense the Roman empire was, with few exceptions, a unified monetary region in which the transfer of large sums of money between different areas was possible.[29]

We will now sketch in more detail the fundamental conditions of *production,* that is, technology and the organization of work (2.2.1) and of exchange and *distribution* (2.2.2). In the last part of this section we will look at the economics of *money* (2.2.3).

2.2.1 Production: Technology and the Organization of Work

A. TECHNOLOGY

We have already indicated that the fundamental technological innovation for the development of agricultural societies is to be found in the invention and production of the iron plow and the exploitation of animal power.[30] Mediterranean societies were also based on this older achievement, and other agricultural implements of iron (hoes, shovels, scythes) were also produced. The processing of grain took place either in simple form in mortars, in which the grain was crushed, or in mills, which ground it into flour. The smaller rotary mills were turned by hand, the larger ones by donkey.[31] Legumes and olives were also processed in mills, wine in winepresses. In or near large cities, such as Alexandria, Rome, Ostia, and Trier, stood grain silos (*horrea*).[32] Even in agriculture we must take into account regional differences in the application of technical devices. In the construction business simple cranes were in use; precise planning was presupposed (say, in the construction of aqueducts and sewers). The use of heat energy for radiant heating in floors is notable, yet ancient heating required a great deal of fuel.

Land Transport and Shipping

Along with the spread of the iron plow, improvements in transportation conditions through ship (sail) and wagon (wheel) also played an important role. Trading ships were mostly single-masted sailboats.[33] Rowboats were also used for inland shipping. "For the 250,000 tons of grain that were consumed each year in Rome, 4500 ship loadings were necessary to transport the grain up the Tiber from Ostia to Rome."[34] The size of the ocean-going freighters varied from 100 to 400 tons.[35] The smaller inland ships held about 70 tons. The building of ships and harbors progressed especially well under the emperors Claudius, Nero, and Trajan.[36] Trade across the seas seems to have been a special domain of Rome. In Horace we often find comments critical of Roman businessmen who seek profits all over the world.[37] And the Revelation to John not only connects Rome with worldwide trade (18:3, 11ff.) but also links this trade especially with ships (18:18-19).

Yet neither wind nor, in principle,[38] water power were yet known as energy sources in the realm of production, with the result that people were solely dependent on human and animal energy. The employment of draft animals in agriculture and transport was largely limited to oxen, since draft harnesses were not adapted for horses, which were capable of greater effort.[39] Donkeys and mules as well as camels in the Near East were superior to oxcarts in land transportation, since narrow streets in poor condition severely limited the use of such teams. In Pompeii, for example, the width of streets varied roughly between three and eight meters.[40] In Rome "even broad exit roads such as the *Via Appia*, the *Via Latina*, and the *Via Ostiensis* displayed a width of only about 4.8 to 6.5 meters. By order of the emperor, vehicular traffic was, with few exceptions, prohibited during the day."[41] Anyone who has traveled the ancient road in Ostia leading toward Rome, which still survives today with its original pavement, can easily imagine how difficult transportation must have been by means of carts equipped with iron-rimmed wheels and pulled by draft animals. It was no doubt only with great effort that people and beasts of burden were able to make progress over the irregular pavement.

One could rent pack animals with or without their handlers (*muliones*). Hillel recounts an anecdote from which we learn that the rental of a donkey for the stretch from Jerusalem to Emmaus cost one denarius, from Jerusalem to Lydda two denarii, and from Jerusalem to Caesarea three denarii.[42] These prices seem realistic, as the costs of land transportation make clear. Food in particular was transported by animals; for unwieldy material (for example, building materials) wagons were also used. Slaves and day laborers (*saccarii*) were used for shorter distances (in warehouses, loading ships in harbors). The development of the network of roads progressed in all areas dominated by the Romans and was improved by the construction of bridges. For example, it was the Romans who expanded the underdeveloped road system in Palestine. This construction activity was in Rome's military and economic interest. From the time of the Bar Kochba rebellion against the Romans, the Babylonian Talmud passes down the following dialogue:

> Then Rabbi Jehuda began and said: "How beautiful are the works of that nation [that is, Rome]: they have laid out roads, built bridges, and constructed baths." Rabbi Yose remained silent. Then Rabbi Shimon ben Yochai spoke and said: "Everything they have built was done in their own interest. They have laid out roads in order to transport whores, constructed baths for their comfort, and built bridges in order to raise the toll!"[43]

The Costs of Transportation

Thus a market-oriented economy was also blocked by the poor conditions for transportation, which raised notable difficulties especially for inland commerce on country roads. This was related to the fact that, in the first place, the means for transporting goods and wares over land were lacking and, second, that the costs of transportation were considerable. From Cato the Elder we know that "the price for an olive press built in Pompeii went up by 73 percent when it was delivered in Venafrum 110 kilometers away."[44] Travel by inland and seagoing ships was, however, of greater importance for the transportation system and hence for the possibility of foreign trade. Yet it was also expensive and dependent on certain seasons. It has been calculated, for example, that the price of a load of wheat doubled when hauled by land 300 miles. To transport a *modius* (a Latin measure of volume equivalent to 6503 kilograms) of wheat over the sea 1250 miles (about the distance from Alexandria to Ostia, the harbor for Rome) cost the same as moving it 50 miles on land, namely, 16 denarii.[45] But transportation by ship required an enormous investment: a ship of 400 tons cost between 250,000 and 400,000 sesterces. Loading it with wheat required another 185,000 sesterces. Hence foreign commerce was obviously a matter for the rich, and it was economically sensible only for necessary goods that the state subsidized for the people, as in the case of wheat from Egypt or North Africa that was desperately needed in Rome.

B. ANCIENT ATTITUDES TOWARD WORK

In the differentiation of ancient attitudes toward work, which could vary according to time, region, and the particular standpoint of the observer, we can nonetheless ascertain that a fundamental distinction prevailed between activities that as bodily or mental effort were directed toward survival (and in principle were held in lower regard socially) and the duties, businesses, and capabilities that were reserved for the elite.[46] Morel comments:

> The essential line of demarcation for the Romans did not run between mental and manual activities but between activities that involved intellectual joys and those that were immediately useful (*animi libera oblectatio/utilitas*), between the *artes liberales*—that is, arts worthy of a free man, say, mathematics, rhetoric, or philosophy—and all others, from handcrafts to medicine and architecture.[47]

Even artists with marvelously developed abilities—as sculptors, for example— were members of a trade in the view of the Roman upper class. They were understood as executors in the service of someone who commissioned them. That is, for the Romans the real creator of a work of art was the one who commissioned or sponsored it. Even today, the restoration or exhibition of ancient works of art in the Vatican in Rome, for example, is marked by a Latin inscription that names the reigning pope as the restorer or exhibitor. In the deprecation of the crafts, physical labor in general, and work performed for a wage, Plato, Aristotle, and Cicero—to name only three—were united, even if the reasons for their view were different.[48] Xenophon (*Oik.* 4.2-4) held the occupations of artisans (*banausoi*) to be suspicious, because they had time and interest for neither love of friends nor political affairs of the city (for example, in case of war).[49] He, as well as Hesiod, Aristotle, Cato the Elder, and Cicero, held the independent, self-sustaining landowner to be, in a social and political sense, the ideal citizen.[50] An exception, according to Plutarch's presentation, was Solon, who is supposed to have bestowed honor on trades and crafts (*Solon* 22.3). Yet this exception is based on the circumstances. For since the poor farmland could not feed enough people, he encouraged citizens to go into the handicrafts, in order thus to ensure the feeding of the idle masses.[51] In the Old Testament–Jewish tradition, by contrast, work for one's livelihood and work involving bodily exertion seem to have been held in higher esteem, though there were also clear distinctions among the professions.[52]

Disparagement of Working for a Living

Thus, for members of the ancient upper class, work in itself basically had no value; that is, it was always judged in connection with the status of the person working.[53] Any work done to earn one's livelihood was disparaged on principle. Yet agricultural work seems to have been more positively valued. Nevertheless, a social perspective also reigned in evaluating work on the land. The crucial question was whether a farmer could live from the land he owned.[54] The more positive estimation of agricultural work also had traditional grounds and resulted from the fact that the elite of ancient societies were especially distinguished by large landholdings. Yet these large landholders did not work themselves. The standpoint of the Roman elite is demonstrated by a well-known text from Cicero:[55]

> Another word about the various skills and occupations. On the question of which of them are appropriate for a free man and which are called dirty, the following view is traditional. First, one may regard as taboo all of those occupations, such as tax collector and usurer, that only result in making one hated by one's fellow human being. Furthermore, ignoble and unclean is the occupation of all untrained day laborers, who are paid not for their skills but for the work completed. What they receive as wage is a lump sum for their labor. Also considered among the dirty occupations are the middlemen who immediately resell what they buy from the wholesaler. They would not earn anything if they did not resort entirely to mendacity. There is nothing more disgraceful than unreliability. All craftsmen also fall in this unclean category: what can there be about a workshop that is noble? Least of all can one condone occupations that serve only sensual pleasures. "Fishmongers, butchers, cooks, poultry dealers, fishermen," as Terence says. In my opinion one can also include quacks, dancers, and the whole scantily clad theater. Those occupations, however, that require more thorough training and strive for higher usefulness—such as the healing arts, architecture, and the teaching of the noble sciences—are worthy of those for whose station they are fitting. The retail trade, however, is to be classified with the unclean businesses, whereas the capital-intensive wholesale business, which transports consumer goods from all over the world and honestly makes them available to the masses, is above reproach. One may even rightfully praise the wholesaler when he has taken care of himself and, satisfied with what he has acquired (which is often the case), withdraws from the high seas into the harbor and from there immediately retires to his own land in the countryside. Of all the kinds of occupation, agriculture is the best, the most productive, the most agreeable, and the most worthy of a free man.

A detailed analysis of this text is not required here.[56] It is indeed notable, on the one hand, that for Cicero the acquisition and possession of land conveys the highest social status. On the other hand, he disdains not only the odious occupations (such as tax collector and usurer) but also the many and varied craft, trade, and service occupations, even if to varying degrees. Even the "arts" (*artes/artificia*), such as healing and architecture, are honorable only for those whose status is appropriate. Here also the view of the Roman elite apparently reigns, probably because such "arts" were frequently practiced by Greeks (whether free, former slaves, or slaves). And it is presupposed that these "arts" are practiced as a way to earn one's livelihood, not to demonstrate the capabilities of a man who otherwise lives from his property or wealth. A far more detailed list of morally reproachable occupations is offered by Dion of Prusa (*Or.* 7.110).[57]

On the acquisition of property, Cicero is apparently not thinking of agricultural work but of the free landowner. He would still have thought very little of the agricultural work of small farmers, tenant farmers, slaves, and wage earners, as did Jesus Sirach, who writes about work on the land and by hand (Sir 38:24-34):

> The wisdom of the scribe depends on the opportunity of leisure; only the one who has little business can become wise. How can one become wise who handles the plow, and who glories in the shaft of a goad, who drives oxen and is occupied with their work, and whose talk is about bulls? He sets his heart on plowing furrows, and he is careful about fodder for heifers. So too is every artisan [*tektōn*] and master artisan [*architektōn*] who labors by night as well as by day; those who cut the signets of seals, each is diligent in making a great variety; they set their heart on painting a lifelike image, and they are careful to finish their work. So too is the smith. . . . So too is the potter. . . . All these rely on their hands, and all are skillful in their own work. Without them no city can be inhabited, and wherever they live, they will not go hungry. Yet they are not sought out for the council of the people, nor do they attain eminence in the public assembly. They do not sit in the judge's seat, nor do they understand the decisions of the courts; they cannot expound discipline or judgment, and they are not found among the rulers. But they maintain the fabric of the world, and their concern is for the exercise of their trade.

Sirach grants to farming and handicrafts a certain value (settling the cities), yet for him farmwork and crafts seem to go along with lack of education (or meager knowledge of the Torah) and lack of political power in decision making. "Only one who is completely free of all physical toil can become a student of scripture and act as judge, counselor, and scripture interpreter. Farmers, shepherds, and craftsmen are not suited for it."[58] If this represents the viewpoint of the "scholar/wise man" (*grammateus*), then in the text cited earlier Cicero probably had in mind the life situation that determined the course of a (large) landowner's day. We learn about him from Pliny the Younger in a brief to Fuscus:[59]

You ask me how I divide my day in Tuscany in the summer. I wake up when I want, mostly around the first hour, often earlier, seldom later. . . . I consider what work I have at the moment, consider it as if I were writing it down word for word and correcting it. . . . Then I call my secretary, let in the daylight, and dictate to him what I have planned. . . . When the fourth or fifth hour has arrived—I don't have a firm, precisely measured division of time—I move onto the terrace, if the weather makes it advisable, or into the parlor, consider further matters, and dictate them. Afterward I get into the wagon. There I also do the same thing as in walking or reclining. The mental tension is maintained, renewed by the change. Then I take a short nap and later go walking again; afterward I read a Greek or Latin speech, loud and clear, less because of the voice than the stomach; naturally, the voice is thereby strengthened at the same time. Another walk, then massage, exercise, and bath. At table, when my wife or a few friends are present, I have something read from a book; after the meal, some comedy or lute playing; afterward a stroll with my people, including educated men. Thus the evening is spent in varied discussions, and even the longest day flies by. . . . Sometimes I go hunting, yet not without something to write on, so that when I don't catch anything, I can still bring something home. I also devote my time to my tenants [coloni], yet not enough in their opinion; their peasant complaints make me think longingly of our studies [litterae] and the activity [opera] in the city.

Nothing here is meant to be disparaging of Pliny's literary activity; rather, the course of his day recalls the utopian society of which Karl Marx dreamed. For Pliny work is writing and study, and it is circumscribed by his (political) activity (opera) in the city. Even the large landowner's contacts with his tenants seem to have been reduced to a minimum and were felt as a burden. Thus Pliny does not contribute much toward the picture of work in antiquity.

As we briefly sketch work in ancient societies, we limit ourselves here largely to activities that are again subdivided into higher and lower kinds, yet are fundamentally distinct from the activities of the elite. Terminologically, it is especially the Latin words *industria, munus, occupatio, officium,* and *tractatio* that refer to the duties and occupations of the upper class. By contrast, work for one's livelihood is indicated by terms such as *ars, artificium, labor, negotium, opera, opus,* and *quaestus.*[60] The corresponding Greek terms are *ponos* (toil, labor), *kopos* (tiresome drudgery), *mochthos* (heavy, laborious work), *ergasia* (daily work), and their derivatives. We will now take a closer look at work in the country and in urban regions.

C. WORK ON THE LAND:
SMALL FARMERS, TENANTS, SLAVES, WAGE EARNERS

Work on the land is considered the epitome of all work.[61] Most workers were also employed in the agricultural sector. Naturally, at harvesttime there was a greater demand for available workers. Agricultural work was performed by (small) farmers and their families (including women and children), tenants, wage earners or day laborers, and slaves. We must also note that on account of the accumulation of property by a few, the number of independent small farmers constantly decreased, while the number of unpropertied wage earners and tenants grew. Also in the villages there were artisans such as carpenters, cobblers, and smiths. They often earned their livelihood in nearby cities (this was perhaps Jesus' situation—see pp. 198–203), and conversely, a portion of the urban population made its living in the cultivation of the fields in the vicinity of a city.[62] Among small farmers, family operations predominated, and even on the larger farms (except for Italy and Sicily) slave labor played no dominant role.[63]

It is true that the ancient Latin writers Cato the Elder, Varro, and Columella, who deal with agriculture in their teaching texts and handbooks, think "essentially of a cultivation of the land by slaves."[64] In fact, reality may well have been different, at least in the first century. For the cultivation of remote and less productive land, Columella (born at the beginning of that century) recommends the use of free tenants instead of managers from the slave class (*De re rustica* 1.74ff.), and the large landowner Pliny the Younger seems to have employed only tenants (*coloni*). Yet we do not have more detailed information about the conditions of slave cultivation and tenancy. "Nonetheless, the tendency is clear: it moved in the direction of an increase in the number of *coloni,* even if this kind of labor was not always easy to find (thus Pliny the Younger, *Epistulae* 3.19.7, also speaks of the *penuria colonorum,* the shortage of *coloni*)."[65]

Of greater importance were the (free) wage earners, above all at harvesttime. Their role is emphasized by Cato the Elder (234–149 B.C.E.) when in his agricultural handbook (*De agricultura* 1.3) he mentions among the requirements for the acquisition of a villa that a sufficient number of workers should be available in the near vicinity. Varro (b. 116 B.C.E.) recommends to his readers the employment of day laborers instead of slaves for unhealthy and dangerous work on the land, since the possible death of a day laborer was economically better than that of a slave (*Rerum rusticarum* 1.17.2). Wage earners were apparently needed only in larger agricultural units. In the smaller rural households, the division of work was determined by the organization of household, which in principle distinguished between the duties of men, women, and children (and possibly slaves). Men were involved throughout the year with the cultivation of the soil; women took care of meals, clothing, and the raising of children. At least at harvesttime, women and (older) children were naturally also drawn into work on the land. Additional help was provided by the balanced reciprocity of the individual households of a village.

This means the mutual assistance of village neighbors who helped each other out with material resources (for example, seeds), tools (also draft animals), and labor (cf. here also 2.2.2a "Reciprocity" below). Thus the smaller farms were family operations.

The Number of Workers and the Quantity of Goods
For the number of workers needed on the larger agricultural properties, Duncan-Jones has compiled the data from ancient writers.[66] According to Cato the Elder (*De agricultura* 10.1), an olive orchard of 240 jugers (ca. 150 English acres; 1 *iugerum* equals ca. 0.622 acre) required 13 workers: 1 overseer (*vilicus*), 1 woman head of household (*vilica*), 5 workers, 3 plowmen, 1 muleteer, 1 shepherd, and 1 swineherd. Wine production apparently required even more labor. A vineyard of 100 jugers (ca. 62 acres) needed a staff of 16 workers (*De agricultura* 11.1). The information from ancient authors on the average labor requirement in terms of land area cultivated by one worker varies between 7 and 10 jugers.[67] The land area named here can also serve as the average value for medium-sized operations.[68] Thus Horace, for example, had a small farm (*agellus*) of about 125 acres, on which 5 tenant families lived.[69] Even large landowners seldom controlled a giant contiguous estate (*latifundia*) but rather had a collection of more moderate holdings of about 150 to 300 jugers.[70] Thus, based on these numbers (see Table 1), the average farm would have kept only about 10 to 30 people occupied.

TABLE I: SIZE OF A FARM AND NUMBER OF WORKERS

	SIZE OF FARM	PRODUCT	NUMBER OF WORKERS
Cato the Elder	240 jugers (150 acres)	olives	13 people
Idem	100 jugers (62 acres)	wine	16 people
Average	7–10 jugers (4–6 acres)	mixed	1 person
Horace	200 jugers (125 acres)	mixed	5 families

D. WORK IN THE CITIES: ARTISANS AND MERCHANTS

We have already indicated that the ancient city was the center of consumption. For into the cities, as the residence of the rich, propertied upper stratum, flowed part of the needed agricultural goods as profit or taxes.[71] Naturally the lower classes in the cities were also dependent on agricultural production for their food. Yet the thesis advocated since Sombart and Weber, and especially by Finley,[72] that the ancient city was a place of consumption—in distinction to the medieval city, which served as a center of production—does not mean that in the cities there was neither craft nor trade. Rather, in the urban centers of the Roman empire there was a remarkable specialization of work.[73] In addition to artisans, merchants played an important economic role (as we will see). For coming into consideration more as consumers than as producers are the various service occupations: from teachers and doctors to barbers and workers in public institutions (such as baths). We must, however, also think of workers in urban administrations performing quasi-police functions (such as *lictors*) or financial duties. Their numbers also included slaves. In nearly all areas women were also employed (see Part Four).

Artisans

Urban working life was shaped above all by handicrafts, which in principle were always connected with small business. Well over one hundred specialized trades can be distinguished here. Naturally, on the one hand, this enormous specialization is an expression of highly developed skill, but on the other, it is also the result of training that is oriented toward rather narrow qualifications. The diversity of tasks that in our day are carried out by an ironworker were in ancient times divided among various individual vocations: "The *scutarius* makes shields, the *laternarius* lanterns, a *vascularius* vessels, the *gladiarius* swords, and a *cultrarius* knives."[74] Here we cannot discuss in detail the diversity within corresponding occupations. Without doubt there was a predominance of small businesses that as family operations perhaps employed one or two wage earners or slaves. Larger businesses, which are also often called factories, were the exception. We know, for example, that in Arezzo a certain Rasinius and a P. Cornelius owned businesses with 60 and 57 slaves, respectively.[75] In the larger operations the handicrafts could also produce considerable profit; in the smaller ones and especially in the smallest, however, one probably had to be satisfied with modest income. As a result, trade and business played a subordinate role and did not contribute substantially to the gross national product.[76]

Nonetheless, we must also recognize that a few cities drew a considerable part of their economic production from the handicrafts.[77] Certain cities were known for the products of special crafts. Cato the Elder writes in the second century:

> Tunics, togas, blankets, smocks and shoes should be bought in Rome; caps, iron tools, scythes, spades, mattocks, axes, harness, ornaments and small chains at Cales or Minturnae; spades at Venafrum, carts and sledges at Suessa and in Lucania, jars and pots at Alba and at Rome; tiles at Venafrum, oil mills at Pom-

peii and at Rufrius's yard at Nola; nails and bars at Rome; pails, oil urns, water pitchers, wine urns, and other copper vessels at Capua and at Nola; Campanian baskets, pulley ropes and all sorts of cordage at Capua, Roman baskets at Suessa and Casinum.[78]

Profit was hardly achievable through a technologically rationalized mass production. At best the exploitation of the labor of family members and slaves or day laborers could produce a (usually modest) result. At the same time, families and households strove for autonomy; that is, they tried to produce the goods needed for use and for consumption themselves. Thus small crafts doubtless prevailed. Products that were produced for "export" or at least had significance in the region and larger area were rarely found.

> In the transregional markets success was possible only for goods that were of high quality and whose manufacture required special skills and the knowledge of certain production techniques (glass from Syria, cloth from the East, ceramics from Arretium). Characteristic of the Roman economy is the fact that even in important production centers like Arretium, work places with more than fifty slaves were rare.[79]

In particular, pottery and textiles seem to have been produced in large quantities. Itinerant artisans—for example, the apostle Paul—promoted the spread of special skills and were welcomed as specialists. Handicrafts and business were at the same time connected with small business, which in larger operations was handled by people especially assigned to the task.

The Areas of Activity of Urban Workers
Naturally, the great building activity in the cities—the construction of private homes, public buildings (temples, amphitheaters), and other projects (bridges, aqueducts, streets)—required workers from a variety of occupations. This is attested, for example, by Plutarch (*Pericles* 12.4), who held public construction activity to be especially profitable for all kinds of tradesmen. Likewise, Herod the Great employed many people with his great building projects (for example, the Jerusalem temple). According to Josephus, 18,000 construction workers, who became unemployed after the completion of Herod's new temple project, were employed by Agrippa II to pave the streets of Jerusalem with marble.[80] This number is presumably exaggerated, for one of the greatest builders of antiquity, Crassus, employed only about 500 building experts and construction workers. Naturally, goldsmiths and silversmiths were needed for the furnishing of Herod's magnificent buildings.

Similarly, many people were occupied with the business of providing the population with the necessities of daily life: food (bakers, butchers, etc.), clothing (spinners, weavers, fullers, tanners, cobblers, etc.), houses (potters, carpenters, furniture makers, construction workers, etc.). Here we should also mention skilled artisans (for example, jewelers and potters) and those providing services (such as barbers and servants in bathhouses). The size of handicraft operations was also dependent on the size of a city, for example, in Rome:

> In providing food in the cities, bakeries were very important, for in the cities of the Imperium Romanum bread was the chief means of feeding the population; in the bakeries, not only was bread baked, but also grain was ground by rotary mills driven by donkeys. An impression of a large bakery in Rome is conveyed by the relief on the gravestone of Eurysaces: the making of bread was already divided into individual work processes and the work of specialized slaves. Slaves spent the whole day on a particular job: some operated the mills; others kneaded the dough and shaped the bread. The finished bread was carried by bearers to a scale, where it was turned over to the officials of the city of Rome. . . . Also evident on the Eurysaces monument is the differentiation between the working slaves and the overseers, who stand out because of their better clothing.[81]

The great bakery in Rome described here was without doubt an exception. Even in the realm of commerce, family businesses predominated, perhaps employing some slaves or free wage earners. The urban regions were supplied with necessary products by the resident artisans, and for this reason there was almost no transregional need for goods.

Merchants

We will go further into the realm of the exchange of goods in the next section. Here trade will be briefly mentioned solely as an area of activity of the urban organization of work. First, we will make a few observations on the ancient *evaluation* of trade.

Based on the text from Cicero quoted on page 25, we can infer clear prejudices regarding small traders and middlemen. Especially despised are the middlemen, because they "immediately resell what they buy from the wholesaler. They would not earn anything if they did not resort entirely to mendacity." For Cicero, no substantiation is needed for the disparagement of small traders. By contrast, "the capital-intensive wholesale business, which transports consumer goods from all over the world and honestly makes them available to the masses, is above reproach" and even to be praised. The term *work* itself is problematic in the realm of commerce. *Activity* is perhaps a more appropriate expression than *work*, for in antiquity the prejudice was widespread that the merchant did not actually accomplish work but rather raised the price of a product in a superfluous way. The interplay of supply and demand, which determines price according to the economic theory of marginal utility, was unknown to the ancients.[82] Trade was not work (in the sense of the Latin *labor* or the Greek *ponos*); rather, the troubles of merchants were seen to be at most in danger (say, in travels abroad, above all by sea) or in the possibility of business loss.[83] Small traders and middlemen were despised above all, but wholesalers were not judged positively in every case. Plato places wholesalers beside small traders (and innkeepers) but holds that trade in itself is meaningful and honorable when it is not misused for one's own profit (*Leg.* 918b–d). Suspicions of merchants as idlers who raised the price of a product without increasing its value were accompanied by ethnic prejudices. If foreign trade was based on "international" activities, contacts with foreign merchants promoted negative projections, which were applied to whole foreign populations, who were suspected of possessing the negative character traits connected with commerce. As early as Homer, the Phoenicians were suspect both as traders and as robbers (likewise in Herodotus); Caesar alleged that the Gauls especially worshiped Mercury, the god of commerce and thieves. The Syrians were also considered avaricious traders. Then in late antiquity the Jews also came under this suspicion, which has accompanied them down to the present.[84] The disparagement of allegedly avaricious and deceitful merchants corresponds to the idealization of so-called silent trade. Herodotus reports such trade between Carthaginians and inhabitants of the coastal area in "Libya." The Carthaginians put their products on the beach, returned to their ships, and sent smoke signals. Then the coastal residents came and on their part put down gold for the goods. When the amount was satisfactory, the Carthaginians took away the gold; the coastal residents, the goods (*Hist.* 4.196). Something similar is reported by Philostratus about trade between Ethiopia and Egypt (*Life of Apollonius* 6.2). Naturally, reality was a different matter.

Merchants and wholesalers (*emporos, mercator*) are to be fundamentally distinguished from small retailers and shopkeepers (*kapēlos, tabernarius*), above all in connection with occupations. (In addition, there were peddlers.) In general, wholesale trade was foreign trade. Nevertheless, local trade naturally defined everyday life. MacMullen estimates its share at "a good three-quarters of the value of all goods exchanged in the economy as a whole."[85] It took place in the towns and villages, but also in certain places in the country where farmers met on market days. Here, above all, women also seem to have been involved. Yet we also find them at the urban markets. In the cities there were, in addition to artisans who also carried on trade, specialized merchants who sold certain wares (textiles, ceramics, wooden objects).

The Importance of Trade

How important was trade? Naturally, it presupposes, on the one hand, a surplus of production not used by the producing unit and, on the other, a corresponding demand that is capable of paying. Yet large parts of the population seem to have existed in poverty. This mass poverty also meant, to be sure, that there could be no mass demand. Moreover, technological possibilities placed narrow restrictions on production in large quantities. Even researchers who give great importance to transregional trade do not posit an economically regulated exchange between, for example, agrarian regions and commercial centers of production.[86] In any case, transport and trade were feasible only for wares and goods that were severely lacking in certain regions—above all, naturally, in the cities. This was true for urban areas in regard to basic foods (grain and oil, as well as wine and salt). In addition, however, there was also a need for materials like metal and wood for building and burning. The urban regions were supplied with the most essential products by local workers, and therefore there was almost no transregional need for commercial goods. Thus the subordinate role of trade and commerce generally corresponds to its low social valuation, as already discussed. Neither merchants nor artisans normally belonged to the urban upper class.

2.2.2 Distribution: Reciprocity, Redistribution, Markets

Fundamentally there are three types of exchange; that is to say, we can distinguish three types of distribution or movement of goods and services.[87] Basic considerations regarding this topic have been presented above all by Polanyi (followed by Sahlins).[88] He distinguishes between *reciprocity, redistribution,* and *market exchange.*[89] Polanyi later adds to these three economic institutions the operation of the household (here we regard the distributive mechanisms within a household or clan as a form of family reciprocity). This division makes it possible to present the central distributive mechanisms of Mediterranean societies in the first century also as the foundation of the concomitant social inequality.

A. RECIPROCITY

The most elementary form of the exchange of goods is *reciprocity,* the exchange of gifts between individual persons, households (families), or clans (relatives). This network of mutual production among persons and social groups with comparable status rests ultimately on reciprocity (quid pro quo) and is not oriented toward profit (*balanced reciprocity*). Thus, in principle reciprocity presupposes symmetry or balance of exchange and is connected with a careful calculation of exchanged goods and services. Equivalents do not always have to correspond with each other directly but can also be granted the giver (on a delayed basis) through prestige or loyalty (say, in the relationship of patron and client). This form of exchange is called *general reciprocity.* If we can perceive a certain element of delay in the balance of quid pro quo in general reciprocity, balance is lacking altogether in *negative reciprocity,* which is ruled not by the ethic of the golden rule but by an interest in doing to another what one does *not* want done to oneself. This is the ethic of hostility against enemies and all groups of people with whom one is not in a reciprocal relationship.[90] Thus, for example, the form of balanced reciprocity within a small circle—the family, household, clan, and even neighbors—is not granted to strangers. Hence, relations with strangers are dominated by the *negative* form of reciprocity, in which self-interest and profit are permitted to dominate.

Reciprocity, naturally, especially shapes tribal societies, but it is also found in the societies of the Roman empire, above all in the rural regions in which a potentially endangered existence and a scarcity of monetary means favor reciprocal solidarity. It includes especially the exchange of (modest) goods and services between households and kinship groups.[91] In general, on the level of ideas this system corresponds to the consciousness of limited goods that are available in a manageable social form and which evoke social envy when, because of this limitation, a relatively rich neighbor possesses a greater share of goods.[92] A more or less rudimentary form of general reciprocity is also found in the social relationships of narrow kinship groups and of patrons and clients. The fundamental idea of the patron-client relationship is that a powerful personality (*patronus*) exerts his or her influence on dependent, lower persons (*clientela*) and in return can count on their loyalty in political or economic matters.

Thus, if we may generalize, reciprocity rules above all in rural areas, and beyond village and kinship solidarity, negative reciprocity with unrelated people and strangers makes possible a modest amount of profit.[93] The accompanying overview (Table 2) presents four forms of reciprocity (familial, balanced, general, and negative), names the potentially involved persons (or groups), and presents the possible expressions of solidarity and the most important ethical concepts and social forms.

B. REDISTRIBUTION

Whereas on the level of reciprocity we cannot really speak of the distribution of goods and services—and thus an economic dynamic can hardly develop—redistribution makes possible a new division and thus at the same time favors greater social inequality. *Redistribution* is based on the principle of a central or institutionalized gathering of goods and their (re)distribution. In its basic form, it is shaped by the division of commonly acquired yields from the hunt or the harvest. Yet as soon as, say, a chieftain controls the division, inequalities can arise. This institutionalization of control over distribution can then be transferred to centers of administration (temples, kings, property owners, tax collectors, etc.) and, in the form of rent, duties and taxes, tributes, tithes, and the like, develop into a system of levies guaranteed or implemented by the

TABLE 2: TYPES OF RECIPROCITY

Form of Solidarity	Ethical Concepts—Social Forms

Familial Reciprocity

household—kinship—clan (*oikos—syngeneis*)

brotherly love

Balanced Reciprocity

(same status, symmetrical relationship)

fellow villagers—neighbors—friends (*geitones—plēsion—philoi*)

general good deeds and borrowing	love of neighbor
(exchange of goods and services)	love of friend
invitations or formal contracts	doing good/kindness
as mutual agreements	(*kalon poiein/agathopoiein*)
buying/selling	hospitality
marriage	

General Reciprocity

(unequal status—asymmetrical relationship)

patron-client, teacher-student, rich-poor

general good deeds (but client cannot	patron-client
repay like with like, offers	allegiance/discipleship
homage and loyalty or political	
support or information, etc.)	
	compassion
	(*eleos/eleos poiein*)
	alms (*eleēmosynē*)
relationship to God/gods	love of God (*eusebeia/pistis*)

Negative Reciprocity

strangers—enemies (*xenoi—echtroi*)

	hospitality
	love of enemy

state, which are imposed on real and personal property, on people (head tax) and animals, and on services and the yields of productive work. The beneficiaries can be state and religious institutions or private individuals. For an agricultural society the process of redistribution means an increasing concentration of land ownership and wealth yet, conversely, an ever-growing number of poor and dependent tenants. To the degree that actual or legal power favors a few privileged individuals, there is a corresponding increase in social hierarchy, or the difference between top and bottom, and in antagonism between the classes. In the Mediterranean societies of the Roman empire, it was above all the redistribution system that established and stabilized the enormous concentration of *power and wealth* in the relatively small upper class in urban centers, but at the same time held the great mass of the population in poverty and made it ever poorer, especially in the country. The centers of the redistribution system—the Roman state itself, emperors and the imperial house, senators and nobility, *decurioni* in the cities, (large) leaseholders, and the like—were in principle also the landowners, who through leases and the administration of the farms controlled the possibility of a production that exceeded the subsistence needs of their households and brought supplementary profit on the market. Thus we may note with good reason that from the standpoint of the elite the dominant exchange system was redistribution. This means that the taxes and rents from the rural producers flowed into the cities and above all into the hands of the elite.[94] The annual state income under Emperor Vespasian, for example, was estimated to be around 1,200,000 to 1,500,000 sesterces.

C. MARKETS

Market exchange presupposes the organization and legal or authoritative guarantee for the exchange of resources, wares, work, services, and even real estate with the help of an equivalent value, usually money, and in principle also the use of writing. In principle, market exchange[95] is also connected with certain localities, although the term is generally an abstraction for something like an "exchange arena," a system that produces prices and regulates supply and demand. Markets are interested less in exchange itself than in the profit or advantage that participating buyers and sellers can (or believe they can) derive from the exchange. Hence it is above all economic interests that drive economic behavior here. Yet *in this sense* there were hardly any markets in the ancient societies of the Mediterranean area. Above all the purchase and sale of land was extremely restricted, since the right of ownership—whether by institutions or individuals—was as a rule passed on through administration (institutions) or inheritance (families). Significant changes in land ownership came about primarily through legacies and conquests but were also possible through the successive appropriation of the property of small farmers on account of their indebtedness. A *labor market* in the modern sense of the word did not exist in ancient societies, if one does not regard as such the slave markets and the seasonally conditioned employment of free wage earners (an example is Matt 20:1ff.). The demand for labor in rural areas was generally limited to harvesttime and came above all from the larger estates. The smaller house-

holds mobilized all their members and helped each other through the reciprocal exchange of workers. Even slave markets could hardly have had an economic importance because of the relatively high cost of slaves (Alföldy
calculates an average price of 800 to 2500 sesterces, depending on age, sex,
and training.)[96] The predominance of the subsistence economy, poor transportation conditions, and lack of buying power among the popular masses
also permitted only a minimal economic relevance of *product markets,* at
which only the few products not made at home had a chance of being mar-
keted.[97] Only the provisioning of the urban population with basic means of
nutrition constituted an important market factor and created a suction effect
by which the cities became the centers of consumption. Accordingly, there
was state oversight in the politically sensitive area of the food supply of cities.
This is described by Jones:[98]

> Economically, the most important interest of a normal city was to make sure
> that the basic means of nutrition, and especially bread, were offered on the mar-
> ket at reasonable prices. This was one of the most important duties of the
> *aedilis* or *agoranomos;* a number of interesting inscriptions from the market-
> place at Ephesus report on the prices that were usual for bread and oil under the
> successful *agoranomoi* "under whose oversight there were abundant and favor-
> able offerings." Sometimes the city authorities sought to control prices by
> decree. . . . Yet such methods seldom proved effective in the long term, and the
> cities usually tried more gentle, if also more expensive, methods. Thus it is occa-
> sionally reported that *agoranomoi* underbid the traders in that they themselves
> offered wine or oil under the market price and at their own loss; the cities also
> had . . . special funds and officials for the purchase of grain.

Thus even in this central area of market economic mechanisms, state
interventions (including the emperors' gifts of grain and subsidization of the
Roman population) made it impossible for a free interaction of market forces
to develop.

2.2.3 Money: Its Function and Its Worth

The direct exchange of goods for services, or payment in kind, is usually
called bartering. If, by contrast, money serves as a medium of exchange, or
taxes and other levies (including fines) are paid with money, one speaks of a
money economy.[99] Yet we should also note that both possibilities can exist
side by side, as was the case in the Roman empire. It has already been pointed out that in a certain sense the Roman empire was a unified monetary area,
and this facilitated the transfer of large sums of money between individual
regions. Yet this was not supported by any special financial or monetary decisions or instruments. The emperors merely ensured that counterfeiting was
prevented and that the metallic value of individual coins and their relation-

ship to each other remained more or less stable.[100]

A. COINS

The coins that were in circulation were not issued from a central location. Rather, they were made in a system of imperial, provincial, local, and counterfeit (or "barbarized") coinages. The kinds of Roman coins were *aureus* (gold), *denarius* (silver), *sesterce* and *dupondius* (brass), and *as* (copper). An aureus was equivalent on average to 25 denarii; a denarius was worth 4 sesterces; a sesterce, 2 dupondii, and a dupondius, 2 asses. In everyday life one calculated mostly in sesterces or denarii but especially needed dupondii and asses. As a reckoning unit the *quadrans* was also used; as the name suggests, it was equivalent to one fourth of an as, but this value was rarely minted.

Function

Money was not primarily a medium of exchange for daily use but a means of payment. It was also a means of preparing for the future and accumulating wealth, as well as measuring value.[101] For exchange and loans there were banks and lenders. Crawford has shown that money was used as a medium of exchange only in the cities of the empire, and that this was an "accidental consequence of the existence of money, not the result of state measures."[102] Therefore, among coin artifacts those of the smallest nominal value are rather rare. The minting of coins itself also occurred not for economic reasons but in order to enable the Roman state and the emperor to make necessary payments—for example, to the army. And they, conversely, then got this money back again as payment for taxes and other levies; that is, the coinage of money had "financial reasons."[103] Thus it would be mistaken to connect the minting of Roman coins with monetary or economic intentions. If there were monetary interests at all, these were the personal interests of the emperors.[104] In a special way, the existence of money benefited the buying, selling, and trading of real estate, whose value could be determined in sums of money. Also for tribute payments, taxes, and perhaps also rents and fines, money served as a measure of value. Similarly, the members of the *ordines* (senators, noblemen, city officials) were divided into tax classes with certain minimal income, which was measured in money (sesterces) (see pp. 73–74 below). Money was kept in a money bag on the belt or on a cord around the neck or arm, or at home in a box, basket, sack, or urn.[105]

The Circulation of Money

From Pompeii, which fell victim to an eruption of Vesuvius in 79 C.E., we know something about the normal *circulation of money* in a city of the Roman empire. The coins found near the bodies and in houses give us an interesting picture of normally present monetary resources as well as the social situation in Pompeii. Twenty-six discoveries vary approximately between 1000 and 10,000 sesterces. Since the *locations* of these caches indicate wealthy citizens, one can infer that the normal money supply of rich (!) Pompeiians had an average value of between 1000 and 3000 sesterces. Only a few exceeded that range. The highest amount found came to 9448 sesterces. In order to give some understanding of the value of these sums, we offer here a brief preview of our calculations of the cost of living given below (see 3.5.1b). With the highest amount of money (which corresponds to ca. 2500 denarii), the average family in the country could have lived about 10 years. An elevated living standard for an urban household with 4 slaves—which Juvenal thought a worthy goal—could have been financed by this sum for half a year. About 60 other finds contained for the most part no more than the value of 200 sesterces. This could have supported an average family in the country for about 3 months. Yet the most numerous finds show that the average inhabitant of Pompeii seldom possessed more than the value of 30 sesterces. "Poor people—and there were many of them—had only a few asses [coins] in their purse; this had to suffice for their food."[106]

B. THE VALUE OF MONEY: COSTS AND PRICES

Another way of perceiving the *value* of these sums is to compare them with some prices and costs in Pompeii. From Pompeiian graffiti we know the price of a *modius* (6503 kilograms) of wheat: 30 asses, that is, almost 2 denarii. A tunic cost 15 sesterces; a mule, 520 sesterces (130 denarii). Two slaves cost 5048 sesterces (1262 denarii). From a kind of household ledger Etienne[107] has also calculated the cost of living of a family of 3, including a slave. The result is an average daily expense of 25 asses. If one extrapolates this figure to one year (365 days), the result, for the cost of living of a 3-person family, is an annual outlay of around 2280 sesterces, that is, 570 denarii. This total amount confirms what can be derived from the purchases themselves and the cost of living calculated by us (see 3.5.1b), namely, "that here we are dealing with Pompeiians who lived in modest circumstances."[108] Measured against this, the caches of the wealthy can be called rather realistic. An inscription from the imperial period (*ILS* 7478) from Aesernia (central Italy) gives us an idea of the prices travelers had to pay for overnight lodging: "Hostess, let's add this up. You have one *sextarius* [about a pint] of wine and bread: one as; [meat]: two asses—OK—one girl: eight asses—also OK—hay for the mule: two asses—this animal will be the end of me."

Duncan-Jones gives an outstanding overview of the various prices and costs in the Roman empire as a whole, differentiated according to regions and individual products or other values, services, and expenses.[109] Here we can offer only a few examples. The prices of slaves in Rome and Italy were apparently extremely variable.[110] A particularly high slave price presupposed certain abilities. Calvisius Sabinus, for example, owned 11 slaves; each of them knew by heart the work of a Greek poet and was supposed to have cost 100,000 sesterces (25,000 denarii). By contrast, Pliny the Elder (*Nat. Hist.* 9.67) names a usual price of 2700 sesterces (675 denarii) for a slave cook in Rome. For uncultivated land suitable for growing grapes, Columella, in his work on agriculture (*De re rustica* 3.3.8), mentions a price of 1000 sesterces (250 denarii).[111] Especially large sums were named for the expenses of holding games (sometimes as much as 200,000 sesterces), the erection of statues (up to 100,000 sesterces), the burial costs of wealthy people (up to 100,000 sesterces), and the financing of public buildings and streets (up to 2,000,000 sesterces).

TABLE 3: SAMPLE COSTS AND PRICES*

1 loaf of bread	1 as
1 liter of wine	ca. 1 as
meat at an inn	2 asses
spices from the East	
1 lb. ginger	6 denarii
1 lb. pepper	4–15 denarii (according to quality)[112]
1 lb. cinnamon	10 denarii
1 lb. incense (*tus*)	3–6 denarii (including 2 denarii for shipping and customs)[113]
simple dishes	1–2 asses
1 tunic	ca. 4 denarii
1 outer garment	12–20 denarii
1 mule	130 denarii
hay for a mule	2 asses
prostitute	8 asses
1 *iugerum* of land[114]	250 denarii
1 *modius* of wheat	almost 2 denarii
its shipping costs	16 denarii (for 50 land miles or 1250 sea miles)
slaves	600–25,000 denarii
burial of the rich	up to 25,000 denarii
erecting a statue	up to 25,000 denarii
holding games	up to 50,000 denarii
a ship of 400 tons	50,000–80,000 denarii
financing a public building	up to 500,000 denarii

*Note: Roman coins included *aureus* (gold), *denarius* (silver), *sesterce* and *dupondius* (brass), and *as* (copper). An aureus was equivalent on average to 25 denarii; a denarius was worth 4 sesterces; a sesterce, 2 dupondii; and a dupondius, 2 asses.

2.3 The Characteristics of Ancient Mediterranean Economics

We will now expand in some detail the foregoing comments about economic life. Since the economy of ancient societies was almost purely agricultural, it will receive the most attention. In one subsection on agriculture (2.3.1) we will discuss property and the concentration of property, leasing, and profits from agricultural concerns, and in another the problem of the tax burden and living and working conditions (2.3.2).

2.3.1 Agriculture

A. REAL PROPERTY AND THE CONCENTRATION OF OWNERSHIP

The land of Israel in the time of Herod the Great is calculated to have had a total area of about 2,500,000 acres. About two-thirds of these are assumed to have been agriculturally usable.[115] This would yield approximately 1,700,000 acres of usable agricultural land. Thus one may assume that Jewish Palestine must indeed have been a land shaped predominantly by an agricultural economy. These modern calculations also agree with a comment by Josephus (*Ap.* 1.12): "We Jews of Palestine neither inhabit a coastal land nor do we have the joy of trade and the concomitant intercourse with foreigners. Rather, our cities lie far from the sea, and we occupy ourselves primarily with the cultivation of our excellent soil." If we extrapolate the numbers for the land of Israel to the whole Roman empire of the first century c.e., we can see the enormous importance of agriculture. We may also presume that more than 90 percent of the population lived in rural areas. Not only did the largest part of the population have to be fed here, but also the vast majority of workers were employed in agriculture. Estimates of the share of agriculture in the gross national product vary, but they confirm its overwhelming importance. Ben-David calculates about 70 percent for Palestine. For the later imperial period, Jones estimates the ratio of the economic importance of agriculture to that of trade and manufacturing to be twenty to one.[116] This number is perhaps too high and is not valid until late antiquity.[117] Yet even if we assume only that agriculture in the whole Roman empire, as in Palestine, produced 70 percent of the goods and services, its predominant economic importance is evident. Agriculture was, moreover, the most important basis for wealth and the object of financial investment.[118] Real estate is presented as more economically certain and of higher moral value than, say, trade. This is true of Cato the Elder in his work *De agricultura.* Columella also confirms the superiority of agriculture over trade.[119] This economic activity was more certain and more promising in terms of social aspirations, since over the long term it was possible for freed slaves who became wealthy to rise into the upper class through the purchase of offices of honor or through marital ties with the local aristocracy.[120] It is true that family operations by far predominate, and therefore the household as fundamental economic and social unit, which is essentially based on a subsistence economy, possessed fundamental importance in the ancient economy. Nevertheless, the social and economic pressure toward the expansion of property was doubtless an important economic factor, which at the same time led to an increasingly unjust division of land and concomitant economic opportunities.[121] More and more small farmers lost their property; free farmers became dependent tenants (*geōrgos, colonus,* Heb. *aris*). The socio-economic tendencies of a developmental period of five centuries are summarized by MacMullen in three words: "Fewer have more."[122]

Since land was the basis of wealth, the increased well-being of the wealthy class was possible only through greater possessions of land. Yet here one must make distinctions within the upper class: "1. Local gentry held land more or less entirely in their region of origin. 2. Middle-ranking senators and equestrians of municipal background had, on top of their local estates, one or more additional centres of property. 3. The richest members of the Roman elite possessed a complex of properties in Italy and abroad."[123] Pliny the Elder says that six men owned half of (North) Africa (*Nat. Hist.* 18.35). From information about Leontini in Sicily (in Cicero *Verr.* 2.3.113), Duncan-Jones has calculated that in the year 73 B.C.E., the 70,000 jugers (44,000 acres) of available land belonged to a total of 84 farmers. Thus the average landholding was 830 jugers (over 500 acres). During Verres's time as Roman governor, he reduced the number of landowning farmers to 32, thereby enormously increasing the concentration of property.[124] Duncan-Jones assumes that the largest estates in Leontini comprised between 7000 and 8500 jugers (ca. 5000 acres).[125] In Italy, Greece, North Africa, and Egypt a few landowners held gigantic estates.[126] Lucius Domitius Ahenobarbus (49 B.C.E.) gave land in Spain to an army of around 10,000 soldiers at the rate of 40 jugers per soldier; hence he must have owned at least 400,000 jugers of land.[127] Pliny the Elder (*Nat. Hist.* 33.135) tells about a freedman named Isodorus, who claimed to own 3600 yoke of oxen. With them he could have plowed about 360,000 jugers of land.[128] (On the agricultural lands in Palestine see pp. 110–11.)

B. PROFIT FROM AGRICULTURE (BOSCOREALE)

An example from Campagna shows how lucrative the profit from agriculture was—especially in vinegrowing. Etienne[129] estimates that the famous Campagna estate, the Villa Boscoreale, comprised agricultural lands of around 60 to 100 jugers, 58 of which were in vineyards. The yearly production of wine was 93,800 liters, which, based on the price of the lowest quality of wine, was worth 52,500 sesterces. Yet it was probably a question of a wine of highest quality, and thus one must multiply the income by three. If one includes other yields (1000–1500 liters of olive oil), then the yearly income would come to around 200,000 sesterces (50,000 denarii). Hence a piece of land of about 60 acres used primarily for wine growing would have produced about 800 denarii or 3200 sesterces per acre per year or about 2000 sesterces per year for one juger. According to Columella, the purchase price for a juger of land suitable for wine growing was 1000 sesterces.[130] Thus the land of the Villa Boscoreale was acquired for 100,000 sesterces and was an extremely profitable piece of property. For agriculture in Campagna, Etienne calculates a net profit of 15 percent and estimates a price of 100,000 sesterces for a medium-sized estate.[131]

The largest landowners of the Roman empire in the first century were the emperors themselves, who through confiscation or inheritance acquired gigantic landholdings in Italy and in the provinces. In addition, the richest men of the empire had tremendous fortunes, some of which were worth 400 million sesterces—for example, Cornelius Lentulus and Narcissus, a freedman of the emperor Claudius. The philosopher Seneca amassed 300 million sesterces.[132] The freedman C. Caecilius Isidorus is supposed to have owned "a vast area of arable land and pasturage. On his death in 8 B.C.E. Isidorus bequeathed 3600 pairs of oxen, 257,000 other stock and 4116 slaves, 60 million sesterces in cash."[133] Crassus's landholdings alone are valued at 48 million denarii.[134] Yet even big landowners like Seneca disapprove such large possessions. Nevertheless, the increasing concentration of possessions in the country seldom led to the creation of gigantic, contiguous landed estates (*latifundia*). Even the wealthy commonly owned only "one substantial property" among many small holdings.[135] Because even the real estate of the rich was often a collection of small farms, its cultivation could only be carried out by slaves or tenants.

C. LEASING

The leasing (*locatio/conductio*) of land to free farmers steadily increased from the middle of the first century.[136] The presumed reasons were, on the one hand, the lack of slaves and, on the other, the diminished interest of landowners in troubling themselves with business.[137] It is possible that the *colonus* himself hired the additional workers (slaves, free wage earners). Yet this could also have been done by the owner himself, who kept the lessees under control with an overseer or other personnel (*procurator/actor*).[138] More frequently, a *colonus* and his family probably ran a small farm alone. There were various forms of lease. Either a fixed amount of rent was agreed upon contractually, independent of the harvest's yield, or with the *colonus partiarius* a share of the harvest was determined—say, one-third.[139] From the viewpoint of the landowner, tenants were unreliable people, who were often behind on their rent. Yet the shortage of lessees also compelled caution in the collection of arrears. This situation is clearly evident in a letter of Pliny in which he tells of his intention to purchase a large estate. Although the purchase is advisable because the land is extremely fruitful, Pliny hesitates to acquire the estate:

> This fortunate condition of the soil is offset, however, by the low pro-
> ductivity of the tenants. For the former owner took legal action against
> them more than once and thereby reduced the arrears of the *coloni* for a
> time, but this exhausted their resources for the future and led to new
> increases in their arrears. Thus I would have to replace them with slaves,
> which would cost me more than simple folk, for neither I nor anyone
> else anywhere use forced labor [shackled slaves]. . . . Now you must
> know how cheaply I can probably acquire the estate: for 3 million ses-
> terces, not because it was once worth 5 million, but because, as a con-
> sequence of the shortage of tenants and the general unfavorability of the
> time, the income from estates—and therefore their price—has
> declined.[140]

A graphic example of a landowner's problem with proper accounting in the administration of an estate is also offered by the parable of the dishonest manager (Luke 16:1-9). The story tells of a property manager (the Greek word is *oikonomos*) whose rich master is informed that the manager is misap-propriating the property.[141] The rich landowner has the manager come to him and demands an accounting. He intends to dismiss the manager, who is per-haps a slave (*vilicus*). In any case, the manager finds himself in a situation of being totally without means and socially insecure. For the parable presuppos-es that after his dismissal, he will have no means and will face the alternative of digging or begging. That is, he must face the possibility of joining the ranks of toiling rural slaves or wage earners, or of fleeing the estate and eking out a living through begging. In order to escape this unpleasant choice, the manag-er plans a bit of trickery. Together with certain debtors of his master, he manipulates their bills and reduces their debts considerably.[142] Accordingly, a debtor who owed 100 jugs (*batoi*—one bath=ca. 40 liters) of oil now owes only 50; another must repay 80 *koroi* of wheat (one *koros*=ca. 400 liters) instead of 100.[143] One hundred baths of oil would be almost 40 hectoliters, and if the average yield of an olive tree was, say, 25 liters, the debtor would have borrowed the yield of 160 olive trees. The 100 *koroi* of wheat would be approximately 400 hectoliters or 1200 hundredweight of grain. If we figure, say, 12 hundredweight of wheat an acre, the result would be a cultivated area of 100 acres. In any case, here it is a question of considerable sums, and thus the intention of the *oikonomos* to obligate the two debtors, so that they would welcome him into their homes, seems entirely plausible. The parable of the wicked tenants (Mark 12:1ff. par.) also describes, in exaggerated fashion, the difficulties of landowners in the collection of rents. Here we apparently have a lease on shares. The owner of the vineyard presumably has slaves supervising the harvest, but they then want to take his share too. In principle, the same conditions prevailed in Palestine as elsewhere in the Roman empire (see 4.1).

If from the landowners' viewpoint there were problems collecting their share from the leases, so the tenants, for their part, had problems especially in producing such sums. They were financially or economically dependent on the landlord, even if they were not slaves in the legal sense. In this connection, Garnsey and Saller refer to an inscription[144] that describes the conditions in one imperial domain in Africa. It reveals that subtenants were exploited by the main leaseholders and not only had to pay their rents but also had to make their labor available beyond the period agreed upon. When they defended themselves against this, they were seized by soldiers, who had been sent against them by the imperial governor, beaten, chained, and tortured. Those treated in this way are also supposed to have included Roman citizens. In another example, there is, among the Oxyrhynchus Papyri, a lease contract from the year 87/88 C.E. that details such an agreement and demonstrates above all the disadvantages for the tenants. In this case the land lease was for the cultivation of radishes (from whose seed oil was pressed in Egypt). It is notable that the tenant had to pay the rent even if the crops failed, and he was threatened with a considerable penalty. A woman is named as lessor, who is also the owner of the land, but she can take legal action only with her husband (as her *kyrios,* her legal spokesman):

> Hierakiaina, daughter of Herod, from Oxyrhynchus, with her husband Apollonios, son of Apollonios, grandson of Aunes, as spokesman, leases to Heras, son of Harmiysis, grandson of Mylos, from the village of the Syrians, descendant of Persians, for the present seventh year of the emperor Caesar Domitianus Augustus Germanicus, all the irrigated arourae from the farmland around [the town of] Nesla belonging to her, in order to sow them with radishes for a rent of two artabs per aroura on the basis of [the results of the new] measurement according to right-angled lines. The lease rent is not affected by any danger. The public taxes for the land are the obligation of Hierakiaina, who shall also enjoy the fruits of the land until the rent is satisfied. When the lease agreement is fulfilled, the lessee shall pay Hierakiaina the lease rent in the month of Payni of the same year at the threshing floor of Nesla in fresh, pure, unadulterated, and sifted radish seed, measured in the completely filled four-choenix measure of the lessee, which lies above the serapis measure. If he does not do this, he shall pay her one and a half times what he owes her as penalty . . .[145]

Thus crop failures were the burden of the lessee. The catastrophic consequences of such crop failures are reported to us by Josephus.[146] He describes situations in which people have neither clothing nor seed for the next year.[147] Most of the famines attested by Josephus fall in the first century B.C.E., but there is also a report of a great famine under Claudius in the year 46–47 C.E.. Thus we can generalize that in years of crop failure, farm families starved. Yet we must also realize that not even good harvest years provided sufficient provisions, if we assume that a minimum field of seventeen acres was probably necessary to feed a peasant family of six to nine people (on this see pp. 80–81). In any case, the overwhelming majority of small farmers seem to have been able at best to eke out their own subsistence. Yet we do not know the details here. Small farmers have left us no literary artifacts. In addition, the boundary between free small farmers, tenants, and rural wage earners is hard to draw. Even free small farmers were available to large landowners as a labor reserve at harvesttime.

2.3.2 The Burdening of the Population

THE PROVISIONING OF THE ROMAN MILITARY
AND THE POPULATION OF ROME

The major part of state expenditures—for, among other things, the military and grain for the *plebs* in Rome—was controversial because of the taxation of agriculturally usable land in all the provinces, with the exception of Italy. The Roman soldiers in particular had to be fed in each of the provinces.[148] At the time of Emperor Augustus, there were about 300,000 legionnaires and auxiliary troops under arms. Their basic rations of grain, wine, and meat had to be provided, wherever possible, in the regions where the military was stationed. For 300,000 soldiers with a daily need of one kilogram of grain per person, Garnsey and Saller (1987, 89) calculate an annual requirement of around 100,000 tons of grain for the military. That corresponds to a quantity of grain equal to 15 million *modii*. This amount of grain would correspond to an approximate need of 600,000 to 800,000 jugers or 375,000 to 500,000 acres of land for the basic provisioning of the military with grain. For comparison, Galilee had approximately 125,000 acres of arable land. Thus just for the provisions of the Roman military, an area of about three to four times that of Galilee would have to have been available. However one wants to estimate the numbers, the Roman military meant a great additional burden on the host localities and their rural environment.

The provisioning of the urban population of Rome with the basic means of nourishment was also an economic and political problem. This is shown by an interesting number game, which we offer here in a very simplified form.[149] Rome had about one million inhabitants. In terms of wheat, the food necessary to maintain the Roman population amounted to 200,000 tons a year. This presupposes a daily need of only 1700 calories. At least 200 kilograms of wheat per person per year is used to achieve this caloric value. Thus the provisioning of the population of the capital city with grain would require at least twice the quantity needed for the military. And since the provisioning of both the military and the Roman population[150] had political priority, for this purpose alone approximately 1,500,000 acres of agricultural land in the Roman empire had to be cultivated and to produce about 45 million *modii* of grain. Josephus (*War* 2.38ff.) notes that North Africa covered the grain needs of Rome for eight months, and Egypt took care of the remaining four months. These quantities in themselves were already a great burden on agricultural production capacities, even if the grain needs for Rome and the military were only partly required as a tax paid in kind (*frumentum, annona*).

B. COMPULSORY LEVIES

At times the compulsory taxes for the military were demanded with great harshness. Tacitus's father-in-law Agricola carried out a more moderate collection of compulsory levies in Britain, according to the portrayal by his son-in-law. From this encomium to the father-in-law we learn something about the chicanery of the military (*Agricola* 19.4):

> He [Agricola] moderated the raising of grain and taxes through a balanced allocation of the demands, and he curtailed what was invented only for profit and was harder to bear than the tax itself. For as an insult the people were compelled to sit in front of the locked grain storage bins and, moreover, to buy their own grain and pay a high price for it; detours and distant districts were set, so that the communities had to deliver to remote and inaccessible areas instead of to nearby winter storage, and thus what was available for all became profit for a few.

On this text Büchner comments:

> The farmers who did not have sufficient grain had to purchase grain themselves for delivery to the army. . . . In the process they were further harrassed in that they were made to wait in front of the state barns. And they were required, paradoxically, to atone for the chicanery with money, as if they had incurred a debt.[151]

If this chicanery is related to Roman Britain, we also have in the beginning of the second century complaints about the high and unjust burdening of the population of the land of Israel through the *annona*.[152] Yet it was only one part of the burden that the population had to bear. In fact, the little people were oppressed by a conglomeration of compulsory levies and duties. In this connection, Stenger[153] refers to a statement of Rabbi Jacob ben Jose (*Pesiq. R.* 10): "Thus is the dominion of Esau [that is, Rome]. It collects the *annona*, but before the *annona* is collected, we have the head tax. This is still being raised, and the recruitment levy is already coming." We may also compare here a text from Tacitus (*Agricola* 31.1), which mentions forced labor in addition to the tax levies. Tacitus credits these critical remarks about Rome to Calgacus, the head of the army in Britain: "Estates and wealth become tribute (*tributum*); the annual output of the land becomes a yield tax (*frumentum*); bodies themselves and hands, with blows and insults, are used to make forests and swamps passable."

C. FORCED LABOR

The forced labor of the native population was demanded for public works (building roads, waste water disposal) and obligations to the military (for example, transportation duties). Incidentally, Matt 5:41 ("if anyone forces you to go one mile, go also the second mile") and the compelling of Simon of Cyrene to carry the crosspiece of the cross for Jesus (Mark 15:21) reflect these compulsory duties (*angareuein*). For in general, not only was the labor of people and animals drawn on for forced service, but the populace often had to pay the costs of public building activity:

> The construction and maintenance of the roads that connected all the important places in the gigantic Roman empire with each other, and which also involved many artificial structures such as bridges and viaducts, were paid for by the resident population. The state contributed funds only in the rarest cases and then only in Italy. The repair costs for a Roman mile (1.5 km) in Italy amounted to over 100,000 sesterces.[154]

Yet direct and indirect taxes oppressed the people most.

D. TAXES

The direct taxes alone were considerable and led especially the small farmers to unreasonable burdens and thereby contributed to their increasing indebtedness, which could finally have been followed by the sale of their modest property or even to indebted slavery. Especially graphic is the situation of the populace in the land of Israel (for details see Chapter 4).

The poor rural population in particular fell victim to excessive taxation. Their situation in the first century C.E. is graphically described by Philo (*Spec. Leg.* 3.159ff.):

> So recently a man near us, who was summoned to the tax collector and was in arrears probably out of poverty, fled out of fear of unbearable penalties; his wife, children, parents, and all other relatives were taken away by force, beaten, mistreated, and forced to suffer all kinds of shameful acts of violence, so that they would betray the fugitive or pay his debts—neither of which they could do, the former because they did not know where he was, and the latter since they were no less poor than the fugitive. He [the tax collector] did not release them until

he had punished their bodies with instruments of torture and torment and taken their lives through outrageous means of killing: he tied cords to a basket filled with sand, hung this heavy load on their necks, and placed them in the market under the open sky, so that they were driven to despair by the terrible pressure of the punishments heaped upon them, by wind and sunburn, by shame before those passing by, and by the load with which they were burdened; others, however, who had to witness this punishment, felt the pain in advance. Some of the latter, who saw sharper with their souls than with their eyes and felt themselves mistreated in the person of the others, ended their lives ahead of time through sword or through poison or through rope, since death without torment seemed to them a good thing in their misfortune.

Similar cruelties against tax debtors in Asia Minor are also reported by Plutarch (*Lucullus* 20). For the later period (end of the third century) Lactantius (*De mort. pers.* 23) describes for us the processes of tax registration (*census*) and their consequences:

The misfortune and misery generally began first through the head and property taxes, which were established at the same time for all provinces and cities. The crowd of tax officials spread everywhere and turned everything into an uproar. There were images of horror, as in the attack of enemies and the leading away of prisoners. Fields were measured by the clod; grapevines and trees were counted. Every kind of domestic animal was recorded; for people, the number of heads was noted. In the cities urban and rural people were herded together. All the squares were overflowing with crowds of servants. Everyone was there with children and slaves. Torture and beatings resounded: sons were tortured against the fathers, the most loyal slaves against their masters, wives against husbands. If everything else failed, the owners were tortured against themselves, and if pain triumphed, property that did not exist was recorded. Neither age nor fragility got any consideration. The ill and infirm were dragged in and the age of individuals estimated. Years were added to children and taken away from old people. Everyone was full of misery and sadness. . . . Nevertheless, the official assessors were not trusted, and others were always sent after the first, as if they could find still more, and the initial figures were always doubled. For if the later ones did not find anything, they added something arbitrarily in order not to have come in vain. In the meantime domestic animals decreased in number and people died off. This did not change the fact that taxes also had to be levied for the dead. In short, one could no longer live free of charge or even die. Only the beggars remained, and nothing could be collected from them. Misery and misfortune had protected them against every kind of harm. But look! The kindhearted man [meaning Emperor Galerius, who ordered this imperial census of 293–310] had mercy even on these people, in order to bring their distress to an end. He had them all brought together, put on ships, and sunk in the sea. How compassionate of the man to want to help all the wretched under his dominion! While he wanted to keep anyone from evading

taxes under the pretext of being without property, he has, against every commandment of humanity, killed a large number of really poor people.

D. LIVING AND WORKING CONDITIONS

The vast majority of the rural populace in antiquity lived on the fine line
between hunger and assurance of subsistence.[155] The reasons for this are to be
found in fields that, on average, were much too small, the catastrophic consequences of crop failures, and above all in the overtaxation and overindebtedness of small farmers. Especially the simple rural people—that is, the great
majority of the population as a whole—apparently lived with constant concern about achieving the means of survival. Jesus' famous text in Matt 6:25ff.
("do not worry about your life"; cf. Luke 12:22ff.) must be understood against
this background. There were "in most parts of the empire masses of very poor
peasants without land or means, who sought to assure their existence as day
laborers and seasonal workers on the estates of wealthy farmers, as well as
major landowners, and on the large landed estates."[156] Something can be
learned about the miserable living conditions of many ancient people from a
writing of the physician Galen, *On the Healthy and Unhealthy Characteristics
of Foods* (7.749ff.). This text also shows that especially the simple people in the
country lived on the edge of or even under a minimal existence:

> Famines, which for a number of years in an unbroken series have affected the
> many peoples subject to the Romans, have clearly shown all those who have not
> completely lost their minds what an important role the consumption of
> unhealthy food has played in the occurrence of diseases. For with many of the
> peoples subject to the Romans—say, among the city dwellers—it was custom-
> ary immediately after the harvest to gather and store enough grain for the
> whole year, and to turn over to the people in the country what was left over, for
> example, various legumes, and a large part of these also flowed into the city. In
> the winter the landowner consumed the legumes and consequently in the
> spring had to resort to unhealthy foods; they ate twigs and shoots from trees
> and bushes, as well as bulbs and roots of indigestible plants; they filled them-
> selves with wild plants and also cooked fresh grass.

Galen (b. 129 C.E.) seems to condemn the behavior of rural people as fool-
hardy conduct and poor planning. Yet his text shows that here it is less a problem of proper planning and healthy conduct of life than the catastrophic food
situation of the rural populace. Their "unhealthy" nourishment with twigs
and fresh grass in spring makes it clear that the provisions obviously lasted
only through the winter. In addition, we may presuppose that the majority of
the *urban* population was also poor. It was a problem just to provide them
with grain, their basic means of nourishment, at an affordable price.[157] We
may, however, also assume from this text of Galen that the masses of residents

in the cities did not live on the verge of hunger. This need was apparently met by the magistrates—especially the "market overseers" (*agoranomoi*)—in order to forestall social unrest. The Roman city population in particular seems to have profited from this politically sensitive situation. Perhaps one can generalize that the living conditions in the urban centers in the western part of the Roman empire, and especially in Rome itself (which again and again provisioned itself with grain from Egypt and North Africa), were to some degree bearable. Yet we must also realize that in the eastern parts of the empire, even in cities, the impoverishment of large groups of people continually increased.

Even the working conditions were generally miserable. Sometimes heavy and extremely heavy manual labor was performed, which was detrimental to one's health. Work was also done at night. Slaves in particular suffered under bad treatment. Apuleius (*Metamorphoses* 9.12) describes the situation of slaves in a bakery:

> How many of the people there were marked all over with welts, their backs cut to shreds, more shaded than covered with rags! Some had still thrown a small scrap over their private parts, but most were clothed in such a way that their nakedness was not thereby reduced. What I did not see of people branded, half shorn, chained at the feet with rings! Pale, they came in like shadows. Their eyelashes were singed by the smoke and steam of the oven; they could hardly see out of their eyes. And like fighters in battle covered with dust, they were powdered from head to foot with flour and ashes, and the dirt made them totally unrecognizable.

In the following chapter we will take an even closer look at the social situation of impoverished people.

3

STRATIFICATION AND THE SOCIAL SITUATION IN ANCIENT MEDITERRANEAN SOCIETIES

This chapter contains five main sections. First, the social differentiation of ancient societies will be presented from the viewpoint of some ancient authors (3.1). Then we will discuss the criteria of a modern stratigraphy (3.2) and present our own stratification model (3.3). Finally, we will sketch the social situation of the elite or upper stratum (3.4) and the masses or lower stratum (3.5).

3.1 Social Differentiation in the View of Ancient Authors

Before we go into modern stratification analyses of Mediterranean societies, we first want to sketch briefly the judgments of the social hierarchy by some ancient contemporaries. In general, the sources present only the *view of the elite and of men*.[1] About the views of the broad masses of the population or of women we know precious little.[2] A few examples will suffice to make clear the most important factors in the antique evaluation of social differences. According to Philo of Alexandria[3] noble origin (*eugéneia*), combined with wealth, honor, and office, as well as health and beautiful form, enjoyed the highest regard, even if philosophers repeatedly focused on the greater importance of the virtues over such external matters. Paul also reflects this widespread standpoint when he names the powerful (*dynatoí*) and noble-born (*eugeneís*) as examples of the highest social esteem (1 Cor 1:26).[4] Aelius Aristides expresses "social division with the oppositions rich/poor, great/small, esteemed/unknown, and noble/ordinary."[5] Comparable is the judgment found in the book of Sirach.[6] The attitudes of two ancient authors of the first century will be examined more closely.

A. JOSEPHUS'S VIEW OF THE SOCIAL HIERARCHY

The social differentiations evident in the work of the Jewish historian Josephus are typical of the attitudes of the elite. His fundamental distinction in Jewish society is oriented around the opposition of king or royal house and priests on the one hand, and the people as a whole (*laos*) or especially the simple man or simple woman (*idiōtēs*) on the other.[7] Above all, however, he is interested in the social elite, whom he characterizes with words like *powerful* (*dynatos*) and the closely linked *rich* (*plousios/euporos*). The mass of the population is, by contrast, *weak* (*adynatos/asthenēs*) and *poor* (*aporos/endeēs;* more rarely *penēs/ptōchos*). Naturally, for him the rich and powerful are also especially valuable, prominent or esteemed, and educated personalities (often paraphrased with *axios* or even *episēmos/ouk asēmos*). The masses, who can show only common ancestry, remain unknown (*asēmos*). In addition to the royal house, Josephus includes among the prominent above all the priestly families of Jerusalem. They are distinguished by land ownership, by political and military power, and also by special clothing, choice foods, education (including knowledge of the Torah), and their rhetorical abilities. By contrast, the masses (*plēthos*), the common people, are uneducated, unmannered, unintelligent, and cowardly.[8] Josephus's social attitudes can be summed up and clarified with a single example. In his *Antiquities* (17.278) he writes about a certain Athronges, who sought power as a social bandit (cf. p. 177). But this Athronges neither had important and esteemed ancestors nor was he rich and powerful (only physically strong); in a word, he was a shepherd. Thus for Josephus also, power, wealth, and esteem (based above all on ancestry) characterize the elite.

B. JUVENAL'S VIEW OF THE SOCIAL HIERARCHY

In principle, the satirist Juvenal, who himself probably belonged to the Roman equestrians, shared this evaluation of the social hierarchy. Yet he held that in his time a social transformation had occurred. Previously, (ethnic) ancestry, (noble) birth, esteem, personal freedom, and education had greater importance for a person's social position than property and income. In his time, however, the latter factors played a decisive role. The rich stood at the top of the social ladder, completely independent of their origin, birth, degree of freedom, and occupation. By contrast, the poor stood at the bottom of the social order, entirely independent of the merits and good qualities they might have in other respects.[9] For Juvenal (*Sat.* 1.23ff.) this deplorable social situation was a basis for satire:

> When an effeminate eunuch takes home a wife, when a bare-breasted Mevia throws a hunting spear and kills an Etruscan boar, when one who scratched off my beard in my youth can be compared with aristocrats in wealth, when Crispinus, who comes from the common people of the Nile and was born in Canopus as a slave, pulls his Tyrian robe over his shoulder and his summer gold ring "wafts" on his sweaty finger (for he could not bear a greater load of jewelry), then it is hard not to write satire.

In Juvenal's view, the eunuch who marries and the woman (Mevia) who fights like a man in the arena[10] both behave against the natural order. From Juvenal's standpoint the same is true of the barber who has acquired great wealth,[11] as well as the Crispinus mentioned by name, who not only displays considerable wealth (cf. also *Sat.* 4.1ff.) but perhaps also holds a high social position. In terms of modern sociological theories, the barber and Crispinus are two apt examples of *status inconsistency* (on this see p. 60). A (former) barber—that is, a contemptible person in the view of the elite—is now comparable in wealth to all patricians. Crispinus is subject to contempt on several grounds: he was born a slave (*verna*), belongs to the *plebs* of his hometown Canopus, which is also considered especially immoral (*Sat.* 6.84; 15.46), is an Egyptian and therefore, according to Juvenal's prejudice, belongs to an uncivilized people (cf., for example, *Sat.* 15.46),[12] and, moreover, makes a show of his wealth.[13] For Juvenal, in any case, Crispinus's wealth stands in stark contrast to his background and status. Basically the satirist's viewpoint is based on the following social categories: (ethnic) origin, nobility, personal freedom, wealth, activity, age, and gender.[14] Then there is also a rank ordering within these categories.[15] An old man, Roman, and patrician who was born free, rich, and without professional occupation would, according to Juvenal, stand at the top of the social ladder.

C. SELF-EVALUATION IN THE UPPER STRATUM

Thus the perspective of the elite unmistakably dominates in ancient stratum definitions. And even for knowledge about the experiences and living conditions of lower-stratum groups, we are essentially dependent on the view of members of the upper stratum. Yet the perspective of the elite was also adopted in lower-stratum groups, as the already mentioned example of Paul shows. According to the standards of this world, he counts the members of the Christian community in Corinth among the "despised" (1 Cor 1:28). And he himself is proud of his heritage as a Hebrew (2 Cor 11:22), yet on the whole he apparently has no illusions that he belongs to the socially weak, the anonymous masses (the "unknown" in distinction to the nobility, the "known"), the have-nots (2 Cor 6:9-10; 11:29; cf. 1 Cor 4:10-11).[16]

Thus the social judgment of people shaped by the elite appears again in the consciousness of those who are judged and indeed condemned. Even those who in their craft have achieved something and become rich are often reluctant to present themselves in their self-testimonies only as members of their occupational class, "for economic success alone is not enough to achieve the esteem of their fellow citizens. Their monuments, inscriptions, and other signs identify them as notables, as dialogue partners recognized by their city or the state."[17] The already mentioned owner of a large Roman bakery, Marcus Vergilius Eurysaces, added to his specification of occupation as baker (*pistor*) that he was a *redemptor,* that is, something like an entrepreneur, who was active in the public markets. At Trimalchio's banquet in Petronius's *Satyricon* there is also a stonemason who has his proper place in the social hierarchy not only through his economic success but through the honorary title of a priest of the imperial cult (*sevir*).[18] Also in commerce, social respect—when it is not a question of wholesalers, who seem already to belong (say, as equestrians) to the ranks of the distinguished anyway—seems to convey recognition only through the special usefulness of the activity for the state. An inscription found in Hierapolis honors the merchant Flavius Zeuxis because of his courage and his social usefulness: "Many times he crossed the sea and served his homeland" (*SIG* 1229). Emperor Hadrian recommended to the city council of Ephesus two *nauklēroi* (apparently shipowners active in ocean trade) for a seat in the city council by giving laudatory recognition not only to their courage but above all to their usefulness for the common good (they had, among other things, also carried the emperor himself on their ships).[19] A dealer in goat leather does not fail to mention in his self-testimony that he sold wares "that met the needs of the people" (*CIL* 9.4796). And when those working for their own living could not boast of such merits, other socially acceptable virtues had to balance the lack of social status of their own occupations. The simple merchant is at least "honest," even compassionate, and a "friend of the poor."[20] In this self-designation as "friend of the poor" he is apparently borrowing for himself an attribute of the nobleman who is also distinguished by his *liberalitas*. In general, the adoption of aristocratic values appears not only in the negative self-evaluation of the little people but also in their adoption of the virtues that are ascribed to the elite.[21]

D. SUMMARY OF ANCIENT EVALUATIONS OF THE SOCIAL HIERARCHY

These few examples of ancient views of social hierarchy suggest that in the minds of the people of antiquity, the most important indicators of a person's social position are (noble) birth, participation in the exercise of political power, and material possessions. They clearly lift a person above the masses of people and bestow high esteem. Also presupposed are being born free and having the rights of citizenship. Conversely, where all or most of these traits are missing, we find disdain and contempt, whether based on low birth, activity required to earn a living, a lack of personal rights, or poverty. Table 4, which includes only the dominant variables, makes clear the ancient evaluation of social distinctions:[22]

TABLE 4: SOCIAL DISTINCTIONS

The Elite	*The Masses*
noble	common
powerful	weak
rich	poor
esteemed	disdained

The division of ancient societies appears again in the conceptual distinction between the *honestiores* (more honored) and the *humiliores* (more humble). While it is true that the legal bestowal of privilege on the elite did not come until the second century (since Hadrian), it seems only to have given a legal basis to the already realized special position of certain groups of people.[23] The *honestiores* included senators, equestrians, and urban aristocracy (later also veterans and certain judges and magistrate's officials). Everyone else belonged in the group of the *humiliores,* that is, both slaves and freed slaves, and every man and woman who met none of the criteria for the bestowal of legal privilege: *dignitas* (merit), esteem, high birth, character, and property.[24] Thus this later development also clearly shows that additional factors—such as personal legal status (personal freedom, rights of citizenship), occupational activity, and age—made no fundamental difference in the basic division of society into elite and nonelite (the masses, simple folk) on the basis of the named dominant variables. And even Juvenal, who favored honor bestowed by birth and despised rich and powerful people of unfree background, still has to recognize implicitly that wealth and high political office can make one prominent in the social hierarchy, even if one has the stain of a common birth and a formerly disparaged occupation.

Yet a stratification analysis of Mediterranean societies cannot depend only on ancient views, since these represent something like an opinion poll, as it were, within one small part of the population, about the *social prestige* of certain persons or groups. Social prestige, however, does not always have to be identical with the actual function of a person or group within the hierarchy of the social strata. Subjective factors, which may also be shared by the vast majority of the population, need to be complemented with objective factors, which inquire, for example, about leadership function and the influence of certain persons and groups on a society. At this point we have come to the modern discussion of ancient societies with regard to their social differentiation.

3.2 The Criteria of a Modern
Stratification Analysis of Ancient Societies

A stratification analysis basically presupposes *social inequality.* That is to say, on the basis of certain factors, the members of a society hold different social positions, which in turn decide their esteem and their choices in life. The limited examples of ancient views on the social differentiation of societies have clearly suggested a fundamental division between *elite* and *nonelite* (the masses). At the top of the societies of the Roman empire there was apparently a small elite group that was distinguished in the consciousness of ancient authors by their noble origin, leadership in public office, wealth, and esteem. Thus this elite is to be understood as both a political (the powerful) and economic (the rich) elite and a prestige (the most esteemed) elite.[25] Over against them are the masses of the population, who are defined by the lack of the social traits that mark the elite. Yet as important as this insight into the fundamental structure of ancient societies is, it ultimately offers only a crude orientation framework. For both the elite and especially the masses of the populace were noticeably differentiated. Yet even the terminology with which this differentiation is to be expressed is controversial. One speaks of stratum, status group, class, position, and caste. Here, however, we will not go into the problem of terminology.[26] None of the named terms is clearly defined either sociologically or in everyday speech. Furthermore, the discussion is complicated by the fact that linguistic classification is closely connected with individual stratification models and their criteria, which both form the basis of a stratification analysis. Thus more important than the terminology is a presentation of the criteria of a stratification analysis. We will soon look at these criteria more closely, but first we will briefly give our reasons for primarily using the term *stratum*.

3.2.1 Stratum and Status

One can speak of a *stratum* when relatively large groups within the population of a society share a comparable social situation and this distinguishes them hierarchically from other groups. The central problem of stratum determination is the selection and correlation of the socially relevant factors that make the social situation of individual people comparable. These may include property, political power or influence, esteem, origin, sex, occupational activity, education, and so forth. Since we will soon look more closely at the criteria of our stratification analysis (see 3.2.2), at this point we will give only the result of the weighting of the named factors and thus the stratum definition to be used here:[27] *A stratum comprises all the people of a society who find themselves in a similar social position on the basis of their share of power, privilege, and prestige.*

This concept of social stratum, which is based on *political* and *economic* criteria, seems more meaningful to us than the term *status*,[28] for status is related above all to the *esteem* of a person in the context of social systems. Thus Funk defines the sociological term *status* "as a position that people in a social system (group, association, society) can assume that is related in multiple ways to other positions of social systems and in each system is accompanied by a certain social prestige."[29] Thus the term *status,* on the one hand, implies a strong role for social *esteem* and, on the other hand, serves to locate the social position of a person in relation to *various* social systems in his or her society. The latter makes possible a multidimensional picture of a society and an insight into the manifold interrelatedness of individuals in various social systems (say, family, religious group, association, and so forth).[30] Hence, in various social systems one person can have more than one status.

Let us look at an example. A freeborn Corinthian craftsman has the highest esteem within his household as *paterfamilias* and master of a small workshop. He rules over family members (including slaves and wage earners) and thus also occupies the highest position of power in his household. At the same time, in his city he by no means belongs to the elite, since he has no position of political leadership. Indeed, if he does not even have citizenship, he has no direct influence whatever on the political decisions of his community. In this respect he is ultimately indistinguishable from his slaves and wage earners, as well as from his wife and children, all of whom are, like him, excluded from political power. Yet our artisan, as a member, say, of an artisan's association (*collegium*), may hold certain leadership positions in his "guild" and thereby compensate somewhat for his political deficit. His slaves, however, also have this possibility.

Thus an analysis of the social status of an individual may in most cases lead to the conclusion that a person has not just one but many social statuses. A stratification analysis cannot express this multidimensional social situation, and it does not have to. Strictly speaking, it considers only the social system called *society*—whether it is a particular local community or the social system of the whole Roman empire—and determines the social position of an individual somewhat macrosociologically; thus it involves a supraindividual perspective that sees society as a whole. This is also meaningful, as another example will make clear.

Within the population group that held the legal status of Roman citizenship (*civitas Romana*) and thus also certain privileges, there were again clear and important gradations. We only need to think of the difference between the emperor, senators, and equestrians on the one hand and the "normal" Roman citizens on the other, of whom one hundred thousand were dependent on the imperial dole of grain to ensure their existence. They all had Roman citizenship and thus a status that was even defined legally, but in the overall social system they held positions that were often extremely divergent.

Yet a stratification analysis must also consider status differences within the individual strata and the phenomenon of so-called status inconsistency or status dissonance. On the status distinctions within the various strata, which will be differentiated below, we note here only that in the upper-stratum groups, imperial house and senators are distinguished from equestrians, and these in turn from the decurions. The idea of status inconsistency calls for additional comment.

INCONSISTENCY OF STATUS

The problem of status inconsistency has been intensively discussed sociologically and also applied in detail to ancient societies and to early Christianity.[31] According to our definition *status inconsistency* is basically found when the central traits of stratum membership (power, privilege, prestige) are incongruent. This is especially the case when the prestige of a person does not agree with his or her actual power functions or privileges—when, for example, a slave, on the basis of his individual abilities, occupational training, or position, acquires influence and privileges that considerably go beyond his legally defined status. Here we only need to recall the high functionaries among the slaves in the *familia Caesaris*. The situation is similar for slaves who are commissioned and empowered by their lords to administer landed estates. Also, some emancipated slaves held more political influence than many senators. Yet the odium of unfree birth clung to them through their lives and as such was, naturally, not only a problem of their own self-consciousness but also a social factor. For in the mind of the ancient elite, as we have seen, it was origin, first and above all, that determined status. In full recognition of these problems, however, one should not overestimate the importance of status inconsistency. For the elevated offices in Rome and other cities presupposed not only appropriate citizenship but also membership in the appropriate *ordines* (senators, equestrians, decurions). And subaltern functions (lictors, tax collectors, subordinate "officials") were accessible even to noncitizens. Finally, only Roman citizens (in principle) could serve in the legions, and the officer's career was in principle open only to equestrians.

Thus status criteria play an important role. Yet for the stratification undertaken here, the status concept is, in our view, ill suited. For a stratification analysis proceeds macrosociologically and thus is concerned with an overall picture of social strata, whereas an analysis of status is better suited for microsociological investigations and can thus take, for example, the social situation of individuals or groups into account.

3.2.2 The Criteria of a Stratification Analysis: Power, Privilege, Prestige

Various factors—property, political power or influence, esteem, background, sex, occupational activity, education, and so forth—are significant for social position. Thus a stratification analysis of ancient societies must be clear about the criteria on the basis of which it determines the social position of a person. One of the few social historians of ancient societies who names the criteria of his stratigraphy at all is Alföldy. His two-strata model (upper and lower strata) for Roman society names four main criteria for belonging to the ancient upper stratum:[32] *wealth, power* (that is, the exercise of higher political or social functions), *esteem,* and above all belonging to an *ordo,* that is, to one of the three "orders" (senators, equestrians, decurions). Meeks names as the categories of his analysis ethnic membership, *ordo,* citizenship, personal freedom, wealth, occupation, age, sex, and public offices or honors.[33] For Vittinghoff, who believes that a global analysis of Roman society is impossible, a central characteristic of ancient society is the inequality of personal rights, which overlaps with and helps determine socio-political factors.[34] The authors named here assume, with justification, that the opportunities and social positions of people depend not only on their personal characteristics and abilities but also on the "distribution system"[35] of their society. In other words, in the sum total of social traits there are obviously certain ones that are determined by the structure of society and bring a greater share of a society's gratifications and thus better opportunities. Thus a stratification analysis also presupposes a social theory, which in turn offers the basis for the stratification model, which is reflected in the social inequality of the society to be studied.

Naturally, we cannot go into the complex discussion of these problems here. We assume (with Lenski,)[36] however, that a society's system of distribution is determined by three "basic elements": *power, privilege,* and *prestige.* They are the most important variables in determining the social position of a person in the social system. Here we understand with Lenski the primary variable to be *power,* which "determines how a society's surplus [the excess of production over need] will be divided." Dependent on power are the *privileges,* which are understood as the "possession or control of a part of the surplus that a society produces."[37] Finally, *prestige* is above all a function of power and privilege.

A. POWER AS THE PRIMARY VARIABLE

If the power variable also basically determines the number of privileges, and prestige is a function of these two variables, then it is logical that in a stratification analysis of ancient Mediterranean societies, the factor of power must play a decisive role. Thus ultimately one's share of power decides one's social position and as the most important trait also enables us to distinguish social positions from each other. Yet at this point we must note on what basis and in what form the share of power is manifested in each society. Here we distinguish two bases of the institutionalized form[38] of social power: *Power through position (office or role)* and *power through property (influence).* The two are frequently, but not necessarily, connected.[39] Whereas a certain position or office in society bestows immediate *authority,* that is, "the enforceable right to command others,"[40] property ownership, for example, means *influence,* that is, the possibility of having one's interests prevail against others or influencing the social situation. In modern western industrial societies, power qua property (or income) no doubt plays the more important role for the social position of a person in the society and the distinction between social strata. An office in society seems, by contrast, to be of less importance. In principle, these offices are open to all citizens, are extremely varied (from head of government to office clerk), and are subject, moreover, to extensive control. In the Roman empire, however, the exercise of leading public function was of decisive importance for one's stratum membership. Yet property, as the foundation of social power, also played a role that should not be underestimated.

B. POWER AND PROPERTY (INFLUENCE)

Thus property as the basis of power is also to be taken into consideration. Here property is not only understood as an economic category but also included in its importance for one's share of social power.[41] Also dependent on the factor of power is the "system of acquisition and transmission of property," which Garnsey and Saller understand as the "basis of the Roman framework of social and economic inequality."[42] That is, property and the acquisition of wealth were possible above all for members of the ruling class but also for the slaves and freemen in their service with higher executive functions. Since it was a question of an agrarian society, in which the ownership of land was of decisive importance, property tended mostly to remain in the hands of the same families through inheritance. Furthermore, this ownership was also the central source for the augmentation of wealth. State offices, however, also made larger incomes possible. Garnsey and Saller state:

> In the main, only where the family had died out and there were no adopted heirs, were outsiders able to gain control over valued resources. It was a peculiarity of the Roman system that the outsiders who benefited were characteristically select lower-class dependents (freedmen, slaves), who had won the confidence or affection of their master.[43]

Accordingly, for the stratigraphy of the societies with which we are dealing here, it is necessary to develop social position on the basis of the named variables, of which the share of power plays the first and foremost role, then privilege, and finally prestige. The evaluations of social distinctions by the ancient authors presented above are based on the opposite principle, for they are oriented toward the *result*, as it were, of a social position that is based on power and privilege and expresses itself in a person's prestige. Nevertheless, they also presuppose that prestige is conditioned by social distribution systems, which ultimately give the aristocratic families the most important share of legal or actual power and thus their measure of privileges and finally determine their prestige.

C. COMPARISON WITH ALFÖLDY'S CRITERIA OF STRATIFICATION

As already mentioned, Alföldy names four main criteria for the classification of upper strata in antiquity: *wealth, power, esteem,* and above all membership in an *ordo,* that is, the three "orders" (senators, equestrians, decurions). If we compare these criteria with those named by us, we can immediately classify three of them with the criterion we call power; these are power (in the sense of higher social functions), wealth, and membership in an *ordo.* Yet the criterion wealth, as well as *ordo,* can also be discussed under our criterion of privilege, since members of the *ordines* belong, according to Alföldy, to the "privileged orders." Thus, in modified form, his four criteria can ultimately be reduced to and therefore compared with the three named by us:

Our Criteria	*Alföldy's Criteria*
power	power
(position/property)	social function/wealth/*ordo*
privilege	wealth/*ordo*
prestige	esteem

Since for Alföldy membership in one of the three *ordines* (which we will characterize below in more detail) actually fulfills the remaining traits of the upper stratum, *ordo* becomes for him the ultimate criterion that decides stratum membership in the societies of the Roman empire; that is to say, social function and social rank form the basis of his analysis.[44] Yet in comparison with the criteria recommended by us, in the category *ordo* only *one* form of power becomes the decisive criterion. Thus we also see adopted here a *Roman* perspective, in which one's position in the power system decides one's place in the social hierarchy. Yet Finley has already pointed out that in ancient Rome the institutionalization of political power had progressed to the point where membership in the Roman upper stratum and the exercise of political power were not absolutely identical.[45] Thus for Alföldy Roman society has the character of a kind of "order-stratum structure,"[46] but this especially undervalues property as the (influence-conveying) second institutionalized form of power.[47] One not unimportant consequence of this prominence of order membership is also the implied adoption of the androcentric perspective. In Alföldy's social model, no consideration is given to women.[48]

D. POWER AND PRIVILEGE

Therefore it seems more sensible to us to subordinate the criterion of membership in an *ordo* to the main criterion of power. In general, it seems to us more appropriate to look at the criteria more fundamentally, since we are not interested only in a social stratigraphy of Roman society. In Jewish society, for example, the elite included not only priests and in particular the families of high priests as members of a quasi *ordo,* but also lay families whose membership was based solely on power and property. Just as membership in the *ordines* represents an idiosyncrasy of Roman societies and, strictly speaking, only a specific form of participation in social power, something comparable is also true for the criterion of "wealth." The material possession of personal and real property conveys, on the one hand, a form of power (namely, influence), but is, on the other hand, an (essential) part of the *privileges* that members of the upper stratum enjoy. In addition, on the basis of their positions they frequently also have legal and actual privileges that they foster vis-à-vis the lower stratum. This difference was revealed above all in treatment before a Roman court, as Garnsey and Saller state: not only did criminal law have two tracks, but also different standards were applied before the court. Thus the statements of high-ranking citizens were given more credence.

The dual-penalty system, together with a differential evaluation of legal testimony in accordance with rank, were formally enunciated in law by the end of the second century, but must have long been practiced by judges, for they were deeply rooted in traditional, aristocratic values. Some decades before the earliest reference in the extant legal sources to a formal *honestiores/humiliores* distinction, the younger Pliny advised a provincial governor in Spain to preserve "the distinction of orders and dignity" in legal hearings, because "if these distinctions are confused, nothing is more unequal than equality itself" (*Ep.* 9.5).[49]

Yet, in the determination of privileges, not only is one's share of power of great importance, but so are one's possessions. For example, wealthy or influential members of the provincial upper stratum could bring their legal quarrels to the emperor, even if they could not demonstrate the Roman citizenship that in principle was a necessary legal prerequisite.[50] Thus power as the presupposition for privilege did not come only through the *authority* that the holders of political office had. It could also be conveyed through the *influence* that was at the command, say, of women and family members of the ruling class and also their slaves and freed slaves, who acted for their politically powerful masters in prominent functions. In principle, freed slaves had no access to high political offices on account of their legal status, yet their wealth gave them a political influence that should not be underestimated. What they lacked, however, was prestige. "Even the powerful imperial freedmen were disdained as 'slaves' by the prominent, although the latter behaved often enough in a servile manner in their presence (cf. for example, Tacitus *Ann.* 14.39)."[51]

Thus there were certainly people who because of their property or their position exercised social power, yet who as women, slaves, or freedmen were kept from belonging to the *ordines* and above all from the leadership of high political or military office. In this connection, even Alföldy sensibly does not consistently maintain his central *ordo* criterion. For he includes rich freed slaves (*liberti*), who belonged to no *ordo*, "at least in regard to the economic situation . . . among the upper stratum of Roman society." Likewise it also included, because of their "economic conditions and their position of power . . . the freedmen and slaves of the emperor (*familia Caesaris*)."[52] The criteria that we have proposed could have more easily justified this stratum classification. Finally, we must observe that even within the same status group—say, senators or slaves—social esteem (prestige) does not have to be identical. "Within the senatorial order, which experienced a high turnover of families, those who could boast of consular ancestors, *nobiles*, stood out from the mass of newcomers."[53] There were notable distinctions among slaves: the shackled rural slaves, for example, were considerably different from those who managed estates for their masters. Indeed, some slaves in the imperial administration not only had relatively high political influence but also enjoyed numerous privileges. Repeatedly mentioned in this connection is a certain Muscius Scurranus, who as slave of the emperor Tiberius was "cashier" in Gaul.[54] He had received from the emperor sixteen household slaves, including two cooks, several servants, three secretaries, a doctor, and a "lover."[55] Likewise, there were distinctions among the lower-stratum groups of citizens and noncitizens, slaves, freed slaves, and those born free in terms of their numbers of legal and actual privileges.

3.2.3 The Problem of the Consideration of Women

A higher or lower social status in a society, as well as a person's overall opportunities, can also be affected by one's gender. Indeed, membership in the female sex in the ancient societies of the Mediterranean region placed one on the wrong side of a fundamental social asymmetry, which diminished not only the social status of women but also their possibilities for participation in social power and the acquisition of privileges. In this sense one can say that because of differentiation between the sexes, ancient societies were again divided into two unequal parts, and in some ways the social situations of men and women differed considerably. Naturally, this has its effects on the social model.[56] Under the conditions of the criteria of Alföldy's presupposed two-strata model, women had to be counted among the lower stratum, since only men could hold political office. Women could not be senators or equestrians, city councilors or even city officials, officers or soldiers. Gender identification also disadvantaged women precisely in regard to the opportunity for social mobility. N. Kampen summarizes the situation of women with respect to advancement opportunities as follows:

Although a woman may be born into a senatorial family, have great wealth of her own, and hold important religious or social offices, in a structural sense she lacks crucial attributes which confer *dignitas* on a Roman. She, and her sisters in the lower strata too, can neither vote nor hold political or governmental office, and all women are barred from military service. Thus, two significant means to independent social mobility, access to independent political power and participation in the ideologically important upper class *cursus honorum*, were closed to all women, regardless of their class. A woman's social position depended far more than a man's upon the family into which she was born and that into which she married. If born into an equestrian family, a woman could move up to the senatorial level only by marriage, whereas a man's mobility depended on his record of service *and* his wealth. At the lowest level of society, among slaves upward mobility might come about through a woman's being granted or purchasing her freedom as well as by her spouse's action, and further, a woman might change status by producing three or four children.[57]

The women of elite families in particular could exercise *indirect* power, say, through the bearing of legitimate heirs, the control of real property and other possessions, through manipulation,[58] and in general through their influence on men (see pp. 366–69.). Yet these were only men who then voted in the senate, who became prefects and governors or in the provinces guided the destiny of a city, say, as *duumviri*. Naturally, in terms of wealth, social esteem, and also the possibilities of political influence, the wives of these men were different not only from the women in lower-stratum families but also from the men.

Thus we have the possibility, on the one hand, of classifying women in a certain stratum *through their husbands or fathers*. Without doubt, one can say that basically women (and children) shared the status of their husbands or fathers and in principle also participated in the same privileges and property or suffered under the lack of same like their fathers or husbands. Yet we can say even more, for women living alone can certainly also be considered in our model of criteria. Since power is conveyed not only through authority and therefore via office but also as influence via property, with the help of this criterion we can basically evaluate the social position of women living alone. And although belonging to a particular sex in principle required the fulfillment of a certain role—which hardly leaves any realm of life unconsidered—and the role of women was considered inferior compared to that of men, the harsh criticism of ancient writers precisely against well-to-do women living alone shows that for women also, property opened up the possibility of breaking through the stereotypical role schema. Thus on the one hand we classify here married women and unmarried daughters to particular strata through their husbands or fathers; on the other hand we count women, whether divorced or widowed, among the upper stratum if they were born into or married into it. Moreover, we consider in the upper stratum independent women who were without husband or political office but had significant possessions. Basically, it is more difficult to classify lower-stratum women with the help of the category of influence (or indirect power). For most of them probably had no influence at all. In addition they seldom had the opportunity to reach the upper stratum through marriage. Rather, upward social mobility seems to have affected women in a special way. Especially after the death of the husband, the situation of women (and children) in the lower-stratum group could worsen dramatically. We know of individual cases in which a cobbler's family was able to survive financially only because the daughters were able to provide a family income as prostitutes. In antiquity as now, women who were employed in agricultural operations or manufacturing received less money for the same work.[59] These remarks will suffice here, since the social situation of women will be given special attention later.

3.3 A Model of Ancient Societies:
Elite (Upper-Stratum Groups) and Nonelite (Lower-Stratum Groups)

Basically, the complexities of ancient societies have been reduced to a model of either two or three strata.[60] In principle, for the description of the social stratification of ancient societies, a *dichotomous model* has been maintained, which understands social inequality through the assumption of upper and lower strata or elite and nonelite (the masses).[61] For we must deny the existence in ancient societies of a middle stratum or strata, in which a medial share of the relevant traits of the upper and lower strata is presupposed. The division of power in particular separated societies into a small power elite on one side and the masses of the powerless on the other. This constellation also basically determined the portion of social privileges and personal possessions, as well as legal advantages. Only through a considerable fortune could those without prominent office—including single women and freed slaves—use influence to compensate for their lack of direct sharing of power. Thus those who possessed neither prominent office nor wealth did not belong to the elite of their society.

Thus the necessary presuppositions for the development of a middle stratum were missing.[62] It is true that it would be relatively easy to make out such a stratum if we could transfer to ancient societies modern criteria such as relative well-being ("middle income") or membership in a certain occupational group (master artisans, teachers). Yet this is hardly meaningful. Nor is this situation altered by the very interesting attempt of Karl Christ, who in disagreement with Alföldy wants to gather various social groups into one "group of middle strata."[63] In this group he includes free farmers on their own land, urban freed slaves with small workshops, free artisans in general, and merchants. He also doubts that one can understand Roman citizens who have their own means of production and business capital or legionnaires as members of the lower stratum. In actuality, however, even the ancient authors themselves reveal no awareness of a middle stratum whose status rests between the upper and lower strata.

The model of a three-stratum social hierarchy attempts to do justice to the phenomenon that within the elite and especially among the masses of the populace, there were clear gradations. Therefore Alföldy speaks in the plural of "upper strata" and "lower strata."[64] Yet this makes it problematical to speak of a two-strata model. In order to do justice to this social differentiation within the elite and the masses of the people, we employ here instead the terms *upper-stratum groups* and *lower-stratum groups,* which are synonymous with the terms *elite* and *nonelite.* Where we have these groups as a whole in mind, we use the designations *upper stratum* and *lower stratum,* which are synonymous with the *elite* and *nonelite.*

THE BASIC STRUCTURES OF SOCIAL STRATIFICATION

As a heuristic model for the determination of a person's social position in the societies of the Roman empire we recommend the basic framework that follows (in 3.3.1 and 3.3.2). Fundamental here is the distinction between elite and nonelite. The groups belonging to the elite are designated here as the upper stratum; the people belonging to the masses of the populace are called the lower stratum. Both of these macrosystems, however, could be further differentiated in meaningful ways.

3.3.1 Upper-Stratum Groups

According to our stratification model the upper stratum includes (a) the members of the Roman *ordines* (and their families), as well as members of the ruling houses and the leading priestly and lay families in vassal states and provinces; (b) wealthy people without prominent political offices, regardless of their sex or legal status; and finally what we with Lenski call (c) retainers of the upper stratum, that is, the free individuals, slaves, and freed slaves who as a kind of appendage fulfill prominent functions for the named upper-stratum groups. We must note here that because of the special structures of agricultural societies, the members of the upper stratum generally lived in the cities and only for brief periods in the country. Thus it is meaningful to speak only of an *urban* upper stratum, even if its property provided its essential basis of esteem and economic support.

A. ORDINES AND RULING FAMILIES IN VASSAL STATES AND PROVINCES

The groups in the upper stratum include, first of all, the relatively clearly delineated "imperial aristocracy": emperor and imperial house (*domus Cae-*

saris), senatorial nobility (*ordo senatorius*), and equestrians (*ordo equester*). They have in common a comparable share in power, privilege, and prestige— even if in varying degrees. They exercise *power* as authority in leading politi- cal offices. These offices presuppose wealth, in varying amounts, and their occupants (as well as their families in many respects) enjoyed—also via the possession of wealth—further *privileges,* not least of all before the judiciary. And finally, the members of the named groups enjoyed the highest *prestige*— again in different degrees. We also include the wives and families of these groups in the upper stratum, although they had only a reduced share of the privileges and the social prestige of their husbands and fathers and in princi- ple exercised only influence and not the authority of office. Likewise, the membership of the *decurions* (city councilors) in the *local or provincial* upper stratum is undoubted, since their share in power, privilege, and prestige clear- ly distinguishes them from the remaining population. The same is true for the ruling houses in vassal states and the lay and priestly families of their upper stratum.

B. THE RICH

In addition to the foregoing members of the *ordines* we include in the upper stratum wealthy people without leading political office, whether single women or men, whether born free or made free. On the basis of their con- siderable wealth, they could exercise power in the form of influence on lead- ing political figures and also command their own sometimes large staffs. Furthermore, their income enabled them to lead a privileged lifestyle, which was fundamentally different from the choices open to the masses of the pop- ulace. In general, they could also expect privileged treatment before the judi- ciary, even if this was not based on law. Their social prestige, which was less than that of members of the *ordines,* was to a certain extent compensated by the bestowal of honorary social office (such as functionary of the imperial cult—*Augustales*—or patron or patroness of social organizations). Here we must also consider differences in wealth and differences between Rome and other cities, since they also affected the degree of influence.

C. RETAINERS

As a specific group within the upper stratum we include the free individuals, freed slaves, and slaves who assumed duties for their masters in prominent political positions or performed important administrative tasks in the private sphere.[65] Lenski, in connection with his multidimensional class system of agricultural societies, calls these groups of retainers the "vassal class." This designation is supposed to express the essential characteristic of the class, namely, "its dependence on the political elite."[66] In our strata model, however, it is more meaningful to use the word *retainers,* since we do not use the concept of class. Yet we must deal with a large number of gradations, which are determined by social power, the wealth of the person's master, and finally the person's share of authority and privilege. Without doubt those who stand out here are the members of the *familia Caesaris,* who in Rome itself, but also in the provinces, held influential positions and exercised noteworthy privileges. Even in the country, however, slaves who managed large estates for their masters could benefit from their opportunities, influence, and privileges. We can classify them with the upper stratum, but since their influence and privileges were highly dependent on the goodwill of their masters and could change at any time—especially because of their legal status—we must clearly delineate them from the elite. In a special way these groups point to the limits of the two-strata model, which cannot comprise all the dimensions of social inequality.

3.3.2 Lower-Stratum Groups

The differentiation of the groups in the lower stratum is, on the whole, more difficult. On the basis of their particular place of residence and work, as well as on economic, cultural, and many other grounds (such as their social mobility), they can first be rather simply subdivided socio-geographically, as it were, into *urban* and *rural* lower-stratum groups.[67] Regarded in its totality, however, the lower stratum was extremely heterogeneous. They can, therefore, be differentiated into groups only on the basis of some essential distinctions. In this process we will focus on the above recommended criteria (power, privilege, and prestige), yet in a relativized form. Since even full citizens in the cities generally had only the possibility of acclamation for the decisions made by the city council and magistrates, the criterion of power can be considered only in the sense of (relative) influence.[68] Even if we must take into account the fact that one or another member of the lower stratum could exercise a certain influence on officeholders on account of property or personal relationships, objectification of this influence is problematic. In principle, however, we assume that full citizens of the cities were condemned to a "factual impotence," that is, that "the subdecurional population of the polis was completely excluded from the city government."[69] Thus, for central criteria we can ultimately use only *relative property (income) or privilege* and *relative status or prestige.*

Property (Income)
Those who, in the view of the upper stratum, belonged to the lower stratum were, in principle, people who had to earn a living for themselves and their families through their own work (see, for example, Cicero *Off.* 1.150; cf. p.

25). Even if this subjective criterion is not adequate, it still expresses a decisive characteristic of lower-stratum groups. For it was not only because of their noninvolvement in high political offices and hence their enormous lack of power, but also because of their minimum or total lack of property that they were dependent on their own work to provide their subsistence.[70] In this sense we can apply to the structuring of the lower stratum above all the criterion of (relative) income or property. Because of their property, free farmers with their own piece of land are different from wage earners without property and day laborers (who may be free and have personal rights). In the cities the same is true for artisans with their own business in relation to their employees, slaves, or day laborers. We must, nonetheless, immediately add the restriction that our knowledge of the individual size of property or income is not sufficient to enable us to undertake finer differentiations here. Yet in our opinion one can draw a pragmatic boundary, which we define by the *minimum existence,* concerning which we will make some calculations below (see 3.5). Thus in the lower stratum we include here (a) the relatively poor or relatively prosperous and (b) the absolutely poor.

A. THE RELATIVELY POOR OR RELATIVELY PROSPEROUS ABOVE THE MINIMUM EXISTENCE (*penētes*)

We include here in the lower-stratum group of the relatively poor or relatively prosperous the individuals who, because of their income or property, were in a position to provide at least an adequate subsistence for themselves and their families, that is, an appropriate dwelling and sufficient food and clothing. The minimum existence provides the boundary on the lower end, but drawing a dividing line on the upper end, between relatively prosperous and rich, is a difficult undertaking in particular cases.

B. THE ABSOLUTELY POOR (*ptōchoi*)

Here we classify in the group of the absolutely poor those people who live at or under the level of minimum existence, that is, those who exhibit a fundamental lack of all or some of the goods necessary to achieve subsistence (food, clothing, dwelling). Here we must consider differences between city and country, but also among cities themselves, since the cost of living in the cities was basically higher than in the country and also varied from city to city.

3.4 The Elite: Upper-Stratum Groups

3.4.1 The Various Upper-Stratum Groups

A. THE MEMBERS OF THE *ORDINES*

The members of the *imperial aristocracy,* which was headed by the Roman imperial house and the senatorial nobility (600 senators), also included the

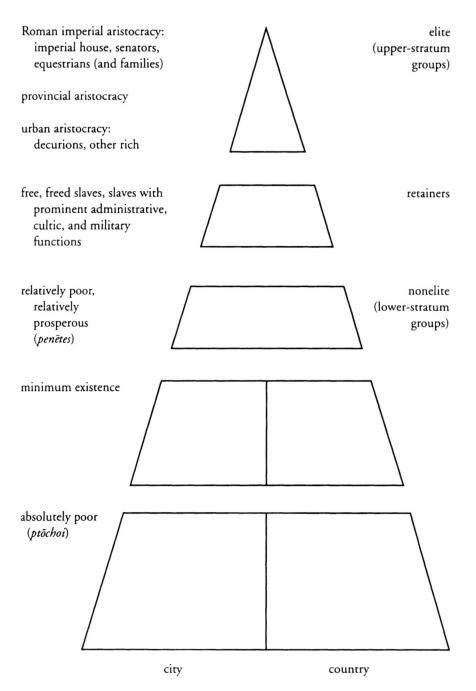

Roman imperial aristocracy:
    imperial house, senators,
    equestrians (and families)

elite
(upper-stratum
groups)

provincial aristocracy

urban aristocracy:
    decurions, other rich

free, freed slaves, slaves with
    prominent administrative,
    cultic, and military
    functions

retainers

relatively poor,
    relatively
    prosperous
    (*penētes*)

nonelite
(lower-stratum
groups)

minimum existence

absolutely poor
    (*ptōchoi*)

city   country

SOCIAL PYRAMID I: OVERVIEW OF SOCIAL STRATIFICATION

equestrians. The minimum wealth of the senators amounted to 1 million sesterces[71] but was far exceeded by most of them.[72] At the same time they were
big landowners (in Italy and the provinces) and probably drew the majority of
their income from their agricultural possessions, as well as from their administration of public offices in the provinces.[73] The senatorial order remained the
most highly esteemed. The toga with the broad purple stripe (*latus clavus*)
made senators and their sons outwardly visible as members of this order. Incidentally, this broad purple stripe could also be worn by equestrians who had
been allowed to apply for senatorial office. The sons of senators could also participate with their fathers in meetings of the senate. In this way Augustus
strengthened the principle of the inheritance of senatorial office, which he had
introduced (Suetonius *Augustus* 38).

In addition to the born aristocracy of the senators, the imperial nobility
included the equestrians (*ordo equester*), who had to be freeborn (under
Tiberius the candidates had to demonstrate free birth in the two preceding
generations). According to Dio Cassius (52.19.4), the equestrian and senatorial orders were comparable, since acceptance into both *ordines* had similar criteria (high birth, outstanding traits of character, and wealth). Nevertheless,
the equestrians were subordinated to the senators in the social hierarchy. The
equestrian order had around 20,000 members with a minimum individual
wealth of 400,000 sesterces. Many of them, however—especially the state
leaseholders (*publicani*) and wholesale merchants—were much richer and,
like the senators, drew their largest income from their real estate. Their numbers included wholesalers, bankers, and holders of leases for taxes and customs
duties. On the whole, this *ordo* was not nearly as homogeneous as the senatorial birth aristocracy. For among the equestrians there were also sons of freed
slaves, aspirants from the military (even as *centurio* one could rise to the level
of officer), and above all members of the provincial upper stratum. For many
equestrians a career in public office (*cursus honorum*) began with the position
of officer. Within the equestrian order, there was a hierarchy. More esteemed
were the equestrians who had an exalted post and a residence in Rome. The
majority of the equestrian order probably belonged to the provincial or local
upper stratum. They stood out from it, however, not only socially but also
through outward signs (golden ring and narrow purple stripe on the toga—
angustus clavus). Since the outward signs of the senatorial and equestrian
orders were of great importance, there were naturally abuses (for example,
through wearing a golden ring: Pliny *Nat. Hist.* 33.32). For in Rome, as well
as in other cities of the empire, members of the imperial aristocracy liked to
parade their position and expected certain privileges (such as reserved seats in
theaters). Augustus was interested in renewing such privileges from the republican period. Suetonius writes:[74]

He issued special regulations to counteract the unordered and accidental system with which spectators reserved seats for these plays. He had been angered by the insulting of a senator whom not one of the spectators offered a seat in the over-filled Puteoli theater. The subsequent senatorial decision provided that at every performance, wherever it took place, the first row of the loge was to be reserved for senators. . . . Its regulations included the separation of soldiers and civilians, the provision for special seats for married commoners, underaged boys and, nearby, their tutors, and the prohibition of wearing dark clothing, which was allowed only in the back rows.

Finally, the group of people with high political functions, considerable property, and esteem also included the aristocracy in the Roman provinces who in the cities formed the *ordo decurionum.* Like the senators and equestrians, these decurions, or councilors, were supposed to demonstrate honorable origin, wealth, and traits of character. They could also be joined, however, by the sons of freed slaves and certain veterans. Important above all here was wealth. For urban offices were offices of honor, which not only did not pay but even meant expenses for their occupants, since contributions of various amounts to the treasury were to be paid when someone joined the city council. In addition, free-will contributions were expected from city councilors.[75] The presupposed minimum income for the provincial aristocracy varied between 20,000 and 100,000 sesterces (in Comum, for example, the minimum income was 100,000 sesterces: Pliny *Ep.* 1.19). Accordingly, their wealth varied considerably, and in many cases they could be called rich only in the context of their local situation. The aim of Roman policy was also to integrate the members of the urban upper stratum in the provinces into the governmental structure of Rome. This goal was pursued especially through the bestowal of Roman citizenship on urban nobility in the provinces. The process of integrating the urban upper stratum into the Roman ruling class was already largely completed toward the end of the first century.[76] Yet even the possession of citizenship (whether in Rome or in the provincial cities) still did not in itself indicate membership in the upper stratum. In the Roman empire there were hardly more than 150,000 to 200,000 decurions in all.

The various privileges of the upper stratum depended not only on their wealth but above all on membership in the *ordines.* Like the senators in Rome, the decurions sat in special seats at the games and in the theater, took part in banquets at the expense of the public budget, and wore their own clothing. They also understood themselves in the moral sense as elite (*boni/honestiores*) and did not suffer the same cruel punishments as the lower stratum (receiving, for example, exile instead of the death penalty).[77]

B. OTHER UPPER-STRATUM MEMBERS

Finally, we also classify in the upper stratum the vassal kings or princes and their families, as well as the upper-stratum families in Rome's vassal states and provinces. Although they could not appeal to their own noble heritage—like, say, the Herodian ruling house in the land of Israel—and never became members of a Roman *ordo,* but only received certain honorary privileges and Roman citizenship, they must still be counted among the elite on the basis of their power, their property, their privileges, and their prestige, which they enjoyed at least in Rome. The criterion of property and power is likewise valid for the families of high priests and laity, who traditionally belonged to the upper-stratum groups in the land of Israel and also enjoyed the esteem of the people.

Based on the character of the upper stratum as *ordo,* wealth alone was not a hallmark of membership in the aristocracy in the view of the members of the senatorial and equestrian nobility. Nevertheless, there were certainly people who were rich and therefore also politically influential. Thus there were

> large numbers of urban citizens who fulfilled the required general qualifications for the decurionate, including wealth, but could not be elected to the council because of the limitation on the number of seats in the curia. Such wealthy citizens—Spanish Gades and Italian Padua are supposed to have had about 500 citizens each with the equestrian wealth of 400,000 sesterces—cannot be classified as lower stratum in contrast to the decurions.[78]

In the group of the rich without prominent political office we must also include the veterans of the Roman army who retired with the rank of a *primipilus* and received a settlement of 600,000 sesterces, or one and a half times the minimum equestrian wealth. Some of them then also became decurions and even rose to positions of leadership on the city council.[79]

Here we must also mention the freed slaves who became rich. The most famous example of this group is a freed slave named Trimalchio, about whom we learn from Petronius in his *Satyricon.* Trimalchio is probably a figure of literary fiction; in many respects he is an overdrawn caricature. Yet from his description we can learn something about this group of rich men without the authority of office and with little esteem. Petronius describes Trimalchio as a very rich man, who was uneducated, dressed and acted like a nobleman, lived a life of luxury, but because of his background enjoyed none of the esteem of a member of the upper stratum. Yet he had considerable political influence, even though he did not belong to an *ordo.* Of some compensation to the rich freed slaves without political office was the possibility of gaining some prestige through honorary offices connected with the cult of the emperor (*Augustales* or *severi Augustales*). The group of the *Augustales* is known to us in Italy through some 3000 inscriptions (likewise in Spain and Gaul). "They had at their disposal a section of reserved seats at local competitions (*ludi*) and spectacles, wore their own insignia of their quasi-official position, and had their own assembly building. Like the decurions they made gifts of money for the benefit of their communities" and in this way shared in good works.[80] But they were not spared the contempt of the nobility. Seneca writes: "In our time there was a certain rich man named Calvisius Sabinus; he had the wealth and the mind of a freedman. I have never seen a man whose fortune was a greater offense against wealth" (*Ep.* 27.5). This Sabinus had paid a great deal of money for slaves who had learned by heart the entire works of Homer and Hesiod, from whom he had then learned a few lines and used them to entertain at banquets. In his satires Juvenal in particular poured out his hatred and scorn on this group of people.[81] Also comparable to them were independent women who did not have to work but lived from their property or wealth (see 12.2.1).

C. RETAINERS

The retainers of the upper stratum included especially the prominent members of the *familia Caesaris*, among them the imperial freed slaves (*Augusti liberti*) with politically privileged position,[82] as well as helpers of the Roman magistracy (*apparitores*), who were probably mostly freed slaves. They performed public and legal activities, worked in archives, in the library, with the census, or in other public projects.[83] Mentioned again and again among the freed slaves of the emperor Claudius with considerable political influence and wealth are Callistus, Narcissus, and Pallas, who according to Pliny the Elder are supposed to have had greater wealth than Crassus (*Nat. Hist.* 33.10.134). Pallas is supposed to have declined a senate bonus of 15 million sesterces for his services.[84] The freed slaves of the emperor, who in their positions exercised prominent executive functions, had not only remarkable power (conveyed by the emperor) but also the opportunity to acquire substantial wealth. Within the imperial administration—especially in the praetorian guard—freed slaves were appointed to important positions. According to Tacitus, they (along with the wives of emperors) pulled the strings behind the scenes of imperial politics and also took part in attempts at political overthrow. Tacitus describes Narcissus and Pallas as powerful men in the court of Claudius.[85] Nonetheless, they also retained the blemish of an unfree birth. Even if they married into noble families, they were personally barred from entering the *ordines*. Yet their sons had the opportunity of attaining high political office. Pliny the Younger (*Ep.* 7.29) writes about one freed slave who was honored with praetorian office:

> Personally I have never thought much of these honors that are bestowed more by accident than by rational decision. Yet this inscription makes clear to me more than anything else how ridiculous a phrase it is when one can throw it

away on such dirt and scum, and that this rabble could have the impudence to accept and reject it.

"The political and in part financial power of many top functionaries from the imperial central offices and also some of the financial governors in the first century exceeded that of many equestrian or senatorial officeholders."[86] Thus in individual cases one may venture to number these top functionaries among the upper stratum not only as retainers but in their own right. Some of the imperial and public slaves for their part also had subordinate slaves (an especially prominent case is that of a paymaster in the Gallic treasury who had sixteen slaves in his service.)[87] On the basis of military position, the category of retainers must also include Roman soldiers in outstanding functions (say, as *centurio* or *primipilus*), as well as priests and priestesses or, in the land of Israel, Pharisees and scribes, as well as lower priestly families. The managers of property (whether free or slave) also belong here.

D. THE UPPER STRATUM AS A PERCENTAGE OF THE OVERALL POPULATION

Estimates of the percentage of the upper stratum in the overall population depend on which total population figure one uses for the Roman empire. If we also include the families, we can set the share of the overall population between 1 and 5 percent. In any case, it is clear that in ancient societies there was only a thin upper stratum.

3.4.2 The Upper Stratum and Wealth

On the whole, the boundary between wealth and poverty was largely identical with that between the upper and lower strata. Yet *wealth* is a relative term. Because of the conditions of the time, one could regard as rich those who had enough to eat, were well clothed, and lived in pleasant circumstances. In any case, those who had it so good could be satisfied. Thus regarded, the living conditions under which we in highly industrialized countries exist today would seem like those of rich people to most of the people of antiquity. Yet these advantages would still fall short of the wealth that was typical of the upper stratum. A yearly income of 20,000 sesterces and the ownership of four slaves was still not wealth even in Juvenal's view. In fact, in North African cities one would have had to lay out between 5000 and 20,000 sesterces merely for the acquisition of an unpaid public honorary office.

A. EXAMPLES OF WEALTH

As already indicated, wealth was expressed above all in the possession of land. Throughout the Roman empire there was a tremendous concentration of ownership. In North Africa, for example, half of the property was in the hands of only 6 large landowners. By contrast, it happened that over 60 peasant families had to share a piece of land of about 2200 square meters (ca. one-half acre).[88] In Jerusalem, Nikodemon ben Gurion was considered an especially rich man. He is supposed to have given his daughter a wedding gift of 1 million gold denarii. Such a gold denarius had the buying power of 300 loaves of bread of 500 grams each. This daughter's bed alone is supposed to have had a value of 12,000 gold denarii. For this amount, 1500 day laborers would have had to work a full year.[89] Naturally, this information may be legendary. Like everywhere else, the rich people in Israel lived in the city (above all in Jerusalem). In many cases they belonged to the priestly aristocracy. There was also wealth among the rabbis. Rabbi Tarphon owned many fields and slaves. He himself called rich anyone who owned 100 vineyards and 100 fields, as well as 100 slaves to work in them.[90] Whittaker calculates that Cato the Younger drew a daily income of 550 to 650 sesterces from his property, which was worth 4 million sesterces.[91] This corresponds to a yearly income of between 200,000 and 240,000 sesterces. According to Tacitus (*Ann.* 13.42), Seneca is supposed to have left property worth 300 million sesterces. In the cities the rich had their palaces (*domus*); in the country, their villas. Most of their houses were luxuriously furnished, and thus the inventory alone represented a considerable sum. The privileged position of the wealthy was clearly and especially evident in their living situation.[92] This was also true of Palestine (see p. 132), even if everything there was on the whole less splendid than in other regions. In the imperial period the city houses—say, of the senators in Rome—increased in number and in their magnificent furnishings (Pliny the Elder *Nat. Hist.* 36.109). An impressive example of the luxurious living conditions of the rich is the palace-like property of the Flavians in Rome, as well as that of the Herodians in the land of Israel.

B. THE FOOD AND CLOTHING OF THE RICH

A special mark of wealth was the convivial banquet, to which rich friends, neighbors, and relatives were invited. They were then offered the most select morsels from all over the empire. Yet even beyond these banquets the lives of the rich were distinguished by their choices of nourishment. For example, only they could generally afford to eat meat. In one Talmudic tractate there is a Tosepta that recommends food regulations appropriate to a person's property, according to which a man who had 10 minas (equivalent to 1000 denarii) should supplement his daily diet with vegetables. With a wealth of 50 minas (5000 denarii), one should eat 340 grams of meat every sabbath. This quantity could be consumed daily by one who possessed 10,000 denarii.[93] The banquet described in Petronius's *Satyricon* is, naturally, an exaggerated caricature. Yet even from it we can discern the enormous importance of good and sumptuous food for the rich. A poor man in the country is apparently proud when he can offer a guest in his house a chicken and eggs (*Satyricon* 46). In contrast to this, the frugal lifestyle of the emperor Augustus is striking. Suetonius, in his biography of the emperor (*Augustus* 76–77) describes his eating habits, which he characterizes as "extremely modest": "He was especially fond of simply bread, small fish, hand-pressed cheese, and fresh figs of the kind that ripen twice a year. He even ate before the main meal, at any time and place, as soon as he felt hungry." The wealthy stood out from the rest of the populace not only through their opulent eating habits but also through their clothing.[94] This difference brings to mind the parable of the rich man and Lazarus (Luke 16:19-31): the rich man was dressed in purple and fine linen and feasted sumptuously every day. Poor Lazarus apparently had no clothing worth mentioning and was starving. A purple-colored garment of wool and an undergarment (*tunica/chitōn*, Heb. *chaluq*) of fine linen signalized wealth and status. Kings dressed that way—and in genuine Tyrian purple—and the rich emulated them. In order to demonstrate his royal claim, the revolutionary Simon bar Giora wore purple and fine linen.[95] Regarding the description of John the Baptist, Jesus asks the people the rhetorical question whether they went out into the wilderness in order to see a man in soft robes. Then he immediately answers the question himself: people who put on fine clothing and live in luxury are in royal palaces (Luke 7:25).

3.5 The Nonelite: Lower-Stratum Groups

3.5.1 The Calculation of Minimum Existence

As already indicated (see 3.3.2), we make a fundamental distinction between people whose property or income was at least sufficient to assure existence and those who lived either constantly at the minimum subsistence level or even had to vegetate below it. This distinction can also be expressed with Greek terms. For, as we will soon present in more detail (see 3.5.3), the named groups can be characterized by the Greek terms *penēs* (plural *penētes*) and *ptōchos* (plural *ptōchoi*) and thus can also be found in the minds of the ancients themselves. Naturally, we must take into account differences between city and country, between regions, and above all between individual cities. Without doubt, the cost of subsistence was higher in Rome than in other cities or in the country, if we only consider that in Rome a rental dwelling could cost about two thousand sesterces (=five hundred denarii) a year. Therefore rent for dwellings was a cardinal problem for the poorer population.[96] The situation in other cities was comparable. Only in the country did the cost of accommodation not play such a significant role. Even with regional differences, it is possible to propose a model calculation for minimum existence.

Cost of Living and Minimum Existence

An outstanding overview of the various calculations and bases of calculations for the determination of minimum existence is provided by Oakman.[97] He assumes that a grown man with a peaceful occupation needs a daily calorie intake of about 2500. The human calorie requirement naturally depends on age, sex, and kind of activity. Nevertheless, the figure of 2500 calories can serve as a standard value. For the attainment of this quantity—if one applies modern conversion values to antiquity—one would need 794 grams of wheat or 756 grams of barley. Extended to the whole year (365 days), one would need, in round numbers, 290 kilograms of wheat or 275 kilograms of barley to cover the daily requirement of 2500 calories per person. If we use the Latin measure of volume, the *modius* (a *modius* of grain=6503 kg), then the corresponding numbers would be about 44 *modii* of wheat or 42 of barley. These figures also correspond approximately to the estimates of Brunt, who calculates 144 *modii* of wheat yearly for an ancient family of four.[98]

A. CALCULATION OF THE
LAND AREA NECESSARY FOR MINIMUM EXISTENCE

What land area is necessary for this yield? We cannot give precise calculations here, since they are not only difficult because of the source situation but also depend on what yield per quantity of seed was attainable from a certain soil.[99] We offer here only a number for comparison. According to Cicero (*Verr.* 2.3.112), in Leontini in Sicily a sowing of 6 *modii* of wheat per juger produced a harvest yield of tenfold in a good year and eightfold on average.[100] We have here, without doubt, especially high yield figures, which would mean in principle that in an average year (with an eightfold yield) a wheat field of one juger would have produced 48 *modii* of wheat. If we subtract the quantity of seed sown, the result is 42 *modii,* which would feed an adult for one year. Yet we know that Polybius and Cato the Elder set the land area necessary to feed an adult for one year at 2 jugers.[101] This figure probably comes closer to the average yield per juger of land.[102] For if one presupposes an average yield of four times the quantity of seed per juger (and again subtracts the invested quantity of seed), then a sowing of 6 *modii* of seed would produce a net yield of 18 *modii* of wheat for consumption. On the basis of Brunt's estimated figure of 144 *modii* for a family of four, their subsistence would require a cultivated area of 8 jugers (5 acres). Hamel also assumes a small harvest yield. According to his calculations the relationship of seed to harvest is 1:3. He estimates that after the subtraction of the seed needed for the following year and the payment of taxes and fees, only one-third (!) remains for subsistence.[103] Likewise, Ben-David presupposes a small yield: a family of 6 to 9 people would have had to cultivate an area of about 7 hectares, or 17.29 acres (=28 jugers), for a subsistence yield.[104] According to Frayn's research, many Roman and Italian small farmers owned or tilled no more than 10 jugers (6 acres).[105] However one evaluates these numbers, they can, in any case, provide a rough idea of the land a family in the country had to cultivate for their benefit in order to assure the survival of family members.

From these calculations we learn that the amount of land necessary for the feeding of one person varies from 2 (Cato/Polybius) to 4.5 jugers (Ben-David). If one figures an average yield of 18 *modii* of wheat per juger and 42 *modii* of wheat yearly to feed one person, the result is a theoretical average of 2⅓ jugers of land that was needed to feed one person for a year. Thus a family of six would, according to our theoretical calculation, have needed for its nourishment a land area of 14 jugers, or about 8 acres (Ben-David estimates twice as much land). Thus the arable land in Israel (ca. 1,500,000 to 1,750,000 acres) would have been able to adequately feed 1.5 million people.

TABLE 5: THE LAND AREA NECESSARY FOR FOOD

	Household	Amount of Wheat	Land Area
Theory	1 person	42 *modii*	2⅓ jugers
Brunt	4 persons	144 *modii*	8 jugers
Cato/Polybius		1 person	2 jugers
Leontini		54 *modii* (10X)	1 juger
Leontini		42 *modii* (8X)	1 juger
average		18 *modii* (4X)	1 juger
Ben-David	6–9 persons		28 jugers
Ben-David	1 person		3–4.5 jugers
Frayn	average area tilled in Italy		10 jugers

Note: 1 juger=ca. 0.622 English acres; 1 *modius*=6503 kg.

B. THE COST OF LIVING

A translation of these calculations into cost of living is made possible by the knowledge of exact prices from Pompeii. There a *modius* of wheat cost 30 asses; that means that 2 *modii* cost 15 sesterces.[106] If we use a value of about 3000 calories for a kilogram of wheat, a *modius* of wheat would produce an energy value of about 20,000 calories. If an average man needs 2500 calories daily, he would have to spend, on the basis of the prices known to us from Pompeii, 3.75 asses a day to reach the necessary calorie ration. For this amount, however, he could have bought 4 loaves of bread in Pompeii, since a single loaf cost almost 1 as there.[107] Yet because we do not know exactly how calorie-rich the bread was, we can hardly draw any further conclusions. Nonetheless, we can go still further, using figures posited by Ben-David.[108] He calculates that a minimal income of 200 denarii for a family of six sufficed to buy 400 loaves of bread yearly for each family member.[109] He sets the calorie value at about 1200–1400 for a loaf of bread,[110] so that according to his calculations, in the Mishnaic period (ca. 200 C.E.) about 2½ to 3 asses were necessary to cover the daily calorie need of 2500.[111] In short, it seems that about 3 asses were required to meet a calorie need of 2500, which would result in a yearly expenditure of about 275 sesterces or 69 denarii.

The price of bread, therefore, is also a good indicator of buying power, since people in antiquity were nourished primarily by bread.[112] Cato the Elder mentions in his work on agriculture that shackled slaves working in the country ate 4 or 5 pounds of bread daily, but hardly anything else (*De agricultura* 56). He also calculates that a field slave cost about 312 sesterces (78 denarii) a year to keep alive and capable of work. For a free worker and his family 1000 sesterces (250 denarii) were required.[113] If one compares these numbers with the value of 144 *modii* given above for a family of four, the result is almost identical with the cost given by Cato. For with a price of 30 asses per *modius* in Pompeii, 144 *modii* of wheat would require a sum of 1080 sesterces (270 denarii).

At this point, however, we have not yet included additional expenditures for nonfood items. In Pompeii a tunic cost 15 sesterces (1 denarius for cleaning) and simple dishes 1–2 asses.[114] For an outer garment (*himation/toga*, Heb. *talith*) between 12 and 20 denarii had to be spent.[115] Above all, however, in this calculation we have omitted the cost of a residence, which comes into the picture for city dwellers, and the tax burden, which was probably considerable for the rural population in particular (presumably at least 20 percent on average). For the situation in Rome, Juvenal offers a certain point of reference for the cost of living. In one satire (9.140ff.) he calls a secured yearly income of 20,000 sesterces (5000 denarii) and ownership of four slaves nothing more than protection against the beggar's staff in old age. Here he has probably also taken into consideration more than just the cost of food. As a further comparison, Cicero stated that a member of the upper stratum needed an annual income of 600,000 sesterces (150,000 denarii) for a sumptuous life. He himself had an annual income of 100,000 sesterces (25,000 denarii).[116] By comparison, the daily wage in Matthew 20 is 1 denarius (4 sesterces). It is also placed at 3 sesterces.[117]

A summary of the information offered here is given in the following tables. The average daily cost for the nourishment of an adult as indicated in these tables is 3 asses. Thus the food for one adult for one year would require the expenditure of almost 70 denarii. If we include the additional costs for clothing and other things, these calculations become comparable to those in the table of household costs. Thus we must assume that the minimum existence of a family of four in the country (including nonfood items and taxes) is to be set at 250 to 300 denarii.[118] In urban regions, especially in Rome itself, even this amount would hardly have sufficed to assure subsistence. There, however, as already mentioned, the citizens enjoyed distributions of food.

TABLE 6: DAILY COST OF FEEDING ONE ADULT:

	Quantity	Calories	Price	Price per daily calorie need
Theory (price for wheat as in Pompeii)	794 grams	2500	3.7 asses	3.7 asses
Pompeii	1 modius	20,000	30 asses	3.7 asses
Pompeii	1 pound of bread	1200	1 as	2 asses
Palestine (Mishnah)	1 pound of bread	1200–1400	1⅓ as	2½–3 asses

TABLE 7: YEARLY HOUSEHOLD COSTS

	Size of household	Yearly cost
Cato the Elder	1 worker and family	250 denarii
Cato the Elder	1 slave	78 denarii
Brunt	4 persons (144 modii of wheat)	270 denarii
Ben-David	6 persons (Palestine)	250–300 denarii
Pompeii	3 persons (and 1 slave)	570 denarii

According to these figures, a slave cost about 80–100 denarii to support (including nonfood items). Thus to buy and support a slave was doubtless a burden that the average household could hardly afford. The above-mentioned example of a family of three in Pompeii, with one slave, which required at least 570 denarii annually for their cost of living, confirms our calculations. Hence this number will serve as a standard value for the subsistence costs of a family of four in *urban* centers. Yet the cost of lodging must be added to that figure, so that for subsistence an urban family of four would need 600–700 denarii annually (at least twice the subsistence costs in the country). On this basis, with the costs that Juvenal gives for a household with four slaves in Rome, we can see that even after taking the high rents into consideration, 5000 denarii yearly would provide a very pleasant life in comparison with the minimum existence. Even this yearly income, however, allowed hardly more than a modest living standard in Rome. For the assurance of subsistence in Rome, in our view, a family of four would require about 900 to 1000 denarii (about three times the costs in the country). The figures named by Cicero (150,000 and 25,000 denarii) make clear the enormous gap in quality of life between the upper stratum and the little people. These numbers, which naturally can be objectified only with reservation as standard values, can again be summarized in the following overview.

TABLE 8: YEARLY MINIMUM EXISTENCE OF A FAMILY OF FOUR

In the country	250–300 denarii
In cities	600–700 denarii
In Rome	900–1000 denarii
Modest prosperity in Rome	5000 denarii
Wealth	150,000 denarii

These calculations show that in general the criterion of property or income for the differentiation of the social groups of the lower stratum is of great significance. Therefore it seems to us justified when, in addition to the division into rural and urban lower-stratum groups, we draw another fundamental line of separation whose distinguishing trait is based on the criterion of property or income and which falls at the level of *minimum existence*. As has become clear, we must consider here the fact that the expenditure for minimum existence varies not only between individual cities but also between city and country. Nevertheless, we can make the fundamental determination that those who cannot guarantee even minimum existence for themselves (and their families) belong to the lower-stratum group that can be called the *absolutely poor*. In this group we number, among others, itinerant and local beggars (especially people with disabilities and the chronically ill), many day laborers in the cities and in the country, runaway slaves, many poor peasants, and tenants. Even among the minor craftsmen, income hardly suffices for the subsistence of families, especially when they could suffer a social catastrophe if they lose their provider through the death of the husband and father. Therefore, among the women of the lower-stratum families it is above all widows who could not enter a new marriage or return to their father's house that we must include in this group of the absolutely poor. Hence it is with good reason that they, together with orphans, are regularly mentioned among the needy or as the beneficiaries of charity.[119] We will discuss in more detail below the important problem of (relative and absolute) poverty in ancient societies.

3.5.2 A Broad Differentiation of Lower-Stratum Groups

Above the line of separation marked by minimum existence, it is difficult to make any further differentiation. For the boundary between relatively poor and relatively prosperous families and individuals is hard to define. Is the earlier example from Juvenal of the possession of four slaves and a yearly income of 20,000 sesterces an expression of relative prosperity or relative poverty? Juvenal himself seems to assume the latter when he places this social situation just above that of a beggar. This evaluation may also apply to the economic and social conditions in Rome, especially in relation to rich members of the upper stratum. In the smaller cities of North Africa, however, even a minimal wealth of 20,000 sesterces was sufficient for membership in the *ordo decurionum* and thus for inclusion in the local upper stratum. Thus the estimation of economic productivity depends on, among other things, social standpoint and the economic conditions of a region or society. Thus here one can only offer hypotheses for differentiating the broad spectrum of lower-stratum groups according to occupational branches with presumably higher and lower prospects of income. In addition, the portion of the population that was not free can only be estimated and is assumed in the urban situation to be a third of the total population.[120]

The overwhelming majority of the populace belonged to the lower stratum, and most of these people lived in the country. On the whole, life was better for the urban lower stratum than for the rural population. More than the differences in status (freed slave, freeborn, slave, citizen or noncitizen, Roman citizen or pilgrim), which conveyed very different privileges, the poverty boundary obviously divided the lower-stratum groups again into two parts. Here we assume that *in the country* most small farmers and their families, small leaseholders, free wage earners, and day laborers constantly lived on the verge of minimum existence. This is confirmed by the already mentioned thesis of Frayn (see p. 81) that the average area of a small farm in Italy was no larger than six acres (=ten jugers). This would have just barely been enough to feed a family of four. It is difficult to say how high one must set the proportion of people living on the poverty line in the city centers. Here too, however, there are many indications of increasing impoverishment, including the families of small artisans and their free wage earners. In addition to them, there were probably also small traders, urban day laborers, and other occasional workers who were constantly on the verge of minimum existence. The regular group of beggars included above all the chronically ill. The army of urban poor was presumably also augmented by the influx of those members of the rural populace who, as nonheirs, could no longer be fed by the meager yields of small plots of land. In the country, however, the freeborn were presumably the most numerous. The situation of rural workers who were not slaves comprised a broad spectrum from indebted servitude to relative independence. In the cities also, slaves (and freed slaves) by no means formed the majority of the population. The *urban lower stratum* included artisans, merchants, doctors (except for the "personal physicians" of the upper stratum), teachers, musicians, administrators of houses and fortunes, harbor workers, day laborers, beggars, and so forth. The few among them who were able to achieve a certain prosperity—for example, richer merchants and tradesmen—compensated for their lack of participation in public power through membership in occupational associations (many honorary offices in these organizations had the same designations as public offices).

Slaves

Particularly among slaves there were important distinctions.[121] An estate manager (*vilicus*) whose master lived somewhere in a city probably looked down on a small farmer, even if the *vilicus* was himself a slave. In contrast to the free farmer, he did not have to work in the fields, for example, and he had a certain amount of social security, even in years of poor harvest. Indeed, a free small farmer may often have envied even the sometimes shackled slaves working in the fields of an estate. They had to work just as hard as he did, but they could count on regular food and clothing. Freed slaves were still bound to their former masters and obligated to perform certain duties. Yet the process could also be reversed: free people could become slaves. That happened mostly as a consequence of military conquests, in which members of the conquered people were turned into slaves. In the time after Augustus, however, this means of acquiring slaves was no longer the order of the day.[122] Thus the sources of replacement remained the offspring produced by slaves themselves, the slave trade—for example, with Germanic tribes and Ethiopians—and the enslavement of free residents of the empire. In addition, abandoned children[123] were raised as slaves, and children of impoverished families were sold into slavery to satisfy indebtedness. Even adults could become slaves in this way.

Being a slave was not absolutely the worst fate that one could imagine, at least not economically or in the face of bare existence. Belonging to a household guaranteed a certain subsistence, for the slave's owner also had an interest in maintaining the slave's ability to work. Finally, developments in the imperial period began to give slaves certain legal protections. Thus in the year 19 B.C.E. a law (*lex Petronia*) was promulgated that required the approval of authorities before slaves could be made to fight with wild animals. And the emperor Claudius regarded it as murder when old or sick slaves were killed. Finally, Domitian prohibited the compulsory castration of slaves. In addition, it became the policy to free slaves in the cities and especially in Rome, so that with the attainment of a certain age they could count on receiving their freedom. This legal act, called *manumissio,* was so generally practiced under Augustus that some feared a danger to the state from these manumissions. And thus there were ultimately laws that were supposed to reduce the number of emancipations. Above all, care was taken to see that freed slaves could not simply "receive Roman citizenship and thereby all too great an influence on public life."[124] Thus the prospect of liberation could also include the bestowal of citizenship, if the slave's owner was a citizen. Naturally, the owner also profited from emancipation, for the slave who wanted to be released had to pay back his purchase price, and that meant acquiring some capital. Thus even as a freed slave he also remained obligated to his master.

The Occupational Activities of Slaves

The occupational activities of slaves (and therefore also of freed slaves) covered a broad spectrum. In the cities slaves were to no small extent involved in occupations that presupposed a certain amount of education or particular capabilities: "Legal advisors, managers of houses or fortunes, doctors, pedagogues, artists, musicians, actors, clerks, engineers, and even . . . philosophers."[125] In production they worked as artisans (for example, in *terra sigillata* workshops). They ran businesses for their masters, and some were busy as cooks, domestic servants, and personal attendants. In the country slaves were naturally involved in agriculture, yet here too in very different positions. Most of them were shamelessly and at times brutally exploited; indeed, even into the imperial period it was the custom to shackle slaves. Emancipation was also less usual in the country than in the cities. Conditions were even worse for slaves in mines than on the land. These were, above all, *damnati,* that is, prisoners. It is also important that slaves in the cities could organize with fellow slaves and with free individuals into occupational or religious associations (*collegia*).

The Flight of Slaves

Yet the phenomenon of flight shows that the living conditions of many slaves were unbearable. According to Bellen[126] the slaves who were inclined to flee were above all those whose masters were cruel and inhuman. These *fugitivi* could count on being able to hide elsewhere, especially in the country, where there was a shortage of labor. In fact, there are even supposed to have been "brokers" for such runaways. In this way the slaves had actually only changed masters, but that could make all the difference. Naturally, there were not only brokers of *fugitivi* but also bounty hunters who chased runaway slaves for reward. There were even arrest warrants for such fugitives.

The treatment of slaves and attitudes toward them varied. There could be cruelty and total discrimination, even racism, but there could also be kindness and generosity, including recognition of slaves as human beings.[127] Seneca held that even slaves were human (*Ep.* 47.1), yet he still presupposed their low social position.[128] The abolition of slavery was not proposed by him or by anyone else—not even by Christians![129]

Slaves and Inconsistency of Status

The phenomenon of status inconsistency was very pronounced precisely in the slave class, which was clearly separable in terms of personal rights. Besides the often extremely hardworking and occasionally shackled slaves on the land and in the mines, there were slaves active in the management of estates. In the cities slaves were active in homes as servants and in the workplace as workers or perhaps as specialists or even as overseers of other slaves. As already mentioned, many performed higher administrative functions in service to aristocrats. Yet common to all was the situation of dependence (even if they all had a reasonable hope of liberation). This dependence often expressed itself in the fact that younger male and female slaves had to be available as sex objects for their masters (and sometimes also for their mistresses). Especially the situation of female slaves, compared to that of males, was generally more uncertain and less hopeful after emancipation.

3.5.3 The Lower Stratum and Poverty

A. ABSOLUTE AND RELATIVE POVERTY—*Penētes and Ptōchoi*

The masses of the people were characterized not only by low birth and the concomitant lack of political power, but also by their poverty. For them "the struggle for material existence and the bare means of survival determined their daily work."[130] The Latin terms for poor, such as *pauper, egens,* and *humilis,* "cannot and should not designate only the beggars and the wretched, but also the somewhat better-situated craftsmen and traders who, compared with the rich, property-owning classes, were without doubt poor."[131] Yet the ancient terminology can also indicate more precise boundaries here. Better than Latin—or even German or English—the Greek language can distinguish between two groups of poor that today we would call relatively or absolutely poor.[132] In a comedy by Aristophanes (*Plutos* 551ff.) this distinction is graphically described: "The nature of the life of the *ptōchos* is to have nothing. That of the *pēnes,* however, is to be frugal and devote himself to work; he has nothing left over, but he also suffers no need." This agrees with a formulation from Martial (11.328): "It is not poverty to own nothing." For he then goes on to describe the most wretched Roman beggars, whom he distinguishes from the poor. But let us return to the text from Aristophanes' comedy. Initially we have intentionally not translated the two Greek terms *ptōchos* and *penēs*. Both can be rendered as "poor." Yet *ptōchos* usually means the poor who live on the verge or even below minimum existence, whereas *penēs* describes an economic situation in which someone can earn a living for himself and his family through work. In principle, this evaluation from the fourth century B.C.E. remained valid for centuries. In the Hebrew these two groups can also be distinguished terminologically: the absolutely poor person is frequently called *ebion,* whereas the usual designation for the relatively poor is *ani.*[133]

More equivocal, however—as already mentioned—are the Latin expressions for *poor.* "Terms like *inopes* (without means), *egentes* (needy), *pauperes* (poor), *humiles* (humble), and *abiecti* (abject, rejected) were used without precision."[134] The Vulgate, for example, translates the beatitude on the poor (Luke 6:20), which has *ptōchoi* in the Greek original, as *pauperes.* But it translates the poor man Lazarus (Luke 16:19ff.), who is likewise a *ptōchos* in the Greek, as a *mendicus,* clearly marking him as a beggar.

However one may judge the use of language in detail, it calls attention to the fact that there was no unified class of poor people. We must, in any case, distinguish between relatively and absolutely poor. This distinction is to be expressed basically in terms of elementary human needs, which in antiquity included nourishment (food and drink), clothing, and lodging. The words of Dion of Prusa (*Or.* 17.21) can be given as an example of many: "Thus we know that our body has only a few needs: clothing, shelter, and food would certainly be named." And we may presume that the great majority of the people of antiquity hardly got beyond a modest realization of these basic needs.[135] This becomes clear if we take as a basis the rough calculations made above for the cost of maintaining a minimum existence (see pp. 79–85.).

Per Capita Income in the Land of Israel

For comparison let us look at one theoretical calculation of the per capita gross annual product in Palestine in the first century. Assuming a population of 1.25 million, Ben-David has estimated the figure to be 49.6 denarii.[136] If we subtract from this figure only 20 percent for taxes and levies—presumably a percentage that is too small—then theoretically (that is, without considering the high concentration of property) each person would have only, say, 40 denarii to live on each year. This figure alone makes it clear that we must take seriously the probability that an enormously large part of the population lived *below* the poverty line. This number is completely realistic. For in Israel (until around the end of the second century C.E.), an annual income of 200 denarii was considered the minimum existence for a family with 5–6 members. In one statement of the rabbis, this sum is described as the boundary of absolute poverty; that is, those who had a yearly income of more than 200 denarii could not expect help from the Jewish charity system.[137] This sum was probably also the amount that a day laborer could earn in one year, if he worked regularly, with feast days and holidays taken into consideration.

If we look at these sobering figures, it is clear that one needed a well-paying occupation in order to feed a family. Was it at all possible for an artisan like Jesus' father to adequately feed his family (which, according to Mark 6:3, included five boys and several girls)? Joseph was a carpenter. Even a trained artisan in a small place like Nazareth in Galilee seldom earned more than a day laborer.[138] Even with 400 denarii a year, Jesus' family probably still lacked what it needed. Yet in this respect they were no different from their neighbors in the country. A small farmer who tilled an area of about 7½ acres, after deducting the most important levies—for example, the tithe—and taxes, received a meager income of about 150 denarii a year.

A work of the church father John Chrysostom makes clear the miserable situation of the rural population (in this case tenants). The text comes from the fourth century but can probably also be applied to the first century. It reveals that in antiquity there was definitely an awareness of the connection between the poverty of the poor and the riches of the rich. In his Matthew commentary (61.3) Chrysostom writes:

> Could there be more unjust people [than the owners of land who draw their wealth from the earth]? For when we examine how they treat the poor and miserable country people, we reach the conclusion that they are more inhumane than barbarians. On the people who must hunger and suffer all their lives they constantly lay impossible levies, burden them with toilsome duties, and use them like donkeys and mules, and even stones; they do not grant them even the least bit of rest but, whether or not the earth produces a yield, suck them dry and give them no consideration whatever. Is there anyone more worthy of compassion than these people when they worry themselves the whole winter, worn down by cold, rain, and night watches, and now stand there with empty hands, still deep in debt, when they then shiver and quake not just from hunger and failure but also from the tormenting of the overseer, from the warrants, the arrests, the calling to account, the foreclosure of the lease, and from the unrelenting demands? Who can enumerate all the things that are done to them, all the advantage that is taken of them? From their work, from their sweat, storage bins and cellars are filled, but they are not allowed to take home even a little bit; rather, [the landowner] hoards the whole harvest in his own chests and throws them a trifling sum as a wage.

B. THE RELATIVELY POOR—*Penētes*

Even the relatively poor (*penētes*) had to work hard (and often engage in unhealthy activities) in order to provide their families with the bare necessities of life. The prosperous among the little people included those who could supply their families regularly with food, drink, and clothing and reside in somewhat acceptable living conditions. The social needs of the urban population are described by the rhetorician Dion of Prusa (*Or.* 7.105–6):

> For these poor it is certainly not easy to find work in the cities, and they are dependent on unfamiliar sources when they must rent a dwelling and buy everything: not only clothing and household items and food but even firewood for their daily need.

Martial (12.32) states that the poor are thin from hunger and cold. And for the satirist Lucian of Samosata, the living conditions of these poor were defined by high levies and debts, freezing in winter, and illness, as well as the experience of being beaten by the powerful (*Cat.* 15). It is this very aspect of violence—even the violent appropriation of property—that shows the poor's lack of power and rights. Assaults of powerful, rich people against their poor neighbors appear as stereotypical complaints in ancient texts,[139] whether it is the rich occupying the property of an orphan (Philostratus *Heroikos* 285) or a rich man acquiring the cottage of a poor man (Apuleius *Metamorphoses* 9.35ff.).[140] The poverty of fishermen was proverbial,[141] and Lucian of Samosata (*Fug.* 13, 17) says that out of hard work artisans, "bent over their work from early morning to evening, cannot earn a living from such endeavors, in spite of their effort and exertion." The Bible confirms this perception, for the itinerant "tent maker" Paul worked longer than usual—from sunrise to sunset—but he still needed the support of others in order to maintain a minimal existence.[142] The situation of artisan families became dramatic when the husband and father died. Here again, Lucian describes the sad conditions for us rather precisely (*Hetaera Dialogues* 6). After the death of a coppersmith in Piraeus, his family experienced a drastic social decline. First, the widow had to sell the work tools and then try to secure a living for the family through spinning, weaving, and sewing; finally, however, the only course left was for the daughter to contribute to the family income as a hetaera. Elementary teachers (*didaskalos/magister*) were notoriously badly paid, and their families lived miserable lives (Juvenal *Sat.* 7.215ff.; Lucian *Hermot.* 10). By contrast, "lawyers" probably had greater opportunities for income, at least in Rome. In his biography of Apollonius, Philostratus presents this occupation as a possibility for transforming poverty into wealth. As lucrative occupations or activities, in addition to owning land, other ancient authors name the credit business, commerce, and the military, as well as being a ship captain, rhetorician, priest, doctor, carpenter, and cobbler.[143]

C. THE ABSOLUTELY POOR—*Ptōchoi*

If the relatively poor could still meet the basic needs of life, the absolutely poor included those who had not even enough to live. In general, the Greek adjective *ptōchos* designates the following situation of the poor: they are hungry and thirsty, have only rags for clothes, and are without lodging or hope. For the necessities of life they are dependent on the help of others, for example, through begging. In addition to beggars, their numbers often include widows and orphans, but also those who are chronically ill or disabled like the blind, the lame, and lepers.[144] Here too, naturally, there were gradations. Poor Lazarus, the deathly ill man who vegetated in front of the house of a rich man and hoped to nourish himself from the food that fell off the table (Luke 16:19ff.), and the beggars who slept under the bridges of Rome, must have envied those who at least got a pauper's burial (Martial 11.328). According to Horace (*Sat.* 1.8.8–16), public slaves walked the streets of Rome, gathering corpses that were thrown out of dwellings (their burial was apparently too expensive for their families). Those who could afford it ensured themselves against such an undignified end by joining burial societies. Even if we do not turn the most crass image of these absolutely poor into a criterion, there were among the poor many individuals who with effort somehow managed to achieve a minimum existence but were constantly in danger of falling into absolute poverty.[145] Some of these were small farmers or tenants, wage earners or day laborers in the country, who perhaps had lodging but not enough to eat; some were small artisans and traders, elementary teachers, day laborers, and itinerant artisans in the cities, who could not adequately feed themselves and their families. And living conditions in the cities were themselves an expression of the poor's miserable situation. Sixteen people sometimes lived in a single small room.[146] In Ostia the still extant, well-preserved rental buildings (*insulae*), which had at least three stories, can convey an impression of the modest living situation. Those who could not even afford such a rental dwelling had to get by living under bridges, under stairs, or in the cellars of apartment houses. Where possible they built huts (*tuguria*). The hygienic conditions, even by the minimal standards of antiquity, were pitiful. In Petronius's *Satyricon* (95), the cockroaches in one *taberna* are impressively described. On one recovered boundary stone, next to the edict of the magistrate ("No one shall throw away excrement here or a dead body"), the following addendum can be read: "Take your shit far away; otherwise you will get it back."[147]

D. THE CLOTHING AND FEEDING OF THE POOR

Clothing was a valuable possession that one either always wore (those who had two tunics wore one over the other) or even stored in a vault.[148] It seems that the possession of two tunics distinguished the better situated of the little people from the poorer. This is indicated by the challenge of John the Baptist to the simple people: "The man with two tunics should share with him who has none" (Luke 3:11, NIV). For the provisioning of rural slaves with clothing Cato the Elder prescribes that every other year they are to get a 3½-foot-long tunic and a wool cloak (*sagum*), along with wooden sandals. Yet the slave had to return this clothing, from which patchwork was then made (*De agricultura* 59). An outer garment was such a valuable possession for the poor that it could serve as security (Matt 5:40) or be stolen (Luke 6:29). Those who wore no outer garment indicated thereby that they were extremely poor or lived outside the usual social norms; in Luke 8:27, for example, the possessed man's lack of a coat indicates either his poverty or his status as an outsider. In this connection the term *naked* (*gymnos*) designates a person who wore no cloak but only an undergarment or rags. In any case, it is an expression of low social status.[149] In connection with its description of the absolutely poor (*ptōchoi*) the New Testament frequently refers to their nakedness (Rev 3:17; Jas 2:16; Matt 25:36; and so forth). A low status, however, is also shown by dark, rough, and worn outer garments, which were considered typical of poor people and slaves (Lucian *Pereg. Morte* 15–16).

A further mark of the absolutely poor is their hunger (and thirst). The connection between lack of clothing and lack of food seems to be typical (Luke 3:11; Matt 25:35-36; Jas 2:15-16). Meat was basically unavailable and was eaten at most on high feast days. Bread and olive oil were the main means of nourishment for the poor,[150] and when possible vegetables (above all onions) or eggs. In one midrash (*Sif. Deut.* 37.76b)[151] we read: "Your father is rich; he feeds you meat, fish, and old wine . . . your father is poor; he feeds you vegetables and legumes." In a price edict of Diocletian (301 C.E.) a pound of pork is limited to 12 denarii; an egg costs 1 denarius. If we compare these numbers with the average day's wage of the time (25 denarii),[152] it is clear that meat could be bought for the enjoyment of a family only on special occasions, if at all. Anyone who consumed about 80 grams of meat and a quarter liter of wine (here imported Italian wine) would have to be called a "glutton and drunkard."[153] Without doubt, a large part of the populace suffered chronic undernourishment,[154] and in times of need[155] many a poor family had no choice but to feed itself with grass and roots (Dionysius Halicarnassus *Ant. Rom.* 7.8.3; cf. the quotation from Galen on p. 51). Thus the poor may have envied slaves who were adequately fed by their masters for economic reasons.

E. SOCIAL MOBILITY

In general, ancient societies were impermeable.[156] MacMullen, who means by the term *social mobility* not only change from one social stratum to another but also change of residence and occupation, posits little mobility, "for in a world in which the small farmer predominated numerically, people seldom changed their residence, and there were only a few who moved up or down socially."[157] Thus the lack of social mobility is connected with the fact that property was ultimately bound to land and hence was, as a rule, passed on through inheritance. Likewise, descent from a prominent family was achieved only through birth (or, more rarely, through adoption). Only membership in the senate of Rome was linked to inheritance, yet membership in the equestrian order was, in fact, also passed on by inheritance in the provincial nobility of the cities. Hence, social ascent into the upper stratum was blocked by almost insurmountable barriers. Nevertheless, there was a certain mobility, above all in the upper-stratum groups. Here ascent into the equestrian or senatorial order was at least possible. And there was the possibility that a man might marry into an aristocratic family, or as a freed slave or even as a slave might come into his own if the family of the slaveholder died out. The most important possibility of acquiring property and social rank outside the fixed social structure was offered by the military. Here it even happened that someone would rise from soldier status via a junior officer's career into the rank of officer (and thus into the upper stratum). The settling of veterans in Roman colonies also led to the promotion, especially in the provinces, of an upper stratum loyal to Rome. In any case, it was possible for someone to receive Roman citizenship through the army (upon exit from the auxiliary troops or upon entrance into the legion). Special opportunities were available to retired centurions. If they had attained the rank of *primipilus*, they could even be accepted into the *ordo* of the equestrians. In an exceptional case, even someone from the broad group of rural workers made a modest social ascent. On this we have a moving document, an inscription from the Roman province of Numidia in Africa:

> I was born as a child of a poor family, of a father without property, who had neither wealth nor a house. From the day of my birth I lived and worked in the fields. Neither the fields nor I myself ever got any rest. If the year brought forth rich fruit, I was the first at the harvest. When the column of scythe-carrying men had harvested the field and then moved on to Cirta in Numidia . . . I was the first of all the reapers in the field and left behind me a thick row of sheaves. I have mowed twelve harvests under burning sun, and then I went from country worker to leader of the column. For eleven years I was the leader of the reaper column, and the fields of Numidia were mowed by us. This effort and a frugal life finally made me a master and gave me a house and estate.[158]

No doubt, things did not go as well for many fellow sufferers as it did for this day laborer. Rather, members of the lower stratum probably experienced further social decline, especially in the country.

F. SOCIAL UNREST

In societies with serious social differences, there is also unrest, conflict, and even rebellion. Appearing repeatedly as the bearers of this unrest, "on whatever level such conflicts were carried out, were slaves, personally free poor people from the cities, and nominally free, but in reality disfranchised, very poor peasants from the provinces."[159] Apparently only in southern Italy were there regular slave rebellions (Tacitus *Ann.* 4.27; 12.65). And only in a few provinces could uprisings against Rome develop with the broad support of the native population (Batavians in 69; the anti-Roman rebellion in Israel, 66–70). In Rome itself, unrest among the hungering *plebs* is attested under the emperors Tiberius and Claudius. At public events there, the masses of people were kept under control by the army. In 32 C.E. Tiberius was cursed by angry theatergoers because he had let the price of grain rise. The emperor asked the senate and magistrature to apply their authority to suppress this demonstration of displeasure (Tacitus *Ann.* 6.15). Public events usually took place only in the presence of troops from the praetorian guard. Nero withdrew the guard from the games (*Ann.* 13.24–25). The Roman military was also used in the provinces to suppress disturbances and rebellions. Nevertheless, the communities themselves were supposed to provide order. Individual citizens also arrested agitators (Acts 18:12-17). Unrest in the populace could have either ethnic or economic causes (Acts 19:23ff.: rebellion of the silversmiths of Ephesus).[160] On the whole, however, the relative "peacefulness" of the poor members of the lower stratum is remarkable.[161] Lucian (*Sat.* 35) marvels that the poor actually so seldom turn against the rich, whose luxury stands before their very eyes.

PART TWO

The Land of Israel,
the Social History of Judaism,
and the Followers of Jesus

Palestine in the First Century

INTRODUCTION

The history of the Jewish people in the land of Israel—that is, in Judea or Palestine[1]—in the last third of the fourth century B.C.E. was shaped by the change from Persian to Greek hegemony, which was exercised at first by the Ptolemaic kingdom in Egypt and at the turn from the third to the second century by the Seleucids in Syria. The rise of Rome hastened the fall of the Seleucid kingdom, so that after the Maccabean revolt, from the middle of the second century on, Judea was able to enter a phase of relative independence under Hasmonean leadership. Not a hundred years later, however, the Hasmonean state fell under the direct sovereignty of Rome and its vassals. In spite of large uprisings during the time of origin of our literature, the Jewish people were no longer able to free themselves from Roman domination.[2] This permanent change of sovereignty had substantial consequences not only for political structure and administration but also for economic and social development in the land of Israel, and naturally also—and not least of all—for religious development. At its center, as in all comparable societies of antiquity, stands the *antagonism between a small minority of members of the ruling elite, who skim off the surplus, and their retainers in the administration and the military, on the one hand, and the great majority of the ruled masses who produce this wealth, on the other.*[3]

The Foundations of Socio-Economic Antagonism

Since in antiquity the backbone of the economy was always agriculture even in the land of Israel, the interests of the (native) farmers were in principle opposed to those of the current ruling stratum. The latter—apart from the period of Hasmonean autonomy—represented primarily the foreign hegemonic powers or their upper stratum, vassals, and retainers. Yet the latter were always supported by members of the native Jewish upper stratum and its retainers, that is, by an "aristocracy" of priestly and lay families. Yet priests and in part members of high priestly families were also in rebellion against the ruling elite, as shown by the Maccabean revolt with its coalition of free farmers and rural priests. Socio-economically, the actual object of the antagonism was *land*, the *crucial factor* of the economy. This was shown, on the one hand, by the fact that the ruling elite always implemented a direct appropriation of real property, not least of all through confiscation, but it also becomes evident, on the other hand, in the manner in which the surplus is skimmed off, that is, in the taxation system, which consisted essentially in taxation of agricultural and other economic products, as well as natural resources. The most striking economic and social consequences of this constellation are the *concentration of land ownership* in the hands of the few, as well as the *overindebtedness* of ever more small free farmers and the concomitant fall that turned many of them into tenants or day laborers and led them into debtor's prison or slavery. Thus the social and economic reality of the Jewish people in the land of Israel was determined by how wide the gap between the current upper and lower strata opened up in terms of the land and the use of its products. The growing problem of debts shows the problem most clearly.

The Religious Presuppositions and Consequences of the Antagonism

Socio-economic antagonism is naturally also reflected in *religious* antagonism. This is true not just because the Jewish people, like other comparable peoples in antiquity, always interpreted their experiences in the context of religious tradition. Rather, this context is itself already determined by socially and economically relevant traditions, which in turn are the consequences of past socio-economic antagonism. In the (written) Torah (the Pentateuch, that is, the five books of Moses), which received its present form in the Persian period, a part of this heritage became the authoritative basis of tradition, so that its social and cultic legislation was binding in the epochs that interest us.[4] Here there is support for the idea that in this tradition a certain balance was achieved socio-economically, especially between the interests of the peasants (for example, in the prohibition of interest and above all in the debt law with its remission of debt regulation) and those of the priests (for example, in the right to tax), and was elevated as sacred legal tradition.[5] Other traditions, such as the prophetic-eschatological and the wisdom, which were hardly or not at all adopted in the Pentateuch, may have already achieved a certain authoritative importance in the time of Hellenistic sovereignty. Still other, later authorized traditions of prophetic-eschatological or early apocalyptic and wisdom-skeptical provenance came into being in this very period.[6]

Thus we can assume that very different traditions influenced the socio-economic antagonism in the land of Israel, and this in turn affected the process of the formation and handing down of tradition. For example, we can relate the ever more broadly flowing stream of *apocalypticism* in this era to the crisis experiences of the Jewish upper and lower strata, even if in very different ways. The same is true for the concentration on certain identity-marking precepts of the Torah and the discussion of halakic (religio-legal) determinations in application to new situations. Examples are the *pikuach-nephesh* regulation in the sabbath halakah (cf. pp. 208–9) and the *prosbol* in the debt law (cf. 4.1). Indeed, even apparently only religiously relevant regulations such as the purity and food halakah reflect a certain—also controversial—reaction to social conditions. Yet even this does not exhaust the socio-historical significance of the religious tradition. For imbedded in the socio-economic antagonism, both the Torah and the prophets and scriptures expanding and interpreting it also influenced identity and direction. As clearly as the Torah offers concrete instructions for the common life, so also are these clearly valid for Israel; that is, in the Torah the unique relationship of the God of Israel to his people and the land of Israel is articulated and constituted. Yet it is quite variously interpreted. This is evident in the Torah interpretations of apocalyptic currents, the Sadducees, the Qumran community, the Pharisees, and not least of all the followers of Jesus. Yet we also see its effects on the Jewish interaction with Hellenism in the land of Israel.

Socio-Economic Factors and Group Formation

Group formation in the land of Israel was especially affected by socio-economic factors, though their influence varied. The members of various groupings all took part in a certain stratum-specific ways in the socio-economic antagonism, but without being reducible to those ways. Rather, it will be seen, especially with the Qumran community and the Pharisees, that their religious interests can conflict with their socio-economic interests, even if in varying ways. These examples also make clear that the process of tradition and interpretation, as pluralistic and antagonistic as it was, was nonetheless not simply wide open, but rather remained related to a fixed entity through its foundation in the tradition of the Torah. For this reason also, as we shall see, religious antagonism and socio-economic antagonism did not simply overlap. As much as, for example, various interests were present among the Pharisees and Sadducees for or against the expansion of the traditional foundation of the Torah through prophetic tradition, these are not simply reducible to their particular socio-economic positions. Rather, we can learn from the history of the Pharisaic movement that the will to balance various directions and interests, which was effective in the constitution of the Torah as a common basis in tradition, was itself a ferment in the ongoing antagonism. These factors that transcend one's social and economic standpoint are also found in movements that, unlike the Sadducees, Pharisees, and Essenes, were not so rooted in the strata of the rulers and their retainers, but rather recruited from the lower stratum. In our view, these movements also include the followers of Jesus.

Jesus' Followers in the Land of Israel

The origin of the religious movement later named Christianity is found in a small group of men and women in which Jesus of Nazareth played the central role. This group, which was active at first in Galilee in the twenties of the first century, and was mostly called the "Jesus movement," belonged to the Judaism of the land of Israel on the basis of its religious self-understanding, its lifestyle, and its social anchoring, and not least of all because of its geographical limitation. There is no question, however, that in regard to their interpretation of the Torah and especially the proclamation of the *nearness* of the kingdom of God, Jesus and the group named after him held a special religious or theological position within the Judaism of the time, which distinguished them from other Jewish groups and at times also led to conflicts with them. Still, the followers of Jesus preserved their Jewish identity even where they differed from other groups. That identity remained constitutively related to the central social institutions of the Israel of their time and was shaped by its experience of the present. *Thus on the basis of religion and social history, the followers of Jesus belonged to the Judaism of the land of Israel.*

After Jesus' death the movement at first continued in the land of Israel itself. On the one hand, we know from the so-called sayings source (a source common to the gospels by Matthew and Luke that they worked into the traditions they adopted from the Gospel of Mark) that a group of "prophets" continued Jesus' proclamation. Yet since this "second generation" of Jesus' followers is hardly distinguishable socio-historically from the original movement, they will not be treated separately here. On the other hand, we learn from the Acts of the Apostles and also from Paul's Letter to the Galatians that in addition to these itinerant prophets, an urban concentration of Jesus' followers first settled in Jerusalem and gave rise to a local community, the so-called Jerusalem early church. We will look at it at least briefly, since it was shaped by its *stabilitas loci,* that is, no longer by the wandering existence of Jesus' actual followers but by the boundary conditions of an urban environment. It became the launching point, as it were, for further churches in Judea, as well as *urban* Christian communities outside of the land of Israel, of which we will speak in Part Three. If the actual followers of Jesus, the Jerusalem early church, and the churches of Judea belong historically to the epoch before the catastrophe of the Jewish people (70 C.E.), the Gospels of Matthew and John represent, in our opinion, urban messianic communities in the land of Israel in the epoch after 70. Thus, under the heading of the followers of Jesus in the land of Israel we combine here the actual Jesus movement, the Jerusalem early church, the churches of Judea, and the messianic communities in Israel after 70 C.E. that we see represented literarily in the Gospels of Matthew and John.

Outline of Part Two

In the fourth chapter we will sketch the economic situation in the land of Israel and then in Chapter 5 give an overview of the social stratification of the society. Chapter 6 will discuss what traces these socio-economic conditions have left behind in Jewish religious history before and outside the Jesus movement. In this chapter we also give an overview of political and socially revolutionary resistance movements in the Herodian-Roman period, which were only partially obligated to an expressly religious agenda. Finally, we will present the followers of Jesus from their origins in the actual Jesus movement (Chapter 7) to the messianic-Jewish communities in Israel after the catastrophe of the First Jewish Revolt (Chapter 8).

4

THE ECONOMIC SITUATION
IN THE LAND OF ISRAEL

The economy of the Jewish people in the land of Israel was determined on the one hand by productive factors, such as agriculture, crafts, trade, and business, and on the other by the political circumstances that determined the kind and extent of taxes, tributes, duties, and other levies that were to be turned over to the various institutions of government, temple, and priesthood. Therefore, we will first present the situation of agriculture, crafts, trade, and business, bringing into the picture the property conditions in regard to land, since it was the basis of wealth in Palestine as well (4.1). Then we will clarify the burdens laid upon the populace by "state" (4.2.1) and "religious" (4.2.2) taxes. In conclusion we will go briefly into the significance of the temple for the economy (4.3). When necessary and possible on the basis of the source situation, we will differentiate according to the particular historical circumstances.

4.1 Agriculture, Crafts, Trade, and Business in the Land of Israel: Decisive Factors in the Economy of the Land of Israel

Palestine's economy, like that of the Mediterranean lands in general, was primarily agrarian in nature.[1] The most important production factors were, accordingly, the soil and human (and animal) energy; these were supplemented with natural resources and, especially in Galilee, fishing. Trade was essentially local. Nonetheless, in the Hellenistic (from the early fourth century B.C.E.) and Hasmonean (from the middle of the second century B.C.E.) periods commercial relations with Egypt and other countries increased. After the separation of the coastal region and the Transjordanian cities by Pompey (middle of the first century B.C.E.), however, the Jewish share of the trade was again reduced. The geographic and climatic conditions were variable. In Galilee, for example, more rain fell on average than in Judea, and northern Galilee was different from southern Galilee. The region around the Lake of Gennesaret was especially fruitful.[2] Josephus also emphasized the productivity of Galilee (*War* 3.41ff.). Nevertheless, the whole land of Israel was used intensively for agriculture, and in Judea terrace farming was employed to make full use of moisture.[3] Technology was also adapted for dry-land farming.

A special plow was used that was not as heavy as the European, since it was merely supposed to scratch the surface of the soil in order to preserve the moisture in the deeper regions.[4] The crops included above all grain and olives but also wine and fruit, vegetables and spices, wood, and not least of all balsam, which was used in the preparation of perfume and medicines. In addition came the production of asphalt and some raising of livestock, in Judea especially for the temple service.[5] We must see the following descriptions from the *Letter of Aristeas* and in Josephus against this background:[6]

> For the efforts in agriculture are strenuous, and their [the Jews'] land is thickly planted with olive groves, grain, and legumes; there is also wine and much honey; their fruit and figs are immeasurable. One also finds many kinds of cattle and abundant pastureland for them. We [Jews] have no coastal region and do not enjoy the trade and commerce with others that it brings. Instead, our cities are built far from the sea, and we devote ourselves to the cultivation of the good earth that is given to us.

The prominent significance that agriculture has for the land of Israel is also seen in traditional Jewish literature (Mishnah, Talmud) and its numerous discussions of agricultural problems, as well as those of property law.[7] At the same time, biblical and rabbinic texts make it clear that Jewish agriculture was subject not only to natural limitations but also to religious precepts (halakic determinations). From the perspective of the pure maximization of profit, these often meant certain restrictions, yet they were developed for the preservation of social peace and the special protection of the weak and dependent, as well as work animals. As an example we mention here only the laws governing the sabbath and the sabbath year. There were also religious norms for other economic areas. The Talmudic regulations for trade, crafts, and business are an impressive testimony of this, even if they, naturally, reflect above all a development after the destruction of the second temple (70 C.E.).[8]

Crafts, business, and—in part independent from them—*trade*[9] flourished in the land of Israel, especially in connection with Hellenization, which also brought a certain urbanization.[10] The spread of the coinage system, which had already begun in the Persian period, also promoted trade.[11] After this time Palestine was also integrated economically into the eastern Mediterranean area and later into the broader area enclosed by the Roman empire.[12] Handicrafts attained a certain specialization and differentiation (see pp. 30–31).[13] They were concentrated particularly in the cities and especially in Jerusalem. Here artisans were sought above all for the expansive building activity.

In the middle of his reign, Herod developed "a downright excessive construction program, which—together with an expansion of the traffic network—no doubt also invigorated the economy of the country."[14] In Jerusalem this included, above all, the building of the temple, the construction of the Antonia fortress northwest of the temple, a palace, a theater, and an amphitheater. In Strato's tower he founded a new city, called Caesarea. Samaria (later Sabaste) was rebuilt, as was Aphek (later Antipatris). The founding of smaller cities included Gaba in western Galilee, Phasaelis in the Jordan valley, and Agrippias near Gaza. Finally, we must mention that Herod had the old Hasmonean constructions in Jericho, Cyprus, Masada, Alexandrium, Hyrcania, and Machaerus refortified and in part finished in luxurious fashion. In addition, south of Jerusalem he build the fortress and residence Herodion, in which he was buried.[15] His followers continued these activities. The building activity naturally gave many people work and income, but it consumed enormous sums. Moreover, the concentration of manpower, as seen, for example, in the temple construction work in Jerusalem, meant an increased potential for social conflict. This is also made clear by the fact that Agrippa II, after the completion of the temple construction, intentionally created work for the newly unemployed by having them pave Jerusalem streets with the help of capital from the temple treasury (Josephus *Ant.* 20.219–21).

In Jerusalem, and especially for the temple construction, there was a need for certain skilled workers, such as special stonemasons, goldsmiths, and silversmiths, but also showbread bakers and producers of incense. And the pilgrim industry required other kinds of handicraft and special tradesmen, for example, glassmakers who produced especially fine glass products,[16] and naturally innkeepers were also needed. Contrary to a certain prejudice, we must ascertain that trade neither was a specifically Jewish activity nor had a special meaning for the economy in the land of Israel. It was quite varied but in no way dominant.[17] Domestic trade involved the most varied wares, although grain, oil, and wine comprised the major portion. Furthermore, it was decentralized; there were markets in many of the larger places and above all in Jerusalem.[18] Yet the trade there was largely limited to the surrounding hinterland.[19] The usual hindrances stood in the way of a greater transregional trade: transportation problems and tariff costs. In addition, after the death of Herod (4 B.C.E.) and the division of the country, there also seem to have been difficulties between the tetrarchies regarding the equivalence of the various small coins.[20]

Nevertheless, there was also a small amount of foreign trade, that is, exports and imports, which linked the country with many urban centers in the Mediterranean world. Yet foreign trade was limited mainly to cities and particularly to Hellenistic (coastal) cities. It involved only a very few goods, such as, naturally, luxury goods like perfumes and common materials that were either not available at all in the land of Israel or available in insufficient quantities, for example, iron, copper, lead, gold, and silver. Thus the *Letter of Aristeas* (114) mentions the Arabian imports "spices, gems, and gold." And in describing the temple gates, Josephus reports that one was of "Corinthian ore," a special bronze casting that exceeded even golden and silver gates in value.[21] Naturally, there could also be the importation of grain in times of crop failure and famine. According to Josephus, in 26 B.C.E. Herod is supposed to have imported a large quantity of grain from Egypt and distributed part of it in the cities of his kingdom.[22] The context in which Josephus reports this makes it clear that Herod was hardly acting out of compassion for his starving subjects but rather out of the most selfish political and economic interests. For the persistent hunger soon threatened even the seed grain and thus the king's future income. Above all, however, the famine had led to anti-Herodian manifestations. It was probably not least of all the consequences for peace and order that frightened even the Romans, for they permitted Herod to purchase Egyptian grain, which was designated only for official Roman use.[23] Thus, on the whole, crafts, business, and trade played only a subordinate role in the economy of the land of Israel apart from the cities, in which they, naturally were of great importance.

ASPECTS OF THE ECONOMY
IN THE CONTEXT OF THE HISTORY OF PALESTINE

Ptolemaic Sovereignty

With the different political sovereignties, the economic situation in Palestine changed, as the kind and scope of property relationships and the taxes, as well as the intensity of land usage and the productivity of various branches of the economy changed. The decisive transformation took place under *Ptolemaic* hegemony.[24] Integrated into the centrally governed, giant Hellenistic territorial state, Palestine also became a subsystem of the state economy that was strictly oriented around the monarch and his ruling house. That means that the monarch and his family represented the center and focus of the economic process. Klort correctly states:

> Not only in theory but also in practice, the king controlled the most property; he owned the most important manufacturing, mines, and quarries; he was the producer and dealer who controlled an effective distribution system on water and on land. As W. Tarn once formulated, "Ptolemy was the greatest grain salesman that the world has ever known."[25]

Quite obviously, however, after this time not only did the productivity of the economy increase, but at the same time, what was produced was also substantially skimmed off by the ruling administrations. Serving especially in this regard was the introduction of the (Greek) tax franchise, that is, the leasing and subleasing of the right to tax to private individuals or companies (see p. 114). One result of this was an intensification of general indebtedness. Finally and above all, however, it was the relationship of the Hellenistic ruler to the land that created the necessary condition for this development. For beginning with Greek sovereignty, the soil of "land acquired by spear" was claimed as royal land, so that ultimately everything that was produced was somehow owed to the king and by some means went at least in part to him.[26] We must distinguish, nevertheless, between the royal land that was also in the possession of royal lease-holders and the released land that was turned over to cities, institutions (such as temples), or private individuals, but which could also be demanded back.[27]

This development had its clearest expression in the concentration of land ownership in the hands of a few large property owners. With perhaps a partial exception in the Hasmonean period, this concentration determined the economic conditions of Palestine in the Roman period, as shown not least of all by the fact that after a change to the sovereignty of a new lord, the land in possession of the old upper stratum was first annexed and then used to build up a new upper stratum. The result was that an unbroken chain of possession can be established from the Ptolemies through the Seleucids to the Hasmoneans and the Herodians and Romans.[28] The transfer of valuable date and balsam plantations near Jericho from Herod to Cleopatra and again back to Herod within a few years may serve as an illustrative example. Presumably these were domains that were previously in Hasmonean hands and whose origins reach back into the Persian period and possibly the period of the Israelite and Judahite monarchies.[29] A similarly impressive example is the history of a domain in the Jezreel valley, which Fiensy has researched.[30] Yet we must note that relatively little land was held directly by Roman upper-stratum families.[31] Archelaus's properties were confiscated after his banishment and then sold (Josephus *Ant.* 17.355).

The Situation of Jewish Peasants under Hellenistic Central States

The consequences of this control of the land of Israel are already evident, on the one hand, in the Ptolemaic period especially in an intensification of the tax burden and, on the other, in the forced exploitation of royal land through the settlement of colonies and the founding of cities.[32] Therefore, in regard to the economic organization of the Ptolemies, Tarn has spoken of a "money making machine."[33] At the same time, however, the rational cultivation of the soil and a strictly organized management also led to a blossoming of Palestine's economy under the Ptolemies, and thus Freyne speaks of an "agribusiness."[34] An eloquent testimony of this is the Zenon correspondence from the middle of the third century (the Zenon Papyri).[35] It also shows how the economic processes operated.

Also notable in this connection is a decree of Ptolemy II "Philadelphus" (283–246 B.C.E.), which was apparently directed against the enslavement of free peasants.[36] It is possible that we have here a conflict of interest between head of state and state leaseholders. The latter, together with the peasants dependent on them, had an interest in the profitability of an operation, and thus the number of partners in the business was reduced by the enslavement of some of their members—which could happen especially through indebtedness. The king, however, had an interest in the largest possible number of free farmers, in whose harvest he could share.[37]

Seleucid Hegemony

After the initial tax liberation of Jerusalem, the Seleucid hegemony hardly changed any of the economic conditions in the land of Israel. As far as the tax policy is concerned, conditions for the Jewish population deteriorated (see p. 114–15). Hengel has assumed that the Hellenistic reform efforts of the Jerusalem upper stratum also had economic motives: they were, namely, supposed to lead to an unrestricted economic exchange with the surrounding Hellenistic world, that is, one free from the restrictions of religious law.[38] That is questionable, nonetheless, since the technological advances had already been introduced earlier.[39] Yet we must note that it was, in any case, the intention of the reformers to secure the economic situation of the upper stratum through the introduction of Hellenistic citizenship.

From the allegedly Aristotelian writing *Oeconomica*[40] we also learn that in the Seleucid period the overall economy of the kingdom was divided into four categories of administration: royal economy, economy of the satraps, urban economy, and private economy. The royal court had the monopoly on coinage, domestic and foreign trade, and expenditures, while the satrapies or provinces administered the state income from leases (*ekphoria*) and the tithe (*dekatē*), that is, the taxes and fees. The income of the provincial economy was drawn above all from the real and other property of the state, from trade and business, from livestock, duties, and taxes of various kinds. The economy of the polis was affected by the administration of income from the property of its territory and likewise from certain taxes. The private economy, finally, involved above all property and moneylending. This enumeration again makes impressively clear, on the one hand, the broad spectrum of the ancient economy, which consisted of landed property and the levying of taxes on it, but also of trade and business and their related taxes. On the other hand, however, we can also see here that rural and urban economies were different. This difference is evident not least of all in the real property situation and the resulting dependency conditions of the peasants. Thus, in addition to royal land, small farmers were also found on the property of the urban upper stratum, and larger estates also occupied day laborers and slaves with a wide variety of functions.

The Situation under the Hasmoneans

Under the Hasmoneans, Jewish small farmers apparently had a relatively tolerable situation, since they were largely liberated from the burden of Seleucid taxes. The Hasmoneans could hardly have regarded all peasants as state tenants on royal land. The Hasmoneans also held their own extensive domains: the balsam plantations near Jericho, for example, were probably Hasmonean property, as was the Jezreel valley conquered by John Hyrcanus. And these were hardly the only properties of the Hasmoneans. Yet they, in contrast to the Hellenistic rulers before them, did not regard the land as their property.[41] As Schalit assumes, landless small farmers were settled by the Hasmoneans in the conquered regions either as leaseholders on royal domains or (what was perhaps even the majority) as owners of the land.[42]

The Changes under Roman and Herodian Rule

In the middle of the first century B.C.E. this situation was abruptly changed by Pompey and his legate Gabinius;[43] that is, they returned conditions to what they had been in the time of Hellenistic sovereignty. Through the separation of the coastal region and the Transjordanian cities from the area of the Jewish state, many Jewish small farmers lost their livelihood and were driven into the remnant state. In addition, the loss of most urbanized regions meant a reduction in trade, which led to additional pressure on agriculture. Joppa alone may have remained a harbor city with a sizable Judean population. Finally and above all, however, the tribute obligation of Judea had considerable consequences for the populace (see p. 116). In one sense Herod the Great emulated the Hellenistic rulers, for he levied high taxes and in the wake of the elimination of the traditional upper stratum, he confiscated enormous land areas (cf., for example, Jos. *Ant.* 17.304ff.). Whether he used these as his own royal domains or gave them to his favorites, the land was now tilled more and more by tenants, day laborers, and slaves. In this way, considerable land passed into the hands of non-Jewish owners, while the number of Jewish leaseholders increased, and this naturally raised the potential for social conflict.

Land Ownership. In a careful analysis of the sources (particularly Josephus, the rabbinical literature, and the New Testament), as well as archaeological evidence, Fiensy has drawn up an overview of moderate and large landownership in Palestine during the Herodian period.[44] He distinguishes between royal and aristocratic estates. Among the non-Herodian large landowners a number of priestly families are also known. Fiensy (with Dohr)[45] divides these operations as follows:

1. small (10–80 jugers=ca. 6–50 acres)
2. medium (80–500 jugers=ca. 50–300 acres)
3. large (over 500 jugers=over 300 acres)

As a result of his analysis, Fiensy summarizes that medium and large land-ownership—that is, property that is large enough that one does not need to work oneself but must engage tenants, day laborers, and slaves—was widely scattered.

The largest estate attested was *Qawarant Beni-Hassan* in the vicinity of Shechem. It was probably over 2500 acres and was first in the possession of the Hasmoneans and then the Herodians.[46] Dar estimates that some 175–200 families lived on this royal domain. Perhaps they were at first owners but then only tenants on their properties. On the northern part of the estate was a building ("palace") of massive stones in the Herodian style; it perhaps stood ready for the owners when they visited the estate. On one hill stood a fortification, which presumably also served the administration of the giant operation. The "Haris" that lay to the east of Qawarat Beni-Hassan was probably the village of Arus mentioned by Josephus, which Herod had given to his minister Prolemaeus of Rhodes (cf. *War* 2.69).[47] This juxtaposition is not atypical, for there are some signs that Herod and his successors, as well as their minions, had large contiguous land holdings almost everywhere in Palestine, with the possible exception of the vicinity of Jerusalem, where non-Herodian upper-stratum families and also the families of the priestly aristocracy, like that of Josephus (cf. *Life* 422), had their estates.[48] Also in the New Testament there are remnants of this situation, especially in the parables (cf., for example, Mark 12:1-12; Luke 15:11ff.; 16:1ff.).[49] In addition, there are indications of landownership near Jerusalem in connection with the followers of Jesus (cf. Matt 27:57ff.; Mark 15:21; Acts 4:36-37; 5:1).

For the most part, we know very little about the general situation of tenants and free small farmers in Roman times. Were the latter still in the majority, or was it now the tenants?[50] Yet even if small farmers were still in the majority, we must assume with Fiensy that the land controlled by Herod, his successors, and the upper strata had an important influence on the economy of Palestine.[51]

Economic Concentration in the Herodian Dynasty. The fact that Herod apparently regarded the entire country as his property is also shown by his settlement policy, whose beneficiaries, in addition to veterans, were Jews from Babylonia and Idumea. This is also made clear by the founding of cities and monumental building activity of Herod and his successors.[52] The construction gave now landless small farmers certain opportunities for work and wages.[53] With the large sums that Herod needed for construction, the army, and administration, as well as for costly gifts, it is understandable that Herod spent more than he had at his disposal, as confirmed by Josephus (*Ant.* 16.154). The same is true of his successors. Under Herod the annual direct income from taxes was at least around 1000 talents (a talent=6000 denarii), and according to Josephus, the state income of the heirs was 900 talents (Herod Antipas 200, Philip 100, Archelaus 600, Salome 60), and the income of Agrippa I came to 1200 talents.[54] To this we must add the yields from crown estates and other sources, such as mines. It is clear that in this way Herod and his successors stimulated the economy of the land but also laid enormous burdens on its population. Without the income that flowed into the land from the Diaspora as temple tax, it would hardly have been possible to support the traditional temple service, the duties associated with the temple, and—not least of all—the enormous building activity in Jerusalem.

The economic changes in Palestine under Roman rule can therefore be characterized (with Applebaum) as an acute lack of land, that is, as a shortage of agriculturally usable land per capita of population.[55] More and more people had to earn their living from less and less land. The result was that the traditional forms of settlement were abandoned.[56] Although the area of cultivated land was expanded wider and wider,[57] more and more small farmers worked less and less land. At the same time, confiscations and the oppressive tax burden narrowed the possibility for self-sufficiency, and thus more and more small farmers lost their land. *Therefore, the indebtedness of small farmers and expropriation of their land are the hallmarks of this Roman epoch.* Hence one can indeed speak of a regular process of pauperization. The decline of free small farmers to small leaseholders, then day laborers, and even beggars was nothing unusual. Thus, on the one hand, the number of those who worked the soil as small leaseholders or even day laborers, and no longer as owners, increased, while, on the other hand, property was increasingly concentrated in the hands of the few. In this way, whole villages became dependent on large landowners, while, conversely, a few individual farmsteads became agglomerations of many smaller houses.[58]

The Problem of Debt. In the Herodian period at the latest, this situation produced the Jewish debt law. For, according to the Mishnah (*Sheb.* 10.2–4), Hillel created, through the introduction of the *prosbol,* the halakic possibility of maintaining a debt beyond the jubilee year through the depersonalization of the promissory note, which could now be turned over to a court.[59] Perhaps he was only regulating an already existing practice,[60] which is presumably also presupposed in an Aramaic papyrus document from Wadi Muraba'at.[61] This drastic change in the debt law of Deut 15:1ff., which prescribes a complete remission of debt in the sabbatical year, probably had its origin in the fact that because of the possibility of debt remission in the sabbatical year, loans to the poor, who were necessarily dependent on them, were hardly or only very reluctantly given, although the Torah makes the giving of credit a duty.[62] Thus Hillel's determination was made in the interest of the oppressed poor, not that of the wealthy lenders. Nevertheless, it naturally also affected the latter and responded to their interest in secure money transactions. Therefore, Goodman has even suggested that the *prosbol* was introduced in the interest of the priestly or lay aristocracy and their investment intentions.[63] It is clear that this pauperization of the peasantry created a considerable potential for robbery and revolutionary movements. Not coincidentally, again and again the now powerless Hasmonean circles recruited from among the small farmers crowds of followers for their struggles against Roman and Herodian powers.[64] For the revolutionary climate, which gave birth to the restructuring of Palestine by Pompey, also remains a socio-political characteristic of the whole epoch up to the First Jewish Revolt, in which it was no accident that the Jerusalem debt records were burned at the very beginning (Jos. *War* 2.427). Here sprouted, as it were, the seed that had been sown more than a hundred years earlier by Pompey.[65]

4.2 Taxation in the Land of Israel

In the land of Israel the criterion of sovereignty, as well as its actual aim, was to raise levies and bring in taxes. Yet the purposes that were connected with it were quite diverse. For foreign Greek and Roman rulers, and for their vassals, the main reasons, naturally, were the maintenance and enlargement of attained positions of power and thus, ultimately, their own enrichment. Often enough this was also the aim of the Jewish upper stratum who shared in this power, but at the same time it was linked more closely with the traditional means of legitimation within the Jewish people. This is true above all for the priestly aristocracy, whose "right of taxation" was chartered through the biblical giving of the law. In our presentation, therefore, we distinguish between "state" and "religious" taxes.[66] Naturally, in many respects that is an artificial distinction. Nevertheless, in the land of Israel, through the concentration of religious taxes on temple and cult, there was something like an manifestation of identity under the very yoke of foreign domination.[67] The various religious taxes (temple tax, tithe, firstling taxes, and so forth), tributes and direct taxes (for example, land tax, head tax), indirect taxes (wreath tax, salt tax, sales tax, and the like), duties (import and export duties, harbor duties, tolls), fees, and compulsory labor (*angaria;*[68] cf. Matt 5:41), which were imposed on the Jewish population in Palestine, are brought together under the term *taxes.*[69] The kind and degree of burden imposed by these taxes were naturally different, yet structurally the system remained relatively the same from the Ptolemies to the Romans.[70]

4.2.1 State Taxes

TAXATION UNDER HELLENISTIC SOVEREIGNTY

With the change from Persian to Greek hegemony, the organization of the tax system also changed. In Judea as elsewhere, the Ptolemies introduced the Greek tax leasing system.[71] This meant that the responsibility for gathering taxes no longer rested directly with the government but was given to entrepreneurs and financiers as leaseholders and subleaseholders. Usually in a cycle of one year, the right of taxation was auctioned to the highest bidder. The tax leaseholders (*telōnēs, telōnai*) could be individuals or collectives. In general the auctioned areas were villages, districts, and even whole provinces, but the majority of leases were small. The tax leaseholders were "middlemen between the taxpayers and the assessors" of the royal finance apparatus.[72] Assessors, together with the finance administrator (*oikonomos*) of a province, watched over the tax leaseholders, who in turn checked on the taxpayers and assessors. The leaseholders and their sureties ultimately bore the risk if they could not bring in the sum that was bid, but if they brought in more than the bid, they made a profit. Josephus gives us a sense of this process when he describes the bidding up of the general tax lease for Syria and Phoenicia by the Tobiad Joseph:

> On the day of the tax leasing, the most prominent of each city bid on its taxes. Eight thousand talents had already been bid on the taxes from Syria, Phoenicia, Judea, and Samaria, when Joseph came and reproached the bidders because they wanted to give so little for the taxes. He himself then promised to give twice as much and to deliver to the king the property of those who proceeded against him, for this was likewise bestowed with the taxes. The king heard this bid with pleasure and gave the contract to Joseph, who wanted so much to increase his income, after asking him whether he could provide sureties.[73]

According to Josephus, Joseph held this general tax lease for twenty-two years, which is supposed to have enabled him to make a legendary climb from poverty (*penia*) to wealth (*Ant.* 12.170). It is not clear what the administrative relationship of the general tax lease of the Tobiads to the tax responsibility of the high priest or Jewish authorities was during this period. During the Seleucid period, in any case, rivals for the office of high priest were also rivals in the bidding for the tax lease. Thus here the responsibility for tax administration lay (again) in the hands of the high priest. We cannot say whether the Ptolemaic system of the small lease was still functioning in the Seleucid period.

The Amount of the Taxes
How great the burden of taxation was in the Ptolemaic period is not known. Yet the decree of the Seleucid Antiochus III (cf. Jos. *Ant.* 12.138ff.) makes it

clear that in addition to the tribute (*phoros*), a head tax, crown tax, and salt tax were customary. It also shows that duties were levied on transported goods such as wood.[74] A certain point of reference is also offered by the information on the time of the alleged *intersacerdotium* (159–152 B.C.E.). At that time Demetrius I claimed one-third of field crops and one-half of the fruit from trees. After the battle of Magnesia, which brought Antiochus III high reparation payments, the tribute, for which the high priest had to take over the grantee, was drastically raised. Though it had already been 300 talents under Seleucus IV,[75] with his "elevation" to the high priest's office, Jason had promised a raise to 360 talents and a further 80, as well as a onetime payment of 150 talents. Menelaus outbid him a few years later by the outrageous sum of an additional 300 talents.[76] The pressure of taxation grew accordingly.[77] The books of Maccabees indicate that between 175 B.C.E., the year when Antiochus IV became king, and 169 B.C.E., the year of the plundering of the temple, almost 4000 talents in tribute payments were given to the Seleucids—this in addition to taxes, duties, and fees.[78] Clearly the outrageous plundering of the temple treasury and forced Hellenization could easily have been the last straw. Thus the Maccabean Revolt should be regarded not least of all as liberation from the Seleucid exploitation of the Jewish people.

TAXATION UNDER THE HASMONEANS

How the situation in Judea changed under Hasmonean leadership with regard to taxes is not entirely clear. Nonetheless, we can be sure of the initially partial (cf. 1 Macc 11:33ff.; Jos. *Ant.* 13.125) and then complete liberation from the Syrian tribute obligation under Demetrius II or Simon in 142 B.C.E. In that year "the yoke of the Gentiles was removed from Israel, and the people began to write in their documents and contracts, 'In the first year of Simon the great high priest and commander and leader of the Judeans'" (1 Macc 13:41-42). Indeed, the expanding Judea itself now made subjugated areas obligated to pay tribute (cf. 1 Macc 15:28ff.; Jos. *War* 1.89). Yet the military actions of the Hasmoneans, which required large armies of mercenaries, caused a large shortage of financial means even after liberation from the Syrian yoke. And thus in principle, the tax system probably remained intact. This is shown by the so-called Pergamum decree, which presupposes a differentiated system of taxes and duties.[79] According to Schalit, under John Hyrcanus or Alexander Jannaeus, the temple tax of one-third shekel, which had been paid since the Persian period, was raised to the then usual half-shekel (see 4.2.2) and in addition was transformed into a "regular state tax for the total Jewish and non-Jewish population, that is, a head tax."[80]

TAXATION UNDER THE ROMANS AND HERODIANS

For the Jewish population of Palestine, nonetheless, the Roman conquest meant a drastic caesura in regard to taxes, as well as in other ways, for once again—as in the pre-Hasmonean period—they were obliged to pay tribute.[81] "Almost like victory booty and war penance," as Cicero aptly characterized the tribute (*Verr.* 3.6.12), the Hasmonean remnant state had to pay the Roman governor of Syria a large sum in money and in kind as a tax for soldiers' pay and war reparations (*stipendium/phoros*).[82] As usual in this connection, Roman tax leaseholders (*publicani*) also came into the country and, beside the already present Hellenistic small leaseholders, collected the various taxes.[83] The former presumably contracted for a share of the direct taxes and the *stipendium,* and also for the land and harbor duties (*portorium*). Yet the publicans' claims to power were considerably restricted by their opponent Gabinius, Pompey's successor as governor of Syria. He seems to have turned the tax collecting over specifically to the "procurator" Antipater and the upper stratum of his five administrative districts (*synedria*).[84] These measures are probably connected with a Roman conflict over the exploitation of the provinces, which had long been brewing between the equestrian order, from whose ranks the publican companies were largely formed, and the senatorial high nobility, who occupied the highest administrative offices in the provinces.[85] Only with the financial reform introduced by Caesar and then carried out under Augustus did the double exploitation—which on the part of the publicans probably meant a literal plundering of the provinces—largely come to an end. In any case, Caesar had already totally forbidden the collecting of taxes in Judea by Roman publicans in 47 B.C.E.[86] He also expressly confirmed that Hyrcanus (and his sons) as high priest, like his forebears, also had claim to the tithe. It is noteworthy that Caesar exempted the sabbath year from the annual tax.[87] The collection now became the responsibility of the Hasmonean ethnarch Hyrcanus II (Jos. *Ant.* 14.200), but in fact probably that especially of his field commander Antipater, who was also officially appointed as procurator of Judea (*Ant.* 14.143; *War* 1.199). Whether the latter also affirmed the services of the Hellenistic small leaseholders is unknown but probable. He depended, however, especially on his sons for the collection of the tribute. This is shown very drastically by the example of Cassius. As the governor of Syria, he tried by every means to extract from Judea the enormous sum of 700 talents of silver by levying different shares from each of the toparchies.[88] Josephus reports that Herod, as military governor of Galilee, was the first to bring in his share, whereas other toparchies apparently could not meet the demand. The result was that Cassius had the magistrates of the other cities, who were apparently responsible for the tribute, and the residents of four cities sold into slavery (cf. *Ant.* 14.271ff.).

Conditions under Herod

After the brief three-year intermezzo in taxes occasioned by the Parthian invasion, with the ascendancy of Herod in 37 B.C.E. the Jewish populace again became obligated to pay tribute to the Romans. Yet it is not completely clear whether the tribute for the Romans was in addition to the taxes that Herod collected for himself or whether it was included in them and thus paid indirectly.[89] In any case, Judea under Herod first had to pay tribute to Antonius and then to Octavian, to whom Herod, after the battle of Actium in 31 B.C.E., also made a gift of the gigantic sum of 800 talents out of gratitude for confirmation as ruler (*Ant.* 15.200). Thus Herod, in fact, served as the Roman procurator, but in so doing he also wore the crown of a king of the Jews, which only meant an additional burden for the people.[90] It is also indicative that after the death of Herod, the wish for relief from the heavy load of taxes came to expression in very different ways.[91] On the one hand, rebellions flared up; on the other, efforts were made to influence the potential successor, Archelaus. In Rome a Jewish delegation even asked the emperor to unite the land of Israel with the Roman province of Syria and let it be administered by its own governor (*Ant.* 17.308), in order in this way to be freed from the essentially unbearable load of Herodian taxes. Yet Augustus left everything much as it was, except that now the division of sovereignty and territory introduced administrative differences.

Taxation in the Province of Judea

Nevertheless, in 6 C.E. the situation changed for one part of the land of Israel when the ethnarchy of Archelaus was transformed into a Roman province. Now the Romans were again the direct recipients of the taxes; that is, for the first time one had to render unto Caesar what was Caesar's. The "census" that was usual in the establishing of a Roman province was carried out, though connected with a routine checking of the tax lists of Syria and also undertaken by the governor there, Quirinius. This is to be inferred from information that is found in Josephus (*Ant.* 18.1-2) and in Luke 2:1ff., although the latter passage falsely assumes a connection with an imperial census by Augustus and as a date the year of Jesus' birth.[92] It is also incorrectly presupposed there that registration in the tax lists could take place only in one's native city. The census meant the assessment of the population for land and head tax (*tributum soli* and *tributum capitis*), that is, entry on lists for future taxation. All male members of a household (*familia* or *oikos*) who were fourteen or older and all female members at least twelve years old were obligated to pay tribute, which probably meant one denarius per head annually (cf. Mark 12:13-17). In the wake of these censuses, which were usually accompanied by brutal hearings, there were also insurrections, for example, the rebellion against the census under Judas Galilean.[93]

The Responsibility of the Jewish Aristocracy for Collecting Taxes

Although the Romans were now directly responsible, in the province of Judaea they apparently neither allowed the publican lease[94] nor collected the taxes directly in other ways through Roman tax collectors. Rather, they turned this task over to third parties. Usually the levies were collected by the provincial upper stratum and highest bidding tax leaseholders, with the Romans providing military force if needed to carry out the task. This could also have been the case in the province of Judaea. According to Josephus, the high priest Joazar was already involved in the carrying out of the census, which, however, was very much to his disadvantage (*Ant.* 18.3, 26).[95] Moreover, the responsibility of the Jewish aristocracy for the collection of taxes can be inferred from a remark in Josephus that refers to the time of the governor Gessius Florus shortly before the First Jewish Revolt. Apparently the toparchy of Jerusalem, the city itself and its hinterlands, had not paid its tribute of 40 talents. According to Josephus, Agrippa II had at first convinced the Jerusalemites not to continue its refusal to pay: "The chiefs (*archontes*) and the councilors (*bouleutai*) spread among the urban districts and gathered in the taxes." Yet he could not exert the same influence in the country. The people turned against him, and he had to withdraw: "He [Agrippa II] sent their leaders together with the most influential citizens (*dynatoi*) to Florus in Caesarea, so that he might appoint from them the tax collectors for the country [that is, the toparchy]."[96] Therefore it could have been good that in accordance with the legally required official policy in the imperial period, the high priest and the members of the Sanhedrin with their wealth had the responsibility for the collection of taxes and thus an immediate interest in their collection.[97] Yet this is only an assumption. For the information from Josephus relates only to the critical phases at the beginning of the province and around the First Jewish Revolt. Therefore the involvement of the high priest in the census could also be part of an administrative tactic of the Romans, who used the upper strata to soften the anger of the people in times of actual or threatened resistance. And the fact that the Jewish aristocracy became involved when the tax payments were refused is easily explained, since they feared violent encounters and wanted to avoid the consequences that did indeed result.

Finally, we must also note that the Synoptic Gospels, for example, say nothing about participation by the high priest or the Sanhedrin in the state taxation of the people. They tell us only that the "tax collectors," that is, the tax leaseholders who bring in the taxes, were all Jews. Thus, according to Luke 18:10-14, a tax collector and a Pharisee go together to the temple to pray, and Jews like Levi/Matthew (Mark 2:13ff./Matt 9:9-13) are referred to as "tax collectors" by Jesus' followers (see pp. 197, 200). Finally, Luke 19:1ff. even mentions a "rich tax collector" (*architelōnēs*) named Zacchaeus in Jericho, who was probably the "head of a tax collector company."[98] Jesus expressly calls him a "son of Abraham," a term that Luke applies exclusively to Jews. Josephus also mentions a rich Jewish tax collector in Caesarea named John (*War* 2.287ff.).

The Extent of the Burden of Taxation

We have no detailed, exact figures about the burden of taxation. Estimates of the tax portion of the gross social product vary between 12 and 50 percent.[99] Applebaum, for example, calculates that Herod collected at least 900 talents in taxes annually, which with an estimated population of 3 million in Palestine would mean a burden of about 3 drachmas or denarii per person.[100] Then one would have to add to this the religious taxes, which were also no small matter. If we consider with Applebaum that a poor Egyptian fellah of the same period had to pay about 60 drachmas from an average income of 210 drachmas, it is clear that a poor Palestinian peasant was hardly better off. If we presuppose that he had to pay taxes for a large family and that his income was close to the minimum existence, the taxes were an unbearable burden. It is possible, however, that Applebaum's estimated population figure is much too high. Broshi, in any case, calculates only 1 million inhabitants.[101] Nevertheless, this means that the tax burden calculated by Applebaum is hardly too high. Even if the occasional change in rulers brought with it certain modifications, the total burden on the population through taxation probably remained relatively constant, that is, always very high. Even Tacitus concedes that taxes in the province of Judaea were a heavy load (*Ann.* 2.42). And more than once Herod apparently had to let up on taxes (Jos. *Ant.* 15.303, 365; 16.64). In general, however, the taxes were relentlessly collected.

4.2.2 Religious Taxes[102]

The rebuilding of postexilic Judaism in the land of Israel also included the organization of the religious taxes. They were centered on the temple and worship but also included the support of priests and Levites everywhere in the country. As a self-obligation Neh 10:32-39 names a yearly tax for temple service (one-third of a shekel), taxes for firewood and firstlings (firstfruits, firstborn animals, and firstborn human males), tithes for the cult personnel (dough, fruit, wine, oil), and other tithes.[103]

TEMPLE TAX

In the Persian period the most important income for the temple—and above all for the cult—came from contributions of the kings. As the already mentioned passage in Nehemiah shows, however, these subsidies were not always assured or sufficient, and thus voluntary contributions had to be added.[104] In accordance with this tradition, when the Seleucid hegemony replaced that of the Ptolemies, Antiochus III promised the Jews contributions to the temple, because he owed them a debt of gratitude (Jos. *Ant.* 12.140–41). According to 2 Macc 3:3, Seleucus IV also assumed the costs of the service of the sacrifices, and Demetrius promised the Hasmonean Jonathan the income from Acco for the temple service (1 Macc 10:39). This information could be interpreted to mean that in the Seleucid period, in any case, there was still no regular temple tax.[105] Yet such a tax is presupposed in the first century c.e. by Josephus, Philo, and the Gospel of Matthew and also expressly for the Diaspora by Josephus and Philo. In agreement with Exod 30:13 and according to Josephus (cf., for example, *Ant.* 3.196; 18.312; *War* 7.218) and rabbinic tradition,[106] it amounted to one-half of a silver shekel or one double drachma (=two denarii), which corresponds to the half-shekel. A double drachma is also attested by Philostratus (*Her.* 186) and the New Testament (Matt 17:24), and two drachmas also had to be paid as *fiscus Judaicus.*[107]

Introduction of the Temple Tax—Presumably under the Hasmoneans

When the payment of half a shekel annually by every male Israelite at least twenty years old was established[108] (even for Jews in the Diaspora) is uncertain.[109] It is probable, however, that the Hasmoneans introduced the temple tax in the true sense.[110] Yet in spite of its introduction, it remained controversial. According to the Talmud, the Sadducees, who appealed to Num 28:4 (because of the second person singular), maintained that the invariable offering of individuals was given voluntarily, whereas the other (Pharisaic?) side countered that Num 28:2 (because of the second person plural) was proof of the obligation of all Israel for the *tamid* offering (*b. Men.* 65a).[111] After 70 c.e. the temple tax was replaced by the humiliating *fiscus Judaicus* for the Jupiter Capitolinus,[112] which taxed men and women between the ages of three and sixty-two.

The Collection of the Temple Tax

In principle one could take one's own temple taxes to Jerusalem. It was more usual, however, in the Diaspora and in the land of Israel for these to be gathered locally by certain reliable people and kept in special trumpet-shaped containers, which made theft more difficult, and then taken by a delegation to Jerusalem.[113] Such collectors of the temple tax are also presupposed by Matt 17:24. Philo (*Spec. Leg.* 1.78) gives us some idea of this process:

> In almost every city there is a treasury (*tameia*) for the holy funds, which one usually seeks out in order to pay the taxes. At certain times emissaries are selected for the holy funds, who are the most capable men, the most respected from each city, in order to safely transport the hopeful gifts. For on the prescribed taxes rest the hopes of the pious.

Josephus even reports that because of the "robber bands of the Parthians," the Jews of Mesopotamia sent the money transports only in the protection of the numerous pilgrims to Jerusalem. The cities in which the gathered money was kept until transfer to Jerusalem were apparently also chosen according to military criteria (*Ant.* 18.311ff.).

Did Everyone Pay the Temple Tax?

Since on the grounds of equality the temple tax came to two denarii for all who were obligated to pay it, whether they were rich or poor, one can imagine that in view of all the other taxes, they were no small burden for many families. In any case, that could explain why 3 Maccabees names as the number one reason for apostasy in Ptolemaic Egypt the abhorrence of contributions for the holy city (3 Macc 2:31). Here the national and religious symbolic value of the temple tax also becomes clear.

It is not accidental then that the Gospel of Matthew, through Jesus and his disciples, also discusses the payment of the temple tax (Matt 17:22-27).[114] At first, Peter expressly maintains to the tax collectors that Jesus paid the double drachma. Yet in the following internal debate Jesus presents this behavior as the avoidance of giving offense. For he (and his disciples) were basically free of this duty. Here a special intimate relationship of Jesus (and his disciples) to God, a special kind of sonship of God, is presupposed as the reason for this freedom.[115] This could be interpreted to the effect that the payment of the temple tax by Jesus' followers was not entirely a matter of course.[116] It is also conceivable, however, that the apothegm projects a discussion of the *fiscus Judaicus* back into the time of Jesus. Notable, in any case, is the pragmatically grounded solidarity with Judaism that the Matthean Jesus required here.[117]

It is also not certain whether the Essenes and the community at Qumran paid the temple tax. According to Josephus, they sent consecrated gifts (*Ant.* 18.19), yet this does not have to mean the temple tax but could mean other voluntary gifts.[118] God-fearers also made such gifts but could not themselves participate in the tax (*Ant.* 14.110). For in principle, non-Jews were excluded from the temple tax.[119] Sometimes it is assumed, however, that the temple tax was paid in addition to consecrated gifts. "They refused only the sacrificial offerings and tithes that were connected with the sabbath and festivals fixed by the calendar, which they used in other ways."[120]

Money Changing in the Temple District

Since the temple tax included—not least of all—the daily *tamid* offering made for the atonement of the whole of Israel, the tax money was considered "holy money" (cf. Jos. *Ant.* 16.27–28, 163–64, 170, and elsewhere) and even "ransom" (Philo *Spec. Leg.* 1.77; cf. Exod 30:15). The required means of payment, because of its constant value, was the Tyrian half-shekel, with an average weight of 7.2 grams of silver.[121] For the exchange of other or normal coins, the temple authorities had hired money changers, who were paid a fee of 8 percent per half-shekel. Such money changers, as is well known, are also mentioned in the scene of the cleansing of the temple in the Gospels (Mark 11:15ff.; Matt 21:12-13; Luke 19:45ff.; John 2:13ff.).[122] Yet here it is presupposed that the money changing and the sale of sacrificial animals took place *in the temple district*. This representation, however, is an extremely tendentious one, especially in the Johannine version, and it is probably not historically accurate. For actually, the animal sellers probably sat "not on the temple mount or, by all appearances, even inside Jerusalem, but outside by one of the city gates,"[123] and the money changers were, in any case, outside the temple district.[124]

The Storage of the Temple Tax

According to Josephus (*War* 5.200), there were several money chambers in the interior rooms of the temple. One of them was *the* treasury (*gazophylak[e]ion*; cf. *Ant.* 19.294; Mark 12:41; John 8:12, 20), which held the temple tax and the freewill offerings. According to the Mishnah (cf. *Sheqal.* 6.5–6), in the women's forecourt there were thirteen trumpet-shaped collection boxes, on which their purpose was written in Aramaic (for example, "New Shekel" for the temple tax for the current year, "Old Shekel" for the tax not yet paid for the past year, and those for the sacrifice of fowl, for burnt offerings, and for freewill offerings). Perhaps this place is meant in the story of the poor widow (Mark 12:41-44; cf. Luke 21:1ff.) who gave two lepta, that is, a quadrans (=¼ of an as).[125] Gifts for the temple could also consist of real property (houses, land); indeed, even slaves were willed to the temple through vows. In each case, however, the equivalent in money was paid, so that the temple itself owned no lands, houses, or slaves.[126]

TAXES FOR THE PRIESTS

In addition to the temple tax, it was above all the taxes for the priests (bread, firstfruits, tithe) and among them especially the "first tithe" or "Levitical tithe" that made a material difference.[127] Originally for the Levites and only a tenth to the priests (cf. Num 18:21-32; Neh 10:38, but different already in Neh 13:4ff.), this tax seems in the New Testament period to have also been levied quite naturally by the priests. In any case, Josephus reports in his autobiography that two of his fellow priests, who had been sent with him to Galilee at the beginning of the uprising in Jerusalem, became rich from the "tithes owed to them" (*Life* 63), whereas he himself, though also a priest, "did not accept the tithes owed to him" (*Life* 80). Yet we may not simply infer from this that all priests were rich. Rather, of the vast numbers of priests in the land of Israel, more than a few probably lived in extremely modest circumstances. A priestly tithe is also presupposed in the book of *Jubilees* (13.24ff.) and in Judith (11:13) and is named by Philo in addition to the Levitical tithe.[128] Among the rabbis it was still disputed whether the tithe belonged to the priests or the Levites.[129] The Hasmoneans, however, seem to have already laid claim to the tithe and to have been expressly granted it by Caesar (cf. Jos. *Ant.* 14.202–3). This tithe may have been completely centralized under the Hasmoneans and then under their supervision a certain portion distributed to the priests.[130] Therefore we must ask whether in the provision of the tithe to Josephus and his fellow delegates, a role was played by the fact that they were in Galilee as a delegation of the high priest. In any case, he also tells of conflicts between the priests and the high priest over the distribution of the tithe, in which the high priests were able to pursue their interests with brute force.[131] Mentioned here by name is Ananias, who is also known in the Talmud (*b. Pes.* 57a) because of his ruthlessness and indeed was responsible for the execution of James, the brother of the Lord.

Tithing
According to the biblical tradition, the first tithe was raised from grain, wine, and oil. According to the oldest rabbinic tradition it was, in principle, to be paid on all agricultural products serving as food.[132] In any case, it probably indicates the special seriousness of the fulfillment of the tax obligation when even "mint, dill, and cumin" (Matt 23:23)[133] or even "all" (Luke 18:12) is tithed, and thus perhaps nonagricultural products as well.[134] For many, the "priestly tithe" was probably not a minor burden. This was all the more true when additional tithes (second tithe, tithe for the poor) could be added, if not annually, then at regular intervals.[135] It is also understandable that not everyone complied—in any case not willingly— with this tax obligation. Therefore the "*demai* law" attempted to guarantee the tithe as much as possible.[136] According to one rabbinic tradition, this law had already been introduced by the Hasmonean John Hyrcanus, but according to another by Jochanan ben Zakkai and thus possibly not until after 70 c.e.

4.3 The Economic Importance of the Temple

The sums that flowed into the temple treasury through the temple tax were not small. Accordingly, they were carefully watched. Furthermore, the removal of money was subject to strict controls (cf. *m. Sheqal.* 3.2–3; *t. Sheqal.* 2.1). Moreover, this encouraged some private individuals to deposit their wealth in the temple. The magnitude of the stored amounts can be inferred not least of all from the numerous attacks and plunderings that are reported.

ATTACKS ON THE TEMPLE TREASURY AND TEMPLE TAX

In 169 B.C.E. Antiochus IV is supposed to have had 1800 talents stolen, in addition to jewelry, silver, gold, and other valuables (1 Macc 1:21ff.; cf. 2 Macc 5:11ff.). Crassus was the first Roman temple robber. According to Josephus, in 54/55 B.C.E. the triumvir "took away all the gold in the temple of Jerusalem, even the 2000 talents that Pompey had not touched," for the financing of the Parthian campaign (*War* 1.179). After the death of Herod in 4 B.C.E. the Roman financial administrator Sabinus plundered the temple treasury (cf. *War* 2.45ff.; *Ant.* 17.261ff.). Pontius Pilate also took money from the "qorban,"[137] that is, probably from the temple treasury designated for the service of sacrifices and for charity; he did this to finance an aqueduct but perhaps also with the intention of enriching himself (*War* 2.175ff.; *Ant.* 18.60ff.). Finally, Gessius Florus embezzled the tax deficit of 17 talents in the year 66 C.E., thereby starting the great revolt (*War* 2.293).

There were also attacks on the temple tax gathered for Jerusalem on the part of authorities and rulers in the Diaspora. In 62/61 B.C.E. Flaccus, the Roman governor of the province of Asia, confiscated the temple money in Apamaea, Laodicea, Adramettium, and Pergamum, apparently the depository cities, in the amount of 120 talents of gold. Incidentally, we learn here that the yield for the temple tax was apparently turned into gold talents. We know that Cicero defended Flaccus in court, since he had been accused in Rome for his behavior.[138] Other attacks are known in connection with reports that mention the assurance of the privileges of the Jews of the Diaspora by Caesar, Augustus, Tiberius, and Claudius, in which the right to gather funds for Jerusalem is sometimes expressly cited (cf. *Ant.* 14.213ff.; 16.163ff.).[139] Finally, this right is also included by Titus in the benefits that Rome granted the Jews (*War* 6.333ff.). The temple tax money of the Diaspora was invaded not only by the Romans. Josephus mentions that Mithridates stole 800 talents from Kos, where the Jews of Asia had taken them out of fear of the king (*Ant.* 14.112–13).[140]

Yet, as Applebaum assumes, Rome probably also had its own economic interest in the temple taxes and in protecting their transference to Jerusalem. For these also guaranteed the influx of hard currency from regions like Mesopotamia that were not under Roman rule, and as soon as the money returned to circulation, it helped to balance payments made for luxury items from the East.[141]

THE ECONOMIC IMPORTANCE OF THE TEMPLE TREASURY

Nevertheless, the economic importance of the temple treasure consisted above all in the fact that it paid for the daily offerings, as well as for the maintenance of various people and groups employed at the temple. In addition, there were expenses for community obligations in Jerusalem (support of construction projects, city walls, water supply, and so forth) and for charitable purposes. It is true that the sums present in the temple were at times considerable, which we know from the occasional plunderings. Here, however, we must also consider the fact that the temple not only held the state treasury but was also used as a depository, as it were, for private fortunes.[142] Yet this should not lead us to conclude that for Jerusalem and its vicinity and beyond, the temple played an enormous and even central economic role in Palestine. For outside of the named, regionally limited projects that were paid for from temple income, the temple treasury represented dead capital that was made economically useful at best sporadically, but which often enough aroused the avarice of foreign conquerors. In this sense, the wealth of the temple was an economic problem, since the redistribution of the funds did not function adequately.[143]

5

SOCIAL DEVELOPMENT
IN THE LAND OF ISRAEL

In the history of Jewish society[1] we see the profound political changes that Palestine experienced in the period of the second temple. This is not only visible in terms of the particular—often foreign—ruler (king, high priest, tetrarch, ethnarch, procurator) but also in the deep tracks left behind in all strata of society. It is evident above all, however, in the transformations that took place in the (Jewish) *upper stratum* of Jerusalem and Judea, as well as the fragmentary Jewish states, under the successors of Herod. While after the Persian period the latter were probably always drawn from priestly and at the same time frequently nonpriestly families, their membership was connected with loyalty to the particular ruling dynasty or foreign sovereign. The revolutionary changes that the Hasmonean and Herodian or Roman hegemonies brought with them are therefore reflected in the Jewish leadership stratum in the rise and fall of certain "good families," in which the loss of power and influence usually also brought with it the loss of wealth and property, and conversely, the gain in power and influence also brought an increase in wealth and property. The priestly aristocracy also remained unprotected from this change, although after the Persian period it traditionally enjoyed not only high esteem but also greater continuity if hereditary succession.

Naturally, even in the land of Israel, the rulers and the upper stratum were supported by a certain officialdom and bureaucracy, that is, *retainers* (see p. 69) who, dependent on the aristocracy, assumed crucial administrative functions. These were recruited from both priestly and nonpriestly Jewish circles, but also and above all from non-Jewish ones. It is noteworthy that precisely in these retainer groups one can ascertain, on the one hand, specific affinities with the ruling houses and the upper-stratum families they served but, on the other hand, corresponding dependencies. If in the leading stratum a large portion of those families sharing power and wealth changed with each new sovereignty, then the lower stratum also experienced such changes. For example, since the Ptolemaic and Seleucid hegemonies, the free small farmers and their families—that is, the largest part of Jewish society—had been confronted with a permanent deterioration of their circumstances, including the radical loss of their land and thus their independence, and with an increase in slavery and poverty. Not until the Maccabean liberation and under Hasmonean sovereignty did their lot take a turn for the better, but it clearly deteriorated again

126

under the Roman and Herodian hegemony. Somewhat better off were the artisans, traders, and businessmen, yet this was naturally very dependent on the craft or field in which one was involved.

5.1 Change in the Upper Stratum
under the Greek Kings and the Hasmonean State

The Jewish Upper Stratum in the Time of the Ptolemies and Seleucids

UPPER STRATUM

At the time of the Greek kingdoms[2] the upper stratum of Judea consisted above all of the prominent priestly families who were descended from Onias I and Simon the Righteous, and who placed the high priests in hereditary succession. Nevertheless, they had to share this power not only with other priestly families but above all with the family of the Tobiads, who had climbed, as it were, from the second into the first rank of respected families. The inclusion of the Tobiads in the Judean elite was traditionally based on extensive land ownership in Ammon and Gilead, political and military power in the Transjordan, and—not least of all—on their control of the tax collections in Syria and Phoenicia, which they had gained under Joseph. This position of power allowed the Tobiads to rival the priestly aristocracy derived from the Oniads and to influence the gerousia.[3]

In a certain sense the Tobiads represent a prototype of the Judean leading stratum of nonpriestly origin in the time of the second temple, in both their rise and their decline. It is significant, first, that here we have a family that had long played a certain role in Judean society on the basis of its property and had its concomitant influence. We must note, second, that for the actual ruler, the Ptolemaic or Seleucid royal house, the Tobiads fulfilled an important function as retainers both economically and politically. Third, however, one must also mention that their destiny was linked more with the destiny of the real, foreign rulers than with the Jewish people. In distinction to the priestly aristocracy, which was a nobility of birth and in a certain sense is comparable to the Roman *ordines*,[4] the Tobiads ascended solely on the basis of their power and property to the upper or leading stratum of Palestine. For the maintenance and possible expansion of their claims to power and property were also their true political aims, and this also explains their openness to the cultural and religious aspects of Hellenism.

RETAINERS OF THE UPPER STRATUM

We can count in the retainer group perhaps all priests and members of the gerousia, but certainly the "officials" occupied with important functions in the temple (temple manager, temple scribes, temple singers), to whom the

Seleucids also granted special tax abatements at the beginning of their hegemony (cf. *Ant.* 12.138–46). This classification also included estate managers and administrators of fortunes, as well as tax leaseholders ("tax collectors"). Noteworthy here is one Arion, who was the financial administrator (*oikonomos*) of the Tobiad Joseph in Alexandria and was given broad powers. The tax money was apparently gathered from him (*Ant.* 12.196ff.).

The insight into Jewish society of that time made possible from the conservative (retainer) perspective of Ben Sira is interesting.[5] For it is clear, on the one hand, that according to him the unquestioned social leadership role was given to the priests. On the other hand, however, Ben Sira also takes into account the influence and power of the laity. Yet he also presents the dangers of wealth, possibly with the thoroughly hellenized Tobiads in mind, and speaks decisively against taking advantage of the poor (*ptōchoi*). Nevertheless, he does not reject wealth in itself and with a certain vanity looks down on peasants, workers, and artisans, who do their job, to be sure, but play no public role because of their lack of "education." Over against them stands his own ideal of the "scribe"[6] or "wise man" (*grammateus*),[7] who is freed from earning a living, spends his life with the study of the Torah and wisdom, conveys learning without pay, and can speak the law and give advice to rulers.[8] Such an ideal, however, can hardly be realized without a certain prosperity or an assured income, which is fitting, say, for a priest (like Ben Sira)[9] in the land of Israel. Therefore it is probably appropriate to include the "scribes" in the retainer group.

The Upper Stratum and the Retainers of the Hasmonean State

With the Maccabean Revolt, which was carried out by peasant and priestly families, the previous Jewish upper stratum largely disappeared, and this included the ruling priestly aristocracy or the house of Onias as well as the Tobiads. Their place was now taken by the priestly family from Modein that led the revolt, whose claim to sovereignty, which was made on the basis of their charismatic leadership of the army, was stabilized through dynasty formation—a rather classic example of Weber's theory of the transformation of a personal into a group charisma. The legitimacy of the assumption of the high priest's office was established on the one hand by decree of the popular assembly and on the other by the fiction of the arrival of the venerable priestly family of the Jehoiarib branch. The Hasmoneans also confiscated the property of the deposed aristocracy. Noteworthy is the grand lifestyle that the Hasmoneans apparently displayed. They used the plain of Jericho for their domain through intensive irrigation. Moreover, to the south of an estate of about 125 acres, a winter residence was built, which during the Hasmonean sovereignty (probably beginning with John Hyrcanus I and ending with

Salome Alexandra) was extensively cultivated and expanded.[10] Since Alexander Janneus, at the latest, the Hasmonean high priests and princes bore the title *king*. Yet under certain circumstances, the high priestly and royal offices could be separated. Thus after the death of Alexander Janneus, Salome Alexandra became queen, while her son Hyrcanus was high priest.

With the Hasmoneans a number of families rose into the upper stratum, including priestly ones such as the family to which the later historian of the First Jewish Revolt, Flavius Josephus, traced his heritage and with which the Hasmonean dynasty was also connected through marriage (cf. *Life* 2ff.). In addition there were some less-tainted members of the old priestly elite and, apparently in the interest of territorial expansion, a number of good families in the border regions.[11] The latter included the family of the proselyte Antipas, whom John Hyrcanus appointed as military governor (*stratēgos*) of Idumea. It was these Idumean "retainers" who then in the second and third generation used a favorable opportunity to finish off the Hasmonean dynasty. The power of the Hasmoneans was based on the (primarily non-Jewish) military and the local elites and in particular on the Jerusalem Sanhedrin, which replaced the earlier gerousia. In the record of the "great assembly of the priests and the people [*laos*]," who confirmed Simon's position, "the rulers [*archontes*] of the nation and the elders [*presbyteroi*] of the country" are named as the deciding entities (cf. 1 Macc 14:28). Perhaps it is a question here of the Jerusalem gerousia and the leading strata of rural Judea.[12] Yet in distinction to the priestly aristocracy, the "priests" or "high priests," members of the non-priestly leading stratum—that is, for example, lay members of the Sanhedrin—can also be called "elders."[13]

Also falling into this period is the rise of the Pharisaic movement, whose basis was probably the already mentioned group of scribes or wise men.[14] We can hardly place them eo ipso in the upper stratum,[15] although they enjoyed high esteem and some of them also sat in the Sanhedrin. Yet we must ask, on the one hand, whether this position was gained on the basis of their membership in the priestly aristocracy and not as scribes. On the other hand, the scribes or wise men most certainly also included men of simple origin and even proselytes. Therefore, Stern is probably correct in saying that the rise of wise men had a significance not encompassed by the old aristocratic distinctions.[16]

5.2 The Structure of Jewish Society under the Romans and the Herodians

The Upper Stratum and Their Retainers

Roman sovereignty over Judea was at first still based on parts of the old Hasmonean dynasty. Nevertheless, Caesar placed the most important responsibilities—namely, the military and financial ones—in the hands of the Idumean retainer of the Hasmoneans, Antipater, and his sons Phasael and Herod. The latter, who was still linked with the Hasmonean dynasty through his second wife Mariamne, had, in the wake of his rise to sole dominion as a vassal of Rome, largely eliminated the old upper stratum and formed his own ruling house.

HEROD'S RULING HOUSE

In Palestine and beyond, in accordance with Augustus's provincial policy, this house developed with many Near Eastern ruling houses into a broad-branched dynasty, which ruled in the land of Israel in one way or another until the death of Agrippa II in the time of Domitian.[17] Members of the ruling house received important administrative posts. Thus Herod's younger brother Pheroras was a tetrarch responsible for Perea; his brother-in-law Castobar administered Idumea, and his cousin Achiab, Judea. Since Herod himself could not occupy the high priest's office, he arranged to have the Hasmonean succession broken off. Then he installed high priests who suited him, and deposed them when reasons of power politics so dictated. Here he turned to descendants of prominent priestly families of the Egyptian and Babylonian Diaspora as he fostered a number of Diaspora families, in particular from Babylonia. Thus the rise of the family of Boethus occurred in the time of Herod. Mariamne, the daughter of the high priest Simon Boethus, became Herod's third wife. In the rabbinic tradition the term *Boethusian* could also refer to the Sadducees.[18] The practice of appointing and deposing high priests was retained by Herod's successors and also by the Roman procurators (*Ant.* 20.249).[19]

The upper and leading stratum was structurally similar under Herod's successors, including especially Agrippa I. Women also played a certain role. In particular, Herod's sister Salome and the daughters of Agrippa I, Drusilla and Bernice, had influential Roman connections. Salome is supposed to have been a friend of Livia, the wife of Augustus. Drusilla married Felix, the governor of Judea. Bernice seems to have had a liaison with Titus (cf. Tacitus *Hist.* 2.2) and been considered his future wife; nevertheless, she had to leave Rome, allegedly because of hostile public opinion (cf. Suetonius *Titus* 7; Dio Cassius 66.15). Yet the Bernice and Titus affair also shows that in spite of all their closeness with the imperial household and the upper stratum of Rome, even the members of the Herodian ruling house always remained merely provincial in the eyes of the top Roman aristocracy. Thus, it is true that Drusilla could marry the Roman equestrian Felix, who was only a social climber as well as a freed slave; but no Judean could enter the *ordo senatorius*. No member of the Herodian royal house was ever voted into the senatorial order (or even into the equestrians).[20] Through Herod's father the Herodians held Roman citizenship. Like other vassal kings, Agrippa I and his son Agrippa II received the *ornamenta praetoria,* the honorary privileges of a member of the senatorial order, but these could be given even to freed slaves. This honor must be strictly distinguished from membership.

RETAINERS OF THE UPPER STRATUM

Herod maintained an enormous administrative staff, in which he employed a number of non-Jewish retainers, such as Ptolemaeus of Rhodes, who was responsible for the financial administration of the kingdom, and Nicholus of Damascus, the most important advisor of the king. The Sanhedrin in Jerusalem was also occupied by Herod's followers and creatures, so that it became a compliant tool in the hands of the king. In addition, there were a number of local magistrates who were in part related to the Herodian ruling house. They were presumably also responsible for overseeing the tax lease-holders or "tax collectors."[21] In any case, we find here the social boundary with the lower retainer group, the officials and managers in service to the royal house, the temple, and local magistrates. They work in administrative positions as secretaries ("scribes," *grammateis*), as managers and overseers of estates, as tax collectors, and also in the army as officers. Under the Herodians the latter were mainly, if not exclusively, non-Jews. Naturally, the numerous household and estate managers (in Greek mostly *oikonomos,* occasionally *epitropos;* Latin *vilicus*), who were in charge of the remaining personnel and the whole household staff, were also included in the *retainers,* as were the accountants, trustees, and urban treasurers.[22]

The responsibilities of these administrators—who, incidentally, could also be slaves (cf. Matt 24:45; Luke 12:42)—were highly variable.

> Whereas in Luke 12:42 *oikonomos* is the designation of a slave with personal responsibility for a limited area, who after being tested is rewarded with the overall management of the property (12:44), 16:1ff. presupposes that the one called *oikonomos* . . . already holds this position and is authorized to take legal actions for or against his master; and thus he not only has this function in internal areas but also holds the position of one authorized to deal with the outside world (16:5–8).[23]

The term *epitropos* in Matt 20:8 means a treasurer or manager who corresponds to the one in 12:42, but in Luke 8:3 ("Herod's steward Chuza") it means a representative of the king. Naturally, this could mean a high official function in the Herodian court ("procurator") or only that of a manager of a small or large estate (corresponding to Matt 20:8). The latter seems to us more likely (cf. also p. 378).

We also include local judges (cf. Luke 12:58; 18:2; *War* 2.571)[24] and priests in the *retainer* group. Some individuals in this group were certainly able to acquire some wealth and esteem. Josephus mentions among the "influential [*dynatoi*] of the Jews" of Caesarea a "tax collector John" (*War* 2.287) who, together with eleven others, was able to gather the considerable sum of eight silver talents (48,000 denarii!) for the procurator Florus.[25] Similarly, the "chief tax collector" Zacchaeus in Jericho (Luke 19:1-10) was probably also rich, but whether we can also make that assumption of Jesus' follower Levi or Matthew (cf. Mark 2:13-17; Luke 5:27-32; Matthew 9) is questionable. He was more likely a small tax leaseholder. Since, however, these people—like, for example, all soldiers—were exclusively in the service of the ruling strata, we must count them in the lowest level of retainers. Nevertheless, the soldiers of the Herodian mercenary troops were probably only rarely of Jewish heritage. Finally, we must also include in the retainer stratum, if not in the upper stratum, the wholesalers and foreign traders (*emporos*)[26] who, in contrast to the small traders, shopkeepers, and peddlers (*kapelos*), could be very prosperous and because of the structure of their trade were necessarily dependent on a close relationship with the ruling stratum.[27]

LAND OWNERSHIP AND BUILDINGS OF THE UPPER STRATUM

In addition to sharing in power, membership in the ruling house or the upper stratum also meant wealth and especially landownership. Thus Herod and his successors not only possessed much property themselves but also gave large estates to their officials and favorites.[28] Even women in the royal house owned estates and small villages.[29] And considerable property was also held by members of the priestly aristocracy, presumably above all in the vicinity of Jerusalem.[30] The wealth of the Herodians was also displayed in buildings. Herod himself had built "most of the Hasmonean desert castles into impressive luxury residences."[31] These include Machaerus, Masada, Cypros, and Alexandreion, whereas the Herodian castle Herodeion was a new construction that was planned by Herod himself as a mausoleum. In addition, the royal house also maintained monumental palaces or luxury residences, for example, in Jerusalem and Jericho. The archaeologically discernible development in Jericho reflects in an impressive way the rise of Herod from Hasmonean retainer to sole ruler.[32] Not quite as magnificent as the Herodian residences are the houses of the members of the Jerusalem upper stratum that have been recently excavated. Nonetheless, they also attest to the still remarkable prosperity of their owners.[33]

ESTEEM AMONG THE JUDEAN POPULATION

Herod's brutal policies and his dynastic policy in particular led to a situation in which the ruling house and the upper-stratum families and retainers dependent on it were able to enjoy little or no prestige among the people.[34] That had consequences especially for the province of Judaea, since after the deposition of Archelaus the Romans could not count on the support of an elite recognized by the people. It is true that some responsibility was again laid in the hands of the high priest and the Sanhedrin. Nevertheless, even the first high priest, Joazar, had made himself impossible through his participation in the census. And his successors were also basically nothing more than marionettes of Rome and were treated accordingly. Thus, in connection with a Judean-Samaritan conflict, the Syrian governor Ummidius Quadratus summarily seized the current high priest, other members of the priestly aristocracy, and the temple manager, and transported them to Rome (cf. *War* 2.243; *Ant.* 20.231). Goodman even presumes that the weakness and failure of the Judean aristocracy form one of the reasons for permanent unrest and, finally, the suicidal war against Rome. The concomitant loss of authority probably also played a role in religious expressions in the land of Israel.[35]

The Lower Stratum

In the lower stratum we include all who do not share in the power and privileges of the ruling stratum and who are not among those in its service. These are above all farmers (and in Galilee also fishermen), agricultural workers or tenants (*geōrgos*), day laborers (*misthios*) and wage earners, indebted servants and slaves, as well as artisans, small traders, and businessmen—the latter especially in the cities. This stratum also includes at the bottom of the lower stratum—that is, below the level of minimum existence—beggars, prostitutes, shepherds, and bandits.[36]

RELATIVE PROSPERITY AND POVERTY

Some of these lower-stratum members were able to achieve a certain prosperity. This idea is supported, in any case, by archaeological evidence such as the grave monuments of artisans who worked on the building of the Jerusalem temple.[37] Yet one can hardly include all construction workers among the well-to-do members of the lower stratum. In their group—but not in the upper stratum or the retainer group—we must also include the type of the "rich man" that we find in Lukan parables (cf. Luke 12:16-21; 16:1-8, 19-31). Here we apparently have only free farmers with relative prosperity (cf. also Luke 15:11–32).[38] Perhaps we could also name here the "householder" or "landowner" (*oikodespotēs*) who appears in Matthean parables (cf. Matt 13:24-30; 20:1-16). In any case, we should not overestimate the number of these prosperous members of the lower stratum. The great majority were probably poor or destitute. This is true of small free farmers and fishermen, who mostly, in Ben-David's estimation, were hardly able to eke out a subsistence living for their families.[39] For if we assume that Ben-David's calculations are more or less accurate, a free farmer in Palestine had to have at least an area of twenty to twenty-five acres in order to achieve a minimum existence for a family of seven (see pp. 80–81). Yet it is unlikely that more than a very few had this much land at their disposal, and thus many lived hardly above the minimum existence. Especially afflicted with poverty and need in the lower stratum were independent women (widows) and children. It is no accident that the Gospels contain special admonitions to take in children, presumably orphans or foundlings (cf. Mark 9:33-37 par.; 10:13-16).[40]

THE PROBLEM OF DEBT

The gap between poor and rich is marked most clearly by the problem of debt. Crüsemann has correctly said that in it "a basic contradiction in society comes to light."[41] Its causes lie, as we have already often mentioned, in the land grabbing of rulers and in the heavy burden of taxation. It is not surprising that we find references to this problem especially in Josephus, in the Synoptic Gospels,[42] and in the Mishnah.

A lively impression is conveyed especially by the parable of the unforgiving servant in Matt 18:23-35.[43] Naturally, a debt of 10,000 talents (=60 million denarii!), which is first named in the parable, is fantastically high and in any case hardly conceivable among private individuals, even if individual private fortunes in this range were known (and far exceeded it, especially in imperial families). Debts of this amount or even higher probably occurred only in connection with war reparations, as tribute levies for subjugated rulers and peoples, and in tax leasehold bids for provinces.[44] Therefore we may presume that the parable is to be understood against the background of such a tax leasehold. Then the underlying idea would be that the whole land was in the possession of the king ("kingdom").[45] The "slave" in the parable who owed 10,000 talents could then be a tax leaseholder, like the Tobiads, or a different highly placed representative of a province,[46] but hardly an individual large landowner or small tax leaseholder.[47] This is also supported by the presupposed situation of the royal settling of accounts (Matt 18:23-24).[48] Not at all unusual, however, are debts in the range of 100 denarii, as named in the second scene of the parable. "It is within the range of such amounts that the overwhelming majority of ancient debt relationships moved."[49]

Measures against Debtors

The spectrum of measures that creditors could take in regard to delinquent or insolvent debtors was broad.[50] It ranged from the remission of debt, which before Hillel's *prosbol* (see p. 112) was actually commanded in sabbatical and jubilee years and could also occur on the occasion of a change in sovereignty,[51]

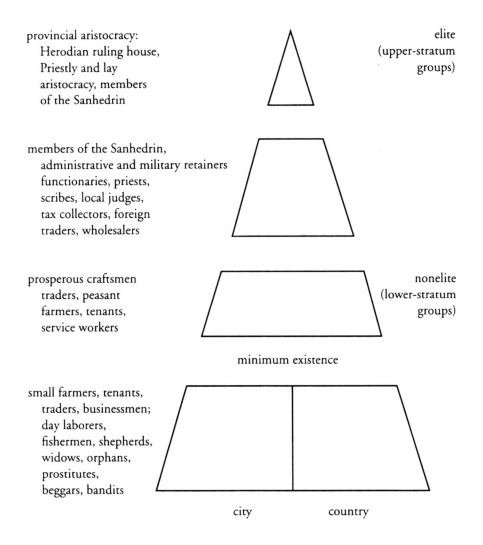

provincial aristocracy:
   Herodian ruling house,
   Priestly and lay
   aristocracy, members
   of the Sanhedrin

elite
(upper-stratum
groups)

members of the Sanhedrin,
   administrative and military retainers
   functionaries, priests,
   scribes, local judges,
   tax collectors, foreign
   traders, wholesalers

prosperous craftsmen
   traders, peasant
   farmers, tenants,
   service workers

nonelite
(lower-stratum
groups)

minimum existence

small farmers, tenants,
   traders, businessmen;
   day laborers,
   fishermen, shepherds,
   widows, orphans,
   prostitutes,
   beggars, bandits

city   country

SOCIAL PYRAMID 2: SOCIAL STRATIFICATION OF JEWISH SOCIETY
IN THE LAND OF ISRAEL (WITHOUT RELIGIOUS GROUPS)

through the moderation of debt or extension of time[52] to the collection of debts through public or private debtor arrest (cf. Matt 5:25/Luke 12:57ff.; Matt 18:30; *War* 2.273),[53] distraint,[54] or debtor slavery,[55] for which particularly the children and wives of debtors had to suffer (cf. Matt 18:25). Whether debtor slavery also existed in Judea is disputed,[56] but in addition to our text and Matt 5:25-26/Luke 12:57ff., Josephus (cf. *Ant.* 16.1ff.) and rabbinic texts suggest that it did. The Essenes, by contrast, seem to have rejected it (cf. Philo *Quod Omn. Prob.* 79). The creditors' means of compulsion could, on the one hand, also include physical force, such as choking (cf. Matt 18:28)[57] and torture (cf. Matt 18:34) and, on the other hand, also involve relatives, neighbors, and friends.[58] What means a creditor employed and whether he resorted to such measures at all depended in part on the social position of the debtor. Means of compulsion were probably more likely to be applied when there was a social difference between creditor and debtor than, say, in debt relationships between members of the upper stratum with equal social status. "Yet Roman governors occasionally did not shrink from such measures in order to move esteemed urban citizens to settle debts."[59] There were only limited legal means that debtors could use when it came time to "settle accounts" (cf. also Luke 16:1ff.) and the debt could not be repaid. In addition to the request for an extension or even a remission of debt, there was the possibility of blocking the creditor's actions through intervention by a person of higher rank or by a court (cf. Matt 18:31). If that failed, the only alternatives were flight or suicide. Therefore it is no accident that in connection with rebellions, we find mention of the annihilation of debt archives.

6

RELIGIOUS PLURALISM
IN THE LAND OF ISRAEL IN THE
HELLENISTIC-ROMAN PERIOD

Fundamental Characteristics

The religion of postexilic Judaism in the land of Israel, as in antiquity in general, was marked by its being embedded in society and its antagonisms. There was no clear boundary between religious and nonreligious areas of life. Compared with the preexilic period with its "monocentrism," the postexilic situation in the land of Israel was shaped by "multicentrism, heterogeneity, and socio-religious multiplicity."[1] This dynamic found clear expression in the Samaritan schism, which in the time of Alexander the Great led to the formation of a more or less independent religious and social entity: the Samaritans.[2] Before and after the resolution of the Jewish-Samaritan conflict, however, there were other divergent conceptions and currents, which also crystallized into specific group formations. Yet in spite of all this pluralism, Judaism in the period of the second temple was always shaped by a number of fixed characteristics and institutions, whose roots reached far back into the preexilic period and its traditions. They included above all *monotheism,* which after the failure of Hellenization was the undisputed mark of Jewish religiosity and even brought from the outside the accusation that Jews were godless. Part of this legacy, moreover, was *faith in the election of the people and the land of Israel.* This interdependence of the God of Israel, the people of Israel, and the land of Israel found its norm in the Torah with its total life-shaping commandments, its striking identity-giving features such as the sabbath, the festal calendar (including the Day of Atonement and the three temple pilgrim feasts: Pesach [Passover], Shabuoth [Weeks], and Sukkoth [Booths], circumcision, and the regulations regarding taxes, food, and purity. Institutionally, the religion of Judaism was supported in the Hellenistic-Roman period especially by the *temple* in Jerusalem. In addition we also find the *synagogue* in the land of Israel, although later than in the Diaspora and not with the same importance. Finally, everyday life was determined by the religious customs of the *family* and its Torah piety. Religious pluralism was ignited not because of the validity of monotheism, faith in election, the Torah, and the institutions themselves, but because of attitudes toward them, which were in turn expressed in different accentuations in the religious tradition and the interpretation of the Torah.

Group Formations, Fundamental Currents, and Charismatic Movements

If we consider the religious developments in the land of Israel in the Hellenistic-Roman period in the context of the social history of the Jewish people, certain group formations ("party factions" such as Pharisees, Essenes, and Sadducees) and fundamental currents become evident as features of this epoch. In addition, in the Roman-Herodian period there were a number of prominent charismatic movements. On the whole, the tendencies here toward identity-preserving delineation and the religious renewal of Jewish society probably overlapped with those of the retreat from its crises.[3] In regard to what we call fundamental currents, in addition to the increasing concentration on the study of the Torah in general, we can mention, on the one hand, the formation of apocalyptic and esoteric mystical or messianic ideas and, on the other hand, endeavors to sanctify life, particularly through a strict observance of the purity laws, and ascetic conceptions of life. These fundamental currents have a certain overarching significance. For they influenced such varied groups as the Pharisees and Essenes, as well as some social-revolutionary resistance and insurrectionist movements and smaller charismatic-ascetic or messianic-prophetic groups, which include those of John the Baptist and, not least of all, his student Jesus of Nazareth.

Yet neither these movements nor the group formations are explained simply by the selective adaptation of fundamental currents. Rather, they represent in each case a specific and original answer to the crisis of Jewish society. In accordance with the already mentioned embedding of religion in socio-economic antagonisms, they are also dependent on their social point of origin; that is, they are stratum-related. Their religio-political character varies accordingly. Thus there are religious reactions to the destruction of Jewish society through the coercions of pagan and semipagan structures of sovereignty, reactions that were only of a more or less indirect or prepolitical kind. In the Hellenistic-Roman period, however, there were also ideas that were more related to religious politics. These differences also reflect the nature of ancient societies, in which sharing in power depended on belonging to the ruling strata and their retainers. Nevertheless, all of this points to the identity-preserving religious potential that was mobilized in the Jewish people by sovereign domination and could be articulated even apart from the great Maccabean and anti-Roman rebellions and occasional smaller socio-revolutionary actions. Yet at the same time, these phenomena meant an unprecedented factionalism of the Jewish social majority. Indeed, even the fact that an influential part of the Jewish upper stratum like the Sadducees is perceived in the tradition as only a faction with its own religious ideas makes evident the deep crisis that this epoch meant for Judaism in the land of Israel.

In this chapter we will first present the relevant religious institutions: temple, synagogue, family (6.1). Then we will attempt to understand some of the named fundamental currents as a reflex of the crisis of Jewish society in the Hellenistic-Roman period (6.2). An overview of group formations, which follows, will make clear that in terms of social history, we are dealing here essentially with phenomena of the upper stratum and retainer group (6.3). By contrast, the charismatic movements in the Herodian-Roman period, as we will show, originated socio-historically in the lower stratum (6.4). The socio-revolutionary resistance movements and anti-Roman insurrectionist groups, which will be discussed in conclusion, overlap in part with the charismatic movements but are distinguished from them because of their specific protest character (6.5). The presentation of the beginnings of the Jesus movement in the land of Israel, which in terms of subject matter belongs here, will for practical reasons receive its own chapter (7).

6.1 Religious Institutions: Temple, Synagogues, and Family

TEMPLE

One can hardly overestimate the importance of the temple as the site of the divine presence and center of national and religious identity for Judaism in the Hellenistic-Roman period.[4] In contrast to the first temple, the second was "not only the place of the cult of sacrifice but also the center of life of the people in all areas of its life, the political and civic as well as the religious and social."[5] Also for Diaspora Judaism, which was bound to the temple through the temple tax and through personal participation in pilgrim festivals, it represented the national and cultic center. The religious concentration on the temple corresponded to its social, political, and in part even economic importance. In the center, naturally, stood the temple service,[6] that is, the cult of sacrifice. Even if a great symbolic, cosmic-mythic, and salvation-historical significance is given to it,[7] the material process of the sacrifice is its indispensable heart. The service of worship in the real sense is the cult of sacrifice of the high priest, who officiated, however, only on high feast days—especially on the Day of Atonement in the Holy of Holies—and occasionally on the sabbath, and of the priests who were responsible for the daily sacrifices, the festal sacrifices, and private sacrifices. A subordinate function was fulfilled by the Levites, who as musicians and singers accompanied worship on the steps of the forecourt but also served as gatekeepers and were responsible for the purity of the temple.

The priests were divided into twenty-four "courses" (Heb. *mishmara*, Gr. *patria* [*Ant.* 7.366] or *ephēmeria* [Luke 1:5, 8]; a part of a course was called a *phylē* [*Life* 2]). Each priest saw service twice a year for one week on a rotating basis and additionally on feast days. For this purpose, most of them went to Jerusalem from their residences and villages in the country, where they lived the rest of the time and perhaps worked as judges, teachers of the Torah, or scribes. Around them were gathered an appropriate representation of Levites and laity (Heb. *maamadot*), so that all the people were involved, at least symbolically, in the temple worship services. Sacrifices were made twice a day, namely, in the morning (Heb. *shaḥarit*) and in the afternoon or evening (Heb. *minḥah*). These *tamid* offerings at the altar for burnt offerings in the priestly forecourt, which consisted of the presentation of a lamb and other sacrifices, were accompanied by smoked sacrifices in the sanctuary (Heb. *hekal;* cf. Luke 1:8ff.), a long room before the Holy of Holies (Heb. *debir*). On sabbaths, new moons, and feast days additional sacrifices (Heb. *musaf*) took place after the morning sacrifice. It is also attested that offerings were made for non-Jews; the cessation of these was, indeed, one of the initial causes of the great anti-Roman rebellion (*War* 2.408–21). One could be a priest or Levite only on the basis of descent from a priestly or Levite family. The temple personnel in the Roman period also included the "temple prefect"[8] (Heb. *sagan,* Gr. *stratēgos [tou hierou]*), who came after the high priest and was his representative, "temple servants" (*hypēretai*),[9] who fulfilled certain security functions, and officials of the temple treasury.[10]

The temple district, however, was not only the cultic center but also a place of learning and teaching, of prayer and worshipful assemblies. The times of prayer were arranged according to the times of sacrifice (cf. Acts 3:1: evening *tamid;* 2:15: morning *tamid?*). Prayers with the recitation of the Shema ("Hear, O Israel . . .") or readings of the Torah were perhaps connected with the daily sacrifices. The temple district perhaps also included a school and a synagogue.[11] In the Gospel of Luke, Jesus appears as a teacher in the temple district (2:41-52; 19:47; 20:1),[12] and according to the Talmud "it is told of R. Jochanan ben Zakkai that he sat and taught all day long in the shadow of the temple" (*b. Pesa.* 26a). Furthermore, there are a number of indications that in the temple district books were stored and copied. According to Josephus (*Life* 418) book rolls and especially the "Law" (Torah scroll, Pentateuch) were seized along with other objects during the plundering of the temple (*War* 7.150, 162). It could also be that "Law" here means the "Book of the Temple" from which, according to the Mishnah, the high priest read on the Day of Atonement and by which copies of the Torah scroll were corrected (cf. *m. Kelim* 15.6; *m. Mo'ed Qat.* 3.4; *y. Sanh.* 2.20c). Yet other books, biblical and nonbiblical, were also stored in the temple district (cf. Jos. *Ant.* 3.38; 4.303; 5.61; *Ap.* 1.33).

SYNAGOGUES

On the basis of Greek inscriptions, we can demonstrate that synagogues[13] existed in the Diaspora in the second half of the third century B.C.E.[14] In the land of Israel the oldest attestations are the Theodotus inscription from Jerusalem and the archaeological findings in Gamla, Herodeion, and the fortress Masada from the middle of the first century C.E.[15] We can therefore assume that synagogues came into existence in the land of Israel rather late, possibly not until the post-Maccabean period.[16] In Josephus, in the New Testament, and also in the Mishnah there are numerous indications of synagogues in Jerusalem and in the land of Israel, namely, in Tiberias, Dor, Caesarea (Maritima), Nazareth, and Capernaum. In contrast to the Diaspora, however, the number of synagogues in Palestine before 70 C.E. was limited. Contrary to what is widely assumed, the roots of the synagogue are probably not to be found in the Babylonian exile but in a postexilic institution "that had the task of administering public duties, including religious functions. Only toward the end of the second temple and above all after its destruction did the importance of cultic functions grow more and more."[17] Nevertheless, the Theodotus inscription, for example, shows that synagogues assumed other functions and that one should be cautious in using the word *cultic* for the main function of the synagogues in the land of Israel. This is also indicated by the Greek word *synagōgē*, which was used mainly for Palestine and can mean both the "assembly" or "congregation" and the building in which the assembly takes place, that is, the synagogue. In the Diaspora, by contrast, the usual Greek term for the synagogue is *proseuchē* ("place of prayer").[18]

As the Greek Theodotus inscription makes clear, synagogues in the land of Israel served both the reading of the Torah and the teaching of the Commandments, as well as the instruction of children, and also, in special rooms, the accommodation of strangers, presumably above all Jewish pilgrims from the Diaspora. Moreover, they could also have been used in Palestine as centers of local assemblies on special occasions (cf. for Tiberias Jos. *Life* 276–77)— that is, to some extent as a city hall—and possibly as a storehouse for various community goods. Whether they, as in the Diaspora, were also places of prayer, common meals, and judicial decisions remains uncertain.

The original content of the (probably weekly) synagogal sabbath "worship service"[19] (cf. Acts 15:21) was the reading of the Torah—presumably with translation into Aramaic (Targum) and occasionally perhaps also Greek— and its interpretation.[20] Luke 4:17 also demonstrates the *haftarah,* the reading of the prophets (cf. also 2 Macc 15:9). It is not certain whether prayer was a part of the liturgy from the beginning. In any case, in *Ant.* 4.212 Josephus is probably referring to the recitation of the Shema (with the following blessings); it is also presupposed by the Mishnah. Other prayers, such as the Eighteen Benedictions (Heb. *tefillah, amida*), the Seven Benedictions, and the adapted parts of the temple liturgy (priestly blessings, *hallel,* and *hoshanot*), may also have been said in the synagogues before the destruction of the temple.

Sometimes synagogues were built through the gifts of prosperous individuals, as the Theodotus inscription shows. Whether there were also God-fearers in the land of Israel who came forward as donors (cf. Luke 7:1-5) is uncertain. Administrative functions lay in the hands of a synagogue leader (Heb. *rosh haknesset, archisynagōgos;* cf. the Theodotus inscription; Mark 5:22, 35-36, 38; Luke 8:49; 13:14). Luke 4:20 also mentions a synagogue attendant (*hypēretēs*).

FAMILY

The importance for Judaism of families or households and thus that of everyday religious life is often overlooked.[21] In fact, however, it was precisely the families that were crucial for religious socialization in the Hellenistic-Roman period. For the everyday was in many ways defined by the Torah and its regulations. They gave shape to the mutual social relationships, the rhythm of everyday life, the sabbath and feasts, and the working world. In particular, the consciousness of Jewish identity was reinforced through the religious structuring of time, daily prayers, the study of the Torah, and, not least of all, purity and food regulations, as well as endogamous marriage strategies.[22] The families and households also gained a special importance through the loss of authority of the Jewish upper stratum, which suffered through its extensive amalgamation with the ruling powers and its luxurious lifestyle, often disregarding Jewish culture. Thus it was perhaps not accidental that already in the early Hellenistic period a personal "Torah piety" began to develop, whose earliest manifestations are found in Psalms 1, 19, and 119.[23] Yet in addition, the traditional Jewish family structures did not remain unaffected by socioeconomic and political tensions. In any case, Goodman maintains that a dissolution of the traditional extended family can be discerned, especially on the basis of archaeological evidence regarding burial customs.[24]

6.2 Basic Religious Currents in the Hellenistic-Roman Period

6.2.1 Purity and Asceticism as Borderline Behavior

In terms of cultural anthropology "purity rules present a sort of grid that covers all aspects of society." They serve the drawing of boundaries between outside and inside and are "concerned with maintaining the wholeness or completeness of the social body," as well as that of the individual.[25] Indeed, individual and social conceptions of purity are interrelated. Such regulations have special identity-preserving importance especially where Judeans were in the minority and subject to strong pressures from majority societies to assimilate, for example, in the Diaspora. Yet even in Palestine there was cause enough for overt sanctification. For, on the one hand, there were regions in which non-Jews comprised a relevant, if not large, part of the overall populace. And, on the other hand, because of the virtually permanent foreign hegemony with its pagan or semipagan governing structures, the urgency of an identity-preserving delineation was not exactly small. In any case, it is not by accident that discussions about purity and food regulations in the New Testament and above all in the Mishnah have important significance;[26] in many respects they are crucial for Pharisees and Essenes. Yet they also shaped the daily life of most Judeans, as attested especially by Josephus (cf. *Ap.* 1.198, 205; but cf. also Luke 2:22-23, 39). This is also indicated, however, by archaeological evidence such as the numerous ritual purification baths (Heb. *mikvaôt*). It is possible that daily washings were already the general custom before and/or after eating or with prayer (cf. Mark 7:2-3 par.; John 2:9-10; *Ep. Arist.* 305–6; *m. Shabb.* 1.4; *Yad.*). There were also occasional (for example, after burials, births, or contact with unclean persons) and recurring purity rites (for example, after menstruation or sexual intercourse). Above all, however, the concern about kosher food probably played a rather large role in the everyday lives of the Jewish people. Naturally, the degree of observance varied and also depended on whether one was a priest, Levite, or Israelite. In addition, there are clear indications that the avoidance of impurity was taken more seriously among Essenes and Pharisees than in other circles in Judaism. Yet there seems to have been no real fundamental questioning of the purity laws, even among Jesus' earliest disciples, even if the accents there were different.[27]

In this connection we should also mention endogamous marriage strategies and incest taboos, as well as the strict rules and taboos regarding sexuality. It is not coincidental that special claims of cultic purity can be combined with sexual asceticism and withdrawal into the wilderness, as shown by the example of charismatic individuals (Bannus, John the Baptist) and especially the Essenes. In general, the sexually ascetic and "economically independent" lifestyle probably represented an overt distance from society and enjoyed special veneration among the people. This is indicated, moreover, by the fact that John the Baptist expected the renewal of Jewish society through a (symbolic) baptism in the Jordan and according to the Synoptic tradition (cf. Mark 6:14ff. par.) suffered martyrdom because of his massive critique of the adultery of Herod Antipas and his illegal marriage (according to Jewish law: Exod 20:17; Lev 20:21) with the wife of his still living brother. The latter corresponds to the restrictive interpretation of the divorce halakah by Jesus (cf.

Mark 10:1ff. par.; Luke 16:18 par.; Matt 5:32) and also in other circles of Judaism in the land of Israel.[28] Finally, we must point to certain analogies to the purity concepts in connection with illnesses and their healing. "Unclean spirits" are the cause of illnesses according to both the Synoptic tradition and the *Testaments of the Twelve Patriarchs*. And exorcism is a common kind of "healing" or "purification."

6.2.2 Apocalypticism as a Phenomenon of Dissidence

Here, with Koch and others,[29] we distinguish between *apocalypse* as a literary genre and *apocalypticism* as the designation of a religious current in the Judaism of the Hellenistic-Roman period and in early Christianity.[30] This in no way denies the fact that apocalypticism extended beyond this epoch both in Christianity and in Judaism.[31] The apocalyptic writings that are grouped together as a genre on the basis of structural similarities stretch back into the third pre-Christian century. Here we will not go into the particularities of the genre. Apocalyptic motifs are quite varied. They include ideas of the present as end time, the increase of evil or desperate times and cosmic catastrophes, and the expectation of the resurrection, a final judgment of all people, and a new age. They also involve the development of mythological conceptions of a heavenly judge figure, such as the Son of Man, and later also messianic redeemer figures.[32] Thus messianic expectations are by no means indispensable for apocalyptic thinking, but when they appear, they develop in rich variation.[33] Apocalyptic elements are also found in other postbiblical and early-Christian literature that does not belong to the literary genre of apocalypses. Therefore it is appropriate to speak of apocalypticism as a religious current. It gained entrance especially into the Qumran writings,[34] the *Testaments of the Twelve Patriarchs,* and the New Testament; all of these writings are in part literarily similar to the apocalypses.[35]

The tradition-historical origin of apocalyptic literature and its motifs is disputed. Substantial roots are probably to be found in the prophetic tradition, but material from other traditions was also adopted. Typical here is the pseudonymity of the seer figures. For apart from the New Testament Apocalypse of John, which gave the whole genre its name, all other apocalypses borrow the name of a biblical figure (for example, Adam, Enoch, Abraham, Moses, Isaiah, Baruch, Ezra). This pseudonymity, as Goodman appealingly presumes, is perhaps also connected with a loss of authority by the leading strata of Jewish society.[36] In any case, it articulates the break with tradition that defines apocalypticism as a whole.[37]

The specifics of the apocalyptic worldview are characterized by Müller as, in comparison to the rest of Israel's tradition, "a completely changed idea of the salvation that is realized in *history*."[38] Such a change is visible mostly in an anthropological sense, as the Qumran writings in particular make clear.[39] A crucial part of the teleological perspective is the collapse of confidence in a salvific development within history, as well as in the continuation and dependability of past salvation history. A turning point is expected only from an abrupt upheaval and the miraculous intervention of God at the end, which is preceded by terrible catastrophic events. This break with tradition is expressed in the fact that one can no longer simply draw meaning and orientation from the biblical tradition but must do so by way of a concept of the revelation of divine mysteries. These are placed in the scriptures by God, according to the apocalyptic view, but they are conveyed or uncovered only through extraordinary revelation. More than just a literary topic, this worldview is also clearly a symptom of the audience of apocalyptic writings and other literature, an audience open to apocalyptic motifs.

SOCIAL ORIGINS OF APOCALYPTICISM

Jewish apocalypticism was not limited to Palestine, but without doubt had its geographic focus in this region. And its worldview was probably primarily a reaction to the socio-economic and political history of Judaism in the Hellenistic-Roman period. Even if apocalypticism was not the direct result of the massive forced Hellenization of Judea under Antiochus IV Epiphanes, but rather had its origins even earlier, the increasingly militant measures of political, economic, and religious coercion after the battle of Magnesia (190 B.C.E.) contributed decisively to the formation of apocalypticism.[40] In this development the party struggles in the Jewish upper strata and the open endeavors of relevant factions toward Hellenization probably played a role. We must also consider the fact that even the Maccabean intermezzo, in spite of initial successes, did not fundamentally change the situation (cf. Dan 11:25) but only further internalized the problems. "The intra-Jewish dispute had to assume increasingly irreconcilable forms as the aims of a consistent and powerful realpolitik on the part of the newly established Hasmonean dynasty already under Simon required an openness to the still resisted 'temptations' of Hellenistic culture."[41] This very constellation basically remained in place in spite of every change in sovereignty under Herodian-Roman leadership. This meant a qualitatively new situation, however, regardless of the Jewish people's previous experiences of catastrophe. For the economic and cultural-religious suppression was combined with the people's actual political impotence, which—precisely because it was suffered in the land of Israel itself and, moreover, was exacerbated by the failure of the Judeans' own elites—made any chance of connecting with traditional concepts of hope extremely unlikely, if not impossible.

THE EXPERIENCE OF IMPOTENCE AND CRISIS

It is this experience of impotence that must be considered when one judges the "eschatologization" of history (Müller), as it occurred in apocalypticism. Therefore it is hardly appropriate to speak of a "dehistoricization" (Bultmann) or fatalistic denial of history. Rather, one can see in radical transcendence a quite emphatic perception of history, yet precisely under the conditions of the experience of the far-reaching hopelessness of the hope for a turn to salvation within history. The understanding of the Torah and Israel's election in apocalypticism must also be evaluated accordingly. For:

> [the] strong *individualization* of salvation or damnation is a historically conditioned consequence of the Jewish struggle over the law in the thirty-four years after 175 B.C.E., in which the time preceding the anticipated last judgment gradually takes on the character of a decision situation for or against the Torah that is no longer interpreted in terms of the people as a whole but only in terms of the individual.[42]

The idea that only the righteous and true will be saved and that the Torah appears above all as the norm of eschatological judgment only reflects in theological terms what had been manifested in practical experience in the crisis of the Jewish people and, not least of all, of its upper stratum. The universality of sin, which was also expressed in the behavior in Israel that was understood as backsliding, shook the traditional idea of election, just as it promoted the idea of a universal judgment that also included Israel. Topoi such as that of a "righteous planting" and a "new covenant," as found in the Qumran literature and elsewhere, underlined the idea that the concept of election centered on Israel was by no means abolished but only modified. Furthermore, such apocalyptic ideas as a "kingdom of God" or the concept of the "Son of Man" and the kingdom of the "holy ones of the Most High" in the book of Daniel, and especially the messianic figures of apocalyptic literature make it clear that the "individualization" of salvation and damnation in no way suppresses the expectation of a society characterized by a just sovereignty. But this is expected in a new age, and participation in it is linked with a radical separation of the spirits.

THE SOCIOLOGY OF THE BEARERS OF APOCALYPTICISM

As clear as apocalypticism is as a reflex of the history of Judaism in the Hellenistic-Roman period, the socio-historical classification of the circles of bearers of apocalyptic literature is very unclear. On account of certain prejudices, some have seen in such writings an antipriest or even anti-Pharisee movement, yet of the sect or conventicle kind.[43] In general, the picture is greatly influenced by sect typology.

Apocalypticism was interpreted in this way already by Weber, according to whom postexilic Judaism, through a process of the increasing exclusion of prophecy in favor of a priestly hierocracy, was also responsible for driving apocalypticism underground. In his view, "the police of priestly power" caused late prophetic-apocalyptic theology to become an "affair of sects and mystery communions."[44] Plöger carries this initiative further in his book *Theocracy and Eschatology* (1968). He regards the apocalyptic circle as a marginalized "conventicle" that maintained the prophetic tradition against the ruling Jewish upper stratum and particularly the priestly aristocracy with its religious affirmation of the status quo, and which therefore found agreement among the simple folk. More recently, Hanson has adopted this model of apocalypticism as an exclusive group standing over against the dominant society.[45]

Certainly in this view the dissident position of apocalypticism has correctly been detected. Yet is questionable, on the one hand, whether the sociological category of the conventicle or sect is an appropriate description and, on the other, whether one can regard Pharisaism or the priesthood as actually in opposition to this current. Actually, priests are not to be excluded as bearers of apocalypticism.[46] The same is true of the scribes. Indeed, there is reason to consider scribal circles in particular as the producers of apocalypses. Not only is this indicated by the literary quality of these writings and their scribal dealings with tradition, but also, the seer Enoch expressly calls himself "scribe of righteousness" (cf. *1 Enoch* 12:3-4; 15:1, as well as *2 Baruch*).[47] Therefore Collins also assumes that "scribes who were distressed by the encroachments of Hellenism and the consequent erosion of traditional customs and aggravation of class divisions" were, in any case, the authors of *Enoch*.[48] Also pointing in this direction is the representation of Daniel as one of "those who are wise" (Dan 12:3, 10).[49] As we have seen, moreover, the scribal and priestly circles overlap, and thus we cannot set up an alternative between the two as the bearers of apocalypticism.

In any case, the origins of apocalypticism are not to be sought in the lower stratum but in the elite: the upper stratum or retainer group. It is conceivable that circles of the upper stratum and retainer group who had lost power and were opposed to the ruling families were the most important bearer groups of apocalypses and apocalypticism. Furthermore, it is therefore not out of the question that they also found sympathy and influence among the people. Nevertheless, we distinguish apocalypticism as an elite literary dissidence phenomenon, as found in the apocalypses but also in other literary witnesses, from prophetic millenarian or chiliastic phenomena such as the repentance movement of John the Baptist and the followers of Jesus, which arose rather in the lower stratum and took shape around charismatic figures in regular movements (see 6.4). Yet the latter, to the extent that they were themselves literarily expressed, also communicated themselves through scribal apocalyptic forms and motifs, as the tradition of John the Baptist and Jesus of Nazareth in the New Testament makes clear. This literary testimony, however, must be distinguished from the historical phenomena themselves. In any case, one can hardly understand the bearers of apocalypticism in the same way as these movements—and not at all like the Pharisees and Essenes—as an internally structured and externally delimited grouping. Rather, we are dealing here with a religio-literary current of the dissident variety that, however, could under certain circumstances become a regular deviance movement with a clear internal social structure and a clear externally delimited identity, which probably actually took place in the case of the Essenes. Nonetheless, this is not a development that came with apocalypticism itself, but rather required certain other catalytic factors.

THE HASIDEANS AS THE MOVEMENT OF ORIGIN

Since Plöger, the apocalyptic circles have been derived from the Hasideans (Heb. *hasidim*, Gr. *asidaioi*), who for many scholars are also supposed to have been the origin of the Essenes and/or the Pharisees. These Hasideans are mentioned in 1 and 2 Maccabees (1 Macc 2:42; 7:13-14; 2 Macc 14:6) in connection with the Maccabean rebellion.[50] According to 1 Macc 2:42, as the "company" (*synagōgē*) of the pious ones, they joined the Maccabeans and as "mighty warriors [*ischyroi dynamei*] of Israel" participated in the rebellion. Moreover, they are characterized here as those "who offered themselves willingly for the law," which was probably also the reason for their being called "pious." According to 1 Macc 7:13-14, they were the "first [*prōtoi*] among the Israelites to seek peace from them" (the Seleucids). Presupposed here is the situation after the rise to power of the Seleucid Demetrius I, who installed Alcimus, a moderately Hellenistically oriented priest, as high priest. Thus, after a certain time, the Hasideans, in contrast to the Maccabeans, apparently sought an accommodation with the Seleucids and recognized Alcimus as the legitimate high priest, although he was not a Zadokite and came only from a simple priestly background. Since immediately before this passage, in verse 12, we read that "scribes" (*grammateis*) appeared before Alcimus and the Syrian governor Bacchides to ask for just terms, Tcherikover[51] and lately especially J. Kampen[52] hold the opinion that the Hasideans are identical with these scribes. Therefore Tcherikover characterizes the Hasideans as a pious, scribal lay group ("scribe class"), who had risen up and become an influential intellectual leadership stratum under the Maccabeans, independently of the priestly aristocracy, on account of their coalition with urban elites. And Kampen sees in the characterization of the Hasideans as *ischyroi dynamei* in 1 Macc 2:42 and as the *prōtoi* in 7:13 an indication of the (high) social status of this group, whom he therefore describes in summary as "leading citizens devoted to the law."[53] This is also indicated, according to Kampen, by 2 Macc 14:6, which mentions that those among the Jews called Hasideans, whose leader was Judas Maccabeus, would not let the war come to an end. Kampen holds that this group is to be regarded as the origin not of apocalypticism but Pharisaism.

There are, however, arguments against these assumptions. First, the opposition presupposed by Kampen between "apocalyptic" and "scribal" or "Pharisaic" is likely to be problematic.[54] In addition, it is rather unlikely that the "scribes" and "Hasideans" mentioned in 1 Macc 7:12 and 7:13-14 are identical. Rather, it is more probable to see here two different groups, who in distinction to the Maccabeans strove for a compromise after the installation of Alcimus. Also, the characterization of the Hasideans as *ischyroi dynamei* hardly points to their social status, but rather to the fact that they were "mighty warriors," that is, to their military importance. Furthermore, the temporal understanding of *prōtoi* in 1 Macc 7:13 is less forced: they were the *first ones* who sought peace with the Seleucids and their minion Alcimus. Finally, the term *Hasideans* in 2 Macc 14:6 (as opposed to 1 Macc 2:42 and 7:13-14?) was probably simply a collective designation for those who rebelled in opposition to Hellenistic coercive measures, as Saldarini assumes: "All genuine opponents of Hellenization were Hasideans and were preservers of Judaism against outside oppression."[55] Therefore, in our opinion, it is hardly possible to define the Hasideans more closely in terms of social history than as a Torah-loyal, anti-Hellenistic resistance movement. Also, it is not plausible to assume that we have here a sect or a conventicle. The same is true of the far-reaching assumption that the Hasideans are the origin of one or even several party factions in early Judaism. This can be true at best in the global sense that the Torah-loyal, anti-Hellenistic circles were the bearers of the basic currents by which the Essenes and Pharisees were also influenced in the Maccabean period. Nonetheless, the idea that the Hasideans represented something like a collective movement that later split into various factions seems to us contrived.

6.3 Group Formation in the Hellenistic-Roman Period

ESSENES, PHARISEES, AND SADDUCEES AS A DEVIANCE PHENOMENON[56]
As we have already seen, the religious pluralism of the Hellenistic-Roman period is not simply equivalent to the main directions of Pharisees, Essenes, and Sadducees, which we have distinguished on the basis of ancient tradition. Rather, ancient Judaism was characterized by a broad spectrum of distinguishable groups, movements, and currents with more or less defined social form. It has therefore also been said that we must speak of "Judaisms" in the plural rather than of "Judaism" in the singular. Yet we consider that term too

far-reaching and impractical. For as we said in the beginning, there are essential features and institutions that are common to all directions and groups, even if they are regarded differently by the various groups.

Nevertheless, it is appropriate for the Essenes (or the community behind the writings found at Qumran), the Pharisees, and the Sadducees to be clearly emphasized as special groupings. The reason for this lies not least of all in the fact that the Pharisees and Sadducees in the New Testament and rabbinic literature, Pharisees, Sadducees, and Essenes in Josephus, and the Essenes in Philo and other ancient authors are expressly mentioned as groups or designated as "directions" or "schools of thought." At this point we will overlook the fact that Josephus also names a "fourth philosophy" for Palestine (cf. pp. 179–80). Nonetheless, we must mention that from one of these main groups—if, in any case, the Essenes are somehow identical with the Qumran community[57]—we also have a considerable literature from various phases of its history. Yet we do not have at our disposal similar self-testimonies for either the Pharisees or the Sadducees. Here we must resort to outside testimonies, which are often rather tendentious.

6.3.1 The Problem of Religio-Sociological Description

One problem is how to describe these directions in terms of the sociology of religion. The Greek word *hairesis,* preferred by Josephus[58] and in the New Testament,[59] is only conditionally expressive. For it comes from Greek culture and presents the Jewish groups in analogy to schools of philosophy; it refers to their teaching or school and thus also to certain collective aspects of these school views.[60] This is certainly in some respects a correct description, since, on the one hand, all three groups have a particular conception of Israel to be found only among these three and, on the other hand, this identity concept of the groups was lived in a more or less circumscribed social form. Nonetheless, there is still the problem, for example, that the Jewish "schools" did not design and live so much a life-historical program for the individual as a concept for the Jewish identity of the entire people. Likewise limited in its expressive power is the often employed modern term *sect,* which goes back to Weber and above all to Troeltsch and is contrasted with the term *church.* The definition of the "church-sect dichotomy" undertaken by Troeltsch[61] is, however, not only discussed critically in modern sociology of religion but also little suited for the description of certain phenomena of early Judaism and early Christianity.[62] Today, therefore, the term *sect* is largely used by Wilson and others in a relatively unspecific way to designate a "religious minority movement."[63] Yet this characterization is too vague to be really expressive in terms of the sociology of religion, for in this sense one could certainly also describe the Pharisees and especially the Essenes as "sects." Then, however, we have failed to capture the specific differences among these groups or their relationship to parts of pluralistic Judaism.

DEVIANCE THEORY

Therefore it seems to us necessary to try other religio-sociological theorems. In particular, we have in mind the so-called *deviance theories,* which have already been successfully applied to the description of the conflict of early Christianity with contemporary Judaism (cf. pp. 244–47). The crucial point here is that this theory describes the process of deviance formation in connection with fundamental crisis situations in societies and group formation as part of a "deviance career" in which initial exclusion as deviants is neutralized. Thus group formation is not merely a consequence of nonconformity or an identity concept that is not (yet) capable of achieving a majority, but also a strengthening of deviant identity itself, since it cannot be stabilized in a group with common convictions, interests, and lifestyles. As above all Erikson has proposed,[64] deviance does not presuppose (in any case, not absolutely) a majority society otherwise regulated by a consensus of norms and in this sense actually secure in itself, as occurs, for example, in the church-sect dichotomy. Nor is the decisive issue the motives of those who regard certain behavior as deviant. Crucial, rather, are the factors that evoke the crisis or the transformation of society and force a new overall orientation and at the same time a drawing of boundaries that mark identity. In this sense, deviance has the possibility under the right circumstances of becoming a majority.

Therefore deviance theories are very fruitful for the description of group formation in the Judaism of the Hellenistic-Roman period because they allow it to be understood as a reaction to the crisis and at the same time explain the various forms. Especially with the Essenes the process of group formation can be understood as the neutralization of delineation processes and as inner stabilization. This is less true of Pharisees and Sadducees, especially since we do not have self-testimonies that could orient us regarding their self-understanding. Nevertheless, here too we find some indications that allow these groups to be described as deviance phenomena.

6.3.2 Essenes, Pharisees, and Sadducees as Deviant Groups

With the Essenes deviance is easily understood. It is seen, for example, in their withdrawal from the majority society and their consolidation after a certain period in a community settlement on the Dead Sea with their own social structure, religious literature, and established rules of community life and of acceptance into the group or exclusion from it. Moreover, the consciousness of separation is also expressed in the Essenes' own self-designation as "community" (Heb. *yaḥad*) and in metaphors—in part also widespread in other apocalyptic writings—such as those of the "holy planting," "planting of right-eousness," "covenant of grace," "covenant of God," and "remnant."[65] Finally, the Qumran community also understands itself as a new, perfect construction (1QS 8:5–6). The withdrawal into "the wilderness" corresponds to a salva-tion-historical symbolism, which was also actualized by other groups (cf. also p. 168). Entrance into the group's "order" meant separation from sin and sin-ners; positively, it meant the forgiveness of sins and, indeed, the "assurance of the everlasting presence of God,"[66] and each year all members were evaluated according to the measure of their knowledge and their way of life and exam-ined in regard to whether they had satisfied the prescripts of the covenant of God.[67] The Qumran community was also organized internally according to a strict hierarchy. At the head were priests, who were also the ultimate deciding authority.[68] Finally and above all, this separation from the majority of the peo-ple is again and again the express topic of the Qumran writings.[69]

It is noteworthy that in 4QMMT (cols. 7–8) this separation from the mainstream of the people is characterized by a form of the Hebrew verb *parash*. For from the same root or its Aramaic equivalent one can also derive the designation of the group called the *Pharisees,* which in the Greek tran-scription is *pharisaioi* (Heb. *perushim,* Aram. *perishaya*), a name probably given to it from the outside "with the derogatory meaning of separatists or sec-tarians."[70] It must be mentioned that in regard to social structure and to com-munity life and its rules, things are not as clear in the case of the Pharisees as with the Qumran community. For it is questionable whether the social forms named in this connection, which according to rabbinic literature can be assumed for the group of the so-called *haverim,* are to be related to the his-torical Pharisees. For this presupposes the controversial equating of the *perushim* (Pharisees) with the *haverim.*[71] In any case, Josephus describes the Pharisees as a political group that is at least outwardly distinguishable. Yet the community life of the Pharisees was without doubt less strictly organized than that of the Essenes, and the boundaries with the majority society were essen-tially more porous for the Pharisees than for the Essenes. Thus deviance in no way automatically has to mean a withdrawal from society and social—sect-like—separation. Rather, it could also be lived aggressively and integrated within the larger society.

The deviance of the Sadducees can be comprehended only indirectly. It is derivable above all from the fact that in the tradition they are also expressly called a *hairesis,* that is, a certain school or direction; in addition, they bear their own party name (*Sadducees* presumably means the "members of the party of Zadok," the Davidic chief priest to whom even the legitimate line of high priests who emigrated to Egypt under Onias IV also appealed),[72] and they are characterized in terms of certain political interests and religious conceptions that conflict with those of the Pharisees. It is also probable that the designation *Sadducees* articulates the claim of continuing the true line of the Zadokites.[73] Moreover, a certain exclusivity is suggested by the presentation of Josephus, according to which he voluntarily "ran through" their school of thought (*Life* 10ff.) and their influence on the people, as well as the priest-hood, was rather small (cf. *War* 3.166; *Ant.* 13.298; 18.17).[74] Finally, the idea of deviance is also supported by the assumption that the Sadducees were by no means identical with the ruling priestly aristocracy but formed a minority even among the priests.[75] This would also be supported by the fact that the Sadducees were perhaps identified in rabbinic tradition with the Boethuse-ans,[76] a name that can probably be traced back to the family of the Alexan-drian priest Boethus, which was one of the four families from which Herod selected his high priests. Yet whether the Sadducees had their own group organization is doubtful. Since, however, they were apparently members of families of the upper stratum and high priesthood, this origin gave them a cer-tain close social structure.

REASONS FOR THE DEVIANCE

The Deviance of the Qumran Community
In contrast to the Qumran community, the basis of the deviance is less clear with both the Pharisees and the Sadducees. For the Qumran community the already mentioned text 4QMMT makes the reason for the separation clear. Here we have a letter (or copies of a letter) to the priestly aristocracy in Jerusalem from the early period of the community, in which the various Torah interpretations that for the community cannot be compromised are summa-rized with regard to some twenty halakic points of disagreement from the "teacher of righteousness" himself or, in any case, from a later influential leader of the community.[77] An important role is also played here not least of all by certain questions of cultic purity, for purity and asceticism basically underline the community's separation from the outside world. Halakic dif-ferences increase in the course of development, so that finally in the Damas-cus Document (CD) there is a comprehensive collection of "the things beyond the biblical scriptures that should have lasting legal validity for the Essenes."[78] This exclusive claim of authoritative interpretation of the Torah implies a charismatic element, as shown by the concentration of this claim on the "teacher of righteousness." It is also expressed in his other designations as "the unique teacher" and simply "the interpreter of the Torah."[79]

This absolute claim with regard to Torah interpretation, however, is at the same time connected with the idea of representing the only legitimate tradi-tion of the cult and the priesthood. Already at the beginning of the separation there was essentially a conflict over the legitimacy of the high priest and the cult calendar, as well as the Jerusalem cult in general. Possibly the revered founder figure of the community, as a legitimate Zadokite, claimed the high priest's office or even possessed it for a certain period after the death of Alcimus until he was deposed by the Maccabean Jonathan (the "Wicked Priest").[80] And in any case, the decisive reason for the secession of the "teacher of righteousness" was probably the rejection of the calendar of the moon, which was first mentioned under the high priest Menelaus in 167 B.C.E. and then introduced by the high priest Jonathan in 152 B.C.E., and the favoring of a calendar of the sun for the temple cult.[81]

Thus the Essene separation meant to a certain extent a total deviance vis-à-vis the Hasmonean or Herodian-Roman-governed Judea, which also expressed itself especially in the strict following of priestly ideas of purity. Accordingly, a claim of sole representation was made in Israel. As "covenant of God" and "temple," they alone represent the "people of God" or "community of Israel," whereas all others belong to the *massa perditionis* that has strayed from the right way. Here the reversal of the community's own deviance is projected on the majority society. "Those who continued to reject this union ultimately excluded themselves from Israel as the people of salvation, disparaged the covenant of God from Sinai, and lost the basis of the Torah, which bound salvation for Israel indissolubly to its existence in God's Holy Land."[82]

This self-understanding is decisively connected with a thoroughly apocalyptically determined view of history, the world, humanity, and the Torah, which underlines the radical claim with dualistic conceptions. Salvation-(or damnation-)historical interpretations of the present as the end time are linked with the consciousness not only of standing on the side of light and truth against darkness and lies, but also of already living in the renewed creation and participating in the heavenly community through worship.

The Deviance of the Pharisees

More difficult to characterize is the nature of Pharisaic deviance. Essentially two reasons are named.[83] One refers to the presentation in Josephus and the New Testament, according to which the Pharisees were particularly known for their accurate Torah interpretation in general and their appeal to special (oral?) traditions not present in the written Torah of Moses itself (cf. *Ant.* 13.297, 408; Mark 7:5; Matt. 15:2). This could also include the polemic against the *dorshe ha-halokot,* the "researchers of smooth things," in Qumran[84] to the extent that they may be interpreted with regard to the Pharisees and as distortion of their appeal to (oral) teaching (*halakot*).[85] The other reason for their deviance involves the references to their strict observance of purity and food laws, as well as the tithes, which are found in the New Testament[86] and are inferred by Neusner from the rabbinic tradition (see below). In this connection the distant relationship of the Pharisees to the 'am ha-ares, the simple people, is also always named.[87]

Here we should perhaps also mention the remarks of Josephus about the Pharisees' simple life averse to any luxury. They hold this interest in ritual purity in common with the Essenes, yet without the latter's ascetic esoteric tendency. In contrast to the Essenes, whose ideal of purity is apparently rooted in their priestly nature, the view of the Pharisees is more like that of the laity. This is also supported by the strict observance of the precepts for tithing. Perhaps the various accentuations in the tradition draw attention to the fact that what appears to be deviant in the Pharisees can be judged differently from different viewpoints. Thus if from the perspective of the ruling strata and particularly the Sadducees they were a group that appealed to their accurate Torah interpretation and patriarchal traditions and represented a different political and religious concept, from the viewpoint of the people they were a group that placed special value on ritual purity and thus represented a line of demonstrative sanctification of life.

Neusner has connected the concentration of the Pharisees on ritual purity and strict tithing with the hypothesis that they formed something like a "table fellowship"—not only on certain occasions but also in daily life. They claimed the ideal of priestly purity and to some extent turned their homes into temples. It was this special purity, which was actually required only in the temple, that set them apart from the normal folk. Josephus characterizes the Pharisees above all as a political interest group that was in conflict with the Sadducees and had influence on the basis of their support among the people, yet the Pharisees were also repeatedly subject to the influence of the Sadducees and then had to experience exclusion and perhaps even persecution under Alexander Jannaeus. Neusner solves this problem with a supplementary hypothesis. Since the latter information relates especially to the early history of the Pharisees under the Maccabeans but the information about the concentration on questions of ritual purity seems to come from the late period of their group history, Neusner holds that in their history the Pharisees developed from a political party to a rather sectarian, quietist religious group in the Herodian period.[88] Yet this assumption is contradicted by the fact that the Pharisees played an influential political role not only under the Hasmoneans but also in the Herodian-Roman period. Moreover, it is methodologically questionable when Neusner claims rabbinic tradition for Pharisaism even when rabbinic traditions do not expressly refer to the Pharisees.[89]

With regard to certain religious convictions of the Pharisees such as belief in the resurrection, judgment, and angels, we can see not only apocalyptic influence but also the openness of the Pharisees to new religious currents. This indicates that the Pharisees were more a reformist than a conservative movement, which comports with the fact that in the question of belief in fate, they took a middle position between the Sadducees, according to whom everything is subject to free will, and the Essenes, for whom everything is predetermined (cf. Jos. *Ant.* 13.171ff.). Josephus in particular describes the Pharisees' unrelenting efforts to influence ruling circles, and this makes it clear that they, in contrast to the Essenes, did not link their deviance with a claim of exclusiveness. Their appeal to "patriarchal traditions" and not to charismatic authority also underlines a program oriented toward institutions. "The Pharisees were not a simple group with a limited, concrete goal but a long, well-connected, voluntary, corporate organization which sought to influence Jewish society and entered into many mutual relationships to accomplish their aims."[90]

The Deviance of the Sadducees

Finally we must ask what were the reasons for the deviance of the Sadducees. In this connection it is often presumed that the Sadducees were an especially hellenized group in the upper stratum.[91] Yet this does not fit in with the group's religious conservatism (discussed below). Indeed, this conservatism even allows the presumption that the Sadducees were an upper-stratum movement that reacted to certain assimilatory or reformist tendencies.[92] We will come closer to the deviance phenomenon if we consider the constellations in which the Sadducees are found. Their competition with the Pharisees for political influence, as presented by Josephus, and their difference from the Pharisees in the judgment of religious questions indicate that the Sadducees are to be regarded above all as an anti-Pharisee group. Thus their deviance is, first of all, a consequence of their reaction to the Pharisees and the latter's influence on ruling circles. That is, the Sadducees developed from the upper stratum as an anti-Pharisaic countermovement. The concentration of the Sadducees on the written Torah and its rejection by Pharisaic traditions, as reported by Josephus, suggests that they held a certain conservative position vis-à-vis the rather reformist stance of the Pharisees.[93] This corresponds both to their rejection of the Pharisaic apocalyptic belief in angels and the resurrection, which developed in the Hellenistic period, and their name *Sadducees,* which expresses a conservative, high-priestly claim to legitimacy. If this brings them close to the Essenes, they are still distinguished from the Essenes by their unapocalyptic character, the recognition of the legitimacy of the high priests in Jerusalem, the missing claim of exclusiveness, and their striving for "system-immanent" influence. This stance was probably not capable of a majority even in the upper stratum. Therefore it is probably appropriate to assume with Saldarini that the Sadducees were not simply identical with the ruling aristocracy but rather possibly represented an especially conservative tendency within the upper stratum.

6.3.3 The Stratum Membership of Essenes, Pharisees, and Sadducees

STRATUM MEMBERSHIP OF THE SADDUCEES

The classification of the three main groups in the strata of Jewish society is rather clear in the case of the Sadducees, for the testimonies in both Josephus and the New Testament suggest that they belonged to the ruling upper stratum of Jerusalem. They are first mentioned by Josephus under John Hyrcanus, who broke with the Pharisees and joined the Sadducees (cf. *Ant.* 13.293ff.). This indicates, in any case, that the Sadducees were close to the ruling stratum. This is also supported by the fact that according to Josephus they gained their followers not from the ordinary folk but from the rich and most respected people (*Ant.* 13.298). It is likewise clear that some members of the high-priestly aristocracy were also included in their numbers; yet Josephus mentions by name only the high priest Ananias (*Ant.* 20.199ff.). Yet we cannot conclude from this that all high priests or even all members of the upper stratum were Sadducees. There is, however, no reason not to accept the converse conclusion. According to the New Testament, the Sadducees, as an influential group of the Sanhedrin, are included in the upper stratum and are named in the same breath with the high priest (cf. only Acts 5:17).

STRATUM MEMBERSHIP OF THE PHARISEES

Whether the Pharisees, by contrast, also belonged to the upper stratum is questionable. It is clear, in any case, that they did not simply belong to the lower stratum, even if they had their main following there. Speaking against this is their politically influential role, first under John Hyrcanus and then above all under Salome Alexandra, as well as in the Herodian-Roman period. In general, they made an ongoing attempt to influence the policies of the ruling circles, which apparently also opened them up to persecutions under Alexander Jannaeus. For the Pharisees drew the Seleucids into the intra-Jewish dispute, and for this Alexander took cruel revenge by having eight hundred rebels crucified (cf. *Ant.* 13.379ff.).[94] The Pharisees probably also had some power under John Hyrcanus. For when he joined the Sadducees, the legal regulations introduced by the Pharisees were nullified (*Ant.* 13.296). Indeed, according to Josephus, under Alexandra they not only shared increasingly in power but ultimately even became administrators (*dioiketai*)[95] of the whole state and held the executive authority to implement or abolish banishments and to arrest or set free (*War* 1.110–11; cf. *Ant.* 13.409). Elsewhere he even describes a situation in which Alexandra was nominally the queen but the power was in fact executed by the Pharisees and in the manner of absolute rulers (*Ant.* 13.409). This agrees with the report that the Pharisees tried to persuade Alexandra to kill those who were responsible for the execution of eight hundred insurgents under Alexander Jannaeus (*Ant.* 13.410). Even

Herod seems to have respected the Pharisees as an important interest group.[96] According to Josephus, among the leading and ruling circles of Jerusalem the most respected Pharisees were ultimately ranked beside the high priests at the beginning of the anti-Roman rebellion (cf. *Life* 20ff.; *War* 2.409ff.). Also according to the presentations of the Gospels of Mark and Matthew, the Pharisees were influential members of the ruling circles in Galilee, and also in Jerusalem, according to the Gospel of John and the Acts of the Apostles— especially as members of the Sanhedrin.[97] All of this indicates that some of the Pharisees are to be classified with the retainer group on the basis of their education, and some presumably even with the ruling upper stratum on account of their background.[98] The boundaries between these two groups are fluid, however, since under certain circumstances the members of the retainer group could rise into the class of the ruling upper stratum.

Thus it is no coincidence that Josephus, who himself came from the priestly aristocracy, counted himself for a time among the Pharisees. Whether this means that he was a committed advocate of Pharisaic teachings is very doubtful. It is, in any case, more likely, in view of *Life* 10–12, that Josephus could not have pursued his public career without considering the leading role of the Pharisees.[99] The Pharisee Simon ben Gamaliel, whom Josephus mentions in his autobiography (*Life* 196ff.), also came from an illustrious Jerusalem family and had influence on the high priest Ananias, who was a Sadducee. The same is true of Samias, who at the time of the rise of Herod was a member of the Sanhedrin, a student of the Pharisee Pollion, and probably also a Pharisee himself (cf. *Ant.* 14.163ff.). Acts 5:34 names as a member of the Sanhedrin and a teacher of the Torah highly regarded by the whole people the Pharisee Gamaliel, who is often identified with Gamaliel I (d. 50 C.E.), a descendant of Hillel. Even if the Lukan Gamaliel is only a literary figure, it is still noteworthy that Luke places him in the leading circles.

Finally, two further comments in Josephus give an interesting insight into the social stratigraphy of the Pharisees. He mentions that "the most highly regarded among the Pharisees," together with the high priests and the influential citizens of Jerusalem attempted to ward off the threatening war in 66 C.E. (*War* 2.408ff.). And in *Life* 197ff. he reports on a delegation that was sent from Jerusalem to Galilee in order to relieve him of his command in Galilee. This legation consisted of men of different background (*genos*) but the same education (*paideia*). Two of them, the Pharisees Jonathan and Ananias, came from the general population (*dēmōtikoi*) and the third, Joazar, likewise a Pharisee, was from the priestly lineage, while the fourth, Simon, came from a high-priestly family. Two things are clear: first the difference between Simon and Joazar; both were priests, and one even came from the aristocracy. The second thing to notice is the difference between Jonathan and Ananias on the one hand and Simon and Joazar on the other. The latter were of priestly origin; the former were not. Yet the question is whether Josephus, with the characterization of the Pharisees Jonathan and Ananias as *dēmōtikoi*, is merely pointing out their nonpriestly origin and is trying to say that they were laymen,[100] or whether he also wants to emphasize their humble origins.[101] The latter is suggested, in any case, on the basis of the context and of other usage of the word *dēmōtikos*[102] in Josephus. We must observe, however, that it was hardly totally simple people who were sent in an official delegation from Jerusalem to Josephus. Also speaking against this is the statement that all four were of the same—and here that probably implied "outstanding"—education and that Jonathan, one of the Pharisees expressly characterized as from a lower background, was the leader of the delegation. Therefore we presume that even the Pharisees of more humble birth in this delegation were members of the retainer class. This is also supported by the remaining administrative tasks or noble functions that this delegation to Josephus had.[103]

Thus it must remain basically true that as retainers the Pharisees came from priestly-scholarly circles, were "in the service of the ruling class as bureaucrats, educators and officials," and under Alexandra "they could gain power in the bureaucracy and become part of the ruling class temporarily. . . ."[104] This alone speaks against the idea that women could also be Pharisees.[105]

One special problem is the presentation in the Acts of the Apostles, according to which Paul was also a Pharisee, the son of a Pharisee (23:6), and a student of Gamaliel (22:3), and the Christian community in Jerusalem included "some believers who belonged to the *hairesis* of the Pharisees" (15:5). There are good reasons to regard the latter piece of information as Lukan fiction without historical basis.[106] But is that also true of the characterization of Paul? Even according to his own witness, he was "as to the law, a Pharisee" (Phil 3:5). Yet it is clear that Paul himself is not simply speaking of himself as a Pharisee but merely expressing the idea that according to the law (*kata nomon*), he was a Pharisee. As the context shows, he is thereby describing himself as one who was serious with his Jewish identity and in particular with his observance of the Torah and the concomitant separation from the outside world. Strictly speaking, however, this means only that he led a Jewish life that corresponded to the Pharisaic interpretation of the Torah, and he expresses this in Gal 1:14 by saying that he once lived within Judaism (*ioudaismos*) and advanced in Judaism beyond his contemporaries in that he was especially zealous for the traditions of his ancestors. While it is striking that he speaks here of the "traditions of my ancestors," the reference is hardly to a specific Pharisaic teaching, that is, the appeal to an oral tradition that goes beyond the written Torah, but rather to faithfulness to the traditional Jewish way of life in accordance with the Torah in general.[107] Also the comment that he "advanced

in Judaism beyond many among my people of the same age"[108] probably did
not mean (only) progress in the study of the Torah but, because of the following explanatory participial phrase, above all the practical pursuit of the Jewish
way of life. We must note, moreover, that Paul does not make express reference
here to Pharisaism; instead he uses the term *ioudaismos,* which means the
activity of being a Jew in decisive separation from the outside world. This
could also be a further indication that in Phil 3:5 Paul is styling himself as a
follower of Pharisaic Torah observance in order to emphasize his Jewish identity, which was lived in strict separation from non-Jews. Then the emphasis on
his earlier life in *ioudaismos* in Gal 1:13-14 would correspond to the *kata
nomon Pharisaios* in Phil 3:5. Both passages speak in parallel formulations of
his zeal, which is directed toward the persecution of the *ekklēsia.* It is naturally possible that the information in Acts is accurate in that Paul once belonged
to the Pharisees in Jerusalem.[109] Yet it seems more likely to us that this also
rests on a Lukan fiction. In any case, as a Diaspora Jew Paul hardly belonged
to the *hairesis* of the Pharisees, since, as Hengel has recently shown, we have no
express information about the Pharisees in the Diaspora.[110]

STRATUM MEMBERSHIP OF THE ESSENES

On the basis of the beginnings of the Qumran community, its stratum membership is clearly to be found in the upper stratum of Jerusalem in the Hasmonean period and especially in the priestly aristocracy. The social
relationships no doubt changed in the course of the community's long history, yet it is doubtful that the Essenes were ever a purely lower-stratum movement or even recruited a significant part of their membership from the lower
stratum. Speaking against this idea is not only the yet-to-be-discussed archaeological evidence but also the permanent priestly domination of the community's organizational structure. Also the mention of the Essenes by name in
Josephus points rather to the upper stratum or the retainer group: John is supposed to have been the commander during the rebellion (*War* 2.567; 3.11),
and Menachem and Simon were named as dream interpreters or seers in the
milieu of Herod and Archelaus (*Ant.* 15.373; 17.347–48). Finally, Josephus
came from the priestly aristocracy of Jerusalem, and he studied with the
Essenes, according to his own statements.

Voluntary Poverty and Common Possession of Goods in Qumran?
The frequent self-designation as "community of the poor" (4QpPs 37) or the
"poor" (1QpHab 12:3ff; 1QM 11:8–9, 13; 13:14; 1QH 1:36; 2:32, 34; 3:25;
5:16ff; and elsewhere) and the term "poor of spirit" (1QM 14:3, 7; cf. 1QS
3:8; 4:3), as well as statements about the "mixing of possessions" (see below),
have furthered assumptions that the community lived in voluntary poverty

and held goods in common. Furthermore, since some statements in the Community Rule (e.g., 1QS 1:1ff.) seem to support the ideal of celibacy, the Qumran community has been compared with a monastic order.[111] This also seemed to confirm information about the Essenes in Pliny the Elder, Philo, and Josephus.[112] But since Josephus seems to presuppose both sexually ascetic and married Essenes, it has been assumed that at least the "core community" in Qumran itself was celibate and lived in voluntary poverty.

There are, in the first place, good reasons to assume that the statements about poverty in the Qumran writings are not simply metaphors for the humble spirituality of the community. Yet at the same time, they do not simply indicate material poverty. Rather, "the term *poor* always refers to those who belong to the true Israel and therefore must suffer violence and misery."[113] As Lohfink has made clear, it is the experiences of persecution, humiliation, and marginalization, along with real need and real misery, that shape the sayings about poverty. Stigmatization through membership in the community, but also concrete oppression and hostility, perhaps even robberies (cf. 1QpHab 12:9–10), are all prominent. Nonetheless, it is striking "that poverty never appears expressly as a lack of earthly possessions and that no group of 'rich' ever appears as the opposite of the 'poor.'"[114] Wealth is never disparaged. When the person praying in 1QH 14:20; 15:23 says that he would not like to exchange the truth of God for possessions, then this presupposes the choice of truth or riches, but not a criticism of wealth in itself. And this corresponds to the fact that, for example, in 1QpHab 8:10–11 the "Wicked Priest" is reproached for being faithless because of cupidity. Thus all of this points more to power-deprived members of the upper stratum than to the lower stratum.

Second, the assumption of a commonality of goods that eliminates private property would also be erroneous.[115] It is true that this interpretation is suggested by Philo and particularly by the report of Josephus on the Essenes. Nevertheless, closer examination demonstrates, as Paschen has already shown, that a Hellenistic ideal of social utopia has distorted the perspective.[116] Based on the property statements in the purity catechism of 1QS 5:13–20, Paschen makes it clear that the step-by-step bringing in of property is connected with the community's priestly code of purity. It is not a question of renouncing possessions but of the fact that in intracommunity economic activity, only goods that meet the purity regulations are exchanged.[117] Thus the step-by-step "mixing" of the entering member's assets with the community's property serves the purification of personal property for intracommunity use. Just as entrants themselves undergo a purification procedure that enables them to "approach" the community, so to speak, like a priest approaching cultic worship, so also their possessions. These are introduced into the community's assets and placed under the supervision of the priests. Private property and private usufruct are therefore not excluded. Certainly, there was also community property held in common and managed by a special "overseer." And apparently, according to CD 14:12–117, everyone had to deliver at least two days' wages to the social treasury each month.[118] This indicates that the community also included those in need of support. It is also possible that some entrants were redeemed from slavery to debt.[119] But with regard to the overall community, it cannot be a question of poverty in the material sense or of voluntary poverty.

In the third place, this is also supported by the archaeological evidence.[120] For the remains of the building complex in Khirbet Qumran are distinguished from the splendid buildings of Herod and other upper-stratum members in the land of Israel by their simplicity and lack of ornamentation. From this alone one cannot conclude that it confirms the Essene self-designation as "poor."[121] For really materially poor people could hardly have afforded these domains, which probably included considerable areas of artificially cultivated land,[122] even if they had combined all their assets. Moreover, the high functionality of the operation and above all the technically highly developed water system stand in stark contrast to the lack of ornamentation, which was due more to religious than to financial considerations. The enormous library that belonged to the community also indicates a considerable economic potential. In any case, the settlement was a thriving economic operation, which was able to cover its self-sufficiency through agriculture and trade, as well as its own pottery, tannery, and manuscript copying center.

Thus the social composition of the Qumran community was able to comprise all strata. From the beginning, however, members from the upper stratum and their retainers, priests, and scribes played a decisive role. Women were probably also able to join, yet with more limited rights.[123]

6.4 Prophetic-Charismatic Movements and Individual Figures in the Herodian-Roman Period

In addition to large main currents and basic movements, whose beginnings reach back into the early stages of the Jewish people's disagreements with the Hellenistic kingdoms, there were a number of religious phenomena in the Herodian-Roman period that, like apocalypticism, are interpretable as indirect protest reactions to the socio-economic and religio-political chaos in the land of Israel. Unlike apocalypticism and the main religious groups, however, they found their main supporters not in the elite but in the lower stratum and among the underprivileged. We have in mind here, on the one hand, individual thaumaturgical or prophetic figures and, on the other, the movements of the so-called sign prophets, as well as, finally, that of John the Baptist (and

Jesus). Since Weber these have been described as "charismatic movements" or, in connection with this, ethno-sociologically as "millenarian movements,"[124] which are typical of the situation of colonized peoples with tribal structures of tradition or underprivileged groups on the edge of foreign majority societies. In connection with the followers of Jesus we will go into this in more detail (cf. p. 192). The named individual figures are naturally also charismatically gifted. Yet they mobilized neither masses nor a close group of followers.

In contrast to this, in the prophetic-chiliastic movement large numbers of followers—or as in the case of the Baptist (and Jesus), both a larger following and a narrower circle of disciples—crystallized around charismatically gifted individuals who either through miracles or through exemplary life, through "economic release" (from the world), and not least of all through martyrdom, sought to legitimate themselves as guarantors of the (messianic) hope of redemption. Such phenomena existed not only in the land of Israel but also in the Diaspora, as shown by the example of the weaver Jonathan in Cyrenaica and his movement (cf. *War* 7.437ff.). If the thaumaturgists (miracle workers) represented one answer to individual distress, then the prophetic-charismatic movements developed a liberation concept, as it were, for the internal and external distress of the entire people. Thus they had a "message" that promised the overcoming of the crisis. These messages connected, not coincidentally, with the salvation-historical events of the people of Israel and venerated charismatic-prophetic figures of the past like Moses, Joshua, and Elijah. For Moses and Elijah were connected, especially in popular belief but also in the biblical tradition, with the idea of an eschatological return and thus the repetition of the history of liberation or the hope of the internal and external restoration of the people of the twelve tribes. The reference to the history of salvation could consist in the announcement of the repetition of a "sign" or miracle of the past or, as in the case of the Baptist, in direct identification as Elijah redivivus, that is, with a person from the past. Even if this identity was ascribed to the Baptist only later, this points to the substantial charismatic character of his movement. For in contrast to the "sign prophets," who were able to mobilize a following only for a short time and whose charisma collapsed with the military annihilation and the failure of the promised sign, the Baptist was able to work charismatically even beyond his death and not least of all on the strength of his martyrdom. The same is also true of Jesus and his followers. We will mention again the fact that with the individual thaumaturgical and prophetic figures there are also connections with biblical models, including Elijah.

6.4.1 Individual Thaumaturgical and Prophetic Figures

There were magic healers and miracle workers not only in Palestine. In the first century C.E. Apollonius of Tyana appeared in eastern Asia Minor and Simon Magus in Samaria. Nonetheless, one scholar has with justification spoken of an "East-West slope"[125] in regard to thaumaturgical phenomena. Apollonius and Simon were above all exorcists. In the postbiblical literature, deeds of exorcism are attributed, for example, to Abraham (cf. 1QapGen ar 20.16–19) and Tobias (Tob 6:13ff; 8:1ff.). Josephus also reports on an exorcist named Eleazar (*Ant.* 7.46–47) in connection with a presentation of Solomon that also characterizes him as a miraculous healer. In the land of Israel, two wonder-workers are especially known by name: Ḥoni the Circle-drawer and Ḥanina ben Dosa.[126] Characteristic of them are magical prayer miracles in the tradition of Elijah. This corresponds to many aspects in the presentation of Jesus in the Synoptic tradition.

ḤONI THE CIRCLE-DRAWER

On Ḥoni there are traditions in Josephus (*Ant.* 14.22ff.) and in the Mishnah (*m. Taʿan.* 3.8; cf. *t. Taʿan.* 2.13). By all appearances, Ḥoni was a simple peasant, perhaps even from Galilee. Shortly before the conquest of Jerusalem by Pompey, Ḥoni is supposed to have successfully prayed for rain because of a persistent drought. This recalls Elijah's miracle (1 Kings 17:1). Also in the Midrash, incidentally, there is a connection between Elijah and Ḥoni, even if in a different regard: "No one is equal to Elijah or Ḥoni the Circle-drawer, who brought humankind to serve God" (*Ber. R.* 13.7). Josephus calls Ḥoni a "righteous and godly man," apparently in order to distinguish him from the subsequently discussed "sign prophets," whom he considers tempters. Accordingly, like the Mishnah, he plays down the magical aspect of his activity.[127] Because of his (magical) abilities, Ḥoni was also, according to Josephus, drawn into the power struggle between the sons of Salome Alexandra, Hyrcanus and Aristobulus, during the civil war. The followers of Hyrcanus asked Ḥoni to pronounce a curse on Aristobulus. When Ḥoni refused, he was stoned by "evil ones among the Jews." According to certain information in the Babylonian Talmud, two of his grandsons are also supposed to have been active as magical rainmakers (cf. *b. Taʿan.* 23a–b).

ḤANINA BEN DOSA

Another charismatic miracle worker known by name, Ḥanina ben Dosa apparently lived in great poverty before 70 C.E. in Galilee in the vicinity of Sepphoris. In the Talmud he is named in connection with Yoḥanan ben Zakkai (*b. Ber.* 34b). According to rabbinic tradition, he is also credited with prayer miracles and above all healing miracles. He is supposed to have healed the son of Yoḥanan ben Zakkai. Above all, however, a distant healing is also ascribed to him, as to Jesus. In the context of a nature miracle, there is an indirect reference to Elijah. The idea that he was a miracle worker could also be derived from a tradition of the Mishnah: "When Rabbi Ḥanina ben Dosa died, the men of action ceased" (*m. Sot.* 9.15). Yet there is controversy over whether "men of action" really means "miracle workers."[128]

JESUS BEN ANANIAS

By contrast, one *prophetic* figure mentioned by Josephus (cf. *War* 6.300ff.) is Jesus, son of Ananias, who has more than just the name in common with Jesus of Nazareth. He was "an uneducated man from the country" who, four years before the First Jewish Revolt, came to Jerusalem in connection with a pilgrimage to the Feast of Booths and, beginning in the temple district, repeatedly prophesied the demise of the temple, the city, and the people. Apparently he based his prophecy on Jeremiah (cf. Jer 7:34; 16:4). Attempts of "respected citizens" to silence him culminated in a complaint lodged with the governor, Albinus, who, after subjecting the prophet of doom to a scourging and a brief hearing, set him free again because he was held to be "insane." He would hardly have been able to escape execution had he—unlike Jesus of Nazareth—not been a loner with no disciples and followers, for such always evoked Roman suspicions of revolutionary activities.[129] According to Josephus, Jesus ben Ananias continued his laments and prophecies of disaster until he was killed by a projectile during the siege of Jerusalem by the Romans.

6.4.2 Prophetic-Charismatic Protest Movements ("Sign Prophets")

One can distinguish the charismatic-prophetic movements, on the one hand, from messianic pretenders and their armed resistance, which has clear socio-revolutionary traits, and, on the other, from charismatic-chiliastic or prophetic movements like those of John the Baptist and Jesus, which are characterized by the formation of a close circle of followers. Indeed, they have their charismatic activism in common with the social bandits and the movements of the Baptist and Jesus. Yet because of the programmatic nonviolence of the latter movements, the boundaries of the charismatic-prophetic groups with the Baptist and Jesus are more clearly marked than those with the social bandits or revolutionary groups. This is also shown by the estimation of these "sign prophets"[130] by Josephus and in the New Testament.[131]

    For Josephus both the nearness to and the distinction from socio-revolutionary strivings are instructive. He mentions them in a general note in connection with the sicarii but makes it clear that their "hands were cleaner." Nevertheless, he considers these "prophets" (*Ant.* 10.97, 169; *War* 2.261), whom he, following Deuteronomy 13, can also call "pseudo-prophets" (*War* 2.261), to be "*tempters* and deceivers who under the pretext of divine inspiration evoked unrest and uproar and through their words instilled demonic enthusiasm in the masses. Finally, they led the people into the *wilderness,* where God wanted to show them *signs* of liberation [*sēmeia eleutherias*]." According to Josephus, in the time of the governor Festus an unnamed prophet led his followers into the wilderness in order to give them "redemption and rest from evil" (*Ant.* 20.188). It is noteworthy in regard to the charismatic element that the announcement of a sign miracle meets with an affective, credulous reaction by the followers.[132]

Similarly, Matt 24:4ff. warns against "false messiahs and *false prophets*" who "will appear and produce great *signs* and omens, to *lead astray,* if possible, even the elect" (24:24). And here too the wilderness is the place of eschatological expectation: "So, if they say to you, 'Look! He is in the *wilderness,*' do not go out" (24:26). A clear separation of Jesus from these "sign prophets" is also found in the Gospel of John, where a connection between prophetic-charismatic movements and revolutionary strivings is apparently also presupposed.[133]

It is noteworthy that the Roman governors treated these movements in the same way as they did revolutionaries and social bandits. This was not simply arbitrary but was related to the mobilization of the masses by the sign prophets. Apparently, however, their boundaries with social bandits and revolutionaries were actually fluid, as shown by the examples of "Theudas" the "Egyptian" and of the "Samaritan," which we will briefly discuss below. Finally, Josephus mentions that in the year 52 C.E. a coalition developed between brigands and such prophetic-millenarian groups (cf. p. 176). And he tells of a "pseudo-prophet" in Jerusalem at the time of the First Jewish Revolt who "proclaimed to the people in the city that God commanded them to go up to the shrine and await the signs of redemption" (*War* 6.285).

For Judea we must mention here the movement of a certain Theudas, who appeared during the time of the procurator Cuspius Fadus (after 44 C.E.; cf. *Ant.* 20.97–98). He is also named in Acts 5:36, though chronologically out of order, being placed before Judas the Galilean (Acts 5:37). Yet it is notable that Theudas is placed in a series with this armed resistance fighter, who was the founder of the so-called fourth philosophy or party faction of the Jews according to Josephus, who also says that Theudas is supposed to have announced himself as a prophet and gathered around himself a large crowd. He asserted that he could command the Jordan to divide. Apparently, in a reversal of the taking of the land under Joshua (cf. Joshua 3), he wanted to lead his followers through the Jordan and back into the wilderness, in order from there to bring about emancipation. Cuspius Fadus sent a cavalry unit against this movement, and it killed many and took some prisoners. Theudas himself was beheaded and his head brought to Jerusalem. Thus the Romans made of him an example that was supposed to serve as a deterrent. It is noteworthy that according to Josephus, the followers of Theudas were supposed to take all their possessions with them. This indicates that they were poor people who did not own much and thus did not have much to lose.

A similar movement was that of the "Egyptian" in the time of the procurator Felix, who is likewise mentioned by Josephus (*War* 2.262ff.; *Ant.* 20.169ff.) and also appears in the New Testament (cf. Acts 21:38). Here we probably have a Jew who had come from Egypt to Jerusalem and announced himself as a prophet. He assembled a gigantic following,[134] led them in a roundabout route through the wilderness to the Mount of Olives, and wanted them to bring down the walls of Jerusalem at his command. Obviously, two salvation-historical motifs are combined here, namely, (1) the expectation—also actualized in the Jesus tradition—that the messianic anointed one would move into the city from the Mount of Olives and (2) the remembrance of the end of the wandering in the wilderness and the beginning of the takeover of the land under Joshua with the miracle of Jericho. Naturally, the fact that an Egyptian is involved here also recalls the exodus. This movement was not only wiped out by the Roman governor Felix and his troops, according to Josephus, but also met resistance among the people themselves. Nevertheless, the "Egyptian" was able to flee. In the Romans' view, the similarity to revolutionary movements here was surely created by the mobilization of the masses. But Josephus also presupposes, at least in the passage in *War* 2, that the "Egyptian," as once the Maccabeans, wanted to enter Jerusalem, overpower the garrison on the temple mount, and exalt himself as ruler over the people. This places him in the company of messianic pretenders and social bandits (cf. 3.5.3 below). This corresponds to the fact that in Acts 21:38 the "Egyptian" is characterized as one who stirred up a revolt with four thousand "assassins" (*sicarii*).

Finally, according to Josephus, there was also a comparable movement among the Samaritans in the time of Pontius Pilate (cf. *Ant.* 18.85ff.). Yet it differed from the previously named movements in that—at least according to Josephus[135]—it bore clear military traits[136] and led to an armed revolt. The instigator of this movement, whom Josephus calls the "Samaritan," gathered his followers on the Mount Gerizim and assured them that he would display there the holy implements buried by Moses. This revolt was also put down militarily by the Romans.

JOHN THE BAPTIST

A unique prophetic-eschatological repentance movement was brought to life by John the Baptist.[137] In distinction to the just discussed charismatic-prophetic movements, which shortly after their appearance were annihilated and whose charismatic impulse collapsed, John the Baptist's was apparently not only active for a long time but his charismatic fire was not extinguished even by his martyrdom. For the Johannine charisma apparently persisted first in Baptist groups and then above all through his follower Jesus of Nazareth.

Message and Influence

According to the Synoptic tradition, John came from a priestly family in the rural regions of Judea but worked in Perea on the east bank of the Jordan across from Jericho in the time of Herod Antipas, who had him imprisoned and beheaded in the fortress Machaerus. His place of activity was "the wilderness" (Mark 1:4). If this is already in itself full of symbolism in terms of salvation history, we also know that John baptized in the exact spot "where Joshua once led the people of Israel through the Jordan and into the Holy Land (Josh 4:13, 19)."[138] The motif of the wilderness also occurs, with reference to Isa 40:3, in the biblical tradition of Elijah redivivus (cf. Mal 3:1). Therefore the place of baptism could also have this reference. "For according to 2 Kgs 2:1-18 the prophet Elijah went from Jericho through the Jordan with dry feet at exactly the place where the people of Israel had once moved in the opposite direction into the Holy Land under the leadership of Joshua."[139] And then Elijah's ascension took place beyond the Jordan, so that the Baptist possibly appeared exactly where the return of Elijah could have been expected. Yet this typological connection could have been established only through scribal work in the Synoptic tradition. For the scribes had an interest in identifying John as Elijah redivivus (Mal 3:1, 23-24; Sir 38:10; cf. Mark 1:2ff.; 9:11ff.).

The eschatological symbolism of the place corresponds to the Baptist's way of life, which underlined repentance, as well as his effectiveness, for his clothing and food were suitable for a wilderness-dweller. His clothing, however, also emulated that of the prophet Elijah (cf. 2 Kings 1:8; Zech 13:4). Yet we must ask once again whether this already represents a later scribal interpretation of John by the Jesus movement. The message of the Baptist is the announcement of a universal judgment over Israel, which no one can escape who does not repent and submit to the "baptism of repentance for the forgiveness of sins" (Mark 1:4; Luke 3:3; cf. Acts 13:24; 19:4; Matt 3:7ff./Luke 3:7ff.). The radicality of this announcement of judgment is striking. It is connected with the early Jewish-apocalyptic ideas of a future annihilation judgment from which only the righteous, and not Israel itself, will be saved.[140] John, however, connected salvation for all not to an already present righteousness but to repentance and baptism yet to take place and to a subsequent life of righteousness. Thus he presupposed a situation of universal sin even in

Israel. Yet he preached not only judgment but also the possibility of salvation with baptism.[141] Baptism in the Jordan seems to have been something like a symbolic purification. Those who went out to John at the Jordan left behind them their sinful past and through baptism in the Jordan returned purified into the land of Israel for a new life. Therefore they achieved a conversion in view of the threatening imminent judgment of God, the baptism of fire (Matt 3:11-12).[142] Though the Baptist offered, as it were, a cheaper and, especially for the little people, more affordable version of the forgiveness of sins than the cult in the temple, the eschatological importance of the baptism of John should not be underestimated. Nothing indicates that for John the temple had lost its importance as the place of atonement. Yet it is probably no accident that John was a priest. His activity, however, was eschatologically motivated. Apparently John saw himself as the earthly representative of the coming Judge, as a "voice in the wilderness" (cf. Isa 40:3), who also gave quite concrete instructions for the new life after repentance. In Josephus this preaching is presented according to the Hellenistic-Jewish paraenesis as the demand for piety and righteousness, the chief commandments of the Torah (*Ant.* 18.117). In Luke we find a comparable stylization of the social balance (cf. Luke 3:10ff.), whose historicity, however, is questionable. It is possible that this insisting on the Torah vis-à-vis the Herodian royal house ultimately caused the martyrdom of the Baptist. For he apparently publicly condemned the second marriage of Herod Antipas with his sister-in-law Herodias as incest prohibited by the Torah (Lev 18:16; 20:21; cf. Mark 6:17-18). But there was probably, on the one hand, a topos of the "criticism of rulers" that was a traditional trait ascribed to the prophet,[143] but also an expression, on the other hand, of a certain nearness of John's movement to that of the "sign prophets," in particular through the mobilization of the masses. In any case, it was sufficient cause for the tetrarch Herod Antipas to act.

Followers and Charismatic Character
John was clearly not a loner like the prophet of doom Jesus ben Ananias (Jos. *War* 6.300ff.) but an extremely popular figure because of his serious piety, which is conceded even by Josephus. Nor was he a loner like Theudas or the "Egyptian," who attracted the masses. He had, instead, a certain number of followers and disciples,[144] who also included Jesus. After John's demise some of them perhaps became followers of Jesus, though there were also some who did not (cf. Acts 19:1ff.). According to old Synoptic tradition, Jesus placed an extraordinarily high evaluation on the salvation-historical importance of the Baptist (Luke 7:28/Matt 11:11). This phenomenon of an authority relationship to a following, together with the symbolic clothing and the marginality and extraeconomic nature of the Baptist's lifestyle, point to a certain charis-

matic character of his movement. It probably continued to exist for a certain period even after John's death, both within and beyond the land of Israel.[145]

Stratum Membership

In accordance with his origins in rural priestly circles, John the Baptist must be placed in the lower retainer stratum. Not only did he probably recruit his following primarily from the ranks of the lower stratum, but through his extra-economic, nomadic way of life he also set out on a clear withdrawal from the social and economic living conditions of a retainer. Here is a clear distinction of the Baptist's movement from the followers of Jesus. We cannot say whether this was also the consequence of a personal economic decline. In any case, it is clear that outside of the traditional prophetic critique of rulers, the message of John had no underlying program oriented toward the improvement of the socio-economic conditions of the Jewish masses. The preaching of social reciprocity found in Luke 3 is probably the result of a later interpretation that possibly comes from Luke himself.

6.5 Religio-Political and Socio-Revolutionary Resistance Movements

In principle, faith in the election of Israel and its land implies political autonomy. Nevertheless, if we disregard the direct political influence that Sadducees and Pharisees, as members of the upper stratum or retainer group, had on the ruling class, the behavior of the majority of the Jewish people in the land of Israel in the Herodian-Roman period was rather unpolitical or prepolitical. Yet the above-mentioned prophetic-charismatic movements in particular represented a certain political protest that from the Roman-Herodian view was very much like that of the social bandits and revolutionaries. In addition, however, there were occasionally also acts of direct anti-Roman resistance and mass demonstrations of the nonviolent kind, which were directed especially against massive insults to the religious feelings of the Jewish populace. Finally, there were also direct political and socio-revolutionary actions and insurrectionary movements that were only partially religiously motivated and politically intentioned.

Many things in these movements also remained religiously diffuse and prepolitical in conception and were clarified mainly in the course of social history, that is, in the dynamic that grew out of the colonization of agrarian societies by foreign domination and can also be ascertained in similar societies in antiquity outside the land of Israel. Here we must mention especially the yet-to-be-discussed phenomenon of social banditry. Yet where the resistance adopted a clear political program, the "ideological" foundation was naturally drawn from the religious tradition of the Jewish people. This is to be observed above all in connection with the formation of the so-called fourth party of Judas the Galilean during the census and in the sicarii and Zealots at the time of the First Jewish Revolt. Here it is noteworthy that religio-politically conscious ideas entered the anti-Roman resistance movements often with the participation of members of the *upper-stratum or retainer group* in leadership positions. Purely *lower-stratum movements* were mostly prepolitical; when they had an expressly religious motivation or "ideology," they were nonviolent, but when they offered violent resistance, they were without express religious motivation or "ideology."

Here we will first discuss briefly nonviolent resistance and mass protests (6.5.1) and then give an overview of the variety of resistance movements (6.5.2). Finally, we will present a more detailed discussion of social banditry (6.5.3) and armed resistance and revolutionary movements (6.5.4).

6.5.1 Nonviolent Resistance and Mass Protests

A spectacular individual action took place at the end of the reign of Herod. For religious reasons some young men, encouraged by their teachers, removed the golden eagle from the temple gate, consciously taking into account the possibility of martyrdom, which then became their lot (Jos. *War* 1.648ff.; *Ant.* 17.149ff.).[146] Mass protests, however, were more frequent. Josephus reports on a counter-funeral demonstration following the death of Herod, in which the above-mentioned martyrs were mourned as victims of Herod's violent rule. This demonstration expanded into a small rebellion against Archelaus and was put down only with difficulty (*War* 2.3ff.). And in connection with punitive measures against villages near Bethhoron, which had apparently supported social bandits (cf. below), there was a protest in Caesarea, because a soldier had torn up a Torah roll and thrown it into the fire (*War* 2.228ff.). Only after the guilty man's execution by Cumanus did the Jews quiet down again.

Other mass protests[147] were provoked by intentional anti-Jewish actions by the Romans. Pilate in particular stimulated several such protests. First, against the normal reserve of the governors, he had the field emblems, with their images of emperors, brought to Jerusalem. This blatant insult to the Torah led to an impressive nonviolent demonstration by Jerusalemites and rural Judeans at the governor's residence in Caesarea, in which the Jews finally prevailed, in spite of massive threats from Pilate (*War* 2.169ff.; *Ant.* 18.55ff.). A further cause was the robbing of the temple treasury to build an aqueduct. In this case, however, Pilate brutally broke the resistance (*War* 2.175ff.; *Ant.* 18.60ff.). Especially dramatic was the mass protest that Caligula unleashed when he insisted on erecting a statue of himself in the Jerusalem temple.[148] All accounts make it clear that the spontaneous massive opposition, of Galilean farmers in particular, to the Syrian governor Petronius, whom Caligula had commissioned to carry out his plan, made a deep impression. Petronius feared war or at least a substantial increase in social banditry. The resistance of the Jews stretched into weeks and also included a kind of agrarian strike, for the fields were no longer worked (*Ant.* 18.272): "If, however, the land remained without seed, there would be a harvest of banditry, for the demands of the taxes could not be fulfilled." Petronius hesitated in the carrying out of his commission, and only the murder of Caligula saved him from punishment. Minor events of a similar nature also took place under Cumanus (cf. *War* 2.224; *Ant.* 20.108) and Florus (*War* 2.280).

All these nonviolent manifestations make clear the latent potential for conflict that Roman-Herodian rulership had created in Jewish society. That it came to expression in mass protests in the particularly sensitive area of religious identity is no accident. Yet this points to profound structural problems,[149] as shown not least of all by the armed resistance that was often a possible outcome of nonviolent actions.

6.5.2 The Variety of Religio-Political and Socio-Revolutionary Resistance and Rebellion Movements

Resistance fighters for religious and political freedom and social revolution in the Herodian-Roman period are often brought together under the heading *Zealots*. This, however, is problematical, for at least in Josephus the party name *Zealot* does not designate the totality of those in revolt[150] but only a portion of them that is relatively limited both temporally and socially. Moreover, this broad linguistic usage presupposes a religio-historical unity of Jewish resistance and freedom movements that is very controversial. Finally, we cannot consider the social revolutionaries and anti-Roman movements in the Herodian-roman period simply and only from the perspective of the later First Jewish Revolt. Naturally, it served as a catalyst for certain resistance potentials, which had long been present, and led to coalitions of different groups. Nevertheless, there were, on the one hand, socio-revolutionary resistance movements long before the First Jewish Revolt and independent of it and, on the other hand, substantial conflicts during the First Jewish Revolt between resistance groups that were rooted in their different social compositions and religio-political aims. Nevertheless, Hengel in particular holds both to the designation of the different groups as "Zealots" and to their "relative 'ideological unity.'"[151] Yet he also concedes that "one most certainly must differentiate among the various bands and groups."[152] The more or less clear distinctions within armed resistance are even more strongly emphasized by scholars such as Baumbach, M. Smith, Rhoads, Horsley, and Crossan.[153] These authors regard, for example, sicarii and Zealots as independent movements. Above all, we call attention here to the phenomenon of social banditry, which also occurred in ancient agrarian societies independent of the First Jewish Revolt and outside of the land of Israel.

Even the picture that Josephus draws is contradictory. In his *Antiquities* (18.9, 23) he gives the impression that the whole freedom movement that culminated in the First Jewish Revolt was the outcome of the "fourth school [*hairesis*]" that was founded at the time of the census by Judas the Galilean and the Pharisee Zaddok. In *War*, by contrast, he seems to emphasize that the revolutionary movements themselves were quite varied and not only clearly distinguished from each other but in part also in violent mutual conflict (cf. the delineation of the groups in *War* 7.254ff.).[154] This is also indicated by his terminology. Josephus calls the insurgents either "the Judeans" or "the insurrectionists" (*stasiastai*), adapting the Roman legal term *seditio* (Gr. *stasis*), which means revolt or breach of the peace. The Roman legal tradition also provides a further collective term: *robber* (*lēstai, lēstrikoi*). It characterizes both common robbery and social banditry, as well as insurrectionists in general relative to different eras and regions and of very different persuasions. The Roman term for "robber" (*latro*) can encompass corresponding phenomena, which range "from individual armed highwaymen to the well organized army of a rebellious province."[155] According to Josephus, there was "robbery" not only in and around the time of the Judean-Roman war but also from the beginning of the Roman-Herodian hegemony. Yet in regard to the First Jewish Revolt, he expressly distinguishes five different groups (see 6.5.4 below).

In view of the foregoing information, we will first discuss the phenomena of social banditry and messianic royal pretenders and then the actual anti-Roman insurrectionist groups. Even when the boundaries between these three groups are fluid and clearly overlap, such a delineation is meaningful for socio-historical reasons.

6.5.3 Social Banditry and (Messianic) Royal Pretenders

THE TERM *SOCIAL BANDIT*

The phrase *social banditry* was coined by Hobsbawm[156] in a comparative study of the forms of social resistance in the nineteenth and twentieth centuries and further developed by Blok[157] on the basis of a study of the Sicilian Mafia. Then especially Shaw has shown that social banditry was a widespread phenomenon in the whole Roman empire, even if it varied a great deal in terms of its intensity.[158] The term refers to peasant outlaws, who are to be found in agrarian societies as a reaction to traditional and social destabilization, oppression, and exploitation by heavy tax burdens, famines, and other crises. Social bandits are distinguished from other peasants in that they refuse to submit to and revolt against oppression, and further distinguished from ordinary robbers in that they remain somehow connected with peasant society. A social rebel is often "regarded by the people as a hero, savior, avenger, and fighter for justice; perhaps he is even regarded as a liberation leader or, in any case, as a man whom one must admire and give help and support."[159] Thus it is not primarily a question of class struggle or of nationalistic freedom fighters who are obligated to specific religious, economic, or political programs. "The social brigand appears only before the poor have achieved political consciousness and acquired effective methods of social agitation."[160] Yet social bandits present "a genuine reflection of real life in a world that is ruled by personal power."[161] Those who join them enter, as it were, a kind of "counterworld" (Shaw) that, apart from charismatic leadership, follows egalitarian principles and thus allows a prominent role for individuals. "Thus in a robber society power and character of the individual are worth something. Therefore people in 'normal society' were often especially impressed by the elements of style that were characteristic of the behavior of robbers. Gestures, clothing, language, and appearance identify robbers as a special kind of human being."[162]

SOCIAL BANDITS AND SOVEREIGNTY

If social bandits, through their refusal of loyalty, often gained sympathies and even protection among other peasants, they represented for the rulers a sensitive provocation regarding the latter's claim of subjugation. In a certain sense, indeed, the social bandits themselves raised a claim to power that called into question not only the power monopoly of the state but also its ideological foundation, which was based precisely on the overcoming of anarchic and predatory conditions.[163] Accordingly, Tacitus can place on the lips of the army leader Calgacus of Britain the critique that the Romans are a universal robber band (*Agricola* 30.3ff.). And Augustine writes: "Take away justice and what remains of states except large bandit bands? And what are bandit bands if not small kingdoms?" (*De civitate Dei* 4.4). Not coincidentally, then, we find among Jewish social bandits a tendency toward royal pretension. And conversely, their unrelenting persecution and punishment[164] belong therefore to the criterion of exercising power, and officially it is among the duties of the provincial governor.[165] Accordingly, we find in Josephus, as will soon be shown, reports about social banditry particularly in connection with critical transition phases and changes of hegemony.

CHARISMATIC ASPECTS OF SOCIAL BANDITRY

Brigand leaders rely above all on "a form of personal power that rests on charisma, on the manner of appearance, on unveiled strength, and on interpersonal bonds (relationships of retainers, friends, and clients)."[166] In addition to the impoverished, miserable peasants and destitute former soldiers who were vocationally predisposed to robbery, as it were, shepherds also formed a classic reservoir for social banditry.[167] Often enough, bandits found not only the protection of sympathetic peasant circles but also accomplices and fences among the rich and in the local upper stratum. Their preferred theaters of operation were little accessible regions such as mountains, swamps, forests, and especially "border regions . . . where the jurisdictional power of the governor was uncertain."[168]

SOCIAL BANDITS IN THE LAND OF ISRAEL

In the wake of the civil war confusion at the end of Hasmonean rule and the beginning of Roman rule and a new set of conditions in Palestine, it was not coincidental that it was Herod who on the way to power became prominent especially in fighting social banditry. Josephus mentions that as governor of Galilee, Herod first eliminated the band of the "bandit chief" Hezekiah, who operated in the Syrian border region (*War* 1.204). Assumptions that it was more a question here of deposed Hasmonean aristocrats than of social bandits are not supported by Josephus's account.[169] Yet it is noteworthy that Herod was accused of murder before the Sanhedrin and, according to a parallel account in the *Antiquities* (14.68), the accusation was based on the intervention of mothers of the victims, who demonstrated daily in the temple district of Jerusalem for his punishment. This indicates that Hezekiah enjoyed a certain popularity and sympathy.[170] The second account (*War* 1.303ff.) concerns the beginning of Herod's rise to sole rulership. He devoted enormous military energy in Galilee to eliminating first the followers of the deposed Hasmonean Antigonus and then also (allied with them?) bands that were holed up in caves. In the vicinity of the village of Arbela, northwest of Tiberias, the opposition was defeated militarily, but the escaped bandits apparently offered stubborn and lengthy resistance from their cave fortifications. Since the information about the battle around Arbela refers solely to the cave bandits, this is a further indication that they apparently received the support of an entire village. After this action Josephus reports nothing more about bands in the land of Israel during the entire reign of Herod.

Not until in connection with the census—that is, in the transition of Judea into a Roman province (6 C.E.)—do we hear again of resistance movements. As we know, Josephus mentions here the founding of the fourth party by Judas the Galilean and Zaddok the Pharisee. Yet many things suggest that we should see in this movement "the moment of transition from social banditry to conscious resistance, from a preideological stage to 'political consciousness . . . and more effective methods of social agitation.'"[171] We will therefore discuss it in connection with the sicarii (see below). Brigands are also mentioned in the passion story of the Gospels, above all Barabbas (John 18:40) and the two "bandits" (*lēstai*) who are crucified with Jesus (Mark 15:27). And when Jesus is arrested, they come to him with swords drawn, as though he were a bandit (Mark 14:48). "Ordinary" robbers are probably meant in Luke 10:30. Josephus does not mention social banditry again until the year 44 C.E., and then, with few exceptions, for all governors until the First Jewish Revolt.

When Agrippa I died and Judea was turned back into a Roman province, there appeared under Cuspius Fadus a certain Tholomaeus who, like Hezekiah, operated in the border region (*Ant.* 20.5). Under Cumanus, Josephus mentions an attack on an imperial slave named Stephen near Beth-horon, between Jerusalem and Caesarea (*War* 2.228ff.), which caused the governor to initiate a punitive action against the surrounding villages, in which he presumed there were sympathizers of the bandits. According to the parallel version in *Ant.* 20.113ff., the leading men of the villages were singled out for special punishment. A second incident under Cumanus, in which social bandits under the leadership of one Eleazar, son of Dinai, and one Alexander were involved, took place in connection with the murder of a pilgrim from Galilee by Samaritans.[172] As was typical of social bandits, Eleazar had apparently kept himself hidden for a long time in the mountains (*Ant.* 20.121). What is noteworthy here, however, is that the encounter between Galileans and Samaritans threatened to expand into a regular war. Since Jerusalemites and Judean masses also became involved in the course of the difficulties, the high priest Jonathan and some of the Judean upper stratum had to make energetic attempts to mollify the angry masses. This was not entirely successful, for "many now shifted to robbery because it seemed rather safe; robberies occurred over the whole land, and the most daring even undertook open attempts at rebellion" (*War* 2.238–39). The turmoil did not end until the rigorous actions of the Syrian governor Quadratus, who not only had insurrectionist Jews executed and the high priest Jonathan and other prominent Judeans and Samaritans deported to Rome in chains, but also ordered the governor Cumanus and the chiliarch Celer to Rome to answer for their actions. As a result of the intervention of Agrippa II in Rome, some of the Samaritans were punished by the emperor Claudius, Cumanus was banished, and Celer was turned over to the Judeans. This incident in the year 52 C.E. is with good reason regarded by Crossan to a certain extent as already a Jewish-Roman war carried on by peasants and social bandits before the First Jewish Revolt. Yet here, unlike in the First Jewish Revolt, there was still no participation from the upper stratum and the retainer group on the side of the insurgents.[173]

Under governor Felix, the encounters with social revolutionary bands continued (cf. *War* 2.253, 264–65; *Ant.* 20.160–61). Two points are important here. First, Felix not only killed captured bandits but also had ordinary people punished as their accomplices or sympathizers. Moreover, he had Eleazar ben Dinai, whom he was able to seize, sent as a prisoner to Rome. Second, Josephus mentions a coalition between the followers of prophetic-millenarian groups and brigands. This points, on the one hand, to the already mentioned fluid boundaries between these groupings and, on the other hand, to a new quality of the resistance in the sense of a broader revolt. The latter also suggests the appearance of the sicarii in this period. In any case, after this time social banditry continued to be a problem in Judea. Festus is said to have captured and killed many robbers (*War* 2.271). And Josephus even asserts that Gessius Florus joined forces with the brigands (*Ant.* 20.255ff.), which is not entirely incredible in view of the accomplices and fences mentioned above, whom the brigands also found in the upper stratum. Social bandits were also involved in the First Jewish Revolt itself. John of Gishala in particular seems to have recruited his army from them, but the sicarius Menachem also drew on this reservoir of freedom fighters (see p. 180). Yet they also appeared on the other side, for the residents of Sepphoris, who wanted to remain true to Rome, appealed to the robber chief Jesus and his band, who operated in the border region of Ptolemy, for help against the commandant of the rebellion in Galilee, Josephus (cf. *Life* 104ff.).

SOCIAL BANDITRY WITH (MESSIANIC) ROYAL PRETENDERS

At the transition from prepolitical and preideological social banditry to a more nationally and religiously conscious movement stand the phenomena of the royal pretenders. According to Josephus this was virtually an automatic process with social banditry, yet he mentions by name only Judas the Galilean, Simon in Peraea, and Athronges in Judea, who appeared, not coincidentally, during the period after the death of Herod (cf. *War* 2.55ff.; *Ant.* 17.269ff.). We know that it is a question of social banditry because the objects of their attacks were the royal palaces and the villas of the rich, as well as Roman transports. Josephus reveals, however, that in contrast to the already mentioned brigands, these made a religio-political claim to sovereignty modeled after the charismatic-messianic military leadership of Saul and David. This is most clearly developed with Athronges, who had himself revered as king and installed his brother as governor.[174] Nonetheless, a regular messianic program is not discernible. According to Josephus, the three named royal pretenders were only part of a broader movement of this kind (cf. *Ant.* 17.285).

Josephus first mentions Judas, the son of the robber chief Hezekiah, whom Herod had eliminated. Near Sepphoris in Galilee he brought "a considerable mob together," attacked the royal arsenal, and armed his followers. Above all, however, he coveted royal sovereignty. Yet we learn no more than this. More detail is reported on Simon and Athronges.

Simon apparently came from the retainer class, for Josephus characterizes him as a former slave of King Herod. Particularly emphasized, however, are his charismatic qualities of military leadership, which recall Saul and David: he was good-looking and of great stature. Simon underlined his claim to majesty by wearing a royal diadem and having himself greeted as king (cf. the mocking scene in Mark 15:16ff.). With his band he plundered the royal palace in Jericho and the country villas of the rich, burning them down. A combined Herodian-Roman task force under Gratus brought this movement to an end and killed Simon.

Even clearer messianic claims were articulated by Athronges. His charismatic qualities of military leadership were also emphasized. Like David, he was once a shepherd; he installed his brother as field marshal and satrap. "He himself played the king and devoted himself only to more worthy activities" (*War* 2.61). Athronges also wore a diadem and had himself called king. At Emmaus, for example, his band attacked a Roman cohort that was guarding a shipment of food and weapons. But after a few months these bands were also eliminated by the Herodian-Roman forces. The Passion stories in the Gospels indicate that Jesus of Nazareth was also suspected of social banditry. This is articulated above all in the proceedings before Pilate (cf. Mark 15:1ff. par.), in the mocking scene (Mark 15:16ff. par.), and in the sign on the cross, "King of the Judeans" (Mark 15:26 par.). Moreover, in the Gospel of John the people want to take Jesus and "make him king" (John 6:15). Nevertheless, the Fourth Gospel clearly distances Jesus from this interpretation.[175]

6.5.4 Anti-Roman Insurrectionist Groups

As already mentioned, Josephus distinguishes five different groups of insurrectionists. The *sicarii* appear under Felix (*War* 2.254) or Festus (*Ant.* 20.186). Their leaders were Menachem, a son of Judas the Galilean, and at Masada, Eleazar ben Jair, a grandson of Judas. The *Zealots* are first mentioned in connection with the actual First Jewish Revolt under the leadership especially of Eleazar ben Simon. In addition Josephus names the *Galilean insurrectionist groups* under John of Gishala, who are not further characterized, the *Judean groups* under Simon bar Giora, and a regional group called the *Idumeans*. In addition, there were the people actually responsible for the rebellion in Jerusalem—that is, the group from the aristocracy that, under the leadership of the temple head Eleazar, the son of the former high priest Ananias, encouraged a "sacrifice boycott"—and finally a part of the anti-Roman nobility led by Ananias himself. Here we will examine only some of these groups more closely.

THE SICARII

In *War* 2.254–55 Josephus states that the sicarii appeared in Jerusalem in the time of the governor Felix as a "new genre of robbers." The newness may have lain in their kind of resistance. For "they murdered people in broad daylight and in the middle of the city; especially at festivals they mixed with the crowd and struck down their opponents with small daggers, which they had hidden under their clothes." From this passage and the parallel version in *Ant.* 20.186 it is clear that Josephus not only makes use of the Roman legal term *sicarii* but is also conscious that its coinage was based on a special weapon, a curved dagger (*sica*). Apparently, however, it is the act of *assassination,* accomplished with the dagger and against one's fellow countrymen and especially members of the upper stratum, that is prominent with the term *sicarii.*[176] The first spectacular assassination of the sicarii was the murder of the high priest Jonathan.[177] Yet Josephus credits them with a series of murders of the powerful and rich, combined with acts of plundering and demanding tribute (*Ant.* 20.187; cf. *War* 2.264ff.).

In addition to assassination, the activities of the sicarii also included hostage-taking. Josephus mentions, for example, that they kidnapped the secretary (*grammateus*) of the temple manager Eleazar, the son of the high priest Ananias, and used him to gain the freedom of ten of their confederates (*Ant.* 20.208–9). This too was probably a part of the new kind of robbery by the sicarii in Judea. In any case, this resistance tactic clearly distinguishes them from social bandits, not least of all because they chose as the object of their attacks not the Romans but only the Jewish upper stratum. There is a further difference: the brigands operated mainly in the country and in villages; the sicarii, however, concentrated on Jerusalem. Thus they can be characterized as urban guerrillas or urban terrorists, who sought out symbolic representatives of the Judean ruling class as the object of their actions.

Finally, it is noteworthy that the leaders of the sicarii, Menachem and Eleazar ben Jair, are considered by Josephus to be related to Judas the Galilean (*War* 2.433; 7.275ff.),[178] the founder of the so-called fourth party of the Judeans and leader of the resistance against the census in Judea in the year 6 C.E. (cf. *Ant.* 18.4ff., 23).[179] And in *War* 7.254 Josephus also calls the followers of Judas the Galilean "sicarii." Certainly, he does not mention here tactics like those of the later sicarii. Yet there is an analogy between these groups, since Josephus also ascribes terror against their fellow countrymen to the sicarii of Judas the Galilean: at that time these "sicarii had set themselves against those who were ready to subject themselves to the Romans."[180] If we consider the background of the term in Roman law, we do not necessarily have to assume a unified group of sicarii after the year 6 C.E. Nevertheless, in addition to kinship relationships, other indications also support the idea that the armed opposition formed by Judas the Galilean is closely related to the sicarii at the time of the First Jewish Revolt. For there are obviously clear agreements regarding the religio-political legitimation and programs of these resistance groups.[181] According to Josephus, Judas the Galilean connected the idea of the sole sovereignty of God with the aim of freedom for Israel, for which many had committed themselves and even become martyrs.[182] He ascribes similar things also to Eleazar and to the sicarii who had fled to Egypt.[183] Moreover, when Josephus expressly calls Judas an important "teacher" or "scholar" (*sophistēs; War* 2.118, 433) and the other founder of the fourth party, Saddok, a Pharisee, and sees this fourth party as fundamentally in agreement with that of the Pharisees, this suggests that Menachem, who is also called a *sophistēs,*[184] and Eleazar came from this *retainer group.*

Recruitment of the Sicarii from the Lower Stratum and the Retainers
Thus the sicarii, in contrast to the social bandits, were not a purely lower-stratum movement but were also recruited from the retainer group of the upper stratum. This is supported by their religio-political agenda as well as the fact that their terror was directed against the high-priestly elite in Jerusalem.[185] For this was also the strategic aim of the sicarii during the rebellion, as shown especially by the murder of the high priest Ananias (*War* 2.423ff.). Nevertheless, Menachem also recruited his followers from among rural social bandits (*War* 2.434). This could be the background for the fact that he, like Judas, Simon, and Athronges, appeared in Jerusalem as a (messianic) royal pretender. He entered the city "like a king" (*War* 2.434) and strode "proud and in the decoration of royal clothing to prayer [in the temple], followed by a crowd of armed Zealots" (*War* 2.444). It is noteworthy that Eleazar, the son of Ananias, and his followers rejected Menachem's claim because of, among other things, his low birth, and Menachem was finally killed by them. Afterward the sicarii withdrew to the fortress Masada, where, under the leadership of Eleazar ben Jair, they resisted the Romans until 74 C.E.

THE ZEALOTS

Hengel has shown that when Josephus uses the Greek word *zēlōtēs* in *War* in the plural and absolutely, with a determiner, it is used exclusively as the party name. Several passages make it clear that we have here "an honorable self-designation"[186] of this group (*War* 4.160–61; 7.268ff.) that goes back to Old Testament models such as the zealot Phinehas (Num 25:10ff.) and to the Maccabean freedom movement.[187] This also agrees with the fact that the leadership,[188] if not the majority, of the Zealots consisted of priests who probably came not least of all from the country and, in any case, not from the priestly aristocracy.[189] They are first mentioned by Josephus in the year 66 C.E. as an armed escort of the sicarius with royal claim, Menachem (*War* 2.444),[190] and then in connection with the power struggles among the insurgents (*War* 2.564), in which the sicarii under the leadership of the priest Eleazar ben Simon replaced the more moderate anti-Roman forces from the aristocracy, namely, Joseph ben Gorion and the high priest Ananias, in the leadership of the rebellion in Jerusalem. This constellation is typical, for while the Zealots in both passages seem to function as bodyguards, they represent a purpose clearly directed against the ruling priestly aristocracy, as shown by the concentration on the temple and the election of new priests and a high priest, which we will discuss below. This was probably also the reason why in the beginning they supported the sicarius Menachem.

Nevertheless, Josephus presents the Zealots as the most radical part of the rebellion. With changing coalitions, they carried out permanent civil war-like feuds with the anti-Roman groups from the Jerusalem aristocracy under the leadership of Ananias and entrenched themselves in the temple. "They, however, transformed the temple into a fortress for themselves and a place of refuge that was supposed to protect them from the assaults of a popular uprising; thus the shrine served them as stronghold" (*War* 4.151; there may be an allusion to this in Mark 11:17: "you have made it a cave of bandits"). With the help of John of Gishala, who drew on the support of the Idumeans, the Zealots initially prevailed and initiated a bloodbath among the priestly and lay nobility. Yet because of the splitting off of some of the Zealots, John was then able to seize the leadership for himself.[191] Nevertheless, he himself was soon fought by the Idumeans and ultimately replaced by Simon bar Giora and his followers. Under the leadership of Eleazar, the Zealots broke again with John and when the assault of Jerusalem by Titus began, had to withdraw into the temple building and, finally, even into the underground vault of the temple. They remained to the end a more or less isolated group among the insurgents and disappeared with the end of the war.

All of this suggests that we should regard the Zealots as a group of radical priests who were limited temporally to the period 66–70 C.E.,[192] socially to the mainly priestly context, and religio-politically to the aims of the rebellion. Attempts to free this party of temporal or other limitations are not convincing.[193]

The most spectacular action of the Zealots was their dethroning of the old priestly aristocracy in the year 67 C.E. In spite of the extraordinarily polemical account of Josephus (*War* 4.147ff.), it is clear that to the first temple reform—the boycott of sacrifices by Gentiles and especially the sacrifice to the emperor—by Eleazar ben Ananias and his followers, the Zealots added a second and substantially more radical reform. Namely, they selected a high priest by lot and thus by divine decision. The lot fell on a country priest named

Phineas. Although Josephus uses drastic words to characterize this choice, which in his opinion is obviously illegitimate, he makes it clear that the Zealots themselves observed legitimacy in their sense. For they elected the high priest from one of "the high-priestly tribes, that was called Eniachin" (*War* 4.155). When Josephus immediately adds that this Phineas in no way "fulfilled the requirement of high-priestly origin," this contradiction is probably based on the different views of legitimate origin. In this sense "the temple reform is not just a question of an attempt to dethrone the Jerusalem priestly nobility but actually a reestablishment of temple purity through a return to the only legitimate high-priestly race."[194] This also places the Zealots in the tradition of the anti-Hellenist battle over the purity of the temple at the time of the Maccabeans.

OTHER INSURGENT GROUPS

Among the remaining insurgent groups, we must now mention those of John ben Levi of Gishala and Simon bar Giora.

John ben Levi came from Galilean Gishala and was a Levite,[195] though he originally belonged in the social realm of the retainer class.[196] This is also indicated by his friendship with the Pharisee Simon ben Gamaliel (Jos. *Life* 189ff.). Yet Josephus characterizes him as "poor" (*penēs; War* 2.585) but not destitute (*ptōchos*). In the beginning he was "a loner as a robber; then later he found colleagues for his undertakings," with whom he demanded tribute in Galilee (*War* 2.587, 589). This suggests that he began his "career" as a social bandit on account of the socio-economic decline and likewise recruited his followers from the marginalized circles of peasants from villages in upper Galilee and from rootless refugees from the region of Tyre (cf. *War* 2.588; *Life* 372). Apparently, he was at first an opponent of the rebellion but then after the destruction of Gishala joined it by gathering the already mentioned refugees and becoming the opponent of the commandant Josephus sent from Jerusalem. Like many other revolutionaries, he and his band avoided the Romans, going from Galilee to Jerusalem, where he quickly also got the Zealots behind him and was able to take over the leadership of the rebellion in the city. After the victory of the Romans he was sentenced to life imprisonment (*War* 6.434). This shows that the Romans did not place a very high value on his importance for the rebellion.

Simon bar Giora, as the sobriquet shows, was the son of a proselyte. He came from Gerasa and thus from the Decapolis. First, he seems to have formed a band of rebels who appeared in the Judean border region in the manner of social bandits, where he robbed and plundered the houses of the rich (*War* 2.652). Yet he was politicized, as it were, by current circumstances, for he fled from an army sent by Ananias from the toparchy of Acrabatene and joined the sicarii who had fled to Masada. After the Zealots and the Idumeans had eliminated Ananias, "he strove for sole sovereignty" in Jerusalem and also made a political claim when "he proclaimed freedom for slaves" (*War* 4.508). It is noteworthy that Josephus then also mentions that "his army now no longer consisted only of slaves or robbers but encompassed a sizable number of citizens who obeyed him like a king" (*War* 4.510). Thus he was able to gather around him not only social bandits but also "respected people" (ibid.). And like Menachem and before him Judas, Simon, and Athronges, he laid claim to the role of a royal pretender. Not accidentally, even Josephus mentions Simon's charismatic military-leader motif of outstanding "bodily strength and bravery" (*War* 4.503). Above all, however, there are indications that Simon consciously based his (messianic) royal pretense on the model of David.[197] Thus Josephus reports that in Idumea Simon first took in Hebron, the city of David before his kingship (2 Sam 2:1ff.; 5:3ff.). And remarkably, he often mentions women or Simon's wife in his entourage, as if writing of the retinue of a royal house (*War* 2.653; 4.505, 538). Above all, however, he stylizes his entrance into Jerusalem, where he was called by the opposition of John of Gishala, as the triumphant summoning of a "savior [*sōtēr*] and protector" (*War* 4.575). This messianic-Davidic redeemer claim is perhaps also reflected on the coins of the rebellion, which bear the imprint "Year 4" and "For the Redemption of Zion."[198] In any case, Simon preserved his royal claim until the end, when, after a failed attempt to flee, he went against the Romans with a white undergarment and purple outer robe (*War* 7.29).[199] In fact, the Romans also regarded him as the most important leader of the rebellion when they took him to Rome "as battle victim in the victory parade" and executed him beside the Forum (cf. *War* 6.434; 7.118ff., 153ff.).

SUMMARY OF GROUPS

If we survey the various groups in the land of Israel in the Herodian-Roman period, it becomes clear that a socio-historical classification can throw some light on the pluralism and the antagonism. Basically, we can distinguish the diverse groups according to whether they are to be classified with the elite or retainer stratum or with the lower stratum. If Essenes, Sadducees, and Pharisees belonged to the heart of the elite, then all remaining movements basically came from the lower stratum. It is true that especially with the Pharisees, but also with the Essenes, there were influences on the masses. And conversely, in the lower-stratum movements there were sometimes individual charismatic figures from the (lower) retainer class. Basically, however, the followers in each case were recruited from either the elite or the lower stratum.

Groups from the Elite or Retainer Class

The Sadducees represented a pure, conservatively oriented, and above all high-priestly defined upper-stratum group, whereas the Pharisees were composed more or less of members of the retainer class, who were in part from priestly backgrounds but more especially from lay families. Of the Pharisees we can say that they, like the Sadducees, essentially represented a reformist grouping of the retainer class striving for political power and influence, while at the same time working for an integration of the Jewish people that was to be accomplished in accordance with their religious ideas. The Essenes, by contrast, came from a group of deposed members of the upper and retainer strata, who turned their claim to power into a radical claim to exclusivity in representing the "true Israel." In this sense, they alone of all upper-stratum groups designed a "counterworld" of an apocalyptic nature. Thus charismatic elements can be observed in these elite groups—also in accordance with the interplay of charisma and stigma or experience of impotence that can be observed in terms of the sociology of religion—only in the case of the Essenes and even here only occasionally, namely, in the person of the revered founding figure, the "teacher of righteousness." Yet it is not coincidental that the Essene community was shaped subsequently by apocalyptic concepts, with which they maintained the radical dissidence whose origin lay in apocalypticism but was also politically based, whereas the Sadducees seem to have remained entirely uninfluenced by this current, and the Pharisees merely adapted certain ideas of an eschatological balance inaugurated by apocalypticism. Worthy of mention is the fact that the claim to legitimacy of these groups was in each case articulated in a specific "hermeneutical" program, which gave shape to either a conservative or reformist or radical line in the interpretation of the Torah.

The particular social shape of each group depended either on its stratum membership or the degree of its deviance, which was the result of the crisis of Jewish society or its fractionation. We may presume that the Sadducees, based on their membership in the Jerusalem (high-priestly) upper stratum, were subject to a certain socio-economic separation from the lower stratum. Yet beyond this, whether and how they were also distinguished from other members of the elite is not clear. In any case, they probably presented themselves according to their self-understanding as legitimate representatives of the high-priestly tradition and as guarantors of the continuity of Israel, and thus in the Pharisees they met, not coincidentally, opposition and competition that defined their position as deviant. The Essenes' situation is comparable, except that this group was ruled from its very beginnings by the experience of losing power and being separated from the ruling Jerusalem aristocracy, which it regarded as illegitimate. This situation led to the formation of a complex

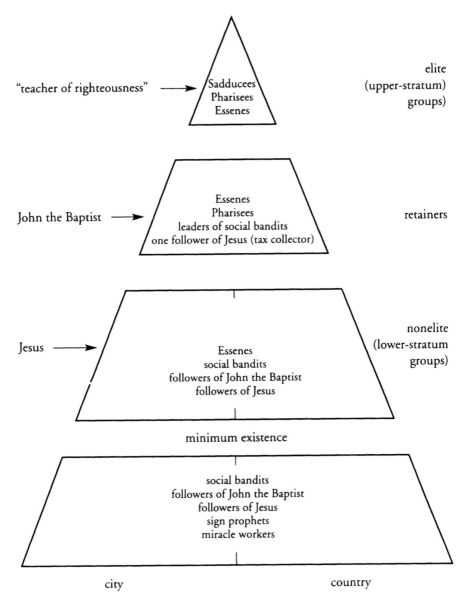

SOCIAL PYRAMID 3:
RELIGIOUS GROUPS IN THE LAND OF ISRAEL,
INCLUDING THE JESUS MOVEMENT

social structure and deviant identity, which made the Essenes the most singular group in Jewish society. For the Pharisees, finally, certain stratum-specific political and common religious interests seem to have given this group its cohesion-promoting impetus. Its deviance is therefore to be seen, on the one hand, from a political perspective to the extent that it resulted from a power conflict and, on the other hand, from a religious viewpoint in that the political conflict was articulated at the same time as a religious one.

Groups from the Lower Stratum

In terms of the sociology of religion, the most striking of the movements among the lower-stratum was probably the charismatic. It not only shaped thaumaturgic individual figures but was also a decisive catalytic element in group formation of the lower stratum. This is shown especially in the short-lived mobilization of the masses by the sign prophets or by the appearance of John the Baptist, which was characterized by both its broad influence and the formation of a smaller group of followers; but it is also seen in the charismatic leaders among the social bandits and insurrectionist movements. These groups, however, are also marked by "economically foreign" lifestyles, as made especially clear by the example of John the Baptist, but also by the social bandits. Also common to these groups is their largely unpolitical or prepolitical character: they designed complete "counterworlds," and in part attempted to live or realize them—for example, in the case of the social bandits and insurrectionists. But apart from the First Jewish Revolt, these movements were not politically influential like the Pharisees and Sadducees. The religious motivations of these movements were fed by linking with great figures of the past (for example, Moses, Joshua, David, Elijah), yet a particular religious conception is evident only in the Zealots and the movement of the Baptist. The latter is clearly shaped by apocalyptic traditions, whereas the former incorporated theocratic ideas.

7

JESUS' FOLLOWERS IN THE LAND
OF ISRAEL IN NEW TESTAMENT TIMES

AN OVERVIEW OF THE FOLLOWERS OF JESUS IN THE LAND OF ISRAEL
Here we will distinguish three groups among the followers of Jesus in the land
of Israel. In our view these groups have their own profile not only for historical but also for sociological reasons:

1. the actual "Jesus movement," that is, the group connected with Jesus during his lifetime, to whose members the Gospels usually applied the term
   disciple (Gk. *mathētēs,* a grammatically masculine term that is somewhat
   misleading, however, since the group also included women);
2. the Jerusalem early church, which arose after Jesus' death, or the "churches of Judea," as Paul calls them (Gal 1:22; 1 Thess 2:14), and expressly distinguished from the "churches of the Gentiles" (Rom 16:4);[1]
3. the messianic churches of the time after 70, as they are represented in our
   view in the Gospels of Matthew and John.

We should at least mention here that after the death of Jesus and approximately contemporaneous with the rise of the local churches of Judea, there
were followers of Jesus who led an itinerant existence. They may be presumed
to be the bearers of the so-called sayings source (Q), the second source that the
Gospels of Matthew and Luke had at their disposal, along with the Gospel of
Mark. It seems to us, however, that the *socio-historical* changes in this group
vis-à-vis the earliest followers of Jesus were only marginal and that therefore a
separate presentation of the so-called logion prophets is unnecessary.[2]

As an overall term for the three religio-social phenomena to be discussed
here we have selected the term *followers of Jesus.* For the group of men and
women followers who were linked with Jesus during his lifetime we use the
term *Jesus movement,* which is quite common today. In terms of the sociology
of religion, however, this term implies a certain prior decision, since it marks
the charismatic element of the phenomenon. For the term *movement* indicates
the opposite of the "institution" and thus also transcends the usual church-
sect dichotomy.[3] Nevertheless, it remains to some extent indefinite sociologically. There is a special problem in that the word *movement* also has negative
connotations because of its use by totalitarian political systems and their
ideologies.[4]

Temporally the followers of Jesus can be delimited by Jesus' presumed date of death in the year 30 c.e. After that came the Jerusalem early church and the churches of Judea, whereas the messianic communities presupposed by the Gospels of Matthew and John are to be placed toward the end of the first century or, in any case, after the destruction of the second temple in 70 c.e.

In terms of both religious and social history, the followers of Jesus are to be understood in the context of the religious pluralism and socio-economic antagonism of the Jewish people in the land of Israel. This is true of the followers of Jesus in the narrower sense, that is, for the Jesus movement, and for the churches in Judea. Yet in many respects a changed situation is to be assumed for the messianic communities presupposed by the Gospels of Matthew and John. There were some new "boundary conditions" for them, since they existed under the religious and socio-economic conditions in the land of Israel in the period after 70. Therefore they were shaped especially by the reformation of Judaism taking place in this period, which sought, among other things, to overcome the previous pluralism. We will look into this in detail below (see Chapter 8).

The churches of Judea, however, were for their part also different from the first Jesus movement. This was related not least of all to their stable location in contrast to the itinerant existence of the followers of Jesus. In general, after the death of Jesus and on account of certain ecstatic visionary experiences, changes were made in the structure of the common life and the leadership of the followers of Jesus. Thus certain functions and leadership tasks were taken over by individuals, such as Peter and the Lord's brother James, and also by "collegia" such as the circle of twelve, the group of the three "pillars" (the Lord's brother James, Peter, and John the son of Zebedee), and the circle of seven composed of Diaspora Jews.[5] Moreover, differentiated forms of the common life were developed, in part with clear religious—including identity-marking—symbolism (baptism, Lord's Supper). These developments were also reflected theologically in terms like *the saints*[6] and *the church of God* (*ekklēsia tou theou*),[7] which characterized the post-Easter followers of Jesus as the divinely elected community of salvation or the eschatological contingent of the people of God from Israel—terms that probably went back to their own self-designations.[8] These names imply an apocalyptic self-understanding that on the one hand is closely related in terms of language and content to that of the Qumran community,[9] yet on the other hand is not found in the older Jesus tradition, in which the term *disciple* (*mathētēs*) predominates.

Nevertheless, in addition to individuals like Peter and the sons of Zebedee, the circle of twelve could have served as a personal and theological bridge between the first followers of Jesus and the churches of Judea. This is true, however, only if the circle came into being not just in connection with vision-ary ecstatic phenomena after the execution of Jesus[10] but was already of pre-Easter origin, which is suggested, to be sure, by the abundant witness of the Gospels.[11] In any case, in apocalyptic tradition the circle of twelve probably expressed the expectation of the gathering and renewal of Israel, the people of twelve tribes (cf. Matt 19:28).[12] Its gradual disappearance after the death of Jesus, which is also indicated in the Gospels by the "historicizing" identifica-tion of the "twelve" with a circle of disciples or the apostles of Jesus, suggests that the apocalyptic self-understanding of the followers of Jesus, which was initially linked with the circle of twelve, merged with that of the "church of God."

In any case, this information from tradition suggests the conclusion that within a few decades a development took place in the Jesus movement that is relevant for the sociology of religion. As we will later present in more detail, it corresponds to the inner dynamic of charismatic movements and specifi-cally to the process of the transformation of the charisma, which is at the same time a process of increasing deviance. This process is also reflected in the New Testament witnesses, yet not only for the time after Jesus' death but already from the beginnings of the story with Jesus himself. This is probably also con-nected with the peculiar character of the sources.

THE QUESTION OF SOURCES

On the Jerusalem early church and the churches of Judea we have information in Acts and the letters of Paul, as well as a note in Josephus about the execu-tion of the Lord's brother James. For the situation of the messianic commu-nities in the period after 70, we draw on the Gospels of Matthew and John, in addition to a few statements in Jewish traditional literature. More difficult is the socio-historical classification of the followers of Jesus. They share the well-known problems of the quest for the historical Jesus. For the source sit-uation this means that the socio-historical quest for the followers of Jesus, like the traditional quest for the historical Jesus himself, essentially must depend on the Gospels. Yet these found their final form at the earliest a generation after the death of Jesus, on the whole probably only after 70 c.e. and in part outside Palestine. In terms of the sociology of religion, this corresponds to the fact that charismatic movements tend to transport their traditions initially in oral form, and written traditions appear only after a certain institutionalized charisma has formed. Thus from a socio-historical perspective we must con-sider the fact that our sources, the Gospels, already reflect a development in the followers of Jesus in which not only their social composition and shape have considerably changed but also their relationship to Judaism, in which they began, is different. For the Gospels and the Acts of the Apostles are shaped by an increasing and, in part, clear deviance experience of the messianic groups in the land of Israel, which especially the Gospels have obviously projected back into their presentation of the genuine followers of Jesus.

In the book of Acts this process is described as a geographic shift and missionary spread of the Christian faith "in Jerusalem . . . and to the ends of the earth" (1:8), as well as a process of progressive differentiation of community life and increasing conflict experience. Moreover, in the characterization of "the Way [of salvation]" (9:2; 14:16; 16:17) or "the sect [*hairesis*] of the Nazarenes" (24:5) and its members as "Christians" (11:26), Luke ascribes to the post-Easter followers of Jesus even before 70 c.e. a clear independent position that is delineated against outsiders and thus deviant in the factional pluralism of Judaism. This is also expressed in the Lukan presentation of increasing conflicts between missionaries of the faith in Christ and Jewish authorities in the land of Israel and the Diaspora, which resulted in demonstrative separations and negative measures. Similar things are predicted in the Gospels as the future destiny of the disciples of Jesus.[13] In addition to Acts, Paul also attests in at least one place that the post-Easter followers of Jesus were subject to certain negative measures in the land of Israel long before 70 c.e. (cf. 1 Thess 2:14). Conflicts of the so-called Jerusalem early church with Jewish authorities are also indicated by the "Antiochene incident" (Gal 2:11ff.). They may also be in the background of the Apostolic Council in Jerusalem (2:1ff.; Acts 15), as well as the arrest of Paul in that city. In any case, however, individual martyrdoms such as those of James, the son of Zebedee, who was executed by Agrippa I (Acts 12:1-2), and the Lord's brother James, whom the high priest Ananias had executed (*Ant.* 20.200), draw attention to the fact that in the forties at the latest the followers of Jesus in the land of Israel came up against measures of defense and exclusion. In addition, it is possible that there were expulsions of individual members from Jerusalem (cf. Acts 8:1-2). Thus we must take into account a certain "career of deviance" of the followers of Jesus even before 70 c.e. in the land of Israel. In the Gospels of Matthew and John we can then discern an increase in these deviance experiences, which is doubtless also connected with the changed circumstances of Jewish society in the period after 70 (see pp. 223ff., 224ff.).

For Jesus himself, however, this deviance experience cannot be simply presupposed. On the contrary, we must assume that later conflicts of the followers of Jesus, conditioned by the genre "gospel," have also influenced the presentation of the life of Jesus. But since charismatic movements have, from their beginnings, sketched a "counterworld" for the overcoming of the crisis in societies, Jesus' initial following already implied a certain genuine deviant position. Without it that following would not have appeared in the first place. Yet this deviance, as we will show, is to be seen especially in what Lipp calls "self-stigmatization." That means that Jesus, as the genuine charismatic, and his early followers not only participated in the sufferings whose overcoming they proclaimed and in part lived, but they also "transfigured them cognitively and normatively with the holy symbols of society."[14] Naturally, this kind of genuine deviance also defined the communities after the death of Jesus in that they understood themselves as the eschatological contingent in the gathering of the people of God. But here they connected themselves, on the one hand, with a certain institutional charisma, which led to a clearer delineation of the movement internally and externally. On the other hand, in the Diaspora and through the leap of the charismatic spark to non-Jews, the followers of Jesus gained a conflict potential that had a lasting influence on the development of deviance.

THE DIVISION OF THE CHAPTER

In this chapter we will first present the origin of the followers of Jesus with Jesus himself and his first men and women followers (7.1); then we will discuss the "churches of Judea" and the so-called Jerusalem early church (7.2). Since the situation of the followers of Jesus before 70 is clearly different from that of messianic communities in the land of Israel, the latter topic will be treated in its own chapter (8).

7.1 The Origins of Jesus' Followers in the Land of Israel

7.1.1 Religio-Sociological Models of Interpretation

Essentially, the oldest followers of Jesus have thus far been interpreted sociologically according to three models: they have been understood as a *sect*, as a *millenarian movement*, and as a *charismatic movement*. The claim of many of these approaches is to describe the phenomenon in terms of the sociology of religion on the basis of comparative methods. Yet all three models contain elements of varying importance that were also abstracted from phenomena of Jewish and Christian religious and social history, so that the comparative claim has only limited validity.

THE SECT MODEL

Of these approaches, the first, the sect model, was for a long time the favorite.[15] It is, however, also the most problematic, since, as already mentioned above, it is either too specialized and anachronistic, because it was gained from the later perspective of the history of Christianity, or too unspecific and general, because it can be used for very different phenomena on account of the modifications that have adapted it to other historical and cultural areas (see pp. 150–51 and esp. pp. 242ff.). Moreover, it presupposes as an opposite a "church," that is, a mainstream or parent body that was to some extent institutionalized, but which did not exist in postbiblical Judaism before the destruction of the second temple. On the contrary, our presentation of group formation in Palestinian Judaism since the middle of the second century B.C.E. at the latest showed that in a basic orientation toward constitutional factors in the Jewish faith, we must take into account a multiplicity of socio-religiously different groups. Yet a mainstream that is in some sense institutionalized is not discernible. To this extent, the traditional church-sect dichotomy is not meaningful for our purposes here. If we understand *sect* more generally in the sense of a religious minority movement (Wilson), one can use it to characterize, on the one hand, the Jesus movement without distinction from its beginnings until far into the history of early Christianity and, on the other hand, a number of the phenomena of early Jewish religious history that, nonetheless, are sociologically distinguishable at essential points from the followers of Jesus. Nor are we aided by modifications that attempt to distinguish certain sect types.

THE MILLENARIAN INTERPRETIVE MODEL

More useful, by contrast, is the millenarian interpretive model, which has been applied to early Christianity especially by Gager.[16] It too bears influences from Jewish and Christian history,[17] yet it can show that in underprivileged strata in different historical and cultural contexts, there are certain typical reactions to comparable political, religious, social, and economic crises. According to Gager, these include the promise of the imminent arrival of heaven on earth, the expectation of an upheaval of social conditions, a community life that can liberate charismatic-emotional energies, and a messianic-prophetic or charismatic authority at the head of this movement. Typical of millenarian movements, finally, is a short life and a subsequent transformation.[18] With the help of these categories, Gager interprets the socio-economic, political, and religious situation of Palestine in Jesus' time as a pre-millenarian crisis. According to Gager, only the initial spark of charismatic authority like that of Jesus was needed in order to ignite a millenarian movement in Palestine, which expected the imminent coming of the kingdom of God to bring about a reversal of social conditions. The fact that the actual following of Jesus lasted for only a short time and after his death transformed itself into a missionizing community fits into Gager's model. Without doubt, this interpretation illuminates essential traits of Jesus' following, yet the explanatory relevance of this model is also limited. For, on the one hand, certain "ideological" aspects of millenarian movements apply at least to early Christianity as a whole, if not also to most early Jewish movements. On the other hand, the sociologically relevant aspects of the "socialization" and transformation of the charisma are apparently explained with reference to Weber's theory of charismatic sovereignty, which is determinative in the third model.[19] Regarded in this way, the millenarian interpretive concept represents a mixture of the charismatic model and "ideological" elements of an apocalyptic or chiliastic nature. Yet it is precisely the abstraction of the concept of charisma from religio-culturally limited aspects that characterizes the third model.

THE CHARISMATIC INTERPRETIVE CONCEPT

The charismatic interpretive model, which goes back to Weber,[20] is presently enjoying considerable favor in the religio-sociological analysis of the Jesus movement. Its application is already found to some extent in Weber himself but has been worked out by Hengel, Theissen, Schütz, Holmberg, Ebertz, Schluchter, Bendix, and others.[21] This model is also influenced by phenomena of Christian-Jewish religious history. It is indebted to the discussion of law and the structure of the church in the nineteenth century and has its paradigm especially in early Christian phenomena.[22]

Nevertheless, Weber, in the context of his sovereignty sociology, built up the concept of charisma into an ideal type—namely, as the antitype of traditional and legal sovereignty—which can be applied to comparable phenomena of quite different religious, political, and cultural provenance. His interest is also valid not only for the unstable beginnings but also in the development of the charisma into and in a movement. For him this process depends on the social situation to which charismatic phenomena are related. He focuses on the process of the transformation of genuinely charismatic movements through the "turning of the charisma into an everyday phenomenon."[23] In terms of social history, this has the advantage that the charisma concept is not exhausted in the interpretation of the extraordinary personality characteristics of certain individuals but is used as a social relational concept. "It is a question of the characterization of situations in which certain characteristics (abilities, powers) of people are capable of social recognition."[24] These situations are determined by an internal urgency, crises in tradition that are evoked by external urgency (that is, political and socio-economic crises), and the "search for persons with supernatural or superhuman characteristics, abilities, or powers,"[25] that is, for the miracle worker who through his charismatic legitimation not only promises a turning point or deliverance from the urgency but also guarantees it through action. Yet this also includes a certain "message" that interprets the new situation, and here the oral mode of handing down this message is primary.[26] But it requires—and this is crucial—proof of the Spirit and of power, that is, verification by unusual miracles or revelation. The charismatic is not a preacher; in order to achieve social recognition, he must provide visible proof of an intimate relationship with the divine. Corresponding to the relational structure of the concept is the necessity of the recognition of the charisma by the "ruled" and their affectively believing devotion to the charismatic.

Thus the crucial point is not only the individual extraordinary characteristic but its social validation through a certain number of disciples. They, along with the genuine charismatic, form a "charismatic movement," in which we must distinguish between a close circle of followers of the genuine charismatic—the "administrative staff"—and a broader group of followers. The structure of charismatic phenomena that breaks through the everyday routine also includes "economic alienation," that is, the renouncing of personal economic concern, which is often connected with "family alienation" and the giving up of the stable location for the narrower circle of the charismatic movement. The lifestyle free of economics is compensated by patronage on the part of the broader following. It is especially this economic alienation that, according to Weber, causes the instability of the beginning charismatic movement and occasions the urgency to "turn the charisma into an everyday phenomenon." Weber regarded this transformation process of a charismatic movement into a lasting social form largely as a process in which the charismatic element is extinguished and charismatic sovereignty is replaced by traditional or legal domination. But he also saw the transformation of genuine charisma into a hereditary or official charisma.

THE FURTHER DEVELOPMENT OF WEBER'S MODEL

The ambivalences immanent in Weber's work have been resolved above all by Bendix,[27] Roth,[28] and Schluchter. Schluchter in particular has made an illuminating recommendation to assume a double outcome of genuinely charismatic movements, namely, one of "making the charisma ordinary," in which the charismatic core is in fact destroyed and replaced by traditional or legal forms of sovereignty, and one of "depersonalizing or objectifying the charisma," in which the charismatic element is retained but separated from a particular person and reshaped into a hereditary or official charisma. That means, however, that the reshaping of the genuine charisma can result in either an ordinary or an extraordinary permanent, structurally stable form: in traditional or legal permanent form, on the one hand, or in personal-charismatic or institutional-charismatic permanent form, on the other.[29]

This ongoing development of Weber's initiative is illuminating not least of all for the interpretation of the history of the Jesus movement and early Christianity. A noteworthy different continuation of Weber is found, in our view, in the works of Lipp,[30] which have already been applied to the Jesus movement by Ebertz—also in adoption of Mühlmann's description of chiliastic movements.[31] Here one aspect of the Weber model in particular is worked out, namely, that charismatic movements have a certain *genuine deviance.* They propose "counterworlds" in which the transformation of the social situation is preached. This deviance does not imply—at least initially—a break with the dominant religious tradition. Rather, that very tradition is called upon to establish the proposed "counterworld." Experienced stigmatizations are negated in a process in which "social inferiority or economic-political inferiority conditions" are reinterpreted with the help of holy tradition "into a condition of election,"[32] whereas the situation of the privileged is negatively evaluated. Crucial here is the "self-stigmatization" (Lipp) of the charismatics; that is, they themselves participate in the evils of the underprivileged, whose overcoming they announce and partially live. This not only strengthens confidence in the message but is also a condition for the survival of the charismatic movement when the charismatic bears the retribution of the rulers in martyrdom.[33] *Thus for charismatic movements the violent death of the genuine bearer of charisma is in no way a catastrophe; rather, it can be the initial spark, as it were, for the development and reshaping of the charisma.*

7.1.2 The Beginnings of Jesus' Following in the Land of Israel

We follow here the interpretation of the genuine followers of Jesus as the beginning of a charismatic movement and combine this with a classification in terms of social and religious history. We will first present the beginnings of the "charismatic career" of Jesus in the circle of the Baptist (a) and Jesus' founding of his own charismatic movement (b). In accordance with Weber's religio-sociological interpretive model, we will develop the charismatic ruling structure of the earliest following of Jesus and then classify it in terms of social history (c). Then comes a description of charismatic effectiveness and message (d), a description of the genuine deviance of Jesus' followers (e), and finally their classification within the religious and socio-historical spectrum of contemporary Judaism in the land of Israel (f).

A. JOHN THE BAPTIST AND JESUS

In the Gospels the beginnings of the "charismatic career" of Jesus in the land of Israel are connected with the eschatological repentance movement of the Baptist.[34] Even if the presentation of the relationship between John and Jesus in these sources is clearly shaped by an interest in salvation-historical timing and the ranking of the two figures, it is still historically probable that Jesus not only was baptized by John but also entered the circle of the Baptist's followers. Possibly this also reflects the name *Nazarene,* which now designates background but may have originally been based on Jesus' membership in the "Baptist's sect" of "preservers" (Aram. *nazren*).[35] "In any case, one must not imagine the relationship of Jesus to the Baptist as only a casual one."[36] That means, however, that before the development of Jesus' own movement, he had already lived in an environment of charismatic prophecy and been shaped by the eschatological message of the Baptist. We will discuss this later in more detail. Whether Jesus himself also baptized alongside the Baptist—that is, before the latter's martyrdom—is not certain, but if the tradition in the Gospel of John (cf. John 3:22—4:3) has a historical basis, it indicates that Jesus assisted in some way for a certain period, together with a circle of other baptismal disciples of John, perhaps on the basis of a commission by John himself. Some other indications of the older Jesus tradition also support the idea that during the lifetime of the Baptist, Jesus was active, together with a group of his own disciples (Luke 7:18ff.; Matt 11:7ff.). Yet we do not assume that the reason for this separate activity was a break between Jesus and John.[37] This is refuted by the high estimation of the Baptist that is ascribed to Jesus in the Gospels (cf. Luke 7:24ff.; Matt 11:7ff.).

The Gospel of Mark connects the independent charismatic appearance of Jesus with the martyrdom of the Baptist: "Now after John was arrested, Jesus came to Galilee, proclaiming the good news of God . . ." (Mark 1:14; cf. Matt 4:12). This does not necessarily contradict the assumption of previous parallel activity by John and Jesus. We presume, rather, that the martyrdom of the Baptist—not untypical in charismatic movements—brought a special charismatic dynamic into Jesus' movement. The violent death of this prophet was understood among his followers not as a denial of his message but as its confirmation and perhaps even a caesura in the eschatological drama. This is shown in an old tradition, the saying in Matt 11:12-13 (cf. Luke 16:16) that connects the appearance of John, and particularly the violent deed against him, with the beginning of the epoch of oppression for all messengers of the coming kingdom of God.[38] The crisis presented by the death of the Baptist is interpreted among the followers of Jesus as a salvation-historically necessary turning point. A later scribal reflex of this is the interpretation of the work and fate of the Baptist as the realization of the promised eschatological mission of Elijah redivivus (cf. Mark 9:11ff.). This also agrees, finally, with the idea that Jesus himself is regarded in the belief of the people as *John redivivus* (cf. Mark 6:14; 8:28). Here we see a direct connection established between the charisma of the Baptist and that of Jesus. Yet Jesus did not simply continue the work of the Baptist and take over his role. Rather, he interpreted his own charismatic experiences, particularly the miraculous healings and exorcisms, as proof of the partial presence of the powers of the coming kingdom of God (Matt 12:28; Luke 11:20).

B. THE DISCIPLES AND FOLLOWERS OF JESUS

The Gospels connect Jesus' independent appearance in Galilee with the calling of the disciples (Mark 1:16-20; 2:13-14 par.; cf. John 1:35-51). "The beginning and core were probably formed by those who were disciples of the Baptist with Jesus and became independent with him."[39] According to the Synoptic Gospels the first called were pairs of brothers, Simon and Andrew and the sons of Zebedee, James and John. The Gospel of John names among the first called two Baptist disciples, one of whom was Andrew. Then comes Simon Peter, with the Zebedee brothers not even mentioned by name until their connection with the Easter appearances (John 21:2). Also mentioned are the calling of individuals, the tax collector Levi/Matthew (cf. Mark 2:13-14 par.) and a rich man, who, however, founders (cf. Mark 10:17-22 par.). After a short time of activity and the gaining of additional followers, the Synoptic tradition reports the creation of a circle of twelve, which includes the four first called and a further eight persons identified by name (cf. Mark 3:14-19 par.).[40] The Gospel of John also presupposes the selection of a circle of twelve (John 6:67), but it does not report on its initiation or include a list of names. Moreover, in the Gospels a special role is ascribed to Simon Peter in the circle of disciples, against whom the "disciple Jesus loved" competes in the Johannine tradition. In the Synoptics, by contrast, a trio of the first called, Peter and the Zebedee brothers, is emphasized in special situations. It is highly probable, however, the latter situation reflects developments after the death of Jesus.[41] The competition between Peter and the favorite disciple also presupposes special Johannine intentions. The group of the "seventy," who are sent out according to Luke's Gospel (Luke 10:1), is completely symbolically motivated.[42]

Even if the first callings and the selection of the circle of twelve are somewhat stylized literarily according to the biblical model,[43] it is clear that here it "is a question of the commission to participate in the ministry of Jesus for the imminent kingdom of God and thus of entering into a *communion of life and fate* with Jesus that is shaped by the kingdom of God."[44] Negatively, this becomes visible in the fact that the calling demands the leaving of families— and *occasionally* also of wives[45]—and generally the giving up of socioeconomic ties (cf. Mark 1:16-20 par.; 10:25 par.; Luke 9:57-62/Matt 8:19-22; Luke 14:26/Matt 10:37). And positively, this is shown by the call to "discipleship" or, in the circle of twelve, selection to be with Jesus, that is, to participate in his "vagabond" lifestyle. Common life, however, also meant in part common activity. This is also shown by the fact that Jesus occasionally sent out the disciples two by two as messengers and "assistants" in his charismatic task (cf. Mark 6:7-13 par.).

The followers included not only the disciples, who were called, but also others who voluntarily joined, such as the healed Bartimaeus (cf. Mark 10:52

par.). Women were also said to have followed after Jesus or accompanied him; two groups of three are mentioned by name: (1) Mary Magdalene, Mary the mother of James the younger and Joses, and Salome (cf. Mark 15:40-41 par.), as well as (2) Mary Magdalene, Joanna the wife of Herod's steward Chuza, and Susanna (Luke 8:2-3). (We will present more of this in Chapter 13.) Remarkably, the Gospels include no one from Jesus' family among his followers. Rather, a certain distancing is reported (cf. Mark 3:20-21, 31-35 par.). It is also true that from the occasional accompaniment of Jesus by a crowd of people, one can say that crowds followed him (cf. Mark 3:7; 5:24; 11:9 and elsewhere). Yet they are not counted among the disciples or followers. The same is true of individual sympathizers, who rendered hospitality to Jesus (cf. Luke 7:36-50; 14; 19:1-10), and also people who on the basis of certain charismatic healing experiences probably belonged to Jesus' following (cf., for example, Mark 1:45 par.; 5:18-20 par.; 7:36). We could probably also understand as a sympathizer Joseph of Arimathea, a respected member of the council, who took care of Jesus' burial (Mark 15:43-46).[46]

Interpretation of Jesus' Earliest Followers with the Charisma Model

Thus regarding the followers of Jesus we will in principle distinguish with Weber between, on the one hand, Jesus the prophet and charismatic authority and, on the other, a broad collection of supporters and sympathizers, as well as a narrower group of disciples and followers. Yet the boundaries between supporters and followers are fluid. Among the followers, moreover, is a circle of disciples that share special tasks with Jesus and thus correspond to those whom Weber calls the "administrative staff." For Jesus and the narrower circle of followers we find the criterion of extraordinariness typical of charismatic movements; it is seen, on the one hand, in alienation from economy and family, along with devotion to the charismatic one, and, on the other hand, in certain miraculous healing experiences. Alienation from the economy is apparently compensated by the patronage of supporters. Faithful commitment and charismatic healing experiences also mark the relationship of Jesus and his followers to the broader circle of supporters. This is made clear especially by the miracle stories, to which the key word *faith* is attached (cf. pp. 203–04). Lacking here, however, is participation in the lifestyle of Jesus and his followers, which is alienated from the economy and the family.

C. THE SOCIAL CLASSIFICATION OF JESUS' FOLLOWERS[47]

At first the followers of Jesus were limited geographically to Galilee and especially to the northern shore of the Lake of Gennesaret (Capernaum, Bethsaida). Most of his disciples of both sexes came from there. The cities of Galilee (Sepphoris and Tiberias) are notably not mentioned as places of Jesus' activity. Although inhabitants of a rural region, Jesus' followers are not described as farmers or as active in any way in agriculture. We have only a small number of prosopographic data, but they, together with other socio-historically relevant information, give us a good insight into social-stratum membership.

Prosopographic Data

One good criterion for the social classification of Jesus and his followers is the information on occupations. According to Mark 6:3, Jesus himself was a *tektōn*, according to Matt 13:55, the son of a *tektōn*, which hardly indicates a shameful distancing but simply corresponds to the style of indicating the occupation of the father.[48] Precisely what is meant by the Greek word *tektōn*, however, is unclear. Was Jesus a carpenter or perhaps a mason? Or did he make tools for farmers, such as plows and yokes?[49] Perhaps we do not have to narrow it down, for the occupational designation *tektōn* could indicate that he was a construction worker who was a "mason, carpenter, cartwright, and joiner all in one."[50] According to our social stratification, in any case, this occupation indicates that Jesus is to be classified with the lower stratum. The economic foundation of a construction worker probably cannot be well imagined. Basically, such a worker belonged to the relatively poor (*penētes*), if not eo ipso to the absolutely poor (*ptōchoi*). Yet this occupation was not safe from crises, as shown by the example of the intentionally created work for temple workers, which is reported by Josephus (cf. p. 106). In general, one must acknowledge that construction workers were not independent and worked for a daily wage.[51] Their low social rank is clearly evident in the text from Sir 38:24ff. quoted above (cf. pp. 26 and 128).

The same is true of the first two disciples called, who were fishermen, according to the Gospels. Certainly, there were also differences in income among fishermen. This is indicated by the calling narrative in Mark. Whereas Simon Peter and Andrew worked without a boat in the waters close to shore with a round or casting net,[52] the Zebedee brothers owned a boat, and they abandoned their father and the rest of the boat's crew, consisting of day laborers. But whether this indicates greater prosperity is questionable. Luke apparently presupposes that the first men called worked with a group of fishermen (cf. Luke 5:1-11). The Lukan parallel version of the first callings also makes it clear, however, that group fishing is not necessarily safer from crises than agriculture.[53] Indeed, it is presupposed here that in spite of great efforts, the nets of the fishermen remained empty. Even if the Lake of Gennesaret held a great wealth of fish, that does not mean that fishing was profitable. For the means of tapping this wealth were relatively primitive technologically. It is no coincidence that Josephus also mentions that "boat owners and those without property" in Tiberias were among the first to join the rebellion (*Life* 66).[54]

Likewise, in the apocryphal *Gospel of the Nazarenes*, Zebedee, the father of John and James, is called a poor fisherman.[55] While the disciples' main occupation was farming, fishing was hardly only a sideline.[56] Moreover, if we compare Mark 1:16-20 with the calling of Elisha by Elijah (1 Kgs 19:19-21), it is noteworthy that Elisha came from quite well-to-do rural circumstances. The economic situation of Jesus' first-called disciples, by contrast, could only be termed modest, if not downright miserable. Nonetheless, Mark 1:29-31 also assumes that Simon and Andrew lived in a house. As the archaeological findings in Capernaum suggest, even this indicates not prosperity but extremely modest conditions.

The tax leaseholder Levi (or Matthew) is to be classified somewhat differently in terms of social history. He was probably a small leaseholder. Since Jesus called him by the lake, we should presumably imagine that he had leased the tax rights for the fish harvest in Capernaum. From this we may also infer that he belonged to local retainer group. In contrast to prosperous tax leaseholders like Zacchaeus in Jericho and the John in Caesarea mentioned by Josephus, Levi was a rather small figure and hardly rich.[57] Yet more important than the economic element in this case is the lack of social prestige of the man called, which can be estimated to be less than that of the previously named disciples of Jesus. For the religious and ethical evaluation of tax leaseholders is negative especially in the New Testament and among the rabbis.[58] In this respect there is no ambiguity in the negative New Testament and rabbinical series, in which tax collectors are named together with prostitutes (Matt 21:31), Gentiles (18:17), and sinners (Mark 2:16-17; Luke 15:1)[59] or with murderers, thieves, usurers, violent criminals, and so forth.[60] In fact, this cliché has some basis in real experiences of the rigorous and even violent execution of the collection of taxes and the unjust enrichment of tax collectors (cf., for example, Luke 19:8). Crucial here for the widespread negative judgment, however, is an ethical criterion and not, say, a political one (collaboration with the Romans), as was often assumed earlier.[61] The calling of a notorious tax collector, as well as the social intercourse of Jesus' followers with such people in general, is therefore probably more significant than their economic and social position. The women in Jesus' retinue mentioned by Mark probably likewise belonged to the lower stratum (see pp. 384–85). The last of the named followers of Jesus is Bartimaeus (Mark 10:46-52). He is described as blind and a beggar (*prosaitēs*) and thus belonged to the group of the absolutely poor; that is, he languished below the level of minimum existence.

A special case is the "respected member of the council," Joseph of Arimathea, who is supposed to have buried Jesus (Mark 15:42-47/Luke 23:50-55) and who belonged to the local upper stratum. When he is characterized as one "who was also himself waiting expectantly for the kingdom of God"

(Mark 15:43), however, this does not mean that he was a disciple or follower of Jesus but only that he was among the pious in the land (cf. Luke 2:25, 38) and perhaps a sympathizer of Jesus' following.[62] Only Matthew and John expressly declare him to be a disciple of Jesus (cf. Matt 27:57; John 19:38). Yet Matthew only says quite generally that he was a "rich man," and John does not characterize his social status at all.

Other Information

If we compare the Lukan presentation of the calling of Peter and the other fishermen (Luke 5:1ff.) with the model of this interpretation in Mark (1:16ff.), we notice immediately that Luke seems to imagine that Peter and the other fishermen belonged to some sort of fishermen's cooperative (cf. only Luke 5:10). As such they would then probably have belonged to the well situated circles of the lower stratum. Accordingly, in the Gospel of Luke they voluntarily gave up *"everything"* to follow Jesus; that is, in Luke's presentation they had possessions to give up (Luke 5:11; 18:28). Nonetheless, we already have here a later interpretation of discipleship to Jesus.[63] It suggests that his disciples *voluntarily* renounced their property and also left their wives. Yet we do not find this ethical radicalism in the oldest Gospel (Mark) or in the so-called sayings source. The narrative on the meaning of wealth shows that forgoing possessions was the demand of *the rich* that led to the failure of their discipleship (Mark 10:17ff.). Therefore, in connection with renunciations by Jesus' followers, it is better to speak of *social renunciation*. That means that in the course of discipleship, the disciples left their extended families (including the duties of their workplaces). Even with Jesus himself, we see that the families were not in agreement with this decision. Jesus' family believed that Jesus was "out of his mind" (Mark 3:21) and wanted to bring him home (3:31ff.).

On the whole, Mark describes for us disciples who are rather poor (in the sense of *ptōchos*). This is presented especially impressively in the contrast between the discipleship of the blind beggar Bartimaeus, who follows Jesus after his healing (10:17ff.), and the failed calling of a rich man (10:46ff.). The bitter poverty of the followers in Jesus' retinue is also seen in the story of the conflict over the sabbath (2:23ff.). Here Jesus defends his grain-plucking followers against the accusation of violating the sabbath when he mentions their material need.[64] The story of the cursing of the fig tree (Mark 11:12ff.) also contains an unmistakable allusion to the hunger of Jesus' people.[65] A corresponding picture is conveyed by the sayings source. Here the disciples of Jesus are expressly addressed and described as absolutely poor people (*ptōchoi*), who hunger and weep (Luke 6:20-21). Their life on the boundary of minimum existence is also presupposed in the speech on "worry." Here it is not a question of the "luxury" cares of the well-to-do but of the survival problems of people who do not know today whether they will have anything to eat tomorrow and who are just barely clothed (Matt 6:25ff./Luke 12:22ff.). Such concern about the basic necessities of life is also presupposed by the petition for daily bread in the Lord's Prayer (Matt 6:11/Luke 11:3). The nomadic existence of Jesus' followers (on homelessness cf., for example, Matt 8:20; Luke 9:58) indicates living conditions on the verge of minimum existence. This picture confirms the relationship of Jesus' followers to the rich and the upper stratum.

Relationship to the Rich

Jesus' followers had a critical relationship to the upper stratum and the rich. They may have had sympathizers there (Mark 15:43), yet our picture of the relations of Jesus' followers with the elite of Jewish society is shaped by criticism of wealth and by Jesus' conflict with the leading stratum of Jerusalem. On the whole, it is striking that the problems of wealth and dealing with riches play a relatively minor role in the Synoptic tradition about Jesus of Nazareth—with the exception of the Gospel of Luke. This underlines once again the distance of Jesus' followers from the rich elite. Without doubt, the oldest Jesus tradition includes the hard saying: "It is easier for a camel to go through the eye of a needle than for someone who is rich to enter the kingdom of God" (Mark 10:25). In the sayings source (using the Aramaic-Phoenician word *mammon*), wealth is plainly condemned as idolatry (Luke 12:13-21; Matt 6:24). Also from the oldest Jesus tradition comes the idea of the reversal of social destinies in the future kingdom of God: the last will be first and the first last.[66] "First" and "last" can also designate social rank. On this basis we can presume that, for example, Luke 1:53 ("he has filled the hungry with good things, and sent the rich away empty") and the parable of the rich man and poor Lazarus (Luke 16:19ff.) also go back to the oldest Jesus tradition. The coming kingdom of God will reestablish a balance between previous social destinies. In it the rich will come out empty, and the poor will no longer hunger and weep. This reversal is also implied in the "woe" to the rich (Luke 6:24-25), whose origin in the oldest Jesus tradition, however, is uncertain. By contrast, the fact that Jesus is called "a glutton and a drunkard" (Matt 11:19; Luke 7:34) is clearly to be understood as unjustified polemic. In the background is the difference between Jesus and John: Jesus eats and drinks, whereas John the Baptist is known as an ascetic. From this we can by no means infer that Jesus "did not see possessions with the fanatically critical eyes of the ascetic rigorist."[67] Also unsuitable, in our view, is the attempt to reduce Jesus' critique of wealth to the selfish *use* of possessions while neglecting love of neighbor.[68] In Jesus' opinion regarding participation in the coming kingdom of God, the rich had a poor prognosis.

Summary

In applying our model of social stratification of ancient societies, it is clear that the overwhelming majority of the members of Jesus' following came from the *rural lower stratum*.[69] Only the tax collector Levi/Matthew is, according to our stratigraphy, to be classified with the retainers of the upper stratum, though apparently to a lower group of the same. He seems to show a notable lack of social prestige. Also among the supporters of the Jesus movement there could have been members of the retainer class. Members of the upper stratum, however, did not belong to the group of followers but at most to the circle of sympathizers (Joseph of Arimathea). We may also attribute to the lower stratum other followers of Jesus who did not belong to his closest group.

Economically, there was a similar spectrum here. It reached from the impoverished through the poor to the relatively prosperous. Yet it is more difficult if one wants to know more precisely whether Jesus' followers belonged more to the upper or lower end of the scale in the lower stratum, since the lower stratum was rather differentiated and in it we find side by side relatively well situated representatives who had their livelihood and many people living on the edge of or below minimum existence. To ask the question differently with the Greek terms for "poor": Did Jesus and his disciples belong to the *penētes* or even to the *ptōchoi*? The latter is suggested at least for the time of their nomadic existence (cf. also Social Pyramid 4 on p. 232).

Discipleship as Self-Stigmatization

Against this background, in the economic and family alienation of the lifestyle of the core of Jesus' following we can see what Lipp calls the "self-stigmatization" of charismatic movements. The abandonment of socio-economic ties by Jesus and his followers meant participation in the fate of the poorest in Jewish society and thus dependency on support. Yet the economic decline that was voluntarily assumed here did not mean a significant renunciation of property. For Jesus and his disciples were already without property, and moreover, the boundaries between relatively poor (*penētes*) and absolutely poor (*ptōchoi*) were fluid. It is noteworthy, nonetheless, that even a former tax leaseholder should have taken this self-stigmatization upon himself. This points to the integrative claim of discipleship of Jesus.

D. THE INFLUENCE AND MESSAGE OF JESUS AND HIS FOLLOWERS

Miraculous Healings

Jesus' charismatic authority rests on his extraordinary powers, which manifest themselves in healings and exorcisms. This connection is expressed terminologically in the tradition of Jesus' words and deeds with the Greek key words *exousia* ("authority"; cf. Mark 1:22, 27; 2:10; 3:15; 11:28ff.) and *dynameis* ("deed of power"; cf. Mark 6:2, 5, 14; Matt 11:20ff.; Luke 10:13). His disciples also receive a share of this authority and power (cf. Mark 3:15; 6:7; Luke 9:1). Although experienced in individual healings and exorcisms, these deeds of power are, nonetheless, also interpreted as eschatological events, namely, as the beginning of the victory over the kingdom of the demons or unclean spirits and thus as a partial presence of the imminent kingdom of God. Accordingly, in the traditional wording the arrival of the kingdom of God is substantiated with a reference to the exorcisms: "But if it is by the finger of God [that is, the power of the Spirit] that I cast out the demons, then the kingdom of God has come to you" (Luke 11:20/Matt 12:28).[70] And, conversely, individual miracles are stylized literarily as battle scenes in which Jesus, as the "Holy One of God," emerges victorious against the kingdom of Satan or of demons (cf. Mark 1:24). Even if the catchphrase *kingdom of God* does not appear in the tradition of Jesus' deeds, a clear connection is nonetheless established in Luke 11:20/Matt 12:28 through the eschatological qualification of the miracles.[71]

Thus it is crucial that Jesus' message comments on his charismatic deeds.[72] In the beginning is the deed. Jesus is not only messenger and preacher but also implementer of the kingdom of God that has come near. And for Jesus' followers the miracles are not signs but events in the kingdom of God. To be sure, the kingdom of God is only partially there in the miracles. Its full realization is still to come. Therefore, in the tradition we find side by side sayings about the arrival of the kingdom of God (Luke 11:20/Matt 12:28; Luke 17:20-21) and its future coming (cf. Matthew 6; Luke 11:2-3; Matt 8:11-12; Mark 9:1; 14:25). The crucial point, however, is that in the miracles it is regarded as having already arrived.

Proclamation of the Kingdom of God

In this regard Jesus goes an important step beyond the eschatological message of John, who preached the nearness of judgment and the necessity of repentance but did not see the eschatological powers as already active in the present. This difference could be the reason that the characteristic key phrase in Jesus' message is *basileia tou theou* ("kingdom of God"). Here the followers of Jesus adopted a catchphrase that was already present in the biblical tradition but is only occasionally found in the eschatological expectation of early Judaism. Apparently it is a symbol actualized especially in critical situations.[73] Jesus did not see the judgment of God as already realized, but saw instead the kingdom of God as having come and, not coincidentally, to people who were in need. It is noteworthy that the kingdom of God is promised, without condition, particularly to the absolutely poor and needy (cf. Luke 6:20-21), as well as to (orphan) children (Mark 9:33-37; 10:14-15).[74] The "poor" here are hardly "a collective designation for Israel."[75] Even if the beatitudes should be in the tradition of the "piety of poverty," the simultaneous naming of those who hunger and weep, as well as the analogous blessing of "children," is a clear indication of the socio-economic situation. Thus it is crucial that the absolutely poor and needy in Israel form the core of the eschatological assembly of the people of God for the kingdom of God. Thus in this way, with holy traditions Jesus "transfigures" the counterworld proclaimed and lived by him.

The key phrase *kingdom of God* accentuates the new situation in which Jesus and his followers saw themselves in the eschatological drama. For this phrase "corresponds to the traditional as well as contemporary ideal of the king who is rescuer and benefactor, not an administrator of affairs."[76] Thus in the idea of the eschatological establishment of the kingdom of God, the positive element of sovereignty—namely, help—stands in the foreground. It is clear that at the same time this implies battle with the demons and victory over them. In any case, however, the idea of the kingdom of God seems to overshadow that of the judgment of God. This does not mean that Jesus did not expect the coming of God also as judge. On the contrary, he also preaches eschatological judgment and in the parables connects the coming of the kingdom with the coming of the judgment (cf. Mark 4:1-34 par.) and miracles as the implementation of the kingdom of God with the call to repentance (cf. also Matt 8:11-12/Luke 13:28-29; Matt 11:21-24/Luke 10:13-15). Like John the Baptist, he presupposes here that all in Israel need repentance. Indeed, he provokingly places the Gentiles over against the "heirs of the kingdom." Historical catastrophes like the massacre of Galilean pilgrims by Pilate serve as monitory examples (Luke 13:1-5). In this sense discipleship with Jesus not only presupposes but also continues the preaching of the Baptist.[77] Yet as John understood himself as the mandatory of the coming judge, so Jesus saw himself and his closest followers as people commissioned for the kingdom of God, as implementers of the kingdom of God. This possibly also implies a future role in the judgment: for Jesus himself as "Son of Man" in regard to his followers (cf. Mark 8:38; Luke 12:8-9 par.) and for "the twelve" in regard to Israel (Matt 19:28). Yet this presupposes that Jesus and the twelve fulfill a mission to Israel that is directed toward the ultimate reconstitution of the old people of twelve tribes.[78]

The self-stigmatization is in harmony with the idea that the ministry and message of Jesus' followers directed especially toward the poorest of the poor and toward those in need. They are not only promised comfort (cf. Matt 6:25ff. par.) but they also experience the nearness of the kingdom of God. This occurs especially in miraculous deeds. Accordingly, wealth is criticized (cf. only Luke 6:24ff.), and wealth is considered anything that exceeds minimum existence (cf. Matt 6:19-21 par.) or makes a life without work possible (cf. Luke 12:16-21). In the prayer petition for "daily bread"—that is, that one may already have today what one can eat tomorrow (Matt 6:11/Luke 11:3)—this perspective on misery becomes impressively clear.[79] Also involved here are Jesus' ethical demands to support the poor (Mark 10:17-22 par.), take in orphans (Mark 9:33-37; 10:13-16 par.), and not oppress debtors (Matt 18:23-34).[80]

Faith in a specific salvation-historical function of Jesus as Messiah seems not to have played any role here. Not Jesus but God himself is the ruler of the coming kingdom. Yet in the tradition the key word *faith*[81] is related to Jesus, above all in the miracle stories. "Faith means to credit Jesus with the miracles that he, with the finger of God, does as an expression of the coming kingdom of God."[82] Jesus, however, probably saw himself as a prophet and was also regarded as such (cf. Mark 6:15; 8:27; Luke 11:49ff.; 13:34-35). It is note-worthy that the message of the imminent kingdom of God also contained the announcement of the forgiveness of sins. Jesus had hardly even promised it himself (but cf. Mark 2:1-12 par.). Perhaps he had contact with notorious yet already repentant sinners, say, in table fellowships (cf. Mark 2:15ff.; Matt 11:19/Luke 7:34). This points again to the integrative character of Jesus' followers. They see the sovereignty of God not only relieving economic and physical need but also healing Jewish society.[83] It is therefore crucial that Jesus' prayer asks for God's forgiveness of sin, for the hallowing of his name, and for the doing of his will in the world (Matt 6:9-13/Luke 11:2-4). In the parables this integrative feature in particular is defended, perhaps in response to criticism (cf. only Luke 15:1ff.; Matt 20:1ff.). In any case, we have here a "counterworld" that promises both to sinners who repent a future in the kingdom of God and to the poor a minimum existence.

E. GENUINE DEVIANCE BUT NOT A BREAK WITH JUDAISM

The charismatic character of Jesus' followers implies a certain genuine deviance and a prepolitical view.[84] Indeed, the interpretation of the present as the time of the inbreaking of the reign of God posits the reality of a counter-world in which the internal and external distress of Jewish society is already partially overcome. Here the core of the gathering of Israel for the kingdom of God is formed by the poorest of the poor and (converted) sinners. It is not least of all this express social connection between the inbreaking of the king-dom of God and the poor and (converted) sinners that shows the deviance of Jesus' followers from some currents in Judaism, even if in its message it exhibits contacts with other directions and groups (see pp. 211–13). It is evi-dent that this eschatological, charismatic self-understanding of Jesus' follow-ers also shaped their relationship with the institutions of Judaism and especially with the Torah. Yet this is often interpreted to mean that already in the beginnings of the Jesus movement there was at least an implicit break with Judaism. In the interpretation of the texts, however, we must consider, on the one hand, that the Jesus tradition was reshaped by later deviance experiences and, on the other, that the history of the reception of Christianity often begins with the premise of Jesus' fundamental break with Judaism. Without doubt, we may assume that under certain conditions, deviance vis-à-vis Judaism was able to increase and ultimately transcend the Jewish context. And we see that this process was in fact completed after the death of Jesus and then especially in connection with extension beyond the intra-Jewish context in the land of Israel through the expansion of the Christian faith to non-Jewish circles in the Diaspora. Only then—and only gradually—did the consciousness of an independent identity vis-à-vis Jews and Gentiles develop (cf. section 9.2.2). For the first followers of Jesus, however, this is not to be presupposed, however salient their position in regard to the institutions of Judaism and particularly to the Torah. We will comment on this briefly in the following paragraphs.

Relationship to the Religious Institutions of Judaism
If we look at the relationship of Jesus' followers to institutions of Judaism, as we discussed them above (see section 6.1), it is immediately clear that the tradition reports quite naturally how Jesus and his followers visited the synagogues on the sabbath (Mark 1:21, 39; 3:1; 6:2; Luke 4:15-16; and elsewhere). There is no critique of any kind. Conditions in regard to the attitude toward the temple seem to have been different. It is true that according to Luke, Jesus, like his parents, goes to the temple as a matter of course, and according to John, he celebrated the pilgrim festivals in Jerusalem (2:23; 5:1; 7:2-11; 10:22). Yet the tradition also reflects a notable critique (cf. Mark 11:1-17 par.; 13:2 par.; 14:58; John 2:18-22). Yet here too, in our opinion, we can ascertain no fundamental questioning of the institution of the temple and the cult of sacrifice but at most a critique of abuses and an announcement of divine punishment. Nevertheless, this was generally the case in the context of the phenomena of temple criticism and prophecies of doom in contemporary Judaism.[85] One can hardly attribute to the Jesus movement an "afamilial ethos," as Theissen does.[86] For the close followers of Jesus, to be sure, the call to discipleship implies a (temporary) abandonment of families. Yet this was not generally true for all his followers. On the contrary, Jesus commanded caring for parents (Mark 7:10-13 par.) and taking in orphans (Mark 9:37 par.), and he prohibited divorce (cf. 1 Cor. 7:10-11; Mark 10:1-12; Luke 16:18 par.; Matt 5:32). If the demands of discipleship involved a break with the principles of familial solidarity and piety (Matt 8:21-22; cf. also Luke 14:26 in distinction to Matt 10:37), this was probably meant hyperbolically or perhaps reflected a later interpretation.[87]

Relationship to the Basic Elements of the Jewish Faith

At no point are the basic elements of the Jewish faith (see p. 137), monotheism and the election of the people, called into question. Confession to one God is taken for granted (cf., for example, Mark 10:17ff. par.; 12:28ff. par.; Matt 23:9). Indeed, the uniqueness of God and the hallowing of his name is called the "foundation of Jesus' message" of the kingdom of God.[88] At the same time, it implies the election of the people, which, however—in accordance with the prophetic-apocalyptic critique—does not automatically serve as a guarantee of salvation (cf. above on the message of judgment). It is true that there are provocative arguments with the witness of Gentiles in the judgment, the participation of Gentiles in the kingdom of God, and the exclusion of the "sons of the kingdom," as well as the exemplary faith of a non-Jew. This presupposes, nonetheless, the election of Israel. There is no programmatic turning of Jesus' attention toward non-Jews.[89] The election of the *land* plays no express role in the Jesus tradition, but one can probably infer that this topos is taken for granted rather than criticized.

Relationship to the Torah

In regard to the relationship to the Torah, we must consider first that basic attitudes toward it in the Jesus tradition are outspokenly affirmative (Matt 5:17–20; cf. Mark 12:28-34). Even if this reflects the positions of a later phase of the Jesus movement, it still calls attention to the fact that as a teacher, Jesus in no way wanted to overcome the Torah. The *interpretation* of the Torah was disputed, but apparently only in certain cases. According to the tradition of the Gospel of Mark, the deviance concerned above all the *sabbath halakah,* the *divorce law,* and the *food and purity laws,* and also, according to the sayings source, especially *love of neighbor* in the context of love of enemies and the forgoing of violence. In every case it seems to us that the charismatic self-understanding of the followers of Jesus as a movement of the poor in Israel is the key to the interpretation of the movement.

Sabbath halakah. In regard to the sabbath halakah, this can be determined in two ways. First, Jesus justifies the behavior of the disciples, who plucked heads of grain on the sabbath (cf. Mark 2:23-28 par.). The basis for the legality of this behavior is the need, the hunger that Jesus' followers suffered as poor beggars (on account of their self-stigmatization). We presume that the principle applied to the beggarly poor here is the one developed in connection with the Maccabean revolt, namely, that life-threatening danger displaces the sabbath (*pikuaḥ nephesh*).[90] Thus from the perspective of the absolutely poor comes the idea that the sabbath is not intended for self-ruination.

In regard to the interpretation of what a life-threatening danger means, socially conditioned viewpoints also played a role, as a comparison will make clear. In Matt 12:11 the rescue of an animal that has fallen into a dangerous situation is permitted. The same can also be demonstrated in rabbinic tradition (cf. *b. Shabb.* 128b). In Qumran, by contrast, the halakah is more rigorous, even in this case (CD 11:16–17).

In other sabbath conflict stories the charismatic authority of Jesus stands at the center of the discussion (cf. Mark 2:1-12; 3:1-6; Luke 13:10-17; 14:1-6; John 5:1-18; 9). There is no question of a violation of the sabbath halakah here, since these healings took place only with words. Thus these stories apparently also reflect "only" conflicts over the authority of Jesus himself. Yet we must also consider here the fact that later distancings from the Jewish way of life had already flowed into the tradition (cf. only Mark 2:28 par.).

Divorce law. The followers of Jesus had great interest in the divorce law, which was interpreted extremely rigorously, namely—similar to the view of the Pharisaic school of Shammai—that divorce was permitted only in extremely exceptional cases (Mark 10:1-12 par.; Luke 16:18 par.; Matt 5:32; cf. 1 Cor 7:10-11). This too is probably best understood in the context of social history. One might conjecture that prophetic "criticism of the ruler" also played a role among the followers of Jesus (cf. pp. 169–70). Nonetheless, the validity of the prohibition of divorce could naturally have covered the broader practice. We may presume, therefore, that the prohibition of divorce relates to certain social phenomena that were caused by the crisis in Jewish society. We have to wonder whether poverty could be a fundamental cause of familial disruption.

Food and purity laws. Statements in the tradition concerning the food and purity laws are clearly shaped by later experiences when they teach the purity of all foods (cf. Mark 7:19). Yet this can hardly be presupposed for Jesus himself. Rather, we must assume that the earliest followers of Jesus basically recognized the purity halakah (cf. only Mark 1:40-45). Otherwise the later conflicts over fellowship meals with non-Jews would hardly be conceivable. If Mark 7:15 should, nonetheless, be an old tradition, it is clear that based on a recognition in principle of ritual purity, an ethical purity of heart is also demanded. This is also found in the Jewish tradition and in that of John the Baptist.[91] Certainly, there is little to suggest that with regard to ritual purity the followers of Jesus were as rigorous as, for example, the priestly influenced Essenes or the Pharisees and later rabbis. They "apparently rejected measures like purifications and the subsequent tithing of possibly untithed agricultural products (Mark 7:1-8 par.; Luke 11:39-42 par.)."[92] Their intention was the ethical, not ritual, sanctification of the people. Yet this also was probably to be interpreted more as the perspective of the wretched lower stratum than as a criticism of the law; that is, it had a motivation similar to that of Jesus' sabbath halakah.

Love of neighbor and the forgoing of violence. Clearly in the programmatic speeches of Jesus (Sermon on the Mount, Sermon on the Plain), there is a design for a "counterworld" whose essence can be traced back to the earliest followers of Jesus (cf. Luke 6:20-49 par.). Decisive here again is the integrative intention of the Torah interpretation.[93] For in the demand to forgo violence, which is apparently also made in regard to compulsory measures by the Romans or other authorities (Luke 6:29/Matt 5:41), there is also a tendency toward balance and defusing conflict situations, just as there was in the requirement to love neighbors even when they are hostile. The same is true of the commandment to forgo judgments. It can be demonstrated in more than one instance that we have in the commandment to love one's enemies only the development of ideas already present in the Torah itself; it is by no means a question of surpassing the Torah.[94] Here, apparently, a basic feature of ancient and especially of Jewish society has been adopted in that the realm of validity of the commandment is expanded. It is notable that the examples of this demand presuppose, among other things, classic balanced and general *reciprocity* (see section 2.2.2a). This is also the basis of concrete situations such as lawsuits (in particular over debts) and lending relations in general—that is, the concrete situations especially of little people. Examples from this realm play a large role especially in the Lukan version.

It is also a part of this design for a "counterworld" that in the circle of disciples "service" is considered a principle of lordship, and thus a reversal of normal relationships is taught (cf. Mark 10:41-45 par.). In general, here and there we hear notes of the eschatological upheaval of present conditions (cf. Luke 1:46-55; 6:20-26). Yet it is notable that, perhaps apart from the question of taxes (cf. p. 121), the message of Jesus' followers can be called at best prepolitical. A discussion of the power politics and socio-economic problems in the land of Israel is lacking, as is a critique of the Jewish elite. Instead, what is criticized is, quite generally, the rich. The conflicts with Pharisees and scribes are, where they do not absolutely rest on retrojections from a later time, not politically but ethically motivated (Torah interpretation).

Jesus' Fate

In connection with a pilgrimage of his movement to Jerusalem, Jesus experiences the fate of a social bandit or revolutionary, that is, a "robber." Such an evaluation of the Jesus movement is not entirely without foundation from the Roman perspective, as we will soon discuss. In the behavior of the Roman authorities there is a certain analogy with the sign prophets and their movements (see section 6.4.2). Such a confusion of roles is also suggested by Jesus' appearance in Jerusalem with a symbolic cleansing of the temple district (cf. Mark 11:15-16 par.), which had a certain effect on the masses. Clearest, however, are the parallels to the fate of the prophet of doom Jesus ben Ananias, who appeared shortly before the First Jewish Revolt (cf. p. 165). In any case, Jesus of Nazareth, perhaps like Jesus ben Ananias on the basis of a slanderous statement from the elite of Jerusalem, was condemned and crucified by the Roman procurator Pontius Pilate as a "bandit." Apparently, because of the nearness of the festival, this quick trial was also supposed to serve as a deterrent and forestall potential disturbances. Yet the presentation of the process in the Passion stories of the Gospels goes far beyond this. It presupposes in part a previous judicial procedure in the Sanhedrin, a betrayer from the ranks of Jesus' close followers, and a pointed interest of the Jewish authorities in Jesus' execution for religious reasons. Moreover, it also tries to give the impression that both the Jewish and Roman authorities were aware of Jesus' innocence. It is without doubt a tendentious presentation, which cannot simply be explained on the basis of later experiences; it reveals, rather, an apologetical interest in warding off the criminalization of Christians in the Roman empire (cf. section 11.1).[95]

F. RELATIONSHIP TO OTHER GROUPS AND MOVEMENTS

In terms of the history of religion, the earliest followers of Jesus have points of contact with numerous tendencies and groups in contemporary Judaism, but in terms of the sociology of religion and social history, only with movements of the lower stratum. In particular, it is the charismatic element that, despite all similarities, distinguishes the followers of Jesus sociologically and religiously from currents and groups of the upper stratum or retainer group. At the same time, however, this constitutes the affinity of Jesus' followers with some movements of the lower stratum. In their focus on the biblical-apocalyptic traditions of the imminent expectation, as well as in the demand for the eschatological purity of the temple, they are close to the Essenes. Here there are also points of contact with insurrectionist groups. The Jesus movement basically shares its integrative trait with the Pharisees, and the confession to the uniqueness of God and his sovereignty also with the sicarii and Zealots. In regard to the meaning of charismatic experiences, not least of all in miracles, Jesus stands close, on the one hand, to individual thaumaturgical figures and, on the other, to the charismatic sign prophets and their movements, whose imminent expectation of liberation, moreover, exhibits analogies to the hope in the kingdom of God of Jesus' followers, even if the catchphrase *kingdom of God* is typical especially of the Jesus movement.

Not least of all, however, there are striking parallels to the social bandits. This is true not only generally in regard to the charismatic phenomenon, which was especially pronounced in the case of the brigand royal pretenders. Rather, the creation of a "counterworld" and the economic and familial alienation and vagabond lifestyle of Jesus' followers—yet at the same time with support from sympathetic, stable local circles—correspond in many ways to the world of the social bandits. Thus it is no coincidence, in our view, that Jesus was executed like a social bandit by the Romans and in the tradition had to be expressly distinguished from sign prophets and the royal pretense of the social bandits (cf. pp. 166, 177). The affinities with social bandits and their "new definition" of a socio-economic career of progressive deterioration can also be understood in terms of social history. Similarly, in terms of social history Jesus and his followers are clearly different from the Pharisees, Essenes, and naturally the Sadducees, who were able to gain sympathizers at most in the lower stratum, but who, nonetheless, were basically recruited from the upper stratum and retainers. By contrast, the earliest followers of Jesus were— like the social bandits but also like the movements of the charismatic sign prophets—a reaction to the crisis of Jewish society in the lower stratum. The "counterworld" that they envisioned was also prepolitical. Nevertheless, their differences from social banditry are likewise clear. The rich were criticized and summoned to compassion and solidarity, but not attacked and robbed. In general, the nonviolence and patient submission of Jesus' followers to foreign power are significant. In general, the charismatic element becomes concrete in powers of healing beneficence, not in bodily distinction and qualities of martial leadership. There is no retreat from society into inaccessible regions, except in prayer situations. The locus of effectiveness remains the public places of the people.

This also distinguishes the Jesus movement from the Essenes. In contrast to them, we also know of no active participation by members of Jesus' following in the First Jewish Revolt. Yet it is often assumed that Simon the Cananaean, one of the twelve (Mark 3:18 par.), was a former Zealot. In our view, however, in Jesus' time there was not yet a revolutionary group called *Zealots* (see pp. 172ff.), and for this reason we see in the sobriquet simply the designation of a religious "enthusiast." Clearly these are also differences from the charismatic movements of the sign prophets. For their charisma collapses when put to the test and also must fail in view of the inordinate expectation of miracles. By contrast, the charisma of the followers of Jesus persisted, since it was oriented toward isolated and individual experiences of healing and integrated from the beginning into an ongoing living community of the charismatic and his followers. Therefore, the violent death of Jesus did not become the catastrophe of his movement. Rather, his followers and especially his close disciples understood his death right away as a further crucial stage in the drama of salvation history (cf. 1 Cor 15:3-4). Later scribal interpretation also comprehended Jesus' martyrdom as an apocalyptic necessity and a biblically foretold fate (cf. Mark 8:31; 9:31; 10:33-34; Luke 24:25-27). His death is interpreted as an effective, sin-forgiving self-sacrifice (cf. Mark 10:45), perhaps prepared by Jesus himself (cf. Mark 14:22-25 par.). Thus, like the earlier martyrdom of John the Baptist, the crucifixion of Jesus did not bring charisma to an end but rather rekindled it in a new way, as the ecstatic visions of the resurrection of Jesus among his followers attest.

7.2 The Communities of God in Judea

CONTINUITY AND TRANSFORMATION
OF CHARISMA AFTER THE DEATH OF JESUS

We see the crucial continuity and at the same time the beginning of the transformation of charisma in the ecstatic, visionary experiences immediately after the death of Jesus among the followers of Jesus, especially in the close circle of Jesus' disciples and followers. According to the earliest tradition, the resurrected One appeared to Simon Peter (Cephas) and the circle of twelve as a whole, then to a larger circle of more than five hundred followers, as well as to James, the brother of Jesus, and all the apostles (1 Cor 15:5-7). In the Gospels, by contrast, it is in part women who are named as the first witnesses of the resurrection (Matt 28:9-10; John 20:11-18; indirectly Mark 16:1–8 par.). Nevertheless, Luke shares with the Pauline tradition the idea of the first appearance to Peter (Luke 24:34). The Gospels also mention the appearance to the circle of twelve (Matt 28:16-0; Luke 24:36-49; John 20:19-23). These epiphanies are understood as appearances of Jesus from heaven. Yet according to the interpretation of his followers, Jesus is not only transported into heaven like John the Baptist and other martyrs before him. Rather, for Jesus' followers his resurrection is at the same time his exaltation to a heavenly position of power at God's right hand as "Son of God" and "Lord" (cf. Rom. 1:3ff.) or, in the scribal adoption of Dan. 7:13, as "Son of Man."

It is probably also in this connection then that Jesus is placed in the messianic tradition of Israel as *Christos*, the Greek translation of the Hebrew *mašiaḥ*, "anointed one" (cf. Mark 12:35-37 par.; 13:26 par.; 14:42 par.; cf. also Matt 28:18). As the resurrected One exalted to God according to the faith of his followers, he stands ready to establish dominion over Israel. Nothing has changed regarding the imminent expectation; it has perhaps become even more urgent. At the same time, from heaven the exalted One is already communicating the eschatological Spirit to his followers. Accordingly, the Gospels link the appearances of the resurrected One to the circle of twelve with renewed commission and mission and with the bestowal of the Spirit.[96] And in the narrative of the outpouring of the Spirit at Pentecost in Jerusalem (Acts 2), which also involved Jews from the Diaspora, the expectation of the eschatological renewal of the people of God is presented in connection with prophetic tradition (Joel 2:28-32; cf. Isa 59:21; Ezek 39:29).

Thus, similar to the martyrdom of John the Baptist, the death of Jesus and his resurrection are apparently understood as a further crucial stage in the drama of salvation history, in which Jesus himself is given an important ongoing role, now played from heaven. In the tradition this "christologization" or "messianization" of Jesus is projected back on the earthly Jesus. At the same time, however, the apostles appear anew among the followers of Jesus, as charismatic miraculous deeds comparable to Jesus' are reported of them (cf. Acts 2:43; 3:1-10; 4:30; 5:12-16; 9:32-43). Indeed, for Paul charismatic deeds are regarded as signs of apostolicity (cf. Rom 15:18-19; 2 Cor 12:12; 1 Cor 2:4; 1 Thess 1:5). Accordingly, some also share Jesus' destiny and in some cases—the sons of Zebedee (Mark 10:35-45; Acts 12:1-2) and later probably also Peter[97] and finally James, the brother of Jesus (*Ant.* 20.200ff.)—they also share his martyrdom. Yet it is noteworthy that Luke most clearly presents an analogy to the passion of Jesus in the martyrdom of Stephen.

APOSTLES

The mission role is underlined above all by the designation *apostle,* which is used, however, in quite different ways in the tradition. It can be both restricted to the circle of twelve (in Jerusalem) and applied (in Antioch and in the Diaspora) to everyone involved in missionary work, including the "church emissaries" provided later to support Paul in the Diaspora.[98] Paul himself seems to distinguish between the apostles who through a vision were directly commissioned by the Lord himself (cf. Gal 1:1; 1 Cor 1:1; 9:1; 15:5-8; Rom 1:1; and elsewhere) and apostles who were commissioned by the churches (2 Cor 8:23). At the same time he makes for himself the claim of being *the* apostle to the Gentiles (Rom 11:13) and compares this with the apostolate of Peter for the circumcised (cf. Gal 2:1-10). The Greek *apostolos* is probably to be understood in terms of the early Jewish *šaliaḥ* institution and the biblical messenger law and marks the emissaries as representatives of their commissioner during his or her absence.[99] This impressively underlines the continuity that was present in the Jesus movement in spite of his death.

THE DEPERSONALIZATION OF THE CHARISMA

Even if later views and theologization have had a stylizing effect, it is still clear how much we have here the "depersonalization" or "objectification" (Schluchter) of the charisma, that is, the transition from the genuine charismatic Jesus to a "personally and institutionally charismatic" movement (cf. pp.

198ff.). Yet this was already prepared in Jesus' earliest following when he gave the twelve a share of his charismatic authority (see pp. 197–98). It is important, nonetheless, that after Jesus' violent death the charisma was transferred, on the one hand, to the entire following, as the mention of the more than five hundred visionaries in Paul and the pouring out of the Spirit at Pentecost show, and, on the other hand, to certain prominent individuals like Simon Peter and the twelve, then later to the Lord's brother James and to all apostles who took over certain missionary and leadership tasks of the exalted One. Notable here is a concentration on Jerusalem as the salvation-historical center of Israel. This does not mean that there were not also other churches in the land of Israel. Especially Judea, however, seems to have become the center.

The charismatic task was related above all to the missionary winning of a broader following in Israel that would now understand itself as the "saints" and the "church of God," that is, as the eschatological assembly of the people of God. Besides the circle of twelve, the core included, first, Simon Peter, regarded as the "rock" (cf. Matt 16:18-19). If the twelve represent the hope of the reconstitution of the people of twelve tribes, then Peter—perhaps on the basis of being the first to see the resurrected One—is given a role similar to the one Abraham had for the first constitution of the people of God, a role in the eschatological assembly of God's people for the kingdom of God. In the tradition this special function is emphasized not only with the honorific Peter/Cephas but also, for example, through his role as spokesman for the disciples.[100] Later a collegium of three—composed of the Lord's brother James, Peter, and John the son of Zebedee— apparently likewise have a salvation-historical function for the eschatological people of God Israel, as suggested by the designation "pillars" (cf. Gal 2:9).[101] Yet this development already presupposes the gradual disappearance of the circle of twelve after the martyr's death of James son of Zebedee under Herod Agrippa I (Acts 12:1-2) at the beginning of the forties. After the separation of Peter from Jerusalem, which was presumably connected with this martyrdom,[102] and possibly after the martyrdom of John son of Zebedee (cf. Mark 10:35-45), the Lord's brother James—until his own martyrdom—seems to have been the only authority in the Jerusalem church, perhaps accompanied by a circle of elders (cf. Acts 15:2, 4, 22-23; 21:18).[103] This development contains certain traits of the reshaping, described by Weber, of genuine charisma into a Gentile charisma.[104] Yet one must observe that this is only a partial aspect of a more extensive "objectification" of the charisma among the followers of Jesus.

THE INSTITUTIONALIZATION OF THE CHARISMA

There is no reason to doubt the ongoing Jewish identity of the followers of Jesus and their loyalty to the institutions and basic convictions of Israel. This is obvious not least of all from the naturalness of their participation in temple worship and its cult of sacrifice, as described by Luke in the Acts of the Apostles.[105] Even if, according to Luke, occasions of worship were also used as opportunities for missionary work, participation in the temple cult is, nonetheless, not to be regarded as merely a tactical basis for Jesus' own sermon. Nor can we yet speak of a "new worship service" here,[106] since worship in the real sense, until the destruction of the temple, was only the cult of sacrifice (and at most the assemblies that took place in connection with it). Even the synagogue gatherings for prayer and reading of the Torah can probably not be called worship before 70 C.E.[107] Nevertheless, certain religious identifying institutions of community life (Acts 2:44) were developed, such as the Lord's Supper and baptism, and specific forms and formulas, like the Lord's Prayer and the *maranatha,* soon influenced the everyday life of Jesus' followers. Yet this is as little to be understood as worship as are the religious manifestations in Jewish families, which took place especially in connection with meals. It corresponds, rather, to the identity-creating function of meals, which was usual in antiquity even beyond Judaism.[108] For it is also in this connection that we read of community and being "together" (*epi to auto;* Acts 2:44; cf. 1 Cor 11:20; 14:23) and "coming together" (*synerchesthai;* 1 Cor 11:17-18, 20, 33-34; 14:23). Accordingly, the Acts of the Apostles also summarizes the lifestyle of the "early church," which was oriented toward temple and home, as follows:

> They devoted themselves to the apostles' teaching and fellowship, to the breaking of bread and the prayers. (2:42)

> Day by day, as they spent much time together in the temple, they broke bread at home and ate their food with glad and generous hearts. (2:46)

Certainly, the self-understanding of the followers of Jesus as *ekklēsia* and communion of the saints—that is, as the Spirit-gifted core of the eschatological gathering of the people of God—means a crucial step toward institutionalization (of the charisma). Here we can see certain analogies to the Qumran community, except that the Jesus community did not separate itself from Jerusalem but was instead concentrated precisely in that locale. And above all, the *place* of their *gathering* was the *house.* Thus, as clearly as we have here to a certain extent the self-identification of the followers of Jesus vis-à-vis the Jews, who did not (yet) share their faith, it is just as clear that their social and religious basis was the house or the family household. Therefore, it is no accident that they have their own socio-religious forms and institutions, namely, *baptism* and the *Lord's Supper,* as well as the development of a specifically symbolic world, a faith, or a doctrine in which membership in the *ekklēsia* is unmistakably expressed. This communal life, however, was also shaped by a certain reciprocity and common ownership of material things. Certainly, all this goes back to particular beginnings with the first followers of Jesus and with the earlier history involving the circle of John the Baptist. And without doubt, there are Jewish and only Jewish traditions that are actualized and further developed here. Nevertheless, this *stabilitas loci,* together with separation from the outside world and an identity-assuring structure within, also represents a process of increasing deviance, which at the same time led to separational measures from the outside.

BAPTISM

With baptism the followers of Jesus after Easter apparently adopted the baptism of John, including its promise of the forgiveness of sins and thus salvation from "this corrupt generation" (Acts 2:40). Yet in distinction to John, the *ekklēsia* no longer baptized in the salvation-historical place beyond the Jordan. It had already passed this stage of the apocalyptic drama. And they baptized "in the name of Jesus Christ" (Acts 2:38; 8:16; 10:48; Matt 28:19). Thus it is not only that one is baptized by the authority of the exalted One, but those baptized are turned over to him and placed under his power.[109] Accordingly, the bestowal of the Spirit is also linked with baptism (Acts 2:38). In contrast to John, who released the baptized again into the people, as it were, the baptism of the Jesus movement made manifest belonging in the *ekklēsia* or to one's Lord. Thus it had a function of identification. This explains how baptism could later come into competition with circumcision.

THE LORD'S SUPPER

The celebration of the Lord's Supper (1 Cor 11:20), the breaking of bread, probably also goes back to the earliest followers of Jesus. It must be seen in the context of the fact that the Jesus movement gathered in homes. This was its most important locus of independent social and religious life. The old expression *breaking of bread* (Acts 2:42; 20:7, 11; 1 Cor 10:16; cf. Mark 6:41; 8:5; 14:22 par.) emphasizes, on the one hand, the most important (and often only) component of the meal for the lower stratum and especially for the poor. On the other hand, it recalls the usual process by which, according to Jewish custom, a meal begins with a eulogy, a word of blessing (Heb. *berakah*), and the breaking of bread. The Lord's Supper also follows the custom of the prayer of thanksgiving, the *eucharistia* (Heb. *kiddush*), over the final cup (Mark 14:23 par.). Hence we do not have here the establishment of an independent cultic process but the expansion of normal Jewish religious customs. At the same time, however, the words of interpretation over the bread and the cup, which show a certain analogy to the Passover meal, call attention to the specifics regarding the meal of the Jesus movement. Thus, in view of the important religious identification function that mealtimes generally had in antiquity,[110] it is quite natural that the Jesus movement secured its faith in the context of meals. In the process, high eschatological expectation found particular expression here, as suggested by the catchwords "glad" or "jubilant" (Acts 2:26, 46) and the Aramaic prayer-like cry *maranatha* ("our Lord, come!"; 1 Cor 16:22; Rev 22:20), which likewise probably belonged to the Lord's Supper (cf. also 1 Cor 11:26).

The gatherings and common meals were perhaps also an occasion to confirm the specific content of the faith of the Jesus movement: its *doctrine*. Here a central role was probably played by the salvation-historical interpretation of Jesus' death and resurrection, as the oldest forms of the tradition,[111] particularly the *pistis* formulas,[112] make clear. Possibly the focus on the tradition of the words of Jesus was also soon added. Even if this naturally goes back to the earliest followers of Jesus, the difference, nonetheless, is that the focus is on the destiny of Jesus himself and his role as guarantor of the salvation-historical process.

THE SOCIO-ECONOMIC SITUATION OF THE *EKKLĒSIA*

After the death of Jesus, the social and economic situation of the followers of Jesus hardly changed significantly. Yet also after a certain time Jews from the Diaspora joined them—perhaps even somewhat prosperous ones, as in the case of Barnabas. When the Acts of the Apostles mentions that a great many priests also became obedient to the faith in Christ (Acts 6:7), this probably corresponded more to the Lukan ideal image of the church than to reality. We would assume that the concentration in Jerusalem also had economic grounds. At first, certainly, it also created new problems, for we may surely exclude the idea that one of the apostles native to Galilee could return to his own house or property in Jerusalem. That means, however, that the apostles were dependent on local supporters, as in the itinerant charismatic period of Jesus' following. This was possible, especially with a material solidarity motivated by an "overheating of community feeling,"[113] only with stability of location. In any case, the economic alienation of the closest followers of Jesus was probably also modified, even if it was still maintained by individual itinerant missionaries. According to the presentation in Acts, the early church lived "together and had all things in common," with the needs of all being met (Acts 2:44-45; 4:32-37). That is without doubt an idealization of the beginnings—going back to Jewish and Greek social utopias—with a paraenetic intention that has its parallels in the ancient presentation of the Essenes. Yet one can hardly doubt that the common life of the *ekklēsia* was defined not only by religious and social but also by a certain amount of economic interaction. This was probably the background of the patronage role that Luke ascribes to the Levite Joseph, called Barnabas, who comes from Cyprus, and—even if with a different significance—to Ananias and Sapphira (Acts 4:36-37; 5:1-11).

Of prime importance, nonetheless, was the fact that poverty was apparently a significant problem in the *ekklēsia* of Jerusalem. This is indicated not only by the differences that Luke mentions between Hebrews and Hellenists regarding the care of widows but also and indeed especially by the intensive collection activity of Paul in the Diaspora for the miserably poor (*ptōchoi*) among the saints in Jerusalem (Gal 2:10; Rom 15:25-29; cf. 1 Cor 16:1-4; 2 Cor 8-9; Acts 11:29).[114] The famine mentioned in Acts 11:27-28 and the sabbath year that followed it (cf. *Ant.* 20.101) probably made the situation of the Jerusalem church especially acute[115] but hardly changed it fundamentally. Perhaps this is also still reflected in the fourth century in the name *Ebionaei,* which Jerome and Epiphanius attest for the Christians in the land east of the Jordan.[116]

THE INCREASING DEVIANCE
AND MISSIONARY INFLUENCE ON DIASPORA JUDAISM

A momentous change in the followers of Jesus in the land of Israel was presented by members who came from Diaspora Judaism. According to Luke, this happened already in the context of the outpouring of the Spirit at Pentecost. In any case, this expansion probably began relatively early, as shown by the calling of Paul outside the land of Israel in the middle of the thirties. Whether or not this process was originally connected with Jerusalem itself, it had, in any case, decisive effects on the house churches there. This is shown by a conflict over the care of the widows of the "Hellenists," that is, the members of the Jesus movement who came from the Diaspora and had Greek as their mother tongue; according to Acts 6:1-6, the issue was resolved through the installation of seven men from the ranks of the Hellenists. This was by no means only a division of labor between apostles and deacons. Rather, the Lukan presentation reveals that with the committee of seven came a separate charismatically led *ekklēsia* of Diaspora Jews alongside the church represented by the circle of twelve or by other groups.[117] In particular, Philip (Acts 8:4-13, 26-40) and Stephen (6:8-7:60) are characterized as charismatics, miracle workers, and missionaries. The mission among non-Jews then also begins with Philip outside Jerusalem. As Luke presents it, this takes place as a result of the disciples' banishment from Jerusalem after the martyrdom of Stephen (Acts 8:1-3). Yet it is interesting to note Luke's mention that the apostles were excepted. Therefore it is more likely that the reason for (and not the result of) the banishment was the mission of the Hellenists among Diaspora Jews and above all among non-Jews. Perhaps that is also the real background of Stephen's martyrdom.

In any case, the Hellenists represent for Luke a connecting link with the mission among non-Jews, which was soon also undertaken by Peter outside Jerusalem. Here the Cornelius episode in particular (Acts 10) suggests that this mission was not the consequence of the apostles' strategic theological deliberations but their reaction to charismatic phenomena among non-Jews. It was probably also not coincidental that the centurion Cornelius was, moreover, a God-fearer (cf. pp. 269–71). Rather, this anticipates the development that in the Diaspora is connected especially with Antioch and Barnabas the Cypriot, as well as with Paul the Diaspora Jew. It is the recognition of the charismatic quality of this mission, demonstrated by the non-Jew Titus at the Apostolic Council (Gal 2:1-10), that overcomes the initially rather hesitant attitude on the subject in the Jerusalem church.

It is significant that the charismatic makeup of the Jesus movement was the basis of both its expansion and its increasing deviance. Accordingly, the spread of the Jesus movement into the realm of Diaspora Judaism and non-Jews is connected especially with increasingly negative measures from the outside. Toward the end of the forties the conflict potential with the churches in the Diaspora increased, especially with the Syrian Antioch church, which lived in a programmatic way the table fellowship of Jews and non-Jews in house churches (see section 9.2.2). This is indicated, on the one hand, by the intervention—influenced by the fear of negative measures—of those from Jerusalem in Antioch (Gal 2:11-14), to which the Jerusalemites Peter and Barnabas then also reacted pragmatically, and, on the other hand, by the "persecutions" in Judea presupposed in 1 Thess 2:14-16 for the period before 50 C.E.

Finally, it was probably not coincidental that Paul, whose name was connected in a special way with this table fellowship transgression in the non-Jewish realm, was arrested in Jerusalem in the middle of the fifties. And when James, among others, also suffered a martyr's death a few years later, this identification with the Diaspora churches probably also played a role. Thus in our opinion it was the charismatic dynamic that separated the Jesus movement more and more clearly from Judaism in Palestine. It is obvious that in the period of the First Jewish Revolt, this meant a special danger. We believe, therefore, that it is entirely conceivable that at the beginning of the rebellion, as Eusebius reports (*Hist. Eccl.* 3.11.1), the church took flight from Jerusalem to Pella beyond the Jordan and thus into the Roman-protected realm of the Hellenistic cities.

8

MESSIANIC COMMUNITIES
IN THE LAND OF ISRAEL AFTER 70 C.E.

"The consequences of the first great war of the Jews against Rome were extremely far-reaching and can hardly be overestimated in their importance for the further history of Judaism."[1] For Judaism in the land of Israel they meant crucial political, social, and economic changes, but also lasting changes in the religious praxis from earlier eras.[2] Judaea remained a Roman province (with praetorian rank), while Jerusalem became the site of a regular encampment of a Roman legion and Caesarea Maritima remained only an administrative center. The land holdings of many Judeans—of all, according to Josephus (*War* 7.216–17)—became the property of the emperor, and thus "most, if not all, Judean peasants thereby became *coloni* [tenants] who worked the land and paid interest."[3] The destruction of the temple brought the end of the cult of sacrifice and many religious activities and duties linked with the temple (for example, pilgrimages to the temple, the blowing of the shofar when the new year came on a sabbath, and certain taxes). The functions of the priests at the temple became obsolete, as did the office of high priest. The traditional duties of the Sanhedrin (*synedrium*), which was based in the temple, came to an end. The temple tax was replaced by the humiliating *fiscus Judaicus*.

The sharp break with former centers of religious and social life required a renewal of religious life. In this process, normative influence was gained by groups generally recognized as moderate, the so-called *wise ones* (Heb. *ḥakamim*), who in an amoral time were generally called "rabbis."[4] In no small degree, they continued the traditions of the Pharisees, from whom they were often express descendants, and of the scribes. The idea—which perhaps had its beginnings earlier—of a transformation of the purity laws that applied to the temple into the realm of the home and table fellowship made a Jewish life possible after the loss of official independence and the destruction of the temple.[5] Things that stood at the center of Pharisaic and above all scribal teachings—the study of the Torah, its application to everyday life, observance of the sabbath, tithing, and faith in the resurrection and judgment—formed the foundations of Jewish existence after 70 C.E., even without the cult of the temple and the Sanhedrin. Thus in connection with the teaching traditions of the so-called scribes (*grammateis*) and other sociologically relevant groups (landowners and merchants), the Pharisees seem to have developed the foundations of a new self-reforming Judaism after the catastrophe of the Judean-Roman war.[6] Little by little, the convictions shared by this "coalition" were extended to all of Israel.[7]

The spiritual center of Judaism became the small town of Yavneh/Jamnia—apparently with Rome's indulgence.[8] Here the religious tradition was given normative form. Of fundamental importance was the fact that the previous "fractionalization" of individual Jewish groupings was also overcome.[9] The school became, as it were, a symbol of the end of previous divisions and the beginning of a new coalition for the reformation of Judaism.[10] Only gradually did institutional authorities (rabbis) also take shape, but a more exact dating is problematic.[11] Widely discussed in connection with the school of Jamnia is the formulation of the so-called *birkat ha-minim* ("heretic benediction"), which involves the twelfth of the Eighteen Benedictions (Heb. *Shemoneh Esreh/Amidah*), in which heretics (Heb. *minim*) are cursed. We will go into this benediction in more detail on pp. 234–35.

The period of Judaism beginning after 70 C.E. is usually called that of "rabbinical Judaism" or even "classical Judaism." Often used, even by German scholars, is the phrase coined by Moore: "formative Judaism."[12] The rendering of the English term *formative* as *formativ* in German usage, however, is problematic. In German we attach rather negative connotations to the word *formativ*, whereas in English it has above all the sense of emphasizing the aspect of taking shape. Thus in the sense of the English technical term, we must also speak of a period of reshaping in Judaism after 70. At the same time, however, we must also speak of an *integrative* process in the Judaism of this period, in which the emphasis is above all on the overcoming of the previous separation of Judaism into groups. The fact that the integration process also resulted in the exclusion of Jewish groups not representing the majority consensus, including the messianic Jesus groups, is demonstrated, for example, by the yet-to-be-discussed new formulation of the so-called *birkat ha-minim*. Here, however, it is apparently a question of a lengthy process that cannot be explained with a single formal and universal act of exclusion.[13] Yet it is already clear that the exclusions are to be understood so to speak as the other side of the integration process and of the sociological logic that results from the new definition of Jewish existence that became necessary in a social and religious crisis. The tension-filled relations between the Jewish majority in the land of Israel and the messianic Jesus communities probably have their *Sitz im Leben* precisely at this point. Of fundamental significance is the fact that the groups of Christ-believers or messianic Jews[14] in the land of Israel doubtless did not belong to the new consensus-bearing coalition. Not only was their essential belief in Jesus as Messiah and Son of God not shared by the Jewish majority, but also the latter's central convictions in regard to the interpretation of the Torah, as well as of the purity laws and the sabbath, were interpreted differently by the Christ-believing communities. With this these groups effectively excluded themselves from the self-shaping mainstream of Judaism.

The composition of the Gospels of Matthew and John must be understood against the background of this conflict with the newly reoriented Judaism of the time after 70. That is to say, their presentation of Jesus and his relationship to Judaism (and vice versa) unmistakably reveal experiences of the messianic followers of Jesus with Judaism in the period after 70 C.E. The exaggerated and polemically distorted portrait of the Pharisees and scribes (especially in the Gospel of Matthew) can be interpreted against this background. Noteworthy here is the fact not only that Pharisees and scribes—that is, the two groups that in a special way headed the coalition of rabbinical Judaism—appear closely connected (Matt 5:20; Matthew 23), but also that they are presented as the leading stratum of Judaism. Both of these points are understandable only in the situation after 70.[15] Also the Gospel of John, in which again and again "the Jews" appear and the Pharisees are virtually identified with them or appear in an authoritative position (for example, in John 9), points to epochal experiences with Judaism after 70. Instructive here is, not least of all, the fact that the Christ-believing communities, in contrast to the integration process within Judaism, have become solidified sociologically in the status of exclusive communities, whereas Judaism had begun to overcome the previous group divisions.

In the following pages we will first discuss briefly the New Testament source situation (8.1). Then we will present the social composition of messianic communities (8.2) and finally go into the conflicts between these communities and the Jewish majority (8.3).

8.1 New Testament Sources

We assume here that the Gospels of Matthew and John (at least in their basic form) originated in the land of Israel and refer to conditions there. The Gospel of Mark can also be brought in here, at least at certain points, since it probably also comes from the regions of Syria bordering on Israel and, in any case, contains some relevant statements on experiences in the context of the First Jewish Revolt; that is to say, it exhibits temporally and geographically a close connection with Israel and with the catastrophe of the First Jewish Revolt.

THE GOSPEL OF MATTHEW

There is a widespread view that the Gospel of Matthew came into being in a Jewish milieu after 70 C.E. In dispute, however, is whether the final redaction was undertaken by a Jewish Christian or Gentile Christian author. The arguments for a Gentile Christian redactor, which Strecker in particular has advanced,[16] have, however, often been refuted.[17] Nor is the "Jewish Christian" character of the Gospel contradicted by the fact that it is composed in good Greek and lends itself to evangelization among non-Jews. In regard to the place of origin of the Gospel, there is a certain older consensus that favors Syria and especially Antioch.[18] It rests above all on the fact that the Gospel of Matthew is written in good Greek and is certainly not a translation. Yet Greek is also the language of Diaspora Jews in the land of Israel, some of whom made themselves known early on to the Christian community (cf. also pp. 219–20). Moreover, there is evidence that the Gospel of Matthew deals with the Judaism taking shape in the land of Israel under the authority of the "wise ones" ("scribes and Pharisees").[19] Therefore, some authors have recently regarded Palestine as the place of origin.[20] This implies the thesis that Matthew and his addressees are to be understood as a deviant group within Jewish society in the land of Israel.

A detailed investigation has recently been offered by Overman. He localizes the Matthean community in Galilee (Tiberias or Sepphoris)[21] and interprets it as a Jewish sect in conflict with the newly reshaped Judaism after 70. Overman assumes an institutionalized independence of the community, for Matthew uses the term *ekklēsia* as a designation of his own group in distinction to "their" synagogues, that is, the places of assembly of the new Judaism. Likewise, Overman assumes special disciplinary capabilities within the community.[22] In this sense, we can speak here of an institutional and organizational separation between the synagogues and the communities that Matthew has in mind. Yet the Matthean community claimed the same tradition, the same authority, and in part even the same "roles" as the new Judaism.[23] Thus the organization of the Christ-believing group seems to have been developed in contrast to Jewish institutions but also in clear dependence on them. For Overman the Matthean community is a minority group that is in sharp conflict with formative Judaism as its parent group. The sectarian language of the Gospel also points to the character of this community as that of a Jewish sect.[24] Like the Matthean sect, however, its parent group, formative Judaism, was also only a minority in Galilee within a territory dominated by Roman sovereignty. Nevertheless, Overman assumes that Pharisaically dominated Judaism had a certain official authority (de facto and de jure). Thus if the Matthean community remains in principle sociologically within Judaism, Overman concedes that some key texts signalize a turning of attention to the Gentiles (21:43; 28:19). Overman holds the composition of the community to be "mostly, if not thoroughly, Jewish" but concedes that it turned toward Gentiles and thereby began to withdraw from formative Judaism.[25]

Saldarini also interprets the Matthean community in the context of Judaism with the help of sociological deviance theories.[26] It is true that in addition to its own religious identity, the Matthean community had its own meetings and had various kinds of conflict with other Jewish groups, yet it continued to be a part of the Jewish world.[27] Its behavior in deviance from the Jewish social majority marks it as an "alienative-expressive group."[28] In sociological deviance theory this means that the Matthean community was a group that focused on social change (alienative) and on the needs of its own members (expressive) and deviated from the majority of society. It offered its members a new Christian Jewish world as an alternative to conventional Judaism.[29] In Saldarini's view, the Matthean community can best be understood as a reforming movement within Judaism, which, in reaction to its rejection, became a sect.[30] Only later—even if only a short time later—did this Jewish group, like most others, become socially a "Christian" one, especially because of its rejection by majority Judaism and because of the dominance of non-Jewish believers in Jesus. They lost their Jewish identity and became an independent, separate group.[31] Yet Saldarini expressly states that a separation of Jewish and Christian communities cannot be presupposed until the middle of the second century.[32]

Both of the foregoing interpretations of the Matthean community as a Jewish "sect" or deviant group rightly note the remarkably close correspondence of many texts of the Gospel of Matthew with phenomena of the newly reshaped Judaism after 70. Both scholars, however, cannot fail to perceive already within the Gospel of Matthew itself signs indicating that the process of separation from Judaism has already begun: the Gentiles/nations (*ethnē*) are already in view. Yet precisely here lies the problem: What role do non-Jews play in the Matthean community? And there is probably a good reason why we can recognize at the end of the Gospel something like a separation of the author from Judaism (Matt 28:15: the rumor of the theft of Jesus' body by his disciples "has spread to this day [!] among Jews" [without the article]). Do not Matt 21:43 and the term *ekklēsia*, as it is used in 16:18; 18:17, show such a separation? This discussion of Matthean texts could be easily expanded.[33] A clear verdict on the question of the participation of the Matthean community in Judaism is without doubt especially difficult and is ultimately to be decided by the problem of whether there were already "Gentile Christians" who belonged to it. Here we will venture no final answer, but we think that it is not only conceivable but also most probable that the community that lies behind the Gospel of Matthew was a part of the messianic Judaism of Israel after 70. The "Gentile Christian" perspective may indicate the actual situation, a "turning point"[34] in history, or a new orientation of the community. This hypothesis forms the foundation of the following evaluation of the

Gospel of Matthew for relations between Christ-believing or messianic Jews and the majority of the Jewish population in Israel.

THE GOSPEL OF JOHN

It is often assumed—not least of all on the basis of early church traditions— that the Gospel of John came into being in Ephesus or Asia Minor, although a Palestinian origin is assumed for the author.[35] Yet this localization presupposes hypotheses and speculations about the identity of the author that are not without problem. It is noteworthy, in any case, that the oldest manuscript evidence of the Gospel comes from Egypt, and the Asia Minor tradition begins substantially later. Therefore, we cannot avoid looking at internal evidence and indications.

Many things support an origin in a Jewish milieu. Recently, moreover, good reasons have been advanced for the provenance of the Gospel of John from the milieu of messianic Judaism in Israel—for example, from Galilee,[36] Judea,[37] or Trachonitis/Batanea.[38] This suggests that the many conflict stories in the Gospel must be understood on the basis of internal Jewish conflict.[39] The so-called *aposynagōgos* passages in the Gospel of John, which reflect the exclusion of confessors of Christ from the synagogue (John 9:22; 12:42; 16:2), probably also point to internal Jewish conflict. We will go into this below. Sanders gives a good overview of other texts of the Fourth Gospel that support such an internal Jewish conflict.[40] He refers first to the tensions perceivable in the Gospel between the followers of Jesus and those of John the Baptist (3:25-26; 4:1-3; 5:31-36; 10:40-42).[41] The various reactions of the Jewish population to Jesus can also be understood as a reflection of the Johannine community's own experiences (7:10ff., 40-44). The Gospel even says that because of Jesus there was a division (*schisma*) in the (Jewish) people (7:43; cf. 10:19). In the discussion on the meaning of Jesus (is he "good" or does he deceive the people: 7:12; is he a prophet or the Messiah: 7:40ff.), Sanders correctly sees a reference to experiences at the time of the writing of the Gospel itself.[42] Especially supportive of this view is verse 7:13: "Yet no one would speak openly about him [Jesus] for fear of the Jews." The motif of the fear of "the" Jews is also found in 9:22; 12:42; 19:38; and 20:19.

The best explanation here is the situation of messianic Jews within a Jewish majority. This is also true of the texts that allege a secret sympathy for Jesus among the leading circles of Judaism (12:42; 19:38; cf. also Nicodemus in 3:1ff.).[43] Furthermore, it is clear that the Gospel of John distinguishes Jesus especially from the sign prophets and from the social bandits and royal pretenders in the land of Israel, and that it characterizes the authorities of the people as false shepherds.[44] Finally, we must also mention that in the Third Letter of John there is an express delineation vis-à-vis nonbelievers (3 John 7).

The foregoing argumentation is not necessarily negated by the fact that the Gospel of John basically reduces the manifold groups of Judaism to "the" Jews, which it, moreover, identifies with the Pharisees.[45] On the contrary, the lack of a division of Jews into various groups and the identification of Judaism with the Pharisees can even be explained better in the time after 70 than in the time of Jesus. And the consciousness of distance that is expressed in the wholesale talk about "the" Jews does not necessarily presuppose a "Gentile Christian" self-understanding, as the Gospel of Matthew shows. This may mean followers of the Jewish majority, who stand over against the Johannine community. The sharp anti-Jewish polemic found especially in the Gospel of John (cf. only 8:31ff.) is best explained as a phenomenon of proximity, that is, of a close relationship to Judaism. These passages obviously deal with conflicts. In the case of John 6:66ff.; 8:31ff., moreover, it may be assumed that it is a question of a reaction of Jews who have fallen away from the Christ-believing confession.[46] In our view, something similar is presupposed by the Johannine letters (cf., for example, 1 John 2:18ff.).[47] Nevertheless, this wholesale talk of "the" Jews is noteworthy, if we presuppose an intra-Jewish situation for the Gospel of John. Likewise, it is notable that no other scripture of the New Testament goes so far in its Christology that, like the Gospel of John, it even predicates Jesus as "God" (John 20:28: "My Lord and my God"; cf. the conflict on this issue in 10:31ff.).

These and other possible objections will not be further explored here. In our opinion they do not suffice to fundamentally call into question the thesis of the origin of the Gospel of John in the milieu of messianic Judaism. Thus we presuppose here that the Johannine community was primarily "Jewish Christian" in nature and is presumably to be sought in the land of Israel. Naturally, we are aware that this can be only a hypothesis.

8.2 The Social Composition of the Messianic Communities

The Matthean Community

In the process of profiling the social structure of the Matthean community, a comparison with Mark is instructive.[48] The result can best be understood by applying our social model (see section 3.3 above):

URBAN MILIEU

The locus of the Matthean community is obviously to be sought in an urban milieu. For it is noteworthy that in the Gospel of Matthew the number of occurrences of *polis* ("city") is considerably greater than in the Gospel of Mark (27 versus 8). Also there is, on the whole, more mention of commerce.[49] Especially notable are the images of children playing in the marketplace (Matt

11:16) and of the vineyard owner who hires day laborers in the marketplace (20:3). An urban milieu is also presupposed by the parable of the wedding banquet, as shown especially by 22:5: one goes away to his farm, another to his business (*emporia*).[50] This milieu is also indicated by a greater differentiation of the retainer group, as well as by the increased references to slaves. In all this, however, we must note that in the Gospel of Matthew the urban situation remains closely connected with the agrarian hinterland. This suggests a small town rather than a metropolis.

UPPER STRATUM

More frequently mentioned than in Mark are members of the lay aristocracy ("elders"), as well as Sadducees, Pharisees, and scribes. These are presented as a critical opposition to the followers of Jesus.[51] Joseph of Arimathea, who is a member of the council in Mark, becomes a rich man in Matthew (27:57).

THE RICH

Joseph of Arimathea also becomes a "disciple of Jesus" (27:57).[52] In the positive image of a rich vineyard owner, the kingdom of heaven is metaphorically transformed (20:1ff.). The Gospel of Matthew basically does not go beyond the critique of the rich adopted from Mark: Matt 13:22; 19:23-24—the rich man has become a rich "young man" (19:22). This is again noteworthy in contrast to the Gospel of Luke and the Letter of James. Indeed, a certain differentiation of the criticism of the rich can be seen in Matt 19:23. While the Markan original (10:23) speaks of how hard it will be for those who have wealth to enter the kingdom of God, Matthew speaks here explicitly of the rich (*plousioi*). In this connection, Matthew's interpretation of the beatitude is also striking: "Blessed are the poor in spirit" (5:3). Naturally, this is not to be understood as a spiritualization of poverty. The addendum "in spirit" is an abbreviated mode of expression for the promise-filled context of this beatitude (cf. Isa 61:1ff.; Matt 11:5).[53] Nevertheless, the difference in the beatitudes between Matthew and Luke, who clearly formulates in a more concrete manner, cannot be overlooked. Apparently Matthew has in mind above all the experience of negative measures of discrimination and disadvantaging, which the disciples of Jesus suffered because of their confession, in spite of their piety and faithfulness to the Torah. This recalls the concept of poverty in Qumran (cf. pp. 160ff.).

RETAINERS

Compared to Mark a larger number of people from the group of retainers of the upper stratum are also mentioned. These include tax collectors,[54] military personnel in general,[55] Roman officers of lower rank (*centurio*),[56] and the high priest's guard.[57]

Noteworthy is the considerable increase in the mention of slaves.[58] Also striking is the mention of prostitutes (Matt 21:31-32).[59]

The Johannine Community

The Gospel of John reveals little concrete information about the social composition of its circle of addressees. Nonetheless, certain indications—such as the basic distinction between sympathizers and followers of Jesus—allow some cautious statements.

SYMPATHIZERS IN THE UPPER STRATUM

The local upper stratum was the source of the sympathizers of Jesus, for example, Nicodemus, a Pharisee and "leader" (*archōn*) of the Jews, that is, a member of the council (John 3:1; 7:50-51; 19:39). A secret disciple (*mathētēs*) of Jesus is Joseph of Arimathea, whose social position is not more precisely characterized (19:38), yet he must have also belonged to the circle of sympathizers from the upper stratum (he is named in the same breath with Nicodemus and had access to the Roman prefect Pilate). John 12:42 presupposes other secret sympathizers of Jesus among the "authorities" (*archontes*). Likewise, we may presuppose for the favorite disciple a social position that is clearly higher than that of the other disciples, since he was "known" to the high priest (18:15). Interestingly, the favorite disciple is also not mentioned among the fishing disciples in John 21 and does not appear until later. For him a different fate is prophesied than for Peter (whose martyrdom is presumably foretold in 21:18). Jesus also transfers to the favorite disciple the social responsibility for his mother (19:26-27). With all the symbolic significance of this scene and the possibility that the figure of the favorite disciple is a literary fiction, the indications of his social background in contrast to that of Peter also throw a light on the Johannine community. Nowhere does John use terms for wealth. The antithesis of rich and poor is not a topic of Jesus' proclamation in the Fourth Gospel.

RETAINERS

It is expressly reported that a royal official (*basilikos*) and his whole household came to faith in Jesus (4:46-53).

LOWER STRATUM

The social background of the circle of disciples (except the favorite disciple) seems initially to remain largely in the dark. One indication comes from the denial scene in which Peter is at home in the circle of the high priest's servants (18:15-17). At the close of the Gospel (21:2-3) we learn that Peter, Thomas, and other disciples are fishing on the Lake of Gennesaret. Nonetheless, on the whole the disciples of Jesus are not presented in a situation of poverty. Judas administers their money (12:6), with which they can, for example, pay for the festival preparations; indeed, from this "common purse" the destitute (*ptōchoi*) are aided (12:5; 13:29). Incidentally, only in connection with the anointing of Jesus in Bethany and the common purse administered by Judas do we find the term for the absolutely poor in the Gospel of John (12:5-6, 8; 13:29); hunger and thirst are used in the figurative sense (4:13-15; 6:35; 7:37). The healings of the lame man at the pool of Bethzatha (5:1ff.) and the man born blind (9:8), who is characterized as a beggar (*prosaitēs*), are noteworthy because of their high symbolic meaning. Their social position as beggars is presupposed or expressly mentioned, but it plays no role in terms of the composition of the circle of disciples. Mary, Martha, and Lazarus convey the impression of having a somewhat prosperous social situation (12:1ff.).[60]

SUMMARY OF THE SOCIAL STRATIFICATION
OF MESSIANIC COMMUNITIES IN ISRAEL AFTER 70 C.E.

When compared with Mark, a number of differences are evident in Matthew. Small differences in the status of the rich cannot be overlooked. While on the whole a critical if not negative attitude is maintained in regard to the rich, it is still interesting that Matthew can present them positively in parables on the kingdom of God. Joseph of Arimathea becomes a rich disciple of Jesus; wealth in itself does not seem to exclude one from the kingdom of God. Thus it is quite probable that rich or at least prosperous people belonged to the Matthean community. Since in the Gospel of Matthew, in contrast to Mark, Joseph of Arimathea is designated as rich but *not* as "a respected member of the council" (Mark 15:43), one would not look for rich or prosperous believers of the Matthean community in decurional or comparable judicial circles. These, like other members of the *ordines* or judicial upper stratum, are missing in Matthew. The Matthean community seems, however, to have gained members from the retainer group. But it is noteworthy here that the tax collector Levi, named as an example, belongs to despised circles. The Matthean community also seems to have recruited predominantly from the urban lower stratum, including, notably, slaves and prostitutes.

In view of the meager indications of social realities in the Fourth Gospel, the characterization of the followers of Jesus is noteworthy. The extremely hazy social portrait of (most) disciples marks them as members of the lower strata, yet they are obviously not destitute and even have some money at their disposal. From this we may conclude that even in the Johannine community there was a predominance of members from the circles of the lower stratum, who lived at least above the level of minimum existence. The favorite disciple, however, seems to stand out above this social milieu. Moreover, in the local upper stratum there are secret followers of Jesus, which could indicate (secret) sympathies for the Christ-believing community in such circles. In spite of John 12:8 ("You always have the poor with you"), the groups of poor living below the minimum existence hardly come into consideration as members of the Johannine community. Even from the viewpoint of the relatively poor disciples, they are seen as recipients of alms but not as members of Jesus' circle of disciples. This hypothesis is supported by the lack of interest of the Fourth Gospel in the social antithesis between poor and rich, which reflects the problem of a latent conflict between lower-stratum members from subdecurional circles, who confess openly to the Christ-believing fellowship, and secret sympathizers in the urban upper stratum.

8.3 Conflicts between Messianic Communities and the Remnant of Judaism in the Land of Israel after 70 C.E.: Basic Considerations

8.3.1 Conflicts Recognizable in the Sources

In this context we will at least suggest what will be discussed later in more detail on pages 338ff. The conflicts between the messianic communities and the rest of Judaism are one aspect of their overall relations, which we believe were on the whole harmonious. The conflicts can be divided into those that took place on the symbolic level (discussions of various religious topics) and those that we call social interactions. With the latter it is to a certain extent a question of the social consequences of religious differences. We also distinguish here socio-geographically between social conflicts in the land of Israel and those in the Diaspora, as well as historically between those in the periods before and after 70 C.E. In this section we deal with conflicts between messianic communities and the rest of Judaism in the land of Israel in the period after 70.

THE SOURCE SITUATION

From Justin's remark that Bar Kokhba threatened messianic Jews with severe punishment if they did not deny Jesus as the Christ, we may conclude that (at least) into this period (132–135 C.E.) there must have been messianic Jews in Israel.[61] This is also indicated by Talmudic traditions, which presuppose contacts with messianic Jews (presumably in Galilee) at the beginning of the second century. Also belonging here is the twelfth of the Eighteen Benedictions, the so-called *birkat ha-minim,* in which heretics are cursed. Of the New Testament scriptures, the Gospels of Matthew and John are included.

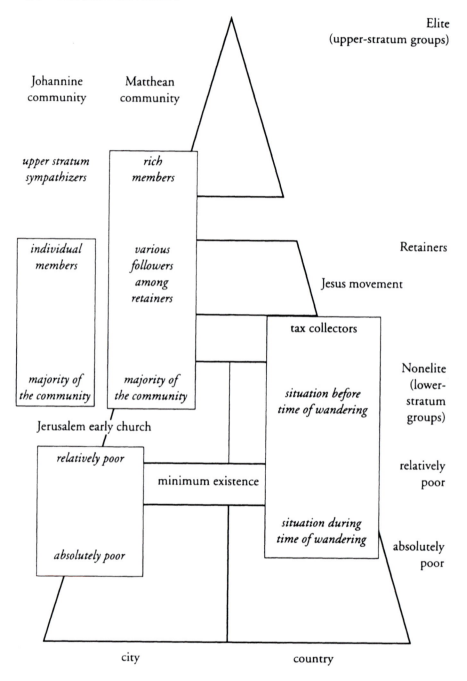

Elite
(upper-stratum groups)

Johannine
community

Matthean
community

*upper stratum
sympathizers*

*rich
members*

*individual
members*

*various
followers
among
retainers*

Retainers

Jesus movement

tax collectors

Nonelite
(lower-
stratum
groups)

*majority of
the community*

*majority of
the community*

*situation before
time of wandering*

relatively
poor

Jerusalem early church

relatively poor

minimum existence

absolutely poor

*situation during
time of wandering*

absolutely
poor

city

country

SOCIAL PYRAMID 4:
OVERVIEW OF THE SOCIAL STRATIFICATION OF THE FOLLOWERS
OF JESUS IN THE LAND OF ISRAEL

The Lukan double volume (Luke-Acts) also contains a variety of statements about the experiences of messianic Jews in Israel, that is, in Jerusalem: in Luke 21:12 Jesus predicts such negative experiences to his disciples. Luke then reports their realization in Acts 4:3; 5:18; 6:8-8:1; 8:2ff.; 9:1ff.; 12:1; 21:27ff.; 22:4-5; 26:9-11. They clearly refer to the period before the first great war and in our view contain no usable information about corresponding Jewish-"Christian" conflicts in Israel *after* 70. Thus they will not be used here. A special problem is presented by possible negative experiences of Christ-confessors in connection with the confusion of the first Jewish-Roman war, which are found above all in the Gospel of Mark (see pp. 235–36).

JEWISH TRADITIONS

In the rabbinic literature (*t. Hul.* 2.20–24)[62] there are a few indications of prohibitions of contact that refer to heretics and also to messianic Jews. One story about Rabbi Eleasar ben Dama reports that he was forbidden to let himself be healed by a certain Jaaqob of Kephar-Sama, apparently a Jew who believed in Christ. The story takes place around 130 C.E. Another story reports that Rabbi Elieser (around 90 C.E.) met a Messiah-confessing Jew named Yaaqob Kephar-Siknin on the street and took pleasure in a heretical saying from him. Both stories presuppose a certain prohibition of contact with messianic Jews, which, however, was temporarily violated here. Yet they describe extraordinary events of outstanding personalities and for this reason provide little indication of everyday experiences. The texts also reveal that the prohibitions of contact with "heretics" were more stringent than those regarding non-Jews. This is confirmed by another text from the Tosephta (*Shabb.* 13.5),[63] which states that interaction with pagans was less offensive than that with heretics. Here Rabbi Tarphon says (ca. 100) that in a situation of persecution he himself would seek refuge even in a temple to idols but by no means in the house of a heretic: "For the idolaters do not know him [God] and deny him, but the [heretics] know him and deny him." A little later in the same treatise Rabbi Yishmael even uses scriptural quotations to justify hate against the heretics. In the story of Rabbi Tarphon we unmistakably have a fictitious, extremely exaggerated situation. Nevertheless, the two comparable texts demonstrate that the attitude toward heretics was more intolerant than toward pagans. It was held that to the pagans' credit, they do not know the true God, whereas the heretics know and deny him. Conversely, we also find a similar intolerance vis-à-vis Judaism in New Testament scriptures. Here, for example, the rejection of Jesus is connected with the rejection of God: "Whoever hates me hates my Father also" (John 15:23); "No one who denies the Son has the Father" (1 John 2:23; cf. Luke 10:16). Sociologically, this intolerance—which even goes to the point of demonizing the Jews (John 8:44)—

can be explained on the basis of a principle from conflict theory: the closer the relationship, the more intense the conflict.

Birkat ha-minim

In connection with the school in Jamnia the formulation of the so-called *birkat ha-minim* ("heretic benediction") was widely discussed. It concerns the twelfth of the Eighteen Benedictions (*Shemoneh Esreh/Amidah*), in which heretics (*minim*) are cursed.

In the recension of the more usual Babylonian Talmud, it reads:[64]

> To blasphemers, however, may there be no hope, and may all who act wickedly instantly be destroyed; may they all soon be eradicated. Uproot the insolent, and smash, topple, and humiliate them soon in our time. Praised are you, Lord, who smash the enemy and humiliate the insolent.

In the Palestinian recension it reads:

> To blasphemers, however, may there be no hope, and may you soon abolish the wicked government in our time, and may [the *Nozrim* (Nazarenes) and] the *minim* [heretics] be instantly destroyed, removed from the book of life, and not written up with the righteous. Praised are you, Lord, who humiliate the insolent.

According to a widespread view in Christian exegesis, the cursing of heretics was formulated under Gamaliel II in the nineties in Jamnia and expressly related to Christ-confessing Jews. Evidence of it is supposedly also seen, for example, in Luke 6:22-23 and above all in John 9:22; 12:42; and 16:2. The new formulation of the *birkat ha-minim* under Gamaliel II is recorded in the Talmud (*b. Ber.* 28a). Yet it is also possible that this story is legendary and goes back to a long process that ultimately culminated in the *birkat ha-minim* and only subsequently was traced back to a single event.[65] Moreover, it is questionable whether the formulation of this benediction was already fixed in its wording before 135 C.E.[66] This is true, for example, of the express mention of the Christ-confessing Jews as *Nozrim* (Nazarenes). The insertion of the *Nozrim* is to be set with greatest probability in the period between 135 and 150 C.E.[67] Presumably only heretics (*minim*) in general were mentioned previously, which, to be sure, could also include Christ-confessing Jews.[68] Actually,

> nothing suggests that it was a question of Christians in the strict sense of the word. A close examination of the individual versions shows that in the *birkat ha-minim* two groups were initially addressed: first, Jewish heretics of varying provenance and orientation and, second, the Roman authorities. It goes without saying that Christians could also be included later among the heretics (they were without doubt originally understood as a Jewish sect), yet this is indeed a

later development that cannot be simply transferred to the introduction of the *birkat ha-minim.*[69]

Even if Christ-confessing Jews were included in the twelfth benediction in the Palestinian version even before the end of the first century, we must note that it could have had only a limited function, namely, to prevent heretics (possibly also Christ-confessing Jews) from functioning as liturgists in the synagogue.[70] In this connection Colpe[71] writes that Christ-confessing Jews "who wanted to sing in the synagogal worship service had to be afraid that in the recitation of the Eighteen Benedictions they might draw the 'benediction against the heretics' upon themselves; for this reason not only they but also community members without liturgical function no longer took part in the Jewish worship service." And Schiffman has emphatically called attention to the fact that while the benediction against the *minim* excluded Christ-confessing Jews from active participation in synagogal worship, its purpose was by no means to drive them out of Judaism. He writes that heresy, however great, was never able to cut off the band of heretics from Judaism. This is also opposed by the halakic criteria regarding Jewish identity.[72] Thus Schiffman notes that it is a question here of a *worship service prayer* and by no means of an instrument of discipline. Its potential effect on believers in Christ presupposed first that they attended the synagogal service *and* had drawn upon themselves the cursing of the *minim;* that is, that they could not join in the praying of the twelfth benediction of the *Amidah* and as the most extreme consequence of this had decided to forgo attending synagogal worship. In Schiffman's view, therefore, it is a question here of something like a negative act of confession. With the presuppositions he mentions, the *birkat ha-minim* could have led at most to the self-exclusion of Christ-confessors from synagogal worship. On this basis, we can exclude on principle the idea that the named New Testament texts refer back to the *birkat ha-minim.* For they presuppose an action on the part of Judaism.

NEW TESTAMENT TRADITIONS

The Confusions of War as Exceptional Circumstances (Gospel of Mark)

In connection with the Jewish-Roman war, there were presumably delations and killings of Christ-confessing Jews (Mark 13:9). Mark indicates that confessors of Jesus were delivered to the Sanhedrin (local Jewish court), beaten in synagogues, and led before governors and kings. We have here a summary in which various experiences are collected: delivery to local Jewish courts, bodily punishment in synagogues, and judicial experiences before kings and (Roman) high officials. "Here Mark is probably summarizing what may have happened to Jewish Christians in the motherland and in Hellenistic cities or the Syrian border regions."[73] The Markan "apocalypse" (Mark 13) suggests that these events are to be found in the environment of the Jewish-Roman war and its effects. Believers in Christ were probably

> doubly affected by the general atmosphere of hate. Caught up in the hatred against Judaism, they cannot, however, count on solidarity with non-Christian Jews, but rather are in many ways in conflict with them. The Jewish synagogal fellowships reject their confession (8:38; 13:9, 11) and their religious practice (cf. 2:6-7; 2:15-16; 2:18; 2:24; 7:2-3). For non-Jewish fellow citizens and Roman authorities, however, they are suspect because they confess their faith in one who was crucified by the Romans as a messianic insurrectionist. Hence they must defend themselves against the suspicion of supporting the Zealot rebellion against Rome (cf. 12:13-17; 15:2-15; 11:17-18).[74]

Justin indicates a similar experience in the context of the Bar Kokhba rebellion (135 c.e.).[75] If we draw on Justin for comparison, however, we find that here it is a question of special experiences limited to the exceptional situation of war. To a certain extent they concern one episode of our epoch and are by no means typical of relations between Christ-confessing Jews and the Jewish majority population.

THE MATTHEAN COMMUNITY

In the Gospel of Matthew we find the following signs of conflict: verbal abuse, floggings in synagogues, deliverance to the Sanhedrin or local courts, persecution or expulsion, and killings. In particular cases it is difficult to decide which statements refer to current events and which to experiences that, from the evangelist's point of view, lie in the past. Yet in our opinion, this is not important for the overall picture.

1. Verbal exclusion (Matt 5:11-12)

In the context of the Sermon on the Mount, the Matthean Jesus blesses his disciples because they are "reviled" and people utter "all kinds of evil" against them (5:11-12). The term *revile* (*oneidizein*) refers to a direct denigration without the involvement of a third party and without specific accusations,[76] whereas the phrase "all kinds of evil against you falsely" presumably means specific reproaches that are made in some kind of public place.[77] Yet this is not necessarily meant judicially; that is, it does not have to mean false witness before a court.[78] On the whole, these negative experiences point to a process of exclusion of members of the Christ-confessing group from the Jewish majority population. The fact that it is mentioned in the same breath with persecution shows that the religious deviance of the messianic groups was the crucial reason for the verbal denigration. The perpetrators of the revilings are not especially characterized. *Thus we can hardly speak of official synagogal acts.*

Rather, it is a question here of a form of "social ostracism" (Hare), that is, the social exclusion of Christ-confessing Jews in everyday life.

2. Floggings in synagogues, deliverance, persecution, and expulsion (Matt. 5:10-12, 44; 10:17, 23; 13:21; 23:34)

Matthew characterizes negative experiences from the Jewish side above all as "persecution."[79] The measures referred to here apparently affected "missionaries"[80] and included their being driven from city to city (10:23; 23:34) and the application of the synagogal punishment of flogging (10:17; 23:34). In each context the mention of being driven from city to city presupposes experiences in Israel. In addition to synagogal flogging, 10:17 mentions deliverance to the local Sanhedrin. Here too it is obviously a question of experiences in the Jewish land.

3. Killings (Matt. 22:6; 23:34)

The general assertion of the killing of the one sent by God (23:34, 37) is hard to evaluate.[81] It is without doubt a generalization and thus also an exaggeration of the rejection of prophets (cf. 1 Thess 2:15). This is especially true where the crucifixion is also mentioned and the fate of Jesus is perhaps also included. In any case, it is extremely problematic to infer from these generalized and wholesale statements anything about the historical experience of the Matthean community.

THE JOHANNINE COMMUNITY

The Gospel of John mentions three negative experiences: exclusion from the synagogue, persecution, and even the killing of confessors to Jesus.

1. Synagogue exclusions (John 9:22; 12:42; 16:2)

John mentions three times the exclusion of confessors of Christ from the synagogue. Here we will quote only 9:22: "His parents said this because they were afraid of the Jews; for the Jews had already agreed that anyone who confessed Jesus to be the Messiah would be put out of the synagogue [aposynagōgos genētai]." The formulation presupposes that an apparently contemporary experience of the addressees of the Gospel of John could have already been made in the time of Jesus, and thus it emphasizes the present.[82] According to John 12:42 many archontes ("authorities") did not confess their faith in Jesus "because of the Pharisees," in order not to be excluded from the synagogue. Finally, in 16:2 it is predicted to Jesus' disciples that they will be excluded from the synagogues. These verses are related either to the synagogal practice of banishment or to the mentioned birkat ha-minim. Both solutions are unconvincing. Banishment concerned a temporary disciplining of synagogue members.[83] A reference of the Johannine verses to the *birkat ha-minim* as a "branding of Jewish Christians as heretics by the developing and prevailing Pharisaic orthodoxy"[84] is, in our opinion, hardly plausible because the *aposynagōgos* texts must involve an active process of exclusion. The *birkat ha-minim*, however, refers to the situation of prayer, especially the prayer of the liturgist, and thus can really mean only an act of self-exclusion or the avoidance of participation in worship. Hence the Johannine statements about exclusion from the synagogue and the *birkat ha-minim* do not mean the same process,[85] quite apart from the problem of whether at the time of the Gospel of John the twelfth benediction already had a clear reference to Christ-confessing Jews as heretics.

M. Smith and Overman offer a compromise solution according to which the Johannine verses reflect an experience that was then later reduced to a concept in the *birkat ha-minim*.[86] This solution avoids the problem that the *birkat ha-minim* is to be dated historically later than the composition of the Gospel of John, and it becomes feasible to posit an experience that resulted in the heretic benediction yet does not have to be interpreted on that basis. That means, in our view, that experiences like that described in John 9:22 preceded the *birkat ha-minim*, which, as a part of the prayers of the worship service, cannot have had a disciplinary function. Nevertheless, it can fulfill its function if the heretics for whom it is intended—possibly also Christ-confessing Jews—are already no longer present in the worship service; thus in the prayer the *birkat ha-minim* assumes an already accomplished separation from heretics. Justin, it seems, also presupposes that the cursing of Christ-believers in the synagogues no longer assumes their presence there.

Which experience, then, is the topic of Johannine texts? It is interesting linguistically that the Greek formulation *aposynagōgon poiein* ("put out of the synagogue") is attested only here, but not in other New Testament scriptures or in writings outside the New Testament. A new linguistic coinage points to a new experience. And since it is hardly possible to relate the *aposynagōgos* statements to a typical synagogal disciplinary situation, we must also posit for this reason an atypical experience: an exclusion from the synagogue that was unforeseen in the context of disciplinary possibilities.

In this context we must clarify which people were affected by exclusion from the synagogue. In the texts they are Jews who confess Jesus as Messiah; namely, *archontes*, disciples, and the parents of the man born blind. Yet since the world of the texts refers to the world of the author and his addressees, this suggests Christ-confessing Jews. And since it is presupposed that they attend synagogal worship, they are presumably people who are on the fringe between the synagogues and the messianic communities. Then the named texts would address a situation in which Jews (who believed in Jesus as the Messiah and belonged to Christ-confessing communities) were forbidden to visit the synagogues or participate in synagogal worship. This excluded the possibility of something like dual membership. Also supporting this is John 12:42, which mentions especially the *archontes* who had come to faith in Jesus yet did not "confess" that faith, so that they would not be excluded from the synagogue (they may also be compared with Nicodemus, who comes to Jesus at night: 3:1).[87] It is noteworthy that the terms *homologeō* and *arneomai,* which mean the public—not necessarily judicial—confession or position on a matter, person, or accusation, are generally found in this context (cf. 9:22; 12:42; 1 John 2:23; 4:2-3, 15; 2 John 7 or 1 John 2:22-23; cf. John 13:38; 18:25, 27). Even if one cannot be convinced by this hypothesis, it is clear that it was initially only a question of the exclusion of Christ-confessors from the synagogal worship service. That this could also involve social consequences is, naturally, to be expected.

2. Persecution (John 5:16; 15:20)

In the Gospel of John negative measures against Jesus and against the disciples are attested in two places with the word *persecute* (*diōkein*), which clearly emphasizes the religious character of the persecution. Moreover, 5:16 clearly shows that the violation of a commandment of the Torah (healing on the sabbath) is the reason for the "persecution" of Jesus. Here persecution is clearly related to religious deviance. In the context of 15:20 it becomes clear that the disciples are persecuted because of the "name" of Jesus. Their persecutors are reproached, furthermore, with the statement that those who hate Jesus also hate the Father (15:23). Hence this could only mean that these are hardly pagan but rather Jewish opponents of Christ-confessing Jews.

3. Killing (John 16:2)

Here the Johannine Jesus predicts to the disciples something that goes even beyond exclusion from the synagogue, namely, killing: "Indeed, an hour is coming when those who kill you will think that by doing so they are presenting an offering [*latreia*][88] to God." The "theological" motivation of this strange verse can be understood against the background of the *Midrash Rabbah* on Numbers (§21).[89] It is questionable whether it corresponds at all to any historical reality.[90] For if one takes seriously the "theological" substantiation of the prediction as the motive of Jewish agents, it can hardly be a question of legal measures of Jewish authorities,[91] in any case, not in the period after 70.[92] If, however, we have here an allusion to vigilante justice,[93] such events would ultimately be possible only with the tolerance of the authorities and thus only with a specific localization of these events.[94] In any case, the idea is worth venturing that John 16:2 was written in view of a feared consequence of the confession of Christ, which for Christ-confessing contemporaries was subjectively not really exclusive.[95]

8.3.2 Conclusions and Sociological Interpretations

The results of our source analyses will first be briefly summarized. Then we will give a sociological interpretation of the conflicts.

RELATIVELY HARMONIOUS EVERYDAY RELATIONS

In regard to the everyday relations between messianic or Christ-confessing Jews and Judaism in the land of Israel we know almost nothing. This deficit, however, allows the assumption that there is absolutely no reason to posit a comprehensive and persistent conflict between these two groups. Even the few Jewish traditions that give an impression of the conflict let us read between the lines a relatively normal everyday relationship. This is made clear by the two texts that presumably refer to experiences in Galilee at the beginning of the second century. The tractate eq *Hullin* in the Tosephta tells how a certain Jacob wanted to heal Rabbi Eleasar, who was bitten by a snake, and to do it in the name of "Jesus" (Yeshua ben Pantera, one of the rabbinic names for Jesus). Nonetheless, another rabbi, Yishmael, did not allow it, although the sick rabbi apparently had confidence in the healing art of the Jesus-confessing Jacob (2.22-23). A little later the same tractate recounts that while on the road Rabbi Elieser met a Jesus-confessing Jew whose (heretical) view he found agreeable (2.24). The two stories show that there were certain restrictions on contact between messianic Jews and other Jews, yet such contacts were without doubt not completely thwarted. And we must also note that prominent rabbis played a role in these stories. What was the situation of the common folk?[96] On the basis of archaeological testimony from Israel, Meyers even comes to the conclusion that in contrast to the impression conveyed to us by the New Testament, Christ-confessing Jews and the Jewish majority in Israel/Palestine lived side by side harmoniously into the seventh century.[97] Even if one places relatively little value on these archaeological testimonies and assumes that our literary sources, which presuppose especially tension-filled Jewish-"Christian" relations, convey a better impression, one cannot, in any case, simply dismiss the assumption that everyday contacts between Christ-confessing Jews and Jews were relatively harmonious.

DISAGREEMENTS AMONG THE JEWS

In the conflicts recognizable in our texts, it is also a question sociologically of disagreements among Jews. In them, accordingly, disciplinary measures of the synagogues play an important role. The negative experiences with the Jewish majority population are also described with the word *persecution* and thus claim for the subjective realm of experience of Christ-confessing Jews a tradition of the rejection of deviant religious convictions. If we set aside statements about killings and the events in connection with the First Jewish Revolt (which, incidentally, could also explain the killing incidents) which are difficult to assess, we are basically left with two negative experiences in the relations of Christ-confessing Jews with the Jewish majority population in Israel after 70. The first is the religious or social exclusion of messianic groups from the Jewish majority population, which culminated in the exclusion from the synagogues and ultimately resulted in the twelfth of the Eighteen Benedictions. Second, Christ-confessing propagandists in the synagogues were punished and in some cases expelled. Both experiences presuppose that Christ-confessing Jews were perceived by the majority population as a deviant religious group within Judaism. We will look at each experience in more detail.

EXCLUSION

The majority population excluded Christ-confessing Jews through verbal abuse (presumably of their deviant religious convictions). This process was also connected with social exclusion (prohibition of contact). The experience can perhaps be best interpreted as a form of social ostracism against those who thought differently. Yet the extent of these exclusions can no longer be determined with precision. The mentioned rabbinic texts lead us to assume that we cannot speak of massive pressure. The culmination of the religious and social exclusion of the Christ-confessors was expulsion from the synagogues, as reflected in the Gospel of John. Without doubt, this expulsion represents an intensification of exclusionary measures and produced secret sympathizers of the messianic groups. In its wake social separation may have also intensified.[98] Certainly noteworthy in regard to exclusion from the synagogues is the fact that it presupposes activities of the synagogues and thus brings an official quality into the disagreement with Christ-confessing Jews. This is also true of the *birkat ha-minim*, which presupposes religious and social exclusion as well as expulsion from the synagogues. It is itself not a disciplinary instrument but implicitly assumes an already accomplished break between the Christ-confessing Jews and the synagogues. That is, we may presume that the heretic benediction is not a part of the exclusionary measures themselves but rather reflects their result, the completed separation.

THE PUNISHMENT OF CHRIST-CONFESSING "MISSIONARIES"

If the named negative exclusionary measures potentially affected all Christ-confessors in Israel, deliverance to the local Sanhedrin and beatings in the synagogue involved the propagandists and prophets of these groups. For this idea is supported by their being driven from city to city and by the context of the corresponding passages (commissioning speeches). In the context of propaganda in Israel, the experiences of floggings in the synagogues ("forty lashes minus one")[99] and deliverance to the local courts also make sense (Matt 10:17).

Sociological Interpretations

The Sociology of Sects. In reference to and dependence on Troeltsch, the sociology of sects has achieved enormous importance in more recent sociological exegesis, above all in the English-speaking world. Scholars have also turned to modern sociological investigations. Scroggs was probably the first to relate this aspect to early Christianity *as a whole.*[100] And the conflict of early "Christianity" with Judaism has recently been understood on the basis of the definition of early Christian communities as "sectarian movements."[101]

The Church-Sect Distinction (Troeltsch, Wilson, Johnson)

In Troeltsch's church-sect distinction,[102] which goes back to previous scholars (for example, Weber), *church* and *sect* are distinguished as "two sociological types." Here we will mention only a few of the distinguishing traits. The church is a "predominantly conservative, relatively world-affirming, all-ruling, and in principle, therefore, universal organization—that is, it claims to encompass everything." Sects are relatively small groups whose members are closely connected with each other and have renounced "winning the world." They behave "indifferently" toward the state and society. Troeltsch, furthermore, sees a stratum-sociological difference between the two social forms in the sense that the sects relate to the "lower strata" or to strata that take a position against the state and society, whereas the churches encompass all strata and especially incorporate the "ruling strata." Initiation into the church happens through birth, whereas one enters a sect through conscious conversion. The organizational methods are also different. The church is a large, hierarchically organized institution; a sect, by contrast, is a small, largely autonomously organized group.

In the modern sociological determination of the sect, as proposed, for example, by Wilson,[103] very important corrections of Troeltsch have been undertaken. Namely, the basic contrast of church and sect is clearly played down by Wilson, since modern sects normally arise not as schismatic or protest movements within and against the churches; they develop, rather, outside the churches. Similarly—and different from medieval Europe—the protest of modern sects, according to Wilson, is directed not against the church but against secular society and the state.[104] *For Wilson sects—largely in agreement with the everyday usage of this term—are "religious minority move-*

ments. "[105] In his sect typology Wilson has worked out the individual character of the tension of the "sectarian movements" with the world as a "response to the world"[106] and distinguished seven types of sects. For Johnson churches are characterized as religious groups by the fact that they accept their social environment, whereas sects reject the social environment in which they exist.[107]

Does the Sociology of Sects Have Explanatory Relevance?
In his distinction, Troeltsch had in mind the differences between sects and the church *of the high Middle Ages.* Only with extensive corrections can this historical model can be transferred to the problem complex under discussion here. Potentially, only the relations between the Christ-confessing Jews and the majority population in Israel are of interest. Here reforming Judaism after 70 would have to be understood as analogous to the universal or state church. Yet even with all the integrative tendencies and dominance of Pharisaic groups, Judaism after 70 was not an entity comparable to the universal or state church. In the internal Jewish conflicts after 70 that are to be investigated here, the decisive role was no doubt played by the tendency of majority Judaism toward unification, in the course of which, on the one hand, the previous fractionation of Judaism was overcome and, on the other hand, new groups that did not go along with the consensus were excluded. Only in the course of this process were Christ-confessing Jews restricted to their own institutional organization. Thus the conflicts analyzed here—verbal and social exclusion, expulsion from the synagogues, punishment in the synagogues—could be interpreted as elements that gave rise to the establishment of Christ-confessing "sects."

Yet this dynamic process itself gains little clarification through the rather static sociology of sects of Troeltsch. For even the stratum-sociological argument is not applicable. Johnson's sect definition is ultimately even less applicable than that of Troeltsch, since the recognizable intra-Jewish conflicts did not produce a rejection of the social environment (here of the Jewish environment in Israel) by Christ-confessing Jews. According to Wilson's definition, every religious minority movement is ultimately a sect. His observations on the origin of modern sects are less convincing when applied to the intra-Jewish relations that interest us here. Thus on the whole, in our opinion, the sociology of sects offers little assistance in the understanding of Jewish-"Christian" relations after 70. It tells us hardly more than that the messianic groups in the land of Israel are to be understood as religious minority movements. And the center of the intra-Jewish conflicts being analyzed here, which we have circumscribed with the term *exclusion,* can be comprehended better sociologically with the help of deviance theories than with the sociology of sects.

DEVIANCE THEORIES

Saldarini, Malina and Neyrey, and Sanders have made deviance theories fruitful for the understanding of the Jewish-"Christian" conflict.[108] They refer to authors such as H. S. Becker, Erikson, and Ben-Yehuda,[109] who in adoption of Durkheim's analyses of society have written about nonconformists, outsiders, and other deviants in their relationship to and function in society. A detailed presentation of the differentiated sociological theories is offered by Sanders, among others.[110] Here we will sketch only a few important aspects.

What is deviance? Every society has norms and structures of behavior that within a broad range of variation are more or less realized and even transgressed. The boundaries of a society define normal and deviant behavior. A basic insight of H. S. Becker is that deviance is created by the society itself: "*social groups create deviance by making the rules whose infraction constitutes deviance,* and by applying those rules to particular people and labeling them as outsiders."[111] The characterization of certain persons as outsiders or deviants is thus not explained by a static definition of the contents and aspects of deviant behavior. Rather, deviant behavior is defined in each case by the majority society.

Becker analyzes a "deviance career," in which the starting point is a deviant act that can be followed by a public labeling as an outsider and, further, an isolation from conventional society, so that deviants finally organize in their own deviance groups. The group formation of the deviants is, conversely, part of their "neutralization" of the exclusion. For the group members have their deviance in common, share a common fate, and thus to a certain extent are in the same boat. In this way a deviant subculture gradually arises. The development of deviant groups ultimately serves to strengthen deviant identity. In the dynamic process of the "deviance career" labeling as deviants can be transferred back to the majority society or to those who force or carry out the public recognition of deviants as deviants. The reasons that certain persons or institutions publicly brand others as deviants lies, for Becker, not mainly in an appeal to certain values. Deviance arises, rather, in a process of interaction between people in which some of them, serving their own interests, set up certain rules that declare others to be deviants. Conversely, others (the deviants) transgress these rules in pursuit of their own interests. Such rules, which give form to certain values, are established in "problematic situations" in which certain areas are classified as "critical" and demand action.[112]

In his theory Erikson emphasizes more than Becker that it is not the motives of those who set up certain rules against deviants that are of crucial importance but rather the specific crisis situations. In his view deviance is a constant element of societies that is not regulated in every case by specific measures. The interest in controlling deviance arises from circumstances that stimulate change in a society (whether on account of internal or external factors). Thus the imposition of the norms of the majority society on deviants is favored by social crises. Deviance control is therefore a form of boundary preservation or boundary drawing in crisis situations. A society gives itself renewed assurance of its identity through the exclusion of others or the intensification of its boundaries.

Ben-Yehuda has extended this idea by noting that deviance is connected in the most intimate way with the identity of a society. It shows where a society draws its boundaries and indicates fundamental structures and values in its social and symbolic system.[113] It should be noted that while deviant positions as such appear outside a society, they are still socially and historically a part of the whole.[114]

The deviance theories just outlined are, in our opinion, extremely helpful in understanding the process of the exclusion of messianic groups in the Jewish majority society. Here we cannot go into the details;[115] we will give attention, rather, to the overall picture. We must begin first and foremost with the fact that the crisis of Jewish society in the land of Israel after the destruction of the temple can without doubt be understood as a situation in which there had to be disagreements about accepted and deviant behavior, about drawing boundaries regarding Jewish identity, and about a corresponding Jewish way of life. The previous multiplicity of diverging groups was replaced by a coalition dominated by moderate Pharisaic groups whose convictions became the core of an ongoing process of integration. The doctrinal school in Jamnia shaped its contours. Even the coexistence of Pharisaic schools still possible before the great war, with their occasionally serious doctrinal differences (Hillel and Shammai), was subjected to greater restrictions.[116] The necessity of the new definition of Judaism included the establishment of boundaries, especially since the threatening of Judaism did not end after the First Jewish Revolt, as shown by subsequent revolts (under Trajan) and finally the Bar Kokhba Revolt.[117]

On this basis we can also understand the exclusion of the messianic groups. In a special way, the ongoing integration process had an excluding effect on Christ-confessing Jews, who had reached deviant conceptions of the central symbols and values of Judaism. Indeed, these groups cultivated programmatic contact with non-Jews that went far beyond normal relations, and in the process they crossed a boundary of Jewish identity that had enormous importance especially for Judaism after 70.[118] For the leaders of Judaism after 70 it was a question not only of the religious identity of Israel but also and especially of its social integrity. Therefore we must agree with Sanders that the exclusion and punishment of deviant Christ-confessing Jews happened not primarily because of divergent teachings or specific christological convictions, but because serious events led the representatives of the identity of majority Judaism to preserve the boundaries of Jewish identity, whereas the Christ-confessing Jews crossed these very boundaries in one way or another.[119]

The dynamic process of the exclusion of Christ-confessing Jews as a deviant group is also still recognizable in the texts. The application of the "forty lashes minus one" is to be interpreted as the punishment of deviants. The mentioned verbal slanders are examples of the public labeling of a deviant group.

This is also indicated by other labelings, of which some are named here. Jesus drives out the evil spirits through Beelzebul (Matt 12:24), and he himself is even regarded as possessed (John 8:48, 52). He is called a "Galilean" (Matt 26:69), a "Nazorean" (Matt 2:23; 26:71; John 18:5, 7; 19:19), and a "Samaritan" (John 8:48).

This process of labeling finds its ultimate embodiment in the *birkat ha-minim,* especially in its relatively late form (cursing of the *Nozrim*). The prohibitions of contact reflect a more or less strict social isolation, which finds its most striking expression in exclusion from the synagogue. Going hand in hand with the experiences of exclusion is the formation of groups of Christ-confessing Jews, through which the exclusion is neutralized. Likewise, a reversal of the labeling is recognizable, for example, when the "Pharisees and scribes" are called "hypocrites" (Matt 15:7; 23:15) and when the demand is formulated for a righteousness that is greater than that of the Pharisees and scribes (Matt 5:20). Is it a coincidence that in these texts the groups who are labeled are precisely those that played a leading role in the newly formed Judaism?

Likewise, it does not seem to us coincidental that the Gospel of Matthew already reveals characteristics of a "secondary deviance."[120] That is to say, the Matthean community finally accepted its deviant status and part of a new integral identity in which Israel was only one people among the nations, and the new people of God recruited its members from Jews and Gentiles. Now the way was clear to go beyond the boundaries of Israel to the nations/Gentiles (*ethnē*), who are to be made "disciples," baptized, and instructed in the teachings of Jesus (cf. Matt 28:16ff.).

The Gospel of John also reflects this new identity in response to exclusion and its acceptance. Prominent here is a strong claim of exclusivity for the revelation of Christ (cf. only John 14:6). It is interesting how the Gospel of John underlines its origin in Judaism (4:22) but at the same time also demonizes Jews (8:44) and expresses an awareness that it is an entity that transcends Judaism. In this it is remarkably oriented toward the classic Jewish-Samaritan schism: a time will come in which the schism between Samaritans and Jews will be overcome, a time "when the true worshipers of God will worship the Father in spirit and truth" (4:21ff.).

Precisely those passages of the Gospels of Matthew and John that as critical objections speak against their origin in Christ-confessing Judaism are best explained by the situation of "secondary deviance." Thus, for example, the tension between, on the one hand, the texts of the Gospel of Matthew in which it formulates a clear limitation of the proclamation to Israel (say, Matt 10:5-6; 15:24) and, on the other hand, the limited statements in which Gentiles come into view (already Matt 2:1ff.; 10:18; 12:18, 21; 21:43; 24:14; 28:19) is to be explained on the basis of the new identity of the Matthean community.

PART THREE

The Social History
of Christ-Confessing
Communities in the Cities
of the Roman Empire

INTRODUCTION

This part deals with the social history of Christ-confessing communities in various cities of the Roman empire outside the land of Israel. These groups are to be distinguished from Jesus' followers in the land of Israel not only on geographical but also on sociological grounds. The difference is expressed linguistically in that we call them *Christ-confessing* communities or churches, whereas we have labeled local groups of Jesus' followers in the land of Israel *messianic* communities. Yet the linguistic differentiation is based merely on practical concerns. For the most important New Testament term for Christ-confessing communities, the Greek word *ekklēsia* ("church"), can be applied to both the messianic communities in Israel and the Christ-confessing communities in pagan cities.

Social Differences between
Christ-confessing Communities and the Followers of Jesus

There are four central social characteristics of the Christ-confessing communities that distinguish them from the followers of Jesus in the land of Israel. First, the Christ-confessing communities are composed of Jews *and* non-Jews, and with the passage of time, these communities become dominated by the membership of former Gentiles—to some extent already in the Pauline era. Second, Jews and non-Jews in these communities programmatically realized an *unrestricted*—though in part controversial—social interaction. Third, the Christ-confessing communities existed as minority groups in the context of the *pagan majority society* of their urban locations. And fourth, *alongside and outside* the Diaspora synagogues, they were the representatives of Judaism outside the land of Israel. Thus socially, the transformation of Jesus' Jewish following from the land of Israel into the pagan cities of the Roman empire was at the same time a movement beyond the boundaries of Judaism. Stated differently, one the one hand, the Christ-confessing communities in the pagan cities of the Roman empire, in contrast to the followers of Jesus in the land of Israel, no longer belonged socially to (Diaspora) Judaism. On the other hand, however, they did not understand themselves as part of paganism.

251

The Independence of Christ-confessing Communities

Generally speaking, it is a question here of groups that are distinguished from other communities in their social environment by common traditions and interests, a feeling of belonging together, a certain institutionalization of their assemblies, and the shaping of the social interaction of their members. According to the self-understanding of these groups, as reflected in the New Testament, the multiplicity of communities was above all reduced to something that was different from Judaism on the one hand and from the pagan majority population on the other. The identity of a collective is often expressed outwardly, in demarcation against strangers, in "asymmetrical antitheses,"[1] recognizable, for example, in the opposites "Israel-nations (Gentiles)" or "Greeks-barbarians." The special nature of the self-understanding of the Christ-confessing communities is shown in the fact that while the idea gradually developed of being something new and different, a third option developed, vis-à-vis Jews and Greeks (or pagans), at the same time that the consciousness of a specific closeness to Judaism was maintained. In the second century this double self-understanding developed into the idea of the church as *tertium genus* ("third classification") and *verus Israel* ("true Israel").

Hints of this, however, are to be found already in the New Testament. For example, 1 Cor 10:32 explicitly demonstrates that the apostle Paul sees in the *ekklēsia* (on this term see section 9.1) a third empirical entity alongside Jews and Greeks (cf. also 2 Cor 11:24-29). Yet at the same time he also refers to the religious tradition of Israel for the self-understanding of non-Jewish, uncircumcised confessors of Christ by speaking of them as "God's beloved" and "called to be saints" (Rom 1:7) and even as descendants of Abraham (Rom 4:11-16). Yet we must note that he distinguishes them from empirical Judaism: "Israel" or "Israel of the flesh" (1 Cor 10:18).[2] Thus Paul speaks of the *ekklēsia of the Gentiles* not as "Israel" or even as the "true or spiritual Israel."[3] He regards it not as a part of Judaism, that is, not as a Jewish movement or sect,[4] but as its own eschatological community called out from the Gentiles.[5] Therefore he can also express the peculiarity of the Christ-confessing group as the abolishing of the ethnic and religious differences between Gentiles and Jews (Rom 3:22; 10:12; Gal 3:28).[6] And if Paul can speak of the *"ekklēsiai of the Gentiles"* (Rom 16:4), this clearly shows that he has in mind the urban Christ-confessing communities precisely on the basis of the religious and ethnic origin of their members and also distinguishes them from, say, the *churches (of God) in Christ in Judea* (Gal 1:22; 1 Thess 2:14), who as a chosen "remnant" represent the eschatological gathering of the people of God but are united with the others in the redemption of all Israel and of all the nations: Romans 9–11).[7]

At first the non-Jewish members seem to have been recruited primarily from the group of "God-fearers," that is, from the sympathizers of Judaism who had not officially converted but stood in a more or less close relationship with the synagogues (see pp. 242–43). This impression is, in any case, conveyed by Acts. According to its presentation, Christ-confessing communities originated outside the synagogues basically from these "God-fearers" and predominantly from former Gentiles. Indeed, the exodus of "Christian" preachers (and their followers) from the synagogues to the Gentiles is generally the first step toward the establishment of the *ekklēsia*.[8] The independence of the Christ-confessing groups is also indicated by the designation *christianoi*,[9] which was presumably applied to them from the outside and identified them as followers of Christ.[10]

Thus we basically presuppose here the existence of independent Christ-confessing communities that are different from the synagogues of the Diaspora.[11] The awareness of their own identity also corresponds to the social experience of believers in Christ.

The Origins of Christ-Confessing Communities

The beginnings of these communities lie largely in darkness. The basic outline can be derived from Acts and a few comments of Paul. According to the presentation in Acts, at some point (in the thirties of the first century) conflicts arose between the Messiah-confessing Jews of Jerusalem and the remaining Jewish population, as well as authorities (Acts 6–8). During the course of these conflicts members of the early church were driven out of Jerusalem (8:1-3) and in Samaria and Judea gained new followers for their messianic faith. Some of the scattered reached Phoenicia, Cyprus, and Antioch, yet at first they preached only to Jews. In Syrian Antioch, finally, they also won "Greeks" for the faith in the Lord Jesus Christ (11:19-20). Nevertheless, Acts reports earlier the exemplary winning of a non-Jew, the Roman centurion Cornelius in Caesarea by the sea, who, together with his household, is baptized by Peter (Acts 10:1—11:18). The historical course of events was presumably somewhat different. The conflicts in Jerusalem apparently concerned, above all, Jews returning from the Diaspora who had joined the messianic community in Jerusalem and were called "Hellenists." Their group was probably represented by the already mentioned committee of seven (see p. 219), one of whose members, the charismatic Philip, is connected with the mission also outside Jerusalem and ultimately even among non-Jews (Acts 8:4-13, 26-40). Nonetheless, beyond individual personalities it is quite certain historically that in Syrian Antioch for the first time a church arose to which "Greeks," that is, non-Jews, also belonged (Acts 11:19-20). Similar processes must have also been taking place in Damascus, for we may reasonably presume that the apostle Paul "persecuted" the Christ-confessing communities of Jews *and* Gentiles there and not in Jerusalem, as Acts recounts. In Damascus he also experienced his calling as apostle to the Gentiles (Galatians 1). The development that began in Antioch in the thirties was then continued in the founding of additional communities outside the greater Palestine (in Syria, Asia Minor, Greece, and on to Rome). The apostle Paul is known to us above all as the founder of many such communities, in which the Gentile Christian element predominated and at times probably became exclusive (cf. only 1 Thess 1:9-10).

The transformation of Jesus' following into the realm of Diaspora Judaism and above all that of non-Jews is thus apparently connected with the radiation of the Jerusalem early church toward Antioch in Syria. This is understandable, because Jerusalem had a lively exchange with the Diaspora Judaism of Antioch, on account of its geographic location as a kind of meeting place for traffic from and to Jerusalem.

The Problem of the Social Interaction of Jews and Non-Jews

The transformation of Jesus' Jewish following in the land of Israel out of Jerusalem and into the realm of Diaspora Judaism and especially that of non-Jews, nevertheless, created a problem in the Pauline era. The issue can be expressed theologically with the question whether Christ-confessing Gentiles must convert to Judaism in order to be able to participate in the messianic salvation of Israel proclaimed to them. Then at the Apostolic Council in Jerusalem (Acts 15; Galatians 2) the Jerusalem early church conceded that Gentiles no longer had to fulfill the central Jewish marks of identification (such as belonging to the covenant people Israel and the concomitant circumcision and obedience to the Torah) as conditions for participation in the future salvation and in table fellowship. This problem had its real basis in the programmatically experienced social (table) fellowship of Jews and non-Jews, which was probably first experienced in Antioch. The problem had also become urgent above all because of the transformation of Jesus' Jewish following (in the land of Israel) into the realm of Diaspora Judaism and the influence of non-Jews back on the Jerusalem early church and the churches of Judea. For the social fellowship of Jews and non-Jews in Antioch seems to have been offensive to non-Christ-confessing Jews and to have had corresponding effects even on the early Jerusalem church (see pp. 268–69). This is indicated by the intervention of the Jerusalemites—caused by fear of negative measures—against the table fellowship of Christ-confessing Jews and Gentiles in Antioch (Gal 2:11-14), to which the Jerusalemites Peter and Barnabas reacted pragmatically; but it is likewise indicated by the "persecutions" in Judea presupposed in 1 Thess 2:14-16 for the period before 50 C.E.

Further Development after 70 *C.E.*

Toward the end of the first century the problem of the social fellowship of Jews and non-Jews in Christ-confessing communities seems to have lost its importance. This was due not least of all to the ethnic and religious composition of Christ-confessing communities, in which the membership of Jews had by then become the exception. In general, after the catastrophe of the Jewish people in the First Jewish Revolt, their situation seems to have changed in many respects. This event also and especially shaped the relationship of Christ-confessing communities to Diaspora Judaism and to paganism, as well as to its official courts. The situation of believers in Christ in this period became even more precarious than in the prewar era of Pauline Christendom, not least of all because of political measures, especially under Emperor Domitian. Thus within the development of Christ-confessing communities in the cities of the Roman empire we can discern a certain caesura, for which the year 70 C.E. stands as a symbolic date.

Overview of Judaism in the Diaspora

Since Christ-confessing communities were repeatedly in contact with the synagogues of the Diaspora, we will offer here at least an overview of Diaspora Judaism.[12] According to Acts 15:21, "Moses has had those who proclaim him, for he has been read aloud every sabbath in the synagogues." In fact, the presence of synagogues in the Diaspora can be demonstrated through inscriptions and papyrus documents since the second half of the third century B.C.E., but there was probably already a Judaism in the Diaspora in the sixth century B.C.E.[13] The term *Diaspora* designates the Jewry living outside the land of Israel. It was already common in ancient times (2 Macc 1:27; cf. also John 7:35) and actually means "scattering." Within the Roman empire in New Testament times there were Jewish Diaspora communities in Syria, Asia Minor, Greece, on Crete and Cyprus, in Egypt and Cyrenaica, and finally also in Italy. The most important were in Syrian Antioch, Alexandria, and Rome.

Share of the Population and Social Situation

Estimates of the proportion of Diaspora Judaism in the total population are problematic; most of them range from 10 to 15 percent of the population, that is, around 5 or 6 million Jews.[14] Philo estimates for Egypt alone 1 million Jews (*Flacc.* 43), which is doubtless an exaggeration.[15] In this connection, Tcherikover indicates that of approximately 1300 papyri that were found in the so-called Zenon archive of Philadelphia, only 1 percent refer to Jews or Judaism.[16] Probably more realistic, therefore, is a number for the province of Asia, where according to calculations by Smallwood, about 50,000 male adults belonged to Jewish communities.[17] The social position of the over-whelming majority of Diaspora Judaism was without doubt that of the ancient lower stratum.[18] This is shown, for example, by significant attestations for artisans of quite varied occupations; these are found in literary and inscriptional texts, as well as in papyri.[19] Yet among the Jewish residents of pagan cities there were also (but probably only a few) merchants, as well as, for example, shipmasters. Certainly, there were also rich people among the members of Diaspora synagogues. Nevertheless, no Jew belonged to the senatorial nobility, and Josephus presupposes Jews as members of the *ordo equester* only in the land of Israel.[20] And there were also individual Roman citizens among Jewry abroad (cf. pp. 310–11), yet before the third century C.E. there was no Jewish member of a municipal decurional council in Asia Minor.[21] This is probably also related to the fact that the rise of individuals into the political elite (*ordines*) outside the land of Israel was connected with falling away from Judaism. Thus in general one will find Jews neither in the elite of imperial Rome nor in the urban elite of the provinces (presumably Egypt was an exception). The lower-stratum situation of the overwhelming majority of Diaspora Judaism corresponds to the fact that the ancient literary elite connected synagogues and Jews with poverty and in part even with extreme poverty.[22] The few rich members of the synagogues, as well as those with Roman citizenship, presumably had a certain influence on the local leadership strata. In this connection, however, the so-called God-fearers also played an important role for the Diaspora synagogues, as well as for the relations between Jewish and Christ-confessing communities.

"God-fearers"

More than just sympathizers of Judaism, God-fearers[23] adapted themselves in varying degrees to the Jewish way of life but, in contrast to proselytes, did not become Jews. In the Acts of the Apostles they are called *phoboumenoi* or *sebomenoi (ton theon)*,[24] a terminology not attested by inscriptions. They can, however, also be designated by the term *theosebēs*.[25] Yet even this is by no means a technical term; rather, one must always decide from the context whether it is basically a statement about the piety of a person (whether a Jew or non-Jew) or designates a God-fearer.[26] The inscriptional evidence for God-fearers (*theosebeis*) on the marble pillar of Aphrodisias speaks against the view expressed by Kraabel and others that the existence of God-fearers was an "invention" of the author of Acts.[27] On this pillar are 125 personal names given as sponsors of the synagogue and that can be further characterized prosopographically: there are, on the one hand, Jews (68 or 69 names) and, on the other, proselytes—Gentiles who converted to Judaism—and finally 54 personal names that are explicitly designated as *theosebeis* and probably rank behind the Jews in the ranking order of the synagogue, although some of them apparently belong to the local elite.[28] Most of these *theosebeis* have names that are not Jewish but clearly Gentile.

From the Acts of the Apostles we can learn some traits of this group of people that reveal a certain profile in the context of other information about them. Luke mentions or presupposes that the God-fearers attend the synagogue on the sabbath[29] and also hold to Jewish prayer customs (Acts 10:2) and—to a not clearly defined extent—to the Torah. Cornelius is called an "upright" man.[30] Yet he is also considered "unclean" and is a non-Jew whose house a Jew may not visit.[31] A limited observance of the Torah or halakah corresponds to a limited participation in the religious customs of Judaism.[32] God-fearers can also distinguish themselves through good deeds for the Jewish people.[33] In any case, they are different from proselytes: they are uncircumcised and do not hold completely to the Torah. To this extent there are limits to association with them (cf. esp. Acts 11:3), whereas even in Luke's view, proselytes fully belong to Judaism (Acts 2:11; 6:5; 13:43 remains problematic). By contrast, however, they were probably also distinguished from "sympathizers" like Sergius Paulus, who was not a God-fearer in the narrower sense: he did not, for example, attend the synagogal worship service (this is immediately evident on the basis of his social position).[34] God-fearers are significantly more often women than men.[35]

Local Political Influence through God-fearers

The local political influence that the synagogues were able to have in the polis through God-fearers is clear from both inscriptional and literary evidence. On the previously mentioned marble pillar of Aphrodisias nine of the God-fearers are characterized by the additional term *bouleutēs*, that is, members of the senate of the city of Aphrodisias. An important role is also played here above all by women,[36] even if it is not always clear whether a particular person belongs in the group of God-fearers or in the broader group of sympathizers. Thus an inscription (*CII* 766; ca. 80–90 c.e.) from Acmonia in Asia Minor mentions a certain Julia Severa who erected and furnished the local synagogue. Since she was a priestess of the cult of the emperor, belonged to the local elite of the city, and was even related to senatorial families, she was hardly a Jew or, indeed, even a God-fearer.[37] We may presume, however, that Capitolina, who is characterized on an inscription from Tralles (*CIG* 2924) as a benefactor of the local synagogue and a *theosebē̄s*, was a God-fearer. Luke also reveals the influence of God-fearing women (Acts 13:50). Similarly, according to Josephus (*War* 2.559–61), the inhabitants of Damascus planned to kill the locally resident Jews, whom they held locked up in the local school. Yet they did not dare to carry out their plan openly, since they feared their own wives,

who with few exceptions were devoted to the Jewish worship of God. Therefore they kept their shameful plan secret from their own wives and suddenly
attacked all the Jews. Even if one considers the numbers that Josephus gives
to be exaggerated (10,500 Jews were murdered; almost all women of Damascus were supposed to be God-fearers), this text still unmistakably reflects the
local political influence of God-fearing women. Also in a midrash (*Deut. Rab.*
2.24) the specific influence of a woman for the benefit of Judaism is emphasized. She persuades her husband, who is a God-fearer (and senator!) to kill
himself in order thereby to negate a senate decision against Judaism. Also
comparable is the importance of women proselytes, for example, the women
in the retinue of Izates, the crown prince of Adiabene (including his mother
Helena).[38] This confirms the hypothesis that among the God-fearers there
were also members of local elite families who were not able to convert to
Judaism and become proselytes—in all probability precisely because they
belonged to the elite and therefore also had to perform certain (cultic) duties.

Synagogues: Concept and Functions

In the oldest testimonies for Diaspora synagogues the term used is not *synagogue* but *proseuchē* (place of prayer),[39] which is generally customary for
synagogues in the Diaspora,[40] whereas for Palestine the word *synagogue* predominates. An exception is the language of the New Testament, in which *synagogue* is also used most often for the Diaspora. The word *proseuchē* is
connected first of all with the concept of prayer in a particular place or building, whereas *synagogue,* based on its original sense, means an assembly or the
synagogal fellowship. Nevertheless, both terms can at times also contain the
primary sense of the other word. In the New Testament itself synagogue frequently means (also) the synagogue building. Private houses or certain rooms
in private houses, as well as special buildings, could serve as places of assembly; more rarely, communities probably also gathered in the open.[41] One of
the most important synagogue buildings was the great synagogue in Alexandria (a five-naved basilica).[42] Synagogues served cultic purposes (prayer, reading of the Torah, singing of hymns) and above all teaching. Yet they were also
available for secular purposes, such as lodging; in fact, in a certain sense they
served—as Hengel maintains regarding the Alexandrian synagogue—as "the
agora of Judaism," that is, also for commercial purposes.[43]

Legal Status and Privileges

A detailed historical overview of the legal status of the Jewish Diaspora population is given by Applebaum.[44] There was in the Roman empire a legal status that was the same for all Jews living abroad: they were basically foreigners

except for the few Jews who had Roman citizenship (and here and there also the citizenship of their particular cities). In this respect they did not differ from the absolute majority of the population in the Roman empire. Yet the Jews of the Diaspora had some privileges, which, however, are not to be understood in the sense of the older scholarly opinion as a kind of general religious freedom of Judaism (*religio licita*).[45] Actually, there were—in part also locally and personally—different privileges,[46] like, for example, the permission as a Jew not to have to appear in court or perform any public functions on the sabbath, as well as the freedom of Jews with Roman citizenship from military service.[47] Trebilco[48] ascertains the following privileges for the Jewish Diaspora in Asia Minor: (1) the right to assemble in the synagogue, which was significant especially in connection with the prohibition of *collegia;* (2) the related right to erect synagogue buildings; (3) the right to collect the temple tax, combined with state protection of its transport; (4) the freedom from military service of Roman citizens among the Jews; (5) the right to observe sabbath and food regulations and to live according to ancestral laws.

Yet from case to case these privileges were also called into question. As an example we will mention here only the experience of the Jewish community in Sardis, where apparently the previously granted privilege of assembly and a certain freedom of the Jewish community to hold its own courts were first revoked in the middle of the first century B.C.E. and then, however, reconfirmed. Afterward the Jewish residents were again permitted to gather "on certain days," and it became possible for Jews "to be allowed to fulfill all the arrangements commanded of them by their laws." They were also "given a place where they could gather with their wives and children and offer their traditional prayers and sacrifices to God."[49] The privileges of Jewish Diaspora communities were called into question only when there were serious tensions between the synagogues and the majority population.[50]

Organization: Politeuma or Collegium

Some scholars, such as Smallwood, hold the view that the standard political organization of Jewish communities abroad was the (Gr.) *politeuma.*[51] This means an association of fellow countrymen in foreign cities; this was probably some kind of legally recognized, semiautonomous "corporation" that was granted to certain groups of immigrants and not only Jews.[52] The term occurs as a characterization of the Jewish community in Alexandria (*Ep. Arist.* 310; cf. *Ant.* 12.108)[53] and Sardis (*Ant.* 14.235);[54] likewise, it appears, for example, in two Jewish inscriptions from Berenice in Cyrenaica (*CPJ* 153).[55] This legal organization can also be presumed for other Diaspora communities—Antioch and perhaps also Caesarea[56]—yet this legal status should by no means be generalized. It is more likely to be expected where the Jewish communities went back to older (military) settlements. Moreover, this status apparently was not able to prevail everywhere.

Hengel[57] shows a change from *politeuma* to synagogue in the inscriptions of the Jewish community of Berenice. In an inscription from the first century B.C.E. the local Jewish community as *politeuma* honors a Roman governor; then in 56 C.E., however, there is no more mention of a *politeuma* but of the *synagogue* of the Jews in Berenice. "The form of the Jewish community in Berenice seems to have changed in the period between the two inscriptions. Instead of the *politeuma* of fellow countrymen, which went back to a Ptolemaic military colony, an ethnic-religious association now appears."[58]

Actually, it seems more meaningful for the epoch in which we are interested to presume a structural commonality of legal constitution and synagogal organization in the fact that Diaspora Judaism more and more assumed the character of voluntary associations (*collegia*) and was judged as such.[59] This also involved certain privileges, such as common assembly and the establishment of a fund that served community purposes. Under Caesar, and in the context of a general prohibition of *collegia*, these privileges were expressly formulated for the synagogues: the right to gather for worship services and common meals, to observe the sabbath and feasts, to follow the other demands of the Torah, and to build synagogues.[60] The synagogues were different from the *collegia* in that they were responsible for the community life of local Jewry as a whole, not for a certain organizational purpose (say, for religious assemblies), and membership was reserved exclusively for Jews (and converts).[61]

Organizational Form

The organization of Jewish Diaspora communities did not follow a standard model, but it seemed in principle to be based on the normal Jewish community in Judea.[62] There was probably a basic distinction between a kind of council, represented by *archontes* or elders (*presbyteroi*), and the executive (frequently represented by a so-called *grammateus*, which did not mean a scholar but a kind of secretary), although it is not clear whether some of the *archontes* or *presbyteroi* had executive functions. A *hypēretēs* ("servant") functioned in gatherings for worship. At the head of the synagogal fellowship stood a synagogue leader (*archisynagōgos*), who had a kind of spiritual, intellectual, and administrative leadership role. The office could be acquired on the basis of a corresponding agreement, an election, or even inheritance.[63] Whether the leader belonged to the *archontes* is not certain. A kind of honorary title was the designation *father* or *mother* of the synagogue.[64] The larger the synagogues were, the more we must assume other functionaries, such as teachers. In Diaspora synagogues women also performed official functions within the community, such as *archisynagōgos* or "elder."[65] This contradicts the common opinion that women played no active role in synagogal meetings.[66] The opinion of the wise cited in this connection (*b. Meg.* 23a), according to which women out of respect for the assembly are not to read from the scripture, makes it implicitly clear that there was no corresponding prohibition.[67] The synagogues were the meeting places—on the sabbath and on feast days[68]—of men, women, and children.[69] Against the general opinion that women did not take part in the public life of Jewish communities, there is broad evidence of their presence. By contrast, there is no clear evidence for a separate sitting arrangement for women or a so-called women's gallery, apart from the Therapeutae described in Philo (see p. 371). On the contrary, from inscriptions and also from archaeological knowledge about ancient synagogues we are more likely to conclude that women and men participated together in synagogal meetings.[70] Synagogal buildings could belong to individual persons and groups or especially to the Jewish community as a whole.[71]

The Division of Part Three

In Chapter 9 we will present the social form and basic features of Christ-confessing communities. Then in Chapter 10 the social composition of these communities will again be analyzed. Finally, in Chapter 11 the external conflicts of the Christ-confessing communities with the pagan majority population and its political representatives and with Diaspora Judaism will receive their own detailed discussion.

9

THE CONCEPT AND BASIC CHARACTERISTICS
OF CHRIST-CONFESSING COMMUNITIES

9.1 The Concept of *Ekklēsia*

The most important New Testament term for Christ-confessing communities
is the Greek word *ekklēsia;* it is applied to individual house churches, to the
area churches that perhaps consist of several house churches, and to all believers in Christ. Its translation into modern languages varies.[1] Here we will most
often use the terms *community, congregation,* and *community assembly* or retain
the Greek term *ekklēsia* (with a capital *E*).[2] A social history must focus on the
description of the *ekklēsia* as a *social* or *empirical* entity in which certain people come together who, however, also maintain community connections
beyond the actual assemblies. The New Testament linguistic usage also contains both aspects of the *ekklēsia:* assembly and community.

A. THE *EKKLĒSIA* AS AN ACTUAL ASSEMBLY
The use of the Greek word *ekklēsia* as the self-designation of Christ-confessing groups is apparently pre-Pauline, but we will concentrate here on its literary usage since the letters of Paul. The word can also be used in combination
with the genitive of God or Christ: the *ekklēsia* of God or of Christ.[3] These
genitive combinations are particularly helpful in the semantic clarification of
the New Testament usage of the word and have been examined in terms of
etymology and the history of traditions. They have been traced back to the
Old Testament terms *qehal 'elohim* ("congregation of God") and *qehal yhwh*
("congregation of Yhwh"; or their Greek translations in the Septuagint) or to
the designation *qehal 'el* ("congregation of God") used in Qumran.[4] On this
tradition-historical basis the New Testament usage of the term then involved
the conscious claim of early Christendom that it saw itself, in contrast to
Israel, as the "true" people of God.[5] Combined with this semantic content of
ekklēsia is a separation of the special New Testament meaning from the general usage,[6] in which *ekklēsia* means (primarily) the political assembly of all
(male) voting citizens in a city.[7] Yet this view is also rightly contradicted, and
with good reason.[8] At this point we cannot go into the details of the theological and tradition-historical discussion that has been carried on in this
connection.

262

In a semantic analysis it seems to us more meaningful to begin not with the named genitive combinations but with the absolute use of the word. It seems clear that in the extrabiblical usage of the term by pagan[9] or Jewish writers,[10] as well as in the biblical usage (Hebrew Bible and Septuagint),[11] the term *ekklēsia* (or Heb. *qahal*) is connected first of all with the meaning of a gathering together. Thus the *ekklēsia* is an (actual) assembly. This very meaning is also prominent in the New Testament texts.[12] That is, the basic meaning of the word is also to be found in the linguistic usage of early Christendom (including the apologists and church fathers) in the idea of an *assembly.* And even if not all New Testament occurrences of the word are semantically unambiguous, this meaning seems to predominate.[13] Thus the semantic difference between the conventional usage and that of the new Testament, which was emphasized in this regard by the older scholarship, lacks a basis in the texts.[14] Moreover, it seems to us that the passages that encompass the Christ-confessing assembly explicitly as *ekklēsia* of God or of Christ, or make a reference to God or Christ,[15] are explainable out of the Old Testament tradition, where assemblies (*qahal/ekklēsia*) are, similar to here, presupposed to have the purpose of hearing the word of God or of worshiping God.[16] Just as little of the basic meaning of an assembly is given up here, we can hardly conclude from these determinations that vis-à-vis Israel, the Christ-confessing communities understood themselves as the eschatological people of God who were replacing the empirical Israel. Yet from the relationship of the communities to God or Christ we can conclude that the believers in Christ claimed a divine origin for their communities. The term probably gained its usefulness in early Christianity because it designated an assembly both in Jewish and Greek culture. The Christ-confessing addressees of the letters of Paul, who were addressed by him as the *ekklēsia* of God (in Corinth, Galatia, or Thessalonica),[17] were hardly able to derive from the term a whole "theology" of Christ-confessing community in relation to Israel or Judaism. It is more likely that in the pragmatic context of their social experience they were able to establish an analogy to the popular political assemblies of their cities.[18]

Naturally, it goes without saying that the Christ-confessing community understood itself as a special assembly of politically different people who were identified by their relationship to the one God and to Christ.[19] Nevertheless, beyond its tradition-historical development, the usage of the term remains understandable only against the background of the general linguistic usage. This semantic link appears notably, for example, in the salutation of the oldest Pauline letter to the church in Thessalonica. Paul writes to "the church [*ekklēsia*] of the Thessalonians" (1 Thess 1:1). The connotations of the assembly of citizens are evident. For the term *ekklēsia* is used here in connection with the name of the people (Thessalonians) and thus means the *assembly of the Thessalonians.* The citizens' assembly of the polis of Thessalonica could also have been addressed in this way. Yet through the addition of "in God the Father and the Lord Jesus Christ" it is clear the addressee here is the assembly of believers. The conclusion of the letter (5:26-27) also suggests that the term *ekklēsia* in the address means the *assembly* of believers. Also conclusive is the linguistic usage in Acts in which the same word *ekklēsia* is used to designate political (19:32, 39, 41) and Christ-confessing assemblies (11:26; 14:27). Only once is the Christ-confessing *ekklēsia* more closely characterized by the genitive "of God" (20:28). Thus in each case the context told the readers of the letters of Paul and the New Testament in general which kind of assembly was meant.

B. THE *EKKLĒSIA* AS COMMUNITY

In addition to the character of the *ekklēsia* as an (actual) assembly of believers, a second constitutive aspect can be derived from New Testament linguistic usage. For we learn from some texts that the *ekklēsia* is also understood as a group or community, for example, in connection with statements about the "persecution" of the *ekklēsia*.[20] That is to say, the term can also designate individuals or a group, independent of whether they are gathered together or not. This usage corresponds to other circumlocutions for believers in Christ (such as those "called to be saints")[21] and to terms that suggest that the Christ-confessing community can be understood as a house fellowship or family (see pp. 277–78).

Thus the New Testament term *ekklēsia* is connected with two constitutive characteristics that are fundamental for its analysis as an organizational form: the Christ-confessing *ekklēsia* is an assembly in which its members come together, and it is a community or group whose members are bound together even outside their actual meetings through reciprocal social interaction.[22] We will return to this point in the following section when the Christ-confessing communities are located in the spectrum of ancient organizational forms. First, however, two fundamental socio-historical aspects of the Christ-confessing communities must be presented in more detail, namely, their spread in the urban milieu and the unrestricted social interaction of their members.

9.2 The Urban Milieu and Unrestricted Social Interaction

Christ-confessing communities established themselves in urban regions of the Roman empire (9.2.1). They were composed of Jews and (in the majority) Gentiles and enjoyed a more or less unrestricted religious and social interaction between their Jewish and non-Jewish members (9.2.2).

9.2.1 The Urban Milieu

The first distinguishing characteristic of Christ-confessing communities of the Diaspora to be discussed here concerns their development in the urban milieu. Even with all the geographic uncertainty regarding the details, one can basically say that Christ-confessing communities came into being in various *cities* of the Roman empire. More precisely, it is a question of the region that, from the perspective of Jerusalem, stretches in the West to Rome and in the East from Macedonia and the coast of Greece and Asia Minor to Syria. Presumably, the great Mediterranean islands of Cyprus (Acts 13) and Crete (Titus) were also involved. The extent of Christ-confessing communities in the East basically encompassed at first only the urban centers of Syria and of the western and southern coastal region of Asia Minor, yet Bithynia in northwestern Asia Minor was added toward the end of the first and the beginning of the second century.[23] Further to the southeast Arabia formed the boundary of the sphere of influence (Gal 1:17).

Yet a precise geographic demarcation is difficult. We know details about Paul and his extended journeys, which led him into many important cities of the Mediterranean world (such as Antioch, Damascus, Ephesus, Philippi, Thessalonica, Corinth, and Rome), where we find the Christ-confessing communities that were founded by him or, in the case of Rome, attributed to his realm of influence as the apostle to the Gentiles.[24] This trend stabilized in the period after Paul. It can be directly inferred, for example, from the salutations and closing statements of the epistolary literature, when such information is revealed at all (Ephesians, Colossians, 2 Thessalonians, 1 and 2 Timothy [to Ephesus], 1 Peter [from Rome]), as well as from Revelation (seven letters to cities in Asia Minor). We find further indications in the presentation of the spread of the gospel in many Mediterranean cities (from Antioch to Rome) in Acts and indirectly in the Gospel of Luke. Thus in Luke's Gospel the Greek term *polis* ("city") is used 39 times (versus 8 occurrences in Mark)—even for villages such as Nazareth and Nain (Luke 1:26; 7:11). It is also noteworthy that Luke calls Bethlehem a "city" (Luke 2:4), whereas John 7:42 speaks of Bethlehem as a "village" (*kōmē;* likewise, Bethsaida is a "city" in Luke 9:10; versus Mark 8:23: "village"). In Luke the implicit situation of many narratives about Jesus and even that of Jesus' parables (for example, Luke 14)[25] is also adapted to urban conditions. In Luke's writings the rural population is not completely overlooked, yet it appears, in relatively wholesale fashion, primarily as the recipient of the proclamation, without really having a profile of its own (Luke 5:17; 9:52, 56; 17:12; Acts 8:25).[26] Frequently, however, we have no direct information about the place of origin of New Testament writings or the homelands of their addressees. Where, for example, was the Letter to the Hebrews written? Where did its addressees live? Where was the home of the author of the Letter of James? This letter is addressed to the twelve tribes in the Diaspora (1:1) and thus, in principle, is envisioned for the whole Mediterranean world in which Jews lived. This comprehensive geographical perspective is also recommended for the following presentation.

Probably starting in the thirties, therefore, Christ-confessing communities emerged in the Mediterranean societies of the Roman empire. And it is noteworthy that we basically find them only in urban regions.

There is, nonetheless, disagreement on the location of the Christ-confessing communities to which the apostle Paul's Letter to the Galatians is addressed. These churches were located either in small cities in the interior of Asia Minor, say, in the region in which Ankara lies today (Tavium, Pessinus, Ancyra), or in cities on the southern coast of present-day Turkey (Pisidian Antioch, Ikonion, Lystra, Derbe in the Roman province of Galatia).[27] Pliny's letter regarding the trials of Christians (ca. 117 c.e.) explicitly assumes that the ruinous superstition of the Christians had spread not only through the cities but also through the villages and the country (*Ep.* 10.96.9). Even if the Roman governor is exaggerating here in order to reinforce the danger to Christians, we can by no means exclude the idea that at the beginning of the second century villages in the vicinity of urban Christianity were also seized by it. Nevertheless, this does not affect the basic insight that Christ-confessing communities probably expanded at first into the cities of the Roman empire (cf. also Tertullian *Apol.* 1.7; 37.4).

Therefore, as Meeks correctly notes, the fact that Christianity "was preeminently an urban phenomenon after the first beginnings in Palestine is now generally recognized."[28] Yet one should not place too much stress on its demarcation vis-à-vis the country.[29] In fact, ancient cities were surrounded by many smaller or larger villages (does this situation form the real background for the spread of the Christian faith according to Pliny's presentation?). Likewise, one must presuppose that the social relations between urban and rural areas were extremely complex. The more recent archaeological research into antiquity calls into question the simplified and generalized distinction between city and country.[30] In a noteworthy study Osborne, for example, shows the close web of relationships between city and country and especially the dependence of the cities on the rural regions.[31] This and other studies not only warn against transferring the modern concept of "city" to antiquity but also suggest that one should presuppose broad social communication between city and country. Yet this insight does not change the fact that with regard to both the social composition of Christ-confessing communities and their sociological form, as well as their external conflicts, the urban milieu should be regarded as the framework of interpretation.

9.2.2 Unrestricted Social Interaction
between Jews and Gentiles in the Christ-confessing Community

Whereas the Jewish character of the followers of Jesus in the land of Israel is also shown in the religious and ethnic origin of its members, in the urban communities we also find former Gentiles alongside Christ-confessing Jews. This trend begins in Syrian Antioch, as shown in both Galatians 2 and Acts 11:20ff. And it is no accident that in the Acts of the Apostles the thus constituted group in Antioch is connected for the first time with the name *christianoi*, "followers of Christ" (Acts 11:26). This tendency was subsequently reinforced, and thus in the period after 70 it is primarily non-Jews who are to be found in the Christ-confessing communities outside the land of Israel. Accordingly, from the very beginnings of these groups there were problems related to their Jewish-Gentile composition. One issue was whether the non-Jewish believers in Christ had to convert to Judaism in order to be able to participate in the messianic salvation of Israel that was proclaimed to them. At the so-called Apostolic Council in Jerusalem (Acts 15; Gal 2:1ff.), after prior irritations, the Jerusalem early church conceded that believers in Christ no longer had to fulfill the central Jewish mark of identity, circumcision, as a condition for participation in the future redemption. Here we will not go into this widely discussed theological and salvation-historical problem. Yet the combining of Jews and Gentiles in Christ-confessing communities also had importance for everyday life. For the unlimited social interaction between Jews and non-Jews in the community was apparently also problematic in the view of some Christ-confessing Jews. Paradigmatic is the so-called Antiochene incident (Gal 2:11ff.). It describes a conflict between Paul on the one side and Peter and other Christ-confessing Jews on the other, in which the question of social intercourse with non-Jews was open to debate.

A. THE ANTIOCHENE CONFLICT (GAL 2:11-18)

Underlying the Antiochene conflict was a difference in opinion between Paul and Peter regarding the participation of (Christ-confessing) Jews in common meals with non-Jewish believers in Christ. Like the other Jewish members of the Antiochene *ekklēsia*, Peter had at first eaten with believers of Gentile background. But after a few delegates of the Lord's brother James appeared in Antioch, he drew back, together with other Jewish members of the community, and separated himself from the non-Jewish confessors of Christ (Gal 2:12-13). According to a comment by Paul, this process of separation occurred "for fear of the circumcision faction" (2:12), which perhaps means that Peter and the Christ-confessing Jews wanted to avoid giving offense, because of their fellowship with Gentiles, to the other Jews—either in Antioch or in Jerusalem or both. Yet beyond these possible outside influences on behavior within the community, the conflict shows not only a fundamental theological but also a social problem that is of constitutive importance for the sociological definition of Christ-confessing communities: the problem of *unrestricted* social interaction of Jews with non-Jews.

The Issue of Common Meals

It is no accident that this problem became acute in regard to the issue of common meals. For on the one hand, common meals are a fundamental element of ancient group sociology.[32] Families and various groups came together for banquets, which consisted of the actual meal (*deipnon*) and the following symposium (*symposion*), which was made of philosophical dialogues or certain forms of entertainment (music, singing). Common meals were also of great importance for the social gatherings of both Jews (on the sabbath or at certain feasts) and non-Jews.[33] Pagan Hellenistic meals were held by social organizations and various mystery religions on cultic occasions (combined with sacrifices and religious offerings), but also for the cult of the dead. The banquets of social organizations also had religious implications. On the other hand, social meals replicate the social positions and relationships of people and prove especially lethargic vis-à-vis social change.[34] Thus meals can be understood as mirrors of social systems and social relationships. They reflect the fundamental values and thus the related boundaries of groups.[35] Table fellowship is therefore also one of the most effective possibilities for defining and differentiating oneself through social groups. In no society is it permitted in any place, with anyone, and on any occasion to eat all possible foods.[36] Thus not only occasions, places, and people but also foods themselves play an important role. In this connection, anthropologist Douglas states that food itself can be understood as a "code" that makes it possible to decipher the social structures expressed in it. The message contained in the food code reveals something about the levels of social hierarchy, about inclusion in or exclusion from groups, about social boundaries, and about transactions across these social boundaries. Thus specific foods are encoded social events.[37]

B. THE SYMBOLIC SIGNIFICANCE
OF COMMON MEALS FOR SOCIAL INTERCOURSE

Galatians 2:11ff.

In the case of the "Antiochene conflict," the text is not clear enough on the surface to discern whether the problem of common meals concerns the participating *people* or the *foods*. Peter and other Jewish community members give up their previous practice of eating with non-Jews/Gentiles. On the motives of this change in behavior we can only speculate. Yet the reason given in the text—"for fear of the circumcision faction"—suggests that on account of the programmatic table fellowship in the Antiochene *ekklēsia* the Christ-confessing Jews in Jerusalem (and in Antioch?) are considering negative measures. Thus Peter and "the other Jews" probably avoided eating with non-Jews for pragmatic reasons to the extent, in any case, that such meals took place in the houses of non-Jews or involved foods that did not satisfy Jewish food laws.

Why were the Jews offended by the table fellowship of Jews and non-Jews? For help in interpretation we can turn here to the conventional behavior of Judaism in the Diaspora. It reveals that one can by no means assume that in principle Jews in the Diaspora avoided any social contact at all with Gentiles or at least tried to avoid it.[38] In the everyday praxis of ancient cities, there was a broad spectrum of public and private social interaction between Jews and Gentiles, the intensity of which depended on the degree of strictness of the religious attitudes of participating Jews.[39] In general, the existence of the so-called God-fearers also speaks against an absolute prohibition of contact with Gentiles. Yet there were areas in which contact was subject to restrictive commandments. These areas included above all the realm of sexuality. Thus sexual relations between Jews and non-Jews, as well as intermarriage, were taboo. In addition, there were specific problems of social interaction with non-Jews with regard to participation in common meals, especially when they were held by Gentiles.[40] The social problem seems to have been caused not so much by the participating individuals (because of a general impurity of Gentiles) but rather by the foods offered (meat, wine, and oil).[41] Yet impurity was also linked in part with people who ate unclean foods.[42] Jews themselves could function without difficulty as hosts of Gentiles, but they could accept Gentiles as hosts only if the latter offered Jewish foods.[43]

Thus it could be that the irritations over the table fellowship of Jews and non-Jews in the Antiochene *ekklēsia* had their basis in the fact that non-Jewish believers in Christ functioned as hosts and in the suspicion that problematic foods were served. Supporting this idea is Paul's reproach of Peter (Gal 2:14) that he had previously lived in Gentile fashion and now wants to compel the Gentiles to live as Jews (*ioudaizein*), if we can infer from this that Peter wanted to continue the table fellowship of Christ-confessing Jews with non-Jews under the condition that the latter hold to *Jewish* food laws.[44] This would also correspond to the conventional praxis of Judaism. Yet it would ultimately be realizable only if either Jews were the hosts or non-Jews lived like Jews.

Acts 10–11

This "symbolic" significance of the food laws is reflected even more clearly in the Cornelius episode (Acts 10:1—11:18). Here, however, the problem is discussed not only in regard to the foods but also to people. Cornelius is even presented as a devout and righteous God-fearer. In a vision Peter sees many kinds of animals that were unclean in the sense of the *kashrut* (Jewish food laws), and a divine voice orders him to eat. From this experience he then decides to change his traditional Jewish social behavior toward non-Jews 10:28-29); he enters the house of Cornelius, eats there, and baptizes the whole household. Basically, the story extrapolates from the symbolic example of the lifting of the boundaries of Jewish food laws to the divine-willed lifting of the boundaries of social interaction between Jews and non-Jews (10:34). Nonetheless, it also follows "that I should not call anyone profane or unclean" (10:28), because "God shows no partiality" (10:34). Yet this impartiality of God's is apparently linked with the presupposition that one "fears him and does what is right" (10:35)—that one behaves in principle as the God-fearers do. Above all, however, in the Cornelius episode it is a question of the idea that these non-Jews are also seized by the Spirit and therefore worthy of baptism (10:44). This is also confirmed in 11:2-3, where the Christ-confessing Jews reproach Peter for visiting Gentiles and eating a common meal with them. Here a non-Jew's explicit conversion and reception of the Spirit as a prerequisite of baptism—the first was an Ethiopian who, like a Jew or God-fearer, had made a pilgrimage to Jerusalem (8:26ff.)—is connected with the problem of common meals without regard to the *kashrut* and with the fundamental problem of social intercourse with Jews and Gentiles. In this connection we should also note that Paul regards Christ-confessing non-Jews as having been "washed" and "sanctified" by God (1 Cor 6:11). Therefore he requires the Corinthian church "to have no fellowship—especially no table fellowship—with those who lead a life of vice (cf. 1 Cor 5:11)."[45] We must also see here the background of Jesus' conflicts especially with Pharisees over table fellowship with sinners and tax collectors.

Even if in Antioch it was a question of the problem not of people but of food, table fellowship with non-Jews still concealed a fundamental shift in mentality and a basic change regarding the definition of group boundaries. That is to say, the common meals of Jews and non-Jews in the *ekklēsia* reflect a comprehensive lifting of the boundaries of social intercourse. The Cornelius episode has the same significance. Also in the sense of the anthropological reflections of Douglas, the previous praxis (before the conflict) of Antiochene believers in Christ is to be interpreted as a transaction across the existing group boundaries (of Judaism). The same is true of the Cornelius episode, in which, however, it is noteworthy that Peter, as it were, plays the role that Paul takes over in the "Antiochene conflict." In any case, it is true that the conventions of Diaspora Judaism were changed in the Christ-confessing communities at a crucial point: through the *unrestricted* table fellowship of *Jews* with non-Jews.

It is true that there was also social intercourse with Gentiles in the Diaspora synagogues. And the God-fearers, for example, adapted their lifestyles to the religious prescriptions of Judaism—even if in varying degrees—and this apparently also included the food laws.[46] Here, however, it is a question of the gradual assimilation of non-Jews to Jewish customs, and therefore in regard to the social intercourse of God-fearers with Jews of the Diaspora, we may assume that their table fellowship took place only under the conditions of *Jewish* food laws.[47] Thus in the social interaction with Gentiles in the synagogal fellowship, this aspect of Jewish exclusivity was preserved.

The situation was different, however, in the Christ-confessing community in Antioch. As the Pauline text shows, the practice of table fellowship meant a change in *Jewish* customs. He even notes that before returning to the traditional Jewish way of life, Peter lived "like a Gentile" (Gal 2:14). That is, in Antioch (Christ-confessing) Jews crossed over the previous boundaries of Judaism (regarding food laws). And to the extent that Jewish food customs were an important element of their distinction from non-Jews, even in the view of the Gentiles,[48] the table fellowship of Christ-confessing Jews and non-Jews without regard to Jewish food laws is to be understood as a manifest deviation from Jewish social behavior. Thus even when only the foods and not the people in themselves presented the problem for table fellowship, eating together in the *ekklesia* must have still been understood as a clear change in the Jewish way of life and as the giving up of exclusive group identity. In the view of Judaism, the common meals of Jews with non-Jews without regard to Jewish food laws could also be understood as a kind of fraternization with paganism.[49]

C. CHARISMA AS A BASIS
FOR DEVIATION FROM JEWISH SOCIAL BEHAVIOR

If we look for the reasons for the deviant behavior of Christ-confessing Jews vis-à-vis (Christ-confessing) non-Jews in the *ekklēsia,* caution is advisable, in our view, with regard to later rationalizations and theologizations. It was not a question of emancipation from the Torah, however substantiated. Rather, it seems to us that the origin of the transcendent mode of behavior was the pneumatic or charismatic character of the Jesus movement. The powers of the Spirit were also seen to be at work among the God-fearers, the non-Jews. Precisely this vaulting of the charismatic fire over the socially well-defined boundaries between Jews and non-Jews, which first took place in the circle of God-fearing sympathizers of Judaism, probably required the Christ-confessing Jews to come to terms with traditional modes of behavior. Historically this happened at the Apostolic Council (Gal 2:1-10), in that through the "Greek" Titus it becomes paradigmatically manifest that the same Spirit that worked among Jews was also at work among non-Jews in the mission of Paul. Theologically this process is reflected in the Cornelius episode in Acts 10 and the Lukan presentation of the Apostolic Council (Acts 15). Accordingly, there is a "revaluation" that is typical of charismatic movements. "Instead of the 'Spirit' being controlled by the 'law,' the 'Spirit' now controls the 'law.'"[50] Thus the experience of the giving of the Spirit, which involved non-Jews but not the (antinomian) interest in an emancipation from the Torah, led to a more flexible treatment of the traditional frame of reference.[51] Indeed, the renunciation of circumcision for Christ-confessing non-Jews is based on this charismatic character of the Christ-confessing communities (cf. Gal 3:1ff.). Yet we must concede that from the Jewish perspective, this could also be perceived as antinomianism. According to the self-understanding of Christ-confessing Jews like Paul, however, just the opposite process was occurring. For him faith in Christ upholds the Torah eschatologically, also and particularly for non-Jews (cf. Rom 3:27-31). This validation of the Torah through faith applies not only in terms of salvation history but also ethically. Indeed, it must even be said that in principle the fulfillment of the Torah—also through non-Jews in the *ekklēsia*—could almost be the ideal of believers in Christ. The indifference of persons, which is demonstrated for Paul on the basis of charismatic gift, is manifested in a complete transformation with the support of the Spirit and in correspondence to the demand for righteousness of the Torah (Rom 8:1ff.), so that "in Christ" neither circumcision nor lack of circumcision counts, but only a "new creation," and at the same time that means keeping the commandments (cf. Gal 5:6; 6:15; 1 Cor 7:19). Yet it is clear that Paul connects the fulfillment of the Torah to a certain extent with its ethical systematization or sublimation.[52] For just as he is clearly guided materially by the Torah in his individual paraeneses, so also he clearly systematizes or sublimates it in the commandment of love (cf. Rom 13:4; Gal 6:14).

D. NO COMPLETE RENUNCIATION OF JEWISH CONVENTIONS

Thus the Antiochene incident revealed a basic problem of the newly developing communities of Jew and non-Jews. At first their unrestricted social intercourse provoked irritations but at the same time shows a serious difference between such freedom and Judaism's self-understanding and social praxis. Thus the new dimension of the Christ-confessing community of Jews and Gentiles expressed itself not only in the fundamental renunciation of circumcision for Gentiles but also in the ignoring of the *kashrut*. In principle Paul himself held fast to the nonobservance of the *kashrut*. No food is in itself unclean for him (Rom 14:14). Nonetheless, he advocates forgoing certain foods if they are offensive to the "weak." Even the eating of meat offered to idols is not offensive to him per se but only out of consideration for the conscience of Christ-confessing sisters and brothers (1 Cor 8:1ff.; 10:24, 28-29). Yet the transgressing of the conventions of Jewish identity is not total even for Paul. For example, he forbids the worship of idols—the cultic adoration of pagan gods (1 Cor 10:7, 14)—apparently, like Diaspora Judaism, in the interest of the exclusivity of the Christ-confessing cult.[53] Likewise, generally prohibited is sexual immorality (1 Cor 10:8). He explicitly imposes a ban of exclusion on a Corinthian believer because he had entered a sexually immoral relationship not permitted by the Torah (1 Cor 5:1ff.; cf. also, in delineation from the Gentiles, 1 Thess 4:3ff. and 1 Cor 7:2). The writer of Revelation also urges the avoidance of sexual immorality; but in distinction to Paul, he also criticizes the eating of meat offered to idols (Rev 2:14, 20; cf. also *Did.* 6.3). The so-called apostolic decree (Acts 15:20, 29) even requires the observance of several of Judaism's marks of exclusivity (avoidance of idol worship, fornication, meat of animals not slaughtered in a kosher manner, and the drinking of blood), even for Christ-confessing Gentiles—perhaps in order to facilitate social intercourse with Jews. This is indicated by the substantiation of the decree in Acts 15:21. Yet one may also hazard that the eating of (sacrificial) meat—either in the temple or at banquets after it had been slaughtered according to pagan ritual and been placed in the market[54]—brought with it the suspicion of fellowship with pagan gods.[55]

9.3 Ancient Analogies to the Christ-confessing Communities

In order to determine the sociological or organizational form of the urban Christ-confessing communities, various models of ancient group formation have been drawn on for comparison: the model of the ancient house, ancient associations (*collegia*), the schools of philosophers, the synagogues, the fellowship (*communitas*), and even the *ekklēsia* as a popular political gathering.[56] In addition there have been attempts, with the help of modern sociological and socio-psychological research to describe early Christianity as, among other things, a "millennium movement,"[57] a "sect,"[58] a new "cult,"[59] or relatively neutrally as a "group" or "small group."[60] Methodologically we should first distinguish between the classification systems of modern analyses and ancient analogies. Turning to ancient analogies raises additional problems. For example, it seems to us fundamentally problematical to use literary testimonies of the early church (of the second and third centuries) as additional sources of information. The corresponding texts reveal the specific (apologetical) situation of their authors, which cannot be simply transferred to the New Testament epoch. Yet this points to a further problem: the self-understanding of believers in Christ as a community was different from the view of outsiders.

Tertullian (*Apol.* 38–39) will serve as an example. To describe the organizational form of Christ-confessing communities, the author combines various concepts that could be used in connection with associations as well as with schools of philosophers: *factio, illicita factio, secta, disciplina, corpus, curia, coitio.*[61] Nevertheless, it is Tertullian's concern to counter the accusation that Christians were an illegal party (*illicita factio*). The analogies are only analogies and an attempt to clarify to outsiders in terms of their social experience the social structure of Christ-confessing communities and prove their "harmlessness." Tertullian did not think that the Christian communities were identical with the *collegia* or philosophical schools.

From the viewpoint of the non-Christ-confessing population and its functionaries, the Christ-confessing communities were understood probably already in the New Testament as *factio* (a kind of political club or forbidden party formation). The Roman governor Felix accuses Paul of being "a ringleader of the sect [*hairesis*] of the Nazarenes" (Acts 24:5), that is, as the leader of an insurgent party within Judaism that was opposed to the fundamental values and principles of order of Rome. In Acts 17:6-7 the members of the Christ-confessing communities are likewise suspected as members of a worldwide anti-Roman insurrectionist movement who wanted to overturn the social and political order.[62] In the second and third centuries these suspicions of Christ-confessing communities increased ominously and culminated in the accusation that Christians were a group of "conspirators."[63] Yet this is clearly an outside view. In a further example, at the beginning of the second century Christians were condemned by Roman authors (Suetonius, Tacitus, Pliny) as members of a moral-ruining foreign religion (*superstitio*), that is, a cult community that harmed the traditional religious and moral norms and values of the majority society.[64] This view as well was hardly shared by the Christians themselves.

When classifying the *ekklesia* in the spectrum of ancient group formations, one must be careful not to describe its organizational form from the viewpoint of outsiders but to compare the structures emerging from the New Testament data themselves with other ancient organizational forms. This must again be distinguished from the application of modern sociological concepts; we will go into this context in a later section (9.4). Four ancient organizational forms have been, as it were, models for various aspects of the empirical form of the *ekklesia*: the popular assembly (9.3.1), the ancient household or nuclear family (9.3.2), the voluntary associations (9.3.3), and the Diaspora synagogues, which we have already discussed (see pp. 255ff.).

9.3.1 The Christ-confessing Assembly and the Popular Assembly

We are convinced that the analogies of the Christ-confessing *ekklēsia* to the like-named (popular) assemblies of the Greek city-states (and in certain variations also of Judaism) are of great significance for the understanding of the organizational form of the Christ-confessing communities.

A. COMPARISON BETWEEN
AN ASSEMBLY OF THE PEOPLE AND THE *EKKLĒSIA*

In the realm of secular experience, the *ekklēsia* is "the assembly of the *demos,* the popular assembly: as in Athens, so in all Greek States."[65] Thus "normally" the word means the popular assembly of all voting free men, the full citizens of a polis.[66] The members of the *ekklēsia* were the citizens. Nevertheless,

> the citizens never comprised the total population of a Greek polis; probably there was no single city-state where even a quarter of the residents enjoyed the status of citizens. . . . Women, children, and slaves were in any case excluded. Their place was in the home. . . . They were members of the household but not of the polis; it was their hometown, but they remained excluded from public life.[67]

The same was true of foreigners. Such assemblies (*ekklēsia*) took place regularly or extraordinarily, and "mostly early in the morning."[68] They began after sacrificial activities (in order to enhance the prospect of a good outcome) and prayers;[69] their agenda was fixed in advance.

A fixed component of the *ekklēsia* was the so-called *hiera,* that is, the "acceptance of reports on the carrying out of the offering presented in the interest of the state by authorized persons" and also commendations of individuals, as well as the bestowal of citizenships.[70] After agreement on the agenda, the assembly itself embarked on discussions of individual points. Taking part were both secular and cultic officials, as well as any voting citizen as rhetor.[71] The individual speakers also customarily prayed before their speech.[72]

Thus in the context of the popular assemblies, *cultic* aspects (sacrificial activities), the *praise* of outstanding personalities, and *debates* about specific topics all played a role; that is, they were also shaped by the speech and response of the participating men. This aspect of the assembly also determined the linguistic usage of the New Testament, and thus already at this point a fundamental analogy of the Christ-confessing to the urban assembly is suggested.[73] "The early Christian '*ekklēsia*' is also constituted by the fact that people 'came together.'"[74] It consisted of prayers,[75] a wide variety of speech forms (speaking in tongues, prophetic speech, instructional speech),[76] and even debates (instructional dialogues?).[77] An analogy to praise (*epainos*), one of the most important elements of the Greek-Hellenistic popular assembly, can be seen in the praise of God (Acts 2:47; cf. 14:27; 1 Cor 14:26), as well as the commendation of believers in Christ (1 Cor 11:2, 17, 22; 2 Cor 8:18).[78] This context also includes criticism and admonition.[79] The assignment of "elders" to the *ekklēsia*,[80] official missions (Acts 14:23; 2 Cor 8:19), and the making of decisions (Acts 15:22) also have analogies in political assemblies.[81] It is against this background that one must understand the *prin-*

ciples of order of the Christ-confessing assembly that Paul had in mind when he admonished the Corinthians that their assemblies should proceed "decently and in order" (1 Cor 14:40). In this connection a problem seems to have arisen regarding the division of roles between men and women in debates and teaching dialogues in the assembly of believers in Christ (see pp. 399–401). Thus in various kinds of details the assembly of the saints was shaped in analogy to the popular assembly.

Yet even with all the analogies, the *specific purpose* of each kind of assembly seems to be different. Popular assemblies come together in order to consider and act upon affairs of the city, decisions about war and peace, official commendations, bestowals of citizenship, and the like. All of these decisions may have varying degrees of significance for the common life in the polis and the well-being of its residents. Yet a common purpose for the assembled as a community is not discernible or is, in any case, rather minimal. By contrast, the purpose of the Christ-confessing assembly is directly related to the assembled as a *community.* It serves the strengthening, preservation, development, confirmation, and manifestation of the community itself as well as of the individuals in it. Even the "psalms" (which were probably sung) in the community gathering, which are supposed to serve the praise of God, have at the same time an instructional and "emotional" function for the gathered.[82] The New Testament term used in this connection is *upbuilding (oikodomē)*;[83] it circumscribes the growth and progress of the community of believers and points to a second fundamental organizational form of antiquity, the house or household, with which the Christ-confessing community also has a fundamental analogy. Before this is discussed, however, we will very briefly describe the recognizable places of assembly and the possible number of community members.

B. PLACE OF ASSEMBLY AND NUMBER OF PARTICIPANTS

The Christ-confessing assemblies probably took place primarily in private houses, as suggested by the term *house church* per se.[84] There were also several house churches in a city, meeting in certain private homes (1 Cor 16:15-16; Rom 16:23). We may assume, however, that assemblies of believers in Christ also met in the open (Pliny *Ep.* 10.96) or in rented rooms or buildings (Acts 20:7; cf. 19:9: *scholē /schola*). They had no building (church) of their own for sacral functions.[85] The possibilities that a private home offered as a place of assembly suggest that the number of members of Christ-confessing communities corresponded to spatial capacities. In Corinth there were perhaps four or five house churches.[86] If one accepts as a basic number for comparison purposes the fact that in the letters ascribed to Paul (except for the pastoral letters) 65 people are mentioned in addition to Paul,[87] including coworkers and traveling companions of Paul,[88] one will estimate the number of members in Christ-confessing communities to be rather low. Banks assumes an average number of 40–45.[89] A similar number (between 30 and 40, or 50 at most) is also reached by Murphy-O'Conner on the basis of calculations of spatial capacities.[90] How often and on which days the believers in Christ gathered are likewise difficult questions to answer.[91] Weekly meetings are possible but not certain. Perhaps the believers in Christ of a *city* met once a month, like many associations and cultic groups.[92]

9.3.2 Ekklēsia *as Community: Household and Family*

A. LINGUISTIC ANALOGIES TO HOUSEHOLD AND FAMILY

The home, the fundamental socio-economic unit of ancient societies, is of eminent importance both in the social context of early Christian communities and in New Testament linguistic usage.[93] Gülzow says correctly that households are the "nucleus" of Christian communities.[94] "From 1 Cor 16:15 [the members of the household of Stephanas were the first Christians in Achaia] we can infer that the history of Christianity in a city began as a rule with the conversion of a household."[95] Moreover, the Christ-confessing communities are generally discussed with terms from this realm of social experience. They are even explicitly called the "household" (*oikos*) of God (1 Tim 3:15)[96] or its members as members of the household (*oikeioi*) of God (Eph 2:19)[97] or members of the family of faith (Gal 6:10).[98] The apostle Paul can paraphrase his proclaiming office as *oikonomia:* the commission of the leadership and stewardship of a household (1 Cor 9:17). In 1 Cor 4:1-2 he uses for his missionary activity further terms from the social realm of the household: he is servant (*hypēretēs*) of Christ and steward (*oikonomos*) of God's mysteries. In a similar way, in Col 1:25 he calls himself *diakonos* (household slave who serves at table) for God's commission (*oikonomia*). Titus 1:7-8 prescribes for a leader of the Christ-confessing communities the code of honor of a steward (*oikonomos*).[99] Also composing a part of this context are the ethical texts of the New Testament that are oriented toward the division of roles in the ancient household (as we will see below). Since in addition to the actual family members the ancient household also encompassed slaves, freed men and women, wage earners, and other coworkers, one can again distinguish family terminology in the narrower sense from the terms for the Christ-confessing community, which adopted the conception of the household. By far most frequently, Paul calls his addressees *adelphos,* "brother," or *adelphē,* "sister" (Rom 16:1); in a few places he also refers to himself explicitly or implicitly as "father" (1 Cor 4:15; 1 Thess 2:11; Philemon 10). Occasionally believers in Christ are also called "children" and "sons" or "daughters" of God (Rom 8:16-17 and elsewhere; Acts 2:17), as brothers and sisters "beloved" by God (1

Thess 1:4, 6), or simply as "beloved." The tone is sometimes emotional and exuberant.[100] Also, the acceptance of a believer into the fellowship of the *ekklēsia,* which was linked with baptism, can be circumscribed with the image of adoption (by God as Father: Gal 4:6; Rom 8:15-17). The concept of the familial fellowship of believers can also be traced back in general to Jesus (Mark 3:31ff. par.).[101]

B. ETHICAL ADMONITIONS IN THE CONTEXT OF HOUSE AND FAMILY

The household and family metaphors also correspond to ethical admonitions to love of neighbor and to brotherly love.[102] These are oriented, each in its own way, toward ancient norms of reciprocity, whereby brotherly love represents the behavior of solidarity within the nuclear family or kinship, and love of neighbor the balanced reciprocity among neighbors and friends. Also falling into this context are New Testament allusions to love of friends, which can overlap with love of neighbor as well as with brotherly love. In Acts (2:42ff.; 4:32ff.)[103] the ideal model of the ancient love of friends serves to describe the community life of the Jerusalem early church. Moreover, Paul seems to interpret love of neighbor as brotherly love.[104] *Hospitality* is also a form of solidarity in the context of balanced reciprocity (cf. also the overview on p. 36).[105] Based on the ancient economy the ethical texts of the New Testament that are oriented toward the division of roles in the ancient household become more understandable.[106] Especially the *household rules* in the strict sense presuppose as a basis of their argumentation the social structure of a household, and they structure their admonitions with a view to the internal division of roles (man-wife, father-children, master-slave).

The connection of ethical admonitions with the terminology of the household and family shows that we have here something like a real-metaphorical use of language; that is, in the everyday reality of believers in Christ, their social relationships are oriented toward the norms of solidarity of familial groups and of the household.[107] In this process the norms for the nuclear family could also be applied within a household to its other (Christ-confessing) members. This seems, however, to have been rather the exception.

Paul, for example, challenges Philemon to receive his slave Onesimus, who has fled and in the meantime been converted to the faith by Paul, no longer as a slave but as a "brother" (Philemon 15-16).[108] Yet this instruction seems to have been the exception, since other texts (Col 3:22-23; Eph 6:5ff.; cf. 1 Cor 7:21-24)[109] do not touch the social relationships between (Christ-confessing) masters and slaves but rather only motivate the particular role behavior in a "Christian" manner.[110] Also, we cannot explicitly derive from Paul's instruction to Philemon a request for the manumission of Onesimus by his master.[111] Paul apparently expects a change in the social status of Onesimus within Philemon's household (Onesimus is to become a "brother" or "partner" of his master), but not the abolition of his legal status as a slave.

C. ORIENTATION TOWARD THE ANCIENT HOUSEHOLD, BUT NOT STRUCTURAL EQUIVALENCE

Thus the historical significance of ancient households for the recruiting of believers and for the solidarity of their social relationships cannot be overestimated. Yet we must note that the Christian community "is not simply identical with a household whose head has converted to Christianity."[112] This is shown already by the Letter to Philemon, which presupposes that a member of Philemon's household (the slave Onesimus) is converted to the faith only later, under the influence of Paul. Furthermore, in some cities there were several Christ-confessing house churches that also met together as the *ekklēsia*, had contacts with Christ-confessing communities in other cities, and felt connected with them. In this way it was possible for the developing Christ-confessing groups to be "inserted into or superimposed upon an existing network of relationships, both internal—kinship, *clientela,* and subordination—and external—ties of friendship and perhaps of occupation."[113] In the houses of fellow believers missionarily active believers in Christ (but probably not only they) received hospitality and sometimes even financial support.[114] The social relations among believers were also based on neighborly and familial solidarity. Thus we can say that Christ-confessing communities, in their self-understanding and social relationships, were based on the model of the ancient household or nuclear family. Yet they were not simply organized and structured like ancient households or families. They neither fulfilled the latter's central purpose (the subsistence of an extended family), nor was their organizational form a crude imitation of the household or family's institutional forms. This is also shown precisely by statements about the leadership functions of the communities.

D. LEADERSHIP FUNCTIONS

It was especially true of the Pauline churches that they contained no developed *institutional* leadership functions. In this context one cannot speak of "offices." The recognizable diversified functions are rather to be understood as "roles" in the context of charismatic groups: apostles, prophets, teachers (1 Cor 12:28); *episcopoi* (functionaries for the administration of community and perhaps financial affairs) and deacons (Phil 1:1).[115] They are based not on the division of roles of an ancient household but at most (as in the case of the *episcopoi* and deacons in Philippi) on that of associations and synagogues. Ultimately unspecific is 1 Thess 5:12 (cf. Rom 12:8; 16:2), where the leading function (*prohistēmi, prostatis*) recalls the duties of patronage. Thus the terms that come from the realm of the household for the designation of certain functions are probably used in the Pauline letters only in a figurative sense (see above). This metaphorical use of language is also clear in the Gospel of Luke. There in a parable (!) the apostles are addressed as administrators and servants of God (Luke 12:35ff.; cf. 17:7-10). Interestingly, in the concrete paraenesis to the representatives of the Christ-confessing communities (Acts 20:17ff.) this terminology does not appear. Also, the hierarchical social structure of an ancient household (with the *paterfamilias* at the head) is not recognizable in the Pauline churches.[116] Yet this situation seems to have changed by the end of the first century (pastoral letters). In 1 Tim 3:15 the *ekklēsia* is explicitly called the "household of God,"[117] and in 2 Tim 2:21 God is understood as its master (*despotēs*). The leader or overseer (*episkopos*)[118] of a church is supposed to head the divine household like a steward (*oikonomos:* Titus 1:7) and to have proved himself through good management of his own household (1 Tim 3:1ff.). He must also know how one behaves in a house and should treat older and younger members of the church like fathers and mothers, brothers and sisters (1 Tim 5:1-2). The *ethical admonitions* of the pastoral letters are also based on the internal division of roles in a house (husbands and wives, old and young, master and slave, also widows).[119] Thus if there is no doubt that the ethical admonitions of the pastoral letters—whether for community leaders or in general for the lives of believers in Christ—are based on the ancient economy, this does not mean, however, that the organizational form of Christ-confessing communities was modeled after the social structure or institutional organization of the ancient households of their time.

9.3.3 Ekklēsia *and Ancient Associations*

In the beginnings of the Roman empire, voluntary organizations of certain social groups experienced a "luxuriant growth."[120] In his standard work on the formation of ancient associations, Waltzing enumerates some one hundred different types.[121] These associations can be labeled as *collegium, corpus, curia, factio, hetaeria, thiasos, eranos, synhodos,* and so forth. Best known are above all the organizations of certain branches of crafts and businesses (bakers, shipmasters, and the like), also of traders and merchants, as well as the burial societies of lower-stratum members (*collegia tenuiorum*), which guaranteed its members an honorable burial. All of these associations had a certain guardian divinity and celebrated cultic rituals, yet they are probably to be distinguished from the actual cultic organizations (*cultores*), which carried certain divinities in their names (such as Jupiter, Hercules, Isis, and Mithras).[122] In their social composition, the associations contained mainly members of the lower stratum, both the poor and the prosperous, and especially for the occupational groups, members of the upper stratum assumed patronage functions.

Slaves and women were most likely to be found in religious or cultic organizations.[123]

> Since the members of the associations as a rule did not meet the preconditions for election to the city magistrature or for cooptation into the *ordo decurionum,* for many the *collegium* may have not only fulfilled a social need to get together in a group of like-minded, similarly interested people, present offerings, and celebrate feasts, but also meant a self-affirmation in a small circle, especially if one had additionally assumed some sort of function.[124]

Thus it is noteworthy that the function designations of many organizations assimilated those of city officeholders (*"prytanis,* treasurer, secretary, *decuriones, quinquennales,* and so on").[125] The assemblies of the associations took place once a month, either in private rooms, even at inns, or if the organizations were prosperous, in dedicated assembly buildings (*schola*).[126]

A. *EKKLĒSIA* AND ASSOCIATION: SIMILARITIES AND DIFFERENCES

Already in the second and third centuries the Christ-confessing communities were understood as a form of the ancient association,[127] and in modern scholarship this comparison has sporadically appeared from the end of the nineteenth century until the present.[128] Like the *collegia,* the Christ-confessing communities were also small, manageable groups in which personal contact with members was possible. Here too, membership was voluntary, and meetings were connected with "cultic" rituals and common meals. Nevertheless, the Christ-confessing communities were significantly more exclusive regarding their membership[129] and not as homogeneous in their social composition as the associations were. From the standpoint of membership (including slaves and women) and the explicit relationship of the Christ-confessing communities to the one God or Christ (*ekklēsia* of God/Christ), they would perhaps be best compared with cultic organizations (*cultores*). In particular, however, it is striking that the "hierarchy of offices," which was a part of the institutional organization of many associations and which connected them closely with the hierarchy of urban functions, was completely lacking in the Christ-confessing communities.[130] Only the regular meetings, which were connected with common meals, could suggest an analogy with the ancient associations. Yet, as we will now show, even this analogy is not unambiguous. It could as easily be modeled after the practice of table fellowship in ancient households.

B. COMMUNITY MEAL

One specific social experience of early Christendom has not yet been discussed: the common meals (including the Lord's Supper) of the gathered. Also in ancient households, there were common meals with the reciprocal invitation of guests. The idea is worth considering that the brief remarks about the "breaking of bread" in Acts 2:42, 46 reflect, *house by house,* the common meals (including the Lord's Supper in 2:46?) of believers in Christ and thus are linked to normal table fellowship in homes. Even with the meals of believers, which took place in house communities, the analogy with reciprocal guest invitations in houses cannot be ruled out (cf. 1 Cor 11:17ff.). Yet also within the associations, individual members appear as hosts of such meals; in addition, these were paid for by patrons or from the association treasury. The few New Testament texts that inform us about the early Christian meal fellowship (Acts 20:7, 11; cf. 1 Cor 10:14-22; 11:17-34) give us no *unambiguous* conclusion as to which model of ancient meal fellowship corresponds to the practice of the *ekklesia.* Yet an analogy to the praxis of the associations is at least indirectly attested in Pliny's letter regarding the trials of Christians, which presupposes that believers in Christ came together in Bithynia for common meals yet had discontinued this practice on account of the prohibition of political associations (*Ep.* 10.96.7). Thus the Bithynian believers in Christ themselves either understood their common meals in analogy with ancient associations or feared that they could be thus understood. Yet since the Pliny letter also reveals a regular assembly of believers in Christ on a set day (*stato die*), a comparison with the practice of ancient associations is probable. Moreover, their fellowship meals had a *ceremonial* character; that is, they took place regularly, and the number of participants was fixed, as was the table arrangement (including the community member who had the function of "presiding" at the meal). In this sense, they also confirmed roles and positions of status within the group.[131] In the community meals the common interests of each particular group were expressed, and they served to consolidate its social cohesion. At the same time, however, the common meals also had a restricting function in that they excluded all who were not invited.[132]

C. THE COMMUNITY MEAL AND THE LORD'S SUPPER

If, as we may presume, the reality of Christ-confessing assemblies at the end of the first century is reflected in Acts 20:7ff., then we can infer from this text that the meetings of believers in Christ took place regularly (on the first day of the week) and were connected with a common meal. The meeting described there takes place in a room on the second floor of a rented house in Troas. The "breaking of bread" appears to be the main purpose of the gathering. It is connected with a regular meal (20:11). Before the meal Paul gives a kind of lecture (in this case, very detailed), which, however, probably also included a dialogue or a disputation with the remaining participants. The same word (*dialegomai*) is also used to designate lectures of Paul in synagogues and at the forum. These talks can refer to the Holy Scripture and proclaim the kingdom of God (17:2, 17; 18:4; 19:8). Also during the meal Paul holds an (educational?) "discussion" (20:7, 11). Moreover, it is he who presides at the common meal. It is not entirely clear whether the "breaking of the bread" connected with the regular meal refers to the Lord's Supper.

The formulation *breaking of bread* (cf. also Acts 2:42, 46; Luke 24:35) is, in any case, an abbreviation for something ceremonial; that is, it is connected with a blessing or prayer of thanks, probably also including an offering gesture by the one who presides over the meal (Luke 24:30; Acts 27:33ff.). This ceremony is to be understood on the basis of the Jewish meal custom but is also connected by Luke especially with Jesus (Luke 24:31, 35).[133] Here, however, reference is also made to the institution of the Lord's Supper (Luke 22:14-20 par.). Yet the ceremonial act does not always have to include the recitation of the so-called words of institution. Especially in the situation described in Acts 27:33ff., this is not to be expected. Yet the fellowship meal held there under the leadership of Paul also contains central elements of the ceremony, and the meal is given a "salvific" character (27:34). In Acts 2:46 the "breaking of bread" is connected with jubilation, which probably means joy over the anticipated eschatological salvation (cf. also the eschatological aspect in the Lord's Supper wording, for example, in 1 Cor 11:26: "until he [Christ] comes"). According to 1 Cor 10:14ff., sharing in the cup and the bread at the Lord's Supper brings exclusive communion with Christ, which excludes participation in other cultic rituals. This "cultic" aspect of the common Lord's Supper reinforces in a prominent way the specific, somehow divinely ordained cohesion of the Christ-confessing group, which is defined metaphorically in the image of one "body" of many believers in Christ (1 Cor 10:17).

The connection of the fellowship meal with the Lord's Supper is thus found explicitly in 1 Cor 11:17-34. The Lord's Supper (*kyriakon deipnon*) also occurs in the context of a gathering of believers in Christ (1 Cor 11:17ff.) and is connected with a regular meal (11:21), which takes place between the words over the bread and those over the cup (1 Cor 11:25: the words over the cup are spoken after the meal).[134] Yet in Corinth the group reinforcement function of the Lord's Supper seems to have suffered. Instead of the "unity" of the members as the ("mystical") body of Christ, the assemblies produced divisions (1 Cor 11:18), and the social differences between church members were apparently manifested in the table fellowship itself. Possibly Christ-confessing hosts placed better (and more) food before their more prosperous guests than before the others.[135]

A clear understanding of the conflict is difficult, for the formulations that circumscribe the problem are ambivalent. Nonetheless, we hold the interpretation of varying hospitality for Christ-confessing guests to be the most likely. First Paul states that the meetings are not really for eating the Lord's Supper (1 Cor 11:20). And as substantiation he adds: "For when the time comes to eat, each of you goes ahead with your own supper, and one goes hungry and another becomes drunk" (11:21). This could be interpreted to mean that the Christ-confessing hosts—in agreement with social conventions[136]—offered different foods (perhaps some of the more prosperous guests also contributed to the meal). The manifested social differences among believers in Christ can be avoided, in Paul's opinion, if the more prosperous believers (who have their own houses) eat at home (11:22). For in the criticized practice, the believers in Christ who have no houses (slaves and other members of nonbelieving households) are discriminated against socially. Moreover, the well-to-do believers seem to begin the meal before the poorer ones (or some of them) are present (11:33). The temporal aspect ("wait for one another": 11:33) is connected with the social aspect. Then we may presume that the introductory formulation ("When you come together, it is not really to eat the Lord's supper": 11:20) is a description of the real circumstances in Corinth.

In any case, this conflict among Corinthian believers in Christ reflects differences in the social status of the gathered that run counter to unity in Christ in Paul's sense.[137] Hence the Corinthian praxis is a textbook example of the previously discussed recognition that in common meals and in their etiquette and foods, differences in social status are replicated, and this social structure proves to be especially resistant to social change. In the Christ-confessing community of Corinth, *internal group* roles seem to have not yet really become fixed; rather, the common meals reflected the status criteria that prevailed outside the Christ-confessing assembly. This could be seen as an indication that the meetings and table fellowship of the Christ-confessing communities were different from those of voluntary associations to the extent that in the latter internal group roles were fixed. Yet a definitive decision about the possible analogy of the Christ-confessing fellowship meals—at home or in meetings—is not necessary in order to place the early Christian meal praxis in terms of social history. For basically, the structure of the Greco-Roman banquet is the model for all table fellowships, whether on the occasion of family get-togethers, invitations from house to house, burials, meetings in philosophical schools, artisans' associations (*collegia*) or other voluntary group formations, and religious (including Jewish) communities, as well as on the occasion of Jewish feasts.[138]

9.4 The Sociological Placement of the *Ekklēsia* in the Context of Ancient Analogies

A. MODERN SOCIOLOGICAL CLASSIFICATION OF THE *EKKLĒSIA*

In the terms of modern sociology the Christ-confessing communities are basically "groups" or "small groups" whose members meet on certain occasions and potentially have personal communication and interaction with each other.[139] If we want to differentiate the group character more precisely, we could call the ancient Christ-confessing communities *interest groups* in that their members shared specific interests and values that they regarded as typical for the group and as fundamental to its existence, its ability to function, and its growth. And since the interests of this group are also formulated in religious terms and thus directed toward a supernatural end—say, the kingdom of God or the future existence of new people after the resurrection—we can speak of the *ekklēsia* as a *religious* group.[140] The self-understanding of a group also includes its relationship with outsiders, that is, a collective self-consciousness ("we" in distinction to "the others"),[141] which can also be demonstrated for the Christ-confessing communities.[142] Not meaningful to the same degree, yet also not completely excluded, would be an understanding of the *ekklēsia* in the sense of modern sociological terminology as a *faction* or *social movement,* to the extent that these include unions of people that deviate structurally from social principles or as social movements pursue the goal of social change.[143] The term that seems least convincing to us is *sect,* when it says no more than that the entity it designates is a minority group.[144] If, however, it is meant in the sense of the view shaped by Weber and Troeltsch, it is not appropriate because it presupposes an opposite (for Troeltsch, church; more neutral is the term *parent body*), which in this case would have to be, say, Judaism (or its local representation in the Diaspora synagogue) or pagan society (or its local manifestation in a certain polis). But for the *ekklēsia* neither Diaspora Judaism nor pagan society had this function of a parent body. Nor is a corresponding self-understanding of Christ-confessing communities discernible either in Paul or in most of the other writings of the New Testament.[145] Only in the Lukan double volume do we find traits of the *ekklēsia* as a kind of Jewish "sect" in the sense of the sect sociology developed by Troeltsch.[146]

B. "EMBEDDED" RELIGION

These modern sociological evaluations of the *ekklēsia* lead to understanding the phenomenon of the Christ-confessing communities in the cities of the ancient Mediterranean world from the perspective of modern viewpoints and the social experience of modern societies. It seems to us, therefore, more meaningful to locate the historical form of the *ekklēsia* within the basic social structures of their ancient societies.[147] Here it is of fundamental importance that in antiquity two distinct social spheres shaped the common life of people: the sphere of the *politeia,* that is, the public life of the polis community to which the residents of a city belonged in legally different ways, and the sphere of the *oikonomia,* the household, to which one either belonged by birth or was added to in some other way. Also embedded into these social spheres was economic life, which as redistribution and market exchange was constitutively connected with the realm of the *politeia* and as reciprocity with the realm of the household and the family. Just as in ancient Mediterranean societies there was no such thing as a pure economy—that is, an economic activity unrelated to the public and household social spheres, so also there was no free-floating social institution that could be designated as "religion" or a purely religious communion or group, nor any difference between church and state or church and family. For the ideas connected with the modern conception of religion can hardly encompass those of the people of antiquity.[148] Yet the latter problem will not concern us here; for now we must focus on the fact that ancient religion was embedded religion, that is, that the structures of ancient religious groups have to be understood on the basis of the fundamental structures of the ancient social system. More precisely, the common religious convictions and practices of ancient people were embedded in the context of comprehensive social relationships that were pregiven either through kinship and family (of household), through membership in a certain people, or through the political structures. As further social institutions of religious practice, one can also name the Roman army and the voluntary associations.

C. *EKKLĒSIA* AS FICTIVE POLITICAL INSTITUTION AND FICTIVE KINSHIP GROUP

It is not surprising that the New Testament texts exhibit no relationships of the *ekklēsia* to the army or to membership in a certain people.[149] By contrast, analogies to the household or nuclear family, to the political structures of the polis, and to voluntary associations play a dominant role. Indeed, our analysis of the linguistic usage, self-understanding, and social praxis of the *ekklēsia* showed that the Christ-confessing communities in various cities of the Roman empire, through their regular meetings in one place and through their community ties during these meetings and beyond them, exhibit specific relationships to the ancient popular assembly and to the ancient household/family or to voluntary associations. The institutional character of the *ekklēsia* can best be compared with the popular assemblies; the character of fellowship is best compared with the ancient household or nuclear family. The connection of meeting and meal fellowship suggests an analogy with the associations. The social community *ekklēsia*, within the context of the social system of its time and its society, bears traits of a *fictive kinship group*, whether in the narrower sense of the family or in the broader sense of a household.[150] Its actual assemblies, by contrast, show the traits of a fictive political institution[151] and, indeed, here and there even those of a fictive polis (city). The fictive political orientation of the *ekklēsia* is also suggested by some further metaphors, not yet discussed, for example, when Paul designates the eschatological future of the believers in Christ as a heavenly *politeuma*, that is, a kind of heavenly citizens' union (Phil 3:20; cf. 1:27; Acts 23:1), or when he relates them to the heavenly Jerusalem (Gal 4:26; cf. esp. Heb 11:10; 12:22-23; 13:14; Rev 21:2, 10ff.). The characterization of the community of believers in Christ as an organism in which the individual members of the body of Christ work together can also have a political aspect.[152] For the metaphor of the body and its members could also be used politically.[153] Even the metaphorical designation of the Christ-confessing community as the temple of God suggests a public, political sphere in the context of ancient religious praxis (1 Cor 3:16-17; 6:19; 2 Cor 6:16; Eph 2:21). Yet we must not underestimate the importance of the differences between the Christ-confessing *ekklēsia* and the political popular assembly. In the latter only certain persons were admitted: free citizens of a city and only men. The Christ-confessing *ekklēsia* gathered together men and women, free and slave, and members of various peoples (cf. Gal 3:28).

10

THE SOCIAL COMPOSITION
OF CHRIST-CONFESSING COMMUNITIES

This chapter offers first a brief overview of some research positions (10.1). We will then discuss the social composition of the Pauline churches and Paul's social status (10.2) and that of the urban Christ-confessing communities after 70 c.e. (10.3).

10.1 The Present State of Research

Toward the end of the nineteenth and in the early twentieth century, the social composition of the Christ-confessing communities in the New Testament period attracted the interest of theological scholars, in part because of current social issues. Then for decades this issue almost completely disappeared from view. Since the 1960s, however, it has drawn increasing attention.[1] In the older research there was, in regard to the social stratification of early Christianity, a broad consensus that the majority of believers in Christ came from the lower social stratum. In more recent research, by contrast, the predominant opinion seems to be that men and women from all strata of the population became believers and, indeed, that in principle the members of the urban elite played a dominant role.[2] We will briefly sketch these antithetical positions.

OLDER RESEARCH POSITIONS

The essence of the older consensus is expressed, for example, in a lecture by Deissmann: "Simply overwhelming is the impression of the close interweaving of early Christianity with the lower (illiterate) strata."[3] Until well into the second century, the Christ-confessing communities were composed "to a very great degree of little people, slaves, emancipated slaves, and craftsmen," maintained Harnack.[4] And where those outside of theological studies discussed the social situation of early Christianity out of decidedly political interests, those like Kautsky emphasized its "proletarian character," since it "was composed of almost exclusively proletarian elements" and a "proletarian organization."[5] This "politicization" of early Christianity was, naturally, disparaged by theologians.[6] Troeltsch, for example, energetically fought against making "Christianity a purely social movement." He emphasized, on the contrary, that early

288

Christianity was essentially a *religious* movement.[7] In spite of the political and philosophical differences, on the one hand, between social democrats and Marxists like Kautsky, who advanced the proletarian character of early Christianity positively for the present, and like F. Engels, who in remarkable contradiction to his class-warfare consciousness wanted to defame the proclamation of early Christianity as a "religion of slaves, exiles, outcasts, and the oppressed" and as "nonsense,"[8] and in spite of most theological scholars, on the other hand, who wanted to hear nothing about a politicization of early Christianity, there was agreement, nonetheless, that the overwhelming majority of early communities belonged to the lower strata. In principle, Troeltsch also held this position, yet he was also of the opinion that faith in Christ reached into the highest levels of society:

> It is true that the communities long consisted mainly of slaves, freedmen, and craftsmen, but . . . in view of the caution exercised in the acceptance of slaves, one must not exaggerate their participation; in any case, particular care was taken to stay away from slaves desirous of emancipation. Already from the very beginning, however, members of the upper stratum were not lacking. . . . Under Domitian Christianity penetrated even the highest court circles, and the famous letter of Pliny speaks expressly of *multi omnis ordinis*. Since Commodus, then, the participation of the upper stratum increased starkly. All of this is no more than natural with the presupposition that it was essentially a question of a religious movement, and it is clear counterevidence against the view that it was a "class movement of the proletariat" or a religious "reshaping of ancient socialism."[9]

Newer Research Positions

In more recent discussions the so-called older consensus has been widely called into question by, among others, the Marxist side. For according to Kreissig, Christianity of the first century "spread not so much among 'proletarians' or craftsmen working alone or even small farmers, but rather in the urban circles of well-situated craftsmen, traders, and members of free occupations."[10] Even the opposite of the lower-stratum thesis of the older research is asserted. According to Judge, namely, the believers in Christ by no means came from a "socially suppressed stratum"; rather, "the predominant element came from the self-conscious upper stratum of the large cities." The lower-stratum members in the Christ-confessing communities were drawn mainly from the households (slaves/clients) of these urban elite.[11] Thus here membership in the Christ-confessing communities is even declared the exception for those from the lower stratum. In adopting Judge, Gülzow states: "The Christian communities were distinguished from the very beginning by the fact that they were joined by people from all possible stations."[12] Against the older "romantic" conception, according to which Christianity spread above all among slaves, Gülzow emphasizes the importance of well situated "God-fearers."[13] Eck also holds the social composition of the Christ-confessing communities even in New Testament times to be "almost a mirror image of the general social stratification."[14] And Hengel assumes that "members of the Christian churches are to be found in *all* strata of the population, from slaves and freed men and women to the local aristocracy, indeed, from the decurions to perhaps even the senatorial nobility."[15]

The Troeltsch quotation above shows that the so-called older consensus about early Christianity as a lower-stratum movement was not shared by everyone even at that time. And it is also noteworthy that in principle Troeltsch's position is also advocated by the so-called newer research consensus.

Troeltsch's critique of the politically motivated "proletarianization" of early Christianity is continued here, in that attribution to the lower stratum, advocated even today, is covertly regarded as attribution to the "proletariat," even when the term does not appear. Thus Meeks writes: "The notion of early Christianity as a proletarian movement was equally congenial, though for quite different reasons, to Marxist historians and to those bourgeois writers who tended to romanticize poverty."[16] Without doubt terms such as *proletarian* and *class movement* are little suited to the task of expressing the social composition or the specific interests of early Christ-confessing communities. In principle, they presuppose a Marxist social model, whose ability to describe ancient societies is problematic (see pp. 7–8). Yet one should also not confuse the term *lower stratum* with the term *proletariat*.

Nevertheless, in the newer research the social stratification of early Christianity is actually still disputed. Gager, for example, is not convinced by the newer consensus.[17] He and Scroggs hold fast to the idea that the majority of believers in Christ came from the lower stratum. Scroggs explains the differences between the old and new consensus, drawing from the same data, by saying that some representatives of the new consensus place too high a value on certain writings in the New Testament (for example, Acts).[18] The differences, however, can also be traced back to the different stratification models (to the extent that one is at all discernible) or to the diverging criteria for judging social position. Thus some scholars posit the existence of middle strata[19] or understand (literary) education, for example, as a sign of the upper stratum.[20]

The Object of Stratification

Here we will analyze separately the Pauline churches, for which only the authentic letters of Paul will be considered (Romans, 1–2 Corinthians, Galatians, 1 Thessalonians, Philippians, Philemon). The Acts of the Apostles, in our opinion, offers above all information about the time of its author. Thus it will be utilized in the section in which the social context of the *ekklēsia* in the period after 70 is presented. We have attributed the Gospels of Matthew and John to the land of Israel and discussed them separately. The remaining eighteen New Testament writings are evaluated differently in their contributions to social history. From some writings we can derive almost no data[21] or only general information[22] on the social position of the addressees. Some offer at least individual data (1–2 Timothy, Titus, 1 Peter, Revelation). Most productive are the Letter of James and above all the Acts of the Apostles. Hard to evaluate are the Gospels of Mark and Luke. They contain only indirect testimonies of their Christ-confessing communities, for their narrative world is the world of Jesus. Nonetheless, in connection with data from the other scriptures, we can draw from them certain conclusions about the social world of their addressees.

Criteria
The underlying structural traits of ancient societies that were established in Chapter 3 will serve for the following stratification of Christ-confessing communities outside the land of Israel: the distinction between elite and nonelite, the differentiation of the elite into members of the *ordines,* rich without *ordo* membership, and retainers of the upper stratum, as well as the fundamental separation of the lower stratum into relatively poor/relatively prosperous and absolutely poor. The situation of women will be treated in Part Four. Since we have already discussed the fact that the communities were located in urban regions, this criterion does not need to be discussed here separately.

10.2 The Social Composition of the Pauline Communities

The social composition of the Pauline communities and to a lesser extent the social status of Paul himself have been the objects of many investigations.[23] Yet the stratification models, as well as the evaluations of Paul's social status in particular, vary remarkably from one another (the scale reaches, roughly speaking, from the upper stratum through the middle to the lower stratum). This is not surprising, since various textual foundations are utilized (in addition to the Pauline letters recognized as authentic, also the Deutero-Paulines and above all Acts) and it is not always clear which criteria are used in measuring social positions. The differences, however, are also connected with the fact that we only rarely have very detailed and concrete information. Ultimately, from the meager prosopographic data (that is, indications of the origin, status, or financial situation of individuals that are connected with personal names or other information) and from indirect data in Paul's letters, we can gain only a relatively hypothetical picture of the social stratification of the Pauline communities. For in general, even the prosopographic data contain only indications of the ethnic (or religious) background of the person in question (for example, for Andronicus and Junia, Herodion and Jason, it is clear from Rom 16:7, 11, 21 merely that they belong to Judaism). Sometimes one can infer the social or legal status from the name (for example, typical slave names are Ampliatus, Urbanus, and Tertius: Rom 16:8-9, 22). On the whole, the general insight is also true here that it is hardly possible to grasp the ancient lower stratum with the help of prosopography.[24] Yet the fact of deficient prosopographic data in itself says a great deal. For the comparison with Acts, in which prosopographic statements also appear regarding members of the upper stratum, among others, results in the heuristic thesis that members of the elite are in principle recognizable as such prosopographically. The information deficit of prosopographic data can also be balanced by further indirect information—for example, the Pauline linguistic usage for rich and poor—though not completely. Nevertheless, it can offer further auxiliary arguments.

10.2.1 The Pauline Communities in General

Extremely helpful is the careful and detailed analysis by Meeks, who utilizes prosopographic and indirect evidence.[25] This means that the individual data about individuals, which are amassed in the greetings lists of Romans (16:1ff.) and the closing passages of 1 Corinthians (16:10ff.), no longer need to be discussed here in detail. Meeks comes to the following conclusions.[26] The resulting sketch of Paul shows people from several social levels side by side, yet the highest and the lowest levels of the Greco-Roman social scale are lacking. The fact that on the one hand, there are no big aristocratic landowners, no senators, no *equites,* and also no decurions (with the possible exception of Erastus) in the communities is not surprising. Yet on the other hand, there are also no concrete indications of people from the strata of the population totally without means, such as hired servants and independent artisans. The poorest of the poor, the peasants, the rural slaves, and the day laborers hired for agriculture apparently were not found in the urban environment of the Pauline communities. It is entirely possible that there were members in the Pauline communities who lived on the edge of minimal existence, yet we learn nothing about them.

By contrast, according to Meeks, all levels between these two extremes are to be found, even slaves, though we cannot say how numerous they were. The "typical" Christian, nevertheless, was a free artisan or small trader. Even in these occupational groups there were people who owned houses and slaves, who had the opportunity to travel, and who showed other signs of prosperity. Some of these rich housed individual Christians or entire groups, made meeting rooms available to them, or supported them in other ways. They practically fulfilled the function of patrons.

A short time later Meeks designates this social composition as a "generally representative cross section of the urban society of the time."[27] Yet this conclusion contradicts his own summary of the social stratification of the Pauline communities. For if the members of the *ordines* and the strata of the population totally without means were lacking, then this is hardly to be called a *representative* cross section of society.[28] In addition to this fundamentally different consequence of the analysis of Meeks, we will discuss in the following pages some individual problems regarding the use of socially relevant data in Paul's letters.

OVERVIEW

Prosopographic Data for Ordo *Members and Retainers*
Theoretically, only the Erastus from Corinth, who is mentioned in Rom 16:23 and called the "city treasurer" (*oikonomos tēs poleōs*), is possibly a Christ-confessing member of an *ordo*. Theissen[29] identifies him with an inscriptionally attested aedile of the same name and posits that the Erastus mentioned by Paul later had a different career and was elected aedile (one of the four most important positions of the magistrature). Yet it is questionable, on the one hand, whether the Erastus named in Romans 16 is identical with the aedile attested by an inscription. In any case, this can be asserted only hypothetically. On the other hand, the title *oikonomos tēs poleōs* commonly designates municipal "officials charged with administering public funds or property; the title is also applied in some cases (in Chalcedon and on Cos, for example) to persons who apparently were public slaves."[30] Thus we can say with certainty only that the Erastus mentioned in Romans 16 at least belonged to the (lower) bureaucracy of Corinth. He could have been a slave but was not necessarily one.[31] Hence, in our opinion, he belonged to the group of retainers of the upper stratum. This group also includes the believers in Christ from the *familia Caesaris* mentioned in Paul's greetings in Phil 4:22, yet we do not know either their specific rank within the group of imperial servants or whether they were slaves or freed individuals.

Finally, membership in the group of retainers is also possible for a few believers that Paul greets in Rom 16:10-11: members of the house of Aristobul and the house of Narcissus. The people mentioned by name are not greeted; they apparently do not belong to the community. Those who are greeted are probably slaves of members of the city of Rome's upper stratum: Aristobulus could belong to the Herodian dynasty and reside in Rome. Narcissus is perhaps identical with the notorious freedman of the emperor Claudius.[32] Thus, in our opinion, there were no members of the upper stratum with *ordo* membership who belonged to the Pauline communities. Yet it remains noteworthy that some members must be included in the group of retainers.

Indirect Information

This picture is not be changed by indirect statements. The well-worn verses of 1 Cor 1:26ff. are indeed often understood to say that among the Corinthians there were some, though not many, who were "powerful" (*dynatoi*) and "of noble birth" (*eugeneis*).[33] Taken literally, this must mean that the Corinthian church included some members of the social elite. Therefore Wuellner holds that "the Corinthian Christians came from by and large fairly well-to-do bourgeois circles with a fair percentage also from upper-class people as well as the very poor."[34] Yet since we do not have even one prosopographically unambiguous testimony for a believer in Christ from the noble and political elite of Corinth, Paul's formulation must be understood rhetorically.[35]

Prosopographic Data for the Rich

If there is no convincing evidence of *ordo* membership among confessors of Christ in the Pauline communities, the question remains whether they contained other rich upper-stratum members. Meeks seems to answer this question positively, for he identifies some of the free artisans and small traders as "rich people." Yet this classification on the basis of the possession of a house or slaves or on the ability to undertake journeys is not at all sufficiently substantiated. That is to say, neither Stephanas with his house in Corinth (1 Cor 1:16; 16:15, 17), Philemon in Colossae (Philemon 2), Prisca and Aquila (Rom 16:3; cf. Acts 18:2, 18, 26), nor Gaius (Rom 16:23; 1 Cor 1:14) can be regarded as rich local members of the upper stratum because they own houses or slaves or have traveled. On this data alone we can make no clear judgment about the wealth of the persons mentioned. Hence we need broader criteria in order to mark the social position of the named individuals more clearly.

One possibility is a relatively high social status, in the sense that these persons are to be regarded as *patrons*—Meeks: "protectors"—of their particular Christ-confessing house churches. This is worth considering especially for Phoebe, who was, according to Paul, *prostatis* for him and many believers in Christ (Rom 16:1-2). For the term *prostatis* could be equated with the Latin *patrona* and thus involve a certain amount of support (of a financial, social, or legal nature), which Phoebe provided for the members of the Christ-confessing community of Cenchrea.[36] Thus we must, in any case, assume a relationship of social inequality between Phoebe as patron and her Christ-confessing clientele, although the degree of social difference can no longer be discerned. Thus it is theoretically possible that Phoebe belonged to the local upper stratum of Cenchrea, had access to wealth, and also wielded a certain amount of influence. Something similar was true of Philemon, who headed a household with (several?) slaves, accommodated Christ-confessing guests, and took on certain protective functions for believers. Paul apparently also trusted him enough to turn over to him one of his slaves (Onesimus).

Yet we can no longer determine with certainty whether all believers in Christ with houses that they made available to the churches for meetings are to be understood as patrons in the narrower sense. In the case of Stephanas, for example, it would then be surprising that Paul has to urge the Corinthians to put themselves at the service of Stephanas (1 Cor 16:15-18). For the patron-client relationship presupposes a reciprocal solidarity, that is, on the side of the client, in any case, a relationship of obligation and subordination. Perhaps at least *relatively* prosperous was Gaius, who bears a typical Roman name and owns a house that was apparently large enough to serve as a place of assembly for all the confessors of Christ in Corinth (in Rom 16:23 he is mentioned as host—*xenos*—of Paul and the whole church; he is presumably identical with the Gaius in 1 Cor 1:14). If he was a citizen of the Roman colony of Corinth and the name *Gaius* (a common Roman name) here represents the first part of a three-part Roman name,[37] then membership in the local Corinthian upper stratum (without official function) is certainly a possibility. In no event, however, did craftsmen like the Jewish couple Prisca and Aquila belong to the local upper stratum.[38] Thus, on the basis of prosopographic data, some rich members of the upper stratum outside the *ordines* cannot be excluded, though they cannot be demonstrated with certainty.

Indirect Information
Not one person Paul names does he call rich. Also lacking in his writings are typical admonitions to the rich, for example, to deal responsibly with wealth.[39] It is noteworthy in general that Paul never uses terms of wealth in the socially concrete sense but only figuratively for God, Christ, and believers.[40] Beyond Paul's express involvement for the benefit of the poor in Jerusalem through the organization of a collection, his general requirements of generosity and hospitality (Rom 12:13; cf. 2 Cor 9:6-7), and his various attempts to reduce social tensions within the churches, the letters of Paul reveal no special interest in socio-economic problems and especially none in the topic of poverty and wealth.[41] Additional indirect statements in the Pauline letters, in which economic differences in the background of certain conflicts can be presumed, do not by any means necessarily have to be interpreted in terms of social tensions between rich and poor community members. The disagreements in connection with the Lord's Supper in Corinth can be understood in the context of the differentiated situation of the lower stratum (1 Cor 11:17ff.).[42] That is to say, this conflict by no means has to have been "a conflict between poor and rich Christians."[43] In other words, we may assume that the socio-economic chasm between the members of the commu-

nity was not great. Nor is there a clear and compelling identification of the so-called strong[44] and weak (*astheneis*) in the conflict over the eating of meat offered to idols (1 Cor 8:1ff.) in the sense of a difference of the social status of the participants. In fact, the "strong"—Paul, incidentally, does not express-ly call them such—in 1 Corinthians 8 are characterized by their possession of knowledge (*gnōsis*), whereas the "weak" do not have this knowledge and are weak in regard to their conscience.

Thus some members of the Pauline communities were possibly relatively prosperous and perhaps belonged to the group of the rich of their city. Nonetheless, they lack the decisive signs of status of the upper stratum (noble birth, political power, clear indications of substantial wealth).

Lower Stratum

A not insignificant number of people mentioned by name have typical slave names and also appear to have been slaves or freed individuals (for example, Epaenetus, Ampliatus, Urbanus, Asyncritus, Phlegon, Hermes, Patrobas, Hermas, Philologus, Julia, Tertius, and probably also Andronicus and Junia—all mentioned in Romans 16; cf. also Onesimus in the Letter to Philemon). This is also confirmed by Paul's paraenesis (1 Cor 7:21-24; Philemon; cf. Gal. 3:28). From 1 Thess 4:11-12 we may conclude that the great majority of the community members in Thessalonica worked as artisans.[45] Thus for the Pauline communities as a whole we may assume that with all the differences between and within the individual churches, in which relatively prosperous members found themselves beside small artisans, traders, and slaves, we must posit lower-stratum membership for most members, who probably generally lived above the level of minimum existence. The prosopographic evidence yields not a single indication of absolute poverty. The use of poverty terms in principle confirms this image. It is true that Paul speaks of the "extreme pover-ty" (*ptōcheia*) in the churches of Macedonia (2 Cor 8:2), but we may assume that in this passage he is using the term in an exaggerated way for rhetorical reasons, in order to praise the generosity of the Macedonians as an example to the Corinthians for the benefit of the really impoverished of Jerusalem.[46] Nevertheless, the Macedonians participated in the collection for Jerusalem, and even Paul received financial support from them more than once (Phil 4:14ff.; 2 Cor 11:9). Only the apostle himself and the Jerusalem early church (see pp. 218–19) are described with terms of poverty in the Pauline letters, *and*, moreover, financial support for them is also mentioned.

10.2.2 The Social Position of Paul

A. THE SOCIAL STATUS OF PAUL ACCORDING TO ACTS

Before we speak of Paul's self-assertions, we must first look at the Lukan picture of Paul in the Acts of the Apostles. On the whole, Luke sketches a picture of Paul that in many respects characterizes him as an outstanding figure and almost a divine human being (*theios aner*). For the Lukan Paul performs miracles of punishment, healing, and salvation, all certainly for the building up of his readers (Acts 13:9ff.; 16:16ff.; 19:11-12). In addition he is distinguished by great rhetorical ability (see, for example, 17:16ff.; 19:9-10), and he speaks Greek, Hebrew, and Aramaic (21:37; 22:2). Paul is the ideal embodiment of an exemplary Jew who is true to the Torah and a believer in Christ; at the same time, however, he is also a loyal subject of the Roman empire. He is equipped with the best Torah education that one can imagine (with Gamaliel in Jerusalem: 22:3); he has authority from the high priest (in regard to the "persecution" of the early church: 9:1ff. and elsewhere); he is a Pharisee and by birth a Roman citizen, as well as a citizen of his hometown Tarsus (22:27; 21:39), a man who knows how to deal with the aristocracy and the elite (with Roman governors and a king; he has friends among the "Asiarchs" in Ephesus; leading personalities of Roman Judaism visit him; and so forth: cf. only 13:6ff.; 19:31; 28:7). His speeches astonish philosophers (17:31ff.) and attract the inhabitants of whole cities (Antioch in Pisidia) and regions (in Ephesus).

Can all this be gained from historical sources? This heroic figure in Acts, in any case, hardly matches Paul's self-image as we are able to derive it from his letters. Debatable, for example, are above all his Jerusalem education and his persecutory activity there, as well as his social status.[47] Here we will examine only the question of social status by first attempting—without regard to the question of the historical authenticity of the Lukan picture of Paul—to present his social status as it is to be discerned from the texts of the Acts of the Apostles.

From the two Lukan assertions that the apostle was educated as a Pharisee in Jerusalem and that he was active in persecution there, we may conclude in regard to the social status of the Lukan Paul that in Jerusalem he must have belonged to the group of retainers of the upper stratum. Yet the question is whether according to the presentation in Acts, his social position must not be placed even higher. Crucial here is the question of Paul's Roman citizenship—as well as of Tarsus—both of which are presupposed by Luke (Acts 16:37-38; 22:25ff.; 23:27; cf. 25:10-11; 21:25-26; 28:19). For according to everything we know about the bestowal of Roman citizenship on provincials in the early imperial period, this was limited to the urban elite. Thus in Paul's hometown Tarsus, possession of Roman citizenship in the early imperial period was equivalent to a sign of upper-stratum status.

Inscriptional evidence from Pergamum shows how Roman citizenship had spread in the leading aristocratic families of this city in Asia Minor in the period between Augustus and Hadrian.[48] In the time of Augustus none of the 5 *stratēgoi* (the highest officials of the magistrature) held Roman citizenship. Under Trajan (98–117 C.E.) we find, in addition to 3 *cives Romani,* 2 foreigners. In 3 different years during Hadrian's rule (117–38 C.E.), all the top municipal officials were *cives Romani.* Other inscriptions in Pergamum show the same picture. The ratio of 5 Roman names to 19 foreigners is still found in the early imperial period. Then under Trajan more than half were *cives Romani,* and in the time of Hadrian's rule almost all leading families (34 of 38) held Roman citizenship. Politically, this practice of Rome's meant a feeling of solidarity and a close connection between the Romans and the traditional upper stratum of the provinces. Sociologically this showed, especially for the eastern areas of the empire, the "class character of Roman citizenship."[49] Yet members of the lower stratum also had the opportunity, after 25 (or more) years of service in the auxiliary troops or the fleet, to retire with Roman citizenship. "Perhaps over two million 'foreigners' were adopted in this way into the Roman citizenry by the middle of the second century C.E."[50]

Even the bestowal of Roman citizenship on long-serving veterans in the auxiliary troops of the Roman military (or the payment of a relatively high settlement) could lead to a situation where at least the higher ranks later belonged to the local elite of their place of service. If Paul's father acquired the privilege of citizenship as the freedman of a Roman citizen,[51] he could have belonged to the elite of his hometown Tarsus, which, in any case, would have been an astonishing if not impossible career for a Jew. Ethnically the father of Paul—and also Paul himself—would have been considered a Roman, which, however, would have raised a few problems in Tarsus. For the participation of Roman citizens of the local elite in the pagan cultic events could hardly have been accomplished by a Torah-true Jew—to say nothing of a Pharisee. In the long run, however, it could not have been avoided. Yet against this objection, one could point out that according to Acts 22:3 it may be presumed that while Paul was born in Tarsus, his parents later moved to Jerusalem, where he then grew up. There strict loyalty to the Torah would probably have been possible even for a Jew with Roman citizenship. Likewise the Philippi episode (Acts 16), which tells of a sharp conflict between Jews and Roman citizens, does not seem to endanger the Lukan picture of Paul's possession of Roman citizenship and his simultaneous membership in Judaism, since Paul at first spreads messianic propaganda *secretly* among Jews and resorts to his Roman citizenship only after the conflict makes it necessary. Also in Jerusalem, Paul appeals only at the last moment to his Roman citizenship (when he was already tied up for flogging: Acts 22:25ff.) and likewise uses it in the trial procedure only in the "emergency" of the threatening transfer of his case to Jerusalem (25:10). Thus the author of Acts makes sure that the possession of Roman citizenship while maintaining loyalty to Judaism will seem plausible to his addressees.

Yet the Lukan picture of a Paul who comes from the local elite of Tarsus seems to be contradicted by the fact that Paul works as an artisan with Aquila and Prisca in Corinth. The text of Acts, however, allows a way out here also. While Luke says that Paul practiced the same craft as the couple (as a *skēnopoios*, "tentmaker": Acts 18:3), Paul does not seem to make his living with this activity. As Luke presents the situation, Paul comes from Athens to Corinth and finds there the married couple Aquila and Prisca, and because he has mastered the same craft, he remains with them, works there, and preaches on the sabbath. Then later he seems to have had to give up this work because he was completely busy with preaching (Acts 18:5). It is also not indicated here that for his livelihood he was dependent on other fellow believers. This allows the presumption that in Luke's opinion Paul's activity in his craft was not necessary for his subsistence and that he had at his disposal financial means on which to live. Thus the work with Aquila and Prisca in their workshop could have had "tactical missionary" reasons. Also supporting the financial independence of Paul is the fact that in Ephesus he used and thus (presumably) rented a philosophers' school for his missionary activity (Acts 19:9), as well as the fact that as a prisoner in Rome he could afford to live in a rented dwelling (28:30). Since such rented quarters in Rome were very expensive and Paul had a privileged prisoner status, the reader must assume that the apostle had considerable means. Consequently, nowhere in Acts do we read that Paul had to work for a living or had to resort to the financial means of others.[52]

In summary, regarding Paul's social status according to the presentation in Acts, we may say that Paul had several characteristics of the upper stratum. On the basis of his familial background and the concomitant legal status of a Roman citizen, he came from the local elite of Tarsus (yet probably above the decurion class); as the executive organ of the high priest in Jerusalem, he had a high status as retainer of the priestly aristocracy there. He apparently had at his disposal considerable financial means to provide his livelihood even as a propagandist of the messianic Christian community. This elite status corresponds to his Jewish and Greek education and his interaction with leading members of the Jewish, Roman, and other provincial elite.

B. THE SOCIAL STATUS OF PAUL ACCORDING TO HIS SELF-TESTIMONY

Paul's noteworthy social position according to Acts has no basis in the apostle's own letters. Nowhere does Paul mention his Roman citizenship. Especially 2 Cor 11:24-25 seems to speak against the possession of this privilege, since Paul reports that he had to undergo the synagogal punishment ("the forty lashes minus one") five times and flogging by Roman authorities three times. For one of the privileges of a Roman citizen included having a free "back," and ancient authorities could not have violated the law so often. We would also have here the historically unique case of a Roman citizen being subject to a synagogal beating. He would not only not have been obligated to do this; on the contrary, a Roman citizen (to say nothing of the synagogues) could hardly have afforded such demeaning treatment in synagogues. The idea that for religious reasons (suffering for the sake of the proclamation of the gospel) Paul forewent the privileges of a Roman citizen and therefore not only did not speak of his status but also underwent dangerous corporal punishment eight times—especially in the case of the Roman floggings—is nothing more than a speculation.

From the Pauline letters, and also in contrast to the picture of Paul in Acts, we do not get the idea that the apostle has considerable wealth at his disposal for financing his journeys, as well as for his living expenses. On the contrary, *all* corresponding self-expressions of Paul strongly suggest that the apostle worked as an artisan to earn his subsistence *and* was dependent on financial support. His occupational activity is not more exactly specified (according to Acts 18:3, he was a *skēnopoios*, "tentmaker"),[53] but it is described as hard work (*kopos, kopian;* 1 Cor 4:12; 2 Cor 6:5; 11:23; 1 Thess 2:9). And according to 1 Thess 2:9, he worked from before sunrise until after sunset. Hock has correctly called attention to the fact that occupational activity was by no means of peripheral but rather of central importance for the life of Paul: "More than any of us has supposed, Paul was *Paul the Tentmaker.* His trade occupied much of his time. . . . His life was very much that of the workshop . . . of being bent over a workbench like a slave and of working side by side with slaves."[54]

Moreover, since Paul worked in various workshops, we may conclude that in his occupation he worked for a daily wage[55] and also evangelized while engaged in this activity (1 Thess 2:9).[56] In this sense he can also understand his hard work as a part of his suffering for his apostolic service. Especially the catalog in 1 Cor 4:8-13 (cf. 9:8ff.; 2 Cor 11:7-11; 12:14-16) reflects typical negative experiences of ancient craftsmen.[57] The modern view of "independent craftsmen"[58] is not only anachronistic; it also leads one astray to such curious ideas as Paul's having "economic independence" and the "opportunity to freely divide his time."[59] Such an evaluation is incomprehensible in view of Paul's assertion that he began his work before sunrise and was still at work after sunset. It contradicts not only our knowledge of the social situation of ancient artisans but also Paul's self-testimonies about a life defined by need.

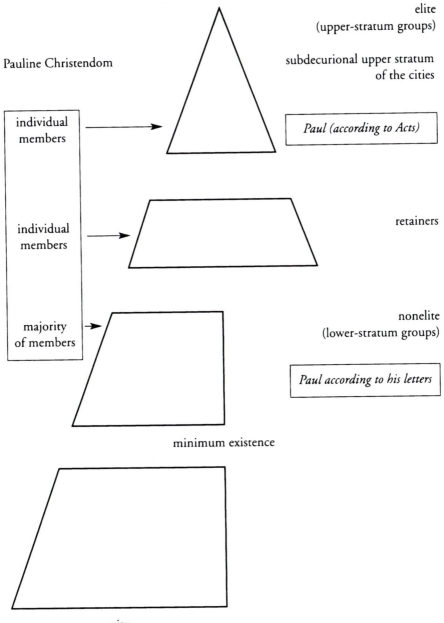

SOCIAL PYRAMID 5:
SOCIAL COMPOSITION OF PAULINE CHRISTENDOM BEFORE C.E. 70

From 1 Cor 4:8-13 we also learn that the apostle suffered hunger and thirst, was poorly clothed, experienced violence, sat in prison, survived all kinds of dangerous adventures on his journeys, was in mortal danger, and was reviled (cf. 2 Cor 6:4ff.; 11:7ff., 23ff.).

Apparently, through his occupational activity he could hardly live more than an extremely meager life[60] and was dependent on the financial support of fellow believers (2 Cor 11:8-9; Phil 4:10ff.).[61] This dependence on financial support, in addition to other statements by Paul, indicates that at times he lived below the level of minimum existence: hunger, thirst, poor clothing (1 Cor 4:11); he is sorrowful (*lypoumenos*) and poor (*ptōchos*), having nothing (2 Cor 6:10). Yet we may presume that this situation of need was also connected with his missionary activity and only at times defined his existence. Hence the socially relevant data from the Pauline letters seem to us to characterize the apostle basically as a member of the lower stratum above minimum existence. His self-testimonies offer no indication of membership in relatively prosperous upper-stratum groups. His (Jewish and Greek) education is considerable but by no means a dominant indication of stratum.[62] The Lukan image of Paul as a radiant speaker, incidentally, does not match his self-testimony: "For they say, 'His letters are weighty and strong, but his bodily presence is weak, and his speech contemptible'" (2 Cor 10:10).

C. A COMPARISON: ACTS AND THE PAULINE LETTERS

Our brief analysis of the social status of Paul has come to the conclusion that according to Luke's presentation, the apostle must have belonged to the local elite of his society. An examination of Paul's self-testimonies, by contrast, strongly suggests that Paul belonged to the ancient lower stratum (above minimum existence, relatively poor) and also understood himself in that way.[63] A balancing of the two literary testimonies is problematic: the idea that Paul gave up a higher social status and his handicraft work was a "sacrifice" in order to identify himself with the small people of his missionary propaganda[64] can, in our opinion, be derived neither from Acts nor from 1 Cor 9:19 and 2 Cor 11:7. Hence the crucial question for the evaluation of the historical Paul is, To what extent is Acts historically reliable in regard to its assertion that Paul was a Roman citizen and was so wealthy that he could support himself?[65] In our view, the Lukan picture of Paul represents a literary fiction, and for the estimation of the social position of the historical Paul, his own letters have priority. The historical Paul was a citizen of neither Rome nor Tarsus.

D. SUMMARY OF THE SOCIAL
STRATIFICATION OF THE PAULINE CHURCHES

There were no *ordo* members from the upper stratum who belonged to the Pauline communities. We have no clear evidence of rich believers in Christ, yet we cannot exclude the possibility that some community members were active in the function of patrons for their fellow believers and belonged to prosperous circles and perhaps even to the local upper stratum below the decurional nobility. Some believers could be identified as retainers of the upper stratum, even if it is not clear on which level this group is to be placed. The overwhelming majority belonged, without doubt, to the lower stratum, that is, to the relatively poor or relatively prosperous. Their occupational activities are only rarely discernible (craft workers like Prisca and Aquila); many were slaves or former slaves. The social position of the apostle Paul himself corresponds to that of the overwhelming majority of his addressees. The group of the absolutely poor is apparently not represented in the Pauline communities.

10.3 The Social Composition
of Urban Christian Communities after 70 C.E.

In this section we will arrange the socially relevant data of all the appropriate New Testament writings according to the criteria established in Part One (section 3.3). Some individual assertions of texts are not clearly interpretable, but this does not change the fundamental picture. The most productive for a sociological analysis is without doubt the Acts of the Apostles. Yet its information about upper-stratum members requires a critical evaluation.

10.3.1 Lower-Stratum Groups

A. ABSOLUTE POVERTY (*ptōchoi*)

It is difficult to clarify unambiguously whether or not the Christ-confessing communities included members of the absolutely poor (*ptōchoi*); the term does not occur in Acts, for example. From *prosopographic* information we know that certain people were slaves (cf. only Rhoda, Acts 12:13; Tychicus, 20:4; Eutychus, 20:9; Onesimus, Col 4:9). Yet nothing indicates that they lived below minimum existence. Further references to slaves can also be thus interpreted.[66] Among women widows are given separate mention. Here one may presume a suggested relegation to the absolutely poor (1 Tim 5:3ff.; Mark 12:40ff.; Jas 1:27), but not necessarily (Acts 9:39, 41). Also uncertain is the characterization of the Christ-confessing community in Smyrna found in Rev 2:9 (they are praised because of their poverty—*ptōcheia*).

The indirect information in the Gospel of Luke and the Letter of James requires its own discussion. Both writings treat in detail the opposition of *poor* and *rich* and therefore raise the question whether their interest in this topic is sociologically useful for the respective addressees.

Indirect Information in Luke and the Letter of James

The Gospel of Luke

In no other Gospel do criticism and concern vis-à-vis the rich (1:53; 6:24-25; 8:14; 12:13-21; 16:14-15, 19-31), exhortation to forgo possessions (5:11, 28; 12:33-34; 14:33; 18:18-30) and do good deeds (3:10-11; 6:33–36; 8:1-3; 16:9; 19:1-10; 21:14), and promises for the poor (1:53; 4:18-19; 6:20-21; 7:22) play as important a role as in Luke.[67]

The prominent significance of the topic of wealth and poverty in the Gospel of Luke is most meaningfully understood sociologically, although there is disagreement on whether it can be traced back to a corresponding stratum-specific situation of the Lukan communities. Esler concludes that among the members of the Lukan communities there were representatives of both the leading groups of the upper stratum and the lowest group of the lower stratum (*ptōchoi*).[68] Here we advocate the thesis that the Lukan communities included rich people, though probably not members of the political elite, as well as relatively poor people (*penētes*), but not representatives of the absolutely poor (*ptōchoi*). Luke 14:7ff., probably the most important text regarding the question of membership of the absolutely poor in the Lukan communities, indicates, in our opinion, that the Christ-confessing addressees of Luke included *no* absolutely poor.[69]

All three banquet parables (Luke 14:7-11, 12-14, 15-16, 21ff.) presuppose the urban milieu and address either the participants or the hosts of banquets. Thus we find ourselves in a milieu that is clearly above that of the absolutely poor. The fact that the host is then asked to invite—instead of the usual guests (friends, brothers, relatives, rich neighbors)—the absolutely poor and disabled (14:12-13) presupposes that from the standpoint of the parable the latter are outsiders. It is not a question of their integration into the social milieu of the host. Also in the parable of the great dinner, the poor and disabled are only substitute guests.

The kingdom of God belongs to the absolutely poor; they are the recipients of the beneficence demanded by Luke. Yet he distinguishes them from the followers of Jesus, who in the Lukan presentation have *voluntarily* become poor. Also speaking against the membership of the absolutely poor in the Lukan communities is the fact that we have no evidence for it from Acts. An evaluation of the social structure similar to the one we have presented here is also found in Moxnes:

. . . the community was a non-elite group that looked with suspicion upon the rich elites in their surroundings. This does not, however, exclude the possibility of social and economic differences within the community, and even people of some wealth among its members. The non-elites in Hellenistic cities consisted of many diverse groups: slaves of different categories, freedmen, foreign merchants and craftsmen, free, but poor citizens, etc. The first Christian communities probably were made up of members from these groups, maybe with some women of higher status.[70]

The Letter of James. The antithesis between rich (*plousioi*) and absolutely poor (*ptōchoi*) is also an important theme of the Letter of James (1:9–11; 2:1ff.; 5:1ff.). Does this reflect a social conflict among the addressees? We must ask the fundamental question, Does this scripture offer any concrete information about Christ-confessing communities?[71] Even the salutation—"To the twelve tribes in the Dispersion" (1:1)—remains vague. The individual relevant texts also advise against applying the social statements of the paraenesis directly to the social structures and problems of the addressees. For precisely where they make reference to the communities themselves, they give the impression of being hypothetical. The author seems to want to underline his paraenetic intentions through the construction of especially "crass individual cases."[72]

James 2:2ff. describes one such flagrant case. A rich person and poor person come into the community assembly and are treated differently. The social contrast is striking. The rich individual reminds one of a Roman "equestrian" (he wears a gold ring and fine clothes); the poor person wears dirty clothes, is labeled with the Greek word *ptōchos,* and is thus absolutely poor. Both are presented only as *visitors,* not as members of the Christ-confessing community. This hypothetical example uses a crassly constructed case to make the sin of partiality graphic as a transgression of the commandment of love (2:8-9). In a further example, faith without works is made graphic in behavior vis-à-vis the poor (2:14ff.). Here again it is a question of a hypothetical example in which absolutely poor individuals (people without clothing and daily nourishment) are given only a blessing but not fundamental assistance. This example assumes that the poor are believers in Christ (brothers and sisters). Yet this is supposed to underline that the blessing ("Go in peace; keep warm and eat your fill": 2:16) is inadequate. Whether it is a question of an actual community experience is likewise doubtful.

There is much support for the idea that James presupposes a social situation in which neither members of the social elite nor absolutely poor people are to be found. Nonetheless, the author seems to deal theoretically with the idea that absolutely poor fellow believers in Christ will come into the community, but not with the reality that they belong to one of the communities he addresses.

B. RELATIVELY POOR AND RELATIVELY
PROSPEROUS LOWER-STRATUM MEMBERS (penētes)

Much prosopographic evidence and also indirect information suggest that the overwhelming majority of believers in Christ in the epoch under consideration here belonged to the part of the lower stratum above minimum existence. The social situation varied between relatively poor and relatively prosperous but in most cases cannot be clarified in detail.

Prosopographic Evidence

Only for a few of the people mentioned by name[73] can we draw conclusions about social position or background. Onesimus, who is also mentioned in Philemon, is a slave (Col 4:9); Mark (John), a cousin of Barnabas (4:10), is a Jew. His mother Mary has a house in Jerusalem (Acts 12:12). A smith (*chalkeus*) named Alexander is mentioned in 2 Tim 4:14 (cf. 1 Tim 1:20). Onesiphorus (2 Tim 1:15) has a house church, as does a woman named Nympha (Col 4:15). None of them show any social traits that would lift them above the lower stratum, which must also include the synagogue official Crispus in Corinth and his whole house (Acts 18:8), as well as Jason, the host of Paul and Silas in Thessalonica (17:9), and Lydia, the dealer in purple cloth, and her household in Philippi (16:14ff.).[74] Also probably belonging there are Barnabas, a Levite from Cyprus (4:36), the "tentmakers" (*skēnopoioi*) Prisca and Aquila (18:2-3), some house and property owners in Jerusalem (4:32ff.; Ananias and Sapphira 5:1ff.), Tabitha (9:36ff.), Jerusalem widows (6:1ff.), and the tanner Simon (9:43; 10:6). Last to be mentioned are the apostles Peter and John, who are called "uneducated [*agrammatos*] and ordinary [*idiōtes*] men" (4:13). Peter has no gold or silver that he can give to a lame beggar (3:6), yet neither he nor any other member of the Jerusalem early church (in contrast to Rom 15:26) or the other Christ-confessing communities is ever called or characterized as absolutely poor. Thus they also belong to the relatively poor.

Indirect Information

Some texts presuppose that their addressees include older and younger men, women, children, free and slave, as well as slaveholders or masters (*kyrioi*)

(Eph 5:21ff.; 6:9; Col 4:1; 1 Pet 2:11ff.; 3:1ff., 7; 5:5; 1 John 2:12ff.; 1 Tim 5:1; 6:1-2; Titus 2:1ff.). These statements also imply what is expressly said elsewhere, namely, that whole "households" believed in Christ (cf. only Col 4:15 and 2 Tim 1:16). In this connection, Verner has pointed out that only around a fourth of the free families in the Roman empire were rich enough to be able to afford slaves.[75] And based on the fact that in some Deutero-Pauline letters slaveholders are admonished, he draws conclusions about the socio-economic situation of the communities receiving these letters. He understands the addressees of the pastoral letters as communities of considerable size and social diversification, including people with noteworthy financial means. The leading members of the communities were probably even recruited from a group of prosperous landlords.[76] Yet they hardly climb above the level of the well-situated lower stratum. The requirement that women dress themselves modestly (1 Tim 2:9-10) also presupposes a certain prosperity but must not be overvalued. The formulation of 2 Thess 3:11-12 (some community members who are not working are commanded to work and earn their own living), which recalls 1 Thess.4:11, hardly means believers in Christ who "can live from their money."[77] This interpretation does not fit with the assertion that they are not eating their own bread. It is a question here, rather, of the problem that they claim support as preachers of the gospel.

C. SUMMARY OF THE LOWER-STRATUM GROUPS

Even if the overall picture must remain vague, there are still many indications that the absolutely poor did not belong to the urban communities of the epoch after 70 C.E., which at most might have included widows. Most of the prosopographic evidence and indirect information points to a lower-stratum situation above the poverty level.

10.3.2 Upper-Stratum Groups

A. ORDINES

According to the presentation of Acts, by the forties and fifties faith in Christ had already penetrated the highest levels of the Roman imperial aristocracy and also reached decurional circles. The governor of Cyprus, Sergius Paulus, who had come to the faith (Acts 13:6ff.), must be ranked with the senatorial nobility. A comparably high position was held by the Ethiopian financial official whom Philip baptized (8:27-39). Dionysius belonged to the decurional nobility; he is a member of the Areopagus in Athens (17:34). Since this picture does not agree with the social structures recognizable in the letters of Paul in the epoch before 70, we have not considered the Pauline communities in this connection. The question is whether it is valid for the period after 70 and thus for the realm of experience of the author of Acts and his community situation (ca. 90 C.E.).

Hindrances for Ordo *Members as Believers in Christ.* Doubt is justified above all in the case of the legendary scene with the proconsul Sergius Paulus (Acts 13:6ff.).[78] His many obligations, in addition to participation in pagan cultic events, included the holding of sacrifices.[79] Also, on the basis of our knowledge about the "penetration of Christianity into the senatorial order before Constantine the Great,"[80] the inclusion of the proconsul Sergius Paulus in the Christ-confessing community is extremely improbable. Nevertheless, it is historically possible that a Roman governor had sympathies for Judaism (and in this case also for believers in Christ).[81] Flavius Clemens and his wife Domitilla, members of the Roman upper stratum who were put on trial by Domitian because of inclination toward "the Jewish way of life" (Dio Cassius 67.14), were probably sympathizers of Judaism; in the older research they were even held to be Christians.[82] Thus in our view, the historical element of the legendary story about Sergius Paulus is to be seen at best in the idea that at the end of the first century there were also persons in the Roman upper stratum who harbored a certain receptiveness (Sergius Paulus is called "an intelligent man") or even *secret* sympathy for believers in Christ.[83]

It is hardly realistic that a member of the urban decurional nobility (Dionysius: Acts 17:34) openly joined the Christ-confessing community. Such a step would have had notable social consequences, and it is no accident that we hear nothing about them. Again, participation in what Jews and Christians would call the worship of idols would have been an insurmountable obstacle, for the duties of the urban magistrate included, among other things, the holding of and participation in sacrificial celebrations.[84] The corresponding obligations (all the duties connected with the organization of the public cult, including the preparation of sacrificial animals) are unimaginable for a believer in Christ. Nevertheless, it is possible that members of the *ordo decurionum,* especially those who were not involved in the magistrature, sympathized (secretly) with the confessors of Christ. This thesis is confirmed by the fact that in later times the assumption of local offices of honor was virtually forbidden for Christians because of the danger of idolatry.[85] And even the presentation of Acts itself raises the question whether Luke really means to assert that Sergius Paulus or Dionysius became adherents of the faith in Christ in the sense of *social membership* in the Christ-confessing community.

Actually Luke speaks only of their coming to faith (Acts 13:12; 17:12, 34). Neither their baptism nor social consequences are mentioned. The lack of baptism in particular, however, is striking for Acts (cf. the baptisms in 2:38-

41; 8:12–13, 16, 38; 9:18; 10:47-48; 16:15, 33; 18:8; 19:5). It was without doubt a ritual process of conversion that symbolized faith or the act of confession as a social process. It is also noteworthy that the baptisms of the Ethiopian, of the *centurio* Cornelius and his household, of Lydia and her household, of the prison guard and his household, of Corinthians (18:8) and the disciples of John in Ephesus (19:5), and, not least of all, of Paul are specifically mentioned. If one overlooks the Ethiopian, of all the members of the upper stratum who came to belief in Christ in Acts, it is asserted only of the women from prominent circles in Thessalonica beyond their faith that they "joined" Paul and Barnabas (17:4).

This conclusion also agrees with the fact that we find adherents to faith in Christ in the highest levels of society, the imperial aristocracy, at the earliest at the end of the second or beginning of the third century.[86] An analogous situation is offered by the phenomenon of Judaism in the Diaspora. If only a very few Jews (such as the nephew of Philo, Tiberius Alexander) belonged to the equestrians and reached the highest levels of political leadership (he became a prefect), this presupposes, nonetheless, a falling away from Judaism.

The Social Stratification of the "Christians" Condemned by Pliny

A further confirmation of our analysis comes from a statement by Pliny the Younger in his letter to the emperor Trajan regarding the trials of Christians (*Ep.* 10.96.9):[87]

> The matter seems worthy of your consideration, especially in light of the number of persons accused. For numerous persons of every age and every class, both genders, are being brought to trial, and this is likely to continue [*multi enim omnis aetatis, omnis ordinis, utriusque sexus etiam, vocantur in periculum et vocabuntur*]. It is not only the towns, but villages and countryside as well which are infected through contact with this perverse superstition. I think that it is still possible for it to be checked. . . .

Pliny is clearly speaking here of the danger (!) that the Christian superstition could take over all the *ordines*. This does not mean, however, that there were already believers in Christ among members of the *ordines* at the beginning of the second century.[88] On the contrary, since from Pliny's formulation we can see his interest in underlining the importance of the matter by noting that all *ordines* are in danger of being seized by the Christian superstition, he would hardly have missed the opportunity to mention such a case if there had been one. Thus in Pliny's time faith in Christ had not even penetrated into the *ordo decurionum*. Again, an analogy is offered by the phenomenon of Diaspora Judaism. For in the period under consideration here, no Jews are known among the local decurions of Asia Minor.[89] As we have already explained, that is hardly a coincidence, since Jews (like believers in Christ) could not have fulfilled the cultic obligations that follow from membership in the *ordo decurionum*.

Believers in Christ as Roman Citizens

Nevertheless, Pliny's letter reveals that the accused *Christians* included Roman citizens (*Ep.* 10.96.5), who were marked by the governor for transfer to Rome. This indication is quite instructive in terms of social history, since we can assume that in this period in the provinces Roman citizenship was granted almost exclusively to the urban upper stratum[90] or to veterans of the military (auxiliary troops) after their discharge. Moreover, veterans of the legions could also have settled in the cities of Asia Minor. Thus, based on what we know of the practice of bestowing Roman citizenship on provincials, it is theoretically possible that the *Christians* with Roman citizenship mentioned by Pliny belonged to the local upper stratum of Bithynia—indeed, even to the decurions. But if there were decurions among the *Christians,* would Pliny have missed the opportunity to communicate this to the emperor? Therefore it is more likely that the Roman citizens mentioned by Pliny came from subdecurional circles; that is, they belonged to the local upper stratum but not to the *ordo decurionum.*

Here again the spread of Roman citizenship among the Jews of Asia Minor offers an analogy. According to Josephus (*Ant.* 14.228), already in the middle of the first century B.C.E. there were Jews with Roman citizenship, for example, in Ephesus. The discussion about the historical credibility of this assertion is widely divergent.[91] The two known inscriptions that offer evidence for the period in question come from the eighties or nineties of the first century. One mentions a certain Publius Tyrronios Klados in Acmonia, who is also called an *archisynagōgos* (synagogue official).[92] The second refers to the family of Titus Flavius Alexander, likewise from Acmonia, which presumably had Roman citizenship since the end of the first century.[93]

Thus even among the Jews of Asia Minor there were some Roman citizens, yet none of them belonged to the circle of the decurions. Also those believers in Christ with Roman citizenship who were marked by Pliny for transport to Rome may have belonged to a socially respected group of local upper-stratum families, yet not to the political elite. It is also possible that they were (relatively) rich. Likewise, we cannot exclude the possibility that the *Christians* with Roman citizenship mentioned by Pliny came from the largest group by far of new Roman citizens, namely, from the military (see the exemplary Gentile Christian Cornelius in Acts 10–11; cf. pp. 269–71).

B. THE RICH AND OTHER UPPER-STRATUM MEMBERS

Again, *prosopographic information* is found only in Acts. Silas and Paul are called Roman citizens (16:37; 22:25); Paul is also supposed to be a citizen of his native city Tarsus (21:39). This would have made Paul a member of the elite of his native city Tarsus (see p. 297). The local elite of Thessalonica also includes the wives of leading (*protoi*) citizens who allow themselves to be convinced by the preaching of Paul (17:4). In Berea even prominent (*euschemōn*) *men* and women are won (17:12). Menachem, who is mentioned in Acts 13:1 as *syntrophos* of the tetrarch Herod, could also be classified with the upper stratum, if we are to understand here something like a youthful companion of Herod.[94]

Indirect information about the rich is found, for example, in the Gospel of Luke. One may presume that the detailed criticism and paraenesis toward the rich (for texts see p. 304) is directed toward Christ-confessing addressees.[95] A rich chief tax collector (Zacchaeus) is interested in Jesus and becomes a model for the proper behavior of the rich (Luke 19:1ff.). Yet he does not belong to the respected circles of the upper stratum but rather remains despised in spite of his riches (19:7, 10). Women from prosperous and socially respected circles of the upper stratum also play a role: according to Luke 8:1-3 they support Jesus financially. This assertion, which is found only in Luke, is apparently a reflection of his own experience (see p. 378).

A paraenesis for the rich is also found in the Letter of James (5:1ff.). This announcement of judgment to the rich, however, hardly concerns believers in Christ, for the rich are accused of having condemned and murdered "the righteous one" (5:6). Even if this does not refer to Jesus, it is still clear that the negative eschatological fate of the rich is fixed; repentance is neither anticipated nor demanded (cf. by contrast the paraenesis in 4:13-17). Nor are the rich reminded of the ideal of the Christ-confessing existence. The addressees of the letter themselves are clearly distinguished from the rich: "Is it not the rich who oppress you? Is it not they who drag you into court? Is it not they who blaspheme the excellent name that was invoked over you?" (2:6-7). Yet James 1:9-11 gives the impression that the author is dealing with rich believers. For here the brother who is lowly (*tapeinos*) is exhorted to boast of his high worth (*hypsos*), the rich one of his lowliness (*tapeinōsis*). Yet the rich man is not expressly designated as a brother. The clear distance from the rich, on the one hand, and the clear warning against the temptation of wealth, on the other—the temptation, ultimately, to give up the standards gained in the faith (no favoritism, election of the poor by God: Jas 2:1, 5)—could lead to a real discussion in which the issue is the readiness of Christ-confessing communities to open themselves to the rich.

Also 1 Timothy contains admonitions to the rich (*plousioi;* 6:17-19). Yet they are kept so general ("those who in the present age are rich": 1 Tim 6:17) that they cannot necessarily be applied to Christ-confessing community members. Comparable is Rev 3:17, where the church in Laodicea is called rich, but this is hardly more than a reference to a certain prosperity. The wealth of the Christ-confessing community in Laodicea was not, in any case, significant, since it is explained in more detail: the church is not in need of anything. Also in the context of 1 Timothy readers are warned against wanting to be rich (*ploutein*) and against the accompanying dangers of the love of money (*philargyria*). By contrast, the letter recommends to the faithful an ideal of sufficiency, which is marked by a modest living situation, having "food and clothing" (6:6ff.). That means that in both 1 Timothy and Revelation, wealth is described as a social situation in which one can procure one's subsistence and has no shortage in the basic needs of life. This is the situation of relatively poor people (*penētes*).

In addition, isolated warnings against greed (*pleonexia*)—actually a topic of the criticism of the rich—are found either as a branding of false prophets (2 Pet 2:3, 14), and therefore to be used with extreme caution, or in catalogs of vices or as dangers of a former pagan existence (Eph 4:19; 5:3, 5; Col 3:5). Apparently they are not topical paraeneses for rich believers in Christ.

From the local elite beyond the decurional nobility, women in particular and perhaps some rich individuals may have belonged to Christ-confessing communities. Yet not only the lack of prosopographic evidence but also the indirect information advise against overevaluating the paraeneses for the rich in Luke, James, and 1 Timothy as the reflection of a significant number of believers in Christ from this upper-stratum group.

C. RETAINERS OF THE UPPER STRATUM

Colossians 4:14 mentions a certain Luke, who is called a physician (*iatros*). "Doctors were often slaves; we might speculate that Luke had been a *medicus* in some Roman *familia*, receiving the name of his master (Lucius, of which Lukas is a hypocorism) on his manumission."[96] If he worked for the upper stratum, he belonged to the retainers. Also a retainer was Zenas, a lawyer (*nomikos;* Titus 3:13); but it is not entirely clear whether he was a teacher of the Torah or a (Roman) lawyer. This category would also include the Jerusalem priests who, according to Acts 6:7, accepted the faith, if we could be sure that we do not have here a fictitious statement. The same is true of the converted Pharisee mentioned in Acts 15:5. The Roman centurion Cornelius, who headed the Italian cohort in Caesarea, would also have been a retainer.

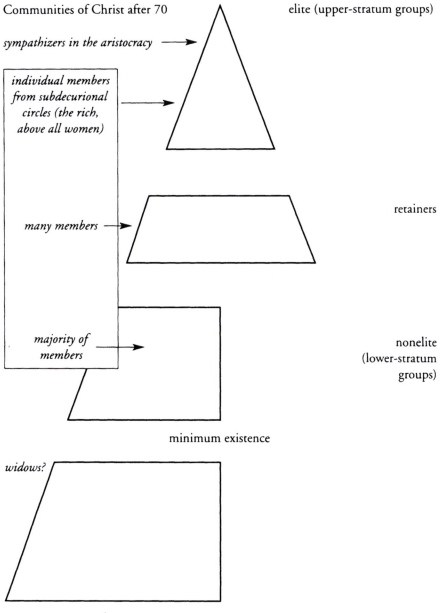

Communities of Christ after 70

elite (upper-stratum groups)

sympathizers in the aristocracy ⟶

individual members from subdecurional circles (the rich, above all women) ⟶

retainers

many members ⟶

majority of members ⟶

nonelite (lower-stratum groups)

minimum existence

widows?

city

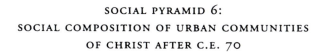

SOCIAL PYRAMID 6:
SOCIAL COMPOSITION OF URBAN COMMUNITIES
OF CHRIST AFTER C.E. 70

He and his household came to faith and were baptized (Acts 10–11), as was the prison guard in Philippi with his household (16:30-34).

Especially noteworthy is the figure of Cornelius. He is described as a God-fearer and benefactor of the Jewish people (Acts 10:2). The Italian cohort he commands (10:1) could mean the *Cohors II. Miliaria Italica Civium Romanorum Voluntariorum,* which was in Syria from shortly before 69 C.E. until into the second century (but not, as the narrative itself suggests, already in the reign of Herod Agrippa I). In his commentary, Haenchen correctly says: "Presumably Luke transferred the conditions of his time to the earlier period."[97] That also means, however, that in Luke's time (end of the first century) it must have been plausible to the readers of his Acts of the Apostles that a Roman junior officer was a God-fearer and had himself baptized. Luke devotes almost two chapters of his work to the conversion of Cornelius (Acts 10:1—11:18). Thus the event apparently serves as an exemplary conversion of a non-Jew (11:18). That it involves a centurion, a member of the group of military retainers (cf. pp. 269–71) is hardly accidental.

The rich chief tax collector Zacchaeus in the Gospel of Luke (19:1ff.) could also be an indication of the increasing importance of believers from the group of the retainers. And already in the Gospel of Mark it is at least suggested that a Roman centurion under the cross (Mark 15:39) confessed Jesus as the Son of God. In the Lukan narrative of the centurion of Capernaum (Luke 7:2ff.; cf. Matt 8:5ff.), he is characterized as a sympathizer and benefactor of Judaism and is also distinguished by his faith in the miracle worker Jesus (Luke 7:5, 9).

D. SUMMARY OF THE SOCIAL COMPOSITION
OF CHRIST-CONFESSING COMMUNITIES AFTER 70

According to the foregoing analysis, one can hardly say that the social composition of the New Testament communities after 70 was something like a "faithful mirror image of the general social stratification" or a "representative cross section" of contemporary society. Lacking were members both from the highest levels of society (*ordines*) and from the group of the absolutely poor (*ptōchoi*), if we assume that the poor widows of the communities were supported. Evidence for rich believers from subdecurional circles is meager but certainly noteworthy.

Lower Stratum
The majority of people in the communities of Christ after 70 came, according to our analysis, from the better placed urban lower stratum (above the poverty line). This conclusion is drawn from almost all the relevant texts. Yet

we have only minimal information about the concrete social situation and occupations of believers in Christ of the lower stratum. We can recognize some occupations (tanner, smith) that are also connected with small business (Lydia, the trader in purple cloth). Yet there also seem to have been wage earners. The community membership of artisans, workers, businesspeople, and traders is also widely attested in the post–New Testament period, for example, artisans (*technitai*) in *Did.* 12.3. Justin also mentions them (*cheirotechnai*), along with quite ordinary people (*Apol.* 2.10). *First Clement* 34.1 mentions a worker (*ergatēs*); Hermas (*Sim.* 9.32.3) a fuller, as well as businesspeople and traders (*Man.* 3.5; 10.1.4–5; *Sim.* 4.5, 7; 8.8.1–2; 9.20.1).[98]

This spectrum can be assumed in the Pauline communities, and in Paul's time there were already slaves[99] in Christ-confessing communities. This tendency seems to have continued as whole households were baptized (Christ-confessing masters as slaveholders and the membership of their slaves in Christ-confessing communities is attested by the paraeneses in Col 3:18ff.; Eph 5:22ff.). Yet there was apparently a change toward the end of the first century when slaves without Christ-confessing masters were also members of the community. "In place of admonitions to slaves in the context of the living arrangements of the Christian household we now have concern for the special needs and difficulties of slaves who have no Christ-confessing masters."[100] Gülzow sees an indication of this already in 1 Pet 2:20ff., since the slaves there are addressed directly; 1 Tim 6:1ff. accepts the fact that some slaves have no Christ-confessing masters. Some slave names support this picture: *Rhoda*, Acts 12:13; *Tychicus*, 20:4; *Eutychus*, 20:9; Col 4:7; Eph 6:21; 2 Tim 4:12; Titus 3:12; *Onesimus*, Col 4:9. On the whole, the *proportion of slaves* in the communities after 70 is hard to quantify; but a great deal of prosopographic evidence indicates that a *considerable number* belonged to this group or participated as emancipated slaves.[101] The lower-stratum mentality of early Christianity in the first century is revealed most clearly in the Letter of James. From the viewpoint of this group the author uses sharp words to criticize the rich: they oppress believers in Christ, drag them into court, and blaspheme Christ (Jas 2:6-7). They live in luxury and hold back the wages of the harvest workers (5:1ff.).

Upper Stratum

We do not have clear prosopographic evidence for believers in Christ from the *ordines*. Occasional sympathy is possible, but hardly membership in the community. Some testimonies—especially from Acts and Luke, as well as the letter of Pliny—suggest that the Christ-confessing communities included rich and respected personalities from the local elite (outside the *ordines*), including above all women. Since wealth is a relative term, this group can hardly be classified more precisely. One indication is Zacchaeus in Luke 19, who is presented as a rich member of the group of retainers. Significant in general is the presence of retainers from the upper stratum.

11

EXTERNAL CONFLICTS OF BELIEVERS IN CHRIST WITH GENTILES AND JEWS IN THE DIASPORA

In this chapter we will first present the external conflicts of believers in Christ with representatives of the Roman and municipal authorities and with the pagan population (11.1). Then social conflicts with Diaspora Judaism will be analyzed and interpreted (11.2). In this section we will often use the term *Christian,* which we have previously avoided because it could be misunderstood anachronistically. Nevertheless, this use of language is justified in the external conflicts to be discussed here, in which believers in Christ, despite their nearness to Judaism, appear as an entity that is quite distinguishable from Judaism and from the pluralistic pagan majority society. Thus we will adopt the terminology that is already found to some extent in the New Testament and in outside sources.

11.1 Discrimination and Criminalization: Social and Legal Conflicts with Paganism

Writers in the early church were the first to label the cruel procedures of Nero against the Roman believers in Christ in the year 64 C.E. as *persecution* and the *institutum Neronianum*[1] as the epitome of Roman measures against Christians. For Eusebius, Domitian (81–96 C.E.) was then the second emperor who at the end of his rule ordered the persecution of Christians.[2] Since Jerome a schema of ten great persecutions is demonstrable.[3] On this basis the term *persecution* has also entered historical research.[4] Popular though it may be, however, it lacks precision.[5] And to the extent that it designates *legally established measures of force against Christians as Christians on the basis of initiatives of Roman authorities,* it is not appropriate for characterizing the experiences of believers in Christ with pagan state courts in the epoch under consideration here. For at the beginning of the second century, when being a Christian was itself regarded as a capital crime, believers in Christ were brought before the court only on the word of informants; Trajan had even expressly forbidden a search (*conquirendi non sunt:* Pliny *Ep.* 10.97.1–2). Thus we will not use the term *persecution* here. Nevertheless, it is clear that in the urban regions of the Roman empire in the epoch in question, as religious and social outsiders believers in Christ experienced *discrimination* on the part of the pagan population and also increasing *criminalization* on the part of Rome.[6] In our opinion, these two terms are best suited to describe the external conflicts of urban Christians with paganism. First we will present the judicial conflicts and their reasons and background (11.1.1). Then we will discuss social tensions with the pagan population (11.1.2).

11.1.1 Individual Judicial Conflicts

First we will present the known conflicts of the urban communities with state courts in the period before 70. On this there is some information in the letters of Paul, which concern the experiences of Paul himself and the community of Thessalonica. Also involved here are the tumult in Rome mentioned by Suetonius and the cruel measures of Nero against Roman believers in Christ. For the epoch after 70 we will utilize some statements from the Revelation to John but above all the texts of the Acts of the Apostles[7] and the letter of Pliny concerning the trials of Christians.

A. CONFLICTS WITH PAGAN AUTHORITIES BEFORE 70

1. Paul

According to 2 Cor 11:25, Paul himself endured flogging three times.[8] In direct connection with this he mentions here (11:23) and in 6:5 that in addition to the beatings, he had endured imprisonment. This probably means the incarceration connected with the floggings.[9] And since in 2 Cor 6:5 Paul also names "riots" (*akatastasiai*) as dangers suffered, one may infer that his arrests and floggings were connected (at least in part) with public riots that arose around him. Unfortunately, this is all we know. And we know no details about his affliction in Asia (2 Cor 1:8-9). He was probably imprisoned for some time in Ephesus and even feared death (cf. Philemon 9, 13; Phil 1:7, 12-14, 30; 2:17). On the whole, the information about his negative experiences with the pagan authorities remains vague. The most likely background of Paul's disciplinary punishments at the hands of the authorities is the *disruption of public order by his propagandistic activities*.[10]

2. The community in Thessalonica

Also comparable in this connection is the conflict experience of the Pauline community in Thessalonica. For according to Paul's presentation, it had experienced oppression and suffering from the pagan side (1 Thess 1:6; 2:14; 3:3-4, 7). Paul himself interprets this as *persecution* (2:14). The instigators are the pagan compatriots of the Thessalonians.[11] We may also presume here that these negative experiences are connected with propagandistic activities of the community in Thessalonica. This is indicated by the imperative to the Thessalonians in 4:11-12 to withdraw from public affairs and work with their own hands, so that believers would not make the wrong impression on outsiders. Supporting this above all, however, are the parallels that Paul draws between the negative experiences of the Thessalonians and those of the Jewish communities, the Lord, the prophets, and the apostle himself in 2:14ff. Thus it is very possible that the sufferings of the Pauline community in Thessalonica were connected with its attempt to promote its cause among the public of the polis. The municipal authorities may have taken administrative measures against the resulting unrest.[12]

3. Rome

The conflict in Rome mentioned by Suetonius (*Claudius* 25.4), according to whom the Jews there were driven to ongoing unrest by a certain *Chrestus* (*Iudaeos impulsore Chresto assidue tumultuantes Roma expulit*), also comes under consideration here. Acts 18:2 also speaks of this conflict and mentions Christ-confessing Jews affected by it (Aquila and Prisca), who are known to us as messianic propagandists. According to Dio Cassius (60.6), the Jewish community of Rome had become so extensive by the year 41 C.E. that they could not be driven out without an uproar (*tarachē*). Instead, Claudius took away their right of assembly. Paulus Orosius dates the expulsion in the ninth year of the government of Claudius, that is, in the year 49 C.E., and bases this on Josephus.[13] Not certain here is whether Dio Cassius on the one hand and Suetonius (or Orosius) on the other have the same event in mind or are referring to different processes. We believe it probable that they are referring to the same event.[14] In any case, it is evident that the Jewish residents of Rome were involved in unrest that presumably was connected with the proclamation of Christ by messianic Jews. Here too, fomenting unrest is the motive for Rome's administrative action.

4. Nero

In the year 64 C.E. the emperor Nero had Roman believers in Christ cruelly punished. The details of these events in Rome are found in the *Annals* written some fifty years later by the Roman historian Tacitus (15.44), who connects the anti-Christian measures of Nero with the burning of Rome. This interpretation is confirmed by the methods of execution which are legal punishments for arson, even if in this case they were staged by the emperor as spectacles of perverse cruelty. The occasion was a catastrophic conflagration of Rome, for which human agents as well as reasons of fate were sought. Since in spite of all official efforts to atone to the gods, the "shame" (*infamia*)—it was believed that the fire was an act of arson—could not be banished, Nero, who was himself under suspicion, in order to put an end to rumors among the populace, placed the guilt for the burning of Rome on the "Christians" (*Chrestiani*).[15] At first the Romans arrested those who had already publicly confessed themselves as "Christians" and then, through their—presumably forced—informing, a large additional group of people. Dressed in animal skins, they were torn apart by dogs or burned as living torches.[16] Tacitus himself believed that the confessors of Christ were not responsible for the fire but that their punishment was justified. Yet he criticized the fact that the means of execution aroused the pity of the population and gave the impression that the victims were sacrificed not to the "common good" but to the cruelty of an individual. It cannot be a question of a somehow legally based *persecution* by Nero of Christians as Christians. The existence of an anti-Christian law that was first put into effect by Nero and that can be inferred especially from Tertullian's writings (for example, *Apol.* 4.4) can be excluded and with good reason.[17] Above all such a law is contradicted by the fact that Nero did not proceed against the *Chrestiani* as such but had them arrested and executed on the basis of a concrete accusation of crime (arson).

B. CONFLICTS WITH PAGAN AUTHORITIES AFTER 70

1. Revelation

The ten-day long oppression (*thlipsis*) and in part imprisonment of the believers in Christ of Smyrna in Asia Minor are predicted in Rev 2:9-10. The church in Pergamum held fast to the "name" of Christ and did not deny its faith in him, even in the days of the martyrdom of a certain Antipas (2:13).[18] One must also ask whether John's stay on the island of Patmos was the consequence of his banishment (1:9).[19] The message to Pergamum suggests that the conflict experience of the church and the death of Antipas were in some way connected with the courts. For here it is emphasized that the church lives "where Satan's throne is": "With 'Satan's throne' (2:13), however, John is probably alluding to the cult of the emperor and his temple. The latter stands at the center of the seer's attacks (cf. Revelation 13)."[20] Also pointing to a judicial experience with the authorities is the imprisonment foretold in Rev 2:10. And because of the reference to the cult of the emperor in Pergamum, we may ask whether the death of Antipas is to be traced back to the fact that "he refused to make a sacrifice before the statue of the emperor, which we find described in detail in the well-known letter of Pliny."[21] Yet more probable than the analogy to Pliny's letter is the idea that Revelation reflects the dangerous situation of Christians under Domitian.[22] Also supporting this idea is a comparison of the experiences of members of the synagogues in Smyrna and Philadelphia with those of the Christ-confessing communities. The intensified collection of the *fiscus Judaicus* under Domitian and the extension of the sacrilege accusation of the "Jewish way of life" by pagans could put believers in Christ in a dangerous situation in cases of conflict (see 11.1.2d). The cause of this conflict could have been the nonparticipation of believers in Christ in the cult of the emperor, since we read nothing of delations in Revelation; also conceivable are "isolated actions brought by local protagonists (for example, the priesthood of the imperial cult),"[23] by which Jews could also have been affected.[24] An attitude that was consciously directed against the imperial cult as the cause of the conflicts would correspond to the sharp opposition of Revelation against the cult and against Rome in general (cf. above all Revelation 13, 17).[25] Thus the Revelation to John possibly reflects *indirectly* an accusation of sacrilege against believers in Christ.

2. Philippi

According to Acts, Paul and Silas are accused by the Romans before the leading magistrates in Philippi, a Roman colony.[26] The substance of the accusation was that Paul and Silas were inciting rebellion in the city and as Jews propagating customs (*ethē*) that Romans were not allowed to adopt (Acts 16:20-21). A regular judicial proceeding (*cognitio*) did not take place. In the ways of the administrative power of the magistrature (*coercitio*), the accused are treated as foreigners and immediately after the accusation, without the pronouncement of a verdict, are flogged and thrown into prison (16:22-23). The accusation has two parts. First, the Jews caused unrest in the city. The sensitivity of Roman and municipal officeholders to this accusation is attested by Acts itself (cf. 17:6; 23:30ff.; 24:5). Yet we should not think here about regular rebellion *(stasis, seditio);* that is, the apostles are by no means accused of a capital crime (rebellion against Rome=high treason, *perduellio*). Yet sufficient for the described quasi-police intervention of officials against Paul and Silas is the understanding of "insurrection" in the sense of incitement of public unrest.[27] The second accusation—propagation of non-Roman (Jewish) customs among Romans—also does not indict the apostles with a legally definable capital crime; the relatively moderate punishment of those concerned bears this out. The accusers themselves emphasize that the adoption of Jewish customs is not allowed for Romans. Here we see the real problem. In the background is the experience, explainable from the period of Domitian's rule, that as a Gentile Christian one could be charged with adopting the "Jewish way of life," an accusation that according to Dio Cassius could have been interpreted during Domitian's rule as sacrilege and therefore as a crime against the state (*crimen laesae maiestatis*—cf. p. 330). Also from the Philippi episode comes indirectly the criminal accusation of sacrilege (*maiestas*) against believers in Christ.

3. Corinth

As described in Acts 18:12ff., the proceedings against the apostle Paul before Gallio, the Roman proconsul of Achaia, go back to "the Jews" (18:12) as accusers.[28] The accusation itself and its treatment by Gallio have an ambivalent character, since Gallio rules that it is a question of an intra-Jewish quarrel over the law (18:14-15). The intention, however, was probably to accuse Paul as a propagandist of un-Roman worship of God (18:13). Here too, it seems to be a question indirectly of the accusation of sacrilege, that is, the adoption of an un-Roman religion. The substance of the accusation reads, namely: "This man [Paul] is persuading people to worship [*sebesthai*] God in ways contrary to the law" (18:13).

4. Thessalonica

According to Acts, Jason, a host of Paul, and some other believers in Christ were dragged by the Jews before the leading magistrates in Thessalonica, since they could not get their hands on Paul himself.[29] In order to bestow the necessary drama on their accusation, they had contrived ahead of time with paid agitators to create unrest in the city (Acts 17:5-6). The accusation, presented by acclamation, alleged that Jason gave shelter to worldwide insurrectionists. This accusation alone could have led to an indictment of high treason and in the period after 70 was especially dangerous, since the Romans feared a revival of the anti-Roman rebellion of the Jews within Diaspora Judaism (see 11.1.2c). The insurrectionist group was further charged with acting against the regulations of the emperor by saying that someone other than the emperor was king, namely, Jesus (17:6-7). This part of the indictment also involved high treason. Obviously, believers in Christ are designated here as worldwide Jewish insurgents and followers of a Jewish royal pretender. The accusation implies the crime of high treason (*perduellio*). As legal background one must consider the *lex Iulia de maiestate*,[30] a law presumably given final form under Augustus,[31] which regulated state crimes or lèse-majesté, that is, crimes against the Roman people or its security. Today we would speak of high treason. The law was intended first of all for Romans themselves, but it was probably extended to all individuals. Such legal proceedings were hardly ever carried out in the provinces, however; the accused—whether Roman citizens or foreigners—were transported instead to Rome.[32] In any case, such a procedure would have had to take place before a sworn court. Noteworthy here also is a formulation of the Roman legal scholar Pomponius. He distinguishes between enemies of Rome and insurrectionists. Enemies are those who publicly declare war on Rome; the other opponents of Rome are *latrones*, bandits.[33] Yet for the people affected, this distinction in terms had no importance. Whether Rome officially declared war and its opponents thereby became "enemies" or Rome proceeded against insurrectionists, in either case the accused felt the full force of a military policy being implemented in order that the interests of Rome might prevail.

5. The trial of Paul

The legendary report in the Acts of the Apostles on the trial of Paul begins with his arrest by the Roman tribune Claudius Lysias in a tumultuous situation in Jerusalem (21:27ff.). He thought Paul was "the Egyptian," the leader of a group of four thousand from the feared anti-Roman resistance group of the sicarii (21:38; on the sicarii cf. pp. 179–80). From his appearance before the Sanhedrin, the Roman officer learned that while Paul had conflicts with the Sanhedrin over questions of the interpretation of the Jewish law (Torah), there was no charge against him deserving death or imprisonment. He transferred Paul to the Roman governor of Judaea, Felix, in Caesarea (23:29-30). The attorney for the Sanhedrin then accused Paul above all of causing worldwide rebellion (*staseis/seditiones*) among the Jews: "We have, in fact, found this man a pestilent fellow, an agitator among all the Jews throughout the world, and a ringleader of the sect of the Nazarenes" (24:5). Felix delayed the trial and passed Paul on to his successor Festus, who also saw only quarrels about the Jewish faith and about Jesus (25:19), but certainly no crime deserving of death (25:25). He did not even know what information about the case of Paul he should pass on to the emperor, to whom Paul had appealed as a Roman citizen (25:27). In a further interrogation of Paul in the presence of the Jewish king Agrippa II and his sister Bernice, Paul's innocence was once more determined, yet he was not released because he had appealed to the emperor (26:31-32). After enduring many sea adventures, Paul reached Rome as a prisoner. We learn nothing about his trial before the emperor. We will not deal further here with the legendary and apologetic character of Paul's trial.[34] The role of the involved representatives of Judaism, including King Agrippa II, is painted in the darkest colors, whereas the Roman officials not only exhibit astonishing understanding for Paul, in spite of the accusation of anti-Roman rebellion, but also want to do the Jews a favor (24:27; 25:9). Neither is historically credible. The presumption harbored against Paul (ringleader of the sicarii) and the accusation made (leader of a worldwide insurrectionist movement among Jews against Rome) apparently reflect experiences after 70. They also involve the punishable crime of high treason (*perduellio*) because of anti-Roman rebellion.

6. The trials of Christians before Pliny

Presumably these trials before Pliny (*Ep.* 10.96–97), the Roman governor of Pontus-Bithynia, took place around 117 c.e.[35] His comment that he has not yet taken part in the trials of Christians (*cognitionibus de Christianis interfui numquam:* 96.1) could imply that Pliny knew of such trials. Yet we have no information about corresponding procedures. The letter to Emperor Trajan reports on private, even anonymous (96.5), accusations against *Christiani* made to the Roman governor Pliny. They set the procedure in motion; the governor himself is not active (96.3). Also according to Trajan's rescript—the written answer to Pliny's letter—the *Christiani* are not to be ferreted out by the state (*conquirendi non sunt:* 97.1), and no anonymous charges are to be considered. "The presupposition of a trial of Christians is thus the charge; therefore the initiative is left to the people."[36] Pliny apparently knows no specific decree or any directive of the emperor in regard to believers in Christ but cites in his letter only the *mandatum* about the prohibition of "associations" (*hetaeriae:* 96.7; cf. 10.33–34). Yet in their letters neither Pliny nor Trajan connects the general prohibition of "political clubs" with the *Christiani*. They are not at all accused of specific crimes—such as the transgression of the edict regarding *hetaeriae* or high treason (*perduellio*)—but *as* "Christians" (*Christiani deferebantur:* 96.3). Accordingly, the central problem in this connection is designated by Pliny's inquiry to the emperor as to whether just the name *Christian* itself (*nomen ipsum*) should be punished even when there is no crime, or whether only crimes (*flagitia*) connected with the name are punishable. Not only the procedures carried out by Pliny but also Emperor Trajan's answer attest that the *nomen ipsum* was sufficient for a trial and for a verdict.[37] Thus in this sense Pliny's letter manifests a new legal praxis of Roman "authorities" against Christians, when here for the first time being a Christian in itself is judged in court. The *Christiani* as a whole are alleged to belong to a pernicious foreign religion (*superstitio prava, immodica*), "which is not only dangerous because of its great expansion and alarming consequences for the religious conditions in Bithynia . . . but in itself . . . deserving of punishment in terms of Roman religious and moral policy."[38]

11.1.2 The Background and Reasons for the Criminalization of Believers in Christ

A. OVERVIEW OF THE DEVELOPMENT OF CRIMINALIZATION

Thus both from the New Testament and from extra-Christian sources we have information regarding penal procedures against believers in Christ before Roman officeholders and provincial magistrates. The texts reveal a development of increasing criminalization of confessors of Christ; though it cannot be sketched in detail, its stages are evident. This is especially true of the preliminary end that this development reached in connection with the trials of Christians before Pliny. For here the very confession of being a Christian (*nomen ipsum*) itself became a punishable offense: those who confessed themselves before Pliny (three times) as "Christian" (*Christianus* or *Christiana sum*) were guilty of a crime deserving death and were executed.[39] Also for Tacitus, a contemporary of Pliny, the criminal character of the people called *Chrestiani* was unambiguous. For in his opinion they belonged to an immoral foreign religion that went back to an anti-Roman rebel who had been executed by Rome. Moreover, he had no doubt that these *Chrestiani* committed "crimes" (*flagitia: Ann.* 15.44). From both Pliny's letter and the comments of Tacitus in his presentation of the Neronian measures against Roman believers in Christ, we learn that by the beginning of the second century, at the latest, being a Christian itself was understood as a crime.[40]

Yet the Roman criminalization of being a Christian has a lengthy prior history, in the course of which believers in Christ were initially not yet accused on account of the *nomen Christianum* but on the basis of *various* other crimes: incitement to public unrest, anti-Roman rebellion (*perduellio*), arson, and adopting or propagating the Jewish way of life. Even if not all these accusations are to be understood as punishable offenses with a definite legal foundation,[41] they still show a clear tendency toward the increasing criminalization of Christians. Here we are making a distinction between the criminalization of being a Christian in itself and a criminalization of believers in Christ on the basis of criminal accusations. In regard to the possible legal foundations[42] of the anti-Christian measures in this epoch, the hypothesis of Wlosok seems to us to be the most convincing. She posits the connecting of "punitive persecution with administrative procedure."[43] That is to say, here and there the application of magisterial police violence in the service of public order (official *coercitio*)[44] may have been a sufficient legal foundation, but believers in Christ were also accused and sentenced on the basis of general penal categories. Yet even for our epoch a firm connection between certain accusations of crime and being a Christian cannot be presupposed.[45]

Not until Pliny and Trajan is being a Christian as such demonstrably elevated as an offense, so that in the course of the second century the Trajan rescript could then become a "general guideline" in procedures against believers in Christ.[46] "This category of crime was unique in Roman penal law."[47] In this way the actions of the Roman high official Pliny are different from those in all other conflict cases named here, in which believers in Christ are accused of concrete, juridically addressable crimes. The report of Tacitus on Nero's measures against believers in Christ in Rome also reflects this distinction. In his opinion the *Chrestiani* are not responsible for the burning of Rome, yet he suspects them of "crimes" (*flagitia*) and believes them guilty because they belong to a degenerate and immoral foreign religion (*exitiabilis superstitio*).

B. THE BASIS AND BACKGROUND OF CRIMINALIZATION

Yet why were there criminal accusations against believers in Christ at all? First, we must consider here the social and religious closeness of Christian communities to, and their origin out of, *Judaism*. With this background believers in Christ drew upon themselves some of the ancient prejudices against the Jews.[48] Vittinghoff correctly says, however, that the transference of anti-Jewish prejudices to believers in Christ cannot explain their criminalization.[49] For there is a decisive difference between them and the Jews in that being a Jew as such was not designated as a punishable crime, whereas being a Christian was—at least since Pliny. Yet the Jews were also burdened not only with prejudices but also with accusations of crime. In this sense, in the development of the criminalization of believers in Christ before Pliny, there are analogies in the behavior of paganism toward Jews. And the negative attitudes and concrete accusations of crimes against believers in Christ are to be explained in part precisely on the basis of their closeness to and identification with Judaism. Yet we do not understand the analogies of anti-Christian accusations as a *wholesale transference* of anti-Jewish prejudices and criminal accusations to believers in Christ. That is, we do not see here a kind of side effect of pagan hostility toward Jews.[50] Rather, anti-Jewish stereotypes are particularized in the specific prejudice of the majority society vis-à-vis believers in Christ as followers of a superstition and an executed insurrectionist.

Tacitus, for example, suspects Christians of a hatred of the human race (*odium humani generis: Ann.* 15.44), as he had alleged of Judaism (*Hist.* 5.5), and he saw in Judaea the origin of the sickness of the Christian superstition. Also in the Acts of the Apostles we can see that believers in Christ were identified with Judaism (cf. only 19:32-33) and, indeed, that they, like the Jews, were alleged to be temple robbers[51] and blasphemers of pagan deities[52] (Rom 2:22; Acts 19:37). Likewise, they—like the Jews (Juvenal *Sat.* 14.96ff.)—were labeled as opponents of the laws and ordinances of Rome. This is the sense, for example, of the accusation against the believers in Christ of Thessalonica, according to which they were acting against the *dogmata* of the emperor (Acts 17:7). Also in this context is the stereotypical accusation of causing unrest, which is made in downright classic fashion in Acts 16:20 against the messianic propagandists Paul and Silas: "These men are disturbing our city; they are Jews." This reproach recalls the previously mentioned comment of Suetonius that Emperor Claudius drove the Jews out of Rome because they, incited by a certain Chrestus, caused constant unrest (*Claudius* 25).

With this, however, we come to what was probably the *decisive reason for the criminalization* of believers in Christ. Apparently they were perceived early on as a special group within Judaism, a group that in the eyes of the Romans was negatively distinguished by its connection with Christ. This special nature was indicated by their designation as "Christians" (*Christianoi, Christiani, Chrestiani*), which we find both in the New Testament (Acts 11:26; 26:28; 1 Pet 4:16), in Pliny (*Ep.* 10.96), and in Tacitus (*Ann.* 15.44).[53] Tacitus derives the group designation expressly from *Chrestus* (=*Christus*) and mentions his execution by the prefect of Judaea under Emperor Tiberius. It is also important for him that the *exitiabilis superstitio* of the faith in Christ ("probably to be translated according to the meaning as *degenerate and immoral foreign religion*")[54] was suppressed for a time by the execution of Christ but then rose up again not only in Judaea but also in Rome (*Ann.* 15.44).[55]

Thus there were two negative characteristics of the group of believers in Christ that made it especially suspicious. The first was its pernicious un-Roman superstition, which also held an attraction for non-Jews and even Romans, as Tacitus laments (*Ann.* 15.44.3).[56] The same accusation is also found in Pliny's letter about the trials of Christians. Pliny also alleges that Christians as a whole belong to a pernicious foreign religion (*superstitio prava, immodica*), "which is not only dangerous because of its great expansion and alarming consequences for the religious conditions in Bithynia . . . but in itself . . . deserving of punishment in terms of Roman religious and moral policy."[57] Clearly discernible here is the xenophobic element, which also played a large role in ancient hostility toward the Jews.[58] Also of some importance is the fact that from the viewpoint of a conservative Roman patrician, Pliny feared the influence of this "superstition" on all social groups. Apparently Tacitus already had in mind something similar in regard to the Jews.[59] The second negative feature of Christians—as suggested by their name—was the fact that they were followers of a certain *Christus/Chrestus*, a *Jewish rebel* executed by the Roman prefect of Judaea, Pontius Pilate. Thus faith in Christ had to be "judged criminal through the person of its 'founder.'"[60]

Both of the criminal accusations constituting the criminalization of believers in Christ are also found in the New Testament. The messianic propagandists Paul and Silas were accused of proclaiming un-Roman customs that Romans were not permitted either to accept or to practice (Acts 16:21); in Corinth, Paul is accused of persuading people to worship God in ways contrary to the law (18:13). In short, it was a question of the accusation of propagating a pernicious un-Roman religion. In addition, we find in Acts the accusation of anti-Roman rebellion and worldwide instigation of unrest, which is connected with the corresponding political interpretation of the confession of Jesus as Christ (17:6-7; 21:38; 24:5). Even if the accused here are not expressly designated as "Christians" but still identified with Judaism, it is nevertheless clear that it is a question of members of a special group within Judaism (24:5: "the sect of the Nazarenes"). The political misunderstanding is revealed, however, in the Lukan passion story, in which Jesus is set before

Pilate as an anti-Roman rebel who is perverting the Jewish people by forbidding them to pay taxes to the emperor and saying that he himself is the Messiah and a king (Luke 23:2). For Luke all these accusations distort the true behavior of Jesus[61] and ascribe to it an insurrectionist meaning. Yet they also reflect an anti-Christian polemic that afterward was repeatedly raised against the Jesus movement as a conspiratorial, anti-Roman, and generally revolutionary group directed against the common good.[62] Thus by presenting Jesus' innocence in the passion story (cf., for example, the "confession" of the centurion: Luke 23:47), Luke is also rejecting the same accusation against the followers who appeal to Jesus.

C. THE IMMEDIATE BACKGROUND OF THE ACCUSATION OF REBELLION

Thus a basic factor in the criminalization of believers in Christ was without doubt their negative identification as a group of anti-Roman rebels coming out of Judaism. Because of the actual situation after the Jewish-Roman war, this accusation had an apparently plausible and dangerous background. As Tacitus remarks: "The notion that only the Jews persisted in their resistance increased the bitterness against them" (*Hist.* 5.10). Their revolt against Rome gave the Jews the general reputation of being rebellious and bellicose.[63] The revolt itself had created a number of difficulties for the Romans, and it was finally put down only through a heavy application of military force.[64] And even afterward, Rome could not be sure that peace had really come to stay. One particular factor in the uncertainty was the worldwide spread of Judaism. This connection between the Jewish motherland and the Judaism of the Diaspora is reflected, for example, in Josephus, who has King Agrippa say in a speech before the outbreak of hostilities that the war would also have an impact on Judaism in the Diaspora.[65] Josephus was already aware of the accuracy of this "prediction."[66] According to him, when the emperor Vespasian heard of the activity of Jewish irregulars, he harbored the suspicion "that revolutionary attitudes among the Jews would never die out. He feared that they would join anew into a unified movement and in the process also add others to their cause" (*War* 7.421). Vespasian's son Domitian, as emperor, pursued an extremely harsh policy against the Jews and like his predecessor feared that a Davidic ruler could rise against Rome.[67]

Thus there was a rather widespread fear of a new flare-up of the Jewish revolt, but now with the additional support of Judaism in the Diaspora. This fear was reinforced by two disturbances, about which Josephus informs us, in Alexandria (*War* 7.407ff.) and in Cyrenaica (7.437ff.; see p. 351). Both conflicts show that the presence of even allegedly insurrectionist movements among the Jewish communities of the Diaspora in the period after 70 could have threatening and possibly fatal implications for the other (loyal) Jews.

They also reveal a conflict in the Jewish communities themselves. (We will return to this later.) In the present context, it is of decisive importance that in the epoch after the Jewish-Roman war, even unarmed fanatical messianic groups were easily in danger of being charged with the crime of anti-Roman rebellion. This opened wide the gate of a corresponding identification of Jesus' followers, the *Christianoi,* as one of the groups of Jewish insurrectionists against Rome that existed in the Diaspora. This suspicion was also based on the execution of the Christ they worshiped.

D. THE PROBLEM OF THE
"JEWISH WAY OF LIFE" IN THE TIME OF DOMITIAN

Thus, particularly in the period after 70, the suspicion of anti-Roman insurrection played an important role in the developing criminalization of believers in Christ. An additional factor must also be seen in the emperor Domitian's policies against Judaism to the extent that this also indirectly affected believers in Christ.[68] In the early nineties, Domitian had intensified the collection of the *fiscus Judaicus* introduced by his father.[69] This tax replaced the Jewish temple tax. In connection with the intensification of the *fiscus Judaicus* under Domitian, the non-Jews who lived a Jewish lifestyle also found themselves in danger. On the one hand, the extremely rigorous collection of the tax by Domitian (Suetonius *Dom.* 12.2) meant the abolition of the previous age limit and, above all, an expansion of the number of groups affected. The tax now also included people who followed a Jewish lifestyle but did not officially confess Judaism, or who had kept their Jewish heritage secret and in this way had previously escaped the supplementary tax levied on the Jewish people. Confessors of Christ could fall into *both* categories.[70]

Yet the problem for believers was not the payment of the tax[71] but the possible expansion of the accusation of following the "Jewish way of life." For Dio Cassius establishes a connection between the accusation of a "Jewish way of life" and the crime of godlessness (*asebeia*). He reports that Domitian had his cousin Titus Flavius Clemens executed and banished the latter's wife Domitilla. They had been accused of "atheism" (*atheotēs*), "a charge on the basis of which many others who had slipped into the Jewish way of life were condemned; some were sentenced to death and others were punished through the confiscation of their wealth" (Dio Cassius 67.14). Domitian's successor Nerva then not only forbade false accusations because of the *fiscus Judaicus,*[72] but also, according to Dio Cassius (68.2), under Nerva's rule "no one was permitted anymore to be charged because of godlessness [*asebeia*] or the Jewish way of life [*Ioudaikos bios*]." The Greek formulation *Ioudaikos bios* here, as similarly in Suetonius (*Dom.* 12.2: *Iudaica vita*), designates the Jewish way of life of Gentiles and perhaps also of proselytes.[73] While the term *atheism* (*atheotēs*) seems to be juridically unspecific, the word *asebeia* ("godlessness") designates a capital crime (*crimen laesae maiestatis*).[74]

The remarkable connection between the accusations of lèse-majesté (*asebeia*) and the "Jewish way of life" should be briefly explained. The problem here is the adoption of the Jewish lifestyle by non-Jews, that is, sympathizers of Judaism (God-fearers) and converts (proselytes). Historically, the Roman administration had reacted extremely sensitively when members of the upper stratum turned in any way toward Judaism (or eastern cults in general). This had possible negative consequences not only for the people involved but also for the Jewish residents of Rome. Although a general prohibition of Jewish propaganda is not demonstrable,[75] there was a practice of anti-Jewish measures that can be connected with Jewish propaganda among the Romans and which affected Jews and their sympathizers.[76] From this we may infer that only a situation that was relevant for Rome—whether conditioned by the large number of sympathizers won to Judaism or by their special social position—led to measures against the Jews or their sympathizers. Important in our context is the fact that when non-Jews became sympathizers with or converts to Judaism, the Romans regarded this as a problem.

Thus under Domitian the connection of the "Jewish way of life" and "godlessness" took on the character of lèse-majesté. The cause of corresponding denunciations could have been the intensified collection of the Jewish tax. Therefore the suspicion of the "Jewish way of life" would have put non-Jews—and especially Gentile Christians—particularly at risk. Non-Jewish confessors of Christ would have already been suspected of a "Jewish way of life" merely by holding to the so-called apostolic decree (Acts 15:20). In this connection the expansion of the cult of the emperor under Domitian no doubt also played a role.[77] At this point, members of synagogal Judaism were more protected (because of their practical liberation from the cult of the emperor) than non-Jews who, like confessors of Christ, could hardly practice the veneration of the emperor because of their convictions.

The New Testament contains some indications that the potential conflict with the cult of the emperor is related to believers' convictions. In addition to Revelation 17–18, Acts 12:20-23—the punishment miracle against Agrippa I in connection with his divine acclamation by the people ("The voice of a god, and not of a mortal!")—is "the clearest renunciation in the New Testament of all forms of royal and imperial cults."[78] Luke, for example, alters his Markan model (Mark 10:42) by critically bringing in the *euergetes* cult (Luke 22:25-26).[79] And from the Lukan formulation of the devil's temptation of "the kingdoms of the world" (Luke 4:5ff.), one must draw the inference "*Roma sedes Satanae*."[80] For according to this passage it is the devil who has bestowed dominion over the *orbis terrarum* (Luke 4:6). Also, it is hardly accidental that the transference of dominion over all kingdoms is linked with the condition of divine adoration of the devil by Jesus and is rejected with a reference to Deut 6:13. In Acts 10:25-26 Peter strictly rejects the quasi-divine adoration given him by Cornelius.[81] The especially drastic experience of Paul and Barnabas in Lystra, where they are confused with Hermes and Zeus and are only barely able to keep the crowd from making sacrifices to them (Acts 14:8ff.), not only reveals the same motivation of those involved as in Acts 10:26 (emphasis of humanity) but also shows clearly their position against any adoration of human beings as divine.

All of this leads to the conclusion that sympathizers of Judaism, converts, and groups like Christians that were identified with Judaism were especially in danger of being charged with godlessness during the reign of Domitian. Outside the New Testament three cases are reported, namely, those of Flavius Clemens, his wife Domitilla, and Acilius Glabrio (who was consul in 91 C.E.). Therefore Williams[82] wants to distinguish between the charge of *fiscus Judaicus* and that of a Jewish way of life qua *asebeia* as stratum-specific, as it were; that is, the latter was brought only against members of the upper stratum (like Flavius Clemens and Domitilla). Yet Dio Cassius indicates that many others were also affected (67.14). In their case it must not have been a question of members of the upper stratum (otherwise, would he not have mentioned them by name?) but of all those who had a special obligation of loyalty to Rome, including, for example, the Roman military. Stenger says aptly: "One may . . . presume that the 'persecutions' of Christians, which seem to lie in the background of some New Testament writings and which are certainly portrayed by later Christian sources in exaggerated fashion, are likewise to be seen in the context of the intensified procedure of the *fiscus iudaicus* under Domitian."[83]

E. BEING CHRISTIAN AS A CAPITAL CRIME: A NEW DIMENSION

Pliny's inquiry to Trajan brings into play a new dimension in regard to the criminalization of Christians, namely, whether they are punishable merely of the basis of the name *Christian* itself, or whether they had to be proven guilty of a "crime [*flagitia*] connected with the name." The question contains the whole problem of the relationship of the Roman authorities to Christians during the period before the Decian persecution.[84] The formulation recalls the Roman administration's dealings, in the late republic and early princeps period, with the adherents of foreign cults, such as those of Bacchus and Isis, and with Druids and magicians;[85] here it was not a case of religious persecutions but of measures against the presumed or actual criminal by-products of these cults. These activities were called *flagitia* or *scelera*. After the prohibition of such foreign cults, the *nomen*—that is, membership in a forbidden cult—was sufficient for condemnation of its members. It was simply assumed that the "crime" associated with the name of the cult was inseparably connected with it.[86] Yet neither Pliny's letter nor Trajan's reply reveals which crime of the Roman state was presupposed to be inseparably bound to the *nomen Christianum*.[87] In this respect, one can speak of "precedents" for the criminalization, under Trajan, of being a Christian,[88] yet the process is legally unique. That is, the trials under Pliny mark the decisive beginning of the criminalization of merely being a Christian.

F. SUMMARY OF THE REASONS FOR CRIMINALIZATION

During the period before 70 there were individual conflicts between urban believers in Christ and Roman or provincial courts, which were probably based on provocation of public disturbances. Here the tensions within Diaspora synagogues caused by messianic propagandists seem also to have played a role. It is noteworthy that already in Suetonius these disturbances were traced back to Christ. Thus the increasing Roman criminalization of confessors of Christ can be understood against the background of the special political situation after the suppression of the anti-Roman rebellion in the land of Israel. Afterward the Jews were regarded as a rebellious people, and it was feared that individual Jewish insurrectionist groups could spread the anti-Roman rebellion worldwide. Confessors of Christ were also especially suspect, for in Jesus Christ they revered the expected Davidic Messiah-king, and his execution by the Roman prefect of Judaea also nourished the suspicion of a rebellious attitude. Under Domitian's rule, Gentile Christians in particular seem to have drawn upon themselves the accusation of *asebeia* because of their membership in a community coming out of Judaism combined with their negative position toward the cult of the emperor. When the Christians were perceived as an independent group, their Jewish origin and their power of attraction also played a certain role even for Romans (Tacitus). At the beginning of the second century, however, the focus of accusations of crime shifted to *Christian faith itself as an immoral foreign religion,* which was connected with crimes *(flagitia)* and then under Pliny became criminal in itself. Thus the path led from the criminalization of believing in Christ to the criminalization of being a Christian.

11.1.3 Conflicts with the Pagan Population

Because of Jesus' name, his followers will be hated by all, predicts Jesus to his disciples (Mark 13:13). This is also the impression of the author of the Gospel of Matthew (10:22), who even says that the followers of Christ will be hated by *all peoples* and indeed by one another (24:9-10). Luke ascertains even more clearly a connection between hate and the judicial experiences of confessors of

Christ, who will be denounced even by their parents and brothers, relatives and friends (21:16). John also notes the hatred of the world for confessors of Jesus (15:18-19; 17:14; 1 John 3:13). Again and again the Acts of the Apostles reports the hostile behavior of the populace toward Christians. Sometimes the rabble is also heated up, or agitators are sent in to stir up public unrest (Acts 13:50; 14:4-5; 16:19ff.; 17:8, 13; 21:27ff.). Acts 19:23ff. describes one such social conflict in great detail. Social tensions between confessors of Christ and their pagan surroundings are also recognizable in 1 Pet 4:12ff. In *Ann.* 15.44.2 Tacitus says that the *Christiani* are hated by the people (*vulgus*) because of their crimes (*flagitia*). For this reason they must also suffer as scapegoats for the burning of Rome. And also from the denunciations that Pliny reports we can infer a negative attitude of the population toward Christians. In New Testament times the hostile attitude of the population—and especially of the rabble—and the number of trials of Christians were clearly increasing.[89] Best known is the martyrdom of Polycarp, in which the governor held a rather friendly position vis-à-vis Christians, while the crowd was hostile to them from the very beginning.

A. CONFLICT IN EPHESUS (ACTS 19:23ff.)[90]

With the help of the conflict in Ephesus, which is described in Acts 19, we can clarify some of the basic mechanisms of the negative attitude of the population toward confessors of Christ. Because of them, a popular disturbance broke out. It was instigated by a certain Demetrius, who blamed Paul's preaching activities for the fact that a considerable number from Ephesus and the entire province of Asia had fallen away from the pagan cult (19:26). This had an impact on the business interests of the makers of devotional items and on their workers (19:24). They feared that their business would fall into disrepute and the temple of Artemis would be scorned. The enraged crowd rushed to the theater, dragging two companions of Paul with them. In the excitement of the assembly a certain Alexander wanted to speak to the crowd and apparently to distance the Jewry of the city from the accusations. When he was recognized as a Jew, the excited crowd professed for two hours their religious convictions ("Great is Artemis of the Ephesians!"). A representative of the city government (*grammateus/scriba*), who was responsible for legal assemblies, succeeded in quieting down the agitated crowd. He pointed out that the Romans might intercede because of the illegal popular assembly and indirectly acquitted the accused (who were "neither temple robbers nor blasphemers of our goddess": 19:37). The illegal assembly finally dissolved. Noteworthy is the identification of the confessors of Christ with Judaism, as the subliminal accusations show.

Comparison with Other Disturbances[91]

Tumults like the mob scene in the theater of the city of Ephesus, as described in Acts 19, were hardly rare.[92] Yet they usually involved conflicts between pagans.[93] In Alexandria and Antioch the Jewish population of the city became involved.[94] Frequently these conflicts had social causes, and the simple folk faced the urban aristocracy.[95] The Ephesian conflict in Acts can be compared with a late second-century inscription found in Magnesia (*Ephesos* II 215), which speaks of a strike of Ephesian bakers that put the city in an uproar. The authorities suspected these bakers of rebellion (*stasis/seditio*).[96] In our case, however, the motif of xenophobia—or hostility to Jews—also plays a role.[97] In this sense, the Jewish-pagan conflicts in, for example, Alexandria and Antioch are also comparable. For even though the Alexandrian conflict had begun in the thirties, it increased in 71 C.E. when Titus stopped in Alexandria on his way back from Palestine.[98] The conflict in Antioch on the Orontes took place at the beginning of the First Jewish Revolt (*War* 7.46).[99] Thus both are close to the time of the writing of Acts.

Antioch. As background of the measures against the Jews of Antioch, Josephus points indirectly to the great attraction of Judaism for the pagan population and above all to the hatred of the Jews in connection with the eruption of the Jewish-Roman war (*War* 7.43ff.). The immediate occasion was the assertion of a certain Antiochus (whose father was a leading member of the Jewish community) that the Jews had decided to set fire to the city (7.47). Apparently the Jews here, like the Christians in Rome during Nero's time, served as scapegoats for an actual fire in Antioch (7.54ff.). In truth, however, some "evil people," who were in debt, had set the fire, according to Josephus (7.61–62). Yet in Antioch the specific behavior of the Jews in regard to their exclusive way of life and the peculiarities of their religion—and thus xenophobia—also played a role in the background of the conflict; this is shown, for example, by the fact that the Jews were forced to make sacrifices in the Greek manner and to break the sabbath commandment (7.50ff.). Thus this conflict in Antioch also basically supports the thesis that ancient hostility to Jews was a particular form of xenophobia.[100]

Yet this interpretation, which is correct in principle, is not sufficient to explain the anti-Jewish pogroms of antiquity. Rather, social and political conflicts also played a considerable role as background in the massive attacks of the pagan populace on Jews. In Antioch the anti-Jewish resentment of the pagan population was to some extent only the feeding ground for the success of the agitation of Antiochus. Without a specific political situation, it would have been impossible for him to make such violent distinctions between the Jewish and pagan populations. This specific political situation was marked by

the early stages of the rebellion against Rome, in the context of which hatred
for the Jews increased and finally erupted in a pogrom. Here the economic
interests of a group of indebted citizens played a key role. They were able to
take the aggressions of the people, which actually should have been directed
toward them as arsonists, and redirect them toward the Jews.

Alexandria.[101] The conflict in Alexandria can be interpreted in a comparable
fashion. "In the thirties of the first century c.e. there was a party of extreme
nationalists that combined opposition to Roman rule with anti-Jewish propaganda. When this grouping gained control of the city for a few months in
the year 38, the previously latent tension and hostility reached its high
point."[102] Not only the "lazy and inactive urban rabble"[103] but also particular groupings ("Egyptians" and nationalistic groups that had been formed
around the secondary school)[104] were represented among the opponents of
the Jews.[105] Perhaps here too a transference of aggression to the Jews formed
part of the socio-psychological background of the pogrom. For the aggression
of the "nationalists" was actually directed against the Romans, but since the
Romans could not be attacked directly, the Jews had to bear the brunt of this
aggression. In the eyes of the nationalistic Alexandrians the Jews were the pro-
tégés of Rome, since in the conflict between the Ptolemies and the Romans
the Jews had taken the Roman side and for this had been granted privileges
(self-preservation, religious freedoms).[106] In addition, in this conflict the
dynamic of the event that sharpened the tensions between the socially hostile
"parties" can, without doubt, only be explained by a specific political constellation.[107] For the ascension of Caligula to power shifted the balance of power
in Alexandria. The Roman governor Flaccus was placed in a difficult position
by Caligula's coming to power, since the latter was considered a friend of the
Alexandrians. Flaccus had been a friend of Tiberius and had played a role in
banishing the mother of the new emperor, Caligula. The nationalistic Greek
upper stratum exploited this "weakness" of Flaccus and drew him to their
side.[108] According to Philo's presentation, leading members of the group of
nationalists in Alexandria offered Flaccus the support of the entire city vis-à-
vis Caligula if Flaccus would in turn "sacrifice" the Jews (Philo *Flacc.*
24.97–103).

   Both of these conflicts between pagan urban populations and Jewish residents, which we have discussed here only briefly, exhibit the following constellation: the social and economic interests of the pagan population or certain
groups in it were able in a specific political situation to lead to a violent eruption of hostility against the Jews that was rooted in xenophobia. In the process
there were apparently also transferences of aggression in which the Jewish
population was made the scapegoat for particular events with an economic

background (fire in Antioch) or political conditions with social consequences (the Romans put an end to the independence of Alexandria). The silversmith episode in Acts 19 also reflects a situation in which the presence of confessors of Christ in a pagan population played an important role in a social conflict.[109] Yet here too the pagan hatred of confessors of Christ is insufficient as the sole explanation for the described uproar. Indeed, the narrative itself reports a concrete social cause of the unrest: the economic loss to silversmiths and their workers. This was the driving force behind the disturbance, and thus in the silversmith narrative we also find a transference of aggression. The primary object of aggression, Paul, was not available. Curiously, his immediate followers also do not play any role in the course of the story. Rather, in the theater a member of the Jewish community, Alexander, is shouted down for two hours by the agitated crowd. Yet we must also observe that the story presupposes that the pagan population did not distinguish between Paul and the Jews of Ephesus.

If, however, this feature of the story expresses a contemporary Lukan experience, one must raise again the question of the primary object of aggression, which is served here by the Jews (and by the "Christians" identified with them). Actually, in this episode it is the Romans who are the primary, subliminal object of aggression. If it is true that in the Roman period the Artemis cult had lost importance because of the cult of the emperor,[110] then on the level of the narrative the Christian/Jewish population in the Ephesus conflict was made the scapegoat for the decline in importance of the cult of Artemis, which had negative economic consequences for the trade in devotional items. Yet in truth, the Romans were in a certain sense responsible for this situation. The town clerk *(grammateus)* uses the threat of Roman retaliation when he tells the crowd that the illegal popular assembly in the theater could be understood as a revolt *(stasis/seditio)*.

B. DISCRIMINATION AGAINST CHRISTIANS (1 PET 4:12ff.)

Like no other text, the First Letter of Peter reveals the hostile attitude of the populace toward confessors of Christ. Already at the beginning of the letter there is a reference to the "various trials" of the addressees (1:6), which are also called "suffering" in the following verses (2:19-20; 3:14, 17; 4:1, 19; 5:10). Following a pragmatic purpose, the text develops various strategies in preparation for negative experiences. Among other things, the author calls attention to the fact that his addressees share their sufferings with confessors of Christ in the whole world (5:9) and also have them in common with the sufferings of Christ (4:1, 13). Adopting Old Testament–Jewish tradition, he also interprets negative experiences as the *alienation* of the elect (1:1, 17; 2:11).[111] As much as the whole letter is shaped by the discussion of the trials and sufferings of the addressees, there is little indication of the extent and the danger of the suffering.[112] Verses 4:15-16 are often assumed to have the background of a judicial conflict: [15]"But let none of you suffer as a murderer [*phoneus*], a thief [*kleptēs*], a criminal [*kakopoios*], or even as a mischief maker [*allotriepiskopos*]. [16] Yet if any of you suffers as a Christian, do not consider it a disgrace, but glorify God because you bear this name." Yet it is hardly a question here of the author warning readers "not to let yourself be judged without contradiction as a criminal."[113] Verse 15 is an ethical admonition, not a report on experienced punitive treatment. The context also suggests that it is at most a question of accusations against Christians. They are "reviled" for the name of Christ (4:14), and when they suffer in this way, they are not supposed to be ashamed. The conceptuality here is to be understood against the background of central Mediterranean notions of "honor and shame."[114] Earlier (2:11-12) the author has already admonished his readers to lead an honorable life so that on the day of judgment the "Gentiles" who malign them as "evildoers" (*kakopoioi*) may glorify God because of their good works. Because they have turned away from the pagan way of life, they are alienated from the Gentiles (4:4). Thus especially discernible here is pagan criticism of the Gentile Christians' *conduct of life* (cf. also 3:13ff.; 4:3ff.), which the author calls maligning, abuse, and reproach (2:12; 3:9, 16; 4:14).

Thus 1 Peter expresses the negative reaction of the pagan populace to Christians. Concrete *judicial* experiences are not discernible.[115] Also, slandering as "evildoers" (2:12; 4:15) designates no specific crime but belongs in the realm of ethically negative behavior, as can be seen above all in 3:17: if one must suffer according to God's will, then it is better to suffer for good deeds than for bad (3:17). Similarly, 4:16 says that if you must suffer because you are a Christian *(hōs Christianos),* then you should not be ashamed but glorify God because you bear this name. Thus the author admonishes his readers not to be provoked to criminal acts by the accusations of the pagan populace. If they must suffer, then let it be as "Christians" and not because of some kind of shameful crime. Thus the sufferings of the addressees of 1 Peter are to be found in the evil suspicions of the pagan majority population, in which group identity *(Christianoi)* no doubt plays a role. For the author these negative experiences are an honorable consequence of being a Christian and an expression of alienage in this world. On the whole, the letter excludes the possibility that its author or readers find themselves "in an officially initiated persecution. Instead it is a question of social discrimination and isolation."[116]

C. SOCIO-PSYCHOLOGICAL INTERPRETATION OF THE CONFLICTS:
XENOPHOBIA AND TRANSFERENCE OF AGGRESSION

Hate, xenophobia, and their specifically anti-Jewish combination in anti-Semitism apparently marked the negative attitude of the pagan population toward the "Christians." In specific crisis situations this structure of prejudice can be mobilized and lead to accusations. In the course of a transference of aggression, confessors of Christ (as well as Jews) are made scapegoats for the economic disadvantages of certain population groups. That is to say, the alleged (Acts 19) or real economic disadvantages of certain population groups (16:19) because of "Christians" led some individuals into judicial conflicts. Tacitus also speaks of "hatred" for *Chrestiani* in connection with the measures implemented under Nero. They become scapegoats for the burning of Rome when Nero skillfully directs the aggressions of the masses against the *Chrestiani.* Social tensions also seem to be behind the accusations against confessors of Christ, as described in the letter of Pliny. For because of the high number of followers of Christ, the (pagan) temples have been abandoned, the cults neglected, and the sales of sacrificial meat reduced.[117] As a motif of the negative attitude of pagans against confessors of Christ, xenophobia in particular plays a crucial role. The strange nonpagan lifestyle of "Christians" causes offense and leads to accusations and slander. Basically, the situation of confessors of Christ is comparable to that of Judaism. Even the First Letter of Peter, which clearly reveals hatred for Christians as Christians, treats this experience of alienation by adopting corresponding Jewish traditions.

D. SOCIOLOGICAL INTERPRETATION: DEVIANCE

In this connection a sociological model of interpretation is offered by deviance theories (see pp. 244–47). Confessors of Christ are labeled as outsiders and deviants (for example, *Christianoi,* evildoers, followers of a pernicious foreign religion, "atheists") who violate the norms and rules of the majority society (this is especially clear in 1 Peter). Yet we can no longer reconstruct in detail the "deviance career" of the confessors of Christ, whose starting point is a deviant act that can be followed by public branding as outsiders and by isolation from the conventions of the majority society, so that deviants ultimately organize into their own deviant groups. The deviance of confessors of Christ seems, however, to have arisen not in connection with particular values and rules but in "problematic situations" in which certain areas are classified as "critical" and demand action.[118] Only in this context is the exclusion of "Christians" possible through an appeal to traditional values. As background one could name the economic loss of certain population groups that can be traced back to confessors of Christ (Ephesus conflict, letter of Pliny). Above all, however, the criminal treatment of confessors of Christ, which is a "degrading of status" in deviance theories,[119] seems to have been determined by the overall political climate after 70, which as a kind of crisis situation promoted the state's interest in the control of deviance.

11.2 The Distancing of Diaspora Judaism from Christ-confessing Communities

The themes treated under this heading are part of the comprehensive topic of Jewish-"Christian" relations in the first century. In this connection it seems appropriate to us to make fundamental distinctions: (1) in terms of the kind of relationship between symbolic and social interactions, (2) socio-geographically between the corresponding relationships in the land of Israel and in the Diaspora, and finally (3) historically between the experiences in the periods before and after 70 c.e. We will discuss the problem of the kind of relationship. The distinction between experiences in the land of Israel and in the Diaspora results, in our view, from the fact that in the land of Israel we have a Jewish majority population to which the messianic Christian communities related as minority groups. In the Diaspora, by contrast, the members of both the synagogues and the *ekklēsia* lived as minority groups in the context of pagan cities. Thus we must always keep in mind that here we have minority conflicts in which the larger entity is either the pagan population or its representatives. Finally, the temporal distinction between the epochs before and after 70 results, on the one hand, from the fact that in the land of Israel in the period after 70 the reshaping of Judaism overcame the previous pluralism and the new self-definition had an exclusionary effect on messianic communities (see pp. 221ff.). In the Diaspora, on the other hand, in the period before 70 Jewish-"Christian" conflicts primarily involved individual experiences in which the political background was rather secondary, whereas in the time after 70 conflicts tended to involve groups (synagogue or *ekklēsia*), and the new overall political climate played an important role.

A. THE DISTINCTION BETWEEN SYMBOLIC AND SOCIAL INTERACTION

The relationships between Jews and "Christians" in antiquity resulted from a complicated religious and socio-historical process.[120] Two levels can be distinguished heuristically: controversies over *religious content and convictions*[121] and *social manifestations and social consequences* of these controversies. The two levels are also distinguished here terminologically as *symbolic* and *social* interaction, although in reality they naturally overlap. For in the context of religion as a comprehensive "cultural system," religious content and convictions also shape values, attitudes, and modes of human behavior. Initially, nonetheless, they can be understood as part of a "symbolic system."[122]

Religious Controversies

At almost every hand the New Testament contains the controversial discourses of its authors with Judaism on the most varied aspects of the "symbolic system," which are also determined by a varied reception of Jewish Holy Scriptures (the Hebrew Bible or its Greek translation, the Septuagint) and Jewish traditions. We cannot begin to give here a complete list of the corresponding themes. Thus the ancient Christian-Jewish conflict can be understood in one sense as a disagreement between diverging symbolic systems based on common traditions.[123] It is sometimes based on real discussions, although this is not always clear. Representative of many examples is Justin's *Dialogue with Trypho* (middle of second century), which is given the form of a religious discourse with a rabbi (Trypho), but there is well-founded doubt about its facticity. The same is true, however, of the disputes and conflict scenes in the New Testament. In scholarly discussion of Jewish-Christian relationships this "symbolic" level of conflict is particularly emphasized. Here we will go into it only tangentially.

Social Conflicts

There is also a social level of the conflict between Jews and confessors of Christ, and it is one theme of a social history of early Christianity. This conflict level can also be connected with "symbolic" interactions, yet they do not take place in the symbolic world but in the context of social systems and institutions. In this sense we call this aspect of Jewish-Christian relations the realm of *social interaction*. Our sources suggest that these involve above all tensions and conflicts, for they give some indications of prominent disturbances in relations—of, so to speak, a process of increasing social distance between confessors of Christ and Jews in which even judicial consequences are mentioned as especially dramatic events.

Presumably, however, the texts convey a false impression. For we know almost nothing regarding the everyday relations between confessors of Christ and Jews in the Diaspora. According to Justin, Jews were allegedly not permitted to speak with Christians.[124] Yet the same author tells us this in his detailed dialogue with a rabbi (Trypho), in which—even if it is a literary fiction—he presupposes that his Christian readers can imagine this dialogue situation. Thus we may presume that everyday relations between confessors of Christ and Jews were relatively harmonious.[125] This can also be inferred, for example, from an analysis of the situation in Rome itself, where confessors of Christ and Jews must have lived in close proximity.[126] And it is also supported by the fact that the New Testament, in principle our only source, contains extremely meager information about *social* conflicts between Jews and confessors of Christ. That there were also social tensions, however, is shown in the case of Rome by the previously mentioned remark of Suetonius that there was persistent unrest among Roman Jews that was caused by one *Chrestus* (*Claudius* 25).

B. CRITICAL DECEPTION OF NEW TESTAMENT TESTIMONIES

Thus, since in principle we have knowledge of the Jewish-Christian conflicts of this epoch only from Christian sources that also exhibit a high degree of emotional involvement in the religious disputes, a critical reception of these testimonies is indispensable. Probably no New Testament author speaks of Judaism *sine ira et studio* (without anger and enthusiasm). If it is not appropriate to reconstruct the *religious* convictions of ancient Judaism from the often polemical texts of the New Testament, it is also inappropriate to derive from them simply and directly a corresponding *historical and social* reality. Yet a sure verdict is hard to reach in individual cases.

Relatively simple is the evaluation of texts that are *openly anti-Jewish* and only imply negative anti-Christian measures. For example, Titus 1:10-14, an especially strange text, shows the whole syndrome of discrimination based on prejudices. Here Jews (or Christ-confessing Jews?)[127] are called "idle talkers" and "deceivers" who for sordid gain upset whole families with their false teachings. The text reveals the anti-Jewish prejudice of its author, yet it cannot be drawn on as a source to support real negative experiences with Jews in Crete. Indeed, it is not even certain whether it might reflect disagreements with Christ-confessing Jews *within* the Christ-confessing community.

More difficult to evaluate are texts that speak *explicitly* of Jewish measures against confessors of Jesus. Acts 9:23-25 will serve as an example. According to this text, "the" Jews of Damascus plotted to kill Paul. They even watched the city gates in order to catch him. Paul, however, was able to escape at night with the help of a basket in which "his disciples" lowered him through the city wall. In 2 Cor 11:32-33, the episode reads differently. There the governor of the (Nabataean) king Aretas had the city watched in order to seize Paul, who was let down through a window in the wall and escaped. In fact, the two accounts are similar. Luke makes the episode even more exciting than Paul himself. More important here, however, is the fact that in Acts the villains are "the" Jews; in Paul the villain is the ethnarch of King Aretas. Attempts to harmonize the two texts so that both Aretas (or his governor) and "the" Jews plot against Paul and thus conspire[128] do not work without additional hypotheses, which are not free of prejudices. Thus Hengel, for example, expands the harmonization with the historical assumption that the "influential and politically powerful Jews of Damascus had a hand in the plot" because they were supposedly disappointed that the Pharisee Paul had become a Christian missionary.[129] Here "the" Jews of Acts have covertly become "influential" and "powerful" Jews, and it is naturally presupposed that Jews want to murder a former fellow believer. Where is the historical proof that "the" Jews were really like that?[130]

It is this very Damascus episode—for which we also happen to have a comment of Paul himself to which we can refer—that suggests that in Luke's presentation of Paul's "mission" he was little concerned with historical precision. Rather, Luke has a clear, repeated tendency to characterize "the" Jews as a critical, rejecting, and indeed persecuting element that was even prepared to plot murder.[131] Therefore everything suggests that we should give priority to the historicity of the Pauline version of the incident, in which Jews play no role, as opposed to the Lukan version. On the whole, we should evaluate critically the recognizable tendency of Acts to characterize Judaism as an anti-Christian force that is prepared to do almost anything.

C. ON THE TERM PERSECUTION

The same is true of the wholesale characterization of the negative experiences that believers in Jesus endured as *persecution* (*diōgmos/diōkein;* for example, in Acts 8:1; Matthew 5–10; Luke 11:49; 21:12; John 15:20; cf. also 1 Thess 2:14-16).[132] In scholarly exegesis this word has almost become a technical term for describing Jewish-Christian conflicts. Above all, it is concluded from the Lukan double volume, which is especially relevant here, that "the" Christians were persecuted by "the" Jews.[133] Or there is an assertion of participation by the Jews in (alleged) Roman persecution, especially in the second century.[134] Tertullian speaks of the synagogues as sources of Christian persecution.[135] Nonetheless, Conzelmann correctly says: "The traditions contain few *facts.*"[136] What is more, for the second century C.E. we cannot speak of direct Jewish participation in Roman measures against confessors of Christ.

When New Testament texts speak in this context of "persecution," they do this with the law of the conceptual generalization of subjective experiences and in the interest of interpreting them in the tradition of the Jewish interpretation of the persecution of prophets (cf. 1 Thess 2:14-16). The New Testament usage of the term *persecution* is thus in the first place only a literary and theological matter.[137] Yet historical research will have to ask more precisely whether this term, which contains very definite social assumptions, is appropriate. It involves a violent procedure against those who think differently, in the context of which the instigators of persecution are in a more powerful position than the persecuted and either can force them to give up their convictions or perhaps, if they persist, inflict upon them harsh punishments, including death. The aim is the extermination of deviant convictions. It is doubtful whether this aim can be attributed to Judaism in the Diaspora, which, in any case, has never found itself in the powerful position necessary for such persecution. In the cities of the Roman empire, the Jewish communities, like the Christian, existed as minority groups that by no means had at their disposal the necessary means of power presupposed by the concept of persecution. The only exceptions here are intrasynagogal disciplinary measures, which presuppose, however, that the ones thus disciplined belong to Judaism and have subjected themselves to its system of discipline.

Thus it is a question of examining the testimonies of the New Testament critically in terms of their social and legal plausibility. In addition to a consideration of the polemical character of the texts, the critical standard of the analysis must in any case be the question whether, based on the social, political, and legal situation, the negative experiences with Jews asserted in the New Testament statements could have been possible. And we would have to ask, among other things, what measures were undertaken—or could have been undertaken—by whom and with what competence.

D. THE SOURCE SITUATION

This critical examination is all the more important in view of the fact that in principle the only literary source for relations between Christ-confessing and Jewish communities in the urban regions of the Roman empire (outside the land of Israel) is the New Testament. We have no Jewish texts from the Diaspora that say anything about relations with believers in Christ in this period. Only the note in Suetonius (*Claudius* 2) can be used here. Moreover, the number of New Testament passages that can be utilized for the problem is limited to a very few texts. In addition to the letters of Paul, the most important and greatest number of statements are found in the Lukan double volume of Luke and Acts; the Revelation to John contains very little data. The remaining scriptures contain no information at all about Jewish-Christian social conflicts, but at most indications of internal problems in relations among the followers of Christ.

The First Letter of John, for example, reflects a situation of the secession of Jewish believers in Christ,[138] and perhaps the Letter of Titus a disagreement between Jewish and non-Jewish believers (see p. 341; some statements in the post–New Testament letters of Ignatius of Antioch are probably also to be understood in this way).[139] Also, a conflict with believers in Christ who hold to the Jewish tradition and especially the Torah could be reflected in 1 Tim 1:6-11. It is possible that some scriptures were written by Christ-confessing Jews (Hebrews, James, perhaps also 1 Peter).[140] Astonishingly, however, even they do not contain any information about real relations between Jews and believers in Christ. The Letter to the Ephesians[141] represents a Gentile Christian standpoint. It understands the communities as a union of Jewish and non-Jewish believers in Christ, in which the hostility between Jews and Gentiles, allegedly based on the Torah, has been overcome; it seems to reject the attachment of Jewish believers to the Torah (the law has been abolished: Eph 2:15).[142] Colossians also contains no information on Jewish-Christian social relations.[143]

11.2.1 Individual Conflicts

A. PAUL

First, we must mention Paul's own behavior (Gal 1:13: "I was violently persecuting the church of God and was trying to destroy it"),[144] which is supposed to have characterized his zeal (Phil 3:6) and his former way of life in Judaism. Presumably, in his "zeal" for the traditions of his ancestors,[145] Paul proceeded against Christ-confessing Jews in the theological tradition of Phinehas (Num 25:6-13).[146] The corresponding presentation in Acts regards the Jerusalem early church as affected by this Pauline "persecution."

In the context of the "persecution" described by Luke (Acts 8:1-3; 9:1-2, 4-5; 22:4-5, 7-8; 26:9-11, 14-15), Paul appears as the real protagonist, who combs Jerusalem house by house for believers in Christ, drags women and men into prison, and finally, with the authority of the high priest, also plans to arrest the Christ-confessing Jews who have fled to Damascus and take them back to Jerusalem. Only his conversion through the appearance of Christ prevents him from doing this.[147] Since outside of Acts we know nothing of this conflict of the early church with the official representatives of Judaism in Jerusalem, it is difficult to evaluate. Theoretically, a partial expulsion of messianic Jews from Jerusalem is not out of the question. Nevertheless, it is curious that according to Acts 8:1 the leading figures, the apostles, remain in Jerusalem. According to everything we know from the writings of Josephus about proceedings against fanatical charismatic groups, the "instigators" were also particular targets. Yet independent of that, the role Luke describes for Paul has little social or legal plausibility and is historically difficult to verify, and this is true not only of the assertion of the systematic eradication of believers in Christ.[148] Rather, the intention attributed to Paul by Luke of exercising police powers as a representative of the Jerusalem high priest in Damascus exceeds by far the possibilities of the Jerusalem high priest outside his jurisdiction.[149] Finally, the idea of Jerusalem as the point of origin of the "persecution" is difficult to harmonize with Gal 1:22, which seems to exclude Paul's negative activity against believers in Christ in Jerusalem (the churches in Judea did not even know him by sight and had only heard of his persecution of Jewish communities). This is supported in 1 Thess 2:14, where Paul mentions the persecution of Jewish communities but does not call himself their persecutor, and in Rom 15:19, where he rather positively connects the origin of his mission activity with Jerusalem.

From Paul's own self-testimonies, we must conclude, rather, that Paul "persecuted" not in Jerusalem but in Damascus.[150] Particular measures, however, are not reported. Paul speaks of persecution or the attempt to destroy the church of God. We have here at most intrasynagogal disciplinary measures, the most extreme form of which was the application of the synagogal punishment of flogging. In any case, this can be inferred from Paul's own later experiences as a missionary.[151] According to 2 Cor 11:24, Paul himself suffered the synagogal punishment of flogging five times. And 1 Thess 2:14-15 reveals that he sees himself, like the prophets, as being persecuted by the Jews (cf. Gal 5:11; 6:12). The immediate context leads one to presume that it was a question of defensive measures against his propaganda activities: "the" Jews hindered him from speaking to the Gentiles so that they might be saved (1 Thess 2:16). It is possible that Paul wanted to win "God-fearers" in the synagogues to his messianic faith.[152] *In this* context, it is possible that he was also punished "disciplinarily" by Diaspora synagogues. In general, Paul's activities as a persecutor and his own corresponding experiences presuppose an *intra-Jewish* conflict in which the instigators and the affected were Jews. From the synagogal point of view, it was a question of excluding (presumed) apostates and their protagonists.

B. THE EDICT OF CLAUDIUS

The measures of Claudius against Jews in Rome (Suetonius *Claudius* 25.2; Acts 18:2)[153] seem to have resulted from tensions within Roman Judaism in which Christ-confessing Jews played a role. This can be inferred from Suetonius's comment that the constant unrest was caused by one "Chrestus" (*impulsore Chresto*) and from Acts, which includes the couple Aquila and Prisca among those expelled. Yet the texts offer nothing more. The alleged expulsion of *all* the Jews of Rome, as reported by Luke, is unlikely.

C. THE REVELATION TO JOHN

The milieu of Revelation is Asia Minor (1:4). The author of this scripture was presumably a Christ-confessor with a Jewish heritage.[154] For against this background his critique of adopting pagan practices (eating meat offered to idols, and fornication: 2:14, 20) is understandable. On the whole, it is notable that Revelation has a critical attitude toward Judaism in only two verses, which contain the strange formulation *synagogue of Satan* (2:9; 3:9). Its interpretation is extremely controversial. Some scholars draw from these verses (and from statements in Acts to be discussed below) the far-reaching conclusion that "the" Jews are behind all the persecutions of "the" Christians. For example, according to Frend[155] the background of Rev 2:9 is a denunciation of believers in Christ before state authorities. Other interpreters understand the author's anti-Jewish polemic as an expression of his conviction that believers in Christ are the true Jews, and thus he regards the ongoing (non-Christian) Jewish communities as not truly Jewish but as communities in which Satan rules instead of God.[156]

On the Question of Denunciation

The formulation *synagogue of Satan* in Rev 2:9; 3:9 is often explained with the Jewish denunciation of believers in Christ before state authorities.[157] It is suggested, in the context of the first passage, that those who say that they are Jews (but in reality are a "synagogue of Satan") are called the originators of slander (*blasphēmia*), and it is assumed that some of the members of the church in Smyrna are about to be thrown into prison (2:9-10). Yet this interpretation is burdened by two problematic presuppositions.

First, it is questionable whether a connection can be established between the statement about the "slander" of the "synagogue of Satan" in v. 9 and the predicted imprisonment in v. 10. The second problem is the semantic concretion of *blasphēmia* as denunciation. On the one hand, there are, in our opinion, good reasons not to understand these two verses as interdependent and mutually interpretable. Verse 10 speaks of future events: future suffering that presupposes imprisonment and a ten-day affliction. Verse 9, by contrast, speaks of an already existing condition of "affliction" and "poverty" within the church and in this context mentions the "synagogue of Satan."[158] On the other hand, speaking against the identification of "slander" with denunciation (imprisonment) is, above all, the language of Revelation. It uses the noun *slander* (*blasphēmia*) and the verb *slander* (*blasphēmein*) elsewhere only in the context of the blasphemy of God (13:1, 5-6; 16:9, 11, 21; 17:3). Thus in connection with the "synagogue of Satan" and based on linguistic usage in Revelation, the catchword *blasphēmia* should be understood first of all as a blaspheming of God.

Finally, with this presupposition, the catchphrase *synagogue of Satan* produces a more precise concretion. In the Revelation to John "Satan" and the "devil" symbolize mythologically a force opposing God (or Christ), a worldwide sovereignty, as it were, that has usurped the legitimate sovereignty of God. This divine counterforce manifests itself in a particular way in the Roman emperor and his divine adoration (cf. above all Revelation 13). This connection is presupposed not least of all in Rev 2:13, which says that the throne of Satan is in Pergamum (apparently meaning the cult of the emperor there).[159] This very antidivine power is also repeatedly connected with blasphemy (for example, in 13:1, 5-6) and its adoration is described (for example, in 13:8). It is also what puts believers in Christ from Smyrna in prison and brings them suffering (2:10: "the devil is about to throw some of you into prison . . ."). Thus the expression *synagogue of Satan* establishes a connection with this antidivine power. In our view, it alludes to the idea that some (!) of those who call themselves Jews (2:9)—and thus by no means "the" Jews—have come to an arrangement with Roman sovereignty and the cult of the emperor, which for the apocalyptist contradicts being a Jew.

This does not have to involve the direct participation of Jews in the cult of the emperor. Rather, for the Seer the adoration of the power of Rome can be expressed even when the power of Rome is accepted, for example, through a dedicatory inscription (13:4: "They worshiped the dragon, for he had given his authority to the beast, and they worshiped the beast, saying, 'Who is like the beast,[160] and who can fight against it?'"). This is "blasphemy" in the eyes of the Seer John and leads him to the polemical conclusion that these Jews can no longer be called Jews, since they are no longer a "synagogue of the Lord" (*synagōgē kyriou:* Num 16:3 LXX) but a "synagogue of Satan" (*synagōgē tou Satana*). Also in accord with this interpretation is the fact that the "synagogue of Satan" in Rev 3:8-9 is contrasted with the steadfast behavior of the church in Philadelphia, which preserves the word and has not denied the name—yet no experiences of denunciation are mentioned here. From this standpoint we can also understand the curious promise in 3:9, where in the context of the second mention of the expression *synagogue of Satan,* the prediction is made that those of the "synagogue of Satan" will bow down before the feet of the church in Philadelphia.

Thus Rev 2:9 and 3:9 reflect *no social disagreement* with Diaspora Judaism. And we have no other indication of such a disagreement in this writing. Rather, it may therefore be a question of Jews being able to withdraw from a conflict with state authorities that threatens believers in Christ.[161] There is also socio-historical evidence on the basis of the different hazards for Jews and believers in Christ briefly presented above (see pp. 329–31) in connection with the *fiscus Judaicus* and the "Jewish way of life." Thus John seems to be speaking of the "synagogue of Satan" because in his view it has submitted itself to "Satan"—the Roman emperor or state. In the named texts there is no mention of the persecution of believers in Christ or their denunciation by Jews.

D. THE GOSPEL OF LUKE AND THE ACTS OF THE APOSTLES

Luke 6:22-23, 26[162] is a key text:

> [22]"Blessed are you when people *hate* you, and when they *exclude* you, *revile* you, and *defame* you on account of the Son of Man. [23]Rejoice in that day and leap for joy, for surely your reward is great in heaven; for that is what their ancestors did to the prophets. . . . [26]Woe to you when all speak well of you, for that is what their ancestors did to the false prophets."

The negative experiences described here refer to the time of Luke himself (they are predictions from Jesus' point of view and hence are different from the other beatitudes). We should also note that Luke, in contrast to the parallel formulation in Matt 5:11-12, does not speak of persecution. The first two terms, "hate" (*misein*) and "exclude" (*aphorizein*), refer to the *disruption* or *breaking off* of community relationships, whereas the last two, "revile" (*oneidizein*) and "defame" (*ekballein to onoma hōs ponēron*, lit. "cast out your name as evil"), mean verbal defamation. Thus the beatitude contains two basic kinds of rejection, which according to the Lukan presentation, believers in Christ experienced at the hands of Diaspora Judaism: (1) verbal and (2) social distancing.

Illustrations of such experiences are found in Acts. From the variety of texts that concern social conflicts with Judaism, the following statements are relevant for the present topic in the realm of urban Christian communities outside the land of Israel: verbal attacks and social distancing (Acts 13:45; 18:4; 19:9; 28:21-22); incitement of the pagan populace or its representatives (13:50; 14:2, 5; 17:5-6, 13); accusations before (pagan) authorities (17:6-7; 18:12ff.).[163] These negative relationships can also be summarized as the *verbal and social distancing* of Christians. According to the Acts of the Apostles, the social distancing climaxes in accusations against believers in Christ before pagan functionaries, which we will treat here as a separate area. All three experiences will be briefly described.

1. Verbal Distancing

The Greek idiom translated as "defame" (Luke 6:22) may refer to a pejorative usage of the designation in Acts 11:26 (cf. 26:28) of the disciples as *Christianoi* or "Nazarenes" (24:5), but we can do no more than speculate at this point. In any case, it is clear that it is not a question of personal insults but of slander against those affected as members of the Christ-confessing community. The more indefinite word "revile" (*oneidizein*) hardly produces a different picture in this context.[164] Verbal distancing is also noted in 13:45; 14:2; 18:6; 19:9, also circumscribed here above all with *blasphēmein/blasphēmia*, which suggests that in the view of those affected, it was a question of negative statements about their religious convictions. The object of this blasphemy is presumably Jesus, as can be inferred from Luke 22:65; 23:29; and Acts 18:6. And the fact that the blasphemy itself represents in a certain sense the *ultima ratio* of the verbal distancing of "Christian" convictions and communities allows a brief comment on Paul's persecutory activity, namely, that through punishment he forced blasphemy, probably with the goal of abjuration (Acts 26:11).[165] The cursing of Jesus in the synagogues, which is often mentioned by Justin,[166] is also understandable as an extreme form of verbal distancing.

Thus the named texts allege that believers in Christ experienced verbal defamation of their convictions of faith on the part of the Jews. We should also note in this connection that Acts assumes statements in the synagogues against "Christian" convictions of faith (cf. 28:22).

The Addressees of Verbal Distancing: The Pagan Population. The previously named activities are on the whole informal and thus do not designate disciplinary measures of the Diaspora synagogues. Nonetheless, according to the presentation in Acts, they seem to be connected with activities of not only individuals but also synagogues, for this experience seems to be characteristic of Paul's relations with Diaspora synagogues, as demonstrated by accounts in Acts of Paul's conflicts in and with synagogues in the Diaspora (13:45; 14:2; 18:6; 19:9). From 13:45; 14:2; 18:6 (and presumably also 19:9) we can infer that the addressees of these blasphemies or slanders are the pagan populace of the particular city. Moreover, it or its representatives are the addressees of the negative activities on the part of synagogues against believers in Christ in Acts 13:50; 14:5, 19; 17:5ff., 13; 18:12ff.[167] And it is notable that in most cases the various activities against Paul from the synagogal side are directly connected with conversion successes among the pagan population. Thus the described conflicts refer to a *distancing of synagogal Judaism from believers in Christ.* That is, since the rejection of believers in Christ was manifested also and precisely in the presence of the pagan populace, this act is understandable as distancing. An intensified form of distancing is mentioned in 13:50; 14:2, 5. Here the incitement of the pagan people against believers in Christ is recounted.

Believers in Christ Identified with Judaism. The verbal distancing of Diaspora Judaism from confessors of Christ presupposes, however, that pagans could confuse or identify members of these communities with members of the synagogues. Yet this very possibility is also reflected in Acts. Paul and Silas, for example, are expressly identified as Jews in Acts 16:20. Likewise, the behavior of the Roman legate of Achaia, before whom Paul was taken by Corinthian Jews, shows that he assumed internal Jewish disputes and thus identified the "Christian" preacher with Judaism (18:15-16). Especially impressive is the bitter experience of an Ephesian Jew named Alexander (cf. p. 333). He attempts to make an apologia before the (illegal) assembly of the people. Yet his attempt at defense is shouted down when the excited crowd recognizes that he is a Jew (19:33-34). Thus here too we may assume that Alexander wanted to defend Ephesian Jews, which would have been quite understandable if he had distinguished the synagogue from the Christ-confessing community.

2. Social Distancing

The verbs *hate* and *exclude* in Luke 6:22-23 address a second dimension of experience. On closer examination *hate* is used as the opposite of love of neighbor or generally of the ancient ethic of reciprocity (6:27ff.). Thus it designates the abolition or failure of social solidarity that may find concrete form in the field of social relationships among neighbors and friends, as well as in intrafamilial relationships (in 14:26, hating "father and mother, wife and children, brothers and sisters" is required as a condition of discipleship). In connection with the verb *exclude* the experience of rejection reflected here can best be understood as a kind of *social ostracism*,[168] that is, an informal rejection expressed through social behavior. This interpretation is again supported by the immediate context (6:26), the woe that parallels the beatitude. It refers to the opposite of such exclusion, namely, to general acceptance ("Woe to you when all speak well of you").

3. Accusations before Pagan Authorities

According to Luke's presentation, the distancing measures culminate in accusations before pagan officials (Luke 12:11-12; Acts 17:5ff. and 18:12ff.). In Luke 12:11-12 Jesus predicts to his disciples that they will be taken before synagogues and "authorities."[169] The verses end with an admonishing of Jesus' disciples to fearless confession. The synagogues themselves exercise no judicial or disciplinary power against the delinquents but apparently play an important role in a dangerous situation that could result in one's appearance before pagan officials. Thus implicit here could be what is then illustrated in the mentioned texts in Acts: the synagogues play a role in one's being brought before (pagan) officials. The term for the "rulers and authorities" in Luke 12:11 (*archai kai exousiai*) circumscribes their official authority but does not give them official titles. In the context of corresponding Lukan linguistic usage, it presumably means Roman and municipal officials with various responsibilities. Thus Luke 12:11 speaks of conflicts between "Gentile Christians" and Diaspora synagogues that are (or could be) ultimately taken before state "authorities." This situation is also described by two texts of Acts (17:5ff.; 18:12ff.) that we have already discussed (see pp. 321–22). They concern accusations against "Christian" missionaries. The legal conflict in Thessalonica, where the affected believers in Christ are accused of being hosts or members of a worldwide movement of Jewish insurrectionists who claim royal dominion for Jesus against the rule of the emperor (17:6-7), clearly implies the cause of the accusations: the suspicion that believers in Christ are followers of a Jewish movement of anti-Roman rebels. Their historical background is revealed in two conflicts within Diaspora Judaism, described by Josephus, that took place in Alexandria (*War* 7.407ff.) and in Cyrenaica (7.437ff.).

In the first conflict insurgents from the feared resistance group of the sicarii who had fled to Alexandria persuaded many of their Jewish hosts to rise up with them for liberty. Some of the most respected Jews opposed them but were killed by the sicarii, who were working hard for revolt. Finally, the leading members of the Alexandrian council recognized the danger to Alexandrian Jews through the sicarii and called together a full assembly, to which it presented the "madness" of the sicarii. It described especially the danger for Alexandrian Jews of becoming involved in these proceedings, even if they had had no share in the deeds of the sicarii. They recommended that the sicarii be turned over to the Romans to justify or defend themselves before the Romans. The crowd was persuaded: six hundred of the sicarii were immediately seized. Apparently the elders and the popular assembly acted with knowledge "of Roman imperial and penal law. . . . Those who socialized with the insurrectionists outside the law were themselves also in extreme danger [kindynos] and had to ponder their own ruin [olethros]—that is, the loss of their own safety under the law—and harsh punishment."[170] The only alternative remained the accusation and handing over of the sicarii to the Romans, in order to justify oneself before the Romans.

The second conflict was initiated by the exodus of a group of Jewish poor (aporoi) under the leadership of the weaver Jonathan. In Cyrenaica he wanted to show the poor marvelous signs. Rich and respected Jews denounced this movement, according to Josephus. This conflict is of importance here especially because the poor led by Jonathan were a group of unarmed religious enthusiasts who were nonetheless reported by Jews to the Roman governor of Libyan Pentapolis and brutally suppressed by him. The arrest of the leader ultimately led to serious consequences for other (especially rich and respected) Jews. Even Josephus, who informs us of this incident, became involved in the conflict himself. For the governor now used the arrest of the weaver Jonathan as a welcome occasion to kill especially rich Jews in Cyrenaica and confiscate their wealth. In this connection, finally, accusations were also made against the most respected Jews in Alexandria (and Josephus in Rome) because of "revolutionary activity" (War 7.447), which, however, were dismissed by Vespasian. Thus in tragic irony, the denunciation of Jonathan and the poor with him led to exactly what it was supposed to prevent.[171]

Especially during the period after 70, one cannot exclude accusations against the followers of Christ, who were connected with Judaism and in the view of the Romans must have been already suspect because of their adoration of Christ, who had been executed as an anti-Roman rebel. This is also suggested by certain indications in the New Testament (cf. pp. 330–31). The Jonathan example shows that even unarmed Jewish enthusiast groups were open to the suspicion of revolution. The two conflicts described by Josephus also reveal that accusations took place in the interest of distancing Diaspora Judaism from these (alleged) rebels, in order to direct possible threatening dangers away from the synagogues.

11.2.2 Conclusions and the Sociological Interpretation of Conflicts between Jews and Believers in Christ

A. CONCLUSIONS

The letters of Paul reveal isolated measures of the intrasynagogal disciplining of Christ-confessing Jews. The so-called edict of Claudius also points to tensions because of Christ-confessing Jews within Roman Jewry. Noteworthy in this case are the perception of the conflict by the Roman authorities and the fact that the Diaspora Judaism of Rome had to bear its social consequences. Of the remaining New Testament writings only the statements of the Lukan double volume are relevant, since even in the Revelation to John no social conflicts between Jews and believers in Christ can be demonstrated. The Lukan double volume reveals above all the verbal and in part also social distancing of Diaspora Judaism from believers in Christ. In two cases this culminates in accusations before pagan officials; they pose an especially difficult historical problem. J. T. Sanders holds them to be historically unbelievable and says that they are only a reflex of theological differences and an expression of Lukan anti-Semitism, since we lack extra–New Testament evidence of corresponding negative experiences.[172] As seriously as this objection must be taken, the New Testament statements, in our opinion, cannot be discounted as totally incredible. Extra–New Testament evidence for such experiences is in principle not to be expected. Even dramatic conflicts, like the pogroms in Alexandria and Antioch that included massive killings and great cruelties against Jews, are known to us only through those affected. The reported conflicts in Alexandria and Cyrenaica also offer historical analogies. Thus, in our view, we cannot, in any case, exclude the possibility of accusations. Nevertheless, it was by no means a matter of typical or frequent experiences, but at most isolated cases. In the special historical situation after 70, delations against believers in Christ are to be understood as Jewish measures of self-protection. Such accusations gave Judaism a chance to distance itself from a messianic movement that was suspected of being anti-Roman.

It is worth noting how few of the New Testament scriptures that are potentially involved here actually reflect social manifestations of the Jewish-Christian conflict. This source situation is in itself already conclusive. It allows the assumption that negative encounters between Christ-confessing groups and Diaspora synagogues took place at most sporadically. And it can even be concluded that only a specific historical situation of danger (after the defeat of the Jewish rebellion or under the rule of Domitian) favored conflicts. Likewise, we can also presume from this source situation that Diaspora Judaism coexisted harmoniously with Christ-confessing communities and, indeed, was in the main officially hardly aware of its existence as such.[173] This state of affairs was doubtless also affected by the increasing dominance of the "Gentile Christian" element in the Christian communities. Our analysis confirms this impression in the sense that in the field of conflict under discussion here, *intrasynagogal* measures are documented only for the period before 70 C.E. After 70 the addressees of the distancing measures are the pagan public or their political authorities.[174]

The situation of urban communities of Christ after 70 is in many respects comparable to that seen in the writings of Justin (middle of the second century). He also knows of no case of a disciplinary measure against a believer of Christ in synagogues or of exclusion from a synagogue. It is true that Justin mentions dangerous measures against Christ-confessing Jews in the context of the Bar Kokhba Revolt,[175] repeatedly mentions verbal "cursings" of believers in Christ in the synagogues,[176] even notes something about a kind of world-wide Jewish counterpropaganda against believers in Christ,[177] and finally calls Jews the instigators of slanderings of believers before pagans.[178] Justin focuses, however, on the judicial measures of pagan authorities, to which he himself ultimately fell victim. In view of his intensive disagreement with Judaism, which approached hostility, this negative finding is notable.[179] Yet it is also in a certain sense natural and understandable in the sense that Justin had in mind the situation of an already consolidated Gentile Christianity that was having trouble with the respect of the Jews who believed in Jesus as Christ.[180] An exception is the case of a Jewish apostle converted to faith in Christ, who after his conversion is supposed to have been flogged in the synagogue (in Cilicia) and finally thrown into the water (Epiphanius *Haer.* 30.11). Yet the historical value of Eusebius's note (*Hist. Eccl.* 5.16: flogging of women by Jews and stoning) is extremely doubtful; the background is probably the death of women followers of Montanus. Moreover, the epistle to Diognetus does not assert that the Jews took part in *persecutions* of believers by pagans (Diognetes 5.17).[181] The same is true of the *Martyrdom of Polycarp* (12.1–3; 13.1; 17.2–18.1: here Jews act alongside pagans against Polycarp).[182]

B. PRESOCIOLOGICAL TERMS AND INTERPRETATIONS

Presociologically in the strict sense, the negative Jewish-"Christian" relationships are called "persecution,"[183] "separation or severance of church and synagogue,"[184] "parting of the ways,"[185] and the problem of "Jewish and Christian self-definition."[186] This terminology implies certain models, as becomes clear especially in the formulation "separation of synagogue and church." Things that have separated must have previously belonged together.

Yet—as we have already presented—the letters of Paul, the oldest literary testimonies about urban "Christian" communities in the Roman empire, presuppose their existence outside the Diaspora synagogues.[187] For this reason alone it makes little sense to imagine Jewish-"Christian" conflicts as a process in the course of which Christ-confessing communities separated from the synagogues.[188] Likewise, the terms *separation, severance, break* (between synagogue and church), and *parting of the ways* suggest particular historical events of separation that are connected with various events and their dates, for example, the turning point after the first Jewish-Roman war (70 C.E., also and especially the flight of messianic Jews to Pella), after the second First Jewish Revolt (135–136 C.E.), or after the so-called heretic blessing, however one dates this formulation historically.[189] Yet because we can name no specific historical events that can mark a separation,[190] more recently there has been talk of the "separation *process*" or of "separation *processes.*"[191] In our opinion, however, one should abandon altogether the term *separation* (and comparable terms like *severance* and *break*). The formulation *parting of the ways* is already better, but it also suggests that there was a gradual process of separation, in which it remains an open question whether social processes or differences in the symbolic world were more important.

The formulation *Jewish and Christian self-definition* emphasizes the discursive level of the conflicts, yet it traces the process of religious differentiation back to a "self-definition" of Jews and Christians that had become necessary in the historical situation (of the last third of the first century) in the interest of gathering and strengthening the identity of the individual communities.[192] In our view, this model is also suited for the understanding of the level of *social* conflicts between urban believers in Christ and Diaspora synagogues. For the concept of "self-definition" presupposes a historically necessary determination of the boundaries of both religious groups (for example, in regard to the question of membership), which at the same time is also connected—at least implicitly—with the exclusion of others. Therefore we advocate here the thesis that the negative aspects of the social relationships between urban Christ-confessing communities and Diaspora Judaism are best comprised by the terms *exclusion* and *distancing*. In the case of Jewish-"Christian" relations in urban regions outside the land of Israel, the process of the *exclusion* can refer only to intrasynagogal measures against individuals or groups with a "Christian" or messianic identity that deviate from the majority of Diaspora Judaism yet still belong to Judaism. In our opinion, this includes only Paul's own activities and his conflicts with synagogues, as seen in his letters. The process of *exclusion*, by contrast, is directed toward the pagan majority population and its political functionaries with the aim of distancing people and groups with "Christian" or messianic identity who do not belong to Diaspora

Judaism. This situation is reflected in the conflicts discernible in the Lukan double volume.

C. SOCIOLOGICAL THEORIES

In principle, three sociological theories have been applied to the interpretation of Jewish-"Christian" relations in the New Testament period: the sect model, deviance theories, and conflict theories.[193] The sect model is not suitable for the conflict situation presented here, for it presupposes that it is a question of *intra-Jewish* conflicts also in the sociological sense. Yet sociologically speaking, urban Christ-confessing communities no longer belonged to Judaism. Theoretically the sect model can be applied at most to the measures carried out by Paul himself against believers in Christ in Damascus.[194] Yet we simply know too little about the groups that he "persecuted." In the case of the negative measures that Paul himself suffered (five synagogal floggings), it is a question of one individual's experience.

Both of the conflict experiences discernible from Paul's letters can be better explained by deviance theory as measures against individuals who deviate from the majority of Diaspora Judaism. These experiences presuppose, on the one hand, deviation by those involved from *Jewish* norms and rules and, on the other, *control* of the synagogues through the implementation of its rules and norms. Nevertheless, in our view, sociological deviance theories are not suited to the interpretation of the "Christian"-Jewish conflicts in the Diaspora *after* 70. In the sense of *intra-Jewish* deviance—in the context of the life, convictions, and values of Diaspora Judaism—Jewish-"Christian" conflicts apparently played a role only in their symbolic representation. That is, "Christian" convictions are contradicted *in* synagogues (cf. Acts 13:45), they are warned against (Acts 28:21), or they are verbally stigmatized (blasphemies: Justin). The Diaspora synagogues did not have any *control* over believers in Christ for the purpose of implementing rules and norms.

Regarding the experiences of urban communities of Christ with synagogues after 70, the texts themselves reveal that the addressees of the measures were mostly the pagan populace or their political authorities. The resulting sociological constellation must assume the values and rules of the *pagan population* as the standard of deviance. The experiences of believers in Christ with paganism were interpreted in this sense (see p. 338). Of significance here is, at most, the point that the distancing measures of the synagogues supported or influenced the social exclusion of believers in Christ. It seems to us that in this respect the presociological term *distancing* selected here seems meaningful, since these conflicts seem to involve a process of Judaism's *exclusion* of Christ-confessing groups. In terms of culture, religion, and sociology, both the synagogues and the Christ-confessing communities were minority groups in

the urban centers of the Roman empire. Thus the conflicts between synagogue and Christ-confessing communities can best be understood as group
conflicts and more precisely as conflicts between minority groups within the
pagan majority society.

Conflict Theory

Gager was the first to take the sociological conflict theory of Coser (based on
Simmel) and apply it to the New Testament.[195] J. T. Sanders[196] continued this
analysis and applied it to "Christian"-Jewish conflicts. In addition to Coser, he
draws above all on the conflict theory of the sociologist Kriesberg.[197]

Conflict theories presuppose that social systems consist of various groups
whose aims and interests may compete and who "therefore use coercive tactics
on each other in order to realize their own goals. Each of the various groups
protects the distinctive interests of its members. Furthermore, relations
between various groups include disagreement, strain, conflict, and force—as
well as consensus and cooperation."[198] For our purposes it is significant that
conflicts can also arise when several groups make comparable claims; that is,
when their interests overlap and compete with one another. And the more
groups resemble each other, the more it becomes necessary to formulate the
specific differences. A group that might be confused with another will distance itself from the other group, especially when the latter is under pressure
or in danger. Gager has also discussed the positive functions of conflicts for
group understanding and formulated four elements of a conflict: (1) conflicts
have a function in group cohesion; (2) ideology intensifies the conflict; (3) the
closer the relations of the groups are, the more intensive is the conflict; (4)
conflicts serve the definition and reinforcement of group structures.

Causes of the Conflict

The Jewish-"Christian" conflicts mentioned in the Lukan double volume
reveal three motifs: (1) defense of messianic believers in Christ against threatening danger from the synagogues, (2) competition for influential clientele in
the cities, (3) limitation of Jewish identity. The third motif is also to be understood in terms of conflict theory on the basis of the limitation of the interests
of another group or in the context of the similarity of the groups that need
distinguishing.

1. Defense against danger and protection of one's own group. In connection with faith
in Jesus as the Messiah of Israel, the possibility of suspecting Christ-confessing
communities as politically dangerous was especially well suited for the transference of the concomitant potential endangerment of believers in Christ to
the Diaspora synagogues. Confessors of Christ could be understood as a world-

wide anti-Roman insurgent movement (Acts 17:6) or as the anti-Roman "sect of the Nazarenes," which causes unrest among the Jews in the region of Roman sovereignty (24:5). Thus by definition, as it were, Diaspora Judaism was affected by the endangerment of believers in Christ. After the defeat of the Jewish rebellions, Jews were considered rebellious and bellicose.[199] Rome's fear that the rebellions would also spread to Diaspora Judaism were not entirely unfounded. In this context the distancing of Diaspora synagogues from the allegedly rebellious messianic followers of Christ is understandable. Its most effective form was without doubt the accusation of supposed delinquents. Yet the two cases of informing reported in Acts (17:5; 18:12ff.), in addition to the two analogies mentioned by Josephus,[200] are apparently exceptions. Thus in terms of conflict theory, distancing can be interpreted in the context of the interest of one's own group, which was necessary on account of the danger threatened by another group because of the confusion of the two groups.[201]

2. Competition. The Acts of the Apostles contains several indications of the competition of Jewish and Christ-confessing groups—namely, for influential persons (cf. 13:6ff.). In Iconium, according to the description in Acts, a regular split developed in the population, so that some sided with the Jews and others with the apostles (14:1ff.). Nevertheless, here, as earlier in Antioch of Pisidia, the synagogue had sufficient influence, especially with the leading personalities of the city, to force the apostles to flee the area (13:50; 14:5). Yet here it is evident that the Jewish reaction to the penetration of a realm of Judaism was distancing vis-à-vis believers in Christ. In the conflicts in Thessalonica and Berea it then becomes especially clear that the conversion successes of "Christian" preachers among the Gentiles—and particularly among the so-called God-fearers[202]—evoked defensive measures by the synagogues (17:5ff., 10ff.). We have already discussed local political influence, especially that of God-fearing women (see pp. 257–58).

Thus competition between believers in Christ and Jews in the pagan polis arose above all from the fact that the "Christian" entered a Jewish realm of influence. Judaism reacted with defensive measures that consisted in contradiction and blasphemy (Acts 13:45), as well as the mobilization of the pagan populace against confessors of Christ. The process of distancing found its most grave expression in accusations (17:6). Thus this second motif, competition, explains the conflict between groups that make comparable claims and whose interests overlap.

3. Limitation of the group identity of Diaspora Judaism. A further motif can clarify the measures of the Jews who distanced themselves from believers in Christ. Here it is a question of the possible limitation of Diaspora Judaism's own religious (or ethnic) identity by the teachings and behavior of confessors of Christ. In two texts we find direct accusations from the Jewish side against representatives of Christ (Stephen and Paul) that express how Judaism is affected by "Christian" convictions: Acts 6:(11,) 13-14 and 21:28. Believers in Christ teach against the law, and they teach against "this holy place" (6:13). By contrast, against Paul we find only the accusation that he is teaching against the people of Israel (21:28; cf. 28:17). These accusations are related to the critical position of believers in Christ against the temple (see only Acts 7), which had to be understood as anti-Jewish especially in the time after the destruction of the Temple and the resulting sorrow in Judaism. The second formulation concerns certain Torah-critical attitudes of believers in Christ, who rejected circumcision and adoption of the Torah by Christ-confessing Gentiles. In the Jewish view the third criticism apparently concerns the same problem (the programmatic inclusion of Gentiles in the salvation of Israel). Along with the other accusations against believers in Christ—they teach against the law and the holy place—this accusation shows that in the Jewish view the Christian community is different from Judaism in its fundamental convictions. This difference can be expressed in the following point: in contrast to the communities of Christ, Diaspora Judaism experienced the present as a time of disaster and Christian convictions as disloyalty vis-à-vis the destiny of Israel. That is, the specifically Jewish view of the churches of Christ is to be understood based on the situation of Israel's catastrophe. This epochal experience influenced not only the above-mentioned massive distancing measures of the synagogues from the churches but also the Jewish interpretation—still discernible in Acts—of confessors of Christ as an anti-Jewish, paganizing movement. In the Jewish view the Christ-confessing community presents itself as a movement that has come forth from Judaism but has abandoned the law of Moses; it has given up the central marks of Jewish identity—circumcision, Torah, temple—in favor of assimilation to paganism and in the epoch after the catastrophic defeat at the hands of the Romans can be comprehended only as a movement directed against Israel.

PART FOUR

The Social Roles and Social Situation of Women in the Mediterranean World and in Early Christianity

INTRODUCTION

The ancient societies of the Mediterranean were shaped not only by the basic differentiation into upper and lower strata (elite and the masses). Also of great significance was a person's membership in the male or female sex. This ancient outlook is thus an example of the cultural anthropological insight that gender is a social construct or is defined socially in the sense that the assignment of roles and division of competence between the sexes are "embedded" in the social and cultural framework of a society.[1] In English one can also make a linguistic distinction between biological (*sex*) and social (*gender*) differences. Ancient Mediterranean societies were characterized by a rather strict differentiation of the social roles and areas of competence assigned to the sexes. They were regarded as grounded in nature and God-given. Accordingly, the expectation of sex-conforming role behavior was extremely high, and the switching of male and female roles or competencies was taboo.

Corresponding to the different role and competence assignments of men and women were stereotypical sex attributes, which were also connected with value orientations and expressed in allegedly typical male and female "characteristics":[2]

men	women
strong	weak
brave[3]	fearful
magnanimous	petty
reserved	loquacious
rational	irrational, emotional
controlled	uncontrolled

These culturally defined antitheses were interwoven in various ways with other discourses. For example, certain characteristics that women allegedly have by nature can also be asserted of men or of particular social groups (such as slaves)—and vice versa. When women exhibited certain ways of behaving that by nature allegedly belonged to men, they were considered manly. Clytemnestra in Aeschylus's tragedy *Agamemnon,* for example, is understood as "manly" because she is especially intelligent and thus apparently possesses a characteristic ascribed to men. Conversely, men can be said to be "effeminate" if they exhibit characteristics or behavior ascribed to women, for example, wearing long hair. This is expressed terminologically in the designation of passively homosexual men, who are called *effeminatus* in Latin and *malakos* ("soft") in Greek.[4]

It is also important in this connection that the value judgments about certain social groups and the allegedly typical behavior of men and women can be mutually interpretive. This is true above all for the behavior of slaves and women on the one hand and that of free men on the other. That is, from the viewpoint of the virtues of a free man—for example, with regard to his discipline in dealing with bodily and sensual excesses—a correspondingly undisciplined behavior was understood as "slavish" (lacking freedom, submissive to the power of the body). Alcoholism and gluttony, as well as sexual excesses, were examples of "enslavement" of a man by his desires.[5] Naturally, the same lack of control over themselves was also ascribed to women; for example, behavior that was understood as slavish could also be regarded as typically feminine. This is shown—to stay with these examples—by the proverbial (alleged) alcoholism of women and their (alleged) lack of sexual control.[6] Just distinguishes for the moral convictions of Athens society three pairs of opposites:[7] freedom and slavery, self-control and incontinence, rationality and emotion. If the behavior of women is placed into these dichotomies, they are regarded mostly as undisciplined, emotional, and thus by nature "unfree" and "slavish." They lack precisely what constitutes a free man: self-determination and discipline. Thus, from the point of view of men, social and legal distinctions are, in fact, explained by the natural makeup of women. These socio-culturally conditioned judgments, which reflect the power structure of ancient societies, were also carried over to sexual relationships between men and women. Gender-specific behavior was generally embedded in the fundamental values of Mediterranean societies and was oriented toward the concepts of honor, shame, and disgrace.[8]

The problems of ancient sexual differences, which are only suggested here, have been widely discussed and have led to substantial insights into the gender-specific discourse of ancient Mediterranean culture and its reflection in the New Testament. Here we will only go into the differentiation of men's and women's spheres of existence, which is especially relevant socio-historically, and the opportunities of women connected with stratum membership. In principle, women are supposed to be limited to the home; by contrast, men have free access to the public places of the polis and ultimately dominate in both realms, although women are granted a greater role in the home. Yet even with all the stereotyping of social roles and areas of competence given by membership in the female sex, we must again distinguish between the opportunities of women of the upper stratum and those of women in the lower stra-

tum. First we will give a basic presentation of these two socio-historically relevant areas (Chapter 12). Then in accordance with the basic differentiation of
early Christianity undertaken above, we will discuss the importance of women
among Jesus' followers in Israel (13) and in urban early Christian communities in the Roman empire (14).

12

GENDER-SPECIFIC SPHERES AND THE SOCIAL STRATIFICATION OF WOMEN IN MEDITERRANEAN SOCIETIES

In the first section (12.1) we will discuss the social significance of the gender-specific spheres of home and public. The second section (12.2) will then present stratum membership of women and its significance for the social situation.

12.1 The Public, the Household, and the "Natural" Separation of the Sexes

The delineation of gender-specific spheres—the public area of the polis on the one hand and the home on the other—offers, as it were, a "structural framework" that makes it possible to differentiate the places of men and women in ancient societies in psychological, cultural, social, and economic respects.[1] Yet the difference should not be simply identified with the modern concepts of "public" and "private."[2] For just as women were not totally excluded from public life and thus the political life of the polis, the home as their central sphere of life was of political importance and not simply a private area beyond public discourses and without influence on them. Nevertheless, we can say that basically the differentiation of the competencies and roles of women and men at home and in public was in principle oriented and organized in terms of gender. That is, independent of their social status, women had, in comparison to men, a clearly restricted access to the various political, economic, and social resources of public life. Here the asymmetry of the sexes and the dominance of men are the most obvious. By contrast, in the home—even with all the de jure dominance of men—the division of competence and roles between women and men seems to have expressed a complementary relationship of the sexes. A short text from Philo (*Spec. Leg.* 3.169ff.) will illustrate the "spatial" opposition of men and women and its political consequences:

> Marketplaces, council meetings, courts, social organizations, assemblies of large crowds of people, and interaction of word and deed in the open, in war and in peace, are suited only for men. The female sex, by contrast, is supposed to guard the house and stay at home; virgins are to remain in the back rooms and regard the connecting doors as boundaries; married women, however, should regard the front door as the boundary. For there are two kinds of urban spheres, a larger and a smaller. The larger ones are called cities, the smaller ones house-

holds [*oikiai*]. Of these two, on the basis of the division, the men are in charge
of the larger one, which is called municipal administration [*politeia*]; women,
of the smaller one, which is called the household [*oikonomia*]. Thus women are
not supposed to concern themselves further with anything but the duties of the
household.

This is without doubt a prescriptive text that shows only how things *should*
be. Actually, women appeared in public in various connections, even before
court, and they also belonged to social organizations (see pp. 369ff.). Yet
direct participation in what Philo calls "municipal administration" (*politeia*)
was the domain of men.

12.1.1 Women and Politics

Thus one central aspect of the distinction of gender-specific spheres consists
in the fact that women were generally excluded from holding public office as
senators, equestrians, decurions, or judges, as well as subordinate positions.[3]
They were not even allowed to belong to the most important political deci-
sion-making body of the polis (except for the magistrates), the popular assembly (*ekklēsia*), in which women could neither vote nor speak.[4] Could they,
nonetheless, at least be present as observers? We do not have an explicit testimony that Greek women, for example, were forbidden to participate in the
popular assembly, but Just infers this prohibition from Aristophanes' comedy
Ekklesiazusae.[5] Further indirect evidence is found in a dialogue in another of
his comedies, *Lysistrata*, which clearly reveals that the wives interrogated their
husbands when they came home from the popular assembly.[6]

Very striking are the reversals of real relationships in the comedies of
Aristophanes. In *Thesmophoriazusae* men have ultimate authority at home
while women, in the manner of men, hold their public assemblies, in which
they speak, elect leaders, and so forth as men normally do, thereby imitating
the popular assembly of the men. This reversal of everyday experience is also
found in the comedy *Lysistrata*. Here the decision about war and peace
becomes the business of women; men are relegated to spinning and weaving.
Women leave their domain, the home, take over the Acropolis, and control
the finances of the polis. It is worth noting that in some texts in the Old Testament–Jewish tradition[7] women (and to some extent children and youth) are
also mentioned as participants in an assembly (*ekklēsia*). But this hardly justifies the general assertion that in Judaism, at least since Ezra, women and children also belonged to the *qahal/ekklēsia*.[8] In no passage do women, children,
or youth participate or vote in the debates.

Men generally ruled extremely sensitively when women became involved
in politics, as can be inferred from an (obviously exaggerated) speech of Cato
the Elder in Livius.[9] In it Cato complains:

I have just come—not without a certain amount of blushing—through a crowd of women to the forum. . . . What kind of a custom is this, going into public, occupying the streets, and speaking to strange men? . . . Our ancestors wanted women not to engage in any activity, not even a private one, without guardian and tutor; they should be under the power of their fathers, brothers, or men. Yet we allow them, if it pleases the gods, even to become eagerly involved in the state's business and to participate in the forum in public meetings and popular assemblies [*contionibus et comitiis*].

From the Livius text we may infer that Roman women appeared in public, even in the forum, and participated in some way in public affairs. Yet it does not suggest any *direct* participation of women in political meetings. Even the speaking of women in public was considered offensive. Valerius Maximus expresses the opinion that the public appearance of women in the forum or in judicial proceedings was appropriate neither to their natural state (*condicio naturae*) nor to the modesty (*verecundia*) of their sex. Accordingly, the three female orators he mentions (Maesia Sentia, Afrania, and Hortensia) are clearly criticized.[10] The gender-specific character of the exclusion of women from the public realm of "municipal administration" (*politeia*) is confirmed by the following insight: the basic free access of all men to the political self-governance of the city was graduated socially and legally. In general, only the urban elite had access to offices of political leadership and decurion status. To the popular assembly of the polis belonged, in addition to the elite, only a limited number of male members of the lower stratum—namely, those with full citizenship. Male members of the lower stratum (free, freedman, and slave) could perform certain subordinate municipal functions as retainers. Yet women, regardless of their social position, were generally barred from access to these political institutions and offices.

According to inscriptional evidence, rich women in Greek city-states were celebrated as benefactors and honored with political functions and titles, such as *gymnasiarch, strategos, prytanis,* and *demiourgos;*[11] yet they neither had a real place in the magistracy of the city nor could vote in the popular assembly.[12] Even the Hellenistic queens—Arsinoe, Bernice, Cleopatra—ruled only with the titular presence of men.[13]

The Political Influence of Women

Yet the fact that women were excluded in principle from the political offices and committees of a polis did not mean that they had no political influence. In the literature of antiquity the political influence of women, especially those from elite families, is presented in an extremely critical and mostly exaggerated way.[14] Especially in the leading families of Roman society, women apparently had a growing influence on politics.[15] It is therefore no accident that

many wives of Roman emperors and leading personalities of the imperial aristocracy were characterized by both a dissolute life and great political influence.
That is to say, the very involvement of women of the elite in the male domain
of politics seems to have especially provoked the caustic criticism of other
aspects of their lifestyles. Some of these women acquired proverbial significance in that they became negative examples for "manly" women because of
their involvement in political affairs and at times also because of their participation in conspiracies and civil wars. Thus, for example, in connection with
the Catilinian conspiracy, Sempronia is supposed to have committed "many
outrages of manly audacity," as Sallust formulates.[16] Also famous and notorious was Fulvia, one of the wives of Mark Antony, of whom it was said that her
body was the only thing feminine about her.[17] Great influence is also attributed to mothers of politically active sons, for example, Servilia, the mother of
Caesar's assassin Brutus.[18]

From the *Annals* of Tacitus one gets the impression that the wives of
emperors and influential freedmen at the imperial court were the real rulers of
the Roman empire (cf. only *Ann.* 11–14). Tacitus attributes everything bad to
(imperial and upper stratum) women. They marry slaves (12.53), are jealous
(13.13) and vain (13.14), immoral, unbridled (13.19), plotting, superficially
virtuous but in truth wanton (13.45), beautiful and flattering (13.46), and
they entice honest men to adultery and divorce in order then to wait for a
richer man (13.44). They are especially dangerous when they combine background, beauty, and an unbridled nature (13.19). Above all, however, they
have a ruinous political influence on their husbands.

This tendentious picture of women shows that one must be careful not to
adopt uncritically the negative judgment of ancient writers.[19] Generalizing
conclusions seem to us to be especially problematic. Messalina, for example,
is called "nymphomaniacal" by modern research, and the political background
of her activities is dismissed as irrelevant, although Tacitus himself, even with
the harshest criticism of Messalina as a person, clearly presents the background of a political plot against Claudius. Even psychologizing evaluations
of Agrippina, who as a child suffered the persecution of her mother and is
supposed to have inherited her mother's "lust for power," naively adopt the
tendentious presentation of Tacitus.[20] The fact that the corresponding parts of
the *Annals* could be relatively easily rewritten into screenplays for Hollywood
films should give us pause.[21] Also the political influence of wives of Roman
governors in the provinces in no way justifies the assertion that "wives of governors in the administration of the provinces interfered so intensively that in
the senate in the year 21 a resolution was proposed that governors be prohibited from taking their wives with them."[22]

In fact, Tacitus (*Ann.* 3.33–34) reports that Severus Caecina proposed a senate action on grounds that concerned the nature of the weak female sex and its lack of discipline. The naturally weaker sex is said to be transformed—when allowed the freedom—into characteristics such as cruelty, ambition, and lust for power. They would involve themselves in military affairs, and in the case of the (financial) oppression of the population by the governors, wives were said to be mostly at fault; likewise the reproach was made that homage was paid to them along with the governors and that they even gave orders. Yet the proposal was not only rejected but its arguments were also in part refuted by Valerius Messalinus. He speaks of the minimal costs for wives and holds their presence to be, in any case, unproblematic in peacetime. Although he concedes the bad influence of wives on their husbands, he paints a true picture when he points out that men also make mistakes. Moreover, he holds that it is more disadvantageous for marriages if husbands are separated too long from their wives and families. In regard to the Tacitus passage, Garnsey and Saller maintain dispassionately: "The governor's wife may have accompanied her husband, but, if virtuous, she did not allow provincials to approach lest they try to influence the governor through her."[23] The book of Acts (25:23ff.) is also realistic when it describes how Bernice, the sister of Herod Agrippa II, participates with her brother and the Roman governor in the interrogation of a Roman citizen (Paul). The direct involvement of Bernice in this procedure is not suggested.

Thus we may certainly assume that (upper stratum) women were active as advisors of their husbands and sons, on whom they exercised influence and with whom they appeared in public, participated in political discussions,[24] and presumably even became involved in political conspiracies.[25] Yet they were always only a "power behind the throne that they themselves could not possess, and their involvement in politics was always accepted with resentment."[26] Women also supported their own husbands or other men in election propaganda, as shown by graffiti in Pompeii.[27] Yet they themselves could not vote in these elections. Furthermore, there are numerous examples of the solidarity of wives who went into exile with their husbands who had fallen into political disfavor,[28] who used sexual means to their husbands' advantage,[29] or even took their own lives.[30] Pliny the Younger reports the fate of a certain Arria who in the hopeless situation of her husband Caecina Paetus stabbed herself in his presence and uttered the famous words: "Paetus, it does not hurt." Then he also stabbed himself.[31] Of greater significance in this connection is the public honoring of women (of the elite), whether through funeral eulogies (*laudationes*), coinages with their portraits, or the bestowing of honorary titles (the latter two for the wives of emperors); here we must always keep in mind that these measures usually also served to increase the prestige of men (husbands and sons).[32] Also the erection of statues of women—in Rome for female members of the imperial houses and for vestal virgins, in the provinces for wives of governors[33] and also for women benefactors of a city[34]—represented a clear presence of women in public.

12.1.2 Women and the Public

The idea that the "formerly reigning view of the 'oriental inaccessibility'" of women in Mediterranean societies has "lost validity" is emphasized above all by Thraede.[35] In fact, the scholarly positions are varied and disputed. On the one side is a rather pessimistic view (the strict limitation of wives to the realm of the home), and on the other, a rather optimistic judgment (greater flexibility in reality).[36] Yet there can be no talk of a general banishment of ancient women from the public areas of the polis, even if the Philo text cited above suggests this opinion. We cannot disregard the fact that in Rome (and elsewhere) women also participated in public events (say, in the theater)[37] or left the house for other reasons (though perhaps in the company of men[38] and in concealing clothing).[39] For we also have inscriptional evidence of this.[40] Nonetheless, women seem to have sat apart from men at public events; in the theater married men, women, and schoolboys sat in separate areas; in the circus they sat as families in order to watch the horse races.[41] Women also appeared in court, even if not as jurists.[42] Yet the participation of women in judicial proceedings was the exception, as a comment in Juvenal reveals (*Sat.* 4.51ff.).[43] Women took part above all in the cultic events of the polis (also as priestesses, for example, in connection with the cult of the emperor; see below).[44] They are also to be found in the meetings of some *collegia* and as participants in banquets. Finally, the occupational activities of many women required their presence outside the household (for example, as market women).[45] This is also true for the agricultural work of women.[46] Thus even on economic grounds a strict maintenance of sexual separation and restriction of lower-stratum women to the home could not be maintained. We will briefly discuss the presence of women in public with two examples, namely, the participation of women in the cult and at banquets.

A. THE PRESENCE OF WOMEN IN THE CULT OF THE POLIS

Women had their place particularly in the cultic celebrations of the polis, even if it was limited in comparison to that of men. They were "so extensively involved in religious life that we can speak of a 'cultic civil right.'"[47] In about half of all festivals in Athens they took part not only passively but also actively, for example in the "choruses"; along with married women, young girls (of the upper stratum) also participated, though seldom in direct involvement with the sacrifice (as basket- or water-bearers).[48] In addition, there were specific ritual communities of women (for example, on the occasion of the thesmophoria festival). Thus priestesses played an important role in the public cult of Greek cities. Like male priests, they were elected or chosen by lot; like the men, they shared in the sacrifice and had to render an accounting upon their departure. "Yet this equality of treatment should not conceal the fact that men elect and decide the priestesses by lot" and that women were not permitted to present the bloody sacrifice themselves.[49] Above all the function of prophecy in Greek city-states was regarded as the domain of women.[50]

Yet even with all the participation of women, the cult in Greece, as in Rome, also remained the privilege of men, and the cultic participation of women in Rome was even more marginal than in Greece. Neither in the public cults in the center of a city nor in the household cult were women prominent. "In the public realm the priestly responsibility always lay in the hands of men."[51] This should not be surprising, since cultic events belonged to the duties of the magistracy. Even in the cultic adoration of female divinities (Ceres and Flora, for example), they were represented by male priests.[52] Thus the vestals were absolutely an exceptional phenomenon of the Roman cult.[53] In the province of Asia women also exercised priestly functions in the cult of the emperor. On the whole, however, women played a rather marginal role in Roman religion or were active only in subordinate functions. Yet as in Greece, women in Rome were also actively or passively involved in the cult.

B. BANQUETS

In the period of the Roman empire, there was, according to Thraede, "basically no social life without women."[54] This was, in any case, supposed to be true in the West. For a difference in practice between Rome and Greece, one may cite Cornelius Nepos (*Praef.* 4–7),[55] who says, on the one hand, that among the Greeks the women lived in the interior of the house (*gynaikōnitis*) and participated in meals only in the presence of their nearest relatives; on the other hand, that Roman women are said to have remained also in the front rooms of the house and even appeared in public (*celebritate versatur*),[56] and that no man considered it a scandal to take his wife with him to the banquet (*convivium*). Yet can we believe this writer uncritically? He also denied pederasty in Rome and is thus guided by an interest in playing Rome off against Greece, as a closer examination shows. Even if one must grant that in Rome wives also took part in banquets,[57] this was true mainly for events in the narrower circle of the family.[58] And even if wives (but in no case unmarried girls) accompanied their husbands to public banquets, they took part only in the actual meal (*deipnon*) and as a rule left the event before the so-called *symposion,* which was devoted to drinking, conversation, and philosophical discussions, but also to erotic aspects. Women who participated in this part of the banquet were regarded as sexually available, as prostitutes, or hetaerae.[59] The "Greek praxis" seems, in any case, to have survived for a long time and also had an influence on Roman behavior.[60] Thus we must make distinctions, for example, between the western and eastern parts of the Roman empire, between city and country, between women of the upper stratum and those of the lower stratum,[61] and also between married women and young girls. For women of the lower stratum, participation in banquets was hardly a gender-specific taboo. They (as well as their husbands) had, on the one hand, little opportunity for this. On the other hand, their participation in banquets of the *collegia,* for example, would also have been problematic, since as slaves or emancipated women, they would have in any case been regarded as sexually available.[62] The (aristocratic) ideal of a Roman wife is formulated, for example, by Pliny the Younger in regard to his (very much younger) wife Calpurnia in a letter to an aunt (*Ep.* 4.19).[63] It is noteworthy that Calpurnia does not participate directly in her husband's entertainment of guests:

> . . . when I recite, she sits quite close to me, separated from me by a curtain [*in proximo discreta velo*] and listens with eager ears to the compliments I receive. She also sings my songs without instruction from a musician, simply out of love [*amor*], which is the best teacher. For these reasons I hope confidently that our agreement [*concordia*] will last forever.

The behavior of Calpurnia recalls the meetings of the *therapeutae,* an ascetic Jewish group on whom Philo reports in *De vita contemplativa.* When the community gathered on the sabbath, the female members sat by themselves, separated from the male members by a wall that did not reach to the ceiling, and thus the women could hear everything but not see the men. Men and women seem to have united only at the Paschal feast, when they sang responsively in choirs.

Ultimately the ancient statements about the presence of women in public leave an ambivalent impression. Women participate passively and actively in cultic celebrations, and they are present at the banquets of their families or social gatherings. Yet their public presence, compared to men, remains limited (also as priestesses or otherwise active or passive cult participants, as well as at banquets), or it is considered inappropriate and brings them the suspicion of sexual availability (above all at banquets).

12.1.3 The Household and the Gender-Specific Division of Roles

Of fundamental importance for the situation of ancient women is no doubt their role in the home and the family. In the present context it is significant that within the household men and women had different gender-specific roles.

Already in Homer's time it was presupposed that women (and even queens) managed the household, in which not only was food prepared but also clothing was made and men were bathed and anointed by women.[64] Centuries later, Xenophon points out in his treatise on the household (*Oikonomikos*) that women in well-to-do circles no longer always carried out this work themselves but engaged slave girls. Nonetheless, he distinguishes certain realms of duty for men and women, which he argues are "natural" or given by the gods: men work outside the house in the fields, cultivating, sowing, harvesting, and subjecting themselves to the cold and the heat; then they bring into the house what they have produced. Women work within the house, raise the children, care for food and clothing, and manage and preserve what is produced. And so that men and women can carry out these different activities, the gods have given them appropriate bodily characteristics. Accordingly, men have a hardier body than women, who work in the protection of the house. Women are weaker than men and have a natural fear that leads them to carefully preserve rations. Men, by contrast, are brave so that outside they can stand their ground. Thus "from the beginning the Divinity has adapted the nature of the woman to indoor work and business and that of men to the outdoors."[65] A similar text is found in Aristotle (1343b–44a), according to which providence created men stronger and women weaker. For the husband must defend the home, and the "fearful" wife watch over it. She is also blessed with patience, which is necessary for manual work, and is responsible for feeding the children, whereas the man is responsible for their education. To behave in a different way would be "unnatural," against what the gods had naturally given, as Xenophon says (*Oik.* 7.31). Columella (12, pref.) writes: "Thus the woman is rightly created to take care of the house, but the man to move about in the market and in foreign parts." Thus what is presented here as "natural" and given by the gods is nothing other than the social division of roles between men and women in the property-owning stratum of classical antiquity.[66] That this ideology has long survived is shown by Schiller's "Lied von der Glocke": "The husband must go out into the hostile world, must work and strive and plant and make. . . . And inside the demure housewife holds sway."[67]

The Home as Woman's Place to Stay

In principle the home is the woman's place to stay. Let us recall here only the Philo text quoted above. According to his presentation, there were in Alexandria women who remained in their houses and whose boundary of movement was the outside door, as well as young girls whose boundary was the connecting door between the front and the back of the house (Philo *Flacc.* 11). Likewise, Philo frequently mentions that women within a house are accorded their own area or wing, which in Greek, for example, is called *gynaikōnitis*. Conversely, men also had their own living area (*andrōnitis*).[68] Although Philo was by no means alone in this opinion,[69] we should not make the mistake of believing that this practice was typically Jewish. It was widespread in antiquity. Indeed, this spatial separation of the sexes was maintained into the Middle Ages, even in northern European lands. It is also presupposed by Xenophon (*Oik.* 9.5-6) and centuries later by Diodorus Siculus (17.50), Josephus (*Ant.* 17.33, 41; 19.130), Lucian (*Gallus* 11), and Strabo, who ascertains, with astonishment, that even the women's wing of the houses of the rich are open to the Sophists (*Geography* 15.65). As early as Menander and Euripides, the front door of the house was designated as the boundary of the territory of a good wife.[70] As far as possible, girls in particular were kept in the house and away from the outside world.[71] The famous orator Lysias once impressed the court with the comment that his sisters and nieces were so correctly brought up that they were embarrassed even in the presence of a man of their own family (Lysias 3.6).[72] This women's wing was sometimes also guarded, as Aristophanes ironically reveals (*Thes.* 414-15).

Yet the actual practice seems not to have corresponded to the ideal of the limitation of women to the house. Social status in particular was probably of considerable importance.[73] That is, an ancient woman could actually fulfill the specific role assigned to her only if she was not compelled to contribute to the maintenance of the family through work outside the house. Even if we can no longer tell with certainty the degree to which the limitation of women to the house was practiced, we should nonetheless assume an orientation in principle toward this idea. Indeed, even into the present time the spatial separation of men and women is the rule in many Mediterranean societies. It also had its meaning in the context of the ancient values of honor, shame, and disgrace. Thus Pitt-Rivers[74] states in general regarding Mediterranean women that the honor of the husband can be damaged by the wife. Not least of all for this reason, the special domain of women was the house and especially its women's quarters, which in principle was out of bounds for men (access was granted at most to relatives, slaves, and people of inferior status). Accordingly, intimate relations were actually possible only between members of the household; also, only here did sexual relations have their legitimate realm. As far as possible, women had to remain in the house, for they were the repositories of male honor. They had to be protected from contacts with men of other households, who might contaminate them.

12.2 The Stratification and Social Situation of Women

12.2.1 Women in the Upper Stratum

We have already indicated that in our stratum model we must also classify the family members—including wives and daughters—of members of the *ordines* with the upper stratum. Even if it is not clear in individual cases whether the wives of the elite controlled their own finances, in many respects they doubtless shared in the material, and in part the legal, privileges of their husbands. Terentia, the wife of Cicero, seems to have been very wealthy herself, so that she also supported her husband financially (Cicero *Fam.* 14). Josephus expressly calls only two Jewish women rich: Mary, the daughter of Eleazar (*War* 6.201) and Bernice (*Ant.* 20.146). We must also note, however, that many women of the Herodian royal house had considerable money at their disposal (namely, Salome, the sister of Herod, who drew from her inheritance a yearly income of sixty talents).[75] The best-known businesswoman of antiquity is Eumachia in Pompeii, who erected a forty-by-sixty-meter building for the guild of fullers (*fullones*), on which the following inscription can be read (*CIL* 10.810): "Eumachia, the daughter of Lucius, public priestess, in her name and the name of her son Numistrius Fronto, had erected at her own costs a gallery, a cryptoporticus, and a portico, and dedicated it herself to the honor of the harmony and piety of Augusta."[76] Her membership in one of the upper-stratum families of Pompeii is undoubted. She was presumably[77] also the *patrona* of the guild (*collegium*) of fullers. Such patronage functions of women (sometimes together with their husbands) are somewhat uncommon but by no means exceptional.[78]

Here we could also name the many female benefactors who are known to us inscriptionally and through their public honors. They belong mostly to the families of the elite but also seem to have considerable funds at their own disposal. They also demonstrate in a special way the stratum model presented here, according to which wealth can in many ways compensate for the lack of direct political power. For many of these women performed cultic functions and were honored with the titles of public offices. Only a few examples can be mentioned here.[79]

Euxenia, a priestess of Aphrodite from Megalopolis in the Peloponnisos in the second century B.C.E., is honored inscriptionally as a female benefactor. She financed a wall around the temple of Aphrodite, as well as a guest house.[80] She belonged to an elite family. Four longer inscriptions report that Menodora (Pisidia, first century C.E.) shared wheat and money with the residents of her native city and in memory of her son gave an endowment of 300,000 denarii for the support of children, not counting the cost for statues of her son.[81] In Aphrodisias a certain Tata financed various festivals and, among other things, also made oil available for the athletes of the public games, a rather costly undertaking.[82]

Inscriptional evidence permits the conclusion that Jewish women also exercised patronage functions in the synagogues. For example, a Jewish woman named Rufina, in a donation inscription from the second century C.E. for the grave of her freed slave, is called "synagogue leader" (archisynagōgos: (CII 741; IGRR 4.1452). From the fourth and fifth centuries there are two further attestations (Sophia Gortynia, who is called presbytera and archisynagōgissa: CII 731c; Theopempte: CII 756). Yet there is some dispute as to whether it is a question here of a functional designation or an honorary title.[83] Further, sarcophagus fragments from Rome that are not precisely datable (CII 523; CII 496: Monteverde catacomb, first century B.C.E. to third century C.E.) and other inscriptional material—in analogy to the male title "father of the synagogue"—name Jewish women "mother of the synagogue" or something similar. In its male form this title could also designate an honorary office.[84] In any case, it is a question here only of women of means, not of women from the upper stratum.

Rich Women

In addition to the mentioned women of the elite, there were wealthy women all over the empire "who did not earn their living by their own work but because of their possessions had others work for them."[85] They independently managed their property, which might consist of real estate, workshops and stores, and even shipping companies and trading vessels.[86] In many cases it is not possible to decide how to estimate the property of these women, and thus a clear stratum classification is difficult.

Women Owners of Property and Businesses

We have already mentioned a property-owning Egyptian woman who leased land (cf. p. 46). There were also Jews among the women who owned property.[87] For one Egyptian village the proportion of property-owning women can be demonstrated to be about one-third.[88] Varro (2.2.20) mentions a certain Domitia Lepida as a property owner, and various property-owning women are also mentioned by name in inscriptions.[89] From Pompeii we must also include Julia Felix, who according to an extant inscription offered a large piece of land for rent.[90] In addition, there were several property-owning women in Ostia.[91] Above all for women owners of brick and lead pipe manufacturing there are numerous inscriptions,[92] regarding, for example, a certain Julia Fortunata in Ostia, who was active in the production of lead pipes (officina plumbaria).[93] Women were also active in the wine business and in shipping (Suetonius Claudius 18, 19). Similarly, we know of women who ran businesses involving bricks and stone masonry.[94] Ummidia Quadratilla (d. 107 C.E.) must have been a wealthy woman, for she owned a whole ballet.[95] Likewise, a certain Caelia Macrina (second century) provided an endowment for the monthly support of about 100 children, which required around 400 denarii (20 sesterces monthly for each boy, 16 for each girl).[96] There were also wealthy women among the emancipated, for example, a certain Lyda who, freed by the empress Livia, owned at least four slaves herself.[97] Emperor Claudius had granted freed women the same privileges as mothers with four children, if they had invested their money for the use of the Roman food supply system, and for emancipated slave women with a wealth of at least 100,000 sesterces, the inheritance regulations also applied. Thus we may presume that also among freed slaves there were rich women.

12.2.2 The Lower Stratum and the Work of Women

Regarding the occupational activity of women of the lower stratum we are relatively well informed.[98] Traders, who perhaps also had a small weaving business, probably belonged to the better situated circles of the lower strata. They included Lydia, a dealer in purple cloth from Thyatira, who headed a house in Philippi (Acts 16:14-15).[99] The poorer groups of the lower strata included bean traders, wreath makers, nail sellers,[100] and fisherwomen.[101] Women like Prisca who worked in craft occupations (Rom 16:13; 1 Cor 16:19; Acts 18:2-3) probably belonged to the poorer circles of the lower stratum.

Areas of Service and Entertainment
The service sector and entertainment branches must be regarded differently. Only a few actresses, dancers, and musicians may have had a reliable income. And they enjoyed little respect (Suetonius *Nero* 27 puts them on the same level with harlots). Many of them were slaves or at best former slaves.[102] Even women who worked as servers in inns and taverns were perhaps not even relatively prosperous. The same applies to the lowest levels of midwives, who were often also regarded as quacks. There were, however, some respected doctors (whether called midwives or doctors).[103] And the nurses (*nutrix*) were especially respected, above all when they raised the children of the upper stratum.

Poor Women of the Lower Stratum
Although there are only a few testimonies for the work of women in agriculture, we can nonetheless infer from known sources that not only did the wives of small farmers and leaseholders work in the fields—and not just in the household—but also women slaves worked as managers and even as fettered slaves.[104] Day laborers were also active in fieldwork.[105] On the whole in the business as well as the service sectors, traditional activities of women, as

described by Xenophon (*Oik.* 7.21), also seemed to dominate in work outside the house.[106] In many male areas of activity women were also to be found, even if certain occupations (for example, working with wood and metal) were reserved for men. Even in mine work (slave) women seem to have been active.[107] Women were active in small business, in food trades (bakers), in the realm of bodily care (barbers, perfume dealers), in the health field as doctors and midwives, in domestic service (nurses, tutors), and even as scribes. We must not forget, however, the many women who had to earn their living as prostitutes and the women who worked as servers in inns and taverns—and in these positions were looked down on like prostitutes. Günther,[108] in her evaluation of inscriptional material (*CIL* 6), comes to the following quantitative result: "Women are most strongly represented in the area of bodily care and personal service," and "typical women's occupations arose, if one can use the term at all, only in the realm of textile production or processing." These occupations were apparently practiced by women who were "at the lower boundary of the slave hierarchy."[109] According to Günther's analysis of the inscriptions, this is the only area of business in which women are also represented, while in the realm of administration women were entrusted only with the management of the household. Many women were also especially occupied in the realm of education and in the medical sector (midwives), according to her analyses. Interesting in this connection are the numbers of Eichenauer,[110] which, even with all the problems of their interpretation, still show that the proportion of freed and slave women in women's occupations was about balanced, whereas free women are hardly mentioned. The doctors, scribes, and nurses tended to belong to the emancipated class, while textile workers and personal servants were mostly slaves. Especially noteworthy is the unusually high proportion of unmarried women. We can draw only vague conclusions about the proportion of women and men in individual occupations, since many women who are named in inscriptions beside their husbands were probably active in the same occupation as their husbands, but this is seldom explicitly stated.[111]

13

WOMEN AMONG THE FOLLOWERS OF
JESUS IN THE LAND OF ISRAEL

13.1 Women in the Jesus Movement

13.1.1 Direct Statements about Women in the Jesus Movement

Feminist theology and exegesis can be given credit for having turned the reconstruction of the early Christian history of women into an object of scholarly research. From the beginning a socio-historical interest has also guided the text analyses to which we will especially refer here. Yet since in dealing with New Testament scriptures it is primarily a question of texts that basically share the ancient androcentric view of tradition, any attempt to reconstruct the participation of women in the charismatic Jesus movement is dependent on a narrow foundation in the sources. The Gospels contain only four texts that *directly* involve the participation of women in the Jesus movement: Mark 15:40-41, with the parallels in Matt 27:55-56; Luke 23:49, and Luke 8:2-3. Of these, the parallel texts of Mark 15:40-41 are demonstrably revisions of their Markan source and therefore add no additional historical information for the Jesus movement itself. Also Luke 8:2-3, according to which several women healed by Jesus accompany and support him, cannot be used for the historical Jesus movement.[1] The two verses clearly reflect Lukan language usage and tendencies and give information about the importance of women for urban communities of Christ outside the land of Israel.[2]

Thus the only *direct* statement remains the text of Mark 15:40-41. This marginal source basis is in itself remarkable and suggests cautious conclusions about the social history of women among the followers of Jesus. R. S. Kraemer correctly writes that feminist research has clearly demonstrated the presence of women as followers of Jesus, while the exact character of their involvement in the Jesus movement is open to discussion.[3] This problem situation is contained in brief in Mark 15:40-41. On the one hand, here in the context of Jesus' crucifixion women are expressly mentioned for the first time in Mark as followers of Jesus; on the other hand, however, their relationship to Jesus is circumscribed with the key word *diēkonoun* ("served," NRSV: "provided for"), whose meaning is controversial:

> There were also women looking on from a distance; among them were Mary Magdalene, and Mary the mother of James the younger and of Joses, and

Salome. These used to follow him and provided for him when he was in Galilee; and there were many other women who had come up with him to Jerusalem. (Mark 15:40-41)

The text presupposes that many women were accompanying Jesus already in Galilee and also followed him to Jerusalem. Among them three women are mentioned by name as followers, perhaps in analogy to the male trio of Peter and the sons of Zebedee, James and John.[4] It is true that neither in Mark nor in the Gospels in general is a woman explicitly called a "disciple" (*mathētria*)[5] of Jesus, yet the word *follow* (*akolouthein*) is used tersely, especially in the Gospel of Mark, to designate the following of Jesus as a disciple.[6] Where the word is used for groups that are at the moment following Jesus (Mark 3:7; 5:24; 11:9), the actual relationship to Jesus is determined by the context. Conversely, Mark 15:40-41 clearly shows that the women following Jesus have been in a continuous relationship to him as followers since Galilee.[7] Thus, in spite of the narrow textual basis, we can determine initially that women also belonged to Jesus' following. In distinction to the male disciples, however, the women of Mark are clearly given a special role vis-à-vis Jesus: they "served," "ministered unto" (KJV), "provided for" (NRSV) him.

Serving (diakonein): A term of discipleship?
The interpretation of the verb *diakonein* ("serve") in Mark 15:41 is strongly disputed. The word often circumscribes the duty assigned to women (and slaves, and less often young men) of serving the table at home. More comprehensively, however, it can also mean caring and providing for people (cf. NIV: "cared for his needs") or serving in the general sense.[8] The usage in the Gospel of Mark covers this spectrum. The word is clearly used in 1:13, 31 in the sense of table service. By contrast, a serving relationship in the broader sense is indicated by *diakonein* in 10:45 (cf. *diakonos* in 9:35; 10:43). Mark 9:35; 10:43-45 show that serving characterizes exemplary behavior for the disciples of Jesus, in imitation of Jesus' own behavior, and thus has a thoroughly positive connotation in the context of discipleship. The conventional hierarchy of ruling and serving is supposed to be reversed in the Jesus movement: the ruling or leading functions are performed in service to all. The idea that this serving leadership is also meant in 15:41 is advocated by, for example, Schüssler Fiorenza.[9] Because of the "fundamental meaning of Mark 10:42-45 par. (and John 13)," Schottroff also understands the verb *diakonein* here "as a designation of discipleship . . . and not in the sense of a gender-hierarchical division of labor as the provisioning work of women."[10] Weiser interprets Mark 15:41 in the broader sense of "helping someone solicitously."[11] Corley, by contrast, holds that the language of Mark 15:41 recalls the image of women who served Jesus at table: the reference of this service

performed by women for Jesus to the preparation of food in the context of meals is unambiguous.[12]

Thus the question is whether *diakonein* in Mark 15:41 is a term of discipleship in the sense of an early Christian semantics,[13] or whether it means general care for someone or special service at table. Methodologically it is meaningful to seek first only a decision in the context of the linguistic usage in the Gospel of Mark. It is noteworthy here that the statements about serving in the sense of exemplary disciple behavior are addressed not to Jesus but to the circle of disciples (9:35: "servant of all"; 10:43: "your servant"). In 15:41, by contrast, Jesus is the recipient of the serving, as in 1:13 and 1:31 (Jesus and Peter), where table service is without doubt intended.[14] The reversal of conventional rank order in the circle of disciples, which is explicit in the context of 9:35 and 10:43, cannot be intended in the formulation of 15:41: "These used to follow him and provide for him when he was in Galilee." For the reference to Jesus as recipient of the serving here excludes the idea of a reversal in rank order. Thus, in our view, the content of the term *diakonein* in 9:35; 10:43, 45 cannot be drawn on as a hermeneutical presupposition for 15:41. And since only here is the term intended in a more general sense, this would suggest understanding 15:41 in analogy to 1:13, 31 as a care-providing activity. This is confirmed not least of all by the identical grammatical construction in all three passages.[15] Hence we are in agreement with Corley's interpretation.[16]

Thus we must state initially that in the context of the only direct evidence of the discipleship of women, their specific relationship to Jesus is described with a conventional term for typical women's activities. By contrast, the male apostles and the circle of the twelve are connected by Mark with proclamation functions and charismatic talents, such as preaching, exorcism, healing, and teaching (Mark 6:7ff., 30-31). Yet this applies for the time being only to the Gospel of Mark, and we must ask whether the focusing of female discipleship on caring activities reflects a secondary interpretation. This is a difficult question to answer. It is notable, however, that in the reception of the Markan statements by Matthew and Luke, the role of women is further relativized.[17] Thus, in our view, we must seriously consider the possibility that this tendency of tradition to relativize the discipleship of women is already present in Mark 15:40-41 and comes form the evangelist Mark himself.[18] For the characterization of the role of women as followers of the historical Jesus, therefore, we do not draw here on the term *diakonein*. Now we must ask whether we can draw from indirect statements information about social background and the relationships of men and women to each other.

13.1.2 Indirect Statements about Women in the Jesus Movement

There are three areas of consideration here: the leaving of the larger family in the wake of discipleship, some prosopographic information about women, and finally the testimony of women followers of Jesus regarding his crucifixion, burial, and resurrection.

Leaving the larger family

Some of the women following Jesus, together with their husbands, presumably left their larger families. For in contrast to the later, clearly tendentious presentation of discipleship by Luke, which includes the leaving of one's wife as a condition of discipleship,[19] the older Gospel of Mark never explicitly says that the disciples leave their wives. The only relevant text in this regard presupposes in its Markan version (10:29-30; Matt 19:29 follows it) the leaving of the larger family (household) and mentions a list of abandoned individuals that includes brothers, sisters, mother, father, and children, but not wife.[20] The text argues implicitly from the perspective of adult men and women—or from that of married couples. It is thus indirect evidence for the inclusion of women among the followers of Jesus. According to 1 Cor 9:5 Peter (Cephas) took his wife along during his preaching activity. If this was also true for the time of discipleship of the earthly Jesus, then his wife was already among the followers of Jesus.

Prosopographic information

Various women are mentioned by name: Mary Magdalene, Mary the mother of James (the younger) and Joses (Joseph), perhaps identical with Mary the wife of Clopas,[21] and Salome (is she the mother of the sons of Zebedee?).[22] Luke (and John) also name Mary and Martha from Bethany (in John she is the sister of Lazarus),[23] and Luke (8:3) mentions Joanna, the wife of Chuza, and Susanna. Mary and Martha are presented as followers of Jesus, though not as disciples who travel with him. In the Synoptic Gospels, in contrast to the Gospel of John, the mother of Jesus does not appear to accompany him. And of the three women mentioned by name in Luke 8:2-3, only Mary Magdalene is also mentioned in the other Gospels. Thus three women can with great probability be named as followers of Jesus already in Galilee: Mary Magdalene, Mary the mother of James and Joses, and Salome.[24] Mary Magdalene (=woman from Magdala) is the only woman follower of Jesus who is connected with a particular place in Galilee,[25] but she is not characterized by her relationship to a man (husband, father, son). This could indicate that she joined the Jesus movement as an unmarried woman. In general, she plays a prominent role among women followers in that she is always named first in the lists of names; in Matthew she (and the "other Mary") meet the resurrected Jesus; in John she is the only one to experience his first appearance.[26] Only Luke mentions that she was healed by Jesus.[27] We have no further prosopographic data on these three women disciples.[28]

Resurrection testimony

Of fundamental importance are the indirect statements about women as followers of Jesus in connection with his crucifixion, his burial, and the story of the empty tomb (Mark 15:47; 16:1ff.). Their Markan presentation is in part clearly expanded in the other Gospels but also shortened,[29] so that here we have only the Markan version as a foundation. It shows that in every case the origin of the resurrection proclamation is connected with women, for they are the first to discover the empty tomb and are the ones to whom the angel proclaims the resurrection of Jesus. The difference of this resurrection tradition from 1 Cor 15:5-8, where apparently[30] only men are mentioned as witnesses to Jesus' resurrection, suggests that Mark 16:1-8 is an older tradition that cannot be ignored.[31] And even if we have only later evidence that the resurrection testimony was considered unbelievable because it came from women,[32] it still shows the great importance of this tradition for the role of women as followers of Jesus.

In the following section we will briefly discuss some further texts that, while not giving direct or indirect statements about women as followers of Jesus, will allow us to make inferences about the relationship of the Jesus movement to women.

13.1.3 The Relationships of Jesus to Women and of Women to Jesus

The healing of women

The Synoptic tradition includes four miracle stories in which women or girls are healed: the mother-in-law of Peter,[33] the woman suffering from hemorrhages, whose healing story is interwoven with the resuscitation of the little daughter of Jairus,[34] and finally the daughter of the Syrophoenician woman, who is healed from a distance.[35] This last miracle story describes Jesus' encounter with a Syrophoenician, or Greek, woman, who is an example of outstanding trust in the healing powers of Jesus. In the sayings source the story is a counterpart of the encounter of Jesus with the centurion from Capernaum. Both stories reflect, in our view, a later problem complex, namely, relations with non-Jews, which had not yet affected the historical Jesus movement itself.[36]

The story of the healing of Peter's mother-in-law sketches a stereotypical scenario.[37] The story links her with the home and the activity of table service, both typical for women.[38] Moreover, she is identified through a man, which likewise shows a conventional androcentric perspective.[39] The woman is hardly characterized here as a disciple "who understood and practiced true Christian leadership."[40] The fact that after her healing she gets up and serves the previously named men first of all confirms her healing, but it is also an indication that her place in the family has been restored; that is, she can now again fulfill her social role.[41]

The woman with hemorrhages likewise remains nameless. She seems to be single and impoverished. Her illness is typical of women and is described as particularly serious (twelve years in length; many doctors could not help her). The culture-specific problem of impurity (cf. Lev 15:25ff.) is not discussed in the text. In the Markan basic version of the story (and the Lukan parallel) the fact that she touches Jesus' cloak is interesting only because of the healing power that went out from Jesus.[42] Fander believes that the miracle story negates the "logic of impurity ideas" and that we find in the "Jesus tradition . . . no trace of the motifs of demonizing menstruation or making it taboo"; indeed, the Jesus tradition sets itself "against conceptions of taboo according to which the powers of fertility and blood have to be banned as dangerous forces. The impurity of the woman is no longer under consideration."[43] Yet such a far-reaching conclusion with an argument from silence is problematic. Actually, we have only prescriptive texts that connect impurity with menstruation or menstrual illnesses.[44] Yet we do not know whether the purity regulations connected with menstruation—for example, the seven-day separation of women and avoidance of contact—were observed in practice.[45] Nor do we know whether menstruating women were actually isolated or generally discriminated against socially. Thus the story of the woman with hemorrhages may, conversely, be evidence that those thus afflicted were *not* isolated or disdained socially. If the story really involves "breaking through the Jewish taboos for menstruating women,"[46] it is in any case amazing that the story itself—in contrast to Mark 1:40ff.; 7:1ff., where the purity regulations are explicitly mentioned—does not say this.

Also in the following awakening of the twelve-year-old girl, Jesus touches a dead person. There is, however, no comment on the resulting problem of temporary impurity (which applies to the touching of all the dead; cf. Num 19:11-13).

Relationship to "public" women
Jesus' anointing by a woman during a meal in the house of Simon the leper is markedly reworked in the Synoptic tradition, as well as in the Gospel of John.[47] From the pre-Markan content of the story[48] we are interested here only in the following element: Jesus accepts anointing by a woman during a meal. The widely held exegetical discussion of this point frequently emphasizes that here "the usual image of women" is abandoned and a woman is

"placed in a purely male tradition, whose continuity is thereby ended."[49] In this discussion the anointment process is related in terms of the history of tradition to messianic anointment or anointing of the dead, while connotations of anointment in connection with meals are rejected.[50] The latter is without doubt inappropriate on account of the described context: a meal. With many references Corley[51] has called attention to the cultural background of this scene: the presence of the woman at the meal and her behavior mark her as a "public" woman, notorious for promiscuity.[52] This also means that the usual picture of a woman is not abandoned here, but we have instead the picture of a woman that does not agree with the conventional values of virtue. It is noteworthy that this state of affairs is not discussed (even by Mark in the oldest literary version).

Comparable behavior that deviates from conventional values in connection with meals is also reflected in Mark 2:15 (Jesus eats with "tax collectors and sinners"). Matt 21:31-32 even explicitly establishes a connection between tax collectors and prostitutes *(pornai):* John the Baptist's followers included tax collectors and prostitutes, and Jesus says that they will go into the kingdom of God before the high priests and scribes.[53] Thus we may presume that the table fellowship of the Jesus movement with "tax collectors and sinners" (Mark 2:15-16) also implies the presence of women with doubtful reputations.[54]

Summary: Lower-Stratum Women of Doubtful Reputation
In spite of the narrow textual basis and the secondary relativizing interpretation by the evangelists, the membership of women among the followers of Jesus is hardly to be doubted historically.[55] In our view, the relativization of their discipleship (accompaniment) and its concentration on typical women's roles (serving) go back to a secondary interpretation by the evangelists. Also against this reduction of women's discipleship is the fact that Galilean women are expressly described in the tradition as witnesses to the crucifixion, burial, and resurrection of Jesus. Their prominent role at the end of Jesus' life is in our view an indication of charismatic experiences of women among Jesus followers. Our analysis has produced two notable socio-historical conclusions: women members of Jesus' following, like the men, probably belonged to the lower stratum of their contemporary society, and their behavior in public lets them appear possibly as women with doubtful reputations.

Stratum Membership
The following arguments suggest the social background of the lower stratum. In no case has the evaluation of prosopographic data and other indirect statements yielded indications of the prominent social position of women disciples. We learn hardly more than their geographic background in Galilee and

in a few cases also individual names. This lack of notable prosopographic information heuristically allows the conclusion of lower-stratum membership. It is also generally supported by an analogy to the male disciples. This low social estimation also accords with the fact that none of the women is characterized as the daughter, wife, or mother of a socially highly regarded man.[56] There is also a lack of socially acceptable categories of "virtuous" or respectable women that let them appear as model daughters, wives, and mothers of legitimate offspring. Mary Magdalene, who was presumably single, is not characterized as the virginal daughter of her father. Nothing is said about the husband of Mary the mother of James the younger and Joses. The women disciples are also not connected with traditional women's roles that would identify them as circumspect, industrious administrators of a household who were concerned about their virtue.[57]

Relationship to the Public

In agreement with this picture is the table fellowship of the Jesus movement with women considered sexually available, as is shown, for example, in the anointment story and probably also in Mark 2:15-16. With a certain probability we can infer from all these statements that the women among the followers of Jesus hardly had good reputations. Their participation in banquets and above all the fact that they belonged to a group of men, with whom they were continually seen in public and with whom they traveled in Galilee and to Jerusalem, allowed them to appear as "public" women with whom promiscuity was also connected.[58] This evaluation can be supported with analogous phenomena of philosophical schools. Corley calls attention to the fact that the term *prostitute* was used as a reproach in debates of philosophical schools because of the participation of women.[59] Epicureans and Cynics, for example, made the mutual accusation that the other group's women members were prostitutes. One example is Hipparchia, who married the famous Cynic Crates and accompanied him in public and at banquets. The doubtful reputation of women who accompany a group of men also emerges indirectly from a text about Apollonius of Tyana:

> On the journey to Mesopotamia the tax collector who stood watch at Zeugma led them to the tax table and asked them what they brought with them. Apollonius answered: "I bring prudence, righteousness, ability, abstinence, bravery, and discipline with me," and listed even more similar names of the feminine sex. Then the tax collector, who already had visions of profit, said: "Write down the names of the slave women for me." "That is not possible," replied Apollonius, "for I bring with me not slave women but ladies."[60]

The tax collector naturally assumed that in the company of traveling men one would expect at best slave women. And the answer of Apollonius also presupposes that women traveling companions of men, if they were not their wives, daughters, or perhaps relatives, would be judged to be unchaste and known for promiscuity.[61]

We must seriously consider this very judgment of the women who belonged to the Jesus movement. Yet the fact that women (and men) in the Jesus movement were not connected with traditional roles does not make them a liberation movement whose conscious aim was the equality of men and women.[62] Their culturally deviant behavior is to be understood rather on the basis of the specific social milieu—a wandering movement that was recruited from the impoverished lower stratum—and the common charismatic experiences of the men and women of this group. It also makes little sense to us to interpret the role of the women in the Jesus movement as a criticism or overcoming of the religious or general patriarchal norms of Judaism. The patriarchal social order, which emphasized and stabilized the predominance of men, was not specifically Jewish but generally common in antiquity. It had to and did lose its defining importance for a group that had left its central social institution, the household and the family. With this loss, both the women and the men of the Jesus movement lacked the institutional framework and the concomitant social necessity of fulfilling traditional roles. Likewise, the exclusive religious precepts for Jewish women, which are known to us from traditional Jewish literature, presuppose orderly household conditions. These include the task of lighting the sabbath lights, the separation or burning of a small part of the bread dough before it is baked (Heb. *ḥallah*), and the purity regulations connected with menstruation.[63] The fact that these precepts that are valid exclusively for women plays no role in the New Testament tradition regarding the genuine followers of Jesus is directly evident from their living conditions outside of households and therefore should not be brought into opposition with the religious practices of Judaism. In the Synoptic tradition we find no indication that the women of the Jesus movement consciously set themselves against the precepts of Judaism related specifically to women.

13.2 Women and the Followers of Jesus in the Land of Israel

For the social situation of women in messianic Jesus communities in the land of Israel after the crucifixion of Jesus we draw on the Acts of the Apostles and the Gospels of Matthew and John. For the period before 70 c.e. only the book of Acts is relevant. Matthew and John reflect the situation of messianic Jesus communities in the land of Israel in the period after the Jewish-Roman war.

WOMEN IN THE JERUSALEM EARLY CHURCH AND OUTSIDE JERUSALEM
ACCORDING TO THE ACTS OF THE APOSTLES

About women in the Jerusalem early church we know only a few things from Acts,[64] whose statements have in part been reshaped in legendary fashion. Acts 1:14 mentions that women, including the mother of Jesus, were gathered in prayer with the group of named apostles. According to 5:14, not only additional men but also women were won as believers. This is confirmed by 8:3 and 22:4, according to which men and women of the Jerusalem community were "persecuted." According to 6:1-2, Hellenistic widows were being overlooked in the daily distribution of food. Of all these women, the few mentioned by name are, in addition to Mary the mother of Jesus, a certain Sapphira (5:1ff.) and Mary the mother of John Mark, as well as the slave Rhoda (12:12-13). Socio-historically productive conclusions can hardly be drawn from these texts. Probably none of the women belonged to the upper stratum, for the fact that Sapphira and her husband bought a piece of property and Mary the mother of John Mark owned a house and a slave cannot be judged to be an indication of significant possession in the sense of wealth.[65] What conflict lies concealed behind the neglecting of the Hellenistic widows can no longer be determined.[66] It is noteworthy, however, that women also belonged to the Jerusalem early church. Perhaps the author of Acts also sees in this very fact a confirmation of the beginning of the end time (2:17-18).

In Samaria women were baptized by Philip along with men (8:12). Tabitha/Dorcas in Joppa (=Jaffe) is described in especially exemplary fashion (9:36ff.).[67] She is called (female) disciple (*mathētria*: 9:36) and characterized by her good works and charity. A prosopographical evaluation of her name and the brief description of her living conditions allow the assumption that she was an emancipated slave.[68] In any case, she is above the minimum existence. Yet the tunics and other clothing she makes for charitable purposes and the mention of her house (lower and upper floors) do not indicate significant wealth.[69]

INFORMATION ABOUT WOMEN
IN THE GOSPELS OF MATTHEW AND JOHN

Basically, the Gospel of Matthew presupposes women in its own community, for the two feeding stories expressly mention that women (and children) also participated in the table fellowship (Matt 14:21; 15:38). Matthew is probably portraying the messianic community here as an assembly of families.[70] The most prominent peculiarity of the Gospel of Matthew, however, is that women of doubtful reputation are often mentioned, and thus Corley pointedly states that Matthew "is the only Gospel to dare to identify explicitly women in its community with the slanderous term *pornai* ['whores']."[71] Even in the family tree of Jesus (1:3, 5-6) there are four women who are by no means known for their virtuous behavior: Tamar, Rahab, Ruth, and the wife of Uriah (Bathsheba). All four women have in common a bad reputation.[72] And only Matthew includes tax collectors and *prostitutes* among the followers of John the Baptist and has Jesus say that they will enter into the kingdom of God before the high priests and elders (21:31-32). The Matthean version of the story of the Syrophoenician woman (15:21-28) also contains some traits that could suggest a doubtful reputation for the woman.[73] At the same time, however, in Matthew she is an explicit example of outstanding faith. Thus, in our view, it is certainly worth venturing that the messianic community of Matthew also included women of doubtful reputation.[74] It is also possible, however, that Matthew is taking an apologetic position with respect to the tradition that he has received.

In the Gospel of John a few women are mentioned by name: Mary the mother of Jesus, Mary and Martha in Bethany, Mary Magdalene, and Mary the wife of Clopas. The Samaritan woman by the well remains nameless. Where the texts go into socio-historically relevant factors at all, they reflect traditional values, for example, when Jesus on the cross entrusts his mother to the favorite disciple, who accepts her into his house (John 19:25-27). The story of the Samaritan woman shows her in a typical woman's activity; Mary also serves while the men lie at table (12:2). By contrast, the fact that Jesus speaks with the Samaritan woman (4:27) is unconventional, and this is expressly noted in the text. Yet it is also noteworthy here that women—like the Samaritan, Mary and Martha, and Mary Magdalene—stand out because of their faith in Jesus. Nevertheless, significant socio-historical knowledge about the situation of women in the Johannine community is not to be derived from the texts.

14

WOMEN IN URBAN CHRIST COMMUNITIES

14.1 The Membership of Women in the *Ekklēsia*

From the beginning women belonged to Christ-confessing communities in the cities of the Roman empire. Indeed, if one follows the presentation of the Acts of the Apostles, they even formed the constitutive core of the communities, and most of them belonged to Diaspora Judaism or to its circle of sympathizers: the mother of Timothy (Acts 16:1), Lydia in Philippi (16:14ff.), and God-fearing women in Thessalonica and Berea (17:4, 12). In Corinth Paul meets the Christ-confessing couple Priscilla and Aquila (18:2).[1] Damaris, who is won to the faith in Athens, is not connected with Judaism (17:34). This may also be true of Christ-confessing women (and children) in Tyre (21:5-6). Paul himself mentions in his letters various women by name,[2] of whom some are clearly identified as Jews (for example, Prisca, Herodiana, and Junia: Rom 16:3, 7, 11). Implicitly, women were also included among the slaves and other members of a household, who are greeted in wholesale fashion (for example, Rom 16:11). Also from 1 Cor 7:1ff.; 11:2ff.; 14:33ff. one may infer that the Corinthian community must have included more than a few women. The conclusion can also be drawn from the so-called household rules and related texts,[3] although it is noteworthy that the post-Pauline letters mention by name only Nympha as leader of a house church in Laodicea (Col 4:15) and Claudia as a greeter (2 Tim 4:21). The trend toward only inclusive mention of women—say, in connection with Christian households—continues in the letters of Ignatius.[4] In addition to these direct statements, many indirect ones point to the membership of women in the Christian communities. As an example we mention here only the story of Mary and Martha (Luke 10:38-42), which probably shifts a discussion situation in the time of Luke back into the time of Jesus.[5]

Unfortunately, an estimate of the proportion of women in the communities is hardly possible. Of approximately eighty prosopographic references that Meeks has collected from the letters of Paul (outside the pastoral letters) and Acts,[6] around one-fifth are women. In the pastoral letters ten coworkers of Paul are mentioned, including one woman.[7] Yet in view of the notorious underrepresentation of women in all historical sources of this period, no demographic conclusions can be drawn from these data.[8] Nevertheless, it

389

seems to us that there are five relevant points that also have significance for the stratum membership of Christ-confessing women:

1. A considerable number of the women belonging to urban communities as Jews or as God-fearers are more or less closely connected with Diaspora synagogues.

2. Most of the women mentioned by name are apparently single. Neither Lydia nor Phoebe nor Nympha, to name only a few, appears to have some relationship to a man. Typical also in this regard is the story of Mary and Martha (Luke 10:38ff.), who are apparently unmarried (in John they have a brother). Only Priscilla is explicitly designated as a wife (Acts 18:2). With other women, like Junia, Julia, and Apphia, a marital or other relationship to a man can only be presumed. The women mentioned collectively in Acts 17:4, 12 were apparently married. Married women as members of the community can also be inferred from 1 Cor 7:1ff., as can single women, including widows. Only a few women are also connected with a man as mothers (for example, Rom 16:13: mother of Rufus; Acts 16:1: mother of Timothy) or sisters (Rom 16:14: the sister of Nereus), and none as daughters. The fact that in our sources the lack of a relationship to men (father, brother, son) clearly predominates cannot be insignificant in a culture that defines free individuals through a connection with a man. This deficit also points to the social status of most women; that is, they are probably slaves or emancipated slaves.[9] For a legal marriage was in principle the privilege of free people, since it was closely linked with property—especially real property. Only Diaspora Judaism is to be judged somewhat differently here, in that it was permitted to live according to patriarchal traditions.[10] It is therefore no accident that the women explicitly designated as married belonged to the upper stratum of their cities (Acts 17:4, 12) or, in the case of Priscilla, to Judaism.

3. Among the single women, widows are explicitly mentioned in 1 Cor 7:8; 1 Tim 5:3ff.; their membership in Christ-confessing communities can also be inferred from Jas 1:27 and Mark 12:40ff.[11] Their social need is a frequent theme in our texts, even if it is not always explicit.[12] This is also true of 1 Tim 5:3ff.; this text probably indicates that the support of needy widows was a burden for the community, and thus their number is not to be estimated as small. The text recommends that widows be cared for first in individual households, and moreover, it sets high requirements for their community support: a "real" widow should be sixty years old, have had only one husband, have done good works, and have raised children. Younger widows, by contrast, should remarry and bear children. If one relates this to the ideal of remaining unmarried in Paul (cf. 1 Cor 7:8), one might see the effect of economic motives and also of adaptation to the con-

vention in 1 Tim 5:3ff. We may also infer from 1 Tim 5:16 that there were Christ-confessing wives who took widows into their households.[13]

4. Some women lead house churches: Lydia in Philippi, Prisca (together with Aquila), Nympha in Laodicea, and perhaps Chloe.[14]

5. Increasingly, women are mentioned only in wholesale fashion or as an afterthought.

14.2 The Stratification of Christ-confessing Women

Here we follow our social model (cf. section 3.3 above) and classify Christ-confessing women in stratum groups on the basis of statements that are relevant for an evaluation of their social situation.

UPPER STRATUM

We find a clear indication of the membership of women of the urban communities in the local upper stratum only in Acts 17:4, 12. Out of the group of God-fearers of Thessalonica "not a few" women of the local elite *(prōtoi)* are supposed to have joined Paul and Silas (17:4). The same is true of Berea, where from the context one may infer that women of prominent *(euschēmōn)* Greek families, as well as men, who came to faith belong to the circle of God-fearers (17:12). It is noteworthy that none of the women is mentioned by name; by contrast, Luke knows even the name of the slave Rhoda, who worked in the house of Mary the mother of Mark (12:12-13). Yet we cannot exclude the possibility that the statements have a basis in reality—not in the world of the narration, that is, in the mission of Paul, but in the Lukan experience. For the readers of Acts they seem plausible, as suggested by the previously mentioned support of the followers of Jesus by some women, which is reported only by Luke (Luke 8:2-3). The Joanna mentioned there, the wife of Chusa, can be classified in the retainer group by way of her husband, an administrator of Herod. It is also likely that the Phoebe recommended by Paul in Rom 16:1-3 also belonged to the local upper stratum of her home city Cenchreae, if her designation as *prostatis* is a technical term and identifies her as a patron of Christ-confessing house churches.[15]

RETAINERS

This group of the upper stratum is indicated in Luke 8:2-3. It is possible that women also can be classified here directly, not by way of their families. Thus women could also have belonged to the people from the *familia Caesaris* who receive the greetings of Paul in Phil 4:22, as well as the members of the houses of Aristobulus and Narcissus in Rom 16:10-11 (cf. p. 293).

LOWER STRATUM

As with men, the overwhelming majority of women belonged to the lower stratum. This classification for Prisca results already from her occupation (Acts 18:2). The same is also true of Lydia (16:14ff.), who apparently owned a small craft business in the area of textile fabrication and who is often placed in the upper stratum. Regarding her house church Richter Reimer has summarized as follows:

> It is possible that Lydia's household included slaves; it is probable that the income of her house made possible an economically better standard of living in comparison with poor beggars. Yet as foreign women from the East who practiced a despised occupation and practiced the Jewish religion in that Roman colony, they still belonged to the *plebs urbana*. . . . They are not comparable with the wholesale merchants of that period.[16]

It is possible that Euodia and Syntyche were likewise businesswomen who lived in Philippi but came from another land.[17] Yet what is true for them and for most of the women mentioned by name is that we can identify them by their names as at most slaves or freed women and can conclude that they belonged to the lower stratum on the basis of the fact that they were mostly single and not related to men. Yet except for a few widows who, we may presume, lived on the verge of minimal subsistence, we have no information about the stratum membership of Christian women below the poverty line.

SUMMARY

From the information that we have thus far we may presume that basically the turning of women to the urban Christ-confessing communities goes back to two "sources": missionary successes within Diaspora Judaism (Jewish and God-fearing women) and the conversion of households. Both could happen at the same time, as in the case of Prisca and Aquila, as well as in the case of Lydia, who was a God-fearer and let herself and her whole household be baptized (Acts 16:14-15). Both mission areas, synagogue and house, generally offered the best opportunity to reach and address women.

In accordance with our general socio-historical data, it is also not surprising that clear indications of upper-stratum membership are extremely rare among Christ-confessing women. It is no accident that the women attributed to the local elite in Acts 17:4, 12 belonged to the circle of God-fearers and sympathizers of Judaism, for this agrees with our general knowledge about the social position of women as sympathizers of the Jewish religion (cf. pp. 257–58). Since they held their high social position because of their families—that is, they were neither single nor the heads of their own households—it is likely that their relationship to the Christ-confessing community, as to the Diaspora synagogue, amounted to a kind of sympathizer status. It is no coincidence that of these women Luke reports no baptisms—in contrast, for example, to Lydia. Nevertheless, the potential influence on upper-stratum circles through such sympathizers of the Christ-confessing communities should not be underestimated. Nor can Phoebe, who was probably single, be attributed with certainty to the local upper stratum. Thus with regard to the stratum membership of Christ-confessing women, the picture is ultimately not different from that of Christ-confessing men: it is entirely possible that some women from families of the local elite were sympathizers of the communities. If among the women belonging to the community there were some from the upper stratum, they were single and belonged to subdecurional circles.

Lower-stratum membership, however, was absolutely predominant among Christ-confessing women. Here the scale of social positions ranged from single women who headed a small business or household to slaves.[18] Socially, the widows were the most needy group. Schottroff correctly calls attention to the fact that 1 Tim 5:16 and Acts 9:36ff. suggest that in the Christ-confessing communities the attempt was made to care for widows within the household. Those provided for in this way apparently returned the favor by working in the community—presumably caring for orphans, visiting prisoners, and providing them with food.[19]

14.3 The Participation of Women in the Communal Life of the *Ekklēsia*

14.3.1 The Participation of Women in the Functions and Roles of the Ekklēsia

Women and men were baptized in the same way, whether with each other (Acts 8:12) or by themselves or together with the whole household (cf. only Acts 16:15; 1 Cor 1:16). There is no discernible gender-specific difference in the baptismal praxis of urban Christ communities. On the contrary, it is of some significance that the same ritual was practiced in the baptism of both sexes; that is to say, a gender-independent "ritual of initiation"[20] could and must have also fundamentally promoted the social integration of women into the new community. At the same time the baptismal ritual was of high symbolic significance and connected with the gift of the Holy Spirit (1 Cor 12:12-13): accordingly, *all* who were baptized into Christ received the same Spirit and belonged to the same "body" (of Christ). Thus in the origin of the Christ-confessing community, baptism symbolized in a special way the unity and basic indistinguishableness of its members in regard to the charisma. The baptismal tradition in Gal 3:27-28 makes this indistinguishableness clear in the abolition of three known oppositions: that of belonging to ethnic groups, the difference in social status, and also the difference of gender:[21] "As many of you as were baptized into Christ have clothed yourselves with Christ. There is no longer Jew or Greek, there is no longer slave or free, there is no longer male and female; for all of you are one in Christ Jesus."

The first opposition shows that it is not just a future eschatological perspective for the baptized that is being sketched here. The further context of Galatians argues on the basis of the equality of Jews and non-Jews: in terms of the gift of the Spirit, the faithful are already demonstrably the offspring of Abraham and God, independent of their membership in God's covenant with Israel and the resulting circumcision (cf. also Gal 6:15: "a new creation"). Likewise, as the Letter to Philemon and 1 Cor 7:17-24 show, Paul seems to affirm an abolition of the status distinction between free and slave *within* the Christ-confessing community: a slave called to faith is a "freed person belonging to the Lord" (1 Cor 7:22). Yet Paul pleads not for a general abolition of slavery but for an annihilation of status differences between free and slave within the *ekklēsia*, which also, as the Letter to Philemon shows, is to have social consequences.[22]

Accordingly, the third opposition pair also involves not just a virtual abolition of the difference of gender. But what is the difference? Gal 3:28c reminds us linguistically of Gen 1:27 LXX in that the neuter formulations "male" (*arsen*) and "female" (*thēly*) are used.[23] This linguistic usage (cf. also Rom 1:27) suggests here an abolition of the sexual differences based on creation, but not, as is often assumed, an abolition of social gender roles.[24] Where the focus is on the social roles of men and women, Paul uses the opposition man-woman (*anēr–gynē*).[25] Thus in spite of the close connection between biological *sex* and social role according to *gender*, Gal 3:28c formulates only an "eschatological antithesis"[26] to the creaturely sex difference. This corresponds to the apocalyptic concept in Mark 12:25/Matt 22:30/Luke 20:35, according to which the dead, after the resurrection, neither marry nor are given in marriage but are (asexual) like the angels in heaven (cf. also *1 Enoch* 15:6-7; 51:4). This is different from the androgynous mythos of Plato, Philo, the rabbis, and Gnosticism, which envision not asexuality but reconstruction of the unity of the sexes.[27] Certainly, for Paul also this sexual difference is actually abolished only with the resurrection or transformation of the body. But in the community the asexual constitution of the new creation has a counterpart when in the present, celibacy and sexual asceticism, for which he himself is the model, represent the ideal way of life (cf. 1 Cor 7:1, 7-9, 26-27, 32-33, 38, 40). Therefore, we do not see it as a contradiction to Gal 3:28c when in 1 Corinthians 11 and 14 the apostle follows quite traditional role models for women (cf. 14.3.2 below).

We must also note, however, that at least some functions and roles within the Christ-confessing communities were assumed not only by men but also by women. Here it is not a question only of functions that resulted from the social status of certain women; that is, that women were, for example, also leaders of Christ-confessing house churches (such as Lydia in Philippi, Prisca—together with Aquila—Nympha in Laodicea, and perhaps Chloe in Corinth). We must note rather that the charismatic equality of the sexes is also revealed in female participation in functions of spiritual leadership within the Christ-confessing communities.

THE LEADERSHIP FUNCTIONS OF WOMEN

Apostles

The only woman who is explicitly designated with the title *apostle* in the New Testament is Junia (Rom 16:7).[28] It probably characterizes her as an envoy legitimated by an appearance of the resurrected Christ. Thus she was one of the earliest itinerant missionaries, even before Paul himself, and she was Jewish. Since she apparently worked with a man (Andronicus), her wandering existence is also socially conceivable (cf. also Prisca and Aquila).

Coworkers in Mission

Paul calls Prisca, Euodia, and Syntyche "coworkers."[29] With this term (*synergos*) he includes the individuals who worked with him "together as commissioned of God in the common 'work' of missionary proclamation."[30] Also to be counted in the circle of women active in missionary preaching are Mary (Rom 16:6), Tryphaena, Tryphosa, and Persis (Rom 16:12), since they are also characterized by the word *kopian* ("toil"), which belongs in the context of mission. All these women apparently played a leading role in the founding of Christ-confessing house churches, a role that also involved the task of proclamation. Some of these women were apparently active not only in their hometowns but also in other cities, as the example of Prisca (and her husband Aquila) suggests and as can be inferred from the greetings list in Romans (Paul must have met the people he greets in Rome somewhere else).[31] The participation of women in missions is easily understandable from the importance of the house for the spread of faith in Christ and the formation of Christ-confessing communities.

Deaconesses[32]

The oldest New Testament attestation for the function of the *diakonos* ("deacon, deaconess") involves a woman! In Rom 16:1-2 Paul recommends a certain Phoebe of the Roman congregation. She is *diakonos* (note the masculine form) of the Christ-confessing community in Cenchreae (a harbor city seven kilometers southeast of Corinth) and presumably the patroness of the congregation there. Philippians 1:1 suggests understanding the term *diakonos* as a designation of a function, which was without doubt connected not only with benevolent but also with preaching tasks. Yet we know no further details. The diaconate at the end of the century seems to have developed to a kind of institutionalized function, as shown by 1 Tim 3:11 and the letter of Pliny to Emperor Trajan regarding the trials of Christians (*Ep.* 10.96.8: slaves were called *ministrae* and tortured). The diaconate was by no means a specialty of women, as shown not least of all by 1 Tim 3:8ff. (vv. 8-10 are directed toward men as deacons).

Widows

In our opinion, there was no "office of widow" as a special function within the *ekklēsia*.[33] There is nothing in the encouragement of widows to pray continually ("night and day": 1 Tim 5:5) to identify the suggestion as a congregational function. Rather, 1 Tim 5:3ff. contains instruction for interaction with widows of the congregation (cf. p. 390). Schottroff correctly writes: "For 1 Tim. 5:3-16 an 'office of widow' is repeatedly discussed. The element of truth here is that widows (and single women), who could not make it alone economically, not only were *recipients* of assistance in the context of the community but also performed respectable work in the congregation."[34]

Elders/Presbyters

It is not entirely clear whether the "older women" (*presbyterai*) mentioned in 1 Tim 5:2 practiced a congregational leadership function. Schüssler Fiorenza concludes from this verse that the leadership of a congregation consisted of men and women presbyters, on the one hand, and deacons and deaconesses, on the other.[35] In fact, 1 Tim 4:14 speaks of a "council of elders" (*presbyterion*). Yet the terminology employed in 5:1-2 does not support the idea that it is a question here of leadership functions. "Older" men and women are juxtaposed with "younger" men and women. The term *diakonos* does not appear. Also the immediately following context (on widows) does not deal with any special congregational function. Thus 1 Tim 5:1-16 speaks generally of interactions with older and younger men and women and with widows. Not until 5:17 is it a question of the function of "elders," which is characterized here unambiguously ("rule . . . labor in preaching and teaching").[36] Whether they include women cannot be clearly determined, but it is rather doubtful. Certainly they do not belong to the group of "elders" who are distinguished through preaching and teaching, for this is contradicted by the express prohibition of teaching by women (2:12). Since women are all admonished to be fully submissive (2:11), we must assume that in the *ekklēsia* that is presupposed by the First Letter of Timothy, women could not perform leadership functions.

Women Prophets

Women are presupposed as prophets in 1 Cor 11:5, as well as in Rev 2:20-23. In the latter case, however, Jezebel, the prophet in Thyatira, is sharply criticized and accused of beguiling servants to practice fornication and eat meat offered to idols. Yet the apocalyptist is not against the fact that she teaches but against the content of her teaching. The harsh castigation of the prophet's false teaching may be based on little more than the concession of believers in Christ in eating meat with their neighbors (meat that normally came from animals slaughtered according to pagan rite).

Functions in the Community Assembly

According to 1 Cor 11:5, women also actively participated in the community assembly by praying and prophesying. Moreover, we may also assume the participation of women in speaking in tongues, its "translation," and the praying (or singing) of psalms (1 Cor 14:2, 26). Indeed, in Corinth women presumably also shared in the "lesson" (*didachē*) in the community assembly (14:26), as may be inferred from Paul's critical comments (14:33-36). This comprehensive active participation of women in community assemblies, however, seems to have been a particular expression of the community in Corinth.[37]

In summary, we may presume—initially for the Pauline communities—that basically women had a share in most of the charismatic gifts of the Christ-confessing communities, whether in the fulfillment of missionary functions, in the performance of tasks in certain areas of competence in the local communities, or in active participation in the assemblies of the *ekklēsia*. In Corinth women also shared in many forms of self-expression in the assembly itself. This indifference to gender with regard to the spiritual leadership of the communities apparently resulted from the charismatic equality of Christ-confessing men and women, which found its social expression in baptism. Thus the charismatic element was egalitarian.[38]

Also of additional significance for the participation of women in leadership functions, however, was no doubt the community form of the *ekklēsia,* which was analogous to the ancient household. When the assembly of the Christ-confessing *ekklēsia,* which belonged in the public realm, took place in the home and understood itself as a familial community, its form of organization also offered women the opportunity for active participation.[39] This is confirmed by the fact that the increasing controversy over the leadership functions of women reached its high point when in the third century c.e. the Christ-confessing communities stopped gathering in private houses and changed to the public area of the polis (basilica).[40] Yet even in the epoch under discussion here, there were already irritations and differences of opinion over the active participation of women in the self-expressions of the *ekklēsia,* which makes it clear that the sexual equality of charismatic status implied in baptism was not simply translated into social reality. This process is already recognizable in the letters of Paul. It seems to have been increasingly reinforced in accordance with the process of the transformation of the charisma.

14.3.2 Restrictions on the Participation
of Women in the Functions and Roles of the Ekklēsia

We have indicated that women—at least in Corinth—also participated in leadership functions in the community assembly (prayer, prophecies, speaking in tongues and its translation, psalms, and teaching). Yet Paul makes two restrictions regarding the Corinthian praxis: he sharply criticizes the fact that women pray and prophesy unveiled (1 Cor 11:5-6, 13-16), and he states that in the community assembly women are to be silent (14:33b-36). In both cases his argument is based on the order set by God—whether that of creation or that of the Torah—as well as on moral conventions.[41]

A. BEING VEILED WHILE PRAYING OR PROPHESYING

Paul reacts rather emotionally to the Corinthian practice of women praying and prophesying *unveiled.* Such a woman might as well have her head shaved. But since it is disgraceful for a woman to cut off her hair or shave her head, she should veil herself (1 Cor 11:5-6). In the background of this argumentation is the subordination of the woman to the man, which is implied in creation (11:3, 8-9). In the same context Paul connects the veiling of women at prayer with (allegedly) natural conditions and the resulting conventions, which for him apparently also go back to creation (11:13-16):

> Judge for yourselves: is it proper for a woman to pray to God with her head unveiled? Does not nature itself teach you that if a man wears long hair, it is degrading to him, but if a woman has long hair, it is her glory? For her hair is given to her for a covering. But if anyone is disposed to be contentious—we have no such custom, nor do the churches of God.

Here we cannot go into the special problem of the veiling of women—also at cultic celebrations. Neither can we cite a general custom for the behavior of Corinthian women nor for Paul's criticism, although for "respectable" women in public, a head covering was generally expected.[42] But "independent of the influences to which the behavior of Christian women in Corinth may be traced back historically, we can still make statements about its significance within the community. The removal of the head covering had to be understood as 'emancipating.'"[43] Thus the point is that in Paul's view, women praying unveiled behave like men[44] and therefore cause confusion in the hierarchy of social sex roles (1 Cor 11:3: "the husband is the head of his wife").[45] This is comparable to his view that men with long hair behave in an unmanly way. The prototype of one such "feminine" man is the *malakos (effeminatus)*.[46] Paul's correction of Corinthian behavior seems, moreover, to be in the interest of a standard behavior for all communities and thus of social control[47] (11:16), which is perhaps also envisioned for the sake of the outside influence of the *ekklēsia*.

B. SPEAKING AND TEACHING IN THE COMMUNITY ASSEMBLY

Extremely controversial is the so-called command of silence for women in 1 Cor 14:33b-36:

> As in all the churches of the saints, women should be silent in the churches. For they are not permitted to speak, but should be subordinate, as the law also says. If there is anything they desire to know, let them ask their husbands at home. For it is shameful for a woman to speak in church. Or did the word of God originate with you? Or are you the only ones it has reached?

There have been numerous attempts to excise this text from First Corinthians and dissociate it from Paul.[48] *Text-critically*, however, this thesis is untenable. It is true that in the text tradition there are transpositions of vv. 34-35 to make them follow v. 40, yet by internal and external criteria, they are not to be regarded as original.[49] Thus there are no text-critical reasons for striking vv. 34-35. This proposal can be supported at most by *literary-critical* considerations that appeal above all to the apparent contradiction between Chapters 11 and 14: the first passage assumes the activity of women as prophets and prayers in worship gatherings; the second commands them to be silent.[50] Nevertheless, there are numerous attempts to reconcile the statements of 1 Corinthians 11 and 14. Most reasonable, in our view, is the attempt to explain that Paul is addressing different roles of women in Chapters 11 and 14. That is, the presumed opposition between 1 Corinthians 11 and 14 dissolves if one notes that in the Christ-confessing *ekklēsia* there were two social experiences that were also judged differently outside the community: on the one hand, acts of worship (praying, prophesying, and the like), on the other, consultations and teaching dialogues (*didachē:* 1 Cor 14:6, 26). A potential public is presupposed for both experiences (14:23-24). From 11:2ff. we learn of the participation of women in acts of worship. In this context, Paul criticizes only the lack of head coverings for women. In 14:34-35, by contrast, the apostle makes a connection between the silence and the learning of women, which is bracketed by the key word *subordinate* and the suggestion that women may ask their own husbands at home.[51]

We support the thesis here that in Paul's opinion (married) women have no right to speak in the *teaching dialogues* or consultations of the *ekklēsia* but are to be silent and ask their husbands at home. Their participation in acts of worship of the community assembly, by contrast, is not discussed here; rather, it is presupposed on the basis of 1 Corinthians 11. This differentiated position of Paul's finds its support in general cultural conventions. For, as already presented above, the concept of the *ekklēsia* is connected first of all with the idea of the full assembly of the men of the polis who have the privileges and the rights of citizenship. In it, only they can speak and vote. Thus when the apostle Paul writes in 1 Cor 14:35: "For it is shameful for a woman to speak in [the *ekklēsia*]," he is without doubt thereby agreeing with the conventions of his society. To behave otherwise would violate ideas of men's honor and of women's shame. This is also confirmed by his previous formulation, whose passive construction is likewise clearly based on convention: (married) women are supposed to be silent in the *ekklēsia,* for they are not allowed to speak (14:34). They are supposed to ask their husbands at home.[52]

This convention is echoed in a text from the comedy *Lysistrata* of Aristophanes. Here Lysistrata inquires of her husband regarding the consultations (506–20):

> In previous times we—being of a moral nature, as we women now are—always endured and were patient in the misery of war, no matter how you men carried it out. You held that we were not permitted to budge. And yet, you were certainly not to be praised! We saw through you well, and we did not expect anything good. And then it often came to our ears, as we sat still at home, how wrongly you handled the most important things! Then, deeply troubled within but still with smiling faces, we asked you: "What have you, in the council of the people, decided this morning for the sake of peace?" . . . "What is that to you?" was the grumbling answer of the husband. "I advise you to be silent!" And I remained silent. . . . Before long we heard again that you made wrong decisions. And so we asked again: "No, tell me, husband: what kind of dumb decisions did you make?" Then he looked at me askance and began: "If you do not remain quietly at your weaving stool, then I will set your stubborn head straight, for war is the business of men."

Women do not take part in the deliberations of men; indeed, they are not even present: they ask their men at home.[53] Yet even there they are brought to silence and directed to their place: the weaving stool. While Paul does not threaten with the weaving stool, he demands in principle what Aristophanes' comedy presupposes as practice. Also influencing Paul here may be the fact that the Christ-confessing assemblies are public; behavior of women that contradicted conventions could have made a negative impression on possible visitors. Not least of all for this reason, he insists that the gatherings should take place "decently" and "in order" (1 Cor 14:40). By contrast, the phenomena of the Greco-Roman world include, as we have seen, the public functioning of women as priestesses, as well as their (active) involvement in the cult. And the participation of Christ-confessing women in the "cultic" acts of the *ekklēsia* is not criticized by Paul.

C. MARY AND MARTHA: SILENT LISTENING AS A MODEL

When we look carefully, we see that the restrictive tendencies vis-à-vis the active participation of Christ-confessing women in the teaching dialogues of the *ekklēsia*, which are already discernible in Paul, increase in the epoch of urban early Christianity after 70 C.E. An example is the Lukan story of Mary and Martha, who receive Jesus in their house during his journey to Jerusalem (Luke 10:38-42). This text is a Lukan construction; it is applicable to the situation of Christ-confessing women in the period after 70. Basically, the interpretation of this story seems to be correct; it reflects the tension between the traditional role of women (table service: Martha) and their assimilation to the role of men as "students" (Mary). Mary sits at Jesus' feet and listens to him (10:39), just as Paul in Acts 22:3 says that he sat at the feet of Gamaliel as a student. By contrast, Martha looks after the table service and complains to Jesus that her sister leaves her alone with this task (10:40). The story, however, by no means plays the housework of Martha off against the role of Mary; rather, Martha is also invited to learn.[54]

Another interpretation of the text has prevailed for some time in Anglo-Saxon feminist exegesis. Schüssler Fiorenza was the first to interpret the story in the context of a conflict over leadership roles in the *ekklēsia*—in analogy to Acts 6:1ff. The basis of the conflict, which is reflected in this story, lies in the question of the leadership function of women in house churches. It sees Martha in such a leadership role, yet in it she is discouraged. That is, the story overlooks the active role of Martha and emphasizes instead the passive role of Mary.[55]

Even if we cannot agree with the alternative interpretation argued by Schüssler Fiorenza because, in our opinion, it is a question here not especially of the leadership functions of women but more generally of their participation in the teaching of the *ekklēsia*, it is still worth noting that the picture of Mary is by no means drawn in an "emancipatory" fashion. Her behavior remains within the conventional framework of Greco-Roman ideology for the behavior of women at private mealtimes: Mary listens to Jesus *silently*. Nor does she lie down at table with Jesus and therefore in no way has a position equal to his.[56] That is, her role in relation to Jesus as teacher is purely receptive: she "listened to what he was saying."[57]

Acts 16:14ff. also describes women (among them Lydia) in purely receptive terms; by contrast, men teach and preach. Lydia herself, who is baptized with her whole household and can thus be called the leader of a house church, offers her services as hostess, but she is not portrayed in any kind of teaching or leading function.

Thus, if the *Sitz im Leben* of the story of Mary and Martha is to be seen basically in the participation of women in the teaching or teaching dialogues of the *ekklēsia*, it continues the restrictive tendency indicated in 1 Cor 14:33b-36. Whereas Paul has to require the silence of (married) women in the teaching dialogues of the *ekklēsia*, Luke himself seems to have to defend this passive behavior of Christ-confessing women against their limitation to the traditional (house)wifely role. For Paul the active participation of women in the teaching dialogues of the *ekklēsia* was the problem; in Luke even their *passive* participation had to be substantiated with the authority of Jesus. This interpretation of the text against the background of an increasing interest in adapting traditional role concepts to women among the followers of Jesus, as well as in the urban Christ-confessing communities, applies not only to the pericope being discussed here. This tendency is also recognizable in many other texts of the Lukan double volume in which women play a role. It was recently presented once again by Corley.[58]

D. GENERAL PROHIBITION OF TEACHING BY WOMEN
AND COMPREHENSIVE CLASSIFICATION UNDER SUBMISSIVE LEARNING

A further intensification of this tendency toward restricting women is found in 1 Tim 2:9-15:

> I desire, then . . . also that the women should dress themselves modestly and decently in suitable clothing, not with their hair braided, or with gold, pearls, or expensive clothes, but with good works, as is proper for women who profess reverence for God. Let a woman learn in silence with full submission. I permit no woman to teach or to have authority over a man; she is to keep silent. For Adam was formed first, then Eve; and Adam was not deceived, but the woman was deceived and became a transgressor. Yet she will be saved through childbearing, provided they continue in faith and love and holiness, with modesty.[59]

This text[60] provides comprehensive rules for the correct behavior of (Christ-confessing) women, not just for their behavior in services of worship. As Schottroff has shown,[61] it falls in the tradition of the "regulation of women," which is also known, for example, through texts by Tacitus and Valerius Maximus.[62] The author of 1 Timothy draws a clear picture of the subordination and inferiority of women, which he substantiates with creation theology. He apparently sees their salvation-historical redemption only in the bearing of children. We are interested here above all in the clear admonition to learn through silence and submissiveness and in the prohibition of teaching. Both are clearly directed toward the behavior of women in the gathered community, but even more fundamentally, the author prescribes for women their behavior in public *and at home*. This is based, first, on the general substantiation of the secondary rank of women (after men) and on their alleged vulnerability to temptation, but also on reasons given in 1 Tim 5:13 (cf. 2 Tim 3:6-7). There we read regarding young widows: "Besides that, they learn to be idle, gadding about from house to house; and they are not merely idle, but also gossips and busybodies, saying what they should not say." The Greek term *argos,* here translated "idle," should not be immediately given a negative connotation (that is, "lazy"). Its Latin counterpart in the Vulgate (*otiosus*) points more clearly to the (male) practice of leisure (*otium*) that is free of duties and devoted to literary education or discussions. Thus in 1 Tim 5:13 it is not a question of the "laziness" of young widows, as also shown by the additional words *gossips* (*phlyaros*) and *busybodies* (*periergos*). In its basic meaning, the word *periergos* describes one who is meddling in things that are not one's concern. Thus the author is criticizing the idea of young widows "gadding about from house to house," devoting themselves to some sort of learning, and thus encroaching on territory reserved for men. What they are doing is, in the eyes of the writer, "gossip"—giving their attention to things that are not the concern of women. In this sense it is again clear that 1 Tim 2:11 must be understood as a *comprehensive* commandment that women are to learn in "silence" (*hēsychia*) with all submissiveness.[63] The restriction on learning corresponds to a *general* prohibition of teaching, which likewise refers not just to the community assembly, as it also becomes clear from the addendum that it is forbidden for women to rule over (*authentein*) men (2:12).[64] The problem seems to be, above all, that women teach *men*.[65] In summary R. S. Kraemer writes about 1 Tim 2:11ff.: "Good Christian women keep their mouths shut, exercise authority only over their households and children and never over men, and generally confine themselves to the private, domestic sphere."[66] Like Schottroff[67] she presumes that the real background of these prescriptions is the exact opposite of the behavior asked of women.

E. REINFORCING THE REQUIREMENT OF SUBORDINATION

If in 1 Cor 11:15; 14:33bff. and Luke 10:38ff. we see a tendency toward the restriction of female participation in the *assemblies* of the community, then the text 1 Tim 2:9ff. discussed above makes clear that this tendency is not limited to the role of women in the public arena of the *ekklēsia*. Apparently by the end of the first century at the latest, the role behavior of Christ-confessing women was even more strongly adapted to that of a traditional ideal woman. This pressure toward the subordination of women is discernible in the pastoral epistles, Colossians, and Ephesians, as well as in 1 Peter. We will go into this here at least briefly.

The so-called household rules (in the narrow sense Col 3:18—4:1 and Eph 5:22—6:9) require the subordination of wives to their husbands. In the same way 1 Pet 3:1, 5-6 also requires the subordination of wives under their husbands; as their special model the passages present, in addition to other saintly women, Sarah, who called Abraham her lord (*kyrios*). The fact that these requirements of obedience are formulated with the same Greek verb (*hypotassesthai*) that Paul uses for subordination to state and to masculine authorities (cf. only Rom 13:1; in regard to women: 1 Cor 14:34) makes it clear that the texts have in mind a *relationship of sovereignty*.[68] Yet here it is a question of order in the household, not in the polis. Nor is patriarchal dominance by the husband basically changed when the subordination of women is compared to the relationship to Christ (or God): "as is appropriate in the Lord" (Col 3:18); "as to the Lord" (Eph 5:22).[69] Yet in each case there is a reciprocal challenge to the husbands to limit their dominion. Col 3:19 commands husbands to love their wives and not be harsh with them. Similarly, moreover, Eph 5:25-29 draws on the model of Christ for the behavior of husbands toward their wives; husbands should love their wives as their own bodies. Husbands are also asked to be considerate of their wives in 1 Pet 3:7.

In comparable pagan texts the subordination of women is balanced with a limitation of male dominion, as shown here with the example of Plutarch *Moralia* 142E:

> This also applies to wives. As long as they subordinate [*hypotattousai*] themselves to their husbands, they deserve praise. But when they set out to rule, they act more inappropriately than those who let themselves be ruled. Nevertheless, the husband is not to rule over his wife like a despot over his property but like the soul over the body, growing together full of sympathy and love.[70]

Wolter's judgment on the reciprocal demands of wives and husbands in the household rules of Colossians applies to both texts: "In terms of content, all of this is naturally not specifically Christian but rather corresponds to the moderate patriarchalism of the economic tradition."[71] Yet what is noteworthy vis-à-vis the economics of, say, a Xenophon is that in the named New Testament texts a positive role description for wives is lacking, whereas Xenophon, for example, formulates the different areas of competence of husbands and wives in a household complementarily, that is, as activities that complement each other for the well-being of the household.[72] The attention of the New Testament texts, by contrast, is given to attitudes, whether of the subordination of wives or the love of husbands. The theme here is no longer the functions, areas of competence, division of work, and significance of behavior within and for the benefit of the whole household. Therefore, even with all the dependence of the texts on the ancient economic tradition, they seem to us to reveal rather the character of a kind of ethic of status roles.

The "household rules" and 1 Pet 3:7ff. are again to be distinguished from the pastoral letters. In them we find on the whole a rather negative picture of women, which is no longer simply understandable as an expression of culturally determined patriarchalism. Titus 2:2-8 admonishes first older men, then older women, younger women, and finally younger men. Whereas the admonitions given in connection with men mostly contain positive virtues, for the women we find terms of vice ("not to be slanderers or slaves to drink"), as well as admonitions for the good management of the household and for submissiveness. Thus women are connected here with slander and drunkenness. The passages already mentioned in 1 Tim 2:9ff. and 5:5ff. (widows), moreover, deal with striving for wealth, sexual vulnerability, unbridled living, gossip, occupation with things that do not concern women (for example, learning), and vulnerability to false teachers in connection with sexual endangerment (2 Tim 3:6).

F. HOW DID THIS REINFORCED RESTRICTIVE DEVELOPMENT COME ABOUT?

In the Pauline communities, especially the community in Corinth, there seems to have been a certain tendency toward a clearer equality of the roles of women and men regarding the various functions in the *ekklēsia* on account of charism. By contrast, however, a certain countertendency toward the limitation of female participation in the self-expressions of the Christ-confessing community was represented already by Paul himself. It can be understood as an assimilation of charismatic experiences in the wake of their becoming common or institutionalized in the structures of the majority society. This probably also determined the post-Pauline development. Moreover, the outward influence of the *ekklēsia* may also have motivated the pressure to adapt internally.

From the *Octavius* of Minucius Felix (third century) we can at least still surmise what accusations were raised against Christ-confessing communities because of their common gatherings. Believers in Christ are characterized there as people who come

> from the lowest ranks of the people . . . ignorant and gullible women who indeed, just because of the weakness of their sex, are easily persuaded. . . . [These] bands of conspirators . . . fraternize in nocturnal assemblies and at solemn fasts and barbarous feasts, not through a holy ceremony, but through an unatonable crime [8.4]. . . . Everywhere they also practice among themselves, so to speak, a kind of cult of sensuality; without distinction they call each other

brother and sister, and through this holy name even the usual immorality becomes incest [9.2]. . . . On a feast day they gather with all children, sisters, mothers, and people of every race and age for a banquet. After an abundant feast the conviviality at table heats up and the glow of impure desire is inflamed by drunkenness. . . . In a darkness that is favorable to shamelessness they are consumed by unspeakable passion, as determined by chance. Thus even if not through the deed, they are incestuous in like manner through their common knowledge [9.6].

In New Testament texts the behavior of women following traditional patriarchal role assignments is understood as a kind of positive advertisement for the Christ-confessing community (1 Pet 3:1-2) or as the cause of possible negative attitudes toward the community (Titus 2:5). In any case it is noteworthy that Paul did not go along with the participation of women in missionary proclamation and cultic activities. Yet here he is in agreement with the conventions of Greco-Roman culture. He requires only the veiling of women; and here he sees himself again in agreement with the contemporary customs and with the feelings of shame and the role behavior given by nature. Likewise, his commandment of silence to women in the assembly of the community corresponds to the conventions of Jewish and Greco-Roman culture. In this sense we may presume that in regard to the external influence of the Christ-confessing communities, Paul was interested in behavior that was in concord with the culture.

In this connection, it is also often pointed out that the Christ-confessing communities' growing longing for recognition by the Roman majority society led to a minimalization of the political and cultural deviance of the Christ-confessing groups.[73] This explanation could also be related to Paul's special restrictions for women or at least for the participation of women in the debates of the *ekklēsia*, for their participation could without doubt be felt to be culturally deviant. Perhaps this is also to be assumed for the problem of veiling, even if in this case a general custom cannot be demonstrated. Both motifs, pressure to adapt and interest in recognition, can still be applied to Luke, for his traditional picture of women may have been determined by this pressure to adapt—whether objective or subjective. Also both motifs can be applied to the pressure toward the subordination of women, which is recognizable in Colossians and Ephesians, as well as in 1 Peter. In our opinion, however, these motifs alone are not adequate to explain the position of the pastoral letters. What Schottroff has proposed seems to us to be carried further here.[74] According to her the authors of these letters were part of an extremely conservative and in part misogynous tradition, as represented in the pagan world by, for example, Tacitus and Valerius Maximus, as well as by Juvenal. Here women are suspected of every possible negative characteristic, ranging from excessive living, drunkenness, striving for luxury, sexual seduction, and proneness to seduction, to lusting for power over men. Conversely, the reaction to these suspicions was an extremely rigid control of women, which in these letters' paraeneses to women found its abstract expression in the demand of a general subordination to men. We may presume that the real background here was an increasing autonomy of women, which—seen in terms of the whole society—was connected with their economic conditions and in the *ekklēsia* in particular with the charismatic experiences of equality in the origin of Christ-confessing communities.

NOTES

Notes to the Introduction

1. On the difficulties of this term see Vouga 1994, 12–13.
2. See p. 3; for more precise differentiations see pp. 187 and 251.
3. On the expansion of Rome cf. the brief overview in Christ 1984, 22ff., 39ff., 62ff.
4. Its boundary on the east is not clearly definable. Thus from certain standpoints we can even speak of an area that with the designation "Middle East" also includes comparable economic and social conditions. Cf. Kippenberg 1991, 220ff.
5. This can be inferred from Pliny's famous letter to Trajan regarding the trials of Christians.
6. Here only a few references to the literature can be given: still fundamental for the milieu of the Mediterranean world are Braudel 1990; Horden and Purcell 1986; Davis 1977; and Pitt-Rivers 1977.
7. We mention here only Malina 1993.
8. Vittinghoff 1980, 31ff. stresses the differences between individual regions and societies in the Roman empire.
9. See also Alföldy 1986a, 71; cf. also the critique of Alföldy by Christ 1980, 214.
10. Alföldy 1986a, 71.
11. Alföldy 1984, 93.

Notes to Chapter 1

1. See, for example, Alföldy 1986b, 47ff.; de Ste. Croix 1981, 210–11; Fiensy 1991, viff.
2. H. Schneider 1981b, 95.
3. Kreissig 1970.
4. Brunt 1971a, 124. Cf. also Alföldy 1984, 117.
5. Kippenberg 1991, 228.
6. Sjoberg 1965, 7ff.
7. On this term (Ger. *Gesellschaftsgeschichte*) see Schluchter 1979, 13, 42.
8. J. H. Kautsky 1982.
9. Ibid., 38.
10. See also the brief treatment and important literature in Kippenberg 1991, 228ff.; for more detail on this discussion see Kolb 1984, 238–60.
11. MacMullen 1974, 49.
12. Marxist social theories are more interested in the factor of the exercise of social power and its significance for the appropriation of assets created through production.

Yet even they cannot avoid the consideration of technological levels in connection with the conditions of social power ("sub-Asiatic mode of production"): cf., e.g., Belo 1980, 21ff.

13. Lenski 1977, cf. also Lenski and Lenski 1987, 176ff.

14. This quotation and the next are from Lenski 1977, 256–57.

15. Cf. Lenski 1977, 393ff.

16. Garnsey and Saller 1987, 43ff.

17. Lenski 1977, 256ff.; cf. Lenski and Lenski 1987, 176ff.

18. Here Lenski refers to Boak 1943 and Mattingly 1959.

19. Sjoberg 1965, 27ff.

20. In Cicero's time a factory in which fifty people worked was regarded as very large. Cf. Cowell 1956, 80.

21. Lenski 1977, 277–78.

22. On ancient literacy see W. V. Harris 1989.

23. For background cf. M. Rostovtzeff 1957; de Ste. Croix 1981; MacMullen 1974.

24. Cf. also Rohrbaugh 1991, 129ff. He refers especially to Leeds 1979; Leeds 1980.

25. Rohrbaugh 1991, 132.

26. Cowell 1956, 290.

27. Cf. here Boak 1943, 200–201.

28. Cowell 1956, 292–93.

29. Boak 1943, 210–12.

Notes to Chapter 2

1. Finley 1974; Ben-David 1974; Carney 1975; Jones 1981; Oakman 1986; Austin and Vidal-Naquet 1984; North 1988; Garnsey and Saller 1987, 43ff.; Kloft 1992; see also the references below in nn. 8, 23, and 24.

2. For more detail on the sources see Kloft 1992, 34ff.

3. Finley 1974, 12.

4. On the last of these see Philo *Spec. Leg.* 3.169ff.

5. Kloft 1992, 3.

6. Cf. on this point Finley 1974, 7ff.; Austin and Vidal-Naquet 1984, 8ff.

7. Finley 1974, 7.

8. Polanyi 1968; also very helpful is the introduction by Humphreys 1979. In critique of Polanyi is Veyne 1988, 67ff.; positively accepting of Polanyi is Austin and Vidal-Naquet 1984, 7–8. An overview of the discussion of "economic anthropology" stimulated especially by Polanyi is given by Carney 1975, 137ff.

9. Polanyi 1979, 39.

10. M. Harris 1989, 122.

11. Polanyi 1979, 206.

12. Cf. Oakman 1991a. It was also possible to invest in buildings, but this was unusual and was limited to large cities (for example, Crassus in Rome).

13. Ibid., 37.

14. Kegler 1992, 17ff.

15. Cf., for example, his comments in Polanyi 1968, 78–115: Aristotle discovered popular economy.

16. Ibid., 81–82, 84.

17. Cf. Finley 1974, 13.

18. Bücher 1903, 101ff.

19. E. Meyer 1924, 79ff.

20. Cf. ibid., 105, 116.

21. M. Rostovtzeff 1957.

22. Cf. Kippenberg 1977, 12–13.

23. Cf. H. Schneider 1981b, 4ff.

24. Jones 1974; Duncan-Jones 1982; Finley 1974.

25. See, for example, H. Schneider 1981b.

26. Also very helpful in this connection is the brief summary of results by Oakman 1986, 17ff.

27. Kloft 1992, 4ff.

28. North (1988) emphasizes the importance of these institutional conditions.

29. Cf. Christ 1988, 481ff.

30. On the problem of technical innovation see Finley 1981b, 168–95.

31. For more details on the mills see H. Schneider 1981a.

32. Kloft 1992, 16.

33. A good overview of technology is given by H. Schneider 1981a, which is our main source here.

34. Kloft 1992, 20.

35. Garnsey and Saller 1987, 49 (with additional bibliography). The Midrash on Genesis (*Mdr. Gen.* 31.10.64) mentions a ship 33 m. long and 11 m. wide, which probably accommodated about 100 tons and was suitable for shallow coastal waters (Ben-David 1974, 280).

36. Marquardt 1986, 2:404.

37. Ibid.

38. At the beginning of the present era, Antipater of Thessalonica extolled a water mill (*Anthol. Pal.* 9.418; cf. Grassl 1982, 98; Kiechle 1969, 115ff.).

39. Cf. also Oakman 1986, 25.

40. Etienne 1978, 324.

41. Christ 1988, 107.

42. Krauss 1910, 2:334.

43. Quoted according to Ben-David 1974, 266 (*b. Shabb.* 33b; cf. *b. Abod. Zar.* 2b).

44. Morel 1991, 263.

45. Jones 1981, 50–51. The numbers are valid for the later imperial period.

46. Cf. the overview on attitudes toward work and the corresponding terminology in Eichenauer 1988, 10ff. Cf. also Burford 1972, 29ff.; Meier 1986; Stroh 1986.

47. Morel 1991, 245.

48. See, for example, Plato *Leg.* 741e; Aristotle *Pol.* 1.5; 3.5; Cicero *Off.* 1.42, 150–51.

49. Cf. Meier 1986, 57–58.

50. Cf. Burford 1972, 29–30.

51. See Grassl 1982, 95–96.

52. Krauss 1910, 2:249ff.; Ben-David 1974, 180ff.

53. Nörr 1965, 69ff.; cf. also, for example, Grassl 1982, 100ff.

54. Hamel 1989, 169.

55. *Off.* 1.150–51.

56. See Finley 1974, 39ff.; Brunt 1973, 26ff. Finley regards Cicero's evaluation as a widespread prejudice; versus Garnsey 1976, 123ff.; cf. also Stroh 1986, 118–20.

57. For further examples from the imperial period see Grassl 1982, 101ff.

58. Stadelmann 1980, 284–85; see p. 128.

59. Pliny *Ep.* 9.36.

60. Eichenauer 1988, 15.

61. Brockmeyer 1968; see also Kolendo 1991, 227ff.

62. For Jerusalem see Ben-David 1974, 370 (n. 185).

63. Garnsey 1975, 226–27; for additional literature see ibid., 233 (n. 8); cf. Alföldy 1984, 121.

64. Martin 1981, 220. Yet we cannot agree with his statement that "especially Columella . . . rejected every other system" (ibid.).

65. Kolendo 1991, 240.

66. Duncan-Jones 1982, 327ff.; cf. idem 1976, 7ff.

67. Duncan-Jones 1982, 327.

68. Garnsey and Saller 1987, 67.

69. Martin 1981, 201.

70. Bleicken 1981, 2:57.

71. See here also Garnsey and Saller 1987, 48; H. Schneider 1981b, 14–15.

72. Finley 1981a; idem 1977, 305ff.

73. See, for example, the differentiation of occupations in Ben-David 1974, 149–50.

74. Morel 1991, 258. On ancient handicrafts see Burford 1972; Garnsey (ed.) 1980.

75. See, for example, Morel 1991, 263.

76. This is the prevailing opinion, which is substantiated by Jones and Finley.

77. Morel 1991, 262; Kippenberg 1991, 228.

78. Cowell 1956, 79; quoted according to Lenski 1977, 274–75.

79. H. Schneider 1981a, 106–7.

80. Jos. *Ant.* 20.219-21.

81. H. Schneider 1981a, 127.

82. See the comments by Veyne (1988, 123).

83. See here and in general on merchants the extremely informative essay of Giardina (1991); see also Garnsey, Hopkins, and Whittaker 1983.

84. Giardina 1991, 279.

85. MacMullen 1981a, 280.

86. Hopkins 1978, 37ff.

87. See the brief summary in Vivelo 1988, 186ff.

88. Polanyi 1968; cf. also Sahlins 1965, 139–236. Sahlins differentiates Polanyi's model by distinguishing balanced, general, and negative reciprocity. We are not entirely convinced by the critique of Polanyi in Veyne 1988, 67ff.

89. See Humphreys 1979, 47ff.

90. See, for example, Sahlins 1965, 148–49, and Oakman 1986, 78.

91. Cf. Oakman 1986, 66.

92. Gregory 1975; Malina 1993, 90ff.

93. See also Oakman 1991b, 156.

94. See ibid.

95. On the following see Carney 1975, 176ff.

96. Alföldy 1984, 117.

97. See Jones 1981, 48ff.

98. Ibid., 63–64.

99. On these brief definitions see the generally helpful information in Bogaert 1976.

100. These needs were met by *nummularii,* who were both money changers and coin inspectors (cf. Herzog 1937).

101. Cf. here Crawford 1981, 258.

102. Ibid., 271.

103. Ibid., 273.

104. Crawford mentions that Tiberius once intervened with an interest-free loan of 100 million sesterces when the moneylenders of Rome demanded repayment of all their loans, in order to protect themselves against the accusations of their debtors.

105. Bogaert 1976, 818, 833. See there also the Greek and Latin terms.

106. Etienne 1978, 214–15.

107. All figures are according to Etienne 1978, 215ff.

108. Ibid., 218.

109. Duncan-Jones 1982, 63ff., 345ff.

110. Ibid., 348ff.

111. Ibid., 48ff.

112. Pliny *Nat. Hist.* 12.28ff.

113. Kloft 1992, 223.

114. See p. 44 .

115. Ben-David 1974, 26–27.

116. Ibid., 304; Jones 1973, 465, 469; cf. Jones 1981, 50.

117. Kippenberg 1991, 230.

118. Cicero *Off.* 1.151; cf. p. 25.

119. Cf. Garnsey and Saller 1987, 45.

120. See the example of Trimalchio in Petronius's *Trimalchio's Banquet* (middle of the first century). As a merchant Trimalchio invested his profit in real estate.

121. See Jones 1974, 114–39.

122. MacMullen 1974, 38.

123. Garnsey and Saller 1987, 64–65; the largest private fortunes are summarized in Duncan-Jones 1982, 343–44.

124. Duncan-Jones 1976, 13.

125. Ibid., 23.

126. MacMullen 1974, 6, with reference to Cicero *Leg. Agr.* 3.14; Pliny *Ep.* 3.19; Petronius *Satyr.* 48.77; Seneca *Ep.* 90.39; *Ben.* 7.10; Dion of Prusa *Or.* 7.11; cf. K. D. White 1967, 62–79; for Palestine see Fiensy 1991, 21ff.

127. Brunt 1971b, 34; Caesar *B. Civ.* 1.17.

128. Cf. Brunt 1971b, 34.

129. Etienne 1978, 185–86, 219.

130. Garnsey and Saller 1987, 76.

131. A detailed discussion of agricultural yields is found in Duncan-Jones 1982, 23ff.

132. Ibid., 343

133. Garnsey and Saller 1987, 67–68.

134. De Ste. Croix 1981, 574.

135. Garnsey and Saller 1987, 69.

136. Garnsey and Saller (1987, 72) also presume a tendency away from slavery toward leasing.

137. Cf. also Wieling 1983, 1184.

138. Pliny *Ep.* 3.19.

139. Ibid.; cf. 9.37; cf. Wieling 1983, 1185.

140. *Ep.* 3.19.

141. Kippenberg (1991, 242) sees in Luke 16:1ff. an example of the conditions that were typical of "royal land."

142. On the debts see also section 2.3.2 and pp. 111–13.

143. On the volume measures see Jos. *Ant.* 8.57; 15.314.

144. *CIL* 8.10570 and 14464; see Garnsey and Saller 1987, 112 (with n. 14).

145. The papyrus (*SB* X 10532) has been printed and translated in Hengstl 1978, 357ff.

146. *Ant.* 14.28; 15.299–300, 365; 16.64; 18.8; 20.101.

147. *Ant.* 15.310, 302–3. Cf. also J. Jeremias 1962, 157–61.

148. See Garnsey and Saller 1987, 88ff.

149. Ibid., 82ff. Cf. also Garnsey 1988.

150. An inscription from Ephesus (second century) presupposes that Rome served itself from the grain stores of North Africa: "It is clear that you will make intelligent use of this agreement, in view of the necessity that the imperial city must first have an abundant supply of wheat, which has been produced and gathered for its markets, and then other cities can also receive rich supplies. If, as we pray, the Nile gives us a normally good flood and an abundant wheat harvest is produced in Egypt, you will be among the first to come home" (*CIG* 29.27, 29.38; cf. Jos. *Ant.* 15.299ff., esp. 305ff.).

151. Büchner 1955, 288–89.

152. Stenger 1988, 36–37.

153. Ibid., 37.

154. Pekary 1979, 105.

155. Oakman 1991b, 167.

156. Alföldy 1984, 123.

157. Jones 1981, 52. The size of the city is hard to estimate. If Rome actually had around 1 million inhabitants, this large number of people would be an absolute exception. In any case, this is the estimate of Garnsey and Saller (1987, 83), for example, on the basis of the grain expenditures of Augustus (*Res Gestae* 15). Yet

ancient figures are problematic. Alexandria and ancient Antioch would, accordingly, have had more than 300,000 residents, and Pergamon about 180,000: Duncan-Jones 1982, 260–61. Rohrbaugh (1991, 133) estimates only 200,000 inhabitants for Rome and holds that only a few cities had over 100,000. Ben-David (1974, 52) calculates for some cities of Israel population figures of about 15,000 (Sepphoris) to 100,000 (Jerusalem). Sepphoris, in whose vicinity Nazareth lies, would then have been about as large as Pompeii.

Notes to Chapter 3

1. MacMullen 1974, 138ff.

2. Vittinghoff 1990, 205–6.

3. Cf., for example, Philo *Virt.* 187ff.

4. He also mentions wise men (*sophoi*), probably as a commitment to an ideal of Judaism.

5. Alföldy 1984, 94: Ael. Aris. *Or.* 26.39, 59.

6. Cf. Wischmeyer 1995, 48ff.

7. On Josephus see the helpful analysis by Hamel (1989, 206ff.). Here we will forego references but refer instead to the Josephus concordance; Hamel also contains many references. Cf. also Mayer-Schärtel 1994, 28ff.

8. Yet we should not underestimate the significance of the fact that Josephus uses the categories "pure" and "impure" extremely seldom (Hamel 1989, 209). This is probably connected, however, with the non-Jewish addressees of his writings.

9. Cf. Reekmans 1971, 121.

10. Cf. also Tacitus *Ann.* 15.32.

11. According to *Sat.* 10.225–26 he owns several country houses.

12. On the general contempt against the Egyptians in antiquity see Smelik and Hemelrijk 1984, 1852–2000; on Juvenal see ibid., 1965–67.

13. Some signs suggest that Crispinus was a Roman equestrian and thus belonged to the *ordo equester* (ring, purple garment), but this is hard to judge: see Reekmans 1971, 142. It may be a question of imitating the appearance of an equestrian; in Petronius's *Satyricon,* for example, Trimalchio imitates the clothing and emblems of the equestrians (*Satyricon* 32): Trimalchio wears a scarlet red coat with broad purple stripes and a lightly gilded ring.

14. Interestingly, for him the *status civitatis* (whether or not one has the rights of citizenship) plays no important role: Reekmans 1971, 123.

15. Ibid., 124.

16. On the details of Paul's social status see section 10.2.2 below.

17. Morel 1991, 251; contra Vittinghoff 1990, 206.

18. Morel 1991, 251.

19. To be found in the *Inscriptions of Ephesus* 5.1487–88; see Giardina 1991, 295–96.

20. Giardina 1991, 299.

21. See, for example, ibid., 300.

22. In principle, these criteria are valid first of all only for men, and thus gender must also be included in the dominant factors of social status. Cf. 3.2.3 below.

23. Vittinghoff 1990, 234.

24. Cf. Garnsey 1970, 221ff.

25. Vittinghoff (1990, 250) emphasizes above all the character of *ordo* members as a "prestige hierarchy."

26. On the discussion of some terms see, for example, Lenski 1977, 108ff.; cf. also Garnsey and Saller 1987, 109ff.; very informative in regard to the theoretical foundations is Rohrbaugh 1984, 519ff.; cf. also Runciman 1968, 25–61.

27. In dependence on Lenski 1977, 109 (who speaks of "class").

28. The term *status* is clearly defined neither in general linguistic usage nor in sociological discussion: Funk 1981, 11; cf. also Lenski 1977, 114.

29. Funk 1981, 11.

30. Meeks (1993, 115ff.) seems for this reason to favor the term *status*.

31. Lenski 1977, 125 (bibliography); Reekmans 1971, 141ff.; Meeks 1983, 55.

32. Alföldy 1984, 94.

33. Meeks 1983, 55 (in reference to Reekmans).

34. Vittinghoff 1990, 172ff.

35. For details see Lenski 1977, 70ff.

36. Ibid.

37. Ibid., 71–72.

38. Here we will not go into the problem of the noninstitutionalized form of power: violence.

39. See Lenski 1977, 89.

40. Ibid., 88 (in adoption of a definition of M. Weber).

41. In this sense Alföldy's implied opposition between economic category and social function seems to us not really apt for stratum definition: he understands "by a social stratum in the *Imperium Romanum* not an economically constituted category but a group of people whose members have an approximately similar social position on the basis of their function and its concomitant evaluation by society" (Alföldy 1986a, 76).

42. Garnsey and Saller 1987, 110.

43. Ibid.

44. See, for example, Alföldy 1986a, 77.

45. Finley 1974, 49; cf. the critique of Alföldy by Christ (1980, 216); cf. also Schöll-gen 1984, 12ff. Thus in this and other respects, Alföldy's model of criteria needs further differentiation. We must point out, however, that Alföldy himself concedes the weaknesses of his analysis discussed here and in part has already expanded on them; cf. Alföldy 1984, 125ff.; 1986a, 72ff.

46. Alföldy 1984, 126.

47. Alföldy's critical comments and rejection of the model of a class society make clear that he, in fact, understands property in principle as only an "economic" category: Alföldy 1984, 126–27; cf. 1986a, 76.

48. Cf. also Mayer-Schärtel 1994, 38–39.

49. Garnsey and Saller 1987, 118.

50. Garnsey 1970.

51. Alföldy 1984, 99.

52. Ibid., 112, 113.

53. Garnsey and Saller 1987, 118.

54. Lenski 1977, 326; Garnsey and Saller 1987, 119.

55. On rich freed slaves and slaves in higher functions cf. also Brockmeyer 1979, 178–79.

56. See Mayer-Schärtel 1994, 38ff.; Blumenberg 1978.

57. N. Kampen 1981, 28.

58. Cf. ibid., 29, which includes references.

59. See, for example, Schottroff 1980, 99–100.

60. Here we will omit consideration of the "class system" proposed by Lenski (1977, 108ff.)

61. See Alföldy 1984; criticism of Alföldy by Christ 1980, 197ff.; Vittinghoff 1980, 31ff.; and acceptance of the criticism by Alföldy 1986a.

62. Garnsey and Saller (1987, 116 and n. 27) also do not posit a genuine middle-class in the sense of a middle group with independent wealth or social standing.

63. Christ 1980, 216–17. For a critique of Christ see Alföldy 1986a, 79.

64. Alföldy 1984, 125; 1986a, 81.

65. Garnsey and Saller (1987, 116) distinguish—both from the elite orders and from the masses—"*apparitores*, lictors, scribes, and other employees of the Roman magistrate"; they also employ the term "dependent of the ruling aristocracy."

66. Lenski 1977, 325ff.

67. See, for example, MacMullen 1970, 30ff.; Alföldy 1984, 114.

68. Langhammer 1973, 49–50.

69. See esp. Plümacher 1987 (the quotation and additional literature are found there on pp. 15–16).

70. On poverty the Greek philosopher Antipater said: "It is not defined by property but by its lack . . . it does not mean possession of little but nonpossession of much"; critically quoted by Seneca *Ep.* 87.39–40.

71. Dion of Prusa *Or.* 54.17.26; Augustus had raised the original minimum wealth of 400,000 sesterces to 1,000,000: Dio Cassius 56.41.3; Augustus *Res Gestae* 8.

72. Seneca is supposed to have earned 300,000,000 sesterces in just four years: Tacitus *Ann.* 13.42.

73. A proconsul in Africa or Asia earned 1,000,000 sesterces in this office.

74. Suetonius *Augustus* 44; cf. Dion of Prusa *Or.* 60.7; Suetonius *Claudius* 21; Tacitus *Ann.* 15.32.

75. On "euergetism" (doing good works) and its connection with social power see Veyne 1988, 101ff.

76. Stahl 1978.

77. Garnsey 1970.

78. Thus, correctly, Vittinghoff 1990, 204–5, in distinction to Alföldy 1986a, 80.

79. Vittinghoff 1990, 241–42.

80. D'Arms 1990, 394; cf. also Vittinghoff 1990, 204–5, 223–24, 250–51.

81. See pp. 54–55 .

82. Weaver 1972, 299–300.

83. Vittinghoff 1990, 190–91.

84. Ibid., 192.

85. *Ann.* 11.34ff.; 13.14; and elsewhere.

86. Vittinghoff 1990, 192–93.

87. Ibid., 192.

88. Alföldy 1984, 95.

89. Ben-David 1974, 313.

90. Ibid., 314.

91. Whittaker 1991, 312.

92. Brödner 1989, 42ff.

93. Hamel 1989, 33.

94. On clothing see the informative overview in Hamel 1989, 57ff.

95. Jos. *War* 7.29.

96. Whittaker 1991, 316ff.

97. Oakman 1986, 57ff.

98. Brunt 1971b, 35.

99. Garnsey and Saller 1987, 77ff.; Oakman 1986, 59ff.

100. Cf. Garnsey and Saller 1987, 79.

101. Oakman 1986, 61.

102. As confirmed by K. D. White (1970, 336), who calculates 7–8 jugers for an average household of 3½ persons.

103. Hamel 1989, 134.

104. Ben-David 1974, 44, 46.

105. Frayn 1979, 15; cf. also Evans 1980, 159ff.

106. Etienne 1978, 215.

107. Ibid., 216.

108. Ben-David 1974, 300–301, 306ff.

109. Accordingly, a loaf of bread (500 g.) in Jewish Palestine in the Mishnaic era cost ca. 1⅓ as, whereas in 79 C.E. in Pompeii it cost ca. 1 as.

110. Cf. Ben-David 1974, 301 (implies ca. 1200 calories) with p. 306 (1400 calories); cf. also Sperber 1965, 250–51: a loaf of bread cost $^{1}/_{24}$ denarius.

111. Yet Ben-David assumes a wheat price equivalent to about 15 asses per *modius* and thus presupposes half of the price that a *modius* of wheat cost in Pompeii. We have used the table in Ben-David 1974, 307, as a basis.

112. For details on means of nourishment and eating customs, see Hamel 1989, 8ff.

113. Cowell 1956, 288, 258, and 104–6.

114. Etienne 1978, 215.

115. Ben-David 1974, 311.

116. Garnsey 1976, 126.

117. Ibid.

118. Ben-David (1974, 292) points out that the Talmud assumes an annual existence minimum of 200 denarii.

119. Bolkestein 1967, 38–39; 281–82; 402.

120. Alföldy 1984, 117; he points out that Galen (5.49) assumes 40,000 citizens for Pergamon in the middle of the second century and gives the number 120,000 for adults, including wives and slaves. Garnsey and Saller assume that since the third century B.C.E. slaves in Italy and Sicily made up a large part of the workforce. In large areas of Africa, however, rural workers were largely free, for example, in Egypt, the second largest breadbasket of the empire. In Gaul and Asia there were other forms of dependent working conditions, but no slavery: Garnsey and Saller 1987, 118ff.

121. From the extensive literature cf. only Finley 1985; Brockmeyer 1979; Bartchy 1973; Gülzow 1969.

122. "Since with suppressed peoples it seldom came to armed resistance against Rome, punished rebels more and more rarely reached the slave market; the enslavement of 97,000 rebellious Jews in the great Jewish war of 66–70 (Jos. *War* 6.420) was rather an exception, as was the rebellion itself": Alföldy 1984, 118.

123. Cf. W. Stegemann 1980, 114ff.

124. Alföldy 1984, 119.

125. Ibid., 116.

126. Bellen 1971.

127. On the attitude of Judaism toward slavery see Gülzow 1969, 18ff.; Urbach 1964.

128. Brockmeyer 1979, 10.

129. Vis-à-vis Christian attempts at self-legitimation in the modern period, Franz Overbeck has without illusion condemned the attitude of early Christianity and the early church toward slavery; cf. Overbeck 1994, 144ff. (and also pp. 11ff. for the history of research).

130. Vittinghoff 1990, 181.

131. Whittaker 1991, 313.

132. On vocabulary see Hamel 1989, 164ff.

133. Ibid., 167.

134. Whittaker 1991, 312.

135. Cipolla 1972, 55.

136. Ben-David 1974, 303. For further calculations on the population density of Palestine see Broshi 1979, 1ff.; Hamel 1989, 137ff.

137. Ben-David 1974, 291ff.

138. Perhaps Jesus and his father found work in the nearby city of Sepphoris.

139. MacMullen 1974, 6ff.

140. See further examples in Grassl 1982, 175.

141. Cf. Vischer 1965, 139–40.

142. On the situation of artisans, much can be learned from Hock 1980.

143. Dion of Prusa *Or.* 80.1; cf. further Grassl 1982, 114.

144. For details see W. Stegemann 1981, 10ff.

145. On the situation in Judaism see pp. 134, 136.

146. Whittaker 1991, 317.

147. Ibid., 322 (*CIL* 6.31614–15).

148. Jos. *War* 6.282.
149. Hamel 1989, 73.
150. Whittaker 1991, 321.
151. Quoted according to Ben-David 1974, 309.
152. For price information see Bücher 1922a, 229–30.
153. Ben-David 1974, 309.
154. Whittaker 1991, 321.
155. On extreme famines see Hamel 1989, 44ff.; Garnsey 1988.
156. Basic here is Vittinghoff 1990, 249ff.
157. MacMullen 1981b, 155.
158. Quoted according to H. Schneider 1981a, 124.
159. Alföldy 1981, 383; cf. also Garnsey and Saller 1987, 157ff.; see also pp. 6.5.3.
160. See also pp. 333–36 .
161. See Vittinghoff 1990, 257ff.

Notes to Part Two, Introduction

1. We alternate here between the biblical designation *Israel,* the term *Palestine—*coined by Roman-Byzantine administrative language to replace the name *Judea,* which was hated by the Romans—and *Judea,* which was the usual term, especially since the Hasmoneans, for the Palestine inhabited by Jews, including Galilee and Perea, and which was also used by Josephus. When we mean the Roman province of the same name, we use the Roman spelling *Judaea.* On the name cf. Avi-Yonah 1973, 322–23; Donner 1976, 11–13.
2. The various sources—literary, epigraphic, and archaeological—are carefully presented by Grabbe (1992) in the two volumes of his work.
3. With some justification J. H. Kautsky (1982, 72) has said that in ancient Mediterranean empires there were no "classes" but two different opposing societies, namely, the ruling and exploiting aristocracy and the ruled and exploited people.
4. Cf. Crüsemann 1992b; Albertz 1992.
5. Cf. Crüsemann 1992a, 393ff.
6. On the history of the canon cf., for example, Beckwith 1985; Mead 1986; and the relevant contributions in Baldermann et al. 1988.

Notes to Chapter 4

1. Cf. here Herzfeld 1894; Krause, vol. 2, esp. 248ff.; Heichelheim 1938; Klausner 1975; Ben-David 1974; Applebaum 1976a; 1977; Sperber 1977; J. Jeremias 1962; Kreissig 1970; Bösen 1990; Oakman 1986; Fiensy 1991; Z. Safrai 1994.
2. Cf. Avi-Yonah 1973, 326ff., 430ff.; Applebaum 1976a, 638ff.; Ben-David 1974, 25ff.; Oakman 1986, 19ff.
3. Reifenberg (1938, 113ff.) estimates that ca. 65–70 percent of the land was cultivated.
4. Cf. Oakman 1986, 25.
5. Cf. Applebaum 1976a, 646ff.; also Sperber 1977; Z. Safrai 1994, 104ff.

6. *Ep. Arist.* 112 (Ger. trans. in Meisner 1973, 60); Jos. *Ap.* 1.60.

7. It has great importance as a source, as Ben-David's work shows; cf. also Z. Safrai 1994.

8. Cf. Ben-David 1974, 176ff.

9. Cf. above all ibid., 143–290; for Jerusalem esp. J. Jeremias 1962; also Z. Safrai 1994, 222ff.

10. Cf. Ben-David 1974, 143; Tcherikover 1961; Z. Safrai 1994, 17ff.

11. Cf. Sperber 1974; Kippenberg 1978, 49ff.

12. Cf. Applebaum 1976a, 631, 667ff.; Z. Safrai 1994, esp. 415ff.

13. For the Talmudic period Ben-David 1974, 149–50, gives a differentiation of around 70 handicrafts; Z. Safrai 1994, 188ff.

14. P. Schäfer 1983, 110; cf. here for detail Schalit 1969, 328ff.

15. Cf. Kuhnen 1990, 141ff.

16. Cf. Avigad 1984, 165, 186.

17. Ben-David 1974, 183.

18. Cf. Z. Safrai 1994, 425–26.

19. Cf. Applebaum 1976a, 662–63.

20. Cf. ibid., 686.

21. *War* 5.201; cf. here n. 69 in the edition of Michel and Bauernfeind (1969, 2/1:252).

22. Cf. *Ant.* 15.299ff.

23. Cf. Jones 1938, 88.

24. J. K. Davies 1984; Kreissig 1978; Kloft 1992, 127ff.

25. Kloft 1992, 131.

26. Cf. M. Rostovtzeff 1955–56, 215ff.; Kippenberg 1978, 78ff.; 1991, 232ff.

27. Cf. Fiensy 1991, 21–22.

28. Cf. ibid., 25.

29. Cf. Hengel 1973b, 41.

30. Cf. Fiensy 1991, 28ff.

31. Salome willed to Augustus's wife Livia territories in Galilee, which Livia then passed on to her son Tiberius (*Ant.* 18.31).

32. Cf. Hengel 1973b, 40–41.

33. Tarn 1959, 179; Hengel 1973b, 68.

34. Freyne 1980, 171.

35. Cf. M. Rostovtzeff 1955–56, 268ff.; Hengel 1973b, 76ff.; Kippenberg 1978, 78ff.

36. Cf. M. Rostovtzeff 1955–56, 270ff.; Kippenberg 1978, 79–80.

37. *Ep. Arist.* 22ff. possibly presupposes this edict; cf. Kippenberg 1991, 245–46.

38. Cf. Hengel 1973b, 505–6; 1976b, 66.

39. Cf. the critique in Bringmann 1983, 76–77.

40. Cf. M. Rostovtzeff 1955–56, 343ff.

41. Cf., for example, Mittwoch 1935, 352ff.; above all Kreissig 1969, 231; Applebaum 1977, 360.

42. Cf. Schalit 1969, 171–72, with addendum, 702ff.; Applebaum 1977, 358–59.

43. This has been emphasized above all by Applebaum (cf. 1976a, 632–33; 1977, 360–61).

44. Cf. Fiensy 1991, 24ff.; other examples are found in Z. Safrai 1994, 355ff.

45. Dohr 1965.

46. Cf. Dar 1986, 230ff.; Fiensy 1991, 38ff. Fiensy presumes on the basis of the layout of the land that the estate was already in existence in the Ptolemaic period.

47. Cf. Dar 1986, 236; Fiensy 1991, 42.

48. Cf. Fiensy 1991, 49ff.

49. Cf. Hengel 1969; Herz 1928; Fiensy 1991, 55–56.

50. Cf. Fiensy 1991, 60 with n. 175, where the advocates of each answer are named.

51. Ibid., 60.

52. Here Momigliano 1934b, 351ff.; Applebaum 1976a, 657–58.

53. Cf. J. Jeremias 1962, 9ff.

54. Cf. Schalit 1969, 262ff.; Applebaum 1977, 375–76.

55. Cf. Applebaum 1976a, 656; 1977, 366–67.

56. Certain archaeological findings can thus be interpreted, at least according to Applebaum; cf. 1976a, 641ff.; 1977, 361ff.

57. Galilee, for example, is supposed to have been used 97 percent for agriculture; cf. Colomb and Keda 1971, 136–40. According to Reifenberg 1938, 113ff., 65–70 percent of the total area of the land was cultivated.

58. Cf. Applebaum 1976a, 643.

59. Cf. the Mishnah tractate *Shebi'it* (Jastrow and Correns 1960).

60. Cf. Neusner 1973, 14ff.

61. Cf. Fiensy 1991, 6ff.

62. Cf. Oakman 1986, 73ff.; Crüsemann 1992b, 268–69.

63. Cf. Goodman 1982; 1987, 57–58.

64. Cf. Schalit 1969, 323–24.

65. Cf. Applebaum 1977, 361.

66. Cf., for example, Stenger 1988.

67. Cf. ibid., 149.

68. Cf. Luz 1985, 293.

69. This corresponds to the ancient perspective as shown, say, by the Greek word *telos;* cf. Herrenbrück 1990, 191.

70. A good overview is found in Stenger 1988; cf. also Herrenbrück 1990.

71. Cf. Herrenbrück 1990, 108ff.

72. M. Rostovtzeff 1955–56, 258.

73. *Ant.* 12.175–77; according to the translation of Herrenbrück 1990, 170–71.

74. Cf. Herrenbrück 1990, 180; Kippenberg 1991, 184ff.

75. Cf. Bringmann 1983, 115, n. 17.

76. Cf. ibid., 115ff.

77. Bringmann (1983, 118) holds that it was higher than in the time of the Romans.

78. Cf. ibid., 119.

79. Cf. Schalit 1969, 265ff.; Herrenbrück 1990, 183–84.

80. Schalit 1969, 262–71.

81. Cf. ibid., 265ff.; M. Rostovtzeff 1955–56, 777ff.; Herrenbrück 1990, 185ff.

82. Caesar's and Augustus's reform of provincial law, through which senatorial and imperial provinces were differentiated, also introduced a distinction in the tribute obligation: senatorial provinces paid the *stipendium,* imperial ones the *tributum.*

83. Thus M. Rostovtzeff 1955–56 and Herrenbrück 1990.

84. Cf. Stenger 1988, 49.

85. Yet certain imperial provinces, including Judaea in particular, received governors from the equestrian order.

86. Cf. Jos. *Ant.* 14.200–201 and M. Rostovtzeff 1955–56, 792–93; Herrenbrück 1990, 186–87.

87. The level of taxation derivable from Jos. *Ant.* 14.202–3 is not clear. According to Heichelheim the annual grain tax was 12.5 percent and in the year after the sabbatical year, which was omitted, double that amount, or 25 percent. For Schalit, by contrast, the normal tax was 20 percent, but 25 percent after the sabbatical year (cf. Grabbe 1992, 335).

88. The sum corresponds to about 7 million denarii. Based on Ben-David's calculations (1974, 303), that would be more than 10 percent of the gross annual product of Palestine.

89. Cf. Grabbe 1992, 337.

90. Cf. Schalit 1969, 162; Stenger 1988, 54.

91. Stenger 1988, 54–55.

92. Cf. *Ant.* 17.355; 18.1–2; *War* 2.117; also Stern 1974b, 372ff.; Stenger 1988, 56ff.

93. Cf. Jones 1974, 164ff.; Stenger 1988, 20–21; and in this book pp. 179–80.

94. A tax collector lease would have meant above all that the organization of the tax system was entirely in the hands of Romans, that is, of equestrians and their employees.

95. Cf. here Stenger 1988, 63; Goodman 1987, 43–44.

96. Jos. *War* 2.405ff.; cf. Herrenbrück 1990, 165.

97. Cf. Stenger 1988, 64.

98. Cf. already M. L. Rostovtzeff 1902, 480; now in more detail in Herrenbrück 1990, 277 and passim.

99. Cf. F. C. Grant 1926, 105; Kippenberg 1978, 126; Oakman 1986, 71–72; Applebaum 1976a, 665; 1977, 376–77; Ben-David 1974, 304; Stenger 1988, 129ff.

100. Applebaum 1976a, 665; 1977, 376; yet according to the calculation by Schalit 1969, 263, inferred from Josephus, 900 talents would be only 9 million drachmas.

101. Cf. Broshi 1979; for discussion see also Z. Safrai 1994, 436ff.

102. Cf. S. Safrai 1976d; Liver 1963; Stern 1974–84, 1:198–99.

103. Cf. Stenger 1988, 149ff.; S. Safrai 1976d; 1981.

104. Cf. Ezra 6:8ff.; 7:15ff.; Neh 10:33ff.; Jos. *Ant.* 11.16ff., 62, 102, 127.

105. In fact, in the literature of this period there is no reference to the temple tax; cf. Stern 1974–84, 1:199.

106. Cf. esp. *m. Sheq.;* also Billerbeck 1961, 1:761–62.

107. On these differences see Stenger 1988, 151ff.

108. According to Exod 30:14; cf. Philo *Spec. Leg.* 1.77. According to Josephus's

rendering of Exod 30:14, the tax obligation lasted from one's 20th to 50th year (*Ant.* 3.196).

109. In Neh 10:32–33 we have a voluntary obligation to a yearly contribution of one-third of a shekel, and Exod 30:11ff. presupposes half a shekel for all male Israelites at least 20 years old, but as a onetime payment. Exodus 30 is also the basis of 4QOrd 6–7; cf. here Schürer 1973–87, 2:271.

110. Cf. Schalit 1969, 262ff.; Stern 1974–84, 1:199; Stenger 1988, 167ff.; Freyne 1980, 279. Liver 1963, 173–98, is critical; only the Pharisees paid the tax, according to Mandel 1984.

111. Cf. S. Safrai 1981, 265. There is also disagreement as to whether priests were obligated to pay taxes; in any case, legal proceedings were not undertaken against them when they did not pay; cf. S. Safrai 1976d, 880; Stenger 1988, 173, 179.

112. Cf. Jos. *War* 7.218; Suetonius *Dom.* 12.2; Dio Cassius 65.7; cf. Stern 1976–84, 2:129–30 and p. 329.

113. Cf. Stenger 1988, 157.

114. Cf. Luz 1990, 527ff.

115. As the children of the king pay no taxes, the children of God are also free from taxes for the house of God.

116. With reference to the Mishnah (*Ned.* 2.4), it is presumed that in Galilee the temple tax was not paid automatically (cf. Freyne 1980, 280; Luz 1990, 531).

117. For discussion of the pericope see also Stenger 1988, 183–84.

118. Cf. S. Safrai 1981, 32–33; Stenger 1988, 173ff.

119. Cf. *m. Sheq.* 1.5; Schürer 1907, 2:362–63.

120. H. Stegemann 1993, 244–45.

121. Cf. Ben-David 1974, 23.

122. In Greek this fee was called *kolbon;* hence such a money changer was a *kollybistēs* (Mark 11:15; Matt 21:12; John 2:15); in Heb. *shulhanim* from *shulhan,* "table"; in the New Testament a banker is generally called a *trapezitēs* from *trapeza,* "table" (Matt 25:27).

123. S. Safrai 1981, 185.

124. Cf. ibid., 187; E. Stegemann 1990a.

125. Since a denarius is about 16 asses, 2 lepta were $^2/_{128}$ of a denarius. One lepton corresponds to the "half peruta" coined under John Hyrcanus II and Herod the Great; it was the smallest coin.

126. Cf. S. Safrai 1976d, 879.

127. Cf. ibid. 1976a, 818ff.; Stenger 1988, 194ff.

128. Cf. S. Safrai 1976b, 821–22; Stenger 1988, 200–201.

129. Cf. Stenger 1988, 203ff.

130. Cf. S. Safrai 1976b, 822.

131. Cf. *Ant.* 20.179ff.; also 20.204ff.

132. Cf. Lev. 27:30; Deut. 14:22, and *m Maʿaś.* 1.1.

133. The parallel in Luke 11:42 names "mint and rue and herbs of all kinds"; at least the herbs are subject to the tithe according to the oldest rabbinic interpretation.

134. This is probably also indicated by *Jub.* 32:2 and CD 14:11ff. and more recent rabbinic tradition (cf. S. Safrai 1976b, 825).

135. Cf. Stenger 1988, 218ff.

136. Cf. S. Safrai 1976b, 822–23; Stenger 1988, 214ff.

137. Greek *korbanas* is a transcription of the Aramaic *qorbana* and designates the temple treasury; cf. Matt 27:6.

138. Cf. Stenger 1988, 159.

139. Cf. ibid., 158ff.

140. S. Safrai holds that this is an exaggerated amount (cf. 1981, 66). Yet we must note that before Mithridates the taxes of many places in Asia Minor were apparently brought to Kos in safety.

141. Cf. Applebaum 1976a, 678.

142. Cf. Schwarz 1919; Tcherikover 1961, 155ff.; Maier 1973, 373.

143. Cf. Goodman 1987, 52–53; Grabbe 1992, 416.

Notes to Chapter 5

1. Cf. Stern 1976a; Goodman 1987. On the strata model cf. pp. 67ff.

2. Cf. Hengel 1973b; Bickerman 1988.

3. Cf. Mazar 1957, 137–45, 229–38; Stern 1976a, 561–62; Grabbe 1992, 192ff.

4. Cf. Jos. *Life* 1.

5. Cf. Tcherikover 1961, 142ff.; Hengel 1973b, 241ff.; Bickerman 1988, 154–55.

6. On the linguistic usage cf. H.-J. Becker 1990, 17ff.

7. Outside of the New Testament, *grammateus* in this sense is found only in the LXX in Ezra; Chronicles; Sir 10:5; 38:24; 1 Macc 7:12; 2 Macc 6:18; but not in Josephus and Philo; cf. J. Jeremias 1933, 740ff.

8. Cf. Stadelmann 1980.

9. Cf. Stern 1976a, 580.

10. Cf. Kuhnen 1990, 54 (bibl.) and esp. the reports of the excavator E. Netzer noted there; cf. also Netzer 1989.

11. Cf. Stern 1976a, 566ff.

12. Cf. P. Schäfer 1983, 75.

13. Cf. Bornkamm 1959, 660–61.

14. Cf. Bickerman 1988, 161ff.; Urbach 1987, esp. 568ff.; J. Jeremias 1962, 264ff.

15. Thus, however, J. Jeremias 1962, 264.

16. Cf. Stern 1976a, 620.

17. Cf. Sullivan 1977; Stern 1974c.

18. Cf. Stern 1976a, 604.

19. Cf. Stern 1974a.

20. Tiberius Alexander, the nephew of Philo, is no exception, since he had given up his Judaism. Also according to Josephus, there were equestrians who were Jewish by origin (cf. *War* 2.308), but only by origin.

21. Cf. Fiensy 1991, 160–61.

22. Cf. Billerbeck 1961, 2:217–18; Michel 1954, 151ff. See also Rom 16:23 and p. 378.

23. Kuhli 1992b, 1219–20; cf. also in section 5.1 the example of the administrator Arion.

24. Cf. Freyne 1980, 198; Fiensy 1991, 163.

25. Cf. Herrenbrück 1990, 211ff.

26. Cf. Matt 13:45 (pearl merchant); Rev 18:3 (named following the kings).

27. Cf. Ben-David 1974, 192.

28. Cf. Fiensy 1991; Ptolemaeus, for example, owned land in Samaria and probably also in Arus (see pp. 110–11).

29. Cf., for example, the information on Bernice and Agrippa II in Jos. *Life* 119; *War* 2.595.

30. Cf. Jos. *Life* 422; *m. Ta`an.* 4.5; *Lam. Rab.* 2 (cf. Fiensy 1991, 36–37, 159).

31. Kuhnen 1990, 144.

32. For Jericho see Kuhnen 1990, 167; Netzer 1989.

33. Cf. Avigad 1984. The Talmud reports a legendary wealth even in regard to the priest Eleazar ben Charsom (*y. Ta`an.* 4.69a; *b. Yoma* 35b); cf. Goodman 1987, 55; Stern 1974–84, 1:33; Fiensy 1991, 36–37.

34. Only Agrippa I, who through his grandmother Mariamne came from the Hasmonean nobility, is something of an exception.

35. Goodman 1987.

36. This includes, in the nomenclature of Lenski 1977, the groups of the unclean and the declassed, as well as the "dispensable."

37. Cf. Fiensy 1991, 164.

38. Cf. Pöhlmann 1993, 183ff.

39. Cf. Ben-David 1974, 297ff.

40. Cf. W. Stegemann 1980, 114ff.

41. Crüsemann 1992a, 94; cf. Kessler 1989.

42. Cf. Matt 5:25/Luke 12:57–59; Matt 5:40; Matt 5:42/Luke 6:35; Luke 4:18; 16:1–8; Matt 6:12; 18:23–35.

43. Cf. above all Sugranyes de Franch 1946, 32ff.; Leutzsch 1992; B. Weber 1993.

44. Cf. Leutzsch 1992, 113ff.

45. Cf. only ibid., 121–22, and B. Weber 1993, 165.

46. Cf. J. Jeremias 1977, 208; Spicq 1961, 55; Derrett 1965, 8. This does not necessarily mean that the parable does not reflect Palestinian conditions.

47. Versus, however, Yoder 1981, 62–63; B. Weber 1993, 166–67.

48. This idea is also supported by the complete remission of debts and perhaps by the designation of debt as *daneion* in Matt 18:27.

49. Leutzsch 1992, 120.

50. Cf. ibid., 108ff.

51. Cf. Kloft 1970, 120ff. Such a remission of debt is probably also suggested by the announcement of the release of captives in Luke 4:18 (Isa 61:1-2); cf. Archelaus's remission in Jos. *Ant.* 17.200ff.

52. Cf. *Test. Job* 11:10.

53. Cf. Leutzsch 1992, 120.

54. A distraint trial is presupposed in Matt 5:25–26/Luke 12:57ff.; also CD 10:18, where seizure on the sabbath is forbidden.

55. Cf. Kippenberg 1991, 141ff., 167ff., 338ff.

56. Cf. J. Jeremias 1977, 179, 209.

57. The choking of a debtor is also attested in *m. B. Bat.* 10.8.

58. "In imperial antiquity tax collectors sometimes resorted to this practice if the tax debtor fled (e.g., Philo *Spec. Leg.* 3.159)": Leutzsch 1992, 110; cf. also Sugranyes de Franch 1946, 62–63.

59. Leutzsch 1992, 122.

Notes to Chapter 6

1. Talmon 1988, 116.

2. Cf. Grabbe 1992, 502ff.

3. Cf. Goodman 1987, 76ff.

4. Cf. S. Safrai 1980, 55ff.; 1976b; 1981; Maier 1973, 371–90; Elbogen 1931; Bachmann 1980, 172ff.; Schürer 1973–87, 2:237ff.

5. S. Safrai 1980, 55.

6. Worship in the real sense is the temple cult; cf. Rom 9:4.

7. Cf. Maier 1973, 383ff.; Grabbe 1992, 539–40.

8. In the Hellenistic period there was a "temple president"; according to S. Safrai (1976b, 875–76) the temple captain could have been identical with the temple prefect named in Talmudic sources.

9. Cf. Mark 15:54 par.; John 18:3, 9, 22; Acts 4:1; 5:24-26; Jos. *War* 6.294. According to Luke 22:4, 52, there were *stratēgoi tou hierou* (literally "captains of the temple"); cf. Schürer 1973–87, 2:278.

10. Cf. Schürer 1973–87, 2:279ff.

11. Cf. *b. Yoma* 13b, but see also Hoenig 1979.

12. According to Acts 3:11ff. Peter also preached in Solomon's Portico (which, however, lay outside the temple district).

13. Cf. Lifshitz 1967; Hengel 1971, 157–84; Hruby 1971; S. Safrai 1976c; Hüttenmeister and Reeg 1977; Hüttenmeister 1993; Levine 1981; Schürer 1973–87, 2:417ff.

14. Lifshitz 1967, no. 92 (Schedia in Alexandrien), no. 99 (Arsinoe/Fajjum).

15. Cf. Hüttenmeister and Reeg 1977, 192–95, 525, 173–74, 314–15; Gutman 1981, 30–41.

16. Cf. Grabbe 1992, 541.

17. Hüttenmeister 1993, 164.

18. Cf. Hengel 1971; Hüttenmeister 1993.

19. Cf. Schäfer 1973, 391–413.

20. Cf. Philo *Quod Omn. Prob.* 12.81–82; *Som.* 2.127; *Vit. Mos.* 2.215–16; *Leg. Gai.* 157; and elsewhere; Jos. *Ap.* 2.175; Luke 4:15ff.; 6:6; Acts 15:21; and elsewhere; John 6:59; 18:20.

21. Cf. above all S. Safrai 1976a–b.

22. Cf. Malina 1993, 117ff.

23. Cf. Amir 1985, 1–34; Albertz 1992, 623ff.

24. Cf. Goodman 1987, 68–69.

25. Malina 1993, 157.

26. Cf. Paschen 1970.

27. Cf. Luz 1990, 414ff.

28. Cf. Amram 1968; Luz 1990, 268ff. (with comprehensive bibliography).

29. Cf. Koch 1970; Koch and Schmidt 1982; cf. also J. J. Collins 1991, 11–32.

30. On the whole topic cf., for example, Hellholm 1983; Lambrecht 1980. A good overview is found in J. J. Collins 1986, 345–70; cf. also J. J. Collins 1979; 1984; A. Y. Collins 1986; K. Müller 1991.

31. Against the classical thesis of the discontinuity of apocalypticism in and after rabbinic Judaism, cf. only Scholem 1992, 23ff.; K. Müller 1991, 35ff.

32. On the rise of the messianic hope cf. K. Müller 1991, 166ff.

33. Cf., for example, Landman 1979; Charlesworth 1992; Lichtenberger 1993.

34. Cf. H. Stegemann 1983, 495–530; J. J. Collins 1990.

35. Cf. on Qumran the foregoing note and Koch and Schmidt 1982, 9–10.

36. Goodman 1987, 77–78.

37. Cf. K. Müller 1991, 195ff.

38. Ibid., 53.

39. Cf. Lichtenberger 1980.

40. Cf. K. Müller 1991, 52ff.

41. Ibid., 92.

42. Ibid., 124.

43. Cf. Koch and Schmidt 1982, 18ff.

44. M. Weber 1920, 3:379ff.

45. Cf. P. D. Hanson 1979.

46. Cf. Lebram 1970, 523–24; H. Stegemann 1983, 504.

47. Cf. Albertz 1992, 636; Saldarini 1989, 258–59, 261.

48. J. J. Collins 1984, 63.

49. Cf. Albertz 1992, 636.

50. Cf. esp. Hengel 1973b, 319–81; J. Kampen 1988.

51. Tcherikover 1961, 125–26, 196ff.

52. J. Kampen 1988.

53. Ibid., 107, 113–14, and elsewhere.

54. Cf. also Albertz 1992, 599.

55. Saldarini 1989, 253.

56. An overview of the extraordinarily extensive literature on these groups is found in Porton 1986, 57–80; Schürer 1973–87, 2:381–82 (Pharisees and Sadducees), 555–58 (Essenes and Qumran community); cf. also Grabbe 1992, 463ff.; Saldarini 1989; Stemberger 1991.

57. Cf. Schürer 1973–87, 2:583ff.; versus the scholars named in Rowley 1981, 27; also Talmon 1989.

58. *War* 2.118, 122, 137, 142, 162; *Ant.* 7.347; 13.171, 288, 293; 15.6; 20.199; *Life* 10, 12, 191, 197.

59. Acts 5:17; 15:5; 24:5, 14; 26:5; 28:22.

60. Cf. Schlier 1933, 180–83; Baumbach 1992, 96–97; Simon 1979; 101–16; Saldarini 1989, 123ff.

61. Kehrer 1988, 158ff.

62. Cf. Holmberg 1990, 108ff. We will go into this later in more detail (cf. pp. 242–43).

63. Cf. Wilson 1973, 11ff.; 1990; Saldarini 1989, 70ff.

64. Erikson 1966.

65. The foreign designation *Essene* perhaps also stresses this separation.

66. Lichtenberger 1980, 138.

67. Cf. Hengel 1973a, 402.

68. Cf. Schürer 1973–87, 2:575–76.

69. Cf. 1QS 8:11–14; 1QSa 1:2–3; 4QFlor 1:14–16; CD 8:16; cf. 7:9–14; 11QMelch 25; 4QMMT.

70. R. Meyer 1973, 13; versus Baumgarten (1983), who understands the name *Pharisee* etymologically as "specifier, interpreter." In the rabbinic literature, not all statements about *perushim* refer to the historic Pharisees; some also refer to a separatist "group that in the period after the temple destruction was distinguished by special continence and asceticism" (P. Schäfer 1991, 130). Nevertheless, in the very designation of this extreme group as "separatists" (*perushim*) the original pejorative character of the term for the historic Pharisees becomes clear once again.

71. Cf. Spiro 1980, 186–216; P. Schäfer 1991, 126; contra, however, for example, Schürer 1973–87, 2:399.

72. Cf. Burchard 1978, 472. It is noteworthy that the Qumran community also called itself *bene Zadok* and thereby expressed its priestly legitimacy, though this name was not conferred upon it from outside.

73. Cf. Baumbach 1973a, 203.

74. Cf. Burchard 1978, 473.

75. Cf. Saldarini 1989, 298ff.

76. Cf. LeMoyne 1972, 332ff.

77. Cf. Schiffman 1992, 35–49.

78. H. Stegemann 1993, 212; cf. Schiffman 1975.

79. Cf. G. Jeremias 1963; H. Stegemann 1993, 206.

80. Thus the assumption of H. Stegemann 1993, 205ff. On the identification of the "wicked priest" with Jonathan, cf. G. Jeremias 1963.

81. Cf. H. Stegemann 1993, 231ff.

82. Ibid., 231.

83. Cf. the brief essay in Porton 1986, 69–70.

84. Cf. 4QpNah 1:2, 7; 2:2, 4; 3:3, 7; 1QH 2:15.

85. Cf. Flusser 1981, 121ff.

86. Cf. Mark 2:15ff./Matt 9:10ff./Luke 5:29ff.; Mark 7:1ff./Matt 15:1ff./Luke 11:37ff.

87. Cf. only Porton 1986, 70.

88. Cf. Neusner 1971; 1973; 1979; also Saldarini 1989, 199ff.

89. Cf. S. Cohen 1984, 27–53; P. Schäfer 1991, 130ff.

90. Saldarini 1989, 284.

91. Aptowitzer 1927, ix; cf. LeMoyne 1972, 334ff.; Saldarini 1989, 302.

92. Cf. Saldarini 1989, 302–3.

93. Cf. R. Meyer 1987; Baumbach 1973a, 211–12.

94. Apparently this brutality of the "angry lion" was not criticized in Qumran, as was at first generally assumed, but rather was fully justified, along with the unusual method of execution; cf. 4QpNah 1:1ff. and also Yadin 1981, 167–84.

95. Here Josephus uses—probably not by accident—the term *dioiket,* which under the Ptolemaic hegemony designated the highest financial and economic administrator of the kingdom after the king.

96. Cf. Saldarini 1989, 98ff.

97. Cf. ibid., 144ff.

98. Cf. ibid., 1989, 94–95.

99. Cf. Mason 1989, 31–45.

100. Thus according to the translation of Clementz 1993, 38.

101. Thus according to the translation of H. St. Thackeray, *Josephus* (Loeb), 1:75 ("from the lower ranks").

102. Cf. Rengstorff 1973, 1:440.

103. They were supposed to call a people's assembly, have over 40,000 silver coins (denarii?) to spend, and be accompanied by 700 armed rebels and 300 other men, who provided them with money and food.

104. Saldarini 1989, 94.

105. The *isha perusha* named in *m. Sot.* 3.4 is not a "Pharisaic" but an extremely continent woman (cf. Schäfer 1991, 129–30).

106. Cf. only Saldarini 1989, 185–86.

107. Betz 1988, 138.

108. Gal 1:14a.

109. Hengel 1991, 222ff.

110. Ibid., 225ff.

111. Cf. above all Siedl 1963.

112. Cf. Adam and Burchard 1972.

113. N. Lohfink 1990, 33.

114. Ibid., 99.

115. According to Hengel 1973a, 40, there is even supposed to have been a "well organized and at the same time forced commonality of goods," which he characterizes as the "Jewish piety of the poor that has become law."

116. Cf. Paschen 1970, 109ff.

117. This is also the background of the "cash buying obligation" of 1QS 5:16–17; cf. Paschen 1970, 102–3.

118. Cf. H. Stegemann 1993, 261ff.

119. Cf. ibid., 262–63.

120. Cf. M. Broshi 1992.

121. Thus, however, Hengel 1978, 335.

122. Cf. ibid., 335ff.

123. Cf. H. Stegemann 1993, 267ff.

124. Cf. Mühlmann 1961; Wilson 1973; Worsley 1968; Gager 1975.

125. Theissen 1974, 251.

126. Cf. Vermes 1993, 45ff.; S. Safrai 1965; Crossan 1994, 198ff.

127. Cf. Crossan 1994, 204–5.

128. Cf. Vermes 1993, 65; versus S. Safrai 1965, 16.

129. Cf. E. P. Sanders 1985, 303.

130. Cf. Barnett 1981; R. A. Horsley 1985; Bittner 1987, 57ff.

131. *War* 2.258ff.; *Ant.* 20.168ff.; in the New Testament esp. Matt 24:23ff.; Mark 13:21-22; Acts 5:36; 21:38. The extensive identical complex of motifs, even in the wording (pseudoprophets, signs, tempt, wilderness), suggests that in both cases the reference is to the same phenomenon.

132. Cf. Hengel 1968, 25–26; Bittner 1987, 63.

133. Cf. Bittner 1987; E. Stegemann 1990b; 1989.

134. According to Josephus there were 30,000 men. Acts 21:38 speaks of 4000 "assassins."

135. Crossan 1994, 227–28, doubts this presentation.

136. Cf. Bittner 1987, 61.

137. Cf. Goguel 1928; Wink 1968; J. Becker 1972; Hengel 1968, 38ff.; Thyen 1970; Lichtenberger 1987; Tilly 1994.

138. H. Stegemann 1993, 296.

139. Ibid., 300.

140. Cf. Brandenburger 1993, 289–338; K. Müller 1994, 23–53.

141. Cf. Reiser 1990, 153ff., 181–82.

142. Cf. Thyen 1970.

143. Cf. Tilly 1994, 224ff.

144. Cf. Mark 2:18; 6:29; Luke 7:18; John 1:35-51; 3:25.

145. Cf. Lichtenberger 1987.

146. Cf. R. A. Horsley 1987, 71ff.

147. Cf. ibid., 90ff.

148. *War* 2.185ff.; *Ant.* 18.261ff.; Philo *Leg. Gai.* 203ff.

149. Cf. R. A. Horsley 1987, 120.

150. Hengel 1976a, 64.

151. Cf. Hengel 1974, 180.

152. Ibid., 181.

153. Baumbach 1965; 1973b; 1985. Cf. M. Smith 1971; Rhoads 1976; R. A. Horsley 1979; 1987; R. A. Horsley and J. S. Hanson 1985; Crossan 1994, esp. 237ff.

154. On the factional fighting among the insurrectionists cf. Goodman 1987, 198ff.

155. Hengel 1976a, 32–33.

156. Hobsbawm 1959; 1985.

157. Blok 1972.

158. Shaw 1984; 1991. For Judea cf. esp. R. A. Horsley (see n. 153 above); Crossan 1994, 237ff.; and Stenger 1988, 136ff.

159. Hobsbawm 1985.

160. Hobsbawm 1959.

161. Shaw 1991, 370.

162. Ibid.

163. Cf. esp. Shaw 1991, passim.

164. On the legal position of bandits cf. Shaw 1991, 360–61.

165. Cf. ibid., 355–56, with reference to *Digests* 1.18.13.

166. Shaw 1991, 339–40.

167. Cf. ibid., 352ff.

168. Ibid., 359.

169. Cf., however, Hengel 1976a, 320; Smallwood 1976, 44; Freyne 1988, 57; contra R. A. Horsley 1979, 54; Stenger 1988, 142; Crossan 1994, 245ff.

170. Cf. R. A. Horsley 1979, 54; Stenger 1988, 142; Crossan 1994, 246.

171. Stenger 1988, 139. Baumbach also sees here an ideologization of social banditry (cf. 1985, 98).

172. Cf. *War* 2.232ff.; *Ant.* 20.118ff.; Tacitus *Ann.* 12.54.

173. Cf. Crossan 1994, 259.

174. Cf. above all R. A. Horsley 1987, 52ff.; Crossan 1994, 275ff.

175. Cf. E. W. and W. Stegemann 1993, 41–56.

176. Cf. Michel and Bauernfeind 1969, 2/2:268–69.

177. According to *Ant.* 20.163ff., the procurator Felix is supposed to have bribed the bandits to kill Jonathan.

178. It is rather unlikely that Judas the Galilean is identical with the royal pretender Judas, the son of the bandit chief Hezekiah; cf., however, Kennard 1945, 281–86; Hengel 1976a, 336ff.; Black 1974, 45–54.

179. The idea that Judas was active in Judea and not in Galilee is suggested not only by the fact that the census was probably carried out only within the area of the province of Judea but also by the sobriquet *the Galilean,* which would be superfluous in Galilee (cf. Hengel 1976a, 342–43).

180. Thus we have here no "anachronistic usage" (thus Rhoads 1976, 56) of the term *sicarii* nor an unspecific expression for insurrectionists in general (which is probably the case in Acts 21:38 for the followers of Theudas).

181. Cf. Hengel 1976a, 93ff.

182. *War* 2.117–18, 433; *Ant.* 18.4ff., 23ff.

183. Cf. *War* 7.323, 327, 341, 372, 406, 410, 418.

184. *War* 2.445; yet the term could also have a pejorative sense: "scribal seducers of the people" (Hengel 1976a, 339).

185. Baumbach (1985, 99) presumes "that Judas united already existing groups of social bandits under a salvation-eschatological program and thereby created an effective, religiously motivated organization that went to work with a purpose" (that is, to free Israel).

186. Hengel 1976a, 68.

187. Ibid., 160ff.

188. Mentioned by name, in addition to Eleazar ben Simon, is a priest named Zacharias, the son of Amphicallus (*War* 4.224).

189. Cf. Hengel 1976a, 64–65; Baumbach 1973b, 278ff.; 1985, 97; Schwier 1989, 142ff.; contra M. Smith 1971, 17ff. ("peasant piety"); R. A. Horsley 1987, 159–92 ("peasants-turned-brigands-turned Zealots").

190. This does not mean that Josephus equated sicarii and Zealots. Rather, it refers back to *War* 2.433–34, where Josephus mentions that "other robbers," including some Zealots, had joined with Menachem (cf. Baumbach 1985, 97).

191. Josephus says that John "joined the Zealots and stopped going his separate way" (*War* 5.250).

192. There is no mention of them in the *Antiquities* of Josephus, which break off before the revolt.

193. Contra Schwier 1989, 131ff.

194. Ibid., 141.

195. Josephus paints the character of John, who was his sharpest opponent in Galilee, in the darkest colors, including the statement that John, although a Levite, allegedly does not keep the food and purity laws (cf. *War* 7.264).

196. When Josephus accuses John of shady activities during the revolt (cf. *War* 2.590ff.; *Life* 71ff.), that is hardly an indication that he is to be classified with Lenski's merchant class (contra Crossan 1994, 269).

197. Cf. Michel and Bauernfeind 1969, 2/1:230; Crossan 1994, 278.

198. Cf. Hengel 1976a, 203.

199. According to Josephus, however, that was Simon's attempt to spread panic through disguise, which was probably also one of the tactics of the social bandits (cf. Shaw 1991, 367ff.).

Notes to Chapter 7

1. Geographically, and because of their composition of Jews and non-Jews, the "churches of the Gentiles" are connected religiously, socially, and historically with Diaspora Judaism and its specific situation on the fringe of non-Jewish majority societies. Before 70 c.e. the churches of Judea, by contrast, included only Jews of the land of Israel and, after a time, some who had come from the Diaspora into Israel. Yet the missionary impulse toward the formation of churches of the Gentiles in the Diaspora came from the ranks of the churches in Judea. And because of personal and social interaction with the churches in the Diaspora, the churches of Judea were also drawn into conflicts of the former with Jewish courts, especially on the basis of the demonstrative table fellowship of Jews and non-Jews (see pp. 267ff.). Yet the difference between the (Christ-confessing) Diaspora churches and those of Judea was always clear, as shown by the differentiation of one apostolate for the circumcised and one for the Gentiles (cf. Gal 2:7-8) and by the emphasis of the salvation-historical preeminence of the Jerusalem churches over the Roman churches (cf., for example, Rom 15:25ff.).

2. For more detail on this group see Schottroff and Stegemann 1990.

3. Cf. Ebertz 1987, 10ff., 27ff.

4. Faber 1990, 135–38.

5. Cf. Schenke 1990, 73ff.

6. Rom 15:26; 2 Cor 8:4; 9:1, 12; cf. Acts 9:13, 32, 41; 26:10.

7. Cf. 1 Thess 2:14; 1 Cor 15:9; Gal 1:13; also Phil 3:6. See also section 9.1.

8. Cf. Roloff 1992, 1001; 1993, 82–83. Yet in the Synoptic tradition, *ekklēsia* is found only in Matt 16:18 and 18:17.

9. Cf. the term *qehal 'el* in 1QM 4:10; 1 QSa 1:25, "the saints of his people" (1QM 6:6), and "man or councillor of holiness" (1QS 5:18, 20); cf. also Roloff 1993, 82–83.

10. Cf. 1 Cor 15:5; Matt 28:16ff.; Luke 24:36ff.; John 20:19ff.

11. Cf. Holtz 1992, 878; Schenke 1990, 75; Roloff 1993, 36–37.

12. Cf. Roloff 1993, 83ff.; also the texts in Billerbeck 1961, 4:902–9, and 1QS 8:1ff.

13. Cf. W. Stegemann 1991, 91ff.

14. Ebertz 1987, 47.

15. Cf. esp. Scroggs 1975.

16. Gager 1975.

17. Cf. above all J. Smith 1978.

18. Cf. Gager 1975, 12; Holmberg 1990, 78.

19. This is the case especially in the studies by Mühlmann (1961) to which Gager refers.

20. Cf. M. Weber 1976.

21. Hengel 1968; Theissen 1991; J. H. Schütz 1979, 222–44; Holmberg 1978; Bendix 1985; Ebertz 1987; cf. Schluchter 1988, 197–260.

22. Kehrer 1990, 195–98.

23. Schluchter 1988, 535–36.

24. Ibid., 538.

25. Ibid.

26. Cf. Bendix 1985, 406–7.

27. Cf. Bendix 1964.

28. Roth 1987, 137ff.

29. Schluchter 1988, 549.

30. Cf. above all Lipp 1985.

31. Cf. Ebertz 1987, 19.

32. Ibid., 47.

33. Cf. Lipp 1985, 14.

34. The prehistories of Matthew and Luke shift the beginnings of Jesus' "charismatic career" back into childhood. This will be omitted here as presumably legendary.

35. Cf. Lidzbarski 1920, xviff.; Black 1982, 197ff.; Rudolph 1960, 112ff.; H. Stegemann 1993, 303–4; Kuhli 1992a.

36. J. Jeremias 1971, 53.

37. But cf. Goguel 1928, 66ff.; Ebertz 1987, 68ff. John 3:25ff. speaks of a quarrel between the Jews and the disciples of John.

38. Cf. Hoffmann 1972, 78–79; Luz 1990, 178–79.

39. Burchard 1987, 35.

40. Yet the lists of names in the Gospels are not identical. It is particularly striking that the tax collector Levi is not mentioned in Mark or Luke.

41. Cf. E. W. Stegemann 1986.

42. Cf. Hoffmann 1972, 251.

43. Cf. above all Hengel 1968, 18ff.

44. Roloff 1993, 39.

45. None of this is mentioned in the Gospels of Mark and Matthew. Only the Gospel of Luke expressly has the disciples also leave their wives, but it seems thereby to be adapting the followers of Jesus to the ideal of the nomadic Cynic philosophers.

46. In Matthew he is made a disciple (27:57).

47. For discussion of this aspect of the Jesus movement see, for example, Theissen 1989f; 1991, 106ff.; Schottroff and Stegemann 1990, 9ff.; W. Stegemann 1979, 94ff.; Burchard 1987, 12ff.

48. Cf. Luz 1990, 384–85.

49. Cf. Bauer et al. 1988, s.v.; Dalman 1967, 79; Bösen 1990, 125. Oakman (1992) calls him a "peasant artisan," a farmer who also practices a (perhaps bivocational) occupation as a craftsman.

50. Hengel 1973b, 34.

51. Cf. Dalman 1967, 79, and the tax decree of Diocletian VII (cf. Bücher 1922b, 210).

52. Cf. Dalman 1964, 7:361.

53. Versus Ebertz 1987, 77.

54. Cf. Theissen 1991, 111.

55. Fragment 33: Schneemelcher 1987, 137.

56. Thus, however, Kreissig 1970, 46.

57. Versus Herrenbrück 1990, 227 and elsewhere.

58. Cf. ibid., 89ff., 198ff., 229ff.

59. According to Herrenbrück the formulation "tax collectors and sinners" in Mark 2:15-16 is to be interpreted epexegetically as "sinful tax collectors" (1990, 228ff.).

60. Cf. the juxtaposition of the series in Herrenbrück 1990, 206.

61. On the history of interpretation cf. ibid., 3ff.

62. Cf. Gnilka 1978–79, 2:333.

63. Cf. Schottroff and Stegemann 1990, 102ff.

64. Cf. ibid., 58ff.

65. Mark 11:12: Jesus is hungry (epeinasen). From a distance he presumes the tree to have figs but confuses the green leaves with ripe fruit. The cursing of the tree would not be in earnest if one were to posit that Jesus had only forgotten to have breakfast in Bethany.

66. Cf. Mark 10:31; Luke 13:30; Matt 19:30; 20:16. On these verses see Schottroff and Stegemann 1990, 38ff.

67. Hengel 1973a, 35.

68. Hengel's interpretation (ibid., 36ff.) leans in this direction.

69. Versus, for example, Hengel 1973a, 34–35: Jesus and his disciples come from the middle class of artisans.

70. On the kingdom of God in Jesus and in early Judaism cf. Camponovo 1984; Merklein 1983; Burchard 1987, 20ff.; Hengel and Schwemer 1991.

71. That the appearance of the kingdom of God means the end of the devil and his dominion is expressly asserted by *As. Mos.* 10:1–2.

72. Cf. Burchard 1987, 29.

73. Cf. Camponovo 1984, 440–41. A connection with martyrdoms is made in *As. Mos.* 9–10.

74. Cf. W. Stegemann 1980, 114ff.

75. Thus, however, Roloff 1993, 35. Cf. in our spirit Crossan 1994, 362ff.

76. Burchard 1987, 23; Cf. Camponovo 1984.

77. Cf. Reiser 1990.

78. Cf. Roloff 1993, 37.

79. Cf. recently Cullmann 1994, 68ff.

80. Cf. Burchard 1987, 46.

81. Cf. Lührmann 1976.

82. Burchard 1987, 27.

83. Cf. Schüssler Fiorenza 1988, 162ff.

84. In our opinion, the prepolitical element in the Jesus movement is overestimated by R. A. Horsley 1989, 105ff.

85. Cf. E. P. Sanders 1985, 61ff.

86. Cf. Theissen 1989f, 83–84 and elsewhere.

87. In Luke there is also a redactional "Cynical interpretation"; cf. W. Stegemann 1979, 94–120. Contra Crossan, who holds Jesus to be a "peasant Jewish Cynic" (1994, 553) and the influence of Greek Cynicism on him to be possible.

88. Cf. Merklein 1987, 13–32.

89. Cf. E. P. Sanders 1985, 212ff.

90. Cf. Schottroff and Stegemann 1979, 58–70.

91. Cf. Burchard 1987, 46–47.

92. Ibid., 46.

93. Cf. ibid., 50–51.

94. Cf., for example, Mathys 1986.

95. Cf. Reinbold 1994.

96. The question of how the number twelve is to be reestablished after the departure of the betrayer Judas, which is raised by the Gospel stories, is answered by Luke: the circle of twelve is restored by Peter on the basis of the election of Matthias through God's decision in Acts 1:15-26.

97. Yet in the Synoptic Gospels this is only presupposed (cf., however, John 21:18-19).

98. Cf. Roloff 1993, 77.

99. Cf. ibid., 78.

100. Cf. ibid., 76.

101. Cf. ibid., 80; Burchard 1983, 600.

102. According to Acts 12:6-18 Peter escapes prison only through a miracle.

103. Cf. Hengel 1985, 71–104.

104. Cf. Colpe 1993.

105. Cf. Roloff 1993, 72–73.

106. Cf., however, ibid., 71.

107. At best, one can perhaps speak of the celebratory gatherings in the Qumran community, which regarded the Jerusalem temple cult as illegitimate, as its own services of worship.

108. Cf. E. Stegemann 1990b.

109. Cf. Roloff 1993, 70–71.

110. Cf. E. Stegemann 1990b.

111. Cf. Vielhauer 1975, 9ff.

112. Cf. Kramer 1963.

113. Colpe 1993.

114. Cf. Georgi 1965; Betz 1993.

115. Apparently the Apostolic Council, at which Paul commits himself to solidarity with the poor, coincided with this sabbath year (47–48 C.E.), which followed the famine.

116. Cf. Colpe 1993.

117. Cf. Löning 1987, 81–82; Schenke 1990, 78ff.

Notes to Chapter 8

1. P. Schäfer 1983, 145.

2. Cf. Stemberger 1979.

3. P. Schäfer 1983, 145.

4. Cf. comprehensively Urbach 1987; also H.-J. Becker 1990, 17ff.

5. Neusner 1970, 166ff.

6. Ibid., 196–99; Neusner 1981, 2:94ff.; see also Urbach 1968, 48–74.

7. Segal 1986, 117.

8. P. Schäfer 1979, 43–101; Stemberger 1979, 54ff.

9. S. Cohen 1984, 27–53.

10. Overman 1990, 43.

11. See only ibid., 43ff.

12. Moore 1954; cf. also Neusner 1979, 3–43.

13. Thus also Overman 1990, 56.

14. We speak here of "Christ-confessing Jews" or "messianic Jews" and not of "Jewish Christians," a term that is problematic in many respects. On the semantics and problems of the term "Jewish Christian" see Colpe 1990, 38ff.

15. For details cf. Overman 1990, 141ff.

16. Cf. Strecker 1971.

17. Cf., for example, Luz 1985, 62ff.

18. Cf. Gnilka 1988, 514–15; also Zumstein 1980, 122–38; Kingsbury 1986, 121. Luz 1985, 73ff., is more careful in regard to Antioch, but "certainly [the place of origin] was a large Syrian city, whose lingua franca was Greek" (75).

19. Cf. H.-J. Becker 1990.

20. Cf., for example, Goulder 1974; Viviano 1979 (Caesarea maritima); Künzel 1978, 251 (suggests Caesarea Philippi); Beare 1982 (including the neighboring northern areas); Overman 1990; for older supporters of this localization cf. Kümmel 1973, 90.

21. Overman 1990, 158–59.

22. Ibid., 152.

23. Ibid., 153.

24. See only ibid., 154.

25. Ibid., 158.

26. Saldarini 1991, 38ff. Similar positions in the same anthology: Segal 1991, 3ff. Cf. also Wire 1991, 87–121. Here it is a question of an extension of the older discussion of the question whether the Matthean community still belonged to the synagogal association (thus, for example, G. Bornkamm) or already stood outside it and was dominated by Gentile Christians.

27. Saldarini 1991, 57.

28. Ibid., 56–57.

29. Ibid., 57.

30. Ibid., 59.

31. Ibid., 60–61.

32. Ibid., 43.

33. On the critique of the Matthean community as a Jewish sect see Gundry 1991, 62–67; cf. also some critical comments by Kingsbury 1991, 259–69.

34. Luz 1985, 66.

35. Cf. Hengel 1993.

36. J. T. Sanders 1993, 40.

37. Brown 1979.

38. Wengst 1992, 157–79. Schenke 1992, 126, believes that Gaulanitis and Batanea were "the original home of the 'Johannine group.'"

39. See, for example, Meeks 1975, 94–104; Segal 1986, 156; J. T. Sanders 1993, 41ff. Schenke also presupposes that the Johannine community was overwhelmingly composed of Christ-confessing Jews, as well as Samaritans and Gentile Christians. Yet as the milieu of the Gospel he prefers a "Hellenistic Judaism that did not have its center in Palestine and Jerusalem": Schenke 1992, 116–18.

40. J. T. Sanders 1993, 41ff.

41. Schenke 1992, 120, is also of the "opinion that the parts of the Gospel of John that present Jesus' disagreement with 'the' Jews had as their real background the controversial theological debates and trials that the 'Johannine' group had with the Judaism of their surroundings."

42. J. T. Sanders 1993, 41.

43. Martyn 1979, 116–18, calls them "secret believers" and Brown 1979, 169, "crypto-Christians"; cf. Wengst 1992, 137ff.

44. Cf. Bittner 1987; E. Stegemann 1989; 1990b.

45. On the problem of this linguistic usage see, for example, Wengst 1992.

46. Jesus speaks here to Jews who *had* believed in him (*pepisteukotas!*): John 8:31.

47. Cf. E. W. Stegemann 1985.

48. Cf. Chapter 12.

49. Matt 10:29; 13:44; 14:15; 19:21; 21:12; 22:5; 25:9-10; 27:7. Matt 13:45-46 does not shrink from comparing the kingdom of heaven with a merchant (*emporos*) in search of fine pearls, who finds one of great price and sells everything in order to possess it.

50. Presumably similar is the parable of the virgins (Matt 25:1ff.).

51. Especially unusual is the combination "Pharisees and Sadducees": Matt 3:7; 16:1, 6, 11-12.

52. Yet in an unusual verbal formulation; cf. also p. 201 .

53. Cf., for example, Stuhlmacher 1982, 289: "If we take Matt. 11:2-6 together with 5:3ff., we can see that the evangelist does not simply spiritualize Jesus' devotion to the poor in the first beatitude, but rather, with a view to Jesus' work, clarifies it in terms of scripture and tradition."

54. Matt 5:46-47; 9:10–11; 10:3; 11:19; 18:17; 21:31-32.

55. Matt 3:14; 5:25.

56. Matt 8:5, 8, 13; 27:54.

57. Matt 26:58; 27:65, 66; 28:11.

58. Matt 8:9; 10:24-25; 13:27, 28; 18:23, 26, 27, 28, 32; 20:27; 21:34ff.; 22:3ff.; 24:45ff.; 25:14, 19, 21, 23, 30; 26:51; *pais*: 8:6, 8, 13; 12:18; 14:2; 17:18.

59. See also pp. 383–84.

60. The anointing oil with which Jesus is anointed in her house has a value of three hundred denarii (John 12:5). This sum, however, probably has mainly symbolic meaning.

61. Justin *Apol.* 1.31; J. T. Sanders 1993, 49ff., also evaluates Justin's *Dialogue with Trypho* with regard to the situation of "Jewish Christians" in Israel.

62. Cf. Kippenberg and Wevers 1979, 200–201. See also a further text from the Babylonian Talmud (*Abod. Zar.* 6a), in which Rabbi Yishmael (d. ca. 135) forbids trade with the "Nazarenes"; cf. Kippenberg and Wevers 1979, 204.

63. Cf. Billerbeck 1961, 4:332.

64. Translations according to Osten-Sacken 1984, 213–14.

65. Overman 1990, 54.

66. Maier 1982, 140–41; Kuhn 1950; P. Schäfer 1975, 54ff., 116ff.; Stemberger 1977, 14ff.

67. Justin *Dial.* 16; Schiffman 1985, 60.

68. J. T. Sanders 1993, 59; Kimelman 1981, 226–44.

69. P. Schäfer 1983, 154.

70. Schiffman 1985, 60.

71. Colpe 1990, 86; with reference to Schiffmann 1981, 115–56.

72. Schiffman 1985, 61.

73. Schenke 1988, 40.

74. Ibid., 41; the most important text in Josephus is *War* 2.461ff.; cf. also Theissen 1989a, 282–83.

75. Justin *Apol.* 1.31.6.

76. Here too we can probably presuppose the so-called heretic benediction of the twelfth of the Eighteen Benedictions.

77. Cf. Hare 1967, 118–19.

78. Thus Lohmeyer 1958, 95. Versus Hare 1967, 119.

79. Matt 5:10-12, 44; 10:23; 13:21; 23:34.

80. Cf. Hare 1967, 99ff.

81. On the extremely uncertain tradition about cases of killing see Hare 1967, 20ff.

82. Thus also Wengst 1992, 52, in addition to many others.

83. See ibid., 53.

84. Thus ibid., 58–59.

85. Thus also Segal 1991, 34: "This is not the same action as the curse."

86. Thus Overman 1990, 54, in adoption of a thesis of M. Smith.

87. Cf. also Wengst 1992, 57, who, however, expounds the problems of the "secret sympathizers" of the Christian churches in the context of the *birkat ha-minim.*

88. On this translation of *latreia* see Strathmann 1942, 65. [The NRSV reads ". . . are offering worship to God." It is slightly altered here because of the German.—Trans.]

89. Cf. Schnackenburg 1982, 139; see also Haacker 1975, 10; on the model of Phinehas, the violent elimination of the apostates can be understood as "sacrifice of atonement"; cf. Billerbeck 1961, 2:565.

90. Hare 1967, 41, rightly asks whether this formulation corresponds to the recognizable tendency of the New Testament to exaggerate in regard to the killing of confessors of Christ. Here we must take into account, rather, the possibility that corresponding expressions are perhaps presented as deeds. In this sense, one could compare this formulation of the Gospel of John with corresponding comments in Justin. For this very reason, it seems to us that the reference to Justin (or *Mart. Pol.* 13.1) in Schnackenburg 1982 (on this passage) is insufficient as possible proof of the historicity of such killings.

91. Thus, however, Martyn 1979, 64ff.

92. Thus correctly Wengst 1992, 51–52.

93. Thus Wengst (ibid.), whereas Hare 1967, 41, holds that we have here a reflection "of Jewish declarations that Christians *ought* to be lynched."

94. Wengst 1992 (ibid.) takes this into account on the basis of his thesis of the location of the Johannine community in Trachonitis or Batanea and the thesis of the Pharisaically occupied Jewish "authorities" there. The same would, in principle, also be true of other Palestinian regions.

95. Cf. E. Stegemann 1989, 116–17.

96. On both texts see also J. T. Sanders 1993, 61ff.

97. Meyers 1988.

98. Yet we believe that Klauck 1985, 198, goes too far: he speaks of "massive external pressure," "economic disadvantages," "the breaking off of social intercourse and trade relations," and "occupational prohibition."

99. Cf. the experiences of Paul in 2 Cor 11:24.

100. Scroggs 1975.

101. Cf. Donaldson 1981; cf. also Esler 1987, 46ff. For Matthew see Overman 1990.

102. Cf. Troeltsch 1977, 364ff. (n. 164).

103. Wilson 1982; 1973.

104. Wilson 1982, 91–92. Yet we should note that Troeltsch, for his part, also discussed the alienation of sects from the world.

105. Wilson 1973, 17, 31.

106. Cf. ibid., 18–26.

107. Johnson 1963.

108. Saldarini 1991, 38ff.; Malina and Neyrey 1991, 97–122; J. T. Sanders 1993, 129ff.

109. H. Becker 1963; Erikson 1966; Ben-Yehuda 1985. For additional literature see Saldarini 1991, 44–45.

110. J. T. Sanders 1993, 130ff.

111. H. Becker 1963, 8–9.

112. Ibid., 131.

113. Ben-Yehuda 1985, 19–20.

114. Saldarini 1991, 47.

115. Ibid., 48ff., applies deviance theories in an extremely differentiated way to the Matthean community.

116. Urbach 1987, 1:594–95.

117. J. T. Sanders 1993, 140.

118. "The thesis developed throughout this study is that the men who stand behind Mishnah-Tosefta were in the process of constructing an Israelite ethnic identity in order to differentiate the Israelites from the gentiles who also populated the Land of Israel": Porton 1988, 1.

119. J. T. Sanders 1993, 141.

120. Thus cogently Saldarini 1991, 60.

Notes to Part Three, Introduction

1. Cf. Kosellek 1979, 211–59.

2. Yet this distinction is hardly expressed in the conceptual designation *ekklēsia* (instead of synagogue) for the Christ-confessing communities—thus, correctly, Berger 1976, 184ff. In Jas 2:2 we find *synagōgos* for the Christ-confessing assembly.

3. The Pauline formulation *Israel of God* (Gal 6:16) could mean Israel itself or the community of God in Judea, that is, the early church; cf. E. Stegemann 1994, 62. Cf. also 1 Pet 2:9, where the honorary title for Israel is transferred to the churches; similarly Heb 3:1; 8:7ff.

4. For the Pauline churches, Theissen 1988, 182, assumes the "stage of a typical sect formation." Thus also Watson, who understands the formation of the Pauline churches as a conscious separation from Judaism (1986, 19, 45, 68); cf. Segal 1990, 271; versus Meeks 1985, 106, and the following note.

5. Cf. Hultgren 1991, 92.

6. In the fellowship of believers in Christ, according to the Letter to the Ephesians (2:11ff.), a difference between Gentiles (*ethnē*) and Israel, uncircumcised and circumcised, in relation to God has been abolished. The "dividing wall" between Jews and Gentiles has been torn down.

7. Cf. E. W. Stegemann 1994, 60ff.

8. Cf. Acts 13:44-48; 18:5-7; 19:8-9; 28:23-28. In the synagogues themselves, in which Paul spent only a few days, there was not yet anything like a Christ-confessing community. Luke also tells nothing about the behavior or the situation of those in the synagogues who had already converted. The act of withdrawal is thus not an act of separation through the exclusion of the Christ-confessing group, which itself leaves the synagogue, nor a self-exclusion of the *ekklēsia* already existing in the synagogues. Not until after the exodus of the preachers and their few followers was the Christ-confessing church established among the Gentiles. The process is described rather clearly in Acts 19:8-9.

9. Acts 11:26; 26:28; 1 Pet 4:16; Ign. *Eph.* 11.2; *Magn.* 4; and elsewhere; outside of the Christian tradition first in Pliny *Ep.* 10.96 (*christiani*) and Tacitus *Ann.* 15.44 (*chrestiani*).

10. Cf. only G. Schneider 1992.

11. Nevertheless, we must remember that the edges were still blurry; that is, the boundaries between the Jewish and Christian communities were still not delineated in a definitive way. Contributing particularly to this blurriness were probably individual Christ-confessing Jews and especially God-fearers who moved from synagogue to Christian community. On this problem see L. M. White 1991, 211–47.

12. Brief information is found in Lang 1991; more detail in Schürer 1973–87, 3/1:1–176; Tcherikover 1961; Hengel 1976b; Smallwood 1976; Kraabel 1979; Meeks 1983, 34ff.; for Asia Minor see Trebilco 1991.

13. For literature see Chapter 6, n. 13; see also Schrage 1964; Frankemölle 1992; S. Safrai 1976c.

14. See only Lang 1991, 420; Meeks 1983, 34.

15. Smallwood 1976, 222.

16. Tcherikover 1961, 293.

17. Smallwood 1976, 125–26.

18. Vittinghoff 1990, 263; Applebaum 1976b, 701–27; cf. also Meeks 1983, 39.

19. Meeks 1983, 39.

20. Cf. p. 130 .

21. Trebilco, 1991, 173. Egypt was probably an exception: see the evidence and literature in Trebilco 1991, 259 (n. 28).

22. Cf. Hengel 1971, 172.

23. Siegert 1973; Simon 1981; Wander 1994, 173ff.

24. Acts 10:2, 22; 13:16, 26; 13:50; 16:14; 17:4, 17; 18:7; cf. Jos. *Ant.* 14.110; cf. 20.34ff.

25. Jos. *Ant.* 20.195; inscriptions: one comes from Pantikapeon (northern coast of the Black Sea) from the first century C.E. (Corpus Inscriptorum Regni Bosporani no. 71=*CII*, 2d ed., 683a); an inscription for the year 210 C.E. from Aphrodisias is published in Reynolds and Tannenbaum 1987.

26. Cf. also Trebilco 1991, 145ff.

27. Cf. only Kraabel 1981; 1982; 1986. A balanced and convincing countercritique is found in Gager 1986.

28. Trebilco 1991, 152–53; Wander 1994, 178–79.

29. Acts 13:16, 26; 15:21; 16:1; 17:4, 17. Cf. also Jos. *War* 7.45; *Exod. Rab.* 30.9; Juvenal *Sat.* 14.96ff.

30. Acts 10:22; cf. Luke 1:6; 2:25; 23:47.

31. Cf. Acts 10:28; 11:3; see also pp. 269–71.

32. *Meg. Ta'an* 1.11: though a God-fearer, Antonius is uncircumcised and thus not permitted to participate in the Passover meal. Cf. Siegert 1973, 116ff.; esp. 117–18.

33. Acts 10:1-2; cf. Luke 7:4-5; cf. also Jos. *Ant.* 14.110.

34. Siegert 1973, 147ff.

35. Acts 13:50; 16:14; 17:4, 12. Jos. *War* 2.560 (almost all women of Damascus); *Ant.* 20.34–48 (here, however, proselyte women); *Deut. Rab.* 2.24 (the wife of a Roman senator).

36. Trebilco 1991, 177: the women of Jewish communities are the clearest example of local political influence; cf. also Kraemer 1992, 106.

37. Trebilco 1991, 59.

38. Jos. *Ant.* 20:34ff.; see also *Ant.* 18:65–84 (Fulvia, a proselyte); Domitilla (a niece of Domitian) may have been a God-fearer or proselyte (but hardly a Christian): Dio Cassius 67.14.

39. Cf. only Frankemölle 1992, 705.

40. Cf. only Hengel 1971, 169ff.

41. The last is presumed, but not certain, in Acts 16:13, 16. Hengel 1971, 175, assumes a synagogue building outside the city of Philippi.

42. Cf. only Hengel 1971, 167–68, and further literature there.

43. Cf. ibid., for example, for arranging employment. On the functions of the synagogue cf. Schrage 1964, 820ff.

44. Applebaum 1974a.

45. The expression goes back to Tertullian *Apol.* 21.1. Smallwood 1976, 135, speaks of the privileges having the *effect* of a *religio licita*. Against the interpretation of Roman privileges in the sense of *religio licita* are, for example, Rajak 1984; Trebilco 1991, 8–9.

46. See only Tcherikover 1961, 301ff.; Smallwood 1976, 120ff.

47. Jos. *Ant.* 16.162–65, 169, 172; 14.190ff.

48. Trebilco 1991, 12ff.

49. Jos. *Ant.* 14.235, 259–61.

50. See the examples from Alexandria and Antioch discussed on pp. 334–35.

51. Smallwood 1976, 226: "the standard political organization of all Jewish communities of any size in the East." Versus, for example, Trebilco 1991, 171.

52. Cf. on interpretation Tcherikover 1961, 296ff.; Smallwood 1976, 139, 225–26, 359–64; Trebilco 1991, 170; Meeks 1983, 36.

53. Cf. Applebaum 1974b, 473ff.

54. Ibid., 477ff.

55. Ibid., 486ff.

56. Trebilco 1991, 257 (n. 14).

57. Hengel 1971, 182–83.

58. Ibid.

59. Cf., comprehensively, Leon 1960, 167–94. A contrary opinion is found in Applebaum 1974b, 502.

60. Smallwood 1976, 134–35. For Rome see Jos. *Ant.* 14.213–16; for Asia, 14.241–46, 256–64.

61. Smallwood 1976, 133.

62. Applebaum 1974b, 491.

63. Ibid., 492–93; Brooten 1982, 5–33; S. Safrai 1976c, 934–35; Trebilco 1991, 104–5.

64. Applebaum 1974b, 497–98.

65. Brooten 1982; Kraemer 1992, 117–18.

66. Cf. S. Safrai 1976c, 921.

67. Cf. Kraemer 1992, 97, Wegner 1988, 158.

68. S. Safrai 1976c, 918.

69. Jos. *Ant.* 14.260; *m. Ber.* 3.3; *b. 'Abod. Zar.* 38b–39a; Acts 16:13; 17:4; and elsewhere; cf. S. Safrai 1976c, 919–20.

70. Brooten 1982, 103–38; Trebilco 1991, 41, 207 (n. 15), 232 (n. 44); Kraemer 1992, 106–7.

71. S. Safrai 1976c, 933.

Notes to Chapter 9

1. The translation "church" seems to us to be not very meaningful, since in modern linguistic usage it can lead to many false connotations. For example, the idea of the church as a building for worshipful assembly has nothing to do with the New Testament *ekklēsia*.

2. Cf. Schmidt 1938, 506.

3. For example, Rom 16:16; 1 Cor 1:2; 4:17; 10:32; 2 Cor 8:1; Gal 1:13; Phil 3:6; 1 Thess 2:14; Philemon 2.

4. Cf. Roloff 1992, 998–1011. The semantics of the New Testament usage of the word are to be explained either on the basis of Old Testament tradition (the *assembly,* the contingent of God) or more specifically on the basis of the Qumran writings, which give an eschatological sense to this terminology: "the eschatological contingent of God, the host of people whom God calls into his service in connection with the eschatological events": Roloff 1993, 83.

5. Stendahl 1959, 1298.

6. The general linguistic usage is either excluded for the New Testament as irrelevant explanation—thus, for example, Stendahl 1959, 1298—or at least regarded as unimportant: for example, Roloff 1993, 83: "This component may, to be sure, also be involved in the earliest Christian language usage. . . ."

7. Brandis 1905, 2163–2200.

8. Berger 1976, 167–207.

9. Cf. only Schrage 1963, 189; see also Banks 1980, 35–37.

10. Cf. briefly Banks 1980, 34–35. This linguistic usage is also found in Greek-speaking Judaism; cf. only Philo *Spec. Leg.* 2.44; Jos. *Ant.* 4.309; *Life* 268; *War* 1.654, 666.

11. For the Septuagint see Deut 4:10; 9:10; 1 Chron 6:3; Ps 106:32; also in the Hebrew Bible *qahal* first means the actual assembly of Israel or of certain groups in Israel: Campbell 1948, 133; cf. Banks 1980, 34–35.

12. 1 Cor 11:17-18, 20; 14:4-5, 12, 19, 23, 28, 34-35; and Acts 11:26; 14:27 (cf. Heb 2:12; 12:23).

13. O'Brien 1993, 124–25.

14. On the older scholarly opinion see only Stendahl 1959, 1298.

15. 1 Cor 1:1; 2 Cor 1:1; cf. 1 Cor 10:32; 11:22; Rom 16:16.

16. Cf. only Deut 4:10; 9:10; 18:16; 31:30; Judg 20:2. Contra, for example, Schrage 1963, 180ff.

17. 1 Cor 1:1; 2 Cor 1:1; Gal 1:1; 1 Thess 1:1.

18. Klauck 1994, 290: "In a city like Corinth, when newly won Christians hear *ekklēsia*, they are reminded of their political heritage, because for them *ekklēsia* means first of all the assembly of the free voting citizens of a community."

19. This aspect is emphasized by Roloff 1993, 98: "in Christ" (1 Thess 2:14; Gal 1:22).

20. Acts 8:1, 3; 9:31; 11:22; 20:17; 1 Cor 11:16, 22; 15:9; Gal 1:13; Phil 3:6; 1 Tim 3:5; and elsewhere; cf. Berger 1976, 187ff.

21. Cf. only 1 Cor 1:2—parallel to *ekklēsia*.

22. The term *synagōgē* ("synagogue") can also mean "assembly" and "congregation," as well as—esp. in the New Testament—the building in which the assembly takes place. Yet in the extracanonical linguistic usage of the Diaspora, the usual Greek word for the synagogue as a building is the term *proseuchē* ("place of prayer").

23. That can be inferred from Pliny's famous letter to the emperor Trajan regarding the trials of Christians (*Ep.* 10.96).

24. Cf. Meeks 1983, 40ff.

25. For more detail on Luke 14 cf. Rohrbaugh 1991, 137ff.

26. Oakman 1991b, 176–77; his thesis is: "Luke's community probably resides in a large town or city somewhere in the Roman Empire" (177).

27. Cf. only Meeks 1983, 42–43.

28. Ibid., 199, n. 10.

29. Meeks 1983, 14–15 (in adoption of MacMullen 1974), probably regards too strictly the delineation between city and country; critical of Meeks is, for example, Rohrbaugh 1991, 127–29.

30. Dyson 1989, 143–46; Greene 1986, esp. 98–141.

31. Osborne 1987.

32. Mack 1988, 81–83; D. S. Smith and H. Taussig 1990, 21–35.

33. Cf. in detail Klauck 1982.

34. Douglas 1971, 61–81; Douglas and Nicod 1974, 744–47; Feeley-Harnik 1981, 6–23.

35. Neyrey 1991, 363.

36. Y. A. Cohen 1968, 508.

37. Douglas 1971, 61; cf. Crossan 1994, 451.

38. On the question of the fellowship of Jews with Gentiles see E. P. Sanders 1990, 170–88.

39. Cf. Dunn 1983, 23; for the social relations of Jews in the Gentile world in general, see also Rajak 1985, 247–62.

40. The *Letter of Aristeas* describes a general meal of Jews with a Gentile king, yet it is clear that the food consumed was Jewish (*Ep. Aris.* 181ff.).

41. Dan 1:3-17; 2 Macc 7:1-2; 3 Macc 3:4, 7; Jdt 10:5; 12:17-19; Tob 1:11; and elsewhere.

42. Cf. *Jub.* 22:16 and *Jos. As.* 7:1; also E. P. Sanders 1990, 177.

43. Dunn 1983, 14.

44. The term *ioudaizein*, however, could also mean that Paul logically expected from Peter the requirement of circumcision for Gentile Christians: E. W. Stegemann 1994, 58 and n. 18 on p. 68.

45. E. W. Stegemann 1994, 58.

46. Juvenal *Sat.* 14.96ff.: the God-fearer eats no pork.

47. Yet according to *Meg. Ta'an.* 1.11 an uncircumcised sympathizer of Judaism cannot participate in the paschal meal.

48. Cf. Esler 1987, 78–80.

49. E. P. Sanders 1990, 186.

50. Schluchter 1985, 12.

51. Yet according to Acts 15:19, for example, the many individual commandments of the Torah represent a burden.

52. On this process cf. M. Weber 1920, 3:349.

53. Meeks 1983, 99; cf. in detail Walter 1979, 425–36. Cf. also the separation from nonbelievers in 2 Cor 6:14ff.

54. Murphy-O'Conner 1983, 161–70.

55. Theissen 1989e.

56. A good overview is offered by Meeks 1983, 74ff.; cf. Judge 1979, 131–64; Wilken 1979, 165–93; Malherbe 1977, 87–91. On *communitas* cf. Sampley 1980. On the popular political assembly see above all Berger 1976; cf. also Klauck 1994, 288–91; Cotter 1994, 369–72.

57. Gager 1979a, 88–130; cf. also pp. 192.

58. Scroggs 1975; cf. pp. 191–92 and 242–43.

59. Stark 1986, 216–25.

60. Meeks 1983, 74.

61. Wilken 1979, 187.

62. On both accusations see pp. 323.

63. Schäfke 1979, 605ff.

64. See pp. 319–20, 323–24.

65. Brandis 1905, 2163.

66. In the New Testament cf. Acts 19:32, 39, 41.

67. Redfield 1993, 193.

68. Brandis 1905, 2172.

69. Ibid., 2173.

70. Ibid., 2187.

71. Ibid., 2191.

72. Schmidt 1938, 518.

73. Cf. also Merklein 1987, 313–14.

74. Berger 1976, 178.

75. Acts 12:5, 12; Rom 15:30; 1 Cor 7:5; 11:4-5; 14:13–15; 1 Thess 5:17; Col 4:2; Philemon 22.

76. 1 Cor 14:26, 35.

77. 1 Cor 4:17; 7:17; 14:19, 28, 34-35; 1 Tim 2:12.

78. Cf. Berger 1976, 178–79.

79. 1 Thess 4:18; 5:11; Rom 15:14.

80. Acts 14:23; 15:4, 22; 20:17; Jas 5:14.

81. Berger 1976, 182–83.

82. 1 Cor 14:26; Col 3:16-17; Eph 5:18-20.

83. 1 Cor 14:3-5, 12, 17, 26; 1 Thess 5:11; Eph 4:11-16.

84. Cf. only 1 Cor 16:19; Rom 16:5; Philemon 2; Col 4:15; Acts 16:15, 31-34.

85. Rordorf 1964, 110-28.

86. 1 Cor 1:12-13, 16; Rom 16:23.

87. Meeks 1983, 55.

88. Cf. the list of names in Theissen 1989d, 255–56.

89. Banks 1980, 41–42.

90. Murphy-O'Conner 1983, 156.

91. Acts 20:7: on the first day of the week; the context suggests that the meaning is Saturday evening (after sunset). According to Pliny *Ep.* 10.96, Christians gathered on a certain day before sunrise. According to Justin *Apol.* 1.67 (cf. *Barn.* 15.9; Ign. *Magn.* 9.1) that day was Sunday.

92. Banks 1980, 41.

93. Cf. only 1 Cor 1:16; 11:22, 34; 14:35; 16:15, 19; Phil 4:22; Rom 16:5; Philemon 2; Col 4:15; 1 Tim 3:4-5, 12; 5:4, 13; 2 Tim 1:16; 3:6; 4:19; Titus 1:11; Acts 16:15, 31-34.

94. Gülzow 1974, 198. On households and house churches cf. Klauck 1981.

95. Wolter 1993, 249.

96. Cf. 2 Tim 2:20-21.

97. Implicitly in 1 Tim 5:8. God as master of the house (*despotēs*) in 2 Tim 2:21.

98. On the household metaphor in the Lukan double volume cf. Elliott 1991, 224ff.

99. Also in 2 Tim 2:19-22 the ancient ideas of the leadership of a household form the background of the instructions for church leaders. Certainly, here are the beginnings of an "institutionalization" of the understanding of the church, according to Roloff 1993, 259–60.

100. As text examples see, for example: 1 Thess 1:4, 6; 2:7-8, 17; 5:13, 26; Phil 2:25ff.; 4:10-11; cf. Meeks 1983, 85–86; Banks 1980, 56–57.

101. The use of family terms can also be found in many pagan associations and cultic communities, as well as in Judaism; cf. only Meeks 1983, 87, and Banks 1980, 59–60.

102. Love of neighbor: Gal 5:14; Rom 13:9; Mark 12:31 par.; Matt 5:43; 19:19; Jas 2:8. Brotherly love: 1 Thess 4:9; cf. 3:12 and Rom 12:10; Heb 13:1; 1 Pet 1:22; 3:8; 2 Pet 1:7; on the latter see Klauck 1990, 144–56; on love of neighbor see W. Stegemann 1987a.

103. Cf. also Luke 7:34; 12:4; Titus 3:15.

104. W. Stegemann 1987a, 71.

105. Rom 12:13; 15:7(?); 16:2, 23; Philemon 22; Acts 10:6, 18, 23, 32; 16:15; 17:20-21; 28:7; 1 Tim 5:10; 1 Pet 4:9; Heb 13:2; cf. Matt 25:35ff.

106. 1 Tim 2:1—6:2; Titus 2:1-10; 1 Pet 5:1-5; cf. also the so-called household rules for the living of a Christian life (Col 3:18—4:1; Eph 5:21—6:9; also similar is 1 Pet 2:13—3:7).

107. Cf., for example, 1 Cor 15:58; Rom 15:14; Phil 3:1; 4:1; Eph 6:10; cf. also Banks 1980, 55ff.

108. Cf. Peterson 1985, 93ff.

109. Titus 2:1ff. and 1 Pet 2:18ff. presuppose non-Christian households.

110. Wolter 1993, 208.

111. Thus, correctly, ibid., 233ff.

112. Ibid., 248.

113. Meeks 1983, 76.

114. Cf. 2 Corinthians 8; 9; 1 Cor 16:2.

115. Cf. Eph 4:11: apostles, prophets, evangelists, pastors, and teachers.

116. Meeks 1983, 76, calls attention to this.

117. Cf. also the image of the church as a building in 2 Tim 2:19-22.

118. Yet the term *episkopos* ("overseer"), also used for the community leader (1 Tim 3:2; Titus 1:7; cf. 1 Pet 2:25; Acts 20:28; Phil 1:1), is not a typical term from the realm of the ancient household. It may designate duties of service and stewardship (particularly in financial matters) and is used both in organizations and for the temple president or head of the synagogue. Cf. only Roloff 1989, 172–73.

119. 1 Tim 2:8-15; 5:1ff.; 6:1-2; Titus 2:1ff. On the specific instructions for women see pp. 402–403.

120. Meeks 1983, 77; cf. also 68–71.

121. Waltzing 1968; there is a brief overview in Vittinghoff 1990, 208ff.

122. Vittinghoff 1990, 210; Ausbüttel 1982, 49ff.

123. Vittinghoff 1990, 211.

124. Ibid.

125. Meeks 1983, 79.

126. Stambaugh 1988, 210; Meeks 1983, 77; Corley 1993, 18.

127. Pliny *Ep.* 10.96: *hetaeria;* cf. Tertullian *Apol.* 38–39: *factio, corpus, curia, coitio.*

128. Heinrici 1876, 464–526; Wilken 1979, 165–93; Malherbe 1977, 87–91.

129. Meeks 1983, 78.

130. Meeks (ibid., 169) posits that only *episkopos* represents an analogy to the *collegia.*

131. On the community meal as ceremony, see in detail Neyrey 1991, 361ff.

132. Stambaugh 1988, 206.

133. Yet the Emmaus disciples do not, as is often assumed, recognize Jesus by this rite.

Rather, during the meal their eyes, which earlier were kept by supernatural power from recognizing him, were opened.

134. Theissen 1989c, 299.

135. For details see Theissen 1989c; Murphy-O'Conner 1983, 158–61.

136. Different foods: Pliny *Ep.* 2.6; Martial *Epigr.* 3.60; 4.85; Murphy-O'Conner 1983, 159–60; Theissen 1989c, 300ff.

137. There do not necessarily have to be differences between strata—between rich (upper stratum) and poor (lower stratum)—cf. p. 295.

138. D. S. Smith 1980.

139. Cf. Meeks 1983, 74.

140. In a certain sense this view is expressed in a modern sociological analysis that tries to distinguish early Christianity (after the death of Jesus) as a new "cult" from the followers of Jesus as a "sect": Stark 1986.

141. Elliott 1993, 130–31.

142. See only 1 Thess 4:12; 1 Cor 5:12-13; Col 4:5.

143. Brief definitions of a *faction* and a *social movement* are in Elliott 1993, 129, 132. Cf. also, for example, Gager's comments on the catchphrase *millenium movement:* Gager 1979a.

144. So strange is the definition of *sect* by Wilson 1973; 1982.

145. Versus Scroggs 1975, for early Christianity as a whole; for the Pauline churches: Watson 1986, esp. 104–5. For 1 Peter: Elliot 1981.

146. The Lukan community is a minority group that one enters through conscious conversion; its leadership seems to be rather charismatic. The author therefore tries to see the Christ-confessing community in a specific relationship to Judaism when, for example, he reduces it positively to the "way" (*hodos:* Acts 9:2; 16:17; 19:9, 23; 22:4; 24:14, 22) or negatively and from the outside as "sect" (*hairesis:* Acts 24:5, 14; 28:22). Both terms are related to Judaism as the parent body. That is, both in the self-understanding of the churches—at least of Luke's community—and also in the outsiders' view of Christians from the perspective of the pagan populations, their leaders, and also members of Diaspora Judaism, the *ekklēsia* appears to be connected somehow with Judaism. Nevertheless, it is always clear to Luke himself as well as to the representatives of Judaism that the church is different from Judaism empirically and in terms of its symbolic system. The Lukan community is understood as "sect" by Esler 1987, 46ff.; Bovon 1985, 128ff.; critical of this is W. Stegemann 1991, 21ff.; J. T. Sanders 1993, 114ff.

147. We base our comments here on the cogent comments of Malina 1986, 92–101.

148. Cf. ibid., 95.

149. Paul avoids the term *people* for the Christ-confessing community. The few New Testament passages are probably not significant (Acts 15:14; 1 Pet 2:9).

150. In the second century then also that of a fictive people or race (*tertium genus*).

151. This is true, although the Christ-confessing assemblies in New Testament times probably took place mostly in private houses, to the extent that localization in the home can be inferred. For the places of assembly generally replicate the institutional character of the group (cf. Malina 1986, 99). Yet we cannot exclude the possibility

that public places of assembly were also used (cf. Acts 19:9 and above all Pliny *Ep.* 10.96). Moreover, it is evident that the *ekklēsia* was basically accessible to the public (cf. only James 2 and 1 Corinthians 14). See also Cotter 1994, 369ff.

152. 1 Cor 12:12ff.; Rom 12:4ff.; cf. Col 1:18-20; Eph 1:22-23.

153. Cf. only Conzelmann 1969, 248–49.

Notes to Chapter 10

1. At this point we will not go into the details of the history of research. An overview of the most important contributions to the problem through the beginning of the 1970s is given by Grimm 1975, 19ff.; for later positions see Holmberg 1990, 28ff.

2. Malherbe (1977, 31) states that in modern studies "perhaps a new consensus has emerged" vis-à-vis the position represented, for example, by Deissmann.

3. Deissmann 1908, 19; cf. 23, 40. Cf. already Hausrath 1875, 396, 405; Lietzmann 1961, 135.

4. Harnack 1924, 559; cf. also Dobschütz 1902; Knopf 1900, 325ff.

5. K. Kautsky 1927, 343, 338.

6. For example, Harnack 1924, 560.

7. Troeltsch 1977, 17, 25; for him the origin of Christianity is basically "to be understood not from social history but from the religious history of antiquity" (25). On Troeltsch see W. Stegemann 1993, 51–79.

8. Marx and Engels 1958, 128–29, 156.

9. Troeltsch 1977, 25.

10. Kreissig 1967, 99.

11. Judge 1964, 58ff.; cf. also Malherbe 1979, 194ff.; Lee 1979, 67–87; R. M. Grant 1981.

12. Gülzow 1969, 28; cf. 1974, 220ff.

13. Gülzow 1969, 26, 174.

14. Eck 1971, 382.

15. Hengel 1973a, 44–45.

16. Cf. only Meeks 1983, 51. Cf. also Hengel 1991, 208. Hengel changes, for example, the classification—favored by some scholars—of Paul with the lower stratum through the designation "propertyless proletariat" (*besitzloses Proletariat*).

17. Gager 1979b, 174–80; 1982, 256–65.

18. Scroggs 1980, 168–71; cf. also W. Stegemann 1981, 26ff.

19. Thus explicitly, for example, R. H. Smith 1980.

20. Cf. only Malherbe 1977.

21. 2 Peter, Jude, Hebrews.

22. Ephesians, Colossians, 2 Thessalonians, 1 Peter, Hebrews, Jude.

23. Cf. only Deissmann 1925; Malherbe 1977; Hock 1978; Judge 1979; 1980; Stowers 1984; W. Stegemann 1985; 1987, 200–229.

24. See here H. Schneider 1981b, 15, and the literature mentioned there.

25. Meeks 1983, 55ff. Yet he also draws on Acts and the Deutero-Paulines (except for the pastoral letters), which we will consider in connection with the analysis of urban Christ-confessing communities after 70.

26. Ibid., 155–56.

27. Ibid., 157.

28. Meeks apparently wants to express his agreement with what Malherbe has called the "new consensus" (ibid.).

29. Theissen 1989d.

30. Meeks 1983, 58; Theissen 1989d, 239.

31. Cadbury 1931, 42–58, considers him a slave. This also seems to be the understanding of the Vulgate translation: *arcarius civitatis.*

32. Cf. Cranfield 1983, 791–92.

33. See only Theissen 1989d, 234; Hengel 1973a, 44–45: "Members of the Christian communities were found in *all* population strata, from slaves and former slaves to the local aristocracy, the decurions, and even sometimes the senatorial nobility."

34. Wuellner 1973, 672.

35. See W. Stegemann 1981, 30–31; cf. Judge 1964, 58–59; Schottroff 1985.

36. Cf. Meeks 1983, 60, and the literature given there. Although Cranfield 1983, 782–83, does not understand *prostatis* as a technical term, even he grants that Phoebe had a certain social position, wealth, and independence. On the patron-client relationship see, for example, Malina 1988.

37. Ramsay 1910, 205, was the first to identify him with the Titius Justus mentioned in Acts 18:7.

38. Thus Hengel 1973a, 46.

39. Yet the apostle does include covetousness in his catalogs of vices (Rom 1:29; 2 Cor 9:5-6; cf. 1 Cor 5:11), although here it is not a question of special admonitions to the rich.

40. 2 Cor 6:10; 8:2, 9-10; 9:10ff.; cf. also 1 Cor 1:5; Rom 2:4; 9:23; 11:12, 33; Gal 4:9.

41. See also Hengel 1973a, 43–44.

42. See here above all Theissen 1989c, 291ff. From the social tensions at the Lord's Supper, Hengel (1973, 46) infers stark social differences within the Christ-confessing community.

43. Theissen 1989c, 297.

44. Thus ibid., 272ff.

45. See only Best 1972, 176.

46. Meeks 1983, 65.

47. On the comprehensive literature on this topic see Burchard 1975, 881–95; Hengel 1991, 180ff.; Niebuhr 1992; W. Stegemann 1994.

48. Habicht 1969, 163–64; for Asia Minor, however, cf. the informative quantitative study of Holtheide 1983.

49. Nörr 1963, 587.

50. Vittinghoff 1990, 1228; on the problem of citizenship in relation to the military cf. also Nicolet 1976, 122ff.

51. Hengel 1991, 203ff.

52. The exception is Acts 20:33-34, where Paul says that he coveted no one's silver or gold or clothing but worked with his own hands to meet his needs and those of his

companions. Paul is therefore presented by Luke as the model of Christian loving activity and of the independence of missionaries. Comparable is the behavior of philosophers, as recommended by Musonius Rufus (frag. 11).

53. For discussion of this occupational activity see only Hock 1980, 20–21: production of leather tents. Richter Reimer 1992, 206ff.; Lampe 1989, 156ff.

54. Hock 1980, 67.

55. Schottroff 1994, 126.

56. Hock 1980; Malherbe 1987, 17ff.

57. Hock 1980.

58. Thus Hengel 1991, 209–10.

59. Ibid., 209.

60. Thus he fared about as well as most artisans: cf. only Lucian *Fugit* 17.

61. But he probably did not expressly adopt this from the Corinthian community (1 Cor 9:12, 15-19; 2 Cor 11:7ff.; 12:13ff.; cf. also 1 Thess 2:9).

62. On the question of literary formation see Malherbe 1977.

63. Thus W. Stegemann 1985, 480ff.; cf. 1987, 226–28; cf. also Saldarini 1989, 139.

64. Thus, for example, Malherbe 1987, 55–56.

65. Cf. W. Stegemann 1987b; versus Hengel 1991, 193–208.

66. Cf., for example, 1 Pet 2:20ff.; Col 3:18ff.; Eph 5:22ff.

67. Radl 1988, 122.

68. Esler 1987, 187.

69. Cf. Schottroff and Stegemann 1990, 129ff.; contra Esler 1987, 186.

70. Moxnes 1991, 267.

71. Dibelius 1964, 7, 162.

72. Thus already ibid., 162.

73. Some examples: Archippus from Colossae (Col 4:17), Aristarchus (4:10-11), Demas (4:14) Epaphras (1:7; 4:12), Jesus Justus (4:11), Tychicus (4:7-8; Eph 6:21-22), Silvanus (2 Thess 1:1; 1 Pet 5:12; often in Acts), Phygelus and Hermogenes (2 Tim 1:15), and Hymenaeus and Philetus (2 Tim 2:17); cf. 2 Tim 4:9ff., 19-21.

74. Cf. Richter Reimer 1992, 123ff., and p. 391.

75. Verner 1983, 60–61.

76. Ibid., 180–81.

77. Thus Kreissig 1967, 98.

78. Cf. only Haenchen 1968, 343, 346.

79. See a list of hindrances in Eck 1971, 400–406.

80. See the essay of Eck 1971.

81. Cf. Publius Petronius, who delayed Caligula's order to set up a picture of the emperor in the temple and exercised his office rather humanely: Philo *Leg. Gai.* 245; see also Jos. *War* 2.184ff.; cf. Siegert 1973, 149.

82. The latter, however, is to be excluded for good reason. See only the basic discussion in Pöhlmann 1966, 56ff.; yet Lampe 1989, 169–70, has recently again held Flavia Domitilla to be a Christian.

83. Counterexamples are Tacitus and Pliny, who openly despised Christians.

84. Langhammer 1973, 64–66.

85. On Tertullian see Schöllgen 1984, 172–73, 189ff.

86. This can be inferred from Tertullian (*Apol.* 37.4; *Scap.* 4.7); cf. only Eck 1971, 383–84.

87. The translation follows Kasten 1968.

88. Thus, for example, Hasenclever 1882, 271. Yet Eck 1971, 383–84, does not include members from the *ordo senatorius* as members of the municipal aristocracy; also correctly opposed to this is Schöllgen 1984, 158–59.

89. Cf. Trebilco's overview of "Jewish involvement in city life" in Asia Minor (1991, 173ff.), according to which Jews held "local offices" in their native cities in Asia Minor only since the third century (173).

90. Cf. pp. 297.

91. Smallwood (1976, 127–28) holds this to be a possibility, yet the number to be "infinitesimally small."

92. On the inscription cf. Trebilco 1991, 58; *CII* 766.

93. Thus Trebilco 1991, 173; *CII* 770.

94. Arguing for a high social status is, for example, Meeks and Wilken 1978, 15. Or was his mother only the wet nurse of Herod? Inscriptional evidence for both possibilities is found in G. H. R. Horsley 1983, 37–38.

95. Cf. Schottroff and Stegemann 1990, 113ff.

96. Meeks 1983, 57.

97. Haenchen 1965, 291.

98. For later times see Origen *Cels.* 1.62; 3.44, 55 (simple, common, dull individuals, slaves, women, children; wool workers, cobblers, fullers, uneducated and unpolished people; wisdom was recently proclaimed in the women's chamber, in the cobbler's workshop, and in the fulling room; even Jesus found followers only among fishermen and tax collectors, who did not know even the rudiments of science); cf. the apologies in Minucius Felix *Octav.* 36.3–7; *Acts of Peter* 23; Justin *Apol.* 2.10.8; Tatian *Or.* 32.

99. On slaves see above all the pioneering work of Gülzow 1969.

100. Gülzow 1974, 207.

101. From post–New Testament writings we then learn that slaves were freed at the cost of the church treasury (*Did.* 18; Ign. *Pol.* 4.3; Aristides *Apology* 15.8; *Martyrium Pionii* 9). Conversely, some individuals sold themselves into slavery in order to redeem or support others: Gülzow 1974, 207.

Notes to Chapter 11

1. Tertullian *Nat.* 1.7.9.

2. Euseb. *Hist. Eccl.* 3.18; cf. 3.20; 4.26; cf. only Speigl 1970, 24. Eusebius's presentation does not go beyond the information that we have from pagan historians (yet not in regard to Christians) and is for this and other reasons correctly called into question: Speigl 1970, 34ff.; Moreau 1971, 37–38. A persecution of Christians by Domitian is also mentioned by Tertullian (*Apol.* 5.4) and Lactantius (*De mort. pers.* 3). Tertullian has Domitian break off the persecution; he probably got his information from Hegesippus, who, like Tertullian, asserts "that through an edict Domitian him-

self ended the persecution previously ordered by him": Moreau 1971, 39. See also Speigl 1970, 33–34, which also names Melito of Sardes.

3. Cf. J. Vogt 1954; Grumel 1956.

4. A persecution of Christians by Domitian is assumed by, for example, Gross 1959, 91–109. J. Vogt (1954a) speaks more cautiously of conflicts of a religious character in Rome and Asia Minor at the time of Domitian; critical of the persecution thesis in reference to Domitian are Christ 1962, 199–206; Speigl 1970, 18ff.; Keresztes 1973; and on the whole Moreau 1971, 37ff.

5. Critical is Overbeck in his "Studien zur Geschichte der alten Kirche" (1994, 2:93ff.).

6. On the term *criminalization* see Vittinghoff 1990, 265ff.; cf. 1984, 331–57.

7. In Luke 12:11-12 Jesus predicts to his disciples judicial conflicts with magistrates (for details cf. W. Stegemann 1991, 77ff.). In Acts 16:19ff.; 17:6-7; 18:12ff. Luke reports corresponding experiences. The arrest and trial of Paul before Roman governors in Syria (Acts 21:27ff. and elsewhere) are likewise to be considered in this connection. On the level of the narrative it is a question of conflicts of the Pauline era, but the contents of the accusations suggest seeing in these stories reflexes of the Lukan period itself and thus of the epoch after 70.

8. According to 1 Thess 2:2, Paul was also mistreated in Philippi. Whether he is referring here to official corporal punishment (as described in Acts 16:22-23) cannot be determined from the formulation. The verb used here (*hybrizō*) is not specific. It can also designate maltreatment by private individuals.

9. Wengst 1986, 94: "Arrest by Roman or urban authorities involved flogging."

10. One cannot exclude the possibility that members of the Diaspora synagogues played a role in this connection. For in 1 Thess 2:16 the apostle writes that "the Jews" hindered him "from speaking to the Gentiles so that they may be saved." In any case, a delational context can be presumed.

11. The conclusion of alleged Jewish persecutors is usually reached through a combination of Acts 17:1ff. with 1 Thessalonians. Cf. Malherbe 1987, 46–47.

12. It is possible that some community members died on account of these measures. This could include the parallels that Paul names in 1 Thess 2:14, the martyrdoms, and perhaps also the treatment of the problem of the deceased in 1 Thess 4:13ff.

13. Orosius *Adversus Paganos* 7.6.15–16. The variety of problems of interpretation will not be discussed here.

14. Arguing for different events are, for example, Smallwood 1976, 210ff., and Bickhoff-Böttcher 1984, 216ff.

15. The reading "Chrestiani" (with the ironic secondary meaning "men of integrity") in the Codex Mediceus II is to be preferred to the reading "Christian," according to E. Koestermann's edition (Leipzig, 1965, 356).

16. In terms of text criticism, crucifixions are doubtful; cf. Wlosok 1982, 286.

17. Cf. only Borleffs 1952.

18. In this context it is also to be noted that the church in Philadelphia, to its credit, did not deny the name of Christ (Rev 3:8).

19. On the problem of the banishment of John see only Pöhlmann 1966, 433ff., and U. B. Müller 1984, 81, with reference to Rev 6:9; 20:4.

20. U. B. Müller 1984, 110; cf. also Pöhlmann 1966, 430ff. This interpretation is supported above all by Rev 13:2: "The dragon, symbol for Satan, gives his power and his throne to the 'beast' from the sea as the symbolic figure for the Roman Empire" (U. B. Müller 1984, 110); cf. also Rev 12:9, which says that the dragon, or the ancient serpent, is called the "Devil" and "Satan."

21. H. Kraft 1974, on the passage.

22. Many interpreters argue for the writing of Revelation in this period; see only the discussion in U. B. Müller 1984, 40–42. On the relationship between Revelation and Domitian see R. Schütz 1933.

23. U. B. Müller 1984, 260.

24. Cf. Jos. *War* 7.46ff.

25. Cf. Pöhlmann 1966, 438ff., and U. B. Müller 1984, 257ff.; Speigl 1970, 50ff.

26. On the officials in Philippi cf. Elliger 1978, 51ff.; on the text as a whole, W. Stegemann 1991, 211ff.

27. Cf. Plutarch *Coriolanus* 19; Jos. *War* 7.41.

28. For details see W. Stegemann 1991, 237ff.

29. Cf. ibid., 226ff., for further discussion of the text.

30. Pomponius in *Digests* 48.4.1, 11.

31. Cf. Rilinger 1988, 209.

32. Ibid., 216, including further literature.

33. *Digests* 50.16.118; cf. Kuhn 1982, 727; also p. 173 .

34. On the historical version of the trial see Tajra 1989, 63ff.

35. Cf. Sherwin-White 1966, 691ff.; Wlosok 1970.

36. Wlosok 1970, 36.

37. On the extensive discussion of the question whether the *nomen ipsum* was already punishable, see the brief weighing of the arguments in Keresztes 1979, 273ff. Keresztes himself holds the *nomen ipsum* to be "a capital crime" (287) and points out that this praxis was also not corrected by the rescript of Trajan (*Ep.* 10.97). Likewise it may be assumed that Trajan's rescript made it possible for the accused who had been Christians in the past not to be punished. More problematic, by contrast, seems the tracing of this practice back to a ban against Christianity initiated by Nero, which via the imperial *mandata* was also known to Pliny (Keresztes 1979, 286; cf. also Molthagen 1970, 25). See also Wlosok 1970, 36–37.

38. Wlosok 1982, 294.

39. Pliny *Ep.* 10.96.3; confirmed by Emperor Trajan: *Ep.* 10.97.1.

40. "Valid at least until 249 was the *confessio nominis,* the confession of the individual Christian that he is a Christian as a punishable state of affairs that called for capital punishment": Freudenberger 1981, 24.

41. Thus the accusation of Jewish propaganda and the adoption of the Jewish way of life are not to be traced back to a corresponding legal prohibition of Rome but to a practice exercised in certain political situations. We will come back to this presently.

42. Cf. only Last 1954, 1208ff.; 1937, 80ff.; Klein 1982, viiff.; Wlosok 1982, 275ff.; 1970; Barnes 1968, 32ff.; Keresztes 1979, 247ff.; Frend 1965, 13ff.

43. Wlosok 1982, 278. The problem of the term *coercitio* has been the object of controversy, since it was learned "that the procedure used in most capital trials was the *cognitio extra ordinem* of the particular bearer of the imperial power," through which the "trial character of the procedure" (Klein 1982, xxvii) receives a greater importance; cf. Sherwin-White 1952, 199ff.; 1964, 23ff. Wlosok 1982, 278–79, however, says (probably correctly): "This last assumption [meaning the connection of punitive persecution with administrative procedure—E. and W. Stegemann] does the most justice to the real state of affairs, especially since in most cases no clear distinction can be made between extraordinary punishment and pure police measures. . . . Hence the procedure can hardly form a criterion. All the more important, then, is the substantiation of the verdict in the individual case, especially where it applies not only to being a Christian but also reveals the real motives of the Roman state for the rejection of Christianity."

44. This hypothesis, advocated since Mommsen, has experienced broad recognition especially in the literature in German, and has been accepted in textbooks on early church history: Lietzmann 1961; yet cf. also Last 1937, 27; Moreau 1971, 61ff.; Wlosok 1982, 279ff. Less probable is the assumption of the older research that Christians were punished on the basis of a special law (*lex, senatus consultum,* or imperial edict), which is traced back to Nero, among others. This thesis guided research of the nineteenth century, above all before Mommsen. More recently it is still advocated by, for example, Keresztes 1979, 286, who assumes a "ban" against Christianity initiated by Nero, which via the "imperial mandates" was also known, for example, to Pliny; see also Molthagen 1970, 25. Further literature is given in Klein 1982, xxvi–xxvii; Wlosok 1982, 276–77. Versus, for example—with good reason—Last 1954, 1208ff.; Wlosok 1982, 277.

45. Thus in the older research. Here the following grounds for punishment are especially mentioned: *maiestas* (treason), *sacrilegium* (sacrilege), *infanticidium* (killing or sacrificing children), *incestum* (sexual immorality), magic, belonging to a forbidden party (*factio illicita*), condemnation in the context of laws regarding the *collegia,* and so forth. The *crimen laesae maiestatis* was understood above all by Mommsen (1890, 389ff.; cf. 1955, 569ff.) as the most important legal reason for the persecution of Christians. In his opinion, confession to Christianity was a crime against the state; Gutermann (1951) sees in participation in unauthorized foreign cults a religious crime, which was prosecuted already in the late Roman republic and then also in the early period of the empire. The problem of the "law of associations"—say, in the context of the *hetaeriae* prohibition—is hardly still favored in the legal-historical discussion. In any case, it is not the problem before or in Pliny's letter regarding the trials of Christians.

46. Cf. Wlosok 1982, 296.

47. Vittinghoff 1990, 267.

48. See the juxtaposition of accusations in, for example, Sevenster 1975, 88ff.; Conzelmann 1981, 43ff.; and more recently Wander 1994, 248.

49. Vittinghoff 1990, 266.

50. Cf. Gülzow 1990, 96–98. Yet it is altogether questionable whether one can speak at all of an ancient pagan anti-Semitism, that is, of an ideologically constructed, generally hostile attitude against the Jews as Jews.

51. On the anti-Jewish accusation of *hierosylie* see only Jos. *Ap.* 1.249; 310; 318; Paul also uses this stereotype (cf. Rom 2:22). Further accusations: ritual murder (Jos. *Ap.* 2.89ff.); not worshiping the emperor's image (*Ap.* 2.73).

52. The accusation of "atheism" (*atheos, asebēs; contemnere deos* or *gens contumelia numinum insignis*) has been made against the Jews since the first century C.E. and was later extended to Christians. In terms of content, it presumably means the rejection of the pagan cult. Cf. Rom 2:22; Jos. *Ap.* 2.148; Diodorus Siculus 34.1; Tacitus *Hist.* 5.5; Pliny *Nat. Hist.* 13.46; *Mart. Pol.* 3, 9; Justin *Apol.* 1.1.6 and elsewhere.

53. Cf. also p. 267.

54. Wlosok 1982, 286.

55. Cf. Vittinghoff 1990, 266.

56. An analogy is again to be found in the attitude toward Judaism. Here too the inclination of non-Jews toward Jewish customs or conversion to Judaism is regarded as especially pernicious (cf. only Juvenal *Sat.* 14.96ff.).

57. Wlosok 1982, 294. Cf. Suetonius *Nero* 16.2.

58. Gager 1985b.

59. Cf. Stern 1964.

60. Vittinghoff 1990, 266.

61. This is shown especially in the problem of the tax obligation, in that the corresponding—previously presented—scene from Jesus' activity shows that this accusation is not correct: cf. Luke 20:20ff.

62. For the early church testimonies see Schäfke 1979, 606ff.

63. Cf. Jos. *War* 2.91–92; *Ant.* 17.314; *Ap.* 2.68.

64. Tacitus *Hist.* 5.1–3; Suetonius *Vespasian* 6; *Titus* 3–4; Dio Cassius 66.1, 4–7.

65. Jos. *War* 2.398–99.

66. Cf. Jos. *War* 2.457ff., 487ff., 559ff.; 7.361ff.; Dio Cassius 66.4; cf. also Hengel 1976a, 374–75.

67. Euseb. *Hist. Eccl.* 3.19–20.

68. On Domitian's "religious policy" see Smallwood 1976, 376ff.; Keresztes 1979, 257ff.; Gross 1959, 91ff.; Speigl 1970, 4ff.

69. On the *fiscus Judaicus* see only Keresztes 1979, 258–59; Smallwood 1976, 371ff.; Stenger 1988, 79ff.

70. See also Smallwood 1976, 376–77; Stenger 1988, 98ff. Juster 1914, 2:284, interprets the expansion under Domitian as according to age or only for apostates but not for "sympathizers." Versus, however, Keresztes 1979, 259.

71. Yet this could lie behind the discussion in Matt 17:22-27; cf. p. 121.

72. Cf. Keresztes 1979, 260; Smallwood 1976, 378: the relief involved only the false accusations, not the tax.

73. Smallwood 1976, 378–79.

74. Ibid., 379.

75. Momigliano 1934a, 29ff.; more precise are Sherwin-White 1952, 81–82, and Smallwood 1976, 130.

76. See Valerius Maximus 1.3.3: Smallwood 1976, 128ff.; Bickhoff-Böttcher 1984, 281–82; and Tacitus *Ann.* 2.85.5; Suetonius *Tiberius* 36.1; Jos. *Ant.* 18.65–84; Dio Cassius 57.18.5: Smallwood 1976, 292ff.; Bickhoff-Böttcher 1984, 284ff.

77. Scott 1936, 88–188.

78. Stählin 1962, 172. The parallel tradition is in Jos. *Ant.* 19.343ff.

79. Cf. Cassidy 1983, 39.

80. Cf. Morgenthaler 1956.

81. See also Tacitus *Ann.* 4.38.

82. Williams 1990, 196–211; cf. also J. T. Sanders 1993, 167–68, 183.

83. Stenger 1988, 108.

84. Sherwin-White 1966, 696.

85. Ibid.; cf. also Moreau 1971, 19ff.

86. Cf. Sherwin-White 1966, 780–81.

87. Ibid., 696–97, presumes that Trajan or his advisers believed that Christians were inclined to commit the crimes of which their enemies accused them: "Thyestean meals" and "oedipal marriages." Yet he can only refer to later anti-Christian accusations; for details see Schäfke 1979, 579ff.

88. Conzelmann 1981, 232.

89. Cf. Schäfke 1979, 466ff.

90. For details and additional literature, see W. Stegemann 1991, 197ff.

91. On the significance of the urban disturbances as a whole see MacMullen 1975, 163ff.; Stahl 1978, 166ff.

92. Cf. Plümacher 1987, 11; cf. also Lee 1979, 67–87.

93. See the listing of these conflicts in Plümacher 1987, 11.

94. Philo *Flacc.* and *Leg. Gai.*; Jos. *War* 2.490ff.; 7.46–62 (Antioch).

95. Dion of Prusa *Or.* 34.21; cf. also *Or.* 39 and 46.48.

96. Plümacher 1987, 20.

97. Wellhausen (1907, 17) was already of the opinion that in Acts 19 Luke adopted an originally anti-Semitic tumult; cf. also Conzelmann 1972, 123, on Acts 19:34: "an impressionistic picture from ancient 'antisemitism'"; on hostility to Jews in Ephesus see Jos. *Ant.* 14.225–30, 234, 237–40, 262–64.

98. Jos. *Ant.* 12.121.

99. See only Kraeling 1982, 150ff.; Downey 1961, 199–200, 204ff.

100. Sevenster 1975, 89ff.; cf. also Bickhoff-Böttcher 1984, 226ff.

101. Cf. Bergmann and Hoffmann 1987, 15ff.

102. Bickhoff-Böttcher 1984, 17.

103. Philo *Flacc.* 33, 38, 41, 66, and elsewhere; *Leg. Gai.* 120, 130, 132.

104. Philo *Flacc.* 17, 29, 34, 93; cf. Jos. *Ant.* 18.257; *War* 2.487, 496; *Ap.* 2.69–70. Cf. Bickhoff-Böttcher 1984, 220ff.

105. The Alexandrian "Acts of the Martyrs" shows this disagreement of the Greek upper stratum of Alexandria with its Jewish residents; cf. Gager 1985b, 47ff.

106. See only Smallwood 1976, 233ff.; Gager 1985b, 44; cf. also Bergmann and Hoffmann (1987, 20ff.), who criticize this theory.

107. Cf. Bergmann and Hoffmann 1987, 29ff.

108. A further shift in the balance of power was then provoked by the visit of the newly appointed Jewish king Agrippa I in Alexandria: Bergmann and Hoffmann 1987, 31ff.

109. The episode itself also reveals anti-Jewish resentment in the population. See only Elliger 1978, 154–55; Lüdemann 1987, 227.

110. Elliger 1978, 89: "The cult of the emperor and faith in oriental gods apparently defined the religious life of the Roman city [Ephesus]. By contrast, the old Greek gods, including the city goddess, seem to have been on the decline."

111. Elliott 1981 supports the thesis that the alienage is to be understood as real (this is entirely possible).

112. See, for example, Speigl 1970, 48: calumnies, trials, suffering, and death (!).

113. Thus Pöhlmann 1966, 406.

114. Cf. only Malina 1993, 28ff.

115. Also a judicial experience can hardly be derived from the author's recommendation (3:15) always to "be ready to make your defense to anyone who demands from you an accounting for the hope that is within you" (presumably because of one's faith); thus also Brox 1989, 29, 159–60.

116. Brox 1989, 220.

117. Pliny *Ep.* 10.96.10.

118. H. Becker 1963, 131.

119. Malina and Neyrey 1991, 107.

120. A good overview of the history of research is found in Wander 1994, 8–39.

121. Conzelmann 1981, 239, speaks in this connection of a "theoretical" disagreement with Judaism.

122. On the definition of religion as a cultural system see Geertz 1987.

123. The distinction between Judaism and Christianity as divergent religions is extremely complex and hard to define in detail; cf. Simon 1948, 95. Schiffman 1985 offers a detailed analysis that results in the following picture: To the extent that Christians distanced themselves from the halakic definitions of Jewish essence, the tannaitic sources show an increasing exclusion of Christians. The final break occurred when Christians became completely "pagan" from the halakic point of view. The halakic definition of a Jew was the reason for the exclusion of Christians from the Jewish community and for the establishment of Christianity as a separate "religion." Schiffman holds the view that after the catastrophe of the Bar Kochba rebellion (135 C.E.)—in connection with which the Jews were banished from Jerusalem and the only Christian groups left there were Gentile Christian—rabbinic Judaism regarded Christians as a separate religion: Schiffman 1985; see esp. 5–7, 76–77.

124. *Dial.* 38, 112.

125. An analogy is the situation in the land of Israel itself, where, according to the (admittedly disputed) archaeologically based thesis of Meyers (1988), Jews and Christians lived harmoniously together into the seventh century C.E. Cf. Gager 1985a, 401; cf. also p. 240.

126. Lampe 1989.

127. Thus, for example, Merkel 1991, 94.

128. Hemer 1989, 182.

129. Hengel (1984, 74) explains the differences by the fact that the same episode was described by Luke and Paul from different perspectives.

130. We will not refer here to the execution of the Lord's brother James at the instigation of the high priest Ananos (Jos. *Ant.* 20.200–203). For on the one hand, it is a question here of an internal Jewish process, which also runs into strong criticism, and of the presumed judicial competence of the high priest. On the other hand, this was a remarkable exception. The execution of James, son of Zebedee, by Herod Agrippa cannot be used here either.

131. Cf. only Acts 13:44ff.; 14:5, 19; 17:5, 13; 18:6, 12; 21:27ff.; 22:22; 23:2ff., 12ff.; 28:17ff.

132. On the terms *diōkein* and *diōgmos* see W. Stegemann 1991, 114–17.

133. Conzelmann 1974b, 61; Reese 1972, 62ff. (who assumes persecution by powerful Jewish leaders).

134. On the traditional image of persecution by Jews see Harnack 1924, 64ff.; Conzelmann 1981, 234; more cautious is Simon 1948, 144ff.; Frend 1965 largely takes the Christian testimonies as factual; warning against this is Riddle 1934, 271ff., among others; very differentiated is Hare 1967, 19ff. and elsewhere; not entirely unambiguous is Maier 1982, 135 (with further literature).

135. *Synagogae Iudaeorum, fontes persecutionum* (*Scorp.* 10.10; cf. *Apol.* 21.20–22; *Adv. Iud.* 13.26; *Nat.* 1.14).

136. Conzelmann 1981, 234.

137. Hare 1967, 1–79.

138. A conflict with Jewish Christians who return to the synagogue is indicated in 1 John 2:19, 22-23: E. Stegemann 1985, 284–94.

139. *Magn.* 8.1; 9.1; 10.3; *Phld.* 6.1.

140. J. T. Sanders 1993, 224.

141. Ibid., 201.

142. This recalls the ancient anti-Jewish stereotype of misanthropy; cf. E. Stegemann 1994, 64.

143. For details cf. J. T. Sanders 1993, 189ff.

144. Cf. Gal 1:23; 1 Cor 15:9; Phil 3:6.

145. Cf. Gal 1:14 with Phil 3:6.

146. Cf. Haacker 1975, 8ff.

147. A collection of the measures described in Acts is found in Wander 1994, 147–49.

148. Cf. Burchard 1970, 47ff. and elsewhere.

149. It is hard to imagine that the persecution resulted from Paul's own initiative, as Wander 1994, 151, 153, holds.

150. Speaking implicitly for Damascus as the place of the Pauline measures is Gal 1:17 (Paul returns to Damascus); see J. Becker 1993, 38, 60; versus, among others, Hultgren 1976, 97ff., who argues for persecution in Judea.

151. See only Hultgren 1976, 108–9.

152. According to the agreement described in Gal 2:9, Paul is to devote himself to the Gentiles, and the Jerusalemites to the Jews. In the specific situation of Diaspora Judaism—if Paul held to this agreement and worked within the realm of influence of the synagogues—only Gentile sympathizers of the synagogues could have been the object of Paul's missionary activities.

153. Cf. Dio Cassius 60.6 (prohibition of assembly for Roman Jews; 41 C.E.); Orosius *Adversus Paganos* 7.6 (49 C.E.).

154. For details see A. Y. Collins 1984, 34–50.

155. Frend 1965, 184.

156. As an example, J. T. Sanders 1993, 169.

157. Cf. only U. B. Müller 1984, 106–7; Pöhlmann 1966, 427ff.

158. An openly anti-Jewish interpretation of this connection has slipped into Hemer 1989, 160; cf. J. T. Sanders 1993, 178.

159. U. B. Müller 1984, 110.

160. Cf. Ps. 35:10: "O Lord, who is like you?"

161. Cf. in this direction also Köster 1980, 689.

162. For individual analysis and additional literature cf. W. Stegemann 1991, 113ff.

163. The trial of Paul, which is described in Acts, has its beginning in Jerusalem, not in the Diaspora.

164. Cf. also 1 Pet 4:14, 16; the verbal slandering of Christians is also mentioned in 1 Pet 2:12; 4:4. See here only Brox 1989, 220ff. and elsewhere.

165. Most clearly expressed in the slandering of Jesus is the verbal distancing of the fellowship of disciples, as attested by Pliny's letter to Trajan (*Ep.* 10.96). In it, the cursing of Christ (*maledicerent Christo*), in addition to the "sacrifice test," was evaluated as the clearest sign that the delinquent was not a Christian. For real Christians could not be forced to do that. Freudenberger (1967) claims to trace the *maledictio* among the Romans back to a "Jewish source" (147, 152)—according to the model of the "sacrifice test," which a Jewish apostate in Antioch recommended against his countrymen and countrywomen (Jos. *War* 7.46ff.). This connection is very unlikely; cf. also Maier 1982, 133–34.

166. *Dial.* 16, 47, 93, 108, 117, 133. It is uncertain whether 1 Cor 12:3 already reflects such a situation.

167. Only in Jerusalem is Paul then accused by Jews from "Asia" to *Jews* themselves. In the Diaspora only Gentiles are ever the addressees of such measures.

168. Hare 1967, 53 (with good reason), who himself argues for an informal act of exclusion.

169. For details see W. Stegemann 1991, 77ff.

170. Michel and Bauernfeind 1969, 281.

171. Whether the religious enthusiast movement of the poor really involved sicarii is extremely doubtful. Neither were they armed nor did they show steadfastness in their interrogation under torture, which otherwise distinguished the sicarii (cf. *War* 7.417ff.). Yet from the Roman viewpoint, this played no role, for even the activities of religious agitators were considered the first step toward insurrection (*War* 2.260; cf. 6.300ff.).

172. J. T. Sanders 1987, 306ff.; cf. 1993, 180ff.; he refers critically to W. Stegemann 1991 (whose interpretation is largely adopted here). Sanders holds that while the historicity of the Jews' accusations of Christians before pagan authorities, as reported in Acts, is not totally out of the question, it is nonetheless questionable. He can imagine them at best as individual cases but by no means as typical measures (1993, 182–83). That it is a question of typical experiences and evidence of a general tendency is not assumed by us either. Yet we cannot follow Sanders's suggestion that sometimes Jewish confessors of Christ denounced Gentile Christians (1993, 186). The details of his critique cannot be discussed here.

173. Thus also J. T. Sanders 1993, 200.

174. Thus correctly also Gülzow 1990, 105.

175. Violent measures in Justin's immediate experience are always formulated only hypothetically: cf. *Dial.* 16, 95, 133; he describes the proselytes as especially fanatical: *Dial.* 122: they want to kill and martyr Christians, but they do not do it. Cf. Maier 1982, 132–33.

176. *Dial.* 16, 47, 93, 108, 117, 133. See only Harnack 1924, 65; Hare 1967, 66ff. Cf. also Segal 1991, 33–34.

177. *Dial.* 17, 108; Maier: "What is quoted here in part in direct speech from the alleged message comes for the most part with certainty from a Christian pen . . . possibly influenced by Acts 26 etc." (1982, 134).

178. *Dial.* 17, 108; cf. also 117.

179. Cf. only Justin *Apol.* 1.37, 39, 43–44, 47, 53, 60. Justin judges the Jews even more negatively than the Gentiles.

180. Cf. only *Dial.* 47, 80; on Justin see Hare 1967, 66ff.; Conzelmann 1981, 272ff.

181. Contra Conzelmann 1981, 272. It is striking that it is said of the "Greeks" that they would persecute *Christianoi,* yet the Jews battle them as "people of other tribes."

182. Cf. also Hare 1967, 69–70.

183. Cf. pp. 342–43.

184. Cf. only Kretschmar 1990, 13; Gülzow 1990, 95–120.

185. Thus already Parkes 1934, esp. Chap. 3: "The Parting of the Ways" (71ff.). Cf. also Rendtorff 1989, 109ff.

186. E. P. Sanders 1980; E. P. Sanders et al. 1981; B. E. Meyer and E. P. Sanders 1982.

187. Thus also Meeks 1985, 106, 108, 114.

188. Also critical of this formulation is Wander 1994, 6.

189. Individual evidence in ibid., 2ff.

190. Cf. Richardson (1969, 2, 48), who correctly points out that the break cannot be traced back to a certain point of time. He presumes a process and various factors.

191. Theissen 1988, 184; Wander 1994.

192. Cf. only Kretschmar 1990, 12.

193. On the sect model see pp. 242–43; on deviance theory pp. 244–47.

194. Theissen (1988, 182) assumes for the Pauline churches the "stage of typical sect formation," as does Watson, who understands the formation of Pauline churches as a conscious separation from Judaism (1986, 19, 45, 68); cf. Segal 1990, 271; versus Meeks 1985, 106.

195. Gager 1975, 79–87; Coser 1972.

196. J. T. Sanders 1993, 125.

197. Kriesberg 1973.

198. Malina 1993, 22.

199. Cf. pp. 328–29.

200. *War* 7.407ff.; 437ff.

201. Too general, in our opinion, is Gülzow 1990, 96–97, who in this connection sees the background basically in pagan hostility toward Jews.

202. This aspect is also emphasized by Gülzow 1990, 109.

Notes to Part Four, Introduction

1. Ortner and Whitehead 1981, 25.

2. Cf. Dover 1974; Just 1991, 153ff.

3. The Greek word for bravery, *andreia,* actually means manliness; it comes from the gender-emphasizing designation *anēr* for man.

4. Cf. 1 Cor 6:9. Philo describes one such type especially dramatically (cf. *Spec. Leg.* 3.37ff.).

5. Cf. only Aeschines 1, Timarchos 42. Further examples are in Just 1991, 171ff.; cf. further the reproach against Jesus in Matt 11:19/Luke 7:34.

6. Cf. Just 1991, 157ff.

7. Ibid., 191ff.

8. See only Malina 1993, 51ff.

Notes to Chapter 12

1. Cf. Rosaldo 1974, 23.

2. Thus correctly Wagner-Hasel 1989; 1988, 11–50.

3. Cf. the later legal fixing in the *Digests* (50.17.2); Schuller 1987, 13.

4. Cf. only Just 1991, 13.

5. Ibid., 281.

6. See p. 400.

7. Neh 8:2; Ezra 10:1; 2 Chron 20:13-14; Jdt 6:16; 7:23; *Par. Jer.* 7.17; Philo *Decal.* 32; 1QSa 1:4.

8. Berger 1976, 172; cf. Thraede 1970, 198, 214.

9. Livius 34.2.8ff. Cf. also Valerius Maximus 3.8.6: "What do women have to do with public assembly? If the patriarchal custom is observed, nothing."

10. Cf. Valerius Maximus 7.3.2; 2.1.3; 3.8.3; cf. Pomeroy 1985, 267ff.

11. See, for example, van Bremen 1983, 238.

12. Lefkowitz 1983, 56–57. Different, however, is Kraemer 1992, 84ff.

13. Lefkowitz 1983, 57–58.

14. A good overview of politically "influential" women is found in Lefkowitz 1983; for Josephus's criticism of the influence of women in the Herodian royal house see Mayer-Schärtel 1994, 53–60.

15. Pomeroy 1985, 283ff.

16. On Sempronia see Sallust *Catilina* 24.3ff.; Balsdon 1979, 51.

17. Cf. Pomeroy 1985, 267, 283–85.

18. Cf. Lefkowitz 1983, 59.

19. In danger of doing this is Balsdon 1979, 107ff.; versus MacMullen 1980, 208ff. For a comprehensive view see Gardner 1986.

20. On both see Schuller 1987, 63, 74.

21. Especially uncritical is Schuller 1987, 64.

22. Ibid., 66.

23. Garnsey and Saller 1987, 134.

24. Ibid., 190, with reference to Cicero *Att.* 15.10ff.

25. Tacitus *Ann.* 15.48 on the participants in the conspiracy of Piso: *senatores eques miles, feminae etiam.*

26. Pomeroy 1985, 290.

27. Lefkowitz 1983, 59.

28. The wife of Lentulus put on men's clothing in order to follow her husband into exile: Lefkowitz 1983, 58.

29. The wife of Coponius had an affair with Mark Antony in order to help her husband (Appian *Bell. Civ.* 4.39–40).

30. There are many examples in Schuller 1987, 65.

31. Pliny *Ep.* 3.16.

32. See the examples in Pomeroy 1985, 279ff., and Lefkowitz 1983, 61.

33. Pomeroy 1985, 282.

34. Wagner-Hasel 1989, 26; van Bremen 1983, 234–35.

35. Thraede 1970, 197–98. Also against this thesis of the "oriental inaccessibility" of women is Wagner-Hasel (1988, 1989), who in general sheds light on the topos from the contemporary historical situation of its origin (1989, 20).

36. For details on the situation in Athens cf. Just 1991, 106ff.

37. Ovid *Ars amatoria* 1.93, 135; Plutarch *Sulla* 33.

38. Seneca *Controversiae* 2.15.

39. Horace *Sat.* 1.2.94.

40. MacMullen 1980, 212.

41. Suetonius *Augustus* 44–45.

42. Thraede 1970, 212–13.

43. In spite of this, Juvenal assumes in his misogynous sixth satire that women are the constant cause of trials and, indeed, write indictments themselves (*Sat.* 6.242ff.). Proverbial as a legal scholar and rhetor is, above all, Afrania (Valerius Maximus 8.3.2); cf. Eichenauer 1988, 134–35; Pomeroy 1985, 267.

44. Cf. Zaidman 1993; Scheid 1993; Pomeroy 1985, 319ff.

45. Aristophanes *Ran.* 576ff.; cf. Schuller 1985, 46ff.

46. Schottroff 1994, 125, with additional literature.

47. Zaidman 1993, 375.

48. Ibid., 381–82.

49. Ibid., 410–11.

50. Plato *Phaedr.* 244B; Lefkowitz 1983, 413.

51. Scheid 1983, 418.

52. Ibid.

53. Kraemer 1992, 81–84.

54. Thraede 1970, 220.

55. Cf. also Balsdon 1979, 223; Schuller 1987, 16, 20; already Marquardt 1975 (reprint of 1886 ed.), 1:59, 66.

56. Balsdon (1979, 223) translates here: "Mittelpunkt des geselligen Lebens" ("center of social life").

57. Cf. Petronius *Satr.* 32, 66.

58. Corley 1993, 29.

59. Ibid., 28, 30, 38ff., 59ff.

60. Cicero *Verr.* 2.1.26.65–27.68. Lucian *Gallus* 11. One should not take Juvenal to be the witness of a thoroughly dissolute life on the part of Roman women (*Sat.* 6.425ff.), for his sixth satire represents a high point in ancient misogyny and is full of false information. In general, the individual data from ancient writers need to be verified in detail.

61. MacMullen 1980, 212–13.

62. Corley 1993, 33, 48ff.

63. Cf. also the idealization of Fannia in *Ep.* 7.19.

64. Pomeroy 1985, 45–46. For this situation of women in the Bronze Age there is also a nonliterary attestation: "In the tablet from Pylos written in Mycenean linear script B, the following tasks of women are listed: fetching water, preparing the bath, spinning, weaving, harvesting, and grinding grain. They also report that at the passing out of meals, the rations of men were two and a half times larger than those of women."

65. Cf. Xenophon *Oik.* 7.1–43.

66. Foucault 1989, 2:202–3, comments on this aptly: "The 'natural' opposition of man and woman and the specialization of their abilities are inseparable from the order of the house; [these abilities] were made for this arrangement and bestowed by it as duties."

67. This is pointed out by Schottroff 1994, 123.

68. Cf., among others, *Migr.* 97; *Som.* 2, 9, 55, 184; *Sac.* 103; *Agr.* 79.

69. From the Old Testament–Jewish realm cf. also 2 Sam 16:22; Sir 25:7ff.; 42:12; Esther 2:3, 9, 14; Tob 2:11; *Ps. Phocylides* 5.215; 2 Macc 3:19; 3 Macc 1:18. Mayer (1987, 85) also calls attention to rabbinic texts.

70. Dover 1988, 267: Menander, fr. 592; Euripides, fr. 521.

71. Dover 1988, 265.

72. Ibid., 267.

73. "The thorough-going segregation of women of citizen status was possible only in households which owned enough slaves and could afford to confine its womenfolk to a leisure enlivened only by the exercise of domestic crafts such as weaving and spinning. This degree of segregation was simply not possible in poorer families . . ." (Dover 1988, 278; cf. also Thraede 1970, 218).

74. Pitt-Rivers 1977, 115ff.

75. *Ant.* 17.147, 321, and elsewhere. On all of this cf. Mayer-Schärtel 1994, 76ff.

76. Translated according to Etienne 1978, 169.

77. Because of a statue of Eumachia that was erected by the *fullones: CIL* 10.813; cf. Etienne 1978, 169.

78. Pomeroy 1985, 311.

79. For details cf. van Bremen 1983; taken up by Kraemer 1992, 84ff.

80. Van Bremen 1983, 223.

81. Ibid.

82. Kraemer 1992, 84.

83. Cf. Brooten 1982, 5ff.

84. Cf. Leon 1960, 194.

85. Eichenauer 1988, 42.

86. Cf. Schottroff 1980, 91ff.; Eichenauer 1988, 42ff.

87. Cf. Schottroff 1980, 91; Eichenauer 1988, 44.

88. Schuller 1987, 23.

89. Eichenauer 1988, 44.

90. Schuller 1987, 23.

91. Ibid., 25.

92. Herzig 1983, 81; additional inscriptional evidence is found in Eichenauer 1988, 45.

93. Eichenauer 1988, 45, with further evidence.

94. Pomeroy 1985, 311; Loane 1938, 103ff.

95. Pliny *Ep.* 7.24.

96. Pomeroy 1985, 316.

97. Ibid., 306.

98. On lower-stratum women in general cf. Pomeroy 1985, 293ff. In addition to the mentioned works (Schottroff 1980, 98ff.; 1994; Eichenauer 1988; and Günther 1987), see also N. Kampen 1981; Treggiari 1976; and Le Gall 1970.

99. Richter Reimer 1992, 123ff.

100. Eichenauer 1988, 83ff.

101. Schottroff 1994, 127, with reference to an inscription: *CIL* 6.9801; cf. also Pliny the Elder *Nat. Hist.* 9.143.

102. See Eichenauer 1988, 60ff.

103. Seneca *Ep.* 66 equates a midwife (*obstetrix*) and a woman doctor (*medica*). For details cf. Eichenauer 1988, 148ff.

104. Schottroff 1980, 97–98; Scheidel 1990; for Josephus see Mayer-Schärtel 1994, 94–95.

105. Schottroff 1994, 150.

106. N. Kampen 1981, 133.

107. Schottroff 1980, 98.

108. Günther 1987, 135ff.

109. See also Mayer-Schärtel 1994, 95–98.

110. Eichenauer 1988, 141ff.

111. Treggiari 1976, 98; Eichenauer 1988, 143.

Notes to Chapter 13

1. The women under the cross mentioned in John 19:25-27 are not called followers of Jesus. Luke 23:55 only repeats the comment of Luke 23:49.

2. Cf. only Fitzmyer 1986, 695–98; Schottroff 1980, 101: "His [Luke's] idea of women of means around Jesus comes not from otherwise buried traditions about the Jesus movement but from later experiences of the young church in the cities of the Roman Empire outside of Palestine (see Acts 16:14-15; 17:4, 12), which he projects back into the time of Jesus."

3. Kraemer 1992, 131.

4. Corley 1993, 84–86, also with abundant secondary literature.

5. Only in Acts 9:36 is Tabitha called *mathētria*.

6. Cf. only Mark 1:18; 2:14; 6:1; 8:34; 9:38; 10:21, 28, 32; and elsewhere.

7. In 23:49 Luke seems rather to weaken the word, since here he uses *synakolouthein,* which has rather the sense of "accompany"; cf. Mark 5:37; 14:51.

8. Cf. only Weiser 1992; cf. also Schottroff 1994, 299ff.

9. Schüssler Fiorenza 1988, 12, 389–90. In her opinion (12), in Mark 15:40-41 "women appear as the true Christian officeholders and witnesses." "They are Jesus' true followers (*akolouthein*), because they have understood that his office consists not in dominion and royalty but in *diakonia,* 'service' (Mark 15:41)."

10. Schottroff 1994, 312–13.

11. Weiser 1992, 727.

12. Corley 1993, 86.

13. Cf. Schottroff 1994, 126: "The mention of the *diakonia* of women in Mark 1:31 par.; Luke 10:40; John 12:2; Mark 15:41 par. must be discussed in connection with the early Christian understanding of serving (*diakonein*)." Yet Schottroff limits this by asking whether Luke 10:40 and John 12:2 mean "the supportive work of women" (ibid.).

14. The interpretation of "serving" in Mark 1:31 (Peter's mother-in-law serves Peter and Jesus after she is healed) as discipleship is, in our opinion, not tenable; cf. also the interpretation of Corley 1993, 87 (with additional literature).

15. The verb meaning "to serve" is linked with a pronoun in the dative.

16. Corley 1993, 86.

17. Matt 27:55-56 establishes an immediate connection between "following" and "serving." That is, in Matthew's interpretation many women follow Jesus of Galilee in order to serve him! Luke 23:49 mentions no women by name but seems to mean the women mentioned in 8:2-3, where the serving behavior of the women is described as a kind of support of the Jesus movement and the term *follow* is avoided. Luke 23:49 uses the term *synakolouthein,* which has rather the unspecific sense of "accompany." This interpretation is supported by Luke 23:55, where the women are characterized again as companions but not as followers (they "went with" Jesus—*synerchesthai*). In Luke 23:49 the women are called "acquaintances" (*gnōstoi*) of Jesus and thus again distanced from the disciples as followers.

18. This is naturally all the more true if Mark 15:41 is Markan: thus recently Fander 1990, 135. Yet in our opinion she goes too far when she says that Mary Magdalene belonged to the Jesus movement at most as an itinerant charismatic.

19. Luke 14:26; 18:29; on the Lukan presentation of discipleship see Schottroff and Stegemann 1990; cf. also Schottroff 1980, 100–101.

20. Cf. also Matt 10:34-37/Luke 12:51-53; also in this text from the sayings source, wives are not mentioned. Note also the difference between Matt 10:37 and Luke 14:26.

21. John 19:25.

22. Mark 15:40, 47; 16:1; Matt 27:56, 61; 28:1; Luke 8:2; 24:10; John 19:25; 20:1, 11, 16, 18.

23. Luke 10:38–42; John 11:11-45; 12:1-8. From John 2:1ff.; 6:42; 19:25-27 one could conclude that Mary, the mother of Jesus, also accompanied him.

24. If she is identical with the mother of the sons of Zebedee (cf. Matt 27:56 with Mark 15:40), then we can infer from Matt 20:20 her membership in the Jesus movement.

25. Magdala is the grecization of Migdal; presumably identical with Taricheia, three miles northwest of Tiberias.

26. In the later Gnostic texts she acquires a special position as, for example, dialogue partner and companion of Jesus, who loved her more than all others and kissed her on the mouth. On this tradition see the brief overview in Vouga 1994, 191–93.

27. Exorcism: seven demons came out of her (Luke 8:2).

28. On the various assumptions and speculations about the women named in Mark 15:40-41 see only Fander 1990, 299ff.

29. A few examples will suffice. According to Mark 15:47, Mary Magdalene and Mary the mother of Joses observe where Jesus' body is buried. In Luke this process is observed by *all* the women who were with Jesus since Galilee (23:55). In the Matthean version (27:61) two women *sit* down across from Jesus' grave. In the story of the empty tomb the Gospels differ not only in regard to the number (John 20:1: only Mary Magdalene; Mark 16:1: three women; Matt 28:1: two women; Luke 24:1, 10: all the women) and names of the women but also in regard to the resurrection experience: Mark and Luke know only something about a proclamation of the resurrection of Jesus by heavenly messengers; in Matthew and John the resurrected Jesus also meets the women (Matt 28:9-10; John 20:14-18).

30. Unless one understands the statements about the appearance of the resurrected One before 500 "brothers" as an expression of inclusive language.

31. Cf. only Kraemer 1992, 130; in general on the resurrection experience of the women cf. Schottroff 1980, 110–12.

32. Origen *Cels.* 2.55; cf. also Luke 24:11.

33. Mark 1:29-31; cf. Matt 8:14-15; Luke 4:38-39.

34. Mark 5:21-43; cf. Matt 9:18-26; Luke 8:40-56.

35. Mark 7:24-30; cf. Matt 15:21-28. Only in Luke do we find the sabbath healing of the woman who was stooped over (13:10-17) and also a general comment to the effect that women healed by Jesus went with him (8:2-3). The two texts are not utilized here for the historical following of Jesus.

36. Cf. more closely Schüssler Fiorenza 1988, 185–86, who emphasizes that the pericope on the Syrophoenician woman is pre-Markan. Does it belong rather to the old-

est Jesus tradition? Critical of Schüssler Fiorenza's interpretation is Kraemer 1992, 132–33. Fander 1990, 74, interprets the pre-Markan tradition to be from "Jewish Christian circles." Corley 1993, 101, holds the story to be obviously Markan.

37. She is presumably a widow, for she is to be found in the house of Peter or Andrew. Yet marriages were patrilocal. Presumably she no longer had any family members who could care for her.

38. Corley 1993, 87–88.

39. In regard to the corresponding linguistic usage of Josephus, see Mayer-Schärtel 1994, 18–21.

40. Thus, for example, Schüssler Fiorenza 1988, 390; Fander 1990, 318–19 and elsewhere; cf. also Schottroff 1994, 313; these interpretations are also criticized by Corley 1993, 88 (esp. n. 20).

41. Malina and Rohrbaugh 1992, 70–71, 181.

42. In the Matthean version the touching of Jesus' coat is not a problem at all. Impurity as the central problem of the healing story is assumed by, among others, Fander 1990 and T. Vogt 1993.

43. Fander 1990, 197, 198, 199.

44. Cf., for example, Lev 15:19ff.; 18:19; 20:18; *m. Zabim* 5.6; *m. Niddah;* Jos. *War* 6.426–27 (a menstruating woman must not participate in the paschal sacrifice).

45. Kraemer 1992, 101ff.

46. T. Vogt 1993, 119.

47. Mark 14:3-9; cf. Matt 26:6-13; Luke 7:36-50; John 12:1-8.

48. Fander 1990, 118ff.: Mark 14:3-8. Mack 1988, 200, reduces the pre-Markan tradition to a chreia: "When Jesus was at table, a disreputable woman entered and poured out a jar of perfumed oil on him. He said, 'That is good.'"

49. Fander 1990, 336.

50. Fander 1990, 130–31, sees references to the messianic anointment and the anointing of the dead but excludes references to anointments in connection with guest meals (128–29). Schüssler Fiorenza 1988, 204, is apparently thinking of a prophetic anointment of Jesus as messianic king; Schottroff 1994, 165, understands the anointment as an "act of—public—solidarity with the Jesus who is going to his crucifixion by the Romans"; for the literature in English see Corley 1993, 103.

51. Corley 1993, 103ff.

52. The anointment of men (even kings) at banquets, as well as the oil used and the vessel, points to courtesans or slave women (Corley 1993, 104). The morally offensive judgment of the woman is already found in Luke (cf. Luke 7:37, 39).

53. In its basic content, this text presumably goes back to the tradition of the sayings source: Corley 1993, 155–56.

54. Ibid., 89ff.

55. Of a different opinion, however, is Fander 1990, 334: "Whether women were also numbered among the itinerant charismatics remains speculative; with Mary Magdalene it could be presumed."

56. Luke seems to presuppose somewhat more elevated and prosperous conditions: the women "ministered to them [the disciples and Jesus] from their substance" (Luke

8:3). Moreover, Luke says that Joanna is the wife of a steward of the tetrach Herod Antipas (*epitropos;* the meaning is perhaps the steward of a royal estate). This comment does not necessarily suggest upper-stratum membership, as Theissen 1989f, 112, assumes; rather, we may presume membership in the retainers.

57. Only the intention of the women disciples to care for the body of Jesus recalls a typical task of women.

58. Corley 1993, 39.

59. Ibid., 63ff.

60. Philostratus *Life of Apollonius* 1.20.

61. Thus Corley 1993, 86.

62. Thus, for example, Schüssler Fiorenza 1988, 189ff. Different, however, is Kraemer 1992, 191: "I am not as confident as some feminist scholars that such egalitarianism was intentionally directed toward the liberation of women, but the practical effect was the same."

63. Cf. Kraemer 1992, 95.

64. Cf. in detail Richter Reimer 1992, 29ff.

65. Versus, for example, Weiser 1983, 166.

66. Is it a question of their active participation at the table or the fact that food for the poor was denied to them? See also p. 219.

67. Richter Reimer 1992, 55ff.

68. Richter Reimer (1992, 60) points out that the name is attested for slave women.

69. Weiser (1983, 166) classifies her with the "economically well-to-do and women of higher social standing."

70. Gundry 1982, 295.

71. Corley 1993, 147.

72. Ibid., 151. Even Jesus' mother, who is likewise mentioned in the genealogy (1:16), is shortly thereafter described as morally suspect: she is pregnant before she has consummated her marriage with her betrothed Joseph (1:18).

73. Cf. in more detail Corley 1993, 165ff. Instead of speaking to Jesus in a house, as in Mark, she addresses him in public; her behavior is offensive (she is apparently running after Jesus' group and screaming, which is criticized by the disciples); she is called by the anachronistic term *Canaanite,* which, on the one hand, characterizes her as a non-Jew; on the other hand, in the biblical tradition Canaanite women are associated with prostitution and other sexual transgressions. Jesus distances himself from the woman more clearly than in Mark; at first he does not react at all to her request and responds only to his disciples.

74. This is not contradicted by the fact that according to Matt 5:32; 19:9, divorce is allowed because of *porneia.* Here it is a question of behavior within marriage.

Notes to Chapter 14

1. Contrary to ancient convention, Priscilla/Prisca is usually named before her husband.

2. Prisca, Phoebe, Mary, Tryphaena, Tryphosa, Persis, Junia, Julia, Herodiana, Euodia, Syntyche, Apphia: Rom 16:1ff.; Phil 4:2-3; Philemon 2.

3. Cf. pp. 278 and 404.

4. Ign. *Smyrn.* 13.1–2 first greets the "houses of my brothers, together with wives and children and the virgins who are called widows," then the "house of Tavia," and finally "Alke" (cf. Ign. *Pol.* 8.3). Dautzenberg 1983, 186: "Here we see the shift (also observable elsewhere) of interest from the house church to the household, in which the women have their place behind their husband, if they do not head it themselves as widows" (Ign. *Pol.* 8.2).

5. See pp. 401–2.

6. Meeks 1983, 55ff.

7. Dautzenberg 1983, 184.

8. Thus correctly Kraemer 1992, 135.

9. Ibid., 136ff.

10. Cf. ibid., 137.

11. Already in the Jerusalem early church and in Jaffa: Acts. 6:1ff.; 9:39, 41; cf. also Luke 2:37; 4:25-26; 7:12; 18:3ff.

12. Josephus also presents them as totally without means. Cf. Mayer-Schärtel 1994, 75.

13. Schottroff 1994, 229.

14. Acts 16:14ff.; Rom 16:3-5; 1 Cor 1:11; 16:19; Col 4:15.

15. Thus, for example, Schüssler Fiorenza 1988, 232; versus G. Lohfink 1983, 325. An inscription from Aphrodisias mentions a *prostatis* of the synagogue (named Jael).

16. Richter Reimer 1992, 142. On Lydia in general and the discussion of her classification in upper-stratum circles, see Richter Reimer 1992, 91ff.

17. Meeks 1983, 57; they have Greek names.

18. Cf. also Wire 1990, 63–66, for the Christ-confessing women in the Corinthian community: "In brief, the social status of the Corinthian women prophets at the time that they are called seems to be mixed on one indicator (free/slave) and low in every other indicator: wisdom, power, rank, ethnic support, and gender" (65).

19. Cf. the cogent comments of Schottroff 1994, 230–31. Note also the reference to Lucian *Pereg. Mort.* 12.

20. Cf. in detail Meeks 1983, 150ff.

21. Cf. above all Thyen 1978, 107–208; Moxnes 1989, 101ff.; Fatum 1989, 61–80.

22. The slave Onesimus, who fled to Paul as spokesman and in the meantime came to faith, is—after his return—supposed to be received by his master (Philemon) no longer as a slave but as a (Christian) brother (Philemon 15-16). On this see only Wolter 1993, 271–72.

23. It should be noted that the formulation is not *ouk eni anēr oude gynē* but *ouk eni arsen kai thēly*.

24. Thus also, for example, Dautzenberg 1983, 217.

25. Cf. only Rom 7:2-3; 1 Cor 7:1-16, 25-40; 11:2-16; 14:34-35.

26. Thyen 1978, 111.

27. Cf. Jervell 1960; Meeks 1973, 165–208; Betz 1988, 344ff.

28. For details on feminine forms of names see Brooten 1978, 148–51. Fàbrega 1984/85.

29. Rom 16:3; Phil 4:2-3; Euodia and Syntyche are, moreover, also characterized as fellow strivers; that is, because of the Christ-confessing community they apparently also had disagreements with Christ-confessing opponents (cf. Phil 1:27-28); see only Weiser 1983, 179.

30. Ollrogg 1979, 67; cf. 1 Thess 3:2; 1 Cor 3:9; Phil 2:25; Philemon 1:24.

31. Cf. also Dautzenberg 1983, 185.

32. For details cf. Schottroff 1994, 222–42.

33. Cf. only Weiser 1983, 169 (with references to additional literature).

34. Schottroff 1994, 230.

35. Schüssler Fiorenza 1988, 349.

36. Schüssler Fiorenza (ibid.) sees here again a special "presiding" group of women presbyters.

37. Cf. 1 Cor 11:16; 14:33b.

38. Cf. Schüssler Fiorenza 1988, 205ff.

39. Similarly Kraemer 1992, 142.

40. Corley 1993, 16.

41. Thus he deduces the veiling of women from the placing of men over women (1 Cor 11:3, 8-9; cf. Gen 2:22-23) or from the proper behavior of women and men (1 Cor 11:5-6, 13-16). The silence of women in the community assembly he bases, on the one hand, on their subordination in accordance with the Torah and, on the other hand, on general customs (1 Cor 14:34-35).

42. For details see Theissen 1983, 161ff. Cf. also Thompson 1988, 99–115, and Küchler 1986.

43. Theissen 1983, 169, with reference to Aristophanes *Lys.* 30–532.

44. Indeed, Paul makes this behavior of Corinthian women similar to that of lesbians. This is shown by a comparison with Lucian. In his *Hetaera Dialogues* (5) we hear about one very masculine homosexual woman from Lesbos. She not only prefers only the masculine form (Megillus) of her feminine name Megilla and regards a woman as her wife but also has short hair, over which she wears a wig. Thus a woman wearing short hair not only behaves like a man but is also suspected of adopting the role of a man in sexual activity. This reversal of roles is also rather crassly condemned by Lucian. The exchanging of roles—that is, the adoption of the female role by men and that of a male by women—is doubtless also the basic problem in the condemnation of homosexuality by Paul (Rom 1:26). Cf. Brooten 1987.

45. Thus also Kraemer 1992, 146–47.

46. Cf. p. 362.

47. See Kraemer 1992, 147.

48. Cf. only Conzelmann 1969, 289–90, who understands vv. 33b-36 as an "interpolation." "This self-contained section goes beyond the context: it interrupts the topic of prophecy and disturbs the flow of the presentation. In content it is in contradiction with 11:2ff., where the appearance of women in the community is presupposed." Other interpolation hypotheses, such as that of Dautzenberg, try to separate not just vv. 34-35 but also 33b-38 (Dautzenberg 1975, 257–74, 290–300). We will not go into that here either.

49. For details cf. Wire 1990, 149–52. Lietzmann's statement is still valid: "The reversal is easily conceivable, because it apparently harshly interrupts here the context of the instructions about prophecy and glossolalia, which are indeed continued in vv. 37-40. It would never occur to someone to explain the situation differently, if the content of the verses did not give one pause: here we have an absolute commandment of silence for women in the community assembly, whereas in 11:2-16 the rule is that a woman must wear a veil when praying or prophesying—an indirect acknowledgement of her right to appear in public": Lietzmann 1969, 75. Thus the decision for the original reading of the text is relatively easy.

50. A brief presentation and cogent rejection of the different interpolation hypotheses is presented in Wire 1990, 229–32.

51. Cf. also Dautzenberg 1983, 195: "The general prohibition of 1 Cor 14:34 is made more precise in 14:35."

52. On the context of "subordination," "silence," and "home" in ancient culture, see also Dautzenberg 1983, 196ff.

53. Cf. also Livius 34.2.10.

54. This interpretation is substantiated above all by Schottroff 1980, 122–24; cf. 1994, 227. Jesus' formulation—"Mary has chosen the good part" (10:42, literal)—produces an opposition between the two women only in its incorrect comparative translation (NRSV: "the better part") or interpretation.

55. Schüssler Fiorenza 1987, 1ff. This interpretation is also shared by Corley 1993, 138ff., among others.

56. Corley 1993, 138. Hence she understands the story of Mary and Martha as an attempt by Luke to support the model submissive role of Mary.

57. We may compare this to the behavior of the Syrophoenician woman, who—with all submission to the authority of the miraculous healer—"discusses" with Jesus.

58. Corley 1993, 108ff.

59. Here we are dependent—yet with some changes—on the translation of Schottroff 1994, 104.

60. For details cf. Küchler 1986. Yet Schottroff 1994, 116 and elsewhere, calls attention to the fact that the interpretation of Old Testament texts in the Jewish tradition, which from today's perspective are negative for women, by no means reveals a specifically Jewish picture of women. Schottroff (116) writes that the "hate-filled propaganda against women's liberation was represented by Roman and Greek writers, as well as by Jewish, Christian, and Gnostic religious writings." On the topic of the sexually seducible seductress, she refers, for example, to Valerius Maximus (4.5; 9.5.3). Cf. also the literature mentioned in Schottroff 1994, 108, n. 20.

61. Schottroff 1994, 105ff.

62. Cf. ibid., 108, with additional literature.

63. We cannot exclude the possibility that 1 Cor 11:3-4; 14:33b-36 provided the model for 1 Tim 2:11-12. Then we would understand learning in silence and submission to be what Paul recommended to women: silence in public and learning at home—under the direction and control of the husband.

64. Then around one century later, Tertullian related 1 Cor 14:33b-36 and 1 Tim 2:11-12 not only to the speaking and teaching of women but also to all other ecclesiastical functions, such as baptism, distribution of the Lord's Supper, and other male duties (*De virginibus verlandis* 9). This general teaching prohibition for women is not contradicted by Titus 2:3, where old women are called good teachers. For the kind of teaching attributed to them here is the instruction of young women "to love their husbands, to love their children, to be self-controlled, chaste, good managers of the household, kind, being submissive to their husbands, so that the word of God may not be discredited" (Titus 2:4-5), in a word: the education of young women for the fulfillment of the traditional roles of women.

65. From the New Testament reference, Clement of Alexandria (*Strom.* 3.6.53) concludes that the apostles took their wives with them and that these women evangelized in the women's quarters (to which foreign men in principle had no access). Thus he does not seem to have a problem with proclamation by women to women.

66. Kraemer 1992, 150–51.

67. Schottroff 1994, 108ff. MacDonald (1983, 54–77) even presumes analogies to the *Acts of Thecla,* that is, the attempt of women who refer to Paul, in order to substantiate their function as teachers and baptizers, to assume the authority of Paul.

68. For details on the catchword *subordinate* cf. K. Müller 1983, 292ff.

69. Ibid., 313–15.

70. Cf. ibid., 297–98; Wolter 1993, 198–200.

71. Wolter 1993, 200.

72. Cf. only *Oik.* 7.19–35, 39–40; see also Foucault 1989, 200ff.

73. Kraemer 1992, 191.

74. Schottroff 1994, 104ff.

BIBLIOGRAPHY

Adam, A., and C. Burchard. 1972. *Antike Berichte über die Essener.* 2d ed. Kleine Texte für Vorlesungen und Übungen 182. Berlin: Walter de Gruyter.

Albertz, R. 1992. *Religionsgeschichte Israels in alttestamentlicher Zeit,* vol. 2. Göttingen: Vandenhoeck & Rupprecht. [ET = *A History of Israelite Religion in the Old Testament Period.* J. Bowden, trans. 2 vols. OTL. Louisville: Westminster/John Knox, 1994.]

Alföldy, G. 1981. "Soziale Konflikte im römischen Kaiserreich." In H. Schneider 1981c, 372–95.

———. 1984. *Römische Sozialgeschichte.* 3d ed. Wiesbaden: Franz Steiner. [ET = *The Social History of Rome.* D. Braund and F. Pollock, trans. Totowa, N.J.: Barnes & Noble, 1985. Reprint ed.: Ancient Society and History Series. Baltimore: Johns Hopkins Univ. Press, 1988.]

———. 1986a. "Die römische Gesellschaft: Eine Nachbetrachtung über Struktur und Eigenart." In idem, *Die römische Gesellschaft: Ausgewählte Beiträge,* 69–98. Heidelberger althistorische Beitrage und epigraphische Studien 1. Stuttgart: Franz Steiner.

———. 1986b. "Die römische Gesellschaft—Struktur und Eigenart." In ibid., 42–68.

Alon, G. 1980/84. *The Jews in Their Land in the Talmudic Age (70–640 C.E.).* 2 vols. Jerusalem: Magnes.

Amir, Y. 1985. "Psalm 119 als Zeugnis eines protorabbinischen Judentums." In idem, *Studien zum antiken Judentum,* 1–34. Bern: Peter Lang.

Applebaum, S. 1974a. "The Legal Status of the Jewish Communities in the Diaspora." In Safrai and Stern 1974, 1:420–63.

———. 1974b. "The Organization of the Jewish Communities in the Diaspora." In ibid., 1:464–503.

———. 1976a. "Economic Life in Palestine." In Safrai and Stern 1976, 2:631–700.

———. 1976b. "The Social and Economic Status of the Jews in the Diaspora." In ibid., 2:701–27.

———. 1977. "Judea as a Roman Province: The Countryside as a Political and Economic Factor." In *ANRW* II 8.355–96.

Aptowitzer, V. 1927. *Parteipolitik der Hasmonäerzeit im rabbinischen und pseudepigraphischen Schrifttum.* Vienna: Kohut-Foundation.

Aram, D. W. 1968. *The Jewish Law of Divorce according to Bible and Talmud.* 2d ed. New York: Hermon.

Astin, M., and Vidal-Naquet, P. 1984. *Gesellschaft und Wirtschaft im alten Griechenland.* Munich: Chr. Kaiser.

Ausbüttel, F. M. 1982. *Untersuchungen zu den Vereinen im Westen des Römischen Reiches.* Kallmünz: M. Lassleben.

Avi-Yonah, M. 1973. "Palestina." In *PRE* supp. 13:322–454.

Avigad, N. 1984. *Discovering Jerusalem.* Oxford: Oxford Univ. Press.

Bachmann, M. 1980. *Jerusalem und der Tempel: Die geographisch-theologischen Elemente in der lukanischen Sicht des jüdischen Kultzentrums.* BWANT 109. Stuttgart: Kohlhammer.

Balch, D. L., ed. 1991. *Social History of the Matthean Community: Cross-Disciplinary Approaches.* Minneapolis: Fortress.

Baldermann, I., et al., eds. 1988. *Zum Problem des biblischen Kanons.* Jahrbuch für Biblische Theologie 3. Neukirchen-Vluyn: Neukirchener.

Balsdon, J. P. D. 1979. *Die Frau in der römischen Antike.* Munich: Chr. Kaiser. [ET = *Roman Women: Their History and Habits.* London: Bodley Head, 1962.]

Banks, R. 1980. *Paul's Idea of Community: The Early House Churches in Their Historical Setting.* Grand Rapids: Eerdmans.

Barnes, T. D. 1968. "The Legislation against the Christians." *JRS* 58:32–50.

Barnett, P. W. 1981. "The Jewish Sign-Prophets—A.D. 40–70: Their Intentions and Origin." *NTS* 27:679–97.

Bartchy, S. 1973. *MALLON CHRESAI: First Century Slavery and the Interpretation of 1 Corinthians 7:21.* SBLDS 11. Missoula, Mont.: Scholars.

Bauer, W., K. Aland, and B. Aland. 1988. *Griechisch-deutsches Wörterbuch zu den Schriften des Neuen Testaments und der frühchristlichen Literatur.* 6th ed. Berlin: Walter de Gruyter.

Baumbach, G. 1965. "Zeloten und Sikarier." *TLZ* 90:727–40.

———. 1973a. "Der Sadduzäische Konservativismus." In *Literatur und Religion des Frühjudentums,* 201–13. J. Maier and J. Schreiner, eds. Würzburg: Echter.

———. 1973b. "Die antirömischen Aufstandsgruppen." In ibid., 273–83.

———. 1985. "Einheit und Vielfalt der jüdischen Freiheitsbewegung im 1. Jh. n. Chr." *EvT* 45:93–107.

———. 1992. "Hairesis, hairetikos." In *EWNT,* 2d ed., 1:96–97. [ET = *EDNT* 1:40–41.]

Baumgarten, A. I. "The Name of the Pharisees." *JBL* 102:411–28.

Beare, F. W. 1981. *The Gospel according to Matthew: A Commentary.* San Francisco: Harper & Row.

Becker, H.-J. 1990. *Auf der Kathedra des Mose: Rabbinisch-theologisches Denken und antirabbinische Polemik in Matthäus 23,1-12.* ANTZ 4. Berlin: Institut Kirche und Judentum.

Becker, H. S. 1963. *Outsiders: Studies in the Sociology of Deviance.* New York: Free Press.

Becker, J. 1972. *Johannes der Täufer und Jesus von Nazareth.* BibS 63. Neukirchen-Vluyn: Neukirchener.

———, ed. 1987. *Die Anfänge des Christentums.* Stuttgart: Kohlhammer. [ET = idem 1993a.]

————, ed. 1993a. *Christian Beginnings: Word and Community from Jesus to Post-Apostolic Times.* A. S. Kidder and R. Krauss, trans. Louisville: Westminster/John Knox, 1993.

————. 1993b. "Paul and His Churches." In idem 1993a, 132–210.

————. 1993c. *Paul: Apostle to the Gentiles.* O. C. Dean, trans. Louisville: Westminster/John Knox.

Beckwith, R. 1985. *The Old Testament Canon of the New Testament Church and Its Background in Early Judaism.* Grand Rapids: Eerdmans.

Bellen, H. 1971. *Studien zur Sklavenflucht im römischen Kaiserreich.* Forschungen zur antiken Sklaverei 4. Wiesbaden: Franz Steiner.

Belo, F. 1980. *Das Markusevangelium materialistisch gelesen.* Stuttgart: Kohlhammer. [ET = *A Materialist Reading of the Gospel of Mark.* M. J. O'Connell, trans. Maryknoll, N.Y.: Orbis, 1981.]

Ben-David, A. 1974. *Talmudische Ökonomie: Die Wirtschaft des jüdischen Palästina zur Zeit der Mischna und des Talmud.* Hildesheim: G. Olms.

Ben-Yehuda, N. 1985. *Deviance and Moral Boundaries: Witchcraft, the Occult, Deviant Sciences and Scientists.* Chicago: Univ. of Chicago Press.

Bendix, R. 1964. *Max Weber—Das Werk.* Munich: Chr. Kaiser. [ET = *Max Weber: An Intellectual Portrait.* Garden City, N.Y.: Doubleday, 1960.]

————. 1985. "Umbildung des persönlichen Charismas: Eine Anwendung von Max Webers Charismabegriff auf das Frühchristentum." In *Max Webers Sicht des antiken Christentums: Interpretation und Kritik,* 404–43. W. Schluchter, ed. Frankfurt: Suhrkamp.

Benko, S., and J. J. O'Rourke, eds. 1971. *The Catacombs and the Colosseum: The Roman Empire as Setting of Primitive Christianity.* Valley Forge, Pa.: Judson.

Berger, K. 1976. "Volksversammlung und Gemeinde Gottes: Zu den Anfängen der christlichen Verwendung von 'ekklesia.'" *ZTK* 73:167–207.

Bergmann, W., and C. Hoffmann. 1987. "Kalkül oder 'Massenwahn': Eine soziologische Interpretation der antijüdischen Unruhen in Alexandria 38 n.d.Z." In *Antisemitismus und Jüdische Geschichte: Studien zu Ehren von Herbert A. Strauss,* 15–46. R. Erb and M. Schmidt, eds. Berlin: Walter de Gruyter

Best, E. 1972. *A Commentary on the First and Second Epistles to the Thessalonians.* HTNC. New York: Harper & Row. [Reprint: Peabody, Mass.: Hendrickson, 1986.]

Betz, H. D. 1988. *Der Galaterbrief: Ein Kommentar zum Brief des Apostels Paulus an die Gemeinden in Galatien.* Munich: Chr. Kaiser. [ET = *Galatians: A Commentary on Paul's Letter to the Churches in Galatia.* Hermeneia. Philadelphia: Fortress, 1979.]

————. 1993. *2. Korintherbrief 8 und 9: Ein Kommentar zu zwei Verwaltungsbriefen des Apostels Paulus.* Gütersloh: Gütersloher. [ET = *2 Corinthians 8 and 9: A Commentary on Two Administrative Letters of the Apostle Paul.* Hermeneia. Philadelphia: Fortress, 1985.]

Bickerman, E. J. 1988. *The Jews in the Greek Age.* Cambridge: Harvard Univ. Press.

Bickhoff-Böttcher, N. 1984. "Das Judentum in der griechisch-römischen Welt: Gesellschaftliche und politische Beziehungen und Konflicte von der Mitte des 1. Jahrhunderts vChr bis zum Ende des 2. Jahrhunderts nChr." Diss., Bochum.

Billerbeck, P. 1961. *Kommentar zum Neuen Testament aus Talmud und Midrasch.* 6 vols. 3d ed. Munich: C. H. Beck.

Bittner, W. J. 1987. *Jesu Zeichen im Johannesevangelium: Die Messias-Erkenntnis im Johannesevangelium vor ihrem jüdischen Hintergrund.* WUNT 2/26. Tübingen: J. C. B. Mohr.

Black, M. 1974. "Judas of Galilee and Josephus's 'Fourth Philosophy.'" In *Josephus-Studien: Untersuchungen zu Josephus, dem antiken Judentum und dem Neuen Testament,* 45–54. O. Betz et al., eds. Göttingen: Vandenhoeck & Ruprecht.

———. 1982. *Die Muttersprache Jesu.* BWANT 115. Stuttgart: Kohlhammer. [ET = *An Aramaic Approach to the Gospels and Acts.* 3d ed. Oxford: Clarendon, 1967. Reprinted with Introduction by C. A. Evans; Peabody, Mass.: Hendrickson, 1999.]

Bleicken, J. 1981. *Verfassungs- und Sozialgeschichte des Römischen Kaiserreiches,* vol. 2. 2d ed. Paderborn: Schoeningh.

Blok, A. 1972. "The Peasant and the Brigand: Social Banditry Reconsidered." *Comparative Studies in Society and History* 14:494–503.

Blumberg, R. L. 1978. *Stratification: Socioeconomic and Sexual Inequality.* Dubuque, Ia.: W. C. Brown.

Boak, A. E. R. 1943. *A History of Rome to 565.* 3d ed. New York: Macmillan.

Bogaert, R. 1976. "Geld (Geldwirtschaft)." In *RAC* 9:797–907.

Bolkestein, H. 1939. *Wohltätigkeit und Armenpflege im vorchristlichen Altertum: Ein Beitrag zum Problem "Moral und Gesellschaft."* Utrecht: A. Oosthoek. [Reprint ed. 1967.]

Borleffs, J. W. P. 1952. "Institutum Neronianum." *VC* 6:129–45.

Bornkamm, G. 1959. "Presbys ktl." In *TWNT* 6:651–83. [ET = *TDNT* 6:651–83.]

Bösen, W. 1990. *Galiläa als Lebensraum und Wirkungsfeld Jesu: Eine zeitgeschichtliche und theologische Untersuchung.* 2d ed. Biblisches Sachbuch. Freiburg: Herder.

Bovon, F. 1985. "Israel, die Kirche und die Völker im lukanischen Doppelwerk." In idem, *Lukas in neuer Sicht: Gesammelte Aufsätze,* 120ff. Neukirchen-Vluyn: Neukirchener. [Orig.: *TLZ* 108 (1983): 403–14.]

Brandenburger, E. 1993. Gerichtskonzeptionen im Urchristentum und ihre Voraussetzungen: Eine Problemstudie." In idem, *Studien zur Geschichte und Theologie des Urchristentum,* 289–338. Stuttgart: Kohlhammer.

Brandis, C. G. 1905. "Ekklēsia." In *PRE* 5:2163–2200.

Braudel, F. 1990. *Das Mittelmeer und die mediterrane Welt in der Epoche Philipps II.* Frankfurt. [ET = *The Mediterranean and the Mediterranean World in the Age of Philip II.* S. Reynolds, trans. New York: Harper & Row, 1972.]

Bremen, R. van. 1983. "Women and Wealth." In *Images of Women in Antiquity,* 223–42. A. Cameron and A. Kuhrt, eds. Detroit: Wayne State Univ. Press.

Bringmann, K. 1983. *Hellenistische Reform und Religionsverfolgung in Judäa.* Göttingen: Vandenhoeck & Ruprecht.

Brockmeyer, N. 1968. *Arbeitsorganisation und ökonomisches Denken in der Gutswirtschaft des römischen Reiches.* Diss., Bochum.

———. 1979. *Antike Sklaverei.* Erträge der Forschung 116. Darmstadt: Wissenschaftliche Buchgesellschaft.

Brödner, E. 1989. *Wohnen in der Antike.* Darmstadt: Wissenschaftliche Buchgesellschaft.

Brooten, B. J. 1978. "'Junia . . . hervorragend unter den Aposteln' (Röm 16,7)." In *Frauenbefreiung: Biblische und theologische Argumente,* 148–51. E. Moltmann-Wendel, ed. 2d ed. Munich: Chr. Kaiser. [ET = "Junia . . . Outstanding among the Apostles (Romans 16:7)." In *Women Priests: A Catholic Commentary,* 141–44. L. Swidler and A. Swidler, eds. New York: Paulist, 1977.]

———. 1982. *Women Leaders in the Ancient Synagogue: Inscriptional Evidence and Background Issues.* BJS 36. Chico, Calif.: Scholars.

———. 1985. "Early Christian Women and Their Cultural Context: Issues of Method in Historical Reconstruction." In *Feminist Perspectives on Biblical Scholarship,* 65–91. A. Y. Collins, ed. SBL Centennial Publications. Atlanta: Scholars.

———. 1987. "Die weibliche Homoerotik bei Paulus." In *Hättest du gedacht, dass wir so viele sind? Lesbische Frauen in der Kirche,* 113ff. M. Barz et al., eds. Stuttgart: Kohlhammer. [ET = "Paul's Views on the Nature of Women and Female Homoeroticism." In *Immaculate and Powerful: The Female in Sacred Images and Social Reality,* 61–87. C. W. Atkinson et al., eds. Harvard Women's Studies in Religion 1. Boston: Beacon, 1985.]

———. 1996. *Love between Women: Early Christian Responses to Female Homoeroticism.* Chicago Series on Sexuality, History, and Society. Chicago: Univ. of Chicago Press.

Broshi, M. 1979. "The Population of Western Palestine in the Roman-Byzantine Period." *BASOR* 236:1–10.

———. 1992. "The Archaelogy of Qumran—A Reconsideration." In *The Dead Sea Scrolls: Forty Years of Research,* 103–15. D. Dimant and U. Rappaport, eds. STDJ 10. Leiden: Brill.

Brown, R. E. 1979. *The Community of the Beloved Disciple.* New York: Paulist.

Brox, N. 1989. *Der erste Petrusbrief.* 3d ed. Neukirchen-Vluyn: Neukirchener.

Brunt, P. A. 1971a. *Italian Manpower 225 B.C.—A.D. 14.* London: Oxford Univ. Press.

———. 1971b. *Social Conflicts in the Roman Republic.* New York: Norton.

———. 1973. "Aspects of the Social Thought of Dio Chrysostom and of the Stoics." In *Proceedings of the Cambridge Philological Society* 199:9–34.

Bücher, K. 1901. "Die Entstehung der Volkswirtschaft." In idem, *Die Entstehung der Volkswirtschaft: Vorträge und Versuche,* 101–78. 3d ed. Tübingen: J. C. B. Mohr.

———. 1922a. *Beiträge zur Wirtschaftsgeschichte.* Tübingen: J. C. B. Mohr.

———. 1922b. "Die Diokletianische Taxordnung vom Jahre 301." In ibid., 179–223.

Büchner, K. 1955. *Publius Cornelius Tacitus: Die historischen Versuche, Agricola, Germania, Dialogus.* Stuttgart: Kohlhammer.

Burchard, C. 1970. *Der dreizehnte Zeuge: Traditions- und kompositionsgeschichtliche Untersuchungen zu Lukas' Darstellung der Frühzeit des Paulus.* Göttingen: Vandenhoeck & Ruprecht.

———.1978. "Sadduzäer." In *PRE* supp. 15:466–78.

———. 1975. "Paulus in der Apostelgeschichte." *TLZ* 100:881–95.

———. 1983. "Joseph und Aseneth." *JSHRZ* 2/4:577–735.

———. 1987. "Jesus von Nazareth." In J. Becker 1987, 12–58. [ET = "Jesus of Nazareth." In J. Becker 1993a, 15–72.]

Burford, A. 1972. *Craftsmen in Greek and Roman Society.* Aspects of Greek and Roman Life. Ithaca, N.Y.: Cornell Univ. Press.

Cadbury, H. J. 1931. "Erastus of Corinth." *JBL* 50:42–58.

Campbell, J. Y. 1948. "The Origin and Meaning of the Christian Use of Ekklesia." *JTS* 49:130–42.

Camponovo, O. 1984. *Königtum, Königsherrschaft und Reich Gottes in den frühjüdischen Schriften.* OBO 58. Göttingen: Vandenhoeck & Ruprecht.

Carney, T. F. 1975. *The Shape of the Past: Models and Antiquity.* Lawrence, Kans.: Coronado.

Cassidy, R. J. 1978. *Jesus, Politics, and Society: A Study of Luke's Gospel.* Maryknoll, N.Y.: Orbis.

Charlesworth, J. H., ed. 1992. *The Messiah: Developments in Earliest Judaism and Christianity.* Minneapolis: Fortress.

Christ, K. 1962. "Zur Herrscherauffassung Domitains." *Schweizerische Zeitschrift für Geschichte* 12:187ff.

———. 1980. "Grundfragen der römischen Sozialstruktur." In *Studien zur antiken Sozialgeschichte,* FS F. Vittinghoff, 197–228. W. Eck et al., eds. KHA 28. Cologne: Bohlau.

———. 1984. *Die Römer: Eine Einführung in ihre Geschichte und Zivilisation.* 2d ed. Munich: Chr. Kaiser. [ET = *The Romans: An Introduction to Their History and Civilization.* C. Holme, trans. Berkeley: Univ. of California Press, 1984.]

———. 1988. *Geschichte der römischen Kaiserzeit: Von Augustus bis Konstantin.* Munich: C. H. Beck.

Cipolla, C. M. 1972. *Wirtschaftsgeschichte und Weltbevölkerung.* Munich: Chr. Kaiser.

Clementz, H. 1993. *Flavius Josephus: Kleinere Schriften.* Reprint ed. Wiesbaden: Franz Steiner. [Orig. ed. Halle: O. Hendel, 1901.]

Cohen, S. J. D. 1984. "The Significance of Yavneh: Pharisees, Rabbis, and the End of Jewish Sectarianism." *HUCA* 54:27–53.

———, ed. 1993. *The Jewish Family in Antiquity.* BJS 289. Atlanta: Scholars.

———. 1997. "Were Pharisees and Rabbis the Leaders of Communal Prayer and Torah Study in Antiquity? The Evidence of the New Testament, Josephus, and the Church Fathers." In *Echoes of Many Texts: Reflections on Jewish and Christian Traditions: Essays in Honor of Lou H. Silbermann,* 99–114. W. G. Dever and J. E. Wright, eds. BJS 313. Atlanta: Scholars.

Cohen, Y. A. 1968. "Food: II. Consumption Patterns." In *International Encyclopedia of the Social Sciences*, 5:508–13. D. Sills, ed. New York: Macmillan.

Collins, A. Y. 1984. *Crisis and Catharsis: The Power of the Apocalypse*. Philadelphia: Fortress.

———, ed. 1986. *Semeia* 36: *Early Christian Apocalypticism: Genre and Social Setting*.

Collins, J. J., ed. 1979. *Semeia* 14: *Apocalypse: The Morphology of a Genre*.

———. 1984. *The Apocalyptic Imagination in Ancient Judaism*. New York: Crossroad.

———. 1986. "Apocalyptic Literature." In *Early Judaism and Its Modern Interpreters*, 345–70. R. A. Kraft and G. W. E. Nickelsburg, eds. Philadelphia: Fortress.

———. 1990. "Was the Dead Sea Sect an Apocalyptic Movement?" In *Archaeology and History in the Dead Sea* Scrolls, 25-51. L. Schiffmann, ed. JSPSS 8. Sheffield: JSOT.

———. 1991. "Genre, Ideology and Social Movements in Jewish Apocalypticism." In *Mysteries and Revelations: Apocalyptic Studies since the Uppsala Colloquium*, 11–32. J. J. Collins and J. H. Charlesworth, eds. JSPSS 9. Sheffield: JSOT.

Colpe, C. 1990. *Das Siegel der Propheten: Historische Beziehungen zwischen Judentum, Judenchristentum, Heidentum und frühem Islam*. ANTZ 3. Berlin: Institut Kirche und Judentum.

———. 1993. "The Oldest Jewish-Christian Community." In J. Becker 1993a, 75–102.

Conzelmann, H. 1969. *Der erste Brief an die Korinther*. Göttingen: Vandenhoeck & Rupprecht. [ET = *1 Corinthians: A Commentary on the First Epistle to the Corinthians*. J. W. Leitch, trans. Hermeneia. Philadelphia: Fortress Press, 1975.]

———. 1972. *Die Apostelgeschichte*. 2d ed. Tübingen: J. C. B. Mohr. [ET = *Acts of the Apostles*. J. Limburg et al., trans. Hermeneia. Philadelphia: Fortress Press, 1987.]

———. 1974a. "Die geschichtliche Ort der lukanischen Schriften im Urchristentum." In *Das Lukas-Evangelium: Die redactions- und kompositionsgeschichtliche Forschung*, 236–60. G. Braumann, ed. WF 280. Darmstadt: Wissenschaftliche Buchgesellschaft.

———. 1974b. "Zur Lukasanalyse." In ibid., 43–63. [Orig. art.: *ZTK* 49 (1952):16–33.]

———. 1981. *Heiden—Juden—Christen: Auseinandersetzungen in der Literatur der hellenistisch-römischen Zeit*. Tübingen: J. C. B. Mohr. [ET = *Gentiles, Jews, Christians: Polemics and Apologetics in the Greco-Roman Period*. M. E. Boring, trans. Minneapolis: Fortress, 1992.]

Corley, K. E. 1993. *Private Women, Public Meals: Social Conflict in the Synoptic Tradition*. Peabody, Mass.: Hendrickson.

Coser, L. A. 1972. *Theorie sozialer Konflikte*. Neuwied am Rhein: Luchterhand. [ET = *The Functions of Social Conflict*. New York: Free Press, 1956.]

Cotter, W. 1994. "Women's Authority Roles in Paul's Churches." *NovT* 36:350–72.

Cowell, F. R. 1956. *Cicero and the Roman Republic*. London: Penguin. [5th ed. 1973.]

Cranfield, C. E. B. 1983. *The Epistle to the Romans*. Vol. 2. ICC. Edinburgh: T. & T. Clark.

Crawford, M. 1981. "Geld und Austausch in der römischen Welt." In H. Schneider 1981b, 258–79.

Croix, G. E. M. de Ste. 1981. *The Class Struggle in the Ancient Greek World.* Ithaca, N.Y.: Cornell Univ. Press.

Crossan, J. D. 1994. *Der historische Jesus.* Munich: Chr. Kaiser. [ET = *The Historical Jesus: The Life of a Mediterranean Jewish Peasant.* San Francisco: HarperSan-Francisco, 1991.]

————. 1998. *The Birth of Christianity: Discovering What Happened in the Years Immediately after the Execution of Jesus.* San Francisco: HarperSanFrancisco.

Crüsemann, F. 1992a. *Die Tora: Theologie und Sozialgeschichte des alttestamentlichen Gesetzes.* Munich: Chr. Kaiser. [ET = *The Torah: Theology and Social History of Old Testament Law.* A. W. Mahnke, trans. Minneapolis: Fortress, 1996.]

————. 1992b. "'. . . wie wir vergeben unseren Schuldigern': Schulden und Schuld in der biblischen Tradition." In *Schuld und Schulden: Biblische Traditionen in gegenwärtigen* Konflikten, 90–103. M. Crüsemann and W. Schottroff, eds. Kaiser Taschenbücher 121. Munich: Chr. Kaiser.

Cullmann, O. 1994. *Das Gebet im Neuen Testament.* Tübingen: J. C. B. Mohr. [ET = *Prayer in the New Testament.* J. Bowden, trans. OBT. Minneapolis: Fortress, 1995.]

Dalman, G. 1964. *Arbeit und Sitte in Palästina.* 7 vols. Schriften des Deutschen Palästinas-Institut. Reprint ed. Hildesheim: G. Olms. [Orig. ed. Gütersloh: C. Bertelsmann, 1928–42.]

————. 1967. *Orte und Wege Jesu.* Reprint ed. Darmstadt: Wissenschaftliche Buchgesellschaft. [4th ed., 1924; ET = *Sacred Sites and Ways: Studies in the Topography of the Gospels.* P. P. Levertoff, trans. New York: Macmillan, 1935.]

Dar, S. 1986. *Landscape and Pattern: An Archaeological Survey of Samaria 800 B.C.E.–636 C.E.* Historical Commentary by S. Applebaum. BAR International Series 308. Oxford: B.A.R.

D'Arms, J. H. 1990. "§4. Italien." In Vittinghoff 1991, 1:375–428.

Dautzenberg, G. 1975. *Urchristliche Prophetie, ihre Erforschung, ihre Voraussetzungen im Judentum und ihre Struktur im ersten Korintherbrief.* Stuttgart: Kohlhammer.

————. 1983. "Zur Stellung der Frauen in den paulinischen Gemeinden." In idem et al. 1983, 182–224.

————, et al., eds. 1983. *Die Frau im Urchristentum.* QD 95. Freiburg: Herder.

Davies, J. K. 1984. "Cultural, Social and Economic Features of the Hellenistic World." In *Cambridge Ancient History.* Vol. 7.1: *The Hellenistic World.* 2d ed. F. W. Wallbank et al., eds. Cambridge: Cambridge Univ. Press.

Davis, J. 1977. *People of the Mediterranean: An Essay in Comparative Social Anthropology.* Library of Man. London: Routledge & Kegan Paul.

Deissmann, A. 1908. *Das Urchristentum und die unteren Schichten.* 2d ed. Göttingen: Vandenhoeck & Ruprecht.

————. 1925. *Paulus: Eine kultur- und religionsgeschichtliche Skizze.* 2d ed. Tübingen: J. C. B. Mohr. [ET = *Paul: A Study in Social and Religious History.* W. E. Wilson, trans. 2d ed. New YorK: Harper & Row, 1957.]

Derrett, J. D. M. 1965. "Law in the New Testament: The Parable of the Unmerciful Servant." *RIDA* 12:3–19.

Dibelius, M. 1964. *Der Brief des Jacobus.* 11th ed. (ed. H. Greeven). Göttingen: Vandenhoeck & Ruprecht. [ET = *James: A Commentary on the Epistle of James.* M. A. Williams, trans. Hermeneia. Philadelphia: Fortress, 1975.]

Dobschütz, E. von. 1902. *Die urchristliche Gemeinden: Sittengeschichtliche Bilder.* Leipzig: J. C. Hinrichs. [ET = *Christian Life in the Primitive Church.* G. Bremner, trans. New York: G. P. Putnam's Sons, 1904.]

Dohr, H. 1965. "Die italischen Gutshöfe nach den Schriften Catos und Varros." Diss., Cologne.

Donaldson, T. L. 1981. "Moses Typology and Sectarian Nature of Early-Christian Anti-Judaism: A Study in Acts 7." *JSNT* 12:27–52.

Donner, H. 1976. *Einführung in die biblische Landes- und Altertumskunde.* Darmstadt: Wissenschaftliche Buchgesellschaft.

Douglas, M. 1971. "Deciphering a Meal." In *Myth, Symbol and* Culture, 68–81. C. Geertz, ed. New York: Norton.

Douglas, M., and M. Nicod. 1974. "Taking the Biscuit: Structure of British Meals." *New Society* 30:744–47.

Dover, K. J. 1974. *Greek Popular Morality in the Time of Plato and Aristotle.* Oxford: Blackwell.

———. 1988. "Classical Greek Attitudes to Sexual Behaviour." In *Sexualität und Erotik in der Antike.* A. K. Siems, ed. WF 605. Darmstadt: Wissenschaftliche Buchgesellschaft.

Downey, G. A. 1961. *A History of Antioch in Syria from Seleucus to the Arab Conquest.* Princeton: Princeton Univ. Press.

Duling, Dennis C. 1997. "Egalitarian Ideology: Leadership and Factional Conflict in the Gospel of Matthew." *BTB* 27:124–37.

Duncan-Jones, R. P. 1976. "Some Configurations of Landholding in the Roman Empire." In Finley 1976, 7–33.

———. 1982. *The Economy of the Roman Empire: Quantitative Studies.* 2d ed. Cambridge: Cambridge Univ. Press.

Dunn, J. D. G. 1983. "The Incident of Antioch (Gal 2:11-18)." *JSNT* 18:3–17.

Dyson, S. 1989. "The Relevance for Roman Archaeologists of Recent Approaches to Archaeology in Greece." *Journal of Roman Archaeology* 2:143–46.

Ebertz, M. N. 1987. *Das Charisma des Gekreuzigten: Zur Soziologie der Jesusbewegung.* WUNT 2/45. Tübingen: J. C. B. Mohr.

Eck, W. 1971. "Das Eindringen des Christentums in den Senatorenstand bis zu Konstantin d. Gr." *Chiron* 1:381–406.

Eichenauer, M. 1988. *Untersuchungen zur Arbeitswelt der Frau in der römischen Antike.* Frankfurt: Peter Lang.

Elbogen, I. 1931. *Der jüdische Gottesdienst in seiner geschichtlichen Entwicklung.* 3d ed. Frankfurt: J. Kauffmann. [ET = *Jewish Liturgy: A Comprehensive History.* R. P. Scheindlin, trans. Philadelphia: Jewish Publication Society, 1993.]

Elliger, W. 1978. *Paulus in Griechenland: Philippi, Thessaloniki, Athen, Korinth.* Stuttgarter Bibelstudien 92. Stuttgart: Katholisches Bibelwerk.

Elliott, J. H. 1981. *A Home for the Homeless: A Sociological Exegesis of 1 Peter, Its Situation and Strategy.* Philadelphia: Fortress; paperback edition with new Introduction, 1990.

———. 1991. "Temple versus Household in Luke-Acts: A Contrast in Social Institutions." In Neyrey 1991b, 211–40.

———. 1993. *What Is Social-Scientific Criticism?* GBS. Minneapolis: Fortress.

Erikson, K. T. 1966. *Wayward Puritans: A Study in the Sociology of Deviance.* New York: John Wiley and Sons.

Esler, P. F. 1987. *Community and Gospel in Luke-Acts: The Social and Political Motivations of Lucan Theology.* SNTSMS 57. Cambridge: Cambridge Univ. Press.

———. 1994. *The First Christians in Their Social World: Social-Scientific Approaches to the New Testament.* London: Routledge.

———, ed. 1995. *Modelling Early Christianity: Social-Scientific Studies of the New Testament in Its Context.* London: Routledge.

Etienne, R. 1978. *Pompeji: Das Leben in einer antiken Stadt.* I Rauth-Welsch, trans. Stuttgart: Reclam.

Evans, J. K. 1980. "Plebs Rusticana." *AJAH* 5:19–47, 134–73.

Faber, R. 1990. "Bewegung." In *Handbuch religionswissenschaftlicher Grundbegriffe,* 2:135–38. H. Canzik et al., eds. Stuttgart: Katholisches Bibelwerk.

Fàbrega, V. 1984/85. "War Junia(s), der hervorrangende Apostel (Röm. 16,7), eine Frau?" *JAC* 27/28:47–64.

Fander, M. 1990. *Die Stellung der Frau im Markusevangelium: Unter besonderer Berücksichtigung kultur- und religionsgeschichtlicher Hintergründe.* Altenberge: Telos.

Fatum, L. 1989. "Women, Symbolic Universe and Structure of Silence: Challenges and Possibilities in Androcentric Texts." *ST* 43:61–80.

Feeley-Harnick, G. 1981. *The Lord's Table: Eucharist and Passover in Early Christianity.* Philadelphia: Univ. of Pennsylvania Press.

Fiensy, D. A. 1991. *The Social History of Palestine in the Herodian Period: The Land Is Mine.* Studies in the Bible and Early Christianity 20. Lewiston, N.Y.: Edwin Mellen.

Finley, M. I. 1974a. *Die antike Wirtschaft.* Munich: Chr. Kaiser. [ET = *The Ancient Economy.* Sather Classical Lectures 43. Berkeley: Univ. of California Press, 1973.]

———, ed. 1974b. *Studies in Ancient Society.* Past and Present Series 2. London: Routledge & Kegan Paul.

———, ed. 1976. *Studies in Roman Property.* Cambridge Classical Studies. Cambridge: Cambridge Univ. Press.

———. 1977. "The Ancient City: From Fustel de Coulanges to Max Weber and Beyond." *Comparative Studies in Society and History* 19:305ff. [Reprinted in idem 1981a, 3–23.]

————. 1981a. *Economy and Society in Ancient Greece.* B. D. Shaw and R. P. Saller, eds. London: Chatto & Windus.

————. 1981b. "Technische Innovation und wirtschaftlicher Fortschritt im Altertum." In H. Schneider 1981b, 168–95. [ET = "Technical Innovation and Economic Progress in the Ancient World." In idem 1981a, 176–95.]

————. 1985. *Die Sklaverei in der Antike.* Munich: Chr. Kaiser. [ET = *Ancient Slavery and Modern Ideology.* New York: Viking, 1980.]

Fiorenza, E. S. 1987. "Theological Criteria and Historical Reconstruction: Martha and Mary; Luke 10:38-42." In *Protocol of the Colloquy of the Center for Hermeneutical Studies in Hellenistic and Modern Culture* 53. Berkeley: Center for Hermeneutical Studies in Hellenistic and Modern Culture.

————. 1988. *Zu ihrem Gedächtnis: Eine feministisch-theologische Rekonstruktion der christlichen Ursprünge.* Munich-Mainz. [ET = *In Memory of Her: A Feminist Theological Reconstruction of Christian Origins.* New York: Crossroad, 1983.]

Fitzmyer, J. A. 1981. *The Gospel according to Luke I–IX.* Anchor Bible 28. New York: Doubleday.

Flusser, D. 1981. "Pharisäer, Sadduzäer und Essener im Pescher Nahum." In Grözinger et al., 1981, 121–66.

Foucault, M. 1989. *Der Gebrauch der Lüste: Sexualität und Wahrheit.* Vol. 2. Frankfurt. [ET = *The History of Sexuality.* 3 vols. R. Hurley, trans. New York: Pantheon, 1978–88.]

Frankemölle, H. 1992. "Synagōgē, episynagōgē." In *EWNT,* 2d ed., 3:702–10. [ET = *EDNT* 3:293–96.]

Frayn, J. M. 1979. *Subsistence Farming in Roman Italy.* Fontwell: Centaur.

Frend, W. H. C. 1965. *Martyrdom and Persecution in the Early Church: A Study of Conflict from the Maccabees to Donatus.* Oxford: Blackwell.

Freudenberger, R. 1967. *Das Verhalten der römischen Behörden gegen die Christen im 2. Jahrhundert: Dargestellt am Brief des Plinius an Trajan und den Reskripten Trajans und Hadrians.* Münchener Beiträge zur Papyrus und antiken Rechtsgeschichte 52. Munich: C. H. Beck.

————, et al. 1981. "Christenverfolgungen." In *TRE* 8:23–62.

Freyne, S. 1980. *Galilee from Alexander to Hadrian: A Study of Second Temple Judaism.* Univ. of Notre Dame Center for the Study of Judaism and Christianity in Antiquity 5. Notre Dame: Univ. of Notre Dame Press; Wilmington, Del.: Michael Glazier.

————. 1988. "Bandits in Galilee: A Contribution to the Study of Social Conditions in First-Century Palestine." In *The Social World and Formative Christianity and Judaism,* 50–68. J. Neusner et al., eds. Philadelphia: Fortress.

Funk, A. 1981. *Status und Rollen in den Paulusbriefen: Eine inhaltsanalytische Untersuchung zur Religionssoziologie.* Innsbruck: Tyrolia.

Gager, J. G. 1971. "Religion and Social Class in the Early Roman Empire." In Benko and O'Rourke 1971, 99–120.

————. 1975. *Kingdom and Community: The Social World of Early Christianity.* Englewood Cliffs, N.J.: Prentice Hall.

———. 1979a. "Das Ende der Zeit und die Entstehung von Gemeinschaften." In Meeks 1979, 88–130.

———. 1979b. "Social Description and Sociological Explanation." *Religious Studies Review* 5:174–80.

———. 1982. "Shall We Marry Our Enemies? Sociology and the New Testament." *Int* 36:256–65.

———. 1983. *The Origins of Anti-Semitism: Attitudes toward Judaism in Pagan and Christian Antiquity.* New York: Oxford Univ. Press.

———. 1985. "Paulus und das antike Judentum: Eine Kritik an Max Webers Interpretation." In *Max Webers Sicht des antiken Christentums: Interpretation und Kritik*, 386–403. W. Schluchter, ed. Frankfurt.

———. 1986. "Jews, Gentiles, and Synagogues in the Book of Acts." In Nickelsburg and MacRae 1986, 91–99.

Gardner, J. F. 1986. *Women in Roman Law and Society.* Bloomington: Indiana Univ. Press.

Garnsey, P. 1970. *Social Status and Legal Privilege in the Roman Empire.* Oxford: Clarendon.

———. 1974. "Legal Privilege in the Roman Empire." *Past and Present* 48:3–24. [Reprinted in Finley 1974b, 141–65].

———. 1975. "Peasants in Ancient Roman Society." *Journal of Peasant Studies* 2:222–35.

———. 1976. "Urban Property Investment." In Finley 1976, 123–36, 190–93.

———, ed. 1980. *Non-Slave Labour in the Greco-Roman World.* Cambridge: Cambridge Univ. Press.

———. 1988. *Famine and Food Supply in the Graeco-Roman World: Responses to Risk and Crisis.* Cambridge: Cambridge Univ. Press.

Garnsey, P., K. Hopkins, and C. R. Whittaker, eds. 1983. *Trade in the Ancient Economy.* Berkeley: Univ. of California Press.

Garnsey, P., and R. P. Saller, 1987. *The Roman Empire: Economy, Society and Culture.* Berkeley: Univ. of California Press.

Geertz, C. 1987. "Religion als kulturelles System." In idem, *Dichte Beschreibung: Beiträge zum Verstehen kultureller Systeme*, 44–95. Frankfurt. [ET = "Religion as a Cultural System." In *The Interpretation of Cultures*, 87–125. New York: Basic.]

Georgi, D. 1965. *Die Geschichte der Kollekte des Paulus für Jerusalem.* Hamburg: H. Reich.

Giardina, A., ed. 1991a. "Der Kaufmann." In idem 1991a, 277–304. [ET = "The Merchant." In idem 1993, 245–71.]

———. 1991b. *Der Mensch der römischen Antike.* Frankfurt. [ET = Giardina 1993.]

———, ed. 1993. *The Romans*, 245–71. L. G. Cochrane, trans. Chicago: Univ. of Chicago Press, 1993.]

Gnilka, J. 1978–79. *Das Evangelium nach Markus.* 2 vols. Neukirchen-Vluyn: Neukirchener.

———. 1988. *Das Matthäusevangelium.* Vol. 2. HTKNT. Freiburg: Herder.

Goguel, M. 1928. *Au seuil de l'évangile Jean-Baptiste.* Paris: Payot.

Golomb, B., and Y. Kedar. 1971. "Ancient Agriculture in the Galilee Mountains." *IEJ* 21:136–40.

Goodman, M. 1982. "The First Jewish Revolt: Social Conflict and the Problem of Debt." *JJS* 33:417–27.

———. 1987. *The Ruling Class of Judaea: The Origins of the Jewish Revolt against Rome A.D. 66–70*. Cambridge: Cambridge Univ. Press.

Goulder, M. D. 1974. *Midrash and Lection in Matthew*. London: SPCK.

Grabbe, L. L. 1992. *Judaism from Cyrus to Hadrian*. Vol. 1: *The Persian and Greek Periods*. Vol. 2: *The Roman Period*. Minneapolis: Fortress.

Grant, F. C. 1926. *The Economic Background of the Gospels*. Oxford: Oxford Univ. Press.

Grant, R. M. 1981. *Christen als Bürger im Römischen Reich*. Göttingen: Vandenhoeck & Ruprecht.

Grassl, H. 1982. *Sozialökonomische Vorstellungen in der kaiserzeitlichen griechischen Literatur (1.–3. Jh. n.Chr.)*. Historia 41. Wiesbaden: Franz Steiner.

Greene, K. 1986. *The Archaelogy of the Roman Economy*. Berkeley: Univ. of California Press.

Gregory, J. R. 1975. "Image of Limited Good or Expectation of Reciprocity?" *Current Anthropology* 16:73–92.

Grimm, B. 1975. "Untersuchungen zur sozialen Stellung der frühen Christen in der römischen Gesellschaft." Diss., Hamburg.

Gross, K. 1959. "Domitianus." In *RAC* 4:91–109.

Grözinger, K. E., et al., eds. 1981. *Qumran*. Darmstadt: Wissenschaftliche Buchgesellschaft.

Grumel, V. 1956. "Du nombre de persécutions païennes dans les anciennes chroniques." *RAug* 7:59–72.

Guijarro, Santiago. 1997. "The Family in First-Century Galilee." In Moxnes 1997, 42–65.

Gülzow, H. 1969. *Christentum und Sklaverei in den ersten drei Jahrhunderten*. Bonn: Rudolph Habelt.

———. 1974. "Soziale Gegebenheiten der altkirchlichen Mission." In *Kirchengeschichte als Missionsgeschichte*. Vol 1: *Die alte Kirche*, 189–226. H. Frohnes and U. W. Knorr, eds. Munich: Chr. Kaiser.

———. 1990. "Soziale Gegebenheiten der Trennung von Kirche und Synagoge und die Anfänge des christlichen Antijudaismus." In *Christlicher Antijudaismus und jüdischer Antipaganismus: Ihre Motive und Hintergründe in der ersten drei Jahrhunderten*, 95–120. H. Frohnhofen, ed. Hamburger Theologische Studien 3. Hamburg: Steinmann & Steinmann.

Gundry, R. H. 1982. *Matthew: A Commentary on His Literary and Theological Art*. Grand Rapids: Eerdmans. [2d ed., 1994.]

———. 1991. "A Responsive Evaluation of the Social History of the Matthean Community in Roman Syria." In Balch 1991, 62–67.

Günther, R. 1987. *Frauenarbeit—Frauenbindung: Untersuchungen zu unfreien und freigelassenen Frauen in den stadtrömischen Inschriften.* Munich: Chr. Kaiser.

Gutermann, L. S. 1951. *Religious Toleration and Persecution in Ancient Rome.* London.

Gutman, S. 1981. "The Synagogue at Gamla." In *Ancient Synagogues Revealed,* 30–41. L. I. Levine, ed. Detroit: Wayne State Univ. Press.

Haacker, K. 1975. "Die Berufung des Verfolgers und die Rechtfertigung des Gottlosen: Erwägungen zum Zusammenhang zwischen Biographie und Theologie des Apostels Paulus." *ThBei* 6:1–12.

Habicht, C. 1969. *Die Inschriften des Asklepieions.* Berlin: Walter de Gruyter.

Haenchen, E. 1965. *Die Apostelgeschichte.* 5th ed. Göttingen: Vandenhoeck & Ruprecht. [ET = *The Acts of the Apostles: A Commentary.* B. Noble and G. Shinn, trans. Philadelphia: Westminster, 1971.]

———. 1968. "Judentum und Christentum in der Apostelgeschichte." In idem, *Die Bibel und wir: Gesammelte Aufsätze,* 2:336–74. Tübingen: J. C. B. Mohr.

Hamel, G. 1989. *Poverty and Charity in Roman Palestine, First Three Centuries C.E.* Univ. of California Publications: Near Eastern Series 23. Berkeley: Univ. of California Press.

Hanson, K. C. 1996. "Kinship." In Rohrbaugh 1996, 62–79.

———. 1997. "The Galilean Fishing Economy and the Jesus Tradition." *BTB* 27:99–111.

Hanson, K. C., and Douglas E. Oakman. 1998. *Palestine in the Time of Jesus: Social Structures and Social Conflicts.* Minneapolis: Fortress.

Hanson, P. D. 1979. *The Dawn of the Apocalyptic: The Historical and Sociological Roots of Jewish Apocalyptic Eschatology.* Rev. ed. Philadelphia: Fortress.

Hare, D. R. A. 1967. *The Theme of Jewish Persecution of Christians in the Gospel according to St. Matthew.* SNTSMS 6. Cambridge: Cambridge Univ. Press.

Harnack, A. von. 1924. *Die Mission und Ausbreitung des Christentums in den ersten drei Jahrhunderten.* 2 vols. 4th ed. Leipzig: J. C. Hinrichs. [ET = *The Mission and Expansion of Christianity in the First Three Centuries.* 2 vols. J. Moffatt, trans. 2d ed. New York: G. P. Putnam's Sons, 1908.]

Harris, M. 1989. *Kulturanthropologie: Ein Lehrbuch.* S. M. Schomberg-Scherff, trans. Frankfurt: Campus. [ET = *Cultural Anthropology.* 4th ed. New York: HarperCollins, 1995.]

Harris, W. V. 1989. *Ancient Literacy.* Cambridge: Harvard Univ. Press.

Hasenclever, L. 1882. "Christliche Proselyten der höheren Stände im ersten Jahrhundert." *Jahrbücher für protestantische Theologie,* 34–78, 230–71.

Hausrath, A. von. 1875. *Neutestamentliche Zeitgeschichte.* Part 2. 2d ed. Heidelberg. [ET = *A History of the New Testament Times.* 2 vols. C. T. Poynting and P. Quenzer, trans. London: Williams and Norgate, 1878–80.]

Heichelheim, F. 1938. *Wirtschaftsgeschichte des Altertums vom Paläolithikum bis zur Völkerwanderung der Germanen, Sklaven und Araber.* 2 vols. Leiden: Brill.

Heinrici, C. F. 1876. "Die Christengemeinde Korinths und die religiösen Genossenschaften der Griechen." *ZWT* 19:464–526.

Hellholm, D., ed. 1983. *Apocalypticism in the Mediterranean World and the Near East.* Tübingen: J. C. B. Mohr. [2d ed., 1989.]

Hemer, C. J. 1989. *The Book of Acts in the Setting of Hellenistic History.* C. H. Gempf, ed. WUNT 2/49. Tübingen: J. C. B. Mohr.

Hengel, M. 1960. "Das Gleichnis von den Weingärtnern Mc 12:1–12 im Licht der Zenonpapyri und der rabbinischen Gleichnisse." *ZNW* 59:1–39.

————. 1968. *Nachfolge und Charisma: Eine exegetisch-religionsgeschichtliche Studie zu Mt 8,21f. und Jesu Ruf in die Nachfolge.* Berlin: A. Töpelmann. [ET = *The Charismatic Leader and His Followers.* J. Greig, trans. New York: Crossroad, 1981.]

————. 1971. "Proseuche und Synagoge." In *Tradition und Glaube: Das frühe Christentum in seiner Umwelt. Festgabe für Karl Georg Kuhn zum 65. Geburtstag,* 157–84. G. Jeremias et al., eds. Göttingen: Vandenhoeck & Ruprecht.

————. 1973a. *Eigentum und Reichtum in der frühen Kirche: Aspekte einer fruhchristlichen Sozialgeschichte.* Stuttgart: Kohlhammer. [ET = *Property and Riches in the Early Church: Aspects of a History of Early Christianity.* J. Bowden, trans. Philadelphia: Fortress, 1974.]

————. 1973b. *Judentum und Hellenismus.* 2d ed. WUNT 2/10. Tübingen: J. C. B. Mohr. [ET = *Judaism and Hellenism: Studies in Their Encounter in Palestine during the Early Hellenistic Period.* 2 vols. J. Bowden, trans. Philadelphia: Fortress, 1981.]

————. 1974. "Zeloten und Sikarier." In *Josephus-Studien: Untersuchungen zu Josephus, dem antiken Judentum und dem Neuen Testament. Otto Michel zum 70. Geburtstag Gewidmet,* 175–96. O. Betz et al., eds. Göttingen: Vandenhoeck & Ruprecht.

————. 1976a. *Die Zeloten: Untersuchungen zur jüdischen Freiheitsbewegung in der Zeit von Herodes I. bis 70 n.Chr.* 2d ed. AGAJU 1. Leiden: Brill. [ET = *The Zealots: Investigations into the Jewish Freedom Movement in the Period from Herod I until 70 A.D.* D. Smith, trans. Edinburgh: T. & T. Clark, 1989.]

————. 1976b. *Juden, Griechen und Barbaren: Aspekte der Hellenisierung des Judentums in vorchristlicher Zeit.* Stuttgart: Katholisches Bibelwerk. [ET = *Jews, Greeks and Barbarians: Aspects of the Hellenization of Judaism in the Pre-Christian Period.* J. Bowden, trans. Philadelphia: Fortress, 1980.]

————. 1978. "Qumran und der Hellenismus." In *Qumrân: Sa piété, sa théologie et son milieu,* 333–72. M. Delcor, ed. BETL 46. Louvain: Louvain Univ. Press; Paris: Duculot.

————. 1983. *Between Jesus and Paul: Studies in the Earliest History of Christiantiy.* J. Bowden, trans. Minneapolis: Fortress.

————. 1984. *Zur urchristlichen Geschichtsschreibung.* 2d ed. Stuttgart: Kohlhammer. [ET = *Acts and the History of the Earliest Church.* J. Bowden, trans. Philadelphia: Fortress, 1979.]

————. 1991a. *The Pre-Christian Paul.* J. Bowden, trans. Philadelphia: Trinity Press International.

————. 1991b. "Der vorchristliche Paulus." In *Paulus und das Antike Judentum,* 177–293. M. Hengel and U. Heckel, eds. Tübingen: J. C. B. Mohr.

———. 1993. *Die johanneische Frage: Ein Lösungsversuch.* WUNT 2/67. Tübingen: J. C. B. Mohr. [ET = *The Johannine Question.* Philadelphia: Trinity Press International, 1989.]

Hengel, M., and A. M. Schwemer, eds. 1991. *Königsherrschaft Gottes und himmlischer Kult im Judentum, Urchristentum und in der hellenistischen Welt.* WUNT 2/55. Tübingen: J. C. B. Mohr.

———. 1997. *Paul between Damascus and Antioch: The Unknown Years.* J. Bowden, trans. Louisville: Westminster John Knox.

Hengstl, J., ed. 1978. *Griechische Papyri aus Ägypten als Zeugnisse des öffentlichen und Privaten Lebens.* Darmstadt: Wissenschaftliche Buchgesellschaft.

Herrenbrück, F. 1990. *Jesus und die Zöllner.* WUNT 2/41. Tübingen: J. C. B. Mohr.

Herz, J. 1928. "Grossgrundbesitz in Palästina im Zeitalter Jesu." *Palästina Jahrbuch* 24:98–113.

Herzfeld, L. 1894. *Handelsgeschichte der Juden des Altertums.* 2d ed. Braunschweig: J. H. Meyer.

Herzig, H. E. 1983. "Frauen in Ostia." *Historia* 32:77–92.

Herzog, R. 1937. "Nummularius." In *PRE* 17/2:1415–56.

Hobsbawm, E. 1959. *Primitive Rebels: Studies in Archaic Forms of Social Movement in the 19th and 20th Centuries.* New York: Norton.

———. 1985. *Bandits.* 2d ed. Harmondsworth: Penguin.

Hock, R. F. 1978. "Paul's Tentmaking and the Problem of His Social Class." *JBL* 97:555–64.

———. 1980. *The Social Context of Paul's Mission: Tentmaking and Apostleship.* Philadelphia: Fortress.

Hoenig, S. B. 1979. "The Ancient City-Square: The Forerunner of the Synagogue." In *ANRW* II 19.1:448–76.

Hoffmann, P. 1975. *Studien zur Theologie der Logienquelle.* 2d ed. NTAbh 8. Münster: Aschendorff.

Holmberg, B. 1978. *Paul and Power: The Structure of Authority in the Primitive Church as Reflected in the Pauline Epistles.* Philadelphia: Fortress.

———. 1990. *Sociology and the New Testament: An Appraisal.* Minneapolis: Fortress.

Holtheide, B. 1983. *Römische Bürgerrechtspolitik und römische Neubürger in der Provinz Asia.* Freiburg.

Holtz, T. 1992. "Dōdeka." In *EWNT,* 2d ed., 1:874–80. [ET = *EDNT* 1:361–63.]

Hopkins, K. 1974. "Elite Mobility in the Roman Empire." In Finley 1974b, 103–20.

———. 1978. "Economic Growth and Towns in Classical Antiquity." In *Towns in Societies,* 37ff. P. Abrams and E. A. Wrigley, eds. Cambridge: Cambridge Univ. Press.

Horden, P., and N. Purcell. 1986. *The Mediterranean World: Man and Environment in Antiquity and the Middle Ages.* Oxford: Oxford Univ. Press.

Horsley, G. H. R., ed. 1983. *New Documents Illustrating Early Christianity.* Vol. 3. Macquarie University.

Horsley, R. A. 1979. "Josephus and the Bandits." *JJS* 10:37–63.

———. 1985. "'Like One of the Prophets of Old': Two Types of Popular Prophets at the Time of Jesus." *CBQ* 47:435–63.

————. 1987. *Jesus and the Spiral of Violence: Popular Jewish Resistance in Roman Palestine.* San Francisco: Harper & Row.

————. 1989. *Sociology and the Jesus Movement.* New York: Crossroad.

————. 1995. *Archaeology, History and Society in Galilee: The Social Context of Jesus and the Rabbis.* Valley Forge, Pa.: Trinity Press International.

————. 1995. *Galilee: History, Politics, People.* Valley Forge, Pa.: Trinity Press International.

Horsley, R. A., and J. S. Hanson. 1985. *Bandits, Prophets, and Messiahs: Popular Movements in the Time of Jesus.* Minneapolis: Winston. [Rev. ed. Valley Forge, Pa.: Trinity Press International, 1999.

Hruby, K. 1971. *Die Synagoge—Geschichtliche Entwicklung einer Institution.* Schriften zur Judentumskunde 3. Zurich: Theologischer.

Hultgren, A. J. 1976. "Paul's Pre-Christian Persecutions of the Church: Their Purpose, Locale, and Nature." *JBL* 95:97–111.

————. 1991. "The Self-Definition of Paul and His Communities." *SEÅ* 56: 78–100.

Humphreys, S. C. 1979. "Geschichte, Volkswirtschaft und Anthropologie: Das Werk Karl Polanyis." In K. Polanyi 1979, 7–12. [ET = "History, Economics, and Anthropology: The Works of Karl Polanyi." *History and Theory* 8 (1969):165–212.]

Hüttenmeister, F. 1993. "'Synagoge' und 'Proseuche' bei Josephus und in anderen antiken Quellen." In *Begegnungen zwischen Christentum und Judentum in Antike und Mittelalter,* FS H. Schreckenberg, 163–81. D. A. Koch and H. Lichtenberger, eds. Göttingen: Vandenhoeck & Ruprecht.

Hüttenmeister, F., and G. Reeg. 1977. *Die antiken Synagogen in Israel.* 2 vols. BTAVO 12/1. Wiesbaden: Reichert.

Jacobs-Malina, D. 1993. *Beyond Patriarchy: The Images of Family in Jesus.* New York: Paulist.

Jastrow, M., and D. Correns, eds. 1960. *Die Mischna: Schebiit.* Giessen: A. Töpelmann.

Jeremias, G. 1963. *Der Lehrer der Gerechtigkeit.* Göttingen: Vandenhoeck & Ruprecht.

Jeremias, J. 1933. "Grammateus." In *TWNT* 1:740–42. [ET = *TDNT* 740–42.]

————. 1962. *Jerusalem zur Zeit Jesu: Eine kulturgeschichtliche Untersuchung zur neutestamentlichen Zeitgeschichte.* 3d ed. Göttingen: Vandenhoeck & Ruprecht. [ET = *Jerusalem in the Time of Jesus: An Investigation into Economic and Social Conditions during the New Testament Period.* F. H. Cave and C. H. Cave, trans. Philadelphia: Fortress, 1969.]

————. 1971. *Neutestamentliche Theologie.* Vol. 1: *Die Verkündigung Jesu.* Gütersloh: Gerd Mohn. [ET = *New Testament Theology.* Vol. 1: *The Proclamation of Jesus.* J. Bowden, trans. New York: Scribner's, 1971.]

———. 1977. *Die Gleichnisse Jesu*. 9th ed. Zurich: Zwingli. [ET = *The Parables of Jesus*. Rev. ed. S. H. Hooke, trans. New York: Charles Scribner's Sons, 1972.]

Jervell, J. 1960. *Imago Dei: Gen. 1.26f. im Spätjudentum, in der Gnosis und in den Paulinischen Briefen*. FRLANT 58. Göttingen: Vandenhoeck & Ruprecht.

Johnson, B. 1963. "On Church and Sect." *American Sociological Review* 28:539–49.

Jones, A. H. M. 1973. *The Later Roman Empire: A Social Economic and Administrative Survey*. 2d ed. Oxford: Oxford Univ. Press.

———. 1974. *The Roman Economy*. P. A. Brunt, ed. Oxford: Oxford Univ. Press.

———. 1981. "Das Wirtschaftsleben in den Städten des römischen Kaiserreiches." In H. Schneider 1981b, 48–80. [ET = "The Economic Life of the Towns of the Roman Empire." In *La Ville* 1:171–85. J. Firenne, ed. Brussels: Librairie Encyclopédique, 1955.]

Judge, E. A. 1964. *Christliche Gruppen in nichtchristlicher Gesellschaft*. Neue Studien 4. Wuppertal: R. Brockhaus. [ET = *The Social Patterns of Christian Groups in the First Century*. London: Tyndale, 1960.]

———. 1979. "Die frühen Christen als scholastische Gemeinschaft." In Meeks 1979, 131–64. [ET = "The Early Christins as Scholastic Community." *Journal of Religious History* 1 (1960):4–15, 125–37.]

———. 1980. "The Social Identity of the First Christians: A Question of Method in Religious History." *JRH* 11:201–17.

Just, R. 1991. *Women in Athenian Law and Life*. London: Routledge.

Juster, J. 1914. *Les Juifs dans l'Empire Romain: Leur Condition juridique, économique et sociale*. 2 vols. Paris: Paul Geunther.

Kampen, J. 1988. *The Hasideans and the Origins of Pharisaism*. SCS 24. Atlanta: Scholars.

Kampen, N. 1981. *Image and Status: Working Women in Ostia*. Berlin: Walter de Gruyter.

Kasten, H. 1968. *Gaius Plinius Caecilius Secundus: Briefe*. Munich: Chr. Kaiser.

Kautsky, J. H. 1982. *The Politics of Aristocratic Empires*. Chapel Hill: Univ. of North Carolina Press.

Kautsky, K. 1927. *Der Ursprung des Christentums: Eine historische Untersuchung*. 14th ed. Berlin: Walter de Gruyter. [Reprint: Hanover: J. H. W. Dietz, 1968.]

Kegler, J. 1992. "Das Zinsverbot in der hebräischen Bibel." In *Schuld und Schulden: Biblische Traditionen in gegenwärtigen Konflikten*, 17–39. M. Crüsemann and W. Schottroff, eds. Munich: Chr. Kaiser.

Kehrer, G. 1988. *Einführung in die Religionssoziologie*. Darmstadt: Wissenschaftliche Buchgesellschaft.

———. 1990. "Charisma." In *Handbuch religionswissenschaftlicher Grundbegriffe*, 2:195–98. H. Cancik et al., eds. Stuttgart: Kohlhammer.

Keresztes, P. 1973. "The Jews, the Christians, and Emperor Domitian." *VC* 27:1–28.

———. 1979. "The Imperial Roman Government and the Christian Church: From Nero to the Severi." In *ANRW* II 23.1:247–315.

Kessler, R. 1989. "Das hebräische Schuldenwesen: Terminologie und Metaphorik." *WD* 20:181–96.

Kiechle, F. 1969. *Sklavenarbeit und technischer Fortschritt im römischen Reich.* Wiesbaden: Franz Steiner.

Kimelman, R. 1981. "*Birkat haminim* and the Lack of Evidence for an Anti-Christian Jewish Prayer in Late Antiquity." In *Jewish and Christian Self-Definition.* Vol. 2: *Aspects of Judaism in the Greco-Roman Period,* 226–44. E. P. Sanders et al., eds. Philadelphia: Fortress.

Kingsbury, J. D. 1986. *Matthew as Story.* Philadelphia: Fortress.

———. 1991. "Conclusion: Analysis of a Conversation." In Balch 1991, 259–69.

Kippenberg, H. G. 1977. "Die Typik antiker Entwicklung." In idem, ed., *Seminar: Die Entstehung der antiken Klassengesellschaft,* 9–61. Frankfurt.

———. 1978. *Religion und Klassenbildung im antiken Judäa: Eine religionssoziologische Studie zum Verhältnis von Tradition und gesellschaftlicher Entwicklung.* Göttingen: Vandenhoeck & Rupprecht.

———. 1991. *Die vorderasiatischen Erlösungsreligionen in ihrem Zusammenhang mit der antiken Stadtherrschaft.* Suhrkamp-Taschenbuch: Wissenschaft 917. Frankfurt: Suhrkamp.

Kippenberg, H. G., and G. A. Wevers, eds. 1979. *Textbuch zur neutestamentlichen Zeitgeschichte.* Göttingen: Vandenhoeck & Ruprecht.

Klauck, H.-J. 1981. *Hausgemeinde und Hauskirche im frühen Christentum.* Stuttgart: Katholisches Bibelwerk.

———. 1982. *Herrenmahl und Hellenistischer Kult: Eine religionsgeschichtliche Untersuchung zum ersten Korintherbrief.* Münster: Aschendorff.

———. 1985. "Gemeinde ohne Amt? Erfahrungen mit der Kirche in den johanneischen Schriften." *BZ* 29:193–220.

———. 1990. "Brotherly Love in Plutarch and in 4 Maccabees." In *Greeks, Romans, and Christians: Essays in Honor of Abraham Malherbe,* 144–56. D. Balch et al., eds. Minneapolis: Fortress.

———. 1994. "Volk Gottes und Leid Christi, oder: Von der kommunikativen Kraft der Bilder." In idem, *Alte Welt und Neuer Glaube: Beiträge zur Religionsgeschichte, Forschungsgeschichte und Theologie des Neuen Testament,* 277–301. NTOA 29. Göttingen: Vandenhoeck & Ruprecht.

Klausner, J. 1975. "The Economy of Judaea in the Period of the Second Temple." In *The Herodian Period,* 179–205. The World History of the Jewish People. M. Avi-Yonah, ed. New Brunswick: Rutgers Univ. Press.

Klein, R., ed. *Das frühe Christentum im römischen Staat.* WF 267. Darmstadt: Wissenschaftliche Buchgesellschaft.

Kloft, H. 1970. *Liberalitas principis: Herkunft und Bedeutung.* Cologne: Bohlau.

———. 1992. *Die Wirtschaft der griechisch-römischen Welt: Eine Einführung.* Darmstadt: Wissenschaftliche Buchgesellschaft.

Knopf, R. 1900. "Über die soziale Zusammensetzung der ältesten heidenchristlichen Gemeinden." *ZTK* 10:325–47.

Koch, K. 1970. *Ratlos vor der Apokalyptik.* Gütersloh: Gerd Mohn. [ET = *The Redis-covery of Apocalyptic.* M. Kohl, trans. SBT 2/22. London: SCM, 1972.]

Koch, K., and J. M. Schmidt, eds. 1982. *Apokalyptik.* WF 365. Darmstadt: Wissenschaftliche Buchgesellschaft.

Koester, H. 1980. *Einführung in das Neue Testament.* Berlin: Walter de Gruyter. [2d German ed. 1995. ET = *Introduction to the New Testament.* 2 vols. Philadelphia: Fortress, 1982.]

Koestermann, E. 1965. *Codex Mediceus* II. Leipzig: J. C. Hinrichs.

Kolb, F. 1984. *Die Stadt im Altertum.* Munich: C. H. Beck.

Kolendo, J. 1991. "Der Bauer." In Giardina 1991a, 227–42. [ET = "The Peasant." In Giardina 1993, 199–213.]

Kosellek, R. 1979. "Zur historisch-politschen Semantik asymmetrischer Gegenbegriffe." In idem, *Vergangene Zukunft: Zur Semantik geschichtliche Zeiten,* 211–59. Frankfurt: Suhrkamp.

Kraabel, A. T. 1979. "The Diaspora Synagogue: Archaeological and Epigraphic Evidence since Sukenik." In *ANRW* II 19.1:477–510.

———. 1981. "The Disappearance of the 'God-fearers.'" *Numen* 28:113–26.

———. 1982. "The Roman Diaspora: Six Questionable Assumptions." *JJS* 33:445–64.

———. 1986. "Greeks, Jews, and Lutherans in the Middle Half of Acts." In Nickelsburg and MacRae 1986, 147–57.

Kraeling, C. H. 1982. "The Jewish Community at Antioch." *JBL* 51:130–60.

Kraemer, R. S. 1992. *Her Share of the Blessings: Women's Religions among Pagans, Jews, and Christians in the Greco-Roman World.* New York: Oxford Univ. Press.

Kraft, H. 1974. *Die Offenbarung des Johannes.* HNT 16A. Tübingen: J. C. B. Mohr.

Kraft, R. A., and G. W. E. Nickelsburg, eds. 1986. *Early Judaism and Its Modern Interpreters.* Philadelphia: Fortress.

Kramer, W. R. 1963. *Christos Kurios Gottessohn.* ATANT 44. Zurich: Zwingli. [ET = *Christ, Lord, Son of God.* B. Hardy, trans. SBT 1/50. Napierville, Ill.: Alec R. Allenson, 1966.]

Krauss, S. 1910–12. *Talmudische Archäologie.* 3 vols. Leipzig: G. Fock. [Reprint ed. Hildesheim: G. Olms, 1966.]

Kreissig, H. 1967. "Zur sozialen Zusammensetzung der früchristlichen Gemeinden im ersten Jahrhundert u.Z." *Eirene* 6:91–100.

———. 1969. "Die landwirtschaftliche Situation in Palästina vor dem Judäischen Krieg." *Acta Antiqua* 17:223–54.

———. 1970. *Die sozialen Zusammenhänge des Judäischen Krieges.* Berlin: Akademie.

Kretschmar, G. 1990. "Die Kirche aus Juden und Heiden: Forschungsprobleme der ersten christlichen Jahrhunderte." In *Juden und Christen in der Antike,* 9–43. J. van Amersfoort and J. van Oort, eds. Kampen: Kok.

Kriesberg, L. 1973. *The Sociology of Social Conflicts.* Englewood Cliffs, N.J.: Prentice Hall.

Küchler, M. 1986. *Schweigen, Schmuck und Schleier: Drei neutestamentliche Vorschriften zur Verdrängung der Frauen auf dem Hintergund einer frauen-*

feindlichen Exegese des Alten Testaments im antiken Judentum. NTOA. Göttingen: Vandenhoeck & Ruprecht.

Kuhli, H. 1992a. "Nazarēnos, Nazōraios." In *EWNT,* 2d ed., 2:1117–21. [ET = *EDNT* 2:454–56.]

―――. 1992b. "Oikonomia, oikonomeō." In *EWNT,* 2d ed., 2:1218–22. [ET = *EDNT* 2:498–500.]

Kuhn, K. G. 1950. *Achtzehngebet und Vaterunser und der Reim.* Tübingen: J. C. B. Mohr.

Kuhnen, H.-P. 1990. *Palästina in griechisch-römischer Zeit.* Munich: Chr. Kaiser.

Kümmel, W. G. 1973. *Einleitung in das Neue Testament.* 17th ed. Heidelberg: Quelle & Meyer. [ET = *Introduction to the New Testament.* Rev. ed. H. C. Kee, trans. Nashville: Abingdon, 1975.]

Künzel, G. 1978. *Studien zum Gemeindeverständnis des Matthäusevangeliums.* Stuttgart: Kohlhammer.

Lambrecht, J., et al., eds. 1980. *L'Apocalypse johannique et l'apocalyptique dans le Nouveau Testament.* Colloquium Biblicum Lovaniense 30. Gembloux: Duculot.

Lampe, P. 1989. *Die stadtrömischen Christen in den ersten beiden Jahrhunderten: Untersuchungen zur Sozialgeschichte.* 2d ed. Tübingen: J. C. B. Mohr. [ET = *From Paul to Valentinus: Christians at Rome in the First Two Centuries.* M. G. Steinhauser, trans. Minneapolis: Fortress, 1999.]

Landman, L., ed. 1979. *Messianism in the Talmudic Era.* New York: Ktav.

Lang, B. 1991. "Diaspora." In *Neues Bibel-Lexikon,* 1:420–23. M. Görg and B. Lang, eds. Zurich: Benziger.

Langhammer, W. 1973. *Die rechtliche und soziale Stellung der Magistratus Municipiales und der Decuriones in der Übergangsphase der Städte von sich selbst verwaltenden Gemeinden zu Vollzugsorganen des spätantiken Zwangsstaates (2.–4. Jahrhundert der römischen Kaiserzeit).* Wiesbaden: Franz Steiner.

Last, H. 1937. "The Study of Persecution." *JRS* 27:80–92.

―――. 1954. "Christenverfolgung II." In *RAC* 2:1208–28.

Le Gall, J. 1970. "Métiers de femmes au Corpus inscriptionum Latinarum." *Revue des études latines* 47:123–38.

Lebram, J. C. H. 1970. "Apokalyptik und Hellenismus im Buche Daniel." *VT* 20:503–24.

Lee, C. L. 1979. "Soziale Unruhe und Urchristentum." In Meeks 1979, 67–87.

Leeds, A. 1979. "Forms of Urban Integration: Social Urbanization in Comparative Perspective." *Urban Anthropology* 8:227–47.

―――. 1980. "Towns and Villages in Society: Hierarchies of Order and Cause." In *Cities in a Larger Context,* 6–33. T. W. Collins, ed. Athens: Univ. of Georgia Press.

Lefkowitz, M. R. 1983. "Influential Women." In *Images of Women in Antiquity,* 49–64. A. Cameron and A. A. Kuhrt, eds. Detroit: Wayne State Univ. Press.

LeMoyne, J. 1972. *Les Sadducéens.* Etudes bibliques. Paris: Gabalda.

Lenski, G. 1977. *Macht und Privileg: Eine Theorie der sozialen Schichtung.* Frankfurt: Suhrkamp. [ET = *Power and Privilege: A Theory of Social Stratification.* New York: McGraw-Hill, 1966.]

Lenski, G. E., and Lenski, J. 1987. *Human Societies: An Introduction to Macrosociology.* 5th ed. New York: McGraw-Hill. [7th ed. with P. Nolan, 1995.]

Leon, H. J. 1960. *The Jews of Ancient Rome.* Philadelphia: Jewish Publication Society. [Rev. ed. with new Introduction by C. Osiek. Peabody, Mass.: Hendrickson, 1995.]

Leutzsch, M. 1992. "Verschuldung und Überschuldung, Schuldenerlass und Sündenvergebung." In *Schuld und Schulden: Biblische Traditionen in gegenwärtigen Konflikten,* 104–31. M. Crüsemann and W. Schottroff, eds. Munich: Chr. Kaiser.

Levine, L. I., ed. 1981. *Ancient Synagogues Revealed.* Jerusalem: Israel Exploration Society.

Lichtenberger, H. 1980. *Studien zum Menschenbild in Texten der Qumrangemeinde.* Göttingen: Vandenhoeck & Ruprecht.

———. 1987. "Täufergemeinden und frühchristliche Täuferpolemik." *ZTK* 84:36–57.

———. 1993. "Messianische Erwartungen und messianische Gestalten in der Zeit des Zeiten Tempels." In E. Stegemann 1993, 9–20.

Lidzbarski, M. 1920. *Mandäische Liturgien.* Berlin: Weidmannsche.

Lietzmann, H. 1961. *Geschichte der alten Kirche.* Reprint ed. Berlin: Walter de Gruyter [Orig. ed. 1932–38. ET = *The Beginnings of the Christian Church.* 3d ed. B. L. Woolf, trans. London: Lutterworth, 1953.]

———. 1969. *An die Korinther.* 2 vols. 5th ed. Tübingen: J. C. B. Mohr.

Lifshitz, B. 1967. *Donateurs et fondateurs dans les synagogues juives.* Paris: Gabalda.

Lipp, W. 1977. "Charisma—Social Deviation, Leadership and Cultural Change." *Annual Review of the Social Sciences of Religion* 1:57–77.

———. 1985. *Stigma und Chrisma: Über soziales Grenzverhalten.* Berlin: Walter de Gruyter.

Liver, J. 1963. "The Half-Shekel Offering in Biblical and Post-Biblical Literature." *HTR* 56:173–98.

Loane, H. J. 1938. *Industry and Commerce of the City of Rome (50 B.C.–200 A.D.).* Johns Hopkins University Studies in Historical and Political Science 56/2. Baltimore: Johns Hopkins Univ. Press.

Lohfink, G. 1983. "Weibliche Diakone im Neuen Testament." In G. Dautzenberg et al. 1983, 320–38.

Lohfink, N. 1990. *Lobgesänge der Armen: Studien zum Magnifikat, den Hodajot von Qumran und einigen späten Psalmen.* Stuttgart: Kohlhammer.

Lohmeyer, E. 1958. *Das Evangelium des Matthäus.* Göttingen: Vandenhoeck & Ruprecht.

Löning, K. 1987. "The Circle of Stephen and Its Mission." In J. Becker 1987, 103–31.

Lüdemann, G. 1987. *Das frühe Christentum nach den Traditionen der Apostelgeschichte: Ein Kommentar.* Göttingen: Vandenhoeck & Ruprecht. [ET =

Early Christianity according to the Traditions of Acts: A Commentary. J. Bowden, trans. Minneapolis: Fortress, 1989.]

Lührmann, D. 1976. *Glaube im frühen Christentum.* Gütersloh: Gerd Mohn.

Luz, U. 1985/1990. *Das Evangelium nach Matthäus.* 2 vols. Vol. 1, *Matt. 1–7; Vol. 2, Matt. 8–17.* Neukirchen-Vluyn: Neukirchener. [ET = *Matthew 1–7.* Continental Commentaries. W. Linss, trans. Minneapolis: Fortress, 1989.]

MacDonald, D. R. 1983. *The Legend and the Apostle: The Battle for Paul in Story and Canon.* Philadelphia: Westminster.

Mack, B. L. 1988. *A Myth of Innocence: Mark and Christian Origins.* Philadelphia: Fortress.

MacMullen, R. 1974. *Roman Social Relations 50 B.C. to A.D. 284.* New Haven: Yale Univ. Press.

————. 1975. *Enemies of the Roman Order: Treason, Unrest, and Alienation in the Empire.* 2d ed. Cambridge: Harvard Univ. Press.

————. 1980. "Women in Public in Roman Society." *Historia* 29:208–18.

————. 1981a. "Markttage im Römischen Imperium." In H. Schneider 1981a, 280–92.

————. 1981b. "Soziale Mobilität und der 'Codex Theodosianus.'" In H. Schneider 1981a, 155–67.

————. 1986. "Women's Power in the Principate." *Klio* 68:434–43.

Maier, J. 1973. "Tempel und Tempelkult." In Maier and Schreiner 1973, 371–90.

————. 1982. *Jüdische Auseinandersetzung mit dem Christentum in der Antike.* Darmstadt: Wissenschaftliche Buchgesellschaft.

Maier, J., and J. Schreiner, eds. 1973. *Literatur und Religion des Frühjudentums.* Würzburg: Echter.

Malherbe, A. J. 1977. *Social Aspect of Early Christianity.* Baton Rouge: Louisiana State Univ. Press.

————. 1979. "Soziale Ebene und literarische Bildung." In Meeks 1979, 194–221.

————. 1987. *Paul and the Thessalonians: The Philosophic Tradition of Pastoral Care.* Philadelphia: Fortress.

Malina, B. J. 1986. "'Religion' in the World of Paul." *BTB* 16:92–101.

————. 1988. "Patron and Client: The Analogy behind Synoptic Theology." *Forum* 4/1:1–32. [Reprinted in idem 1993b, 143–75.]

————. 1993a. *The New Testament World: Insights from Cultural Anthropology.* Rev. ed. Louisville: Westminster/John Knox.

————. 1993b. *The Social World of Jesus and the Gospels.* London: Routledge.

————. 1995. "Pain, Power, and Personhood: Ascetic Behavior in the Ancient Mediterranean." In *Asceticism,* 162–77. V. Wimbush and R. Valantasis, eds. New York: Oxford Univ. Press.

————. 1996. "Mediterranean Sacrifice: Dimensions of Domestic and Political Religion." *BTB* 26:26–44.

————. Forthcoming. *The Social Gospel of Jesus.* Minneapolis: Fortress.

Malina, B. J., and J. H. Neyrey. 1991. "Conflict in Luke-Acts: Labelling and Deviance Theory." In Neyrey 1991b, 97–122.

———. 1996. *Portraits of Paul: An Archaeology of Personality.* Louisville: Westminster/John Knox.

Malina, B. J., and R. L. Rohrbaugh. 1993. *Social-Science Commentary on the Synoptic Gospels.* Minneapolis: Fortress.

———. 1998. *Social-Science Commentary on the Gospel of John.* Minneapolis: Fortress.

Mandel, S. 1984. "Who Paid the Temple Tax When the Jews Were under Roman Rule?" *HTR* 77:223–42.

Marquardt, J. 1886. *Das Privatleben der Römer.* 2 vols. 2d ed. Leipzig. [Reprint ed. Darmstadt: Wissenschaftliche Buchgesellschaft, 1975.]

Marshall, A. J. 1975. "Roman Women and the Provinces." *Ancient Society* 6:110–19.

Martin, R. "Plinius der Jüngere und die wirtschaftlichen Probleme seiner Zeit." In H. Schneider 1981a, 198–233.

Martyn, J. L. 1968 (2d ed. 1979). *History and Theology in the Fourth Gospel.* Nashville: Abingdon.

Marx, K., and F. Engels. 1958. *Über die Religion.* Berlin: Walter de Gruyter.

Mason, S. N. 1989. "Was Josephus a Pharisee? A Reexamination of *Life* 10–12." *JJS* 40:31–45.

Mathys, H. P. 1986. *Liebe deinen Nächsten wie dich selbst: Untersuchungen zum alttestamentlichen Gebot der Nächstenliebe.* Göttingen: Vandenhoeck & Ruprecht.

Mattingly, H. B. 1959. *Roman Imperial Civilization.* New York: Edward Arnold. [Reprint ed. 1967.]

Mayer, G. 1987. *Die jüdische Frau in der hellenistisch-römischen Antike.* Stuttgart: Kohlhammer.

Mayer-Schärtel, B. 1994. "'Die Frau ist in jeder Hinsicht schwächer als der Mann": Eine sozialgeschichtliche und kulturanthropologische Untersuchung zum Frauenbild des Josephus." Diss., Neuendettelsau.

Mazar, B. 1957. "The Tobiads." *IEJ* 7:137–45, 229–38.

Meade, D. G. 1986. *Pseudonymity and Canon: An Investigation into the Relationship of Authorship and Authority in Jewish and Earliest Christian Tradition.* Tübingen: J. C. B. Mohr.

Meeks, W. A. 1973. "The Image of the Androgyne: Some Uses of a Symbol in Earliest Christianity." *HTR* 13:165–208.

———. 1975. "Am I a Jew? Johannine Christianity and Judaism." In Neusner 1975, 163–86.

———, ed. 1979. *Zur Soziologie des Urchristentums: Beiträge zum frühchristlichen Gemeinschaftsleben in seiner gesellschaftlichen Umwelt.* Theologische Bücherei 62. Munich: Chr. Kaiser.

———. 1983. *The First Urban Christians: The Social World of the Apostle Paul.* New Haven: Yale Univ. Press.

———. 1985. "Breaking Away: Three New Testament Pictures of Christianity's Separation from the Jewish Communities." In Neusner and Frerichs 1985, 93–115.

Meeks, W. A., and R. L. Wilken. 1978. *Jews and Christians in Antioch in the First Four Centuries of the Common Era.* SBLSBS13. Missoula, Mont.: Scholars.

Meier, C. 1986. "Arbeit, Politik und Identität: Neue Fragen im alten Athen?" In *Der Mensch und seine Arbeit: Eine Ringvorlesung der Universität München*, 47–109. V. Schubert, ed. St. Ottilien: EOS.

Meisner, N. 1973. "Der Aristeasbrief." JSHRZ 2/1.

Merkel, H. 1991. *Die Pastoralbriefe.* NTD 9. Göttingen: Vandenhoeck & Ruprecht.

Merklein, H. 1983. *Jesu Botschaft von der Gottesherrschaft: Eine Skizze.* Stuttgart: Katholisches Bibelwerk.

———. 1987. "Die Ekklesia Gottes." In idem, *Studien zu Jesus und Paulus*, 296–318. Tübingen: J. C. B. Mohr.

Meyer, B. E., and E. P. Sanders, eds. 1982. *Jewish and Christian Self-Definition.* Vol. 3: *Self-Definition in the Graeco-Roman World.* Minneapolis: Fortress.

Meyer, E. 1924. "Die wirtschaftliche Entwicklung des Altertums." In idem, *Kleine Schriften I.* 2d ed., 79–151. Halle: Niemeyer.

Meyer, R. 1973. "Pharisaios." In *TWNT* 9:11–36. [ET = *TDNT* 9:11–35.]

———. 1987. *Hellenistisches in der rabbinischen Anthropologie.* Stuttgart: Kohlhammer.

Meyers, E. M. 1988. "Early Judaism and Christianity in the Light of Archaeology." *BA* 51:69–79.

Michel, O. 1954. "Oikos, ktl." In *TWNT* 5:122–61. [ET = *TDNT* 5:119–59.]

Michel, O., and O. Bauernfeind. 1969. *Flavius Josephus: De Bello Judaico: Der jüdische Krieg, Griechisch und Deutsch.* 3 vols. Darmstadt: Wissenschaftliche Buchgesellschaft.

Mittwoch, A. 1955. "Tribute and Land Tax in Seleucid Judaea." *Bib* 36:352–61.

Molthagen, J. 1970. *Der römische Staat und die Christen im 2. und 3. Jahrhundert.* Göttingen: Vandenhoeck & Ruprecht.

Momigliano, A. 1934a. *Claudius the Emperor and His Achievement.* Oxford: Oxford Univ. Press. [Reprint ed. New York: Barnes & Noble, 1962.]

———. 1934b. "Richerce sull' organizzazione della Giudea sotto il dominio romano (63 a.C.–70 d.C.)." *Annali della Scuola Normale Superiore di Pisa, Classe di Lettere* 3:183–221, 347–96.

Mommsen, T. 1890. "Der Religionsfrevel nach römischen Recht." *HZ* 64:389–429.

———. 1955. *Römisches Strafrecht.* Reprint ed. Berlin: Akademie. [Orig. ed. Leipzig: Duncker & Humblot, 1899.]

Moore, G. F. 1954. *Judaism in the First Centuries of the Christian Era.* 7th ed. Cambridge: Harvard Univ. Press.

Moreau, J. 1971. *Die Christenverfolgung im Römischen Reich.* 2d ed. Berlin: Walter de Gruyter.

Morel, J.-P. 1991. "Der Handwerker." In Giardina 1991b, 243–76. [ET = "The Craftsman." In Giardina 1993, 214-44.]

Morgenthaler, R. 1956. "Roma—Sedes Satanae." *TZ* 12:289–304.

Moxnes, H. 1989. "Social Integration and the Problem of Gender in St. Paul's Letters." *ST* 43:99–113.

———. 1991. "Patron-Client Relations and the New Community in Luke-Acts." In Neyrey 1991b, 241–68.

———, ed. 1997. *Constructing Early Christian Families: Family as Social Reality and Metaphor*. London: Routledge.

Mühlmann, W. E. 1961. *Chiliasmus und Nativismus: Studien zur Psychologie, Soziologie und historischen Kasuistik der Umsturzbewegungen*. Berlin: Walter de Gruyter.

Müller, K. 1983. "Die Haustafel des Kolosserbriefes und das antike Frauenthema: Eine kritischen Rückschau auf alte Ergebnisse." In G. Dautzenberg et al. 1983, 263–319.

———. 1991. *Studien zur frühjüdischen Apokalyptik*. Stuttgart: Kohlhammer.

———. 1994. "Gott als Richter und die Erscheinungsweisen seiner Gerichte in den Schriften des Frühjudentums." In *Weltgericht und Weltvollendung: Zukunftsbilder im Neuen Testament*, 23–53. H.-J. Klauck, ed. Freiburg: Herder.

Müller, U. B. 1984. *Die Offenbarung des Johannes*. Würzburg: Echter.

Murphy-O'Conner, J. 1983. *St. Paul's Corinth: Texts and Archaeology*. Wilmington, Del.: Michael Glazier. [Reprint ed. Collegeville, Minn.: Liturgical, 1990.]

Netzer, E. 1989. "Jericho und Herodium: Verschwenderisches Leben in den Tagen der Hasmonäer und Herodes' des Grossen." *Judaica* 45:21–44.

Neusner, J. 1970. *A Life of Yohanan ben Zakkai: Ca. 1–80 C.E.* 2d ed. Studia Post-Biblica 6. Leiden: Brill.

———. 1971. *The Rabbinic Traditions about the Pharisees before 70*. 3 vols. Leiden: Brill.

———. 1972. "The Formation of Rabbinic Judaism: Yavneh from A.D. 70–100." In *ANRW* II 19.2:3–42.

———. 1973. *The Pharisees: Rabbinic Perspectives*. Studies in Ancient Judaism. Hoboken, N.J.: Ktav.

———, ed. 1975. *Judaism and Other Greco-Roman Cults: Studies for Morton Smith at Sixty*. 4 vols. SJLA 12. Leiden: Brill.

———. 1979. *From Politics to Piety: The Emergence of Pharisaic Judaism*. 2d ed. New York.

———. 1981. *Method and Meaning in Ancient Judaism*, vol. 2. Chico, Calif.: Scholars.

Neusner, J., and E. Frerichs, eds. 1985. *To See Ourselves as Others See Us: Christians, Jews, "Others" in Late Antiquity*. Scholars Press Studies in the Humanities. Chico, Calif.: Scholars.

Neyrey, J. H. 1991a. "Ceremonies in Luke-Acts: The Case of Meals and Table Fellowship." In idem 1991b, 361–87.

———, ed. 1991b. *The Social World of Luke-Acts: Models for Interpretation*. Peabody, Mass.: Hendrickson.

———. 1998. *Honor and Shame in the Gospel of Matthew*. Louisville: Westminster John Knox.

Nickelsburg, G. W. E., and G. MacRae, eds. 1986. *Christians among Jews and Gentiles: Essays in Honor of Krister Stendahl on His Sixty-fifth Birthday*. Philadelphia: Fortress.

Nicolet, C. 1976. *Le métier de citoyen dans la Rome républicaine.* Paris. [ET = *The World of the Citizen in Republican Rome.* P. S. Falla, trans. Berkeley: Univ. of California Press, 1980.]

Niebuhr, K.-W. 1992. *Heidenapostel aus Israel.* Tübingen: J. C. B. Mohr.

Nörr, D. 1963. "Origo: Studien zur Orts-, Stadt- und Reichszugehörigkeit in der Antike." *Tijdschrift voor Rechtsgeschiedenis* 31:525–600.

———. 1965. "Zur sozialen und rechtlichen Bewertung der freien Arbeit in Rom." *Zeitschrift der Savigny-Stiftung für Rechtsgeschichte, Romanistische Abteilung* 82:67–105.

North, D. C. 1988. *Theorie des institutionellen Wandels.* Tübingen: J. C. B. Mohr.

Oakman, D. E. 1986. *Jesus and the Economic Questions of His Day.* Studies in the Bible and Early Christianity 8. Lewiston, N.Y.: Edwin Mellen.

———. 1991a. "The Ancient Economy in the Bible." *BTB* 21:34–39.

———. 1991b. "The Countryside in Luke-Acts." In Neyrey 1991b, 151–79.

———. 1992. "Was Jesus a Peasant?" *BTB* 22:117–25.

———. 1994. "The Archaeology of First-Century Galilee and the Social Interpretation of the Historical Jesus." In *SBL 1994 Seminar Papers.* Vol. 33, 220–51. Atlanta: Scholars.

———. 1996. "The Ancient Economy." In Rohrbaugh 1996, 126–43.

O'Brien, P. T. 1993. "Church." In *Dictionary of Paul and His Letters,* 123–31. G. Hawthorn and R. P. Martin, eds. Downers Grove, Ill.: InterVarsity.

Ollrogg, W.-H. 1979. *Paulus und seine Mitarbeiter: Untersuchungen zu Theorie und Praxis der Paulinischen Mission.* WMANT 50. Neukirchen-Vluyn: Neukirchener.

Ortner, S. B., and H. Whitehead, eds. 1981. *Sexual Meanings: The Cultural Construction of Gender and Sexuality.* Cambridge: Cambridge Univ. Press.

Osborne, R. 1987. *Classical Landscape with Figures: The Ancient Greek City and Its Countryside.* Dobbs Ferry, N.Y.: Sheridan.

Osiek, C. 1996. "The Family in Early Christianity: 'Family Values' Reconsidered." *CBQ* 58:1–24.

Osiek, C., and D. L. Balch. 1997. *The Family in the New Testament: Households and House Churches.* The Family, Religion, and Culture. Louisville: Westminster John Knox.

Osten-Sacken, P. von der. 1984. *Katechismus und Siddur: Aufbrüche mit Martin Luther und den Lehrern Israels.* Berlin: Institut Kirche und Judentum.

Overbeck, F. 1994. *Werke und Nachlass.* Vol. 2: *Schriften bis 1880, in Zusammenarbeit mit M. Stauffacher-Schaub.* E. Stegemann and R. Brändle, eds. Stuttgart: Metzler.

Overman, J. A. 1990. *Matthew's Gospel and Formative Judaism: The Social World of the Matthean Community.* Minneapolis: Fortress.

Parkes, J. 1934. *The Conflict of the Church and the Synagogue: A Study in the Origins of Antisemitism.* New York: Hermon.

Paschen, W. 1970. *Rein und unrein: Untersuchung zur biblischen Wortgeschichte.* Munich: Kösel.

Pekary, T. 1979. *Die Wirtschaft der griechisch-römischen Antike.* Wiesbaden.

Peterson, N. R. 1985. *Rediscovering Paul: Philemon and the Sociology of Paul's Narrative World.* Philadelphia: Fortress.

Pilch, J. J. 1991. *Introducing the Cultural Context of the New Testament.* New York: Paulist.

———. 1999. *Healing in the New Testament: Insights from Medical and Mediterranean Anthropology.* Minneapolis: Fortress.

Pilch, J. J., and B. J. Malina, eds. 1998. *Handbook of Biblical Social Values.* 2d ed. Peabody, Mass.: Hendrickson.

Pitt-Rivers, J. 1977. *The Fate of Shechem or the Politics of Sex: Essays in Anthropology of the Mediterranean.* Cambridge: Cambridge Univ. Press.

Plöger, O. 1968. *Theokratie und Eschatologie.* 3d ed. Neukirchen-Vluyn: Neukirchener. [ET = *Theocracy and Eschatology.* S. Rudman, trans. Richmond, Va.: John Knox, 1968.]

Plümacher, E. 1987. *Identitätsverlust und Indentitätsgewinn: Studien zum Verhältnis von kaiserzeitlicher Stadt und frühem Christentum.* Biblische-Theologische Studien 11. Neukirchen-Vluyn: Neukirchener.

Pöhlmann, W. 1966. "Die heidnische, jüdische und christliche Opposition gegen Domitian: Studien zur Neutestamentlichen Zeitgeschichte." Diss., Erlangen.

———. 1993. *Der Verlorene Sohn und das Haus: Studien zu Lukas 15,1–32 im Horizont der antiken Lehre von Haus, Erziehung und Ackerbau.* WUNT 2/68. Tübingen: J. C. B. Mohr.

Polanyi, K. 1968. *Primitive, Archaic and Modern Economy: Essays of Karl Polanyi.* G. Dalton, ed. Garden City, N.Y.: Doubleday. [Reprint ed. Boston: Beacon, 1971.]

———. 1979. *Ökonomie und Gesellschaft.* Suhrkamp-Taschenbuch: Wissenschaft 295. Frankfurt: Shurkamp.

Pomeroy, S. B. 1985. *Frauenleben im klassischen Altertum.* Stuttgart: Kohlhammer. [ET = *Goddesses, Whores, Wives, and Slaves: Women in Classical Antiquity.* New York: Schocken, 1975.]

Porton, G. G. 1986. "Diversity in Postbiblical Judaism." In Kraft and Nickelsburg 1986, 57–80.

———. 1988. *GOYIM: Gentiles and Israelites in Mishnah-Tosefta.* BJS 155. Atlanta: Scholars.

———. 1994. *The Stranger within Your Gates: Converts and Conversion in Rabbinic Literature.* Chicago Studies in the History of Judaism. Chicago: Univ. of Chicago Press.

Radl, W. 1988. *Das Lukas-Evangelium.* Darmstadt: Wissenschaftliche Buchgesellschaft.

Rajak, T. 1984. "Was There a Roman Charter for the Jews?" *JRS* 74:107–23.

———. 1985. "Jews and Christians as Groups in a Pagan World." In Neusner and Frerichs 1985, 247–62.

Ramsay, W. M. 1910. *Pictures of the Apostolic Church: Its Life and Thought.* London: Hodder & Stoughton.

Redfield, J. 1993. "Homo Domesticus." In *Der Mensch der griechischen Antike,* 180–218. J.-P. Vernant, ed. Frankfurt: Fischer.

Reekmans, T. 1971. "Juvenal's View on Social Change." *Ancient Society* 2:117–61.

Reese, T. 1972. "The Political Theology of Luke-Acts." *Biblical Theology* 22:62–65.

Reifenberg, A. 1938. *The Soils of Palestine.* C. L. Whittles, trans. London: T. Murray. [Rev. ed. 1947.]

Reimer, I. R. 1992. *Frauen in der Apostelgeschichte des Lukas.* Gütersloh: Gütersloher. [ET = *Women in the Acts of the Apostles: A Feminist Liberation Perspective.* L. M. Maloney, trans. Minneapolis: Fortress, 1995.]

Reinbold, W. 1994. *Der älteste Bericht über den Tod Jesu: Literarische Analyse und historische Kritik der Passionsdarstellungen der Evangelien.* Beihefte zur Zeitschrift für die Neutestamentliche Wissenschaft und die Kunde der älteren Kirche 69. Berlin: Walter de Gruyter.

Reiser, M. 1990. *Die Gerichtspredigt Jesu: Eine Untersuchung zur eschatologischen Verkündigung Jesu und ihrem frühjüdischen Hintergrund.* Münster.

Rendtorff, R., ed. 1989. *Arbeitsbuch Christen und Juden: Zur Studie des Rates der Evangelischen Kirche in Deutschland.* 4th ed. Gütersloh: Gerd Mohn.

Rengstorff, K. H. 1973. *A Complete Concordance to Flavius Josephus.* Vol. 1. Leiden: Brill.

Reynolds, J., and R. Tannenbaum. 1987. *Jews and Godfearers at Aphrodisias: Greek Inscriptions with Commentary, Texts from the Excavations at Aphrodisias Conducted by K. T. Erim.* Cambridge: Cambridge Univ. Press.

Rhoads, D. M. 1976. *Israel in Revolution: 6–74 C.E.: A Political History Based on the Writings of Josephus.* Philadelphia: Fortress.

Richardson, P. 1969. *Israel in the Apostolic Church.* SNTSMS 10. Cambridge: Cambridge Univ. Press.

———. 1996. *Herod: King of the Jews and Friend of the Romans.* Studies in the Personalities of the New Testament. Columbia: Univ. of South Carolina Press. [Paperback ed. Minneapolis: Fortress, 1999.]

Riddle, D. W. 1934. "Die Verfolgungslogien in formgeschichtlicher und soziologischer Beleuchtung." *ZNW* 33:271–89.

Rilinger, R. 1988. *Humiliores-Honestiores: Zu einer sozialen Dichotomie im Strafrecht der römischen Kaiserzeit.* Munich: Chr. Kaiser.

Rohrbaugh, R. L. 1984. "Methodological Considerations in the Debate over the Social Class Status of Early Christianity." *JAAR* 52:519–46.

———. 1991. "The Pre-Industrial City in Luke-Acts: Urban Social Relations." In Neyrey 1991b, 125–49.

———. 1993. "The Social Location of the Markan Audience." *BTB* 23:114–27.

———, ed. 1996. *The Social Sciences and New Testament Interpretation.* Peabody, Mass.: Hendrickson.

Roloff, J. 1989. *Der erste Brief an Timotheus.* EKKNT 15. Neukirchen-Vluyn: Neukirchener.

———. 1992. "Ekklēsia." In *EWNT,* 2d ed., 1:998–1011. [ET = *EDNT* 1:410–15.]

———. 1993. *Die Kirche im Neuen Testament.* Grundrisse 10. Göttingen: Vandenhoeck & Ruprecht.

Rordorf, W. 1964. "Was wissen wir über die christlichen Gottesdiensträume der vorkonstantinischen Zeit?" *ZNW* 55:110–28.

Rosaldo, M. Z. 1974. "Women, Culture and Society: A Theoretical Overview." In *Women, Culture and Society,* 17–42. M. Z. Rosaldo and L. Lamphere, eds. Stanford: Stanford Univ. Press.

Rostovtzeff, M. I. 1902. *Geschichte der Staatspacht in der römischen Kaiserzeit bis Diokletian.* Leipzig: Dietrich.

———. 1955–56. *Die hellenistische Welt: Gesellschaft und Wirtschaft.* 3 vols. Stuttgart: Kohlhammer. [ET = *The Social and Economic History of the Hellenistic World.* 3 vols. Rev. by P. M. Fraser. Oxford: Clarendon, 1959.]

———. 1957. *Social and Economic History of the Roman Empire.* 2 vols. Oxford: Oxford Univ. Press.

Roth, G. 1987. *Politische Herrschaft und persönliche Freiheit: Heidelberger Max Weber-Vorlesungen 1983.* Frankfurt: Suhrkamp.

Roth, G., and W. Schluchter. 1979. *Max Weber's Vision of History, Ethics and Methods.* Berkeley: Univ. of California Press.

Rowley, H. H. 1981. "Die Geschichte der Qumransekte." In Grözinger 1981, 23–57.

Rudolph, K. 1960. *Die Mandäer.* Vol. 1: *Prolegomena. Das Mandäerproblem.* Göttingen: Vandenhoeck & Ruprecht.

Runciman, W. G. 1968. "Class, Status and Power." In *Social Stratification,* 25–61. J.A. Jackson, ed. Sociological Studies 1. Cambridge: Cambridge Univ. Press.

Safrai, S. 1965. "The Teaching of Pietists in Mishnaic Literature." *JJS* 16:15–33.

———. 1976a. "Home and Family." In Safrai and Stern 1976, 728–92.

———. 1976b. "Religion in Everyday Life." In ibid., 793–833.

———. 1976c. "The Synagogue." In ibid., 908–44.

———. 1976d. "The Temple." In ibid., 865–907.

———. 1980. *Das jüdische Volk im Zeitalter des Zweiten Tempels.* 2d ed. Neukirchen-Vluyn: Neukirchener.

———. 1981. *Die Wallfahrt im Zeitalter des Zweiten Tempels.* D. Mach, trans. Forschungen zum jüdisch-christlichen Dialog 3. Neukirchen-Vluyn: Neukirchener.

Safrai, S., and M. Stern, eds. 1974–76. *The Jewish People in the First Century.* 2 vols. Compendia Rerum Iudicarum ad Novum Testamentum. Assen: Van Gorcum; Philadelphia: Fortress.

Safrai, Z. 1994. *The Economy of Roman Palestine.* London: Routledge.

Sahlins, M. D. 1965. "On the Sociology of Primitive Exchange." In *The Relevance of Models for Social Anthropology,* 139–236. M. Banton, ed. New York: Praeger.

Saldarini, A. J. 1989. *Pharisees, Scribes and Saducees in Palestinian Society: A Sociological Approach.* Wilmington, Del.: Michael Glazier.

———. 1991. "The Gospel of Matthew and the Jewish-Christian Conflict." In Balch 1991, 38–61.

Saller, R. P. 1982. *Personal Patronage under the Empire*. New York: Cambridge Univ. Press.

———. 1989. "Patronage and Friendship in Early Imperial Rome: Drawing the Distinction." In *Patronage in Ancient Society*, 49–62. A. Wallace-Hadrill, ed. Leicester-Nottingham Studies in Ancient Society 1. London: Routledge.

Sampley, J. P. 1980. *Pauline Partnership in Christ: Christian Community and Commitment in Light of Roman Law*. Philadelphia: Fortress.

Sanders, E. P. 1985. *Jesus and Judaism*. Philadelphia: Fortress.

———. 1990. "Jewish Association with Gentiles and Galatians 2:11-14." In *The Conversation Continues: Studies in Paul and John in Honor of Louis Martyn*, 170–88. R. F. Fortna and B. R. Gaventa, eds. Nashville: Abingdon.

———, ed. 1980. *Jewish and Christian Self-Definition*. Vol. 1: *The Shaping of Christianity in the Second and Third Centuries*. Philadelphia: Fortress.

Sanders, E. P., A. I. Baumgarten, and A. Mendelson, eds. 1981. *Jewish and Christian Self-Definition*. Vol. 2: *Aspects of Judaism in the Graeco-Roman Period*. Philadelphia: Fortress.

Sanders, J. T. 1987. *The Jews in Luke-Acts*. Philadelphia: Fortress.

———. 1993. *Schismatics, Sectarians, Dissidents, Deviants: The First One Hundred Years of Jewish-Christian Relations*. Valley Forge, Pa.: Trinity Press International.

Schäfer, P. 1975. "Die sogenannte Synode von Jabne: Zur Trennung von Juden und Christen im ersten/zweiten Jahrhundert n.Chr." *Judaica* 31:54–64, 116–24.

———. 1979. "Die Flucht Johanan b. Zakkais aus Jerusalem und die Gründung des 'Lehrhauses' in Jabne." In *ANRW* II 19.2:43–101.

———. 1983. *Geschichte der Juden in der Antike*. Stuttgart: Katholisches Bibelwerk. [ET = *The History of the Jews in Antiquity: The Jews in Palestine from Alexander the Great to the Arab Conquest*. D. Chowcat, trans. Newark, N.J.: Harwood Academic, 1995.]

———. 1991. "Der vorrabbinische Pharisäismus." In *Paulus und das antike Judentum*, 125–75. M. Hengel and U. Heckel, eds. Tübingen: J. C. B. Mohr.

Schäfke, W. 1979. "Frühchristliche Widerstand." In *ANRW* II 23.1:460–723.

Schalit, A. 1969. *König Herodes: Der Mann und sein Werk*. J. Amir, trans. Studia Judaica 4. Berlin: Walter de Gruyter.

Scheid, J. 1993. "Die Rolle der Frauen in der römischen Religion." In *Geschichte der Frauen*. Vol. 1: *Antike*, 417–49. P. Schmitt Pantel, ed. Frankfurt: Campus.

Scheidel, W. 1990. "Feldarbeit von Frauen in der antiken Landwirtschaft." *Gymnasium* 97:405–31.

Schenke, L. 1988. *Das Markusevangelium*. Stuttgart: Kohlhammer.

———. 1990. *Das Urgemeinde: Geschichtliche und theologische Entwicklung*. Stuttgart: Kohlhammer.

———. 1992. *Das Johannesevangelium*. Stuttgart: Kohlhammer.

Schiffman, L. H. 1975. *The Halakhah at Qumran*. SJLA 16. Leiden: Brill.

———. 1981. "At the Crossroads: Tannaitic Perspectives on the Jewish-Christian Schism." In E. P. Sanders, Baumgarten, and Mendelson 1981, 115–56.

———. 1985. *Who Was a Jew? Rabbinic and Halakhic Perspectives on the Jewish Christian Schism*. New York: Ktav.

————. 1992. "The Sadducean Understanding of the Dead Sea Scrolls Sect." In *Understanding the Dead Sea Scrolls*, 35–49. H. Shanks, ed. New York: Random House.

Schlier, H. 1933. "Haireomi, ktl." In *TWNT* 1:179–84. [ET = *TDNT* 1:180–85.]

Schluchter, W. 1979. *Die Entwicklung des okzidentalen Rationalismus: Eine Analyse von Max Webers Gesellschaftsgeschichte*. Tübingen: J. C. B. Mohr.

————. 1985. "Einleitung: Max Webers Analyse des antiken Christentums. Grundzüge eines unvollendeten Projekts." In *Max Webers Analyse des antiken Christentums: Interpretation und Kritik*, 11–71. Idem, ed. Frankfurt: Suhrkamp.

————. 1988. *Religion und Lebensführung*. Vol. 2: *Studien zu Max Webers Religions- und Herrschaftssoziologie*. Frankfurt.

Schmidt, K. L. 1938. "Ekklēsia." In *TWNT* 3:502–39. [ET = *TDNT* 3:501–36.]

Schnackenburg, R. 1982. *Das Johannesevangelium. III. Teil: Kommentar zu Kapitel 13–21*. 4th ed. Freiburg: Herder. [ET = *The Gospel according to John*. Vol. 3: *Commentary on Chapters 13–21*. C. Hastings et al., trans. New York: Crossroad, 1982.]

Schneemelcher, W. 1987. *Neutestamentlicher Apokryphen in deutscher Übersetzung*. Vol. 1: *Evangelien*. 5th ed. Tübingen: J. C. B. Mohr. [ET = *New Testament Apocrypha*. Vol. 1: *Gospels and Related Writings*. Rev. ed. R. McL. Wilson, trans. Louisville: Westminster/John Knox, 1991.]

Schneider, G. 1992. "Christianos." In *EWNT*, 2d ed., 3:1145–47. [ET = *EDNT* 3:477–78.]

Schneider, H. 1981a. "Die antike Sklavenwirtschaft: Das Imperium Romanum." In *Geschichte der Arbeit: Vom Alten Ägypten bis zur Gegenwart*, 96–154. A. Eggebrecht et al., eds. Cologne: Kipenheuer & Witsch.

————. 1981b. "Einleitung." In idem 1981c, 4–28.

————, ed. 1981c. *Sozial- und Wirtschaftsgeschichte der römischen Kaiserzeit*. WF 552. Darmstadt: Wissenschaftliche Buchgesellschaft.

Scholem, G. 1992. *Sabbatai Zwi: Der mystische Messias*. Frankfurt. [ET = *Sabbatai Sevi: The Mystical Messiah*. Princeton: Princeton Univ. Press, 1975.]

Schöllgen, G. 1985. *Ecclesia sordida? Zur Frage der sozialen Schichtung frühchristlicher Gemeinden am Beispiel Karthagos zur Zeit Tertullians*. Münster: Aschendorff.

Schottroff, L. 1980. "Frauen in der Nachfolge Jesu in neutstamentlicher Zeit." In *Traditionen der Befreiung: Sozialgeschichtliche Bibelauslegungen*. Vol. 2: *Frauen in der Bibel*, 91–133. W. Schottroff and W. Stegemann, eds. Munich: Chr. Kaiser.

————. 1985. "'Nicht viele Mächtige': Annäherungen an eine Soziologie des Urchristentums." *BK* 40:2–8.

————. 1994a. "Dienerinnen der Heiligen: Der Diakonat der Frauen im Neuen Testament." In *Diakonie—biblische Grundlagen und Orientierungen: Ein Arbeitsbuch*, 222–42. G. K. Schäfer and T. Strohm, eds. 2d ed. Veröffentlichungen des diakoniewissenschaftlichen Instituts an der Universitäts Heidelberg 2. Heidelberg: Heidelberger Verlagsanstalt.

————. 1994b. *Lydias ungeduldige Schwestern: Feministische Sozialgeschichte des frühen Christentums*. Gütersloh: Gütersloher. [ET = *Lydia's Impatient Sisters: A*

Feminist Social History of Early Christianity. B. Rumscheidt and M. Rumscheidt, trans. Louisville: Westminster/John Knox, 1995.]

Schottroff, L., and W. Stegemann. 1990. *Jesus von Nazareth—Hoffnung der Armen*. 3d ed. Urban Taschenbücher 639. Stuttgart: Kohlhammer. [ET= *Jesus and the Hope of the Poor*. M. J. O'Connell, trans. Maryknoll: Orbis, 1986.]

Schottroff, W., and W. Stegemann, eds. 1979. *Der Gott der kleinen Leute*. 2 vols. Munich: Chr. Kaiser. [Abridged ET = *The God of the Lowly: Socio-historical Interpretations of the Bible*. M. J. O'Connell, trans. Maryknoll, N.Y.: Orbis, 1984.]

Schrage, W. 1963. "'Ekklesia' und 'Synagoge': Zum Ursprung des urchristlichen Kirchenbegriffs." *ZTK* 60:178–202.

———. 1964. "Synagoge ktl." In *TWNT* 7:798–850. [ET = *TDNT* 7:798–852.]

Schuller, W. 1985. *Frauen in der griechischen Geschichte*. Konstanzer Bibliothek 3. Constance: Konstanz Universitätsverlag.

———. 1987. *Frauen in der römischen Geschichte*. Constance: Konstanz Universitätsverlag. [2d ed. Munich: Piper, 1992.]

Schürer, E. 1901/1909. *Geschichte des jüdischen Volkes im Zeitalter Jesu Christi*. 3d and 4th ed. Leipzig: J. C. Hinrichs.

———. 1973–87. *The History of the Jewish People in the Age of Jesus Christ (175 B.C.–A.D. 135)*. Rev. and ed. by G. Vermes and F. Millar. 3 vols. Edinburgh: T. & T. Clark.

Schütz, J. H. 1975. *Paul and the Anatomy of Apostolic Authority*. SNTSMS 26. Cambridge: Cambridge Univ. Press.

———. 1979. "Charisma und soziale Wirklichkeit im Urchristentum." In Meeks 1979, 222–44. [ET = "Charisma and Social Reality in Primitive Christianity." *JR* 54 (1974):51–70.]

Schütz, R. 1933. *Die Offenbarung des Johannes und Kaiser Domitian*. Göttingen: Vandenhoeck & Ruprecht.

Schwarz, A. 1919. "Die Schatzkammer des Tempels zu Jerusalem." *MGWJ* 63:227–52.

Schwier, H. 1989. *Tempel und Tempelzerstörung: Untersuchungen zu den theologischen und ideologischen Faktoren im ersten jüdisch-römischen Krieg (66–74 n.Chr.)*. Fribourg–Göttingen: Vandenhoeck & Ruprecht.

Scott, K. 1936. *The Imperial Cult under the Flavians*. Stuttgart: Kohlhammer.

Scroggs, R. 1975. "The Earliest Christian Communities as Sectarian Movements." In Neusner 1975, 2:1–23.

———. 1980. "The Sociological Interpretation of the New Testament: The Present State of Research." *NTS* 16:164–79.

Segal, A. F. 1986. *Rebecca's Children: Judaism and Christianity in the Roman World.* Cambridge: Harvard Univ. Press. [2d ed. 1989.]

———. 1990. *Paul the Convert: The Apostolate and Apostasy of Saul the Pharisee.* New Haven: Yale Univ. Press.

———. 1991. "Matthew's Jewish Voice." In Balch 1991, 3–37.

Sevenster, J. N. 1975. *The Roots of Pagan Antisemitism in the Ancient World.* NovTSup 41. Leiden: Brill.

Shaw, B. D. 1984. "Bandits in the Roman Empire." *Past and Present* 105:5–52.

———. 1991. "Der Bandit." In Giardina 1991b, 337–81. [ET = "The Bandit." In Giardina 1993, 300–341.]

Sherwin-White, A. N. 1952. "The Early Persecutions and Roman Law Again." *JTS* 3:199–213.

———. 1964. "Why Were the Early Christians Persecuted? An Amendment." *Past and Present* 27:23–27.

———. 1966. *The Letters of Pliny: A Historical and Social Commentary.* Oxford: Oxford Univ. Press.

Siedl, S. H. 1963. *Qumran: eine Mönchsgemeinde im Alten Bund: Studie über Serek Ha-Yahad.* Rome: Desclée.

Siegert, F. 1973. "Gottesfürchtige und Sympathisanten." *JSJ* 4:109–64.

Simon, M. 1948. *Verus Israel.* Paris. [ET = *Verus Israel: A Study of the Relations between Christians and Jews in the Roman Empire 135–425.* H. McKeating, trans. Littman Library of Jewish Civilization. Oxford: Oxford Univ. Press, 1966. Reprint ed. 1986.]

———. 1979. "From Greek Hairesis to Christian Heresy." In *Early Christian Literature and the Classical Intellectual Tradition,* 101–16. W. R. Schoedel and R. L. Wilken. Théologique Historique 54. Paris: Beauchesne.

———. 1981. "Gottesfürchtige." In *RAC* 11:1060–70.

Sjoberg, G. 1965. *The Preindustrial City: Past and Present.* Glencoe, Ill.: Free Press.

Smallwood, E. M. 1976. *The Jews under Roman Rule: From Pompey to Diocletian.* SJLA 20. Leiden: Brill. [2d ed. 1980.]

Smelik, K. A. D., and E. A. Hemelrijk. 1984. "'Who Knows Not What Monsters Demented Egypt Worship?' Opinions on Egyptian Animal Worship in Antiquity as Part of the Ancient Conception of Egypt." In *ANRW* II 17.4:1852–2000, 2337–57.

Smith, D. E. 1980. "Social Obligation in the Context of Communal Meals: A Study of the Christian Meal in 1 Corinthians Compared to Graeco-Roman Communal Meals." Diss., Harvard.

Smith, D. E., and H. Taussig. 1990. *Many Tables: The Eucharist in the New Testament and Liturgy Today.* Philadelphia: Trinity Press International.

Smith, J. Z. 1978. "Too Much Kingdom, Too Little Community." *Zygon* 13:123–30.

Smith, M. 1971. "Zealots and Sicarii, Their Origins and Relation." *HTR* 64:1–19.

Smith, R. H. 1980. "Were the Early Christians Middle-Class? A Sociological Analysis of the New Testament." *Currents in Theology and Mission* 7:260–76.

Speigl, J. 1970. *Der römische Staat und die Christen.* Amsterdam.

Sperber, D. 1974. *Roman Palestine 200–400: Money and Prices.* Studies in Near Eastern Languages and Cultures. Ramat Gan: Bar-Ilan Univ. Press.

———. 1977. "Aspects of Agrarian Life in Roman Palestine I." In *ANRW* II 8:397–443.

———. 1978. *Roman Palestine 200–400: The Land.* Studies in Near Eastern Languages and Cultures. Ramat Gan: Bar-Ilan Univ. Press.

Spicq, C. 1961. *Dieu et l'homme selon le Nouveau Testament.* Paris: Cerf.

Spiro, S. J. 1980. "Who Was the *Haber?* A New Approach to an Ancient Institution." *JSJ* 11:186–216.

Stadelmann, H. 1980. *Ben Sira als Schriftgelehrter: Eine Untersuchung zum Berufsbild des vor-makkabäischen Sofer unter Berücksichtigung seines Verhältnisses zu Priester-, Propheten- und Weisheitslehrertum.* Tübingen: J. C. B. Mohr.

Stahl, M. 1978. *Imperiale Herrschaft und provinziale Stadt: Strukturprobleme der römischen Reichsorganisation im 1.–3. Jh. der Kaiserzeit.* Göttingen: Vandenhoeck & Rupprecht.

Stählin, G. 1962. *Die Apostelgeschichte.* 10th ed. Texte zum Neuen Testament 5. Göttingen: Vandenhoeck & Ruprecht.

Stambaugh, J. E. 1988. *The Ancient Roman City.* Baltimore: Johns Hopkins Univ. Press.

Stark, R. 1986. "The Class Basis of Early Christianity: Inferences from a Sociological Model." *Sociological Analysis* 47:216–25.

———. 1996. *The Rise of Christianity: A Sociologist Reconsiders History.* Princeton: Princeton Univ. Press.

Stegemann, E. W. 1985. "'Kindlein, hütet euch vor den Götterbildern!' Erwägungen zum Schluss des 1. Johannesbriefes." *TZ* 41:284–94.

———. 1986. "Zur Rolle von Petrus, Jakobus und Johannes im Markusevangelium." *TZ* 42:366–74.

———. 1989. "Die Tragödie der Nähe: Zu den judenfeindlichen Aussagen des Johannesevangeliums." *Kirche und Israel* 4:114–22.

———. 1990a. "Das Abendmahl im Kontext antiker Mahlzeiten." *Zeitschrift für Mission* 16:133–39.

———. 1990b. "Zur Tempelreinigung im Johannesevangelium." In *Die Hebräische Bibel und ihre zweifache Nachgeschichte: Festschrift für Rolf Rendtorff zum 65. Geburtstag,* 503–16. E. Blum, G. C. Macholz, and E. W. Stegemann, eds. Neukirchen-Vluyn: Neukirchener.

———, ed. 1993. *Messias-Vorstellungen bei Juden und Christen.* Stuttgart: Kohlhammer.

———. 1994. "Zwischen Juden und Heiden, aber 'mehr' als Juden und Heiden? Neutestamentliche Anmerkungen zur Identitätsproblematik des frühen Christentums." *Kirche und Israel* 9:53–69.

Stegemann, E. W., and W. Stegemann. "König Israels, nicht König der Juden: Jesus als König im Johannesevangelium." In E. W. Stegemann 1993, 41–56.

Stegemann, H. 1983. "Die Bedeutung der Qumranfunde für die Erforschung der Apokalyptik." In Hellholm 1983, 495–530.

————. 1993. *Die Essener, Qumran, Johannes der Täufer und Jesus: Ein Sachbuch.* Freiburg: Herder.

Stegemann, W. 1979. "Wanderradikalismus im Urchristentum? Historische und theologische Auseinandersetzung mit einer interessanten These." In W. Schottroff and W. Stegemann 1979, 2:94–120. [ET = "Vagabond Radicalism in Early Christianity? A Historical and Theological Discussion of a Thesis Proposed by Gerd Theissen." In W. Schottroff and W. Stegemann 1984, 148–68.]

————. 1980. "Lasset die Kinder zu mir kommen: Sozialgeschichtliche Aspekte des Kinderevangeliums." In *Traditionen der Befreiung: Sozialgeschichtliche Bibelauslegungen.* Vol. 1: *Methodische Zugange,* 114ff. W. Schottroff and W. Stegemann, eds. Munich: Chr. Kaiser.

————. 1981. *Das Evangelium und die Armen: Über den Ursprung der Theologie der Armen im Neuen Testament.* Munich: Chr. Kaiser.

————. 1985. "Zwei sozialgeschichtliche Anfragen an unser Paulusbild." *EvErz* 37:480–90.

————. 1987a. "Nächstenliebe oder Barmherzigkeit: Überlegungen zum ethischen und soziologischen Ort der Nächstenliebe." In *Spiritualität: Theologische Beiträge,* 59–82. H. Wagner, eds. Stuttgart: Calwer.

————. 1987b. "War der Apostel Paulus ein römischer Bürger?" *ZNW* 78:200–229.

————. 1991. *Zwischen Synagoge und Obrigkeit: Zur historischen Situation der lukanischen Christen.* Göttingen: Vandenhoeck & Ruprecht.

————. 1993. "Zur Deutung des Urchristentums in den 'Soziallehren.'" In *Ernst Troeltschs Soziallehren: Studien zu ihrer Interpretation.* Troeltsch-Studien 6:51–79. F. W. Graf and T. Rendtorff, eds. Gütersloh: Gerd Mohn.

————. 1994. "Zur neueren exegetischen Diskussion um die Apostelgeschichte." *EvErz* 46:198–219.

Stemberger, G. 1977. "Die sogenannte 'Synode von Jabne' und das frühe Christentum." *Kairos* 19:14–21.

————. 1979. *Das klassische Judentum: Kultur und Geschichte der rabbinischen Zeit.* Munich: Chr. Kaiser.

————. 1991. *Pharisaer, Sadduzaer, Essener.* Stuttgart: Kohlhammer. [ET = *Jewish Contemporaries of Jesus: Pharisees, Sadducees, Essenes.* A. W. Mahnke, trans. Minneapolis: Fortress, 1995.]

Stendahl, K. 1959. "Kirche II. Im Urchristentum" In *RGG* 3d ed., 3:1297–1304.

Stenger, W. 1988. *"Gebt dem Kaiser, was des Kaisers ist . . .!" Eine sozialgeschichtliche Untersuchung zur Besteuerung Palästinas in neutestamentlicher Zeit.* Frankfurt: Athenäum.

Stern, M. 1964. "Sympathy for Judaism in Roman Senatorial Circles in the Period of the Early Empire." *Zion* 29:155–67 (Hebrew).

————. 1974–84. *Greek and Latin Authors on Jews and Judaism.* 3 vols. Jerusalem: Israel Academy of Sciences and Humanities.

————. 1974a. "Jewish Self-Government." In Safrai and Stern 1974, 1:377–419.

————. 1974b. "The Province of Judaea." In ibid., 1:308–76.

———. 1974c. "The Reign of Herod and the Herodian Dynasty." In ibid., 1:216–307.

———. 1976a. "Aspects of Jewish Society: The Priesthood and Other Classes." In Safrai and Stern 1976, 2:561–630.

———. 1976b. "The Jews in Greek and Latin Literature." In ibid., 2:1101–59.

———. 1978. "Die Zeit des Zweiten Tempels." In *Geschichte des jüdischen Volkes*, 1:229–373. H. H. Ben Sasson, ed. Munich: Chr. Kaiser.

Stowers, S. K. 1984. "Social Status, Public Speaking and Private Teaching: The Circumstances of Paul's Preaching Activity." *NovT* 26:59–82.

Strathmann, H. 1942. "Latreuo, latreia." In *TWNT* 4:58–66. [ET = *TDNT* 4:58–65.]

Strecker, G. 1959. "Ebioniten." In *RAC* 4:487–500.

———. 1971. *Der Weg der Gerechtigkeit: Untersuchungen zur Theologie des Matthäus.* 3d ed. FRLANT 82. Göttingen: Vandenhoeck & Ruprecht.

Stroh, W. 1986. "Labor Improbus: Die Arbeit im antiken Rom." In *Der Mensch und seine Arbeit: Eine Ringvorlesung der Universität München,* 111–45. V. Schubert, ed. St. Ottilien: EOS.

Stuhlmacher, P. 1982. "Jesu vollkommenes Gesetz der Freiheit." *ZTK* 79:283–322.

Sugranyes de Franch, R. 1946. *Etudes sur le droit palestinien à l'époque évangélique.* Fribourg.

Sullivan, R. D. 1977. "The Dynasty of Judaea in the First Century." In *ANRW* II 8:296–354.

Tajra, H. W. 1989. *The Trial of St. Paul: A Juridical Exegesis of the Second Half of the Acts of Apostles.* Tübingen: J. C. B. Mohr.

Talmon, S. 1988. "Jüdische Sektenbildung in der Frühzeit des Zweiten Tempels." In idem, *Gesellschaft und Literatur in der Hebräischen Bibel: Gesammelte Aufsätze,* 1:95–131. Neukirchen-Vluyn: Neukirchener.

———. 1989. *The World of Qumran from Within: Collected Studies.* Leiden: Brill.

Tarn, W. W., and G. T. Griffith. 1959. *Hellenistic Civilization.* 3d ed. London: Edward Arnold.

Tcherikover, V. A. 1961. *Hellenistic Civilization and the Jews.* 2d ed. New York: Jewish Publication Society.

Theissen, G. 1974. *Urchristliche Wundergeschichten: Ein Beitrag zur formgeschichtlichen Erforschung der synoptischen Evangelien.* Gütersloh: Gerd Mohn. [ET = *The Miracle Stories of the Early Christian Tradition.* F. McDonagh, trans. Philadelphia: Fortress, 1983.]

———. 1978. *Sociology of Early Palestinian Christianity.* J. Bowden, trans. Minneapolis: Fortress, 1978. [Trans. of 1st ed. (1977) of idem 1991.]

———. 1982. *The Social Setting of Pauline Christianity: Essays on Corinth.* J. H. Schütz, ed. and trans. Philadelphia: Fortress. [A translation of parts of idem 1983b; see also idem 1992.]

———. 1983a. *Psychologische Aspekte paulinischer Theologie.* FRLANT 131. Göttingen: Vandenhoeck & Ruprecht. [ET = *Psychological Aspects of Pauline Theology.* J. P. Galvin, trans. Minneapolis: Fortress, 1987.]

―――. 1983b. *Studien zur Soziologie des Urchristentums.* 2d ed. WUNT 2/19. Tübingen: J. C. B. Mohr. [ET = see 1982 and 1992.]

―――. 1988. "Zur Entstehung des Christentums aus dem Judentum: Bemerkungen zu David Flussers Thesen." *Kirche und Israel* 3:179–89.

―――. 1989a. "Legitimation und Lebensunterhalt: Ein Beitrag zur Soziologie urchristlicher Missionare." In idem, *Studien zur Soziologie des Urchristentums,* 201–30. 3d ed. Tübingen: J. C. B. Mohr. [ET = "Legitimation and Subsistence: An Essay on the Sociology of Early Christian Missionaries." In idem 1982, 27–67.]

―――. 1989b. *Lokalkolorit und Zeitgeschichte in den Evangelien: Ein Beitrag zur Geschichte der synoptischen Tradition.* Freiburg. [ET = *The Gospels in Context: Social and Political History in the Synoptic Tradition.* L. M. Maloney, trans. Minneapolis: Fortress, 1991.]

―――. 1989c. "Soziale Integration und sakramentales Handeln: Eine Analyse von 1 Cor. XI 17–34." In ibid., 290–317. [ET = "Social Integration and Sacramental Activity: An Analysis of 1 Cor. 11:17-34." In idem 1982, 145–74.]

―――. 1989d. "Soziale Schichtung in der korinthischen Gemeinde: Ein Beitrag zur Soziologie des hellenistischen Urchristentums." In ibid., 231–71. [ET = "Social Stratification in the Corinthian Community: A Contribution to the Sociology of Early Hellenistic Christianity." In idem 1982, 69–119.]

―――. 1989e. "Die Starken und Schwachen in Korinth: Soziologische Analyse eines theologischen Streites." In ibid., 272–89. [ET = "The Strong and the Weak in Corinth: A Sociological Analysis of a Theological Quarrel." In idem 1982, 121–43.]

―――. 1989f. "Wanderradikalismus: Literatursoziologische Aspekte der Überlieferung von Worten Jesu im Urchristentum." In ibid., 79–105. [ET = "The Wandering Radicals: Light Shed by the Sociology of Literature on the Early Transmission of Jesus Sayings." In idem 1992, 33–59.]

―――. 1989g. "'Wir haben alles verlassen' (Mc X,28): Nachfolge und soziale Entwurzelung in der jüdisch-palästinischen Gesellschaft des 1. Jahrhunderts n.Chr." In ibid., 106–41. [ET = "'We Have Left Everything . . .' (Mark 10:28): Discipleship and Social Uprooting in the Jewish-Palestinian Society of the First Century." In idem 1992, 60–93.]

―――. 1991. *Soziologie der Jesusbewegung: Ein Beitrag zur Entstehungsgeschichte des Urchristentums.* 6th ed. Munich: Chr. Kaiser. [ET = *Sociology of Early Palestinian Christianity.* J. Bowden, trans. Minneapolis: Fortress, 1978.]

―――. 1992. *Social Reality and the Early Christians: Theology, Ethics, and the World of the New Testament.* M. Kohl, trans. Minneapolis: Fortress. [Translation of parts of idem 1983b.]

―――. 1999. *The Religion of the Earliest Churches: Creating a Symbolic World.* J. Bowden, trans. Minneapolis: Fortress.

Theissen, G., and A. Merz. 1998. *The Historical Jesus: A Comprehensive Guide.* J. Bowden, trans. Minneapolis: Fortress.

Thompson, C. L. 1988. "Portraits from Roman Corinth: Hairstyles, Headcoverings and St. Paul." *BA* 51:99–115.

Thraede, K. 1970. "Frau." In *RAC* 8:197–269.

Thyen, H. 1970. *Studien zur Sündenvergebung im Neuen Testament und seinen alttestamentlichen und jüdischen Voraussetzungen.* Göttingen: Vandenhoeck & Ruprecht.

———. 1978. "'. . . nicht mehr männlich und weiblich . . .': Eine Studie zu Gal 3,28." In *Als Mann und Frau geschaffen: Exegetische Studien zur Rolle der Frau*, 197–208. F. Crüsemann and H. Thyen, eds. Gelnhausen: Burchardthaus.

Tilly, M. 1994. *Johannes der Täufer und die Biographie der Propheten: Die synoptische Täuferüberlieferung und das jüdischen Prophetenbild zur Zeit des Täufers.* BWANT 137. Stuttgart: Kohlhammer.

Torjesen, K. J. 1993. *When Women Were Priests: Women's Leadership in the Early Church and the Scandal of Their Subordination in the Rise of Christiantiy.* San Francisco: HarperSanFrancisco.

Trebilco, P. R. 1991. *Jewish Communities in Asia Minor.* SNTSMS 69. Cambridge: Cambridge Univ. Press.

Treggiari, S. 1976. "Jobs for Women." *AJAH* 1:76–104.

———. 1979. "Lower-Class Women in the Roman Economy." *Florilegium* 1:65–86.

Troeltsch, E. 1977. *Die Soziallehren der christlichen Kirchen und Gruppen: Gesammelte Schriften.* Vols. 1 and 3. Reprint ed. Aalen. [Orig. ed. Tübingen 1922. ET = *The Social Teaching of the Christian Church.* O. Wyon, trans. London: Allen & Unwin, 1931. Reprinted with a new Introduction by H. R. Niebuhr, Chicago: Univ. of Chicago Press, 1981.]

Urbach, E. E. 1964. "Laws Regarding Slavery." In *Papers of the Institute of Jewish Studies, London.* J. G. Weiss, ed. Vol. 1. Jerusalem: Magnes.

———. 1968. "Class, Status, and Leadership in the World of the Palestinian Sages." In *Proceedings of the Israel Academy of Sciences and Humanities* 2:48–74.

———. 1987. *The Sages: Their Concepts and Beliefs.* 2 vols. I. Abrahams, trans. Jerusalem: Magnes.

Vermes, G. 1993. *Jesus der Jude: Ein Historiker liest die Evangelien.* Neukirchen-Vluyn: Neukirchener. [ET = *Jesus the Jew: A Historian's Reading of the Gospels.* Philadelphia: Fortress, 1981.]

Verner, D. C. 1983. *The Household of God: The Social World of the Pastoral Epistles.* SBLDS 71. Chico, Calif.: Scholars.

Veyne, P. 1988. *Brot und Spiele: Gesellschaftliche Macht und politische Herrschaft in der Antike.* Frankfurt: Campus. [ET = *Bread and Circuses: Historical Sociology and Political Pluralism.* Abridged with an introduction by O. Murray. B. Pearce, trans. London: Allen Lane, 1990.]

Vielhauer, P. 1975. *Geschichte der urchristlichen Literatur.* De Gruyter Lehrbuch. Berlin: Walter de Gruyter.

Vischer, R. 1965. *Das einfache Leben: Wort- und motivgeschichtliche Untersuchungen zu einem Wertbegriff der antiken Literatur.* Göttingen: Vandenhoeck & Ruprecht.

Vittinghoff, F. 1980. "Soziale Struktur und politisches System der hohen römischen Kaiserzeit." *HZ* 230:30–55.

———. 1984. "'Christianus sum': Das 'Verbrechen' von Aussenseitern der römischen Gesellschaft." *Historia* 33:331–57.

———, ed. 1990. *Handbuch der europäischen Wirtschafts- und Sozialgeschichte.* Vol. 1. Stuttgart: Kohlhammer.

Vivelo, F. R. 1988. *Handbuch der Kulturanthropologie: Eine grundlegende Einführung.* Munich: Chr. Kaiser.

Viviano, B. 1979. "Where Was the Gospel according to St. Matthew Written?" *CBQ* 41:533–46.

Vogt, J. 1954a. "Christenverfolgung (historisch)." In *RAC* 2:1159–1208.

———. 1954b. "Die Zählung der Christenverfolgungen im Römischen Reich." *Parola del Passato* 9:5–15.

Vogt, T. 1993. *Angst und Identität im Markusevangelium: Ein textpsychologischer und sozialgeschichtlicher Beitrag.* NTOA 26. Göttingen: Vandenhoeck & Ruprecht.

Vouga, F. 1994. *Geschichte des frühen Christentums.* Tübingen: J. C. B. Mohr.

Wagner-Hasel, B. 1988. "Das Private wird politisch: Die Perspektive 'Geschlecht' in der Altertumswissenschaft." In *Weiblichkeit in geschichtlicher Perspektive: Fallstudien und Reflexionen zu Grundproblemen der historischen Frauenforschung,* 11–50. U. A. J. Becher and J. Rüsen, eds. Suhrkamp-Taschenbuch: Wissenschaft 725. Frankfurt: Suhrkamp.

———. 1989. "Frauenleben in orientalischer Abgeschlossenheit? Zur Geschichte und Nutzanwendung eines Topos." *Der Altsprachliche Unterricht* 32/2:18–29.

Walter, N. 1979. "Christusglaube und heidnische Religiosität in paulinischen Gemeinden." *NTS* 25:422–42.

Waltzing, J.-P. 1968. *Etude historique sur les corporations professionnelles chez les Romains depuis les origines jusqu'à la chute de l'Empire d'Occident.* 4 vols. Reprint ed. Hildesheim: G. Olms. [Orig. ed. 1895–1900.]

Wander, B. 1994. *Trennungsprozesse zwischen Frühem Christentum und Judentum im 1. Jh. n.Chr.* Tübingen: Francke.

Watson, F. 1986. *Paul, Judaism and the Gentiles: A Sociological Approach.* SNTSMS 56. Cambridge: Cambridge Univ. Press.

Weaver, P. R. C. 1967. "Social Mobility in the Early Roman Empire: The Evidence of the Imperial Freedmen and Slaves." *Past and Present* 37:3–20.

———. 1972. *Familia Caesaris: A Social Study of the Emperor's Freedmen and Slaves.* Cambridge: Cambridge Univ. Press.

Weber, B. 1993. "Alltagswelt und Gottesreich: Überlegungen zum Verstehenshintergrund des Gleichnisses vom 'Schalksknecht' (Matthäus 18,23-34)." *BZ* 37:161–82.

Weber, M. 1920. *Gesammelte Aufsätze zur Religionssoziologie.* 3 vols. Tübingen: J. C. B. Mohr. [Paperback ed. 1980.]

———. 1976. *Wirtschaft und Gesellschaft: Grundriss der verstehenden Soziologie.* 5th ed. J. Winckelmann, ed. Tübingen: J. C. B. Mohr.

Wegner, J. R. 1988. *Chattel or Person? The Status of Women in the Mishnah.* New York: Oxford Univ. Press.

Weifel, W. 1977. "The Jewish Community in Ancient Rome and the Origins of Roman Christianity." In *The Romans Debate,* 100–119. K. P. Donfried, ed. Minneapolis: Augsburg.

Weiser, A. 1983. "Die Rolle der Frau in der urchristlichen Mission." In Dautzenberg et al. 1983, 158–81.

———. 1992. "Diakoneō." In *EWNT,* 2d ed., 1:726–32. [ET = *EDNT* 1:302–4.]

Wellhausen, J. 1907. *Noten zur Apostelgeschichte.* Berlin: Walter de Gruyter.

Wengst, K. 1986. *Pax Romana: Anspruch und Wirklichkeit: Erfahrungen und Wahrnehmungen des Friedens bei Jesus und im Urchristentum.* Munich: Chr. Kaiser. [ET = *Pax Romana and the Peace of Christ.* J. Bowden, trans. Philadelphia: Fortress, 1987.]

———. 1992. *Bedrängte Gemeinde und verherrlichter Christus.* 4th ed. Munich: Chr. Kaiser.

White, K. D. 1967. "Latifundia." *Bulletin of the Institute of Classical Studies* 14:62–79.

———. 1970. *Roman Farming.* Ithaca, N.Y.: Cornell Univ. Press.

White, L. M. 1991. "Crisis Management and Boundary Maintenance: The Social Location of the Matthean Community." In Balch 1991, 211–47.

Whittaker, Ch. R. 1991. "Der Arme." In Giardina 1991b, 305–33. [ET = "The Poor." In Giardina 1993, 272–99.]

Wieling, H. 1983. "Grundbesitz I (rechtsgeschichtlich)." In *RAC* 12:1172–96.

Wilken, R. L. 1979. "Kollegien, Philosophenschulen und Theologie." In Meeks 1979, 165–93. [ET = "Collegia, Philosophical Schools and Theology." In Benko and O'Rourke 1971, 268–98.]

Williams, M. H. 1990. "Domitian, the Jews and the 'Judaizers'—A Simple Matter of Cupiditas and Maiestas?" *Historia* 39:196–211.

Wilson, B. 1973. *Magic and the Millennium: A Sociological Study of Religious Movements of Protest among Tribal and Third-World Peoples.* London: Heinemann.

———. 1982. *Religion in Sociological Perspective.* Oxford: Oxford Univ. Press.

———. 1990. *The Social Dimension of Sectarianism.* Oxford: Oxford Univ. Press.

Wink, W. 1968. *John the Baptist in the Gospel Tradition.* SNTSMS 7. Cambridge: Cambridge Univ. Press.

Wire, A. C. 1990. *The Corinthian Women Prophets: A Reconstruction through Paul's Rhetoric.* Minneapolis: Fortress.

———. 1991. "Gender Roles in a Scribal Community." In Balch 1991, 87–121.

Wischmeyer, O. 1995. *Die Kultur des Buches Jesus Sirach.* Berlin: Walter de Gruyter.

Wlosok, A. 1970. *Rom und die Christen: Zur Auseinandersetzung zwischen Christentum und römischem Staat.* Altsprachliche Unterricht 13/1. Stuttgart: E. Klett.

———. 1982. "Die Rechtsgrundlagen der Christenverfolgungen der ersten zwei Jahrhunderte." In *Das frühe Christentum im römischen Staat,* 275–301. 2d ed. R. Klein, ed. Darmstadt: Wissenschaftliche Buchgesellschaft.

Wolter, M. 1993. *Der Brief an die Kolosser: Der Brief an Philemon.* Würzburg: Echter.

Worsley, P. 1968. *The Trumpet Shall Sound: A Study of "Cargo" Cults in Melanesia.* 2d ed. New York: Schocken.

Wuellner, W. H. 1973. "The Sociological Implications of 1 Corinthians 1,26-28 Reconsidered." *Studia Evangelica* 6 (TU 112): 666–72.

Yadin, Y. 1981. "Pescher Nahum (4QpNahum) erneut untersucht." In Grözinger 1981, 167–84.

Yoder, J. H. 1981. *Die Politik Jesu—der Weg des Kreuzes*. Maxdorf: Agape. [ET = *The Politics of Jesus: Vicit Agnus Noster*. Grand Rapids: Eerdmans, 1972; 2d ed. 1994.]

Zaidman, L. Bruit. 1993. "Die Töchter der Pandora: Die Frauen in den Kulten der Polis." In *Geschichte der Frauen*. Vol. 1: *Antike*, 375–415. P. Schmitt Pantel, ed. Frankfurt: Campus.

Zumstein, J. 1980. *Antioche sur l'Oronte et l'évangile selon Matthieu*. Linz: SNTU.

INDEX OF NEW TESTAMENT PASSAGES

BIBLE

Printed in the United States
125702LV00001B/100-108/P